THE BATTLE
FOR THE SOULS
OF BLACK FOLK

THE BATTLE
FOR THE SOULS
OF BLACK FOLK

W.E.B. Du Bois,
Booker T. Washington,
and the Debate That Shaped
the Course of Civil Rights

Thomas Aiello

 PRAEGER™

An Imprint of ABC-CLIO, LLC
Santa Barbara, California • Denver, Colorado

Library of Congress Cataloging-in-Publication Data

Names: Aiello, Thomas, 1977– author.
Title: The battle for the souls of Black folk : W.E.B. Du Bois, Booker T. Washington, and the debate that shaped the course of civil rights / Thomas Aiello. Other titles : W.E.B. Du Bois, Booker T. Washington, and the debate that shaped the course of civil rights.
Description: Santa Barbara, California : Praeger, an imprint of ABC-CLIO, LLC, [2016] | Includes bibliographical references and index.
Identifiers: LCCN 2016000777 | ISBN 9781440843570 (hard copy : alk. paper) | ISBN 9781440843587 (ebook)
Subjects: LCSH: Du Bois, W.E.B. (William Edward Burghardt), 1868–1963. | Du Bois, W.E.B. (William Edward Burghardt), 1868–1963—Political and social views. | Washington, Booker T., 1856–1915. | Washington, Booker T., 1856–1915—Political and social views. | African American civil rights workers—Biography. | African American intellectuals—Biography. | African American leadership—History—20th century. | African Americans—Civil rights—History—20th century. | African Americans—Intellectual life—20th century. | Civil rights movements—United States—History.
Classification: LCC E185.97.D73 A84 2016 | DDC 323.092/2 [B]—dc23 LC record available at https://lccn.loc.gov/2016000777

ISBN: 978-1-4408-4357-0
EISBN: 978-1-4408-4358-7

20 19 18 17 16   1 2 3 4 5

This book is also available as an eBook.

Praeger
An Imprint of ABC-CLIO, LLC

ABC-CLIO, LLC
130 Cremona Drive, P.O. Box 1911
Santa Barbara, California 93116-1911
www.abc-clio.com

This book is printed on acid-free paper ∞

Manufactured in the United States of America

The author wishes to thank the following for reprint permission:
Crisis Publishing Co., Inc., the publisher of the magazine of the National Association for the Advancement of Colored People, for the use of material first published in the September 1924, March 1926, July 1927, February 1929, June 1929, and June 1931 issues of Crisis.

University of Massachusetts Press, the publisher of The Correspondence of W.E.B. Du Bois, Volume 1: Selections, 1877–1934. Copyright © 1973 by the University of Massachusetts Press.

Howard University, the publisher of W.E.B. Du Bois (1932). Education and work. The Journal of Negro Education, 1, 60–74.

University of Chicago Press, the publisher of Ida B. Wells, Crusade for Justice: The Autobiography of Ida B. Wells, ed. Alfreda M. Duster. Chicago: University of Chicago Press, 1970, pp. 261–268, 280–281, 321–324, 329–331.

for Soo

A conversation is a dialogue, not a monologue. That's why there are so few good conversations: due to scarcity, two intelligent talkers seldom meet.

Truman Capote

This may look to outsiders as a petty squabble of thoughtless self-seekers. It is in fact the life and death struggle of nine million men.

W.E.B. Du Bois

Contents

Preface

I remember as a student so many years ago first encountering Studs Terkel's *The Good War*. It was a tremendously affecting portrait of World War II for someone who was not tremendously affected by war stories. Unlike other analyses of the conflict, Terkel's gave us a virtually silent narrator, steering the narrative through his questions but otherwise allowing the participants themselves to tell their stories, the collective whole standing as testament to what the fight against fascism was like for so many, from so many places in so many different situations. Although those stories provided his account with a particular intimacy, their combination also had larger arguments to make about the conduct of the war, racism in the military, the tensions that ultimately became the Cold War, and many other aspects of the fight. It was not simply a combination of intimate stories and big ideas. It was the use of intimate stories to find them.

Terkel's was a work of oral history. This is not. But it is still a story told by the participants. Inspired by the work of Studs Terkel, as well as more recent histories by James Andrew Miller and Tom Shales, I have tried to tell the story of the debate between W.E.B. Du Bois and Booker T. Washington by presenting their own voices. In other analyses of the leaders, that debate is treated as one motivating factor in a larger whole that theorizes the role of protest in early century rights debates, economic nationalism in the progressive era, and so many other realities of black life in the wake of Jim Crow retrenchment. Rightly so. Many of those studies appear in the notes to this volume. What this volume is doing, however, is fundamentally different. It seeks, like Terkel, to find those big ideas through intimacy. It tells the story of the ideological and personal battle between Du Bois and Washington through the stories told by them, their allies, aides, and enemies.

Unlike Terkel, of course, and unlike Miller and Shales, I was not able to interview the participants. Instead, I have used their writings and the writings of others, both published and unpublished, public and private, to shape a portrait of the conversation. Oral history, of course, has its own theory and development that is not included here. This is not oral history. But it is, I hope, a completely different way of viewing a controversy that defined the lives of both Du Bois and Washington, set the strategic considerations for how black America would respond to Jim Crow, and created the two distinct theoretical lines that would define the quest for civil rights throughout the 20th century. And it provides the best measure of its two main participants because each is allowed to present his own case.

This book begins by allowing them to introduce themselves, establishing their development in the decades before the seminal year of 1895, when Frederick Douglass died, Washington made his infamous Atlanta Compromise speech at the Cotton States Exposition, and Du Bois completed his doctorate from Harvard. The book moves chronologically from there, Chapter 3 describing the first sustained contact between Washington and Du Bois, when the latter began searching for teaching jobs after the completion of his degree. The first real rift between the two occurred in 1898, when criticism of Washington from Boston rights advocates (and friends of Du Bois) led Tuskegee's leader to resign from the board of an Alabama industrial school founded by a friend of Du Bois. It grew from there. Du Bois felt slighted when he did not get a job recommendation from Washington for a school superintendency in the nation's capital, then Washington plagiarized his National Negro Business League from a format developed by Du Bois and his colleagues at Atlanta University. Washington published his autobiography *Up From Slavery* in 1901, then Du Bois issued a scathing critique of it later that year. In 1903, Du Bois published his *The Souls of Black Folk* and included an essay deriding Washington, then William Monroe Trotter and other Du Bois allies interrupted a Washington address to the Boston chapter of the National Negro Business League later that year.

Chapter 10 describes a summit between the two leaders and their supporters at Carnegie Hall, an attempt at a truce that ultimately fell flat. The conference created a Committee of Twelve to coordinate racial leadership, but Washington excluded Du Bois from meeting preparations and he resigned in response. Washington, for all of his better qualities, lorded power over black political appointments, the black press, and white philanthropy to black causes, and his sensitivity to criticism often made him vindictive, bringing the full force of what became known as the "Tuskegee Machine" to bear on his opponents. The Machine demonstrated that vindictiveness against Du Bois's Niagara Movement beginning in 1905, and against the National Association for the Advancement of Colored People beginning in 1909. That domestic conflict then became international, as described in Chapter 16, when Washington made statements about improving U.S. race relations while on tour in England, and Du Bois responded with an open letter to the British denying his counterpart's optimism.

The conflict would continue in the years that followed, continuing until Washington's death in 1915. As explained in Chapter 19, his death returned the divide between the two leaders back to the front pages and led many to theorize about the Tuskegee leader's complicated legacy. More than anything else, however, his death would allow Du Bois to shape the narrative in the years and decades to come. That narrative would obviously preference Du Bois and hurt the reputation of Washington.

This is the story of a 20-year war of words that helped to shape the course of the 20th-century debate about the role of civil rights activism.

It is the story of a war of words that cauterized the divide in black higher education between a liberal arts curriculum and agricultural and industrial training.

It is the story of a war of words that would frame the conversation about how best to pull the souls of black folk up from slavery.

And it was a good war.

The italicized text is my own, but everything else is original to the designated speaker. Ellipses mark cuts to the contemporary text where that narrative veered into discussions of material ancillary to *The Battle for the Souls of Black Folk*. The notes provide context where appropriate and sources for each individual entry. For purposes of permissions and ease of access, source notes refer to published instances of primary sources, although all correspondence is available as archival material. Archives consulted are listed in the bibliography.

Introduction

On February 20, 1895, Frederick Douglass attended a meeting of the National Council of Women in the nation's capital. He was in his late seventies, but he ambled to the podium with help nonetheless, where the assembly gave him a standing ovation. Douglass was gracious, then ambled back down, then ambled home. That evening, he was felled by a massive heart attack, leaving the women's rights movement, the black rights movement, and minority rights in general badly damaged.

Perhaps even more importantly, his death would leave a power vacuum at the top of the African American political community. It was a coveted position, to be sure, and so later that year a 39-year-old schoolteacher—the president of Tuskegee Institute in Alabama—gave a speech in Atlanta that made him famous. Booker Taliaferro Washington accepted segregation as a temporary accommodation between the races. In return, he wanted white support for black efforts for education, social uplift, and economic progress. "In all things that are purely social we can be as separate as the fingers," he famously argued, "yet one as the hand in all things essential to mutual progress." Washington's Atlanta Compromise (as it came to be known) was not trumpeting permanent second-class citizenship for African Americans. Instead he wanted black self-improvement that would ultimately earn white respect and thus a seat at the negotiating table as equals somewhere down the road.

Many black critics, however, saw Washington's compromise as a slippery slope that would cause more problems than it could ever hope to solve. Born into slavery in western Virginia in 1856 to a black mother and unknown white father, Booker Washington was raised by his mother on a small farm. After a childhood of hard work, diligence, and Christian morality, he attended Hampton Normal and Agricultural Institute, founded in 1868 by white missionary Samuel Chapman Armstrong to teach both African Americans and Native Americans hard work, diligence, and Christian morality. Washington taught there for a couple of years, before moving to Alabama in 1881 to found Tuskegee Institute, built on the Hampton model, an ideal that Washington would champion until the day he died in 1915.[1]

Chief among his critics would be William Edward Burghardt Du Bois, although he would come to his anti-Washington position slowly. In fact, he originally celebrated the speech and had a cordial if not productive relationship with Tuskegee's leader. Du Bois was 12 years younger than Washington, and he did not grow up in slavery, poverty, or southern racism. He grew up in the largely white New England town of Great Barrington, Massachusetts, where he experienced little overt, openly hostile racism. After high school, he went to Fisk, then to Harvard where he became the first black man to earn a PhD. He was a scholar and an activist. He wrote two dozen books, but he was also determined to confront disfranchisement, Jim Crow, and lynching. Unlike Washington, he did not believe in a gradual approach to eliminating white supremacy. And he had little tolerance for black people who were unwilling to demand their civil and political rights.[2] And so by 1898, the relationship started to falter, and the two would become personal and ideological foes whose public battle would engulf the movement for black rights and begin a substantive discussion of how to get them.

Their conflict would ultimately frame the debate about civil rights throughout the 20th century. Despite the common caricature, the two were not divided by conservative and radical politics: if Du Bois in the pre-World War I era is the lynchpin of a lineage that runs from Frederick Douglass to Martin Luther King, it is just as easy to pinpoint Washington as the connective tissue that binds Martin Delany and Malcolm X.

In fact, in the Hegelian reductionist model of black history after Reconstruction, new incarnations of leadership followed a relatively reliable trend. Two leaders emerged, representing two sides of the rights-bearing coin, striving after a revolution in citizenship and voting rights, considered separately. First there was Frederick Douglass and Martin

Delany, struggling to set the agenda of black America following the Fourteenth and Fifteenth Amendments. Last there was Martin Luther King and Malcolm X, setting new agendas that would ultimately lead to the Civil Rights Act of 1964 and Voting Rights Act of 1965. In between these two poles there was Booker T. Washington and W.E.B. Du Bois, struggling for the souls of black folk following the onset of segregation laws and constitutional voting restrictions.

Of course, this kind of problematic oversimplification creates more dilemmas than it solves, omitting the cacophony of voices surrounding these leaders, forgetting the legitimate influential leadership of others, and assuming a two-party bipolar caste to debates involving the best methods for countering white supremacy. Still, such cribs exist for a reason. There were massive numbers of influential backers of Tuskegee, but all tended to defer to Washington on major policy issues. William Monroe Trotter was a Du Bois ally and staunch opponent of Tuskegee, but his radicalism left him far less influential than Du Bois. The same could be said of Ida Wells' gender. (Of course, the voices of the Tuskegee Machine, Trotter, and Wells will all loudly participate in the conversation that follows.) Marcus Garvey is sometimes placed alongside Du Bois and Washington in such debates, but he did not even arrive in the United States until after Washington's death.

And so it was that in the twenty years between 1895 and 1915, two leaders shaped the contours of the struggle for African American rights in the 20th century. This feud is usually treated by biographers of one or the other, always cited, always assumed, but rarely given pride of place in any influential manuscript. August Meier published an early attempt to sketch the debate in the year of Du Bois's death with his 1963 *Negro Thought in America, 1880–1915: Racial Ideologies in the Age of Booker T. Washington.* Hugh Hawkins followed in the next decade with a brief essay collection in the 1970s titled *Booker T. Washington and His Critics.*[3] Hawkins, however, would be eclipsed by Washington's most influential and prolific biographer, Louis Harlan. It was Harlan, along with Du Bois authorities Herbert Aptheker and, later, David Levering Lewis, who ultimately provided our most cogent understanding of the debate.[4]

No matter how cogent the understanding, however, questions persist. Harlan is one of many, for example, who argue that Du Bois "would join the anti-Washington camp" in 1903, presumably with the publication of *The Souls of Black Folk.*[5] Lewis traces the feud back to a 1900 controversy over an appointment to a superintendent position in the Washington, D.C. public school system. This manuscript will revise both of those assumptions, arguing that the split between Du Bois and Washington began as early as 1898.

Regardless, it is clear that a relationship that began with a reasonable dose of mutual respect soured along the way, and the acrimony it engendered fed the distinctions that both camps would draw between the two leaders. And it is ultimately those distinctions that lead to the common caricature of Du Bois as a radical and Washington as an Uncle Tom, neither of which is accurate.

Washington, for his part, viewed himself as a pragmatist. David Levering Lewis portrays him as an inscrutable calculator who guarded his status as a perceived necessity in a racist climate. "Whether or not he truly believed" his regular public jokes about his fellow black Americans is less an issue for Lewis than Washington's belief that they were ultimately a necessity. At various times, for example, Tuskegee's leader jokingly advocated lynching and slavery.[6] This, however, seems an untenable position, as the constant money and effort placed on the destruction of black newspapers and their message, of the organizations put together by Du Bois, and of the intellectual clique so opposed to him centered in Boston go against all pragmatic calculation. The first thing that someone who uses lynching jokes to ingratiate himself to white audiences learns is that it is counterproductive to eliminate a foil, particularly one as relatively harmless as a northern intellectual. It is true that the actual words of Du Bois and Washington leave the Harvard man looking like a disingenuous intellectual bigot in his worst moments, but so too do they leave his Tuskegee counterpart appearing as a distracted, petty megalomaniac with anything but racial pragmatism on his mind.

Of course, there were pragmatic benefits to Washington's actions. In the wake of his Atlanta Compromise speech, white leaders flocked to him as the new Douglass. Andrew Carnegie built 29 buildings on the campuses of HBCUs because of Washington. Julius Rosenwald, the president of Sears, Roebuck, built a series of black secondary schools across the South with Washington's guidance. Between 1913 and 1932, more than 5,300 "Rosenwald schools" were built, at a cost of more than 28 million dollars. In addition, graduates of Tuskegee went all around the South helping industrial and agricultural education proliferate, fundamentally altering the educational landscape for African Americans.[7] At the same time, however, it is harder to defend as pragmatic the Tuskegee Machine's actions against, for example, Du Bois's Niagara Movement. Washington used every means at his disposal to undermine the seminal early civil rights campaign, paying editors to attack Du Bois in print and sending spies to Niagara meetings to report on the group's activities. After its dissolution, he tried to subvert Du Bois's next attempt, the National Association for the Advancement of Colored

People (NAACP), whenever possible. He again employed spies in the organization to discover what it was doing and discredit it. He again paid editors of newspapers to write about him favorably and about the NACCP negatively. Washington was obsessed. He would even alert white newspapers of certain meetings so that white supremacists could have all the information ahead of time.[8] It was behavior that would better be termed mania than pragmatism.

Still, that does not mean that Washington's belief in the role of black activism was not both sincere and valid. "If today, we have fewer political convictions," he argued in 1898, "we have more economic gatherings. If we have fewer political clubs, we have more building and loan associations. If we cherish fewer air-castles, we own more acres of land and more homes than has ever been true in the history of the Negro race. If we have fewer men in Congress, we have more merchants and more leaders in commerce."[9]

He believed that white southern intransigence was such that there was no fundamental advantage for advocating publicly and dramatically for rights. He had many examples at his disposal to prove his point. In such a situation, the only way to fight was to grow stronger within the paradigm, rather than trying to change the paradigm itself, just as a military unit would wait for reinforcements when hopelessly outmanned. "I do not favor the Negro's giving up anything which is fundamental and which has been guaranteed to him by the Constitution," he argued. "It is not best for him to relinquish his rights; nor would his doing so be best for the Southern white man." There was, however, an essential difference between relinquishment and outright advocacy. Overreach could only set everything back.[10]

But advocacy was something Washington was willing to do. He spoke to the Louisiana legislature in 1898, for example, urging them to reconsider the state's grandfather clause. He also organized and raised money for the cause behind the scenes. He did the same for Alabama's voting restrictions in 1901. He provided funds for antidiscrimination railroad suits and for suits challenging jury exclusion. He also funded the successful challenge to southern debt peonage.[11]

Washington's problem was his belief that disagreement with his core philosophy must be the result of jealousy or naiveté. Du Bois, he assumed, was an outsider, and therefore was incapable of an authentic understanding of the black southern experience. As Lewis has explained, although Du Bois was working in the South, his knowledge of the region was that of an explorer. Washington's was that of a native.[12]

Regardless, accommodation failed, only allowing white redeemers to strengthen their position and to disenfranchise almost all black southerners. But black opposition to Washington's policies came well before that failure. Du Bois's frustration with Washington, for example, began with the Tuskegeean's attacks on the liberal arts and higher education. What originally began as Washington's ingratiating jokes about the simplicity of southern blacks morphed in Du Bois's mind into a version of classism, or at least a revulsion against high society. And Du Bois was nothing if not a progenitor of all things high society. That made Washington's assaults seem directed specifically at him. In his 1898 commencement address at his alma mater Fisk, for example, Du Bois told his audience that those trained at industrial schools would supply skilled labor and service industry jobs. Fisk graduates were "gentlemen and ladies, trained in the liberal arts and subjects in that vast kingdom of culture that has lighted the world from its infancy and guided it through bigotry and falsehood and sin."[13]

That being the case, the division of "northern" and "southern" blackness could also be a method of subtly denoting class. It could imply urban and rural distinctions. It could imply divisions of education and culture, all exacerbated by the social context of the debate between Du Bois and Washington. Lewis argues that the debate was inevitable and would have happened even without two powerful leaders to espouse the positions. The arguments of each would represent responses to two different white supremacies in two very different regions of the country at a very specific time and place.[14]

That time and place were dominated by white southern retrenchment in the Gilded Age, prompting black southerners to escape the region in the first wave of what would come to be known as the Great Migration. That retrenchment took many forms, but one of the most significant was a series of electioneering amendments to state constitutions in southern states specifically designed to abrogate the Fifteenth amendment. Literacy tests, property qualifications, and poll taxes ensured that black voters would be disenfranchised, and none of them ever mentioned "race, color, or previous condition of servitude." South Carolina, for example, passed the Eight Box Law in 1882. It required voters to deposit separate ballots for separate election races in the proper ballot box. Illiterate voters could not identify the boxes without white election officials "helping" them.[15]

It was also during these years that states began passing "Jim Crow" laws, mandating segregation in almost all public facilities. That imperative for segregation would take over every facet of southern life, but it began on railroads. In 1889, for example, black Baptists from Savannah bought first-class tickets to travel to a convention in Indianapolis. News was telegraphed ahead, and the black Baptists were confronted by a white mob at a railroad stop in Georgia, where they were threatened and beaten. A white man shoved a pistol into the breast of a black woman who had screamed in fear. He demanded, "You goddamned heffer, if you don't hush your mouth and get out of here, I will blow your goddamned brains out." And so it was deemed necessary to make such things into law. Tennessee mandated segregation on railroad cars in 1881. Florida in 1887. Louisiana took its turn in 1890, when it passed the Separate Car Act, a law that would ultimately lead to the Supreme Court's *Plessy v. Ferguson* (1896) decision, validating the doctrine of "separate but equal."[16]

But along with disenfranchisement and segregation, black life in the Gilded Age was also dramatically affected by continued violence. In Phoenix, South Carolina, in 1898, a white Republican candidate for Congress tried to convince black voters to fill out affidavits claiming they were denied the right to vote. White Democrats responded violently, shooting the candidate, then going on a rampage killing an uncertain number of black men. Such race riots were commonplace, but so too were individual lynchings. Between 1889 and 1932, 3,745 people were lynched, an average of between two and three every week. In the 1890s alone there was an average of more than 180 lynchings per year.[17]

In response to the violence and restrictions, many in the South decided to flee. Thus began the Great Migration. Of course, in the 19th century, most black southerners were far more likely to emigrate to Africa, to the American west, or to urban hubs within the South than they were to large industrial cities in the North. And it was a slow move at first. In the 1910s, for example, 90 percent of black Americans still lived in the South. The larger Great Migration to northern urban industrial hubs did not really begin until the middle of the 1910s. Still, the early migration was significant, inaugurating the massive demographic upheaval that would change so much for black America, economically, culturally, and politically.[18] It was against the backdrop of this white southern retrenchment and the birth pangs of African American demographic upheaval that the ideological contest between Washington and Du Bois would take place.

Adolph L. Reed has argued that the divide between the two "derived largely from the fact that Washington had established a monopoly over access to patronage sources," although Reed still sees any real conflict as impossible without the clear strategic and ideological rifts resulting from the racial mores of the white South.[19]

In Hugh Hawkins' famous 1962 collection of essays concerning Washington "and his critics," he placed the genesis of the public divide in 1903 with the publication of *The Souls of Black Folk*. Hawkins mentioned the

Tuskegee Machine's continual machinations to maintain influence and power but placed Du Bois in the role of instigator, arguing that his frustration with what he saw as Washington's role in the black loss of political rights and the overemphasis on industrial over academic education drove the initial split and continued to widen the gulf as the years progressed. For Hawkins, the growth of the feud between Du Bois and Washington in the years before its public explosion in 1903 occurred simultaneously to Du Bois's move away from academic sociological work and into more activism and writing for popular audiences. It was not a move caused by Washington, but Du Bois's need to serve as a counterweight to what he saw as overtly problematic accomodationism emanating from Tuskegee surely played a role in that transition.[20]

Such analyses lead to the general conclusion that "Du Bois and Washington, in speaking for two dissimilar socioeconomic orders, were really speaking past each other rather than to the same set of racial problems and solutions; but Du Bois, for all his Victorian sensibilities and elitism, had the advantage of speaking to the future, while Washington, business-oriented and folksy, spoke, nevertheless, for the early industrial past."[21]

And thus we have circled back around to the caricature.

Caricature holds sway as it does in the Washington–Du Bois controversy only when the issue being caricatured is consistently treated as tertiary to a broader narrative. There are dozens of books that discuss the rivalry, so many in fact that among black history scholars it is an assumed part of the broader narrative. Those books, however, are biographies of one party or another, they are books about the struggle for rights during the early period of Jim Crow, they are books about Tuskegee or books about the NAACP. More recently, Aldon Morris's pioneering work in *The Scholar Denied: W.E.B. Du Bois and the Birth of Modern Sociology* focuses on Washington's relationship with Robert Park and the case of academic forgetting that all but erased Du Bois's role as a foundational pioneer in the discipline of sociology.[22]

This book, however, is different from its predecessors. It seeks to situate the conversation between Washington and Du Bois in a place of primacy in order to fully examine its contours. In so doing, it comes to some significant new conclusions.

First, the split between the two began much earlier than presumed by most accounts. The nascent onset of the dispute generally appears in most tellings in 1900, in what Du Bois saw as a betrayal by Washington in a recommendation dispute over a school superintendency position in Washington, D.C. That first sign of weakness in the relationship was then exacerbated by the formation of the National Negro Business

League, Du Bois's review of *Up From Slavery*, the Boston Riot of 1903, and the publication of *The Souls of Black Folk*. The relationship between Du Bois and Washington, however, was problematic even before the Washington School District problems of 1900. A relationship that was for all practical intents cordial between 1894 and 1897 felt its first strain two years before Washington, D.C., with the Tuskegee leader's early rhetorical stumbles in Boston and an Alabama controversy surrounding William E. Benson's Kowaliga Academic and Industrial Institute in 1898.

Second, even though it has an earlier beginning than is normally acknowledged, the great battle between the two was really kept aflame by others and events that were out of their control. These pages are filled with advisors, sycophants, and neophytes pressing each of the men to further exacerbate a program against the other. It was such behavior that encouraged broad-brush caricatures of the leaders. Of course, Du Bois was definitely condescending and Washington's victim complex definitely made him overcompensate to the point where he sometimes appeared to be an evil overlord, but even during their debate, there were moments of agreement and contact. Those moments of agreement were opportunities for a broader coalition that could have fostered a rights program that included more than one approach. Although there were real points of theoretical and practical contention between them, the plans of Du Bois and Washington could have coexisted far more easily than their representatives ever allowed.

Finally, those caricatures mentioned earlier, particularly the caricature of Washington, stuck for so long after the death of Washington in 1915 largely because Du Bois lived longer. That Du Bois got such a long-lasting last word shaped the perception of the conflict and allowed him to influence American thinking about the debate and about Washington. That influence ultimately affected the academic narrative just as it did the popular narrative, ensuring that Du Bois would be cast as an uncompromising progressive and Washington would forever be a rude conglomeration of Uncle Tom and Simon Legree. Neither depiction, of course, was wholly accurate.

From the death of Frederick Douglass on February 20, 1895, to the death of Booker T. Washington on November 14, 1915, black America split in two. The conversation between Washington and Du Bois would define the age and lay the foundation for the ideologies of the post-World War II civil rights movement. It was a conversation that included many voices, many opinions. It evolved over time, becoming fiercer and more personal as the years progressed. It produced a cacophony of ideas that made it anything but a bipolar debate, even though it would ultimately shape the contours of two influential biographies and the two dominant strains of activist strategy. But despite its complexities and steadily accumulating bitterness, it was still, at base, a conversation—a contest at the turn of the century to capture the souls of black folk.

NOTES

1. Booker Washington controlled his own biographical narrative during his life, and Du Bois was able to set the agenda in the decades that followed his death. The first real biographical reconsideration of Washington came in 1957, when August Meier published "Toward a Reinterpretation of Booker T. Washington" in *Journal of Southern History* 23 (May 1957): 220–227. The biographical evolution continued from there, led by Louis R. Harlan. For a brief historiographical summary, listed in order of publication, see Harlan, 1970, 1581–1599; Harlan, 1971, 393–416; Harlan, 1972; Strickland, 1973, 559–564; Friedman, 1974, 337–351; Harlan, 1983; Norrell, 2009; Smock, 2009; Boston, 2010; and Zimmerman, 2012.

2. His doctorate was in history in 1895. The biographical material on Du Bois is exponentially greater than that on Washington, due primarily to his increased popularity, his long life, his diverse output and interests, and the broad evolution that his thinking went through in the course of his productive years. What follows is a brief chronological sampling of that work, beginning with Broderick, 1959, published while Du Bois was still alive. See also Rudwick, 1968; Rampersad, 1976; Lewis, 1994; Lewis, 2001; Shaw, 2013; Apiah, 2014; and Morris, 2015.

3. Meier, 1963; Hawkins, 1974. In the 1990s, Cary D. Wintz would continue this effort with an essay collection featuring the work of Washington, Du Bois, Marcus Garvey, and Asa Philip Randolph. Wintz, 1996.

4. For examples of Harlan's influence on the scholarship, see Harlan, 1972; Harlan, 1979, 45–62; Harlan, 1971, 393–416; and Harlan 1957, 189–202.

5. Harlan, *Booker T. Washington*, 225.

6. Lewis, 1993, 238–239.

7. See notes 1 and 4 for more on the positive aftermath of the Atlanta Compromise speech. See also Ascoli, 2006; Hoffschwelle, 2006; and Deutsch, 2011.

8. For more on Washington's behavior in this vein, see the sources in note 1. These machinations are also covered in depth in the pages that follow.

9. Washington, 1972, 28–29.

10. Lewis, 1993, 258.

11. The best source for such examples of Washington's more secretive advocacy can be found in Harlan, 1971, 393–416.

12. Lewis, 1993, 256.

13. Ibid., 261–262.

14. Ibid., 502.

15. See Perman, 2000; Kousser, 1974; Kousser, 1999; Kirby, 1972; and Ayers, 1992.

16. See Woodward, 1955; Woodward, 1951; Cohen, 1991; Cell, 1982; and Klarman, 2004.

17. See Brundage, 1993; Tolnay and Beck, 1995; Waldrep, 2004; Feimster, 2009; Waldrep, 2006; Wood, 2009; and Brundage, 1997.

18. See Berlin, 2010; Wilkerson, 2010; Trotter, 1991; Harrison, 1991; and Baldwin, 2007.

19. Reed, 1997, 60–64.

20. Hawkins, 1978, 19.

21. Lewis, 1993, 502. For further examples of analysis of the onset of the Washington–Du Bois feud, see Kilson, 2000, 298–313; and Bauerlein, 2004–2005, 106–114.

22. Morris, 2015.

1

Before the Cotton States

Booker Taliaferro Washington was born into slavery in western Virginia in 1856 to a black mother and an unknown white father. He was raised by his mother on a small farm before attending Virginia's Hampton Normal and Agricultural Institute, founded by white missionary Samuel Chapman Armstrong. The school's star pupil, he taught at Hampton after graduation before moving to Alabama in 1881 to found Tuskegee Institute, built on the Hampton model. While Washington worked to build Tuskegee, a younger Du Bois worked to get through school, first attending Fisk, then Harvard, then graduate school in Germany. His childhood in Massachusetts was far more comfortable than that of Washington, as was his education. Still, Washington was 12 years older than Du Bois, with a far more direct experience with southern racial intransigence. Du Bois did attend Fisk with the woman who would become Washington's third wife, but the Tuskegee leader's experience and notoriety would ensure that in the years before 1895, the student would be far more aware of the teacher than the other way around.

BOOKER TALIAFERRO WASHINGTON

I was born a slave on a plantation in Virginia in 1857 or 1858, I think. My first memory of life is that of a one-room log cabin with a dirt floor and a hole in the center that served as a winter home for sweet potatoes, and wrapped in a few rags on this dirt floor I spent my nights, and clad in a single garment about the plantation, I often spent my days.

The morning of freedom came, and though a child, I recall vividly my appearance with that of forty or fifty slaves before the veranda of the "big house" to hear read the documents that made us men instead of property. With the long-prayed-for freedom in actual possession, each started out into the world to find new friends and new homes. My mother decided to locate in West Virginia, and after many days and nights of weary travel we found ourselves among the salt furnaces and coal mines of West Virginia. Soon after reaching West Virginia I began work in the coal mine for the support of my mother. While doing this I heard in some way, I do not now remember how, of General Armstrong's school at Hampton, Virginia. I heard at the same time, which impressed me most, that it was a school where a poor boy could work for his education, so far as his board was concerned. As soon as I heard of Hampton, I made up my mind that in some way I was going to find my way to that institution. I began at once to save every nickel I could get hold of. At length, with my own savings and a little help from my brother and mother, I started for Hampton, although at that time I hardly knew where Hampton was or how much it would cost to reach the school. After walking a portion of the distance, traveling in a stage coach and cars the remainder of the journey, I at length found myself in the city of Richmond, Virginia. I also found myself without friends, money or a place to stay all night. After walking about the city till midnight, and I had grown almost discouraged and quite exhausted, I crawled under a sidewalk and slept all that night. The next morning, as good luck would have it, I found myself very near a ship that was unloading pig iron. I applied to the captain for work, and he gave it, and I worked on this ship by day and slept under the sidewalk by night till I had earned money enough to continue my way to Hampton, where I soon arrived with a surplus of fifty cents in my pocket. I at once found General Armstrong, and told him what my condition was and what I had come for. In his great hearty way he said that if I was worth anything he would give me a chance to work my way.

At Hampton I found buildings, instructors, industries provided by the generous; in other words, the chance for me to work for my education. While at Hampton I resolved, if God permitted me to finish the course of study, I would enter the far South, the Black Belt of the Gulf states, and give my life in providing as best I could the same kind of chance for self-help for the youth of my race that I found ready for me when I went to Hampton: And so in 1881 I left Hampton and started the Tuskegee Normal and Industrial Institute in a small church and shanty, with one teacher and thirty students. Since then the institution at Tuskegee has gradually grown, so that we have today over 1,000 students, 88 officers, 26 industries, 42 buildings, 2,267 acres of land, and $300,000 worth of property.[1]

WILLIAM EDWARD BURGHARDT DU BOIS

. . . My name is William Edward Burghardt Du Bois; I was born at Great Barrington, Massachusetts, on the 23rd day of February, 1868, being the sole issue of the marriage of Mary S. Burghardt and Alfred Du Bois.

My paternal great-grandfather was a French doctor in the West Indies, and brought my grandfather and his brother to the United States when quite young. My grandfather settled in Connecticut and afterward removed to New Bedford, Mass. He was a boat steward by trade. My father was one of many children, and a barber by trade. He died when I was young.

My mother was a mulatto, the fourth in direct descent from Thomas Burghardt, who when young, was brought from Africa as a slave to the Dutch in New York state, early in the 18th century. He fought in the Revolutionary war. His son Jack Burghardt had several children, among whom was Othello, my grandfather. Othello and his wife, Sally Lampman, were both born slaves, but freed at majority. My mother was the youngest of several children, and received a good common-school education.

Both grandfathers and my father had good common educations. Alexander Du Bois, as my grandfather was named, had accumulated some property, but most of it went to his maintenance in his old age. There was some property in my mother's family but none of it reached me. My father saved nothing, and after his death we were often near pauperism. Nevertheless my mother kept me in school until she was disabled by paralysis, when I managed to keep on by means of work after hours and on vacation. In 1884 I graduated from the Gt. Barrington High School, and in the fall of 1885 I went south on the advice of friends, and entered the sophomore class at Fisk University. My mother died in the spring of 1885.

I remained at Fisk three years, graduating with the degree of A.B., in 1888. My vacations were spent in teaching country schools. I now determined to come to Harvard and pursue a course for the degree of Ph.D. On the strength of my recommendations I was appointed to $250 of Price Greenleaf Aid at Harvard before coming. During the summer of 1888 I worked in a hotel in the northwest, and in the fall entered the Junior class at this place. I managed to pay the expenses of the first year by the Aid, lecturing, loan fund, and a prize; the next year I was granted a Matthews Scholarship, which added to a series of summer readings and another prize enabled me to finish that year. For the year '90–'91, I was appointed to the H.B. Rogers Memorial Fellowship in Political Science, and re-appointed to the same for 1891–92.

Of the four years spent at Harvard, the first was spent in general studies (e.g. Chemistry, Geology, Ethics, Economics &c), the second year in Philosophy, and Economics, and the last two in History and Political Science. My doctor's thesis has been written and is on the suppression of the slave trade in the United States, including colonial times. My future study will be in political science with especial reference to the history of social problems.[2]

BOOKER T. WASHINGTON

To work from seven o'clock in the morning till six o'clock at night, and then study from seven o'clock till nine or half past nine, is an undertaking that few young men would be willing to stick to through all the seasons of the year. Yet this is just what thirty-five young men at Hampton have done for the past year. All of them came here with no capital but their determination to get an education, and hands that could work for it.

It was thought at first that it would be hard to keep them awake, but a few jokes, their own earnestness, and many interesting questions reduced this supposed obstacle to nothing. It was a rare thing to find one asleep. Their hard work in the day seemed to give them an appetite for study at night. They studied and recited the same night. They digested a good deal of what they studied at night, while at work in the day. Passing by them at work, one could almost always hear them discussing some point in grammar or some problem in arithmetic. They would generally have a number of questions to ask at night, which they had failed to agree upon or to understand during the day. One was noticed to carry a broken piece of slate about with him on which he could work examples while the wheel-barrow of dirt he had loaded, was being emptied. Their books were in their hands at every spare moment. No teacher ever had a more interesting class.

With all their zeal for study, they made excellent workers, and the superintendent of the Industrial works, by whom most of them were employed, showed his appreciation of their services by making each one a nice present at the end of the year . . .

These young men not only enter school with enough knowledge to pay them for this year's work, but they have saved an average of seventy dollars apiece, after buying their clothes. This amount, with their earnings during school and in vacation, will keep them in school two years. Thus, seven have saved enough in one year to graduate them at the institution, and the others enough to take them into their senior year. What these have done, others can do. With such privileges offered to our young men, poverty can no longer be pleaded as an excuse for ignorance. There are thousands of young men all over this country who could, if they would sacrifice a few evenings' pleasure for a while, open the door to a respectable education. How much better this would be than to be compelled by ignorance to spend the remainder of their lives as the lowest kind of servants! They would not then go through the world as mere pretenders to an education, as so many do, nor would they then feel the necessity of spending all their money for fine clothes with which they vainly hope to hide the poverty of the inner man.

Give a man a chance to work out his own education, and, as a general thing, you do far more for him than you would by paying his way in school for three or four years. A man who is not willing to work for his education will do nothing with it after he gets it . . .[3]

ALABAMA LEGISLATURE

An Act to establish a Normal School for colored teachers at Tuskegee.[4]

Section 1. *Be it enacted by the General Assembly of Alabama,* There shall be established, at Tuskegee, in this State, a normal school for the education of colored teachers. Pupils shall be admitted free of charge for tuition in the school, on giving an obligation in writing to teach in the free public schools in this State for two years after they become qualified. The school shall not be begun or continued with a less number than twenty-five pupils, nor shall the school be taught for a less period than nine months in each year.

Sec 2. *Be it further enacted,* There is appropriated out of the general school revenue, set apart to the colored children, the sum of two thousand dollars, annually, for the maintenance and support of the school;

and the apportionment of the general fund for the colored race shall be made to the different counties of this State, after the deduction of the sum of two thousand dollars herein appropriated for the school at Tuskegee.

Sec. 3. *Be it further enacted*, The school shall be under the direction, control and supervision of a board of three commissioners, who shall consist of the following persons, to-wit: Thos. B. Dryer, M.B. Swanson, and Lewis Adams,[5] who may fill any vacancy that may occur in the board of commissioners. The commissioners shall elect one of their number chairman, and they shall report quarterly to the Superintendent of Education, how many pupils have been in attendance, what branches have been taught, and other facts of interest and importance appertaining to the school . . .

Approved February 10, 1881.[6]

SAMUEL CHAPMAN ARMSTRONG *(Armstrong was a Union veteran, the founder, in 1868, of Hampton Normal and Agricultural Institute, and Washington's mentor.)*

[Hampton, Va.] May 31 81

Gentlemen Yours of the 24th is recd.

The only man I can suggest is one Mr. Booker Washington a graduate of this institution, a very competent capable mulatto, clear headed, modest, sensible, polite and a thorough teacher and superior man. The best man we ever had here.

I am satisfied he would not disappoint you.

He cannot well be spared till Oct. 1st.

Could you give him time and how much?

Are the buildings all ready?

Is the appropriation one to be depended on from year to year?

Is his being colored an objection?

He can find first [rate] colored assistants.

I am confident he would not disappoint you.

I know of no white man who would do better.

He has been teaching in this institution the past year & I am ready to promote him because he so richly deserves it . . .

S C Armstrong[7]

BOOKER T. WASHINGTON

Dear friends: I arrived here four weeks ago. Instead of finding my work in a low marshy country as I expected, I find Tuskegee a beautiful little town, with a high and healthy location. It is a town such as one rarely sees in the South. Its quiet, shady streets and tasteful and rich dwellings remind one of a New England village. After my arrival I had one week in which to prepare for the opening of the Normal School. I utilized this time in seeing the teachers and others who wished to enter the school, and in getting a general idea of my work and the people. Sunday I spoke in both churches to the people about the school, and told all who wished to enter to come and see me at my boarding place during the week. About thirty persons called and had their names enrolled, others called whose names, for various reasons, I could not enroll. With the young people many of their parents came. I was particularly impressed with the desire of the parents to educate their children, whatever might be the sacrifice.

On Friday I rode about fourteen miles into the country to visit the closing exercises of one of the teachers. From this trip I got some idea of the people in the country. Never was I more surprised and moved than when I saw at one house, two boys thirteen or fourteen years old, perfectly nude. They seemed not to mind their condition in the least. Passing on from house to house I saw many other children five and six years old in the same condition. It was very seldom that I saw children anything like decently dressed. If they wore clothing it was only one garment, and this so black and greasy that it did not resemble cloth. As a rule, the colored people all through this section are very poor and ignorant, but the one encouraging thing about it is that they see their weakness and are desirous of improving. The teachers in this part of Alabama have had few advantages, many of them having never attended school themselves. They know nothing of the improved methods of teaching. They hail with gladness, the Normal School, and most of them will be among its students. If there is any place in the world where a good Normal School is needed, it is right here. What an influence for good, first on the teachers, and from them on the children and parents.

I opened school last week. At present I have over forty students— anxious and earnest young men and women. I expect quite an increase in September and October. The school is taught, at present, in one of the colored churches, which they kindly let us have for that purpose. This building is not very well suited to school purposes, and we hope to be able to move to a more commodious place in a short time. The place referred to is on a beautiful and conveniently located farm of one hundred acres, which we have contracted to buy for $500. The state pays for tuition. The farm I hope to pay for by my own exertions and the help of others here. As a rule, the colored people in the South are not and will not be able for years to board their children in school at ten or twelve dollars per month, hence my object is, as soon as possible, to get the school on a labor basis, so that earnest students can help themselves and at the same time learn the true dignity of labor. An institution for the education of colored youths can be but a partial success without a boarding department. In it they can be taught those correct habits which they fail to get at home. Without this part of the training they go out into the world with untrained intellects and their morals and bodies neglected. After the land is paid for, we hope to get a boarding department on foot as soon as possible.

The good-will manifested towards the school by both white and colored is a great encouragement to me to push the work forward. I have had many kind words of encouragement from the whites, and have been well treated by them in every way. The trustees seem to be exceptional men. Whether I have met the colored people in their churches, societies or homes, I have received their hearty co-operation and a "God bless you." Even the colored preachers seem to be highly in favor of the work, and one of the pastors here, fifty years old, is one of my students . . .[8]

BOOKER T. WASHINGTON

Editor Southern Workman: Please allow me through your paper to express my heart felt thanks to the "vacation" students of Hampton for their noble efforts in behalf of the Tuskegee Normal School.

We were all no little surprised and gratified when we received a letter a few days ago, from Mr. [Morgan] M. Snowden, stating that the students had raised, through an entertainment $60 or $75 to help us in the purchase of our farm.

To all who in any way aided in raising the money, the teachers at this school join me in words of praise and thankfulness.

With this generous gift and the aid of other friends, we are already nearly able to return the $200 borrowed to make our first payment. We have directed nearly all our efforts towards paying for the land, because this will give us a sure foundation on which to work.

That the colored people begin to help each other, is the best evidence of their progress. I was about to say that every dollar that we can get out of the colored people themselves, for educational purposes is worth two coming from elsewhere.

There is hope for an individual or a race when they begin to look outside of themselves.

In my last letter I reported that the school opened with thirty students. Now we have an enrollment of sixty.

We have made some efforts to interest the people in the different counties, in education. Many of the teachers and others begin to see their deficiencies and new students come in every week.

The people in this state have suffered not so much from the failure of the state to support the free schools, but from incompetent teachers. We hope within a few months to make our humble efforts here felt in the surrounding counties. Of course we have to labor under many disadvantages, not having apparatus, school furniture and suitable buildings. This ought not to be so, for when teachers come here thirsty for knowledge and with only money enough to remain in school a few months, we ought to be able to give them the best advantages at once. Some of these wants are being supplied by friends and we hope in a few months to double the advantages of the school. There is much that is encouraging in the work. The students are anxious to improve and they pin themselves down to study without coercion.[9]

As Washington was developing his reputation and that of Tuskegee, Du Bois was busy being a teenager. He attended an integrated high school, and although he experienced racism as a boy, he was also surrounded by a supportive group of adults in his home, school, and church—many of them white— that black southerners simply did not have. When he decided to attend Fisk University, for example, members of his church took a collection to help defray part of the cost of his tuition.[10]

W.E.B. DU BOIS

New Bedford July 21, 1883.

Dear Mam, I arrived here safely friday after noon [to visit his paternal grandfather, Alexander Du Bois]. It was just noon when I got to Hartford. After eating my lunch & buying my ticket I went up to the capitol which is but a little ways to the depot. The grounds are laid out beautifully and the building is magnificent. It consists of a main part and two wings. The main part is surmounted by a tower & dome, which, by the way, is gilded, & upon this is a bronzed statue. As you go in the main entrance the first thing you see is a very large statue of a woman holding a wreath. On either side in cabinets are the different flags, the floor is of colored marble. The staircases are also of marble, if here is a book to write your names there & of course my illustrious name is there. I looked into the chamber of the House of representatives. It is very nice. The chairs & desks are arranged in a semicircle. The chairmans seat is in the middle. In front are seats for the clerks & at the side for reporters, there is an elevator which anybody can go up & down in when they wish to. The whole building is frescoed splendidly. On the outside there are niches for statues. There is a picture gallery in the state library room. I cannot tell you 1/2 what I saw there. I did not go up in dome fearing that the train would leave me. When I came down to the depot & finding that I had a little time left I took a walk up a street near by. When I got back to the depot the train was gone, & news agent told me there was no other to providence that afternoon, imagine my situation! At last however I found out there was another train out on another road, so I had to sell my ticket which I paid $2.70 for, for $1.50 because I had my baggage checked on it & baggage had gone by the other train. At last I was on the way to providence. The railroad runs down parelal with the Connecticut river & the scenery is beautiful. I saw two or three steamers. After we had got to the coast I changed cars & took the shore line. There the scenery was magnificent the steamers, sailboat, the beautiful seaside resorts &c. I reached providence about 8 pm. & there was no one to meet me, sarah thinking that I would not come because I did not come on the other train I asked a policeman & he directed me to her residence. Providence is a very nice city & I like it very much.

I went around a good deal what little time I was there.

Sarah has a very nice little cottage. I saw the soldiers monument & I will tell you about it when I come. I started on the 8 a.m. train for n.b. & arrive there about 11 a.m. There was no one to meet me & I was mad, very mad. in fact if I could got hold of some one I should have hurt them, but I didn't, by inquiries I found the house which is about half a mile from the depot. The house is white with green blinds & the yard is full of flower gardens. Grandma is about my color & taller than I thought. I like her very much. Grandpa is short & rather thick set. I like him better than I thought I would. He say very little but speaks civily when I say anything to him. Grandma says by and bye he'll talk more I like it very much here & am having a nice time.

Last night Grandma & I took a walk up street & visited some of her friends. I have been walking out this afternoon. We are going on a picnic to onset point next week & down to Martha's Vineyard & to hear the Miss Davis the elocutionist &c. I have not been to Mr. Freedom's yet but will go next week. Tell Jennie not to forget the courier. Tell Grace I would like to slap her once I suppose you are very lonesome. I felt a little home sick this afternoon. Will write soon, with love to all, good by

Your son,
W E Du Bois.[11]

W.E.B. DU BOIS

29 October, 1887

Dear Sir: I am a Negro, a student of Fisk University. I shall receive the degree of A.B. from this institution next June at the age of 20. I wish to pursue at Harvard a course of study for the degree of Ph.D. in Political Science after graduation. I am poor and if I should enter your college next year would probably not be able to raise more [than] $100 or $150. If I should teach a year and then enter I could earn enough to pay my expenses for a year. I wish your advice as to what I had better do. You can see by the catalogue I shall send herewith what our course of instruction is here. I can furnish satisfactory certificates of character and scholarship from the President and Professors of Fisk, and from Western Massachusetts where I was born, and graduated from the public schools. I am also Editor of the Fisk Herald, a copy of which I send. As I said I wish your advice as to whether I had better teach a year or two or come immediately after graduation. I expect to take the special field of Political Economy.

I am, Sir,
Yours,
W.E.B. Du Bois[12]

BOOKER T. WASHINGTON

Lincoln University, Pa., Apr. 26, 1888

. . . It has occurred to me that a few minutes spent in considering the resources of that rich and beautiful country—the South—"Where every prospect pleases, and only man is vile," would not be spent in vain. I come to speak to you of a section of country that has been purchased and paid for ten times over by the sweat and blood of our forefathers. Their two hundred and fifty years of forced and unrequited toil, secured for us an inheritance which at no late day we are going to occupy and enjoy as independent and intelligent citizens.

Perhaps the most important considerations for a successful career are land, men and climate. I would put as the condition of all conditions for success in life, whether it relate to the individual or the race, ownership in the soil—cleavage to mother Earth.

Embracing what are commonly known as the Southern States, we have 877,000 square miles of land that is as well adapted to the sustenance of man as the same sized section found anywhere on the globe. An eminent economist has said that thirty counties in Mississippi properly cultivated could be made to produce last year's cotton crop of 1,200,000 bales. The statement will apply with equal force to other Southern States and to other products.

Can land be secured? Never, I believe, in the history of any state could such valuable property be purchased for so little money as at present in Alabama and other Southern States.

Landed estates which in Antebellum days could not be purchased for $25 per acre can now be had for $4.

Land owners who 20 years ago would not part with their land to the Negro partly because of prejudice and partly because the owners thought that their financial salvation lay in holding on to their lands, are now ready and anxious to sell to black or white, and often it is the old family homestead that has been sacred, where generations of slaveholders have been born and reared that is offered for sale. I do not rejoice at the misfortune of the southern white man, for he is my brother, but I do feel it a duty to urge that his extremity is our opportunity to buy the foundation for a high civilization that is frought with the most favorable conditions.

If the sins of the fathers are visited upon the children to the third and fourth generations, who knows, but what God in His divine goodness means through the enslavers improvidence to repay the enslaved that of which he has been robbed . . .

If the Vanderbilts, Girards, Peabodys, Peter Coopers started out poverty-stricken with untrained minds and in competition with the shrewd and energetic yankee amassed fortunes what superior opportunities open up before our young men who begin life with a college trained mind and in a locality where competition is at its minimum?

To the rank and file of our aspiring youth seeking an opening in life, to me but two alternatives present themselves as matters now stand— to live a menial in the north or a semi-freeman in the South.

This brings us face to face with Northern competition and Southern prejudice and between them I have no hesitancy in saying that the

Negro can find his way to the front sooner through Southern prejudice than through Northern competition. The one decreases, the other increases.

To the really brave, earnest, energetic, ambitious, christian young man the obstacles presented, it seems to me, by prejudice form an apology for not entering this field so weak, so unreasonable as not to merit serious consideration, yet prejudice does keep so large and valuable a class of those who are mentally and morally strong from that field that the question must be considered.

The most effective ammunition with which to fight prejudice is men—men such as are before me—men who in every act, word and thought give the lie to the assertion of his enemies North and South that the Negro is the inferior of the white man.

In advocating the South as a field for a career, I have no sympathy with those who would stoop to sacrifice manhood to satisfy unreasonable whims of the South, but would advise you to be there as here a man—every inch a man, and demand with reasonable patience, with proper judgement and in lawful manner every right that God and the constitution have vouchsafed to us as American citizens. I come to you from a seven years' residence in the "Black Belt" of Alabama—the heart of the South—and I speak as one who has given his strength without reserve to the amelioration of the condition of his race and to a consideration on all sides and under all circumstances of the problems that have grown out of his newly acquired citizenship. I do not wish to create the impression that all these problems have been solved yet, and that everything is just right in the South, but out of my own honest opinion that the rate at which prejudice is dying out is so rapid as to justify the conclusion that the Negro will in a quarter of a century enjoy in Alabama every right that he now does in Pennsylvania, a rate such as to furnish occasion for universal gratitude and thanksgiving to Him who controls the destinies of races. As compared with the great question of the race's acquiring education, character and property the question of prejudice, it seems to me, dwindles into insignificance . . .

Just so sure as the rays of the sun dispel the frost of winter, so sure will Brains and Property and Character conquer prejudice; just so sure as right in all ages and among all races has conquered wrong, so sure will the time come and at no distant day, when the Negro South shall be triumphant over the last lingering vestige of prejudice. To believe otherwise is to deny the existence of Him who rewards virtue and condemns vice.

It is encouraging to note that there is already an entire absence of hostile feeling against business enterprises of blacks, South. A Negro merchant having a quality of goods that is in demand receives the patronage of both races. This applies in almost all branches of business.

A young man with energy, ambition and foresight can get successfully launched into business there on a capital that would not enable him to pay the first month's rent in a Northern city.

In any business enterprise requiring push, snap, tact, and continual and close attention, the wide awake Negro has an immense advantage, for the Southern white man evades as a rule any occupation that requires early rising or late retiring that removes him very far from a shade tree or the sunless side of a house.

For three hundred years the North has been adding value to value, accumulating wealth and experience in every direction and when we, the freemen of a day, enter into competition with this it is not hard to say who will win and who will lose.

In entering the South for a career, you have the advantage of having a large number of our own kith and kin for whom to work, on whom to depend for support and with whom to cooperate. This is an advantage that perhaps outweighs all others. Notwithstanding many assertions to the contrary, I glean from my experience that the Negro is as loyal to faithful and intelligent leadership, is as ready to cooperate, to stand shoulder to shoulder for the common good as any race with no more experience in self government, whose history we know . . .

In pointing you to this field, I do not do so as one who believes that the Negro must rise at the expense of the Southern white man, for whatever his wrongs to us, he is our neighbor and the divine commandment "Love thy neighbor as thyself" is broad enough to include him with all his shortcomings, and wherever by act or word we can benefit him let us not with-hold our help, but at the same time and under all circumstances show him that we know our rights and that we dare maintain them . . .

As to the lines of work, let me be more specific. If you desire school work it seems enough to say that 73% of the colored people south can not read or write. There is a school population of 2,000,000 but not more than 45% of this number now attend school. There are between 16 and 17 thousand school teachers, but not more than 25% are in any degree competent. We have in the South 99 Normal Schools, academies, and 18 so-called colleges and universities, and 13 schools of law, theology and medicine; hence as regards our higher institutions, the demand is not for an increase in number but in efficiency. They need developing upward and downward . . .

But perhaps the most lucrative career is in the line of the professions. What are the chances and opportunities in this field? Let Alabama serve as an example in answering this question. There are in the state 600,000 Negroes. To do the legal business of this number and stand between them and injustice there are but four colored lawyers in the whole state and some of these are far from being brilliant luminaries. Go into any community, examine the deeds (where there are any) of the colored property owners and you will find them of the most defective character, carelessly written by unprincipled lawyers with nothing in view but a fee. Having occasion a short time ago to buy some land from a colored man, I was told by him that a certain white man had a mortgage on it which would have to be paid but on investigating, I found that instead of a mortgage the white man held a deed in fee simple for the land and the hard working Negro had not the scratch of a pen to show his right of possession. Go, if you please, into the jails and penitentiaries and you will find colored men, women, and even boys and girls of tender age serving sentences for crimes of which they have been illegally convicted. Only a few days ago, a colored boy of 15 was found in one of the convict camps of Alabama wearing a chain that had not been taken off his limbs night or day for months and it was so heavy that his legs had swollen twice their natural size. On the same day that this discovery was made the boy had been mercilessly whipped because he did not "jump around fast enough." Often these miserable creatures are sentenced for 12 months but are retained for 15 or 18 months. A perfectly innocent colored man in Alabama was not long ago snatched up in the road and without legal process was taken into Georgia and thrust into a convict camp and kept there six months before opportunity presented itself to inform his friends. I could spend much time in citing similar cases. The white lawyer who will take an interest in his colored client's case farther than to secure his fee is the exception. With such opportunities for work presenting themselves, can those of you who have talent in this direction refrain from going into the South and devoting your lives to seeing that the Negro has justice before the courts? Do this not alone for the financial gain (for there is money to be made by it) but for the real good you can do. In such work you can render acceptable worship to God and high service to man.

Retaining Alabama as an example with 600,000 colored inhabitants there are but six colored physicians in the state. It is my opinion that as a rule the colored physicians have achieved more signal success than any other professional colored men. Patients and money are not long in coming to the dutiful and competent physician. One hundred colored physicians can today earn an independent living in Alabama . . .

As to preachers, the numbers to be found in the South would seem to indicate that we are not in very great need. One church near Tuskegee has a total membership of 200 and 18 of them are said to be preachers. But the character of many of these preachers may be illustrated by what is told of one. It is said that while he was at work in a cotton field in the middle of July he suddenly stopped, looked up toward heaven and exclaimed, "O, Lord, de work is so hard, de cotton is so grassy, and de sun am so hot, I believe dis darkey am called to preach . . ." The call for ministers with trained heart and intellect is pressing and loud.

As the colored population grows larger and more wealthy and intelligent a higher and better class of race literature will be in demand. I have no hesitancy in asserting that the time is not far distant when colored men can devote their lives to literature in the South and receive support and encouragement from the race; that the time will come when literature produced by colored men and of the widest scope—from the daily newspaper to the most select and best edited quarterly reviews—will be in paying demand. But it would be a mistake to attempt to confine our young men to the school room or to professional careers—your services are in demand as planters, as merchants, as operators of mines, as manufacturers and as mechanics. The time has come when the Negro should be in a higher sense a producer as well as a consumer, and where can a field more inviting be found? . . .

Wherever the stars and stripes float, there the sentiment that to be governed implies the right to govern, is cherished and fostered, and this sentiment, like Banquo's ghost, will not down.

I have said that at the close of this century the race will in all probability number twelve millions—twelve million souls,

> "With freedom's soil beneath
>   their feet and
> Freedom's banner waving
>   over them."

Would you tell me that twelve million free people daily growing in wealth, experience and intelligence will long submit to oppression, political disfranchisement and taxation without representation? Will this be submitted to when any considerable number of the masses are intelligent, when schools and colleges exist on every hand, when high-minded, educated and patriotic leaders are in every town and hamlet? No gentlemen, a thousand times—no! Might as well attempt to stop the mighty Mississippi in its onward march to the sea, or to prevent the warmth and moisture of spring from sending forth the flower and fruit of summer . . .[13]

BOOKER T. WASHINGTON

A Stable as a Civilizer

The Tuskegee Normal and Industrial School, at Tuskegee, Alabama, of which Booker T. Washington is principal, has in process of erection a stable which, when completed, will be the largest and most complete in the State of Alabama.

There will also be ample room for storing away feed and sheltering wagons, etc . . .

The barn can be completed for $1,500 cash. It is at present half completed, all the work having been done by the students, and they will do all the work necessary to finish the building; but there are certain cash outlays in the way of material that will amount to $1,500, and these the school is compelled to ask of its friends. This barn will be not only a great means of good to students connected with the school, but a constant teacher for the surrounding country.[14]

As Washington was clearly establishing himself as a leader in the world of black education and the black southern situation more broadly, Du Bois was completing his education. After graduating from Fisk in 1888, he moved on to Harvard, which accepted the graduate as a third-year junior. When he graduated two years later, he would be featured as one of six commencement speakers. His speech would be a study of the "moral obtuseness and refined brutality" of the South, a foreshadowing of his later evaluation of the region.

W.E.B. DU BOIS

Jefferson Davis as a Representative of Civilization

Jefferson Davis was a typical Teutonic hero; the history of civilization during the last millennium has been the development of the idea of the Strong Man of which he was the embodiment. The Anglo-Saxon loves a soldier—Jefferson Davis was an Anglo-Saxon, Jefferson Davis was a soldier. There was not a phase in that familiarly strange life that would not have graced a mediaeval romance: from the fiery and impetuous young lieutenant who stole as his bride the daughter of a ruler-elect of the land, to the cool and ambitious politician in the Senate hall. So boldly and surely did that cadaverous figure with the thin nervous lips and flashing eye, write the first line of the new page of American history, that the historian of the future must ever see back of the War of Secession, the strong arm of one imperious man, who defied disease, trampled on precedent, would not be defeated, and never surrendered. A soldier and a lover, a statesman and a ruler; passionate, ambitious and indomitable; bold reckless guardian of a people's All—judged by the whole standard of Teutonic civilization, there is something noble in the figure of Jefferson Davis; and judged by every canon of human justice, there is something fundamentally incomplete about that standard.

I wish to consider not the man, but the type of civilization which his life represented: its foundation is the idea of the Strong Man—Individualism coupled with the rule of might—and it is this idea that has made the logic of even modern history, the cool logic of the Club. It made a naturally brave and generous man, Jefferson Davis—now advancing civilization by murdering Indians, now hero of a national disgrace called by courtesy, the Mexican War, and finally, as the crowning absurdity, the peculiar champion of a people fighting to be free in order that another people should not be free. Whenever this idea has for a moment escaped from the individual realm, it has found an even more secure foothold in the policy and philosophy of the State. The Strong Man and his mighty Right Arm have become the Strong Nation with its armies. Under whatever guise, however a Jefferson Davis may appear, as man, as race, or as nation, his life can only logically mean this: the advance of a part of the world at the expence of the whole: the overweening sense of the I and the consequent forgetting of the Thou. It has thus happened, that advance in civilization has always been handicapped by shortsighted national selfishness. The vital principle of division of labor has been stifled not only in industry, but also in civilization, so as to render it well nigh impossible for a new race to introduce a new idea into the world except by means of the cudgel. To say that a nation is in the way of civilization is a contradiction in terms, and a system of human culture whose principle is the rise of one race on the ruins of another is a farce and a lie. Yet this is the type of civilization which Jefferson Davis represented: it represents a field for stalwart manhood and heroic character, and at the same time for moral obtuseness and refined brutality. These striking contradictions of character always arise when a people seemingly become convinced that the object of the world is not civilization, but Teutonic civilization. Such a type is not wholly evil or fruitless: the world has needed and will need its Jefferson Davises; but such a type is incomplete and never can serve its best purpose until checked by its complementary ideas. Whence shall these come?

To the most casual observer, it must have occurred that the Rod of Empire has in these days, turned towards the South. In every Southern country, however, destined to play a future part in the world—in Southern North America, South America, Australia, and Africa—a new nation has a more or less firm foothold. This circumstance has, however, attracted but incidental notice, hitherto; for wherever the Negro people have touched civilization their rise has been singularly unromantic and unscientific. Through the glamour of history, the rise of a nation has ever been typified by the Strong Man crushing out an effete civilization. That brutality buried aught else beside Rome when it descended golden haired and drunk from the blue north has scarcely entered human imagination. Not as the muscular warrior came the Negro, but as the cringing slave. The Teutonic met civilization and crushed it—the Negro met civilization and was crushed by it. The one was the hero the world has ever worshipped, who gained unthought of triumphs and made unthought of mistakes; the other was the personification of dogged patience bending to the inevitable, and waiting. In the history of this people, we seek in vain the elements of Teutonic deification of Self, and Roman brute force, but we do find an idea of submission apart from cowardice, laziness, or stupidity, such as the world never saw before. This is the race which by its very presence must play a part in the world of tomorrow; and this is the race whose rise, I contend, has practically illustrated an idea which is at once the check and complement of the Teutonic Strong Man. It is the doctrine of the Submissive Man—given to the world by strange coincidence, by the race of whose rights, Jefferson Davis had not heard.

What then is the change made in the conception of civilization, by adding to the idea of the Strong Man, that of the Submissive Man? It is this: the submission of the strength of the Strong to the advance of all—not in mere aimless sacrifice, but recognizing the fact that, "To no one type of mind is it given to discern the totality of Truth," that civilization cannot afford to lose the contribution of the very least of nations for its full development: that not only the assertion of the I, but also to the submission to the Thou is the highest Individualism . . .[15]

W.E.B. DU BOIS

Cambridge, November 4, 1890

Dear Sir [Rutherford B. Hayes]:

The following clipping from the Boston Herald of Nov. 2nd, has come to my notice:

Negroes in the South

Ex-President Hayes Says Their Chief and Almost Only Gift Is Oratory Baltimore, Md., Nov. 1,1890. Ex-President Hayes said today to the students of Johns Hopkins University, on the subject of negro education in the South:

> "If there is any young colored man in the South whom we find to have a talent for art or literature, or any especial aptitude for study, we are willing to give him money from the education funds to send him to Europe or to give him an advanced education, but hitherto their chief and almost only gift has been that of oratory.
>
> "What you find as historical students, as to their condition in the South, especially in the black belt, is surely not encouraging. They are seen most favorably in what is called the Virginia land district of Ohio. This tract of land, between the Scioto, Little Miami and Ohio rivers, was granted by the state of Virginia to its officers in the revolutionary war, many of whom settled there with their slaves. Most of these were freed, and have increased rapidly with a corresponding increase in education. A careful examination of that region will show a considerable advance in the good qualities of civilization, and proper appreciation of citizenship.
>
> "But I do not despair of the other negroes, but am rather hopeful of their being uplifted in the future."

If this be a true report of your words, I wish to lay my case before you.

I am a Negro, twenty-three years of age next February, (23rd), and a graduate of Fisk University, '88. After leaving there I came to Harvard University and entering the Junior class graduated in 1890. This year I have entered the graduate School and am a candidate for the degrees of A.M. and Ph.D. in Political Science. I have so far gained my education by teaching in the South, giving small lectures in the North, working in Hotels, laundries, &c, and by various scholarships and the charity of friends. I have no money or property myself and am an orphan. My particular field in Political Science is the History of African Slavery from the economic and social stand point. The faculty of Harvard College have seen fit to recognize whatever ability I have by appointing me to Price Greenleaf aid, a Mathews Scholarship and finally for the year 1890–90 [sic] to a fellowship . . .[16]

BOOKER T. WASHINGTON

Few agencies for the uplifting of the colored people have accomplished more good than the negro newspapers. These papers have served to create race confidence, in that they have taught the colored people that the colored man could manage a business requiring the outlay of money, brains and push that a newspaper enterprise demands. The colored editors have rendered most valuable service to the cause of education by constantly stimulating and encouraging our people to educate themselves and their children.

The papers have served as educators to the white race, in matters that pertain to the progress of the negro. The white press readily sees our dark side, but is not disposed, as a rule, to go far out of its way to let the world know of the negro's advancement.

The work of the colored newspapers has thus far been one of love and self-sacrifice, few if any of them paying in dollars and cents; but there has been evident growth, both in the make-up of the papers and in the paid circulation, and I apprehend that the day is not far distant when they will bring in an encouraging revenue. Already Mr. B.T. Harvey is publishing in Columbus, Ga., a colored daily, and he seems to be supported in his efforts to an encouraging degree.[17]

W.E.B. DU BOIS

Cambridge, April 19, 1891 [dated 1890]

Dear Sir [Rutherford B. Hayes]:

You will have received by the time this reaches you, I think, testimonials from President Eliot, Prof. Shaler, Prof. Hart, and Prof. Peabody, of Harvard.

I will give you a brief statement of my case.

I was born in Great Barrington, Berkshire County, Mass., on the 23rd Feb. 1868. My grandparents, on my mother's side, were slaves among the Dutch in New York, on my father's side, among the French in the West Indies. I was educated in the public schools of the town; I supported my self and partially supported my mother during my course thro' the High school (father having died when I was quite young) graduating there in June 1884. I went South to Fisk University in Nashville Tenn. on the recommendation of Rev. C.C. Painter of the Indian Bureau (to whom I am well known) in September 1885. Here I entered the Sophomore class and graduated in June 1888. I was supported while there by the contribution of my own Sunday-school in Gt. B. & three others, and by teaching summer schools in the country. In the fall of '88 I secured a Price Greenleaf aid at Harvard and entered the junior class. I supported myself by lectures, loans and prizes. The next year I rec'd a Matthews Scholarship and another prize which with readings delivered during the summer paid my way. I received my degree here in '90 (A.B., *cum laude*), being one of the Commencement speakers. I then entered the Graduate school to study social science, and was appointed to the Bromfield Rogers Memorial Fellowship. I expect to spend next year here at the same work, after which I wish to spend a couple of years in study in Europe on the same subject.

I am in good physical condition as may be ascertained by the records of the Harvard gymnasium.

I hereby respectfully apply to the board for a fellowship which will enable me to study in Europe one or two years.

Respectfully yours,
W.E.B. Du Bois

P.S. I omitted stating that I am, in blood, about one half or more Negro, and the rest French and Dutch.[18]

BOOKER T. WASHINGTON

To a young man just emerging from slavery with all its demoralizing environments, and entering into the pure, strong, active and unselfish influence of General Armstrong's personality as it was my privilege, with hundreds of others, to do, there came as if by miracle all at once, a new meaning to the possibilities and the object of life, that is hard for most in this audience to understand or appreciate. So, aside from our sense of obligation to General Armstrong for his long years of work for our race, there is a deep and tender love in our hearts for the man himself; a nearness to him, and confidence in him that makes those of us who have been his students not only love but worship him. While at work in the far South for the elevation of our race, when we have grown discouraged at the many difficulties by which we were surrounded, it has been the mental picture of Gen. Armstrong, who knew no discouragement, that has given us strength to go on and conquer. When we have grown selfish and disposed to live for ourselves, the vision of General Armstrong, who never seemed to know aught but to live and do for others, has come and made us ashamed of our selfishness, and when we have been inclined to grow indifferent and inactive, the form of General Armstrong who never seemed to rest night or day, winter or summer, has come before us and given new zeal and new activity.

It has been my privilege while a student at Hampton, as well as in later life, to see something of the way in which General Armstrong has actually worn away his life, not in his cause nor Hampton's cause but for the Nation's cause—your cause. If time permitted I could tell you how in the early days of Hampton when the Institution was sorely pressed for means I have seen him arrive at home at 4 o'clock in the morning from a long Northern tour, begging for funds, speaking at meetings night after night, and filling his days with going from door to door, from office to office. And how, without even going to his room, I have seen him go to his office and plunge into his work of the day while students and teachers were yet in bed.

Future years will show more clearly than these the value of General Armstrong's work. His central idea has been from the first that the salvation of the negro and of the South was in industrial development and in cementing, not tearing asunder the friendships of the blacks and whites. I can remember how, not many years ago, the wisdom of Gen. Armstrong's plan of industrial education found many doubters at the North and many opposers at the South among the most prominent colored men. But now, as the results begin to manifest themselves, how happily has all this changed? What would have been the result supposing that the education of the negro had gone on without industrial training? Without my words you understand better than I that the effect of mental development is to increase one's wants, & sensitiveness to bring about an unrest. General Armstrong saw that there would be danger to the peace of the whole South unless while his wants were being increased by mental training, industrial training at the same time increased his capacity to supply those increased wants.

He saw too that the negro must be prepared to live side by side of his white brother of the South, and that industrial education would create the desire for ownership in land and the ability to develop industries that would make the negro a producer as well as a consumer— industries that would make the white man dependent on the black man for something instead of all the dependence being on the other side.

He saw as this development went on that it would bring about, as it is doing, an interdependence of the races; that their material and business interests in those Southern communities would become so linked together, so interlaced, that the interests of the two races would be identical, and that instead of strife there would come peace and union.

He also saw that it was through such development, such union, that we must finally look for the solution of the political and social troubles that are so far from being settled in the South; and that industrial education would, in the near future, destroy the idea of labor being degrading that has held back and retarded like a nightmare, the progress of both races in the South, and would soon make them see in labor a privilege and blessing instead of a curse.

From the first, in this matter of education at the South, we have had your help and the struggles of the colored people themselves. We are now gradually gaining one other element of strength, I mean the interest and co-operation of the best class of Southern white people. As Hampton, Tuskegee, and other Institutions have been able year after year to present to Southern white people object lessons showing the value of an educated colored man, letting them see that an educated man was a help instead of a hindrance to the progress of the South, and as they have seen year after year, these educated young men and women revolutionize and regenerate whole communities, giving them ownership in homes instead of the rented one room log cabin, and bank account instead of a debt; and six or eight months school taught in a neat frame schoolhouse instead of three months taught in a wreck of a log cabin; a moral stamina instead of habits of moral crookedness and weakness. As the whites have seen this they are changing their feelings and actions towards the education of the Negro.

A few weeks ago as I sat in the office of the Superintendant of education in the State of Alabama, who but yesterday owned scores of black men and women, he said "Mr. Washington, I have grown to this point, if there is any difference in my heart, in my desire to help in the education of the two races, I do not know where to find it." Legal slavery is dead, but there is a mental, moral, and industrial slavery in the South that is not dead, and will not be for years to come. What was 250 years being done cannot be undone in 25 or 30. It seems to me that the vital question that centres in this meeting is: Shall the work and influence of Hampton go on? Hampton is the heart that is sending a constant stream of life-giving blood into every State and County in the South. Shall it flow on? That the American nation might see the value and power of this work, Gen. Armstrong has practically given his life, and now the question that comes to each of us with renewed emphasis as that grand hero lies prostrated, is: What will we give of our service, of our substance, that his work may be continued and perpetuated?[19]

Du Bois's application to the Slater Fund of Rutherford B. Hayes was successful, allowing him to spend much of his time in graduate school studying

in Germany, before returning to the United States in the summer of 1894.
Based at the University of Berlin, Du Bois was able to travel the continent and
study under some of the leading social scientists in the world, including econ-
omists like Gustav von Schmoller and Adolph Wagner.[20]

W.E.B. DU BOIS

Eisenach, 29 Sept. 1892

To the Congregational Sunday-School:

I venture to send you a few words about the German town in which I have been spending the summer, because it is so intimately connected with the life of Martin Luther whom we all reverence. In the middle of Germany, on the north west edge of the famous Thuringian forest stands the town of Eisenach, one of the most beautiful spots of a beautiful region. I shall not attempt to describe the natural beauty of the place, first because I know I could not do it justice, and secondly because the memory of my own blue Berkshire hills tells me that the task would be an unnecessary one. It is however of the rich legacy of history and legend which belongs to these hills that I wish to speak. It is ever a strange experience for an American to walk for the first time in a land, the natural beauty of which is surrounded and enhanced by the thought, legends, and deeds of a thousand years. Such is the case here, and the deeds are all the more interesting because they furthered that freedom of conscience and deeper religion which is the heritage of Gt. Barrington [Great Barrington, Massachusetts, Du Bois's hometown] and of the world. Let us suppose the hills were thrown in somewhat wilder confusion, our shingles turned into red tiles, and our streets crooked a bit; so you could imagine yourselves in Eisenach; now we can take a walk through the old town treading on centuries of footsteps and breathing air full of ancient whispers. Here on the Luther place is the house where Martin Luther, the first Protestant, lived, while he attended school in Eisenach. His father and mother dwelt over the hills yonder to the west, in Mohra—poor ordinary peasants, too poor to keep the boy in school. So Frau Vroula Cotta gave a place at her table and here, in the same decade in which Columbus discovered America, lived the great boy, in this queer old house with its projecting stories and little windows. A little farther on, in the great square market-place, he went to school under the shadow of a huge, unsightly Gothic church, which for half a thousand years has stood there. I attended service here last Sunday: it is a queer place with stiff old pews, great pillars, galleries, ancient gravestones, and an old high gilded pulpit. As I heard the grey-haired preacher in the pulpit, I remembered that 371 years ago, Luther himself had preached in the self-same pulpit, and under the same cherub-bedecked covering. It was on his return from the Diet of Worms in 1521, where, before the Emperor Charles V, and the assembled princes and prelates of Europe he had defended liberty of conscience. Excommunicated by the church and forbidden to preach, he nevertheless defied the edict of the Emperor and preached in this church, and then was spirited away by his friends and for nearly a year hidden from his persecutors—so costly was it to be brave. And where was he hidden? Let us see; imagining still that Gt. Barrington is Eisenach, let us take our stand in the market-place in front of the Town Hall. Look now upon East Mountain, and in place of East Rock, imagine the height crowned by a rambling old castle with great walls, buildings and towers. It is the castle Wartburg, and is very old; when Washington was President it was old; when your great-great-grandfathers stole my great-great grandfather and brought him a slave to America, it was old; when Wycliffe translated the Bible, it was old—indeed, it was at the time William the Conqueror invaded England that Ludwig the Springer, a warrior, saw this height and saving: "Wart Berg! Du sollst mir ein Burg sein" (Wait, mountain! You shall be my fortress), he forthwith builded this castle. Thus for 825 years has it guarded the land, and here Luther found asylum in 1521 when the rest of Christendom was closed against him. Protestantism could have had no more significant cradle . . .

Sincerely yours,
W.E.B. Du Bois[21]

ALABAMA LEGISLATURE

To incorporate the Tuskegee Normal and Industrial Institute and amend an act to amend an act to establish a normal school for colored teachers at Tuskegee, approved Feb. 16, 1883.

Section 1. *Be it enacted by the General Assembly of Alabama*, That an act to amend an act to establish a normal school for colored teachers at Tuskegee, approved February 16th, 1883, be amended so as to read as follows . . .

Sec. 2. *Be it further enacted*, That the purposes of said Tuskegee Normal and Industrial Institute shall be as follows: For the instruction of colored teachers and youths in the various common academic and collegiate branches, the best methods of teaching the same, and the best methods of theoretical and practical industry, in their applications to agriculture and mechanic arts; and for the carrying out of these purposes, said trustees shall have the power to establish and provide for the support of any departments or schools in said institution, and to control the operations of the same, to grant such diplomas and confer such degrees as are customary in other colleges of like grade, to appoint such officers for presiding over and transacting the business of this body as may be necessary and prescribe their duties and obligations, to appoint the time and place for their meetings, to determine their own tenure of office, and to adopt such rules, regulations and bylaws, not contrary to the laws of this state or the United States, as they may deem necessary for the good government of the said Tuskegee Normal and Industrial Institute. The said institute shall not be begun nor continued with a less number than twenty-five (25), nor be taught for a period less than nine (9) months of each year. Pupils from this state shall be admitted free of tuition, on giving an obligation in writing to teach for two years in the public schools of this state after they become qualified . . .

Sec. 6. *Be it further enacted*, That there is hereby appropriated, out of the general school revenue set apart for the education of colored children, the sum of three thousand ($3,000) dollars annually for the maintenance and support of said school, and the apportionment of the general fund for colored children shall be made to the several counties of this state, after the deduction of the sum herein appropriated; the said appropriation shall be under the control of the commissioners hereinafter provided for, and shall be applied in such manner as they deem best to carry out the purpose of this act, and said commissioners shall be members of said board of trustees with the same rights and powers as the other trustees.

Sec. 7. *Be it further enacted*, That the school shall be under the direction and control of a board of three (3) commissioners, which shall consist of the following persons, to-wit: George W. Campbell, S Q Hale, and Lewis Adams, who shall select one of their members as chairman of the board, and shall have power to fill any vacancy that may occur in the board . . . The commissioners shall make an annual written report to the superintendent of education of the condition and progress of the school, the teachers that have been employed, the number of pupils that have been in attendance, the manner in which the appropriation has been expended, the branches that have been taught, and such other facts relating to the school that may be of public interest and importance . . .

Approved December 13, 1892.[22]

BOOKER T. WASHINGTON

Taking Advantage of our Disadvantages

Four years ago a Jew, only a few months from Europe, passed through the town of Tuskegee, Ala., on foot, with all his earthly possessions in a cheap and much-worn satchel which was swung across his shoulder. This Jew, by accident, stopped over night, sixteen miles from Tuskegee, at a common country settlement in the midst of the cotton-raising district. Looking about the next morning with an eye to business, this Jew soon decided to remain for awhile in this community, and he soon found some one to hire him for a few dollars per month. Soon he began renting land to sub-let to others; then followed the opening of a store, and the development and accumulation have gone on to the extent that to-day this Jew does a business of $50,000 a year. He owns hundreds of acres of land; contracts the cotton from all the plantations in that neighborhood; and there is not a man, woman nor child within five miles who does not pay tribute to this Jew. His note or check is honored at any bank, and his credit with wholesale merchants is almost without limit.

What this Jew has done, the blackest Negro in the United States can do in Alabama. "What," says one, "do you mean to say that a black man in the Black belt of Alabama has the same opportunity for business development as a Jew or a white man?" Yes; this is just what I mean to say. I make this assertion with knowledge not based on hearsay, but upon what I have actually come in contact with during the last twelve years in the heart of the South. Of course the black man, like the Jew or white man, should be careful as to the kind of business he selects, as he, like the white man, can succeed in one branch of business better than in another. When it comes to business, pure and simple, stripped of all sentiment, I am constantly surprised to see how little prejudice is exhibited. There are always those who are ready to take advantage of the ignorant. I am not at all unmindful of the fact that the South is full of those (just as it is true of most parts of our country), who are ready to take advantage of the ignorant and unfortunate of any race.

We have made a mistake, I fear sometimes, in not constantly keeping in sight our advantages. We have had any number of conventions and organizations, whose objects were to redress some grievance. This is right and proper; but with a race as with an individual, it will begin to make progress backward if it is continually dwelling on the dark side; is continually grumbling and finding fault; is continually finding a way not to succeed instead of finding a way to succeed. It requires a man with no special gift in brain power to find fault with an individual, organization or state of things. After all, what we want—and it is what America honors—is the man who can teach his fellows how to overcome obstacles; how to "find a way or make one."

While I write I am not unmindful of the fact that we in the South are surrounded by prejudice, deprived of a share in government, in most cases, and are too often shot down and lynched, and denied our just rights on public carriers. It is my firm conviction that every right of which we are now deprived can be secured through business development, coupled with education and character. Suppose in any town in the South there were ten colored men worth a half million dollars each, how much Negro oppression would be practiced in that town? Suppose in Montgomery, Ala., there were ten colored men whose freight bills amounted to $10,000 a year each. Not one of the competing railroads between Montgomery and New York, would dare thrust one of these colored men into a "jim crow" car. No man, North or South, black or white, is respected until he gets something that some body else wants, something of culture, influence or of material wealth. When two individuals stick close to each other, one has something that the other wants. Two nations or races are good friends in proportion as the one has something by way of trade, the other wants. It is surprising to see how quickly sentiment and prejudice will disappear under the influence of hard cash. No street railway in the South will pay if the patronage of the Negro is withdrawn. If the city street cars discriminate, the Negro stops riding as was the case in Atlanta a few months ago. Seeing that the Negro's nickel is necessary to keep the street railway corporation alive, the same white man who refuses to ride in the same steam railway coach when the Negro is perhaps sitting fifty feet from him, will get out of the steam car and sit right beside the same Negro, though black and dirty he may be; the law of necessity makes this respectable, and the time is not far distant for this law to make it respectable for the white and black man to ride in the same railway coach. My advice to the Negro is: Get dollars! get dollars!! and spend them wisely and effectively.

In a recent speech in Washington, Prof. Hugh Brown used this illustration: A certain ship had been lost at sea for many days. Suddenly a sail was sighted, and when the two vessels came into signaling distance, the unfortunate vessel signaled—"water, water." The answer was signaled back—"cast down your buckets where you are." Again the lost vessel signaled—"we want water; we die of thirst." "Cast down your buckets where you are," was signaled back a third and then a fourth time, and finally the captain of the unfortunate vessel obeyed, and the bucket came up full of pure, fresh, sparkling water from the Amazon river. In our effort and anxiety to secure every right that is ours at once, I fear we are often inclined to over look the opportunities that are right about us. We fail to cast down our buckets where we are, thinking that relief is far away. In the first place, a man who does not try to make friends with those among whom he lives, is a fool.

As I said in the beginning the colored man's present great opportunity in the South is in the matter of business, and success here is going to constitute the foundation for success and relief along other lines. We need first an industrial or business foundation. No one, not even in the North, cares much about the rights of a hungry man. We of the Negro race are too hungry and too empty-handed to exert much of an influence. In business, what are our opportunities? The Southern white has not advanced to the point yet where he will invite a Negro to his *prayer-meeting*, but has advanced to the point where he will invite him to the *stock-holders meetings*, as I can prove by numerous examples. If a colored man wants to borrow money on his note or get his note discounted, in no city in the South does the color of the face enter in. It is simply a question of reliability. The black man in this regard is given absolutely the same showing that the white man is given. Any colored man with common sense, a reasonable education and business ability, can take $1,000 in cash and go into any Southern community, and in five years be worth $5,000. He does not meet with that stern, relentless competition that he does when he butts up against the Northern Yankee. The black man can sooner conquer Southern prejudice than Northern competition. There are one thousand places in the South where a colored man can take $600 and open a brickyard, and in a few years grow independent, and when the colored man sells $10,000 worth of bricks to a white man and gets a mortgage on his house, this white man will not drive that Negro away from the polls when he sees him going up to vote, nor will the railroad, over which he ships $25,000 worth of bricks a year, put him into the smoking car.

Land is cheap all over the South; cheaper now than it will ever be again.

Another great advantage that the Negro has in the South, and one that I fear he does not value high enough, is in the matter of trades or skilled labor. Here again, there is almost no color-line drawn. While

I write, within a few yards of me, is a large printing office in charge of a colored man with two Southern white printers under him who work by the side of dozens of colored printers, without a word of objection.

In conclusion, let us stop spending so much of our strength in whining, complaining, fault-finding, but let us go forward conquering and to conquer. If the acquisition of property, education, morality, refinement and religion do not, in God's own time, bring us every political and civil right, then Nature is false, God is false, the teachings of Christ are false, everything is false . . .[23]

NOTES

1. Washington, 1899, 3–6.
2. Du Bois, 1973, 15–16.
3. Washington, 1880, 112.
4. This legislation was sponsored by Arthur L. Brooks, a representative from Macon County and supported in the state senate by Macon County's Wilbur Foster, who traded support for the bill for black electoral support. Regardless, both assumed the school would be a boon to Tuskegee and Macon County. Washington, vol. 2, 1972, 108–109.
5. Thomas B. Dryer and M.B. Swanson were local white businessmen from Tuskegee. Lewis Adams was a freedman who had been born a Tuskegee slave. Though he owned a hardware store in town and served as a Trustee, Adams would also join the Tuskegee faculty. Washington, 1972, vol. 2, 109.
6. "An Act to establish a Normal School for colored teachers at Tuskegee," 1881, 395–396.
7. Washington, 1972, vol. 2, 127–128. Armstrong's institute taught both African Americans and Native Americans hard work, diligence, and Christian morality. It stressed learning trades, like shoemaking, carpentry, tailoring, and sewing. There was little to no emphasis on critical thinking. Students were taught middle-class values. Armstrong cautioned against black involvement in politics, and he never spoke against Jim Crow segregation. See Engs, 1999; and Anderson, 1988, 33–47.
8. Washington, September 1881, 94.
9. Ibid., October 1881, 101.
10. Horne, 2009, 7.
11. Du Bois, 1973, 3–4.
12. Ibid., 6.
13. Washington, vol. 2, 1972, 439–450.
14. Washington, 1889, 47.
15. Du Bois, 1995, 17–19.
16. Du Bois, 1973, 10–11.
17. Penn, 1891, 446–448.

18. Du Bois, 1973, 12–13.
19. Washington, 1974, 199–201.
20. Lewis, 1993, 90–103.
21. Ibid., 19–20.
22. Washington, 1974, vol. 3, 274–277.
23. Washington, 1894, 478–483.

2

The Death of
Frederick Douglass

*The death of Frederick Douglass in 1895 left a power vacuum in black politi-
cal leadership that many scrambled to fill. The initial winner in that contest
was Booker T. Washington, who later that same year gave a speech at the Cotton States Exposition in Atlanta that made him a household name. Black
America was best served by learning skills and being willing to do manual
labor. "No race can prosper till it learns that there is as much dignity in tilling a field as in writing a poem. It is at the bottom of life we must begin, and
not at the top," he told his audience. The idea was that eventually such work
would earn white respect, would build an economic infrastructure, and racism would thus die on the vine on its own. And so, until that happened, Washington was willing to accept segregation as a temporary accommodation in
return for economic and educational concessions from the white South. He
said, "In all things that are purely social we can be as separate as the fingers,
yet one as the hand in all things essential to mutual progress." Although his
white audience loved the speech, it received mixed reviews from the black north.
Among its early supporters, however, was W.E.B. Du Bois. In that seminal year,
Du Bois finished his doctorate in 1895 (becoming the first African American*

to earn the degree from Harvard) and began searching for teaching jobs, even applying to Tuskegee before taking a position at Wilberforce. Du Bois focused on black colleges and universities, knowing that no white college would hire him. He sent letters of inquiry to colleges across the country. One of those inquiries was to Tuskegee, and would constitute the introductory contact between Du Bois and Washington.[1]

WILLIAM EDWARD BURGHARDT DU BOIS

Gt. Barrington, Mass., 27 July '94

President Washington, Sir! May I ask if you have a vacancy for a teacher in your institution next year? I am a Fisk and Harvard man (A.B. & A.M.) & have just returned from two years abroad as scholar of the John F. Slater trustees. My specialty is history and social science but I can teach German, philosophy, natural science, classics &c. You[r] wife knows of me, and I refer by permission to

President Gilman, Johns Hopkins Univ., Baltimore
Secretary Harvard Univ.,
    5 University Hall, Cambridge
President Fisk Univ. Nashville
Rev. C. C. Painter of Indian Rights Association
President Calloway of Alcorn[2]

I can procure letters from any and all of these. Respectfully yours,

W.E.B. Du Bois[3]

Washington's wife did, indeed, know Du Bois. Margaret James Murray was born to a poor sharecropping family. She excelled at school and moved from student to teacher at age 14. At 19, in 1881, she enrolled in Fisk to bolster her ability to teach, and there was a classmate of Du Bois. She became a teacher at Tuskegee in 1889 and Booker T. Washington's third wife in 1892. Although she was devoted to Tuskegee and her husband, she and her former classmate would remain friends despite the differences between Du Bois and her husband.[4]

BOOKER TALIAFERRO WASHINGTON

8/25- 1894

Dated   Tuskegee Ala

To   W.E.B. Du Bois—
          Gt Barrington Mass

Can give mathematics here if terms suit. Will you accept Wire answer

Booker T. Washington[5]

Du Bois ultimately received offers from Lincoln University in Missouri, from Wilberforce, and from Tuskegee. He chose Wilberforce because it offered more money than Lincoln. The Tuskegee offer was the last to arrive, and so was eliminated by default. He later wondered how the trajectory of his life and thought would have changed had he chosen otherwise: "It would be interesting to speculate just what would have happened if I had received the offer of Tuskegee first, instead of that of Wilberforce."[6]

Regardless, in 1895, Du Bois was teaching languages at Wilberforce, but despite his pleas, the university was uninterested in his proposed sociology course. He was frustrated—he had chosen Wilberforce over other offers and felt he was being ill-used—but found relief the following year when he accepted a temporary appointment at the University of Pennsylvania.[7]

NEW YORK TIMES

Death of Fred Douglass

WASHINGTON, Feb. 20—Frederick Douglass dropped dead in the hallway of his residence on Anacostia Heights this evening at 7 o'clock. He had been in the highest spirits, and apparently in the best of health, despite his seventy-eight years, when death overtook him.

This morning he was driven to Washington, accompanied by his wife. She left him at the Congressional Library, and he continued to Metzerott Hall, where he attended the sessions of the Women's Council in the forenoon and the afternoon, returning to Cedar Hill, his residence, between 5 and 6 o'clock. After dining, he had a chat in the hallway with his wife about the doings of the council. He grew very enthusiastic in his explanation of one of the events of the day, when he fell upon his knees, with hands clasped.

Mrs. Douglass, thinking this was part of his description, was not alarmed, but as she looked he sank lower and lower, and finally lay stretched upon the floor, breathing his last. Realizing that he was ill, she raised his head, and then understood that he was dying. She was alone in the house, and rushed to the front door with cries for help. Some men who were near by quickly responded, and attempted to reassure the dying man. One of them called Dr. J. Stewart Harrison, and while he was injecting a restorative into the patient's arm, Mr. Douglass passed away, seemingly without pain . . .

Mrs. Douglass said to-night that her husband had apparently been in the best of health lately, and had shown unusual vigor for one of his years. No arrangements, she said, would be made for his funeral until his children could be consulted.

It is a singular fact, in connection with the death of Mr. Douglass, that the very last hours of his life were given in attention to one of the principles to which he has devoted his energies since his escape from slavery. This morning he drove into Washington from his residence, about a mile out from Anacostia, a suburb just across the eastern branch of the Potomac, and at 10 o'clock appeared at Metzerott Hall, where the Women's National Council is holding its triennial. Mr. Douglass was a regularly-enrolled member of the National Women's Suffrage Association, and had always attended its conventions. It was probably with a view to consistency in this respect that he appeared at Metzerott Hall.[8]

BOOKER T. WASHINGTON

The Atlanta Exposition, at which I had been asked to make an address as a representative of the Negro race . . . was opened with a short address from Governor Bullock. After other interesting exercises, including an invocation from Bishop Nelson, of Georgia, a dedicatory ode by Albert Howell, Jr., and addresses by the President of the Exposition and Mrs. Joseph Thompson, the President of the Woman's Board, Governor Bullock introduced me with the words, "We have with us to-day a representative of Negro enterprise and Negro civilization."[9]

When I arose to speak, there was considerable cheering, especially from the coloured people. As I remember it now, the thing that was uppermost in my mind was the desire to say something that would cement the friendship of the races and bring about hearty cooperation between them. So far as my outward surroundings were concerned, the only thing that I recall distinctly now is that when I got up, I saw thousands of eyes looking intently into my face. The following is the address which I delivered:—

MR. PRESIDENT AND GENTLEMEN OF
THE BOARD OF DIRECTORS AND CITIZENS.

One-third of the population of the South is of the Negro race. No enterprise seeking the material, civil, or moral welfare of this section can disregard this element of our population and reach the highest success. I but convey to you, Mr. President and Directors, the sentiment of the masses of my race when I say that in no way have the value and manhood of the American Negro been more fittingly and generously recognized than by the managers of this magnificent Exposition at every stage of its progress. It is a recognition that will do more to cement the friendship of the two races than any occurrence since the dawn of our freedom.

Not only this, but the opportunity here afforded will awaken among us a new era of industrial progress. Ignorant and inexperienced, it is not strange that in the first years of our new life we began at the top instead of at the bottom; that a seat in Congress or the state legislature was more sought than real estate or industrial skill; that the political convention of stump speaking had more attraction than starting a dairy farm or truck garden.

A ship lost at sea for many days suddenly sighted a friendly vessel. From the mast of the unfortunate vessel was seen a signal, "Water, water; we die of thirst!" The answer from the friendly vessel at once came back, "Cast down your bucket where you are." A second time the signal, "Water, water; send us water!" ran up from the distressed vessel, and was answered, "Cast down your bucket where you are." And a third and fourth signal for water was answered, "Cast down your bucket where you are." The captain of the distressed vessel, at last heeding the injunction, cast down his bucket, and it came up full of fresh, sparkling water from the mouth of the Amazon River. To those of my race who depend on bettering their condition in a foreign land or who underestimate the importance of cultivating friendly relations with the Southern white man, who is their next-door neighbour, I would say: "Cast down your bucket where you are"—cast it down in making friends in every manly way of the people of all races by whom we are surrounded.[10]

Cast it down in agriculture, mechanics, in commerce, in domestic service, and in the professions. And in this connection it is well to bear in mind that whatever other sins the South may be called to bear, when it comes to business, pure and simple, it is in the South that the Negro is given a man's chance in the commercial world, and in nothing is this Exposition more eloquent than in emphasizing this chance. Our greatest danger is that in the great leap from slavery to freedom we may overlook the fact that the masses of us are to live by the productions of our hands, and fail to keep in mind that we shall prosper in proportion as we learn to dignify and glorify common labour and put brains and skill into the common occupations of life; shall prosper in proportion as we learn to draw the line between the superficial and the substantial, the ornamental gewgaws of life and the useful. No race can prosper till it learns that there is as much dignity in tilling a field as in writing a poem. It is at the bottom of life we must begin, and not at the top. Nor should we permit our grievances to overshadow our opportunities.

To those of the white race who look to the incoming of those of foreign birth and strange tongue and habits for the prosperity of the South, were I permitted I would repeat what I say to my own race, "Cast down your bucket where you are." Cast it down among the eight millions of Negroes whose habits you know, whose fidelity and love you have tested in days when to have proved treacherous meant the ruin of your firesides. Cast down your bucket among these people who have, without strikes and labour wars, tilled your fields, cleared your forests, builded your railroads and cities, and brought forth treasures from the bowels of the earth, and helped make possible this magnificent representation of the progress of the South. Casting down your bucket among my people, helping and encouraging them as you are doing on these grounds, and to education of head, hand, and heart, you will find that they will buy your surplus land, make blossom the waste places in your fields, and run your factories. While doing this, you can be sure in the future, as in the past, that you and your families will be surrounded by the most patient, faithful, law-abiding, and unresentful people that the world has seen. As we have proved our loyalty to you in the past, in nursing your children, watching by the sick-bed of your mothers and fathers, and often following them with tear-dimmed eyes to their graves, so in the future, in our humble way, we shall stand by you with a devotion that no foreigner can approach, ready to lay down our lives, if need be, in defence of yours, interlacing our industrial, commercial, civil, and religious life with yours in a way that shall make the interests of both races one. In all things that are purely social we can be as separate as the fingers, yet one as the hand in all things essential to mutual progress.

There is no defence or security for any of us except in the highest intelligence and development of all. If anywhere there are efforts tending to curtail the fullest growth of the Negro, let these efforts be turned into stimulating, encouraging, and making him the most useful and intelligent citizen. Effort or means so invested will pay a thousand per cent interest. These efforts will be twice blessed—"blessing him that gives and him that takes."

There is no escape through law of man or God from the inevitable:—

> The laws of changeless justice bind
> Oppressor with oppressed;
> And close as sin and suffering joined
> We march to fate abreast.

Nearly sixteen millions of hands will aid you in pulling the load upward, or they will pull against you the load downward. We shall constitute one-third and more of the ignorance and crime of the South, or one-third its intelligence and progress; we shall contribute one-third to the business and industrial prosperity of the South, or we shall prove a veritable body of death, stagnating, depressing, retarding every effort to advance the body politic.

Gentlemen of the Exposition, as we present to you our humble effort at an exhibition of our progress, you must not expect overmuch. Starting thirty years ago with ownership here and there in a few quilts and pumpkins and chickens (gathered from miscellaneous sources), remember the path that has led from these to the inventions and production of agricultural implements, buggies, steam-engines, newspapers, books, statuary, carving, paintings, the management of drug-stores and banks, has not been trodden without contact with thorns and thistles. While we take pride in what we exhibit as a result of our independent efforts, we do not for a moment forget that our part in this exhibition would fall far short of your expectations but for the constant help that has come to our educational life, not only from the Southern states, but especially from Northern philanthropists, who have made their gifts a constant stream of blessing and encouragement.

The wisest among my race understand that the agitation of questions of social equality is the extremest folly, and that progress in the enjoyment of all the privileges that will come to us must be the result of severe and constant struggle rather than of artificial forcing. No race that has anything to contribute to the markets of the world is long in any degree ostracized. It is important and right that all privileges of the law be ours, but it is vastly more important that we be prepared for the exercises of these privileges. The opportunity to earn a dollar in a factory just now is worth infinitely more than the opportunity to spend a dollar in an opera-house.

In conclusion, may I repeat that nothing in thirty years has given us more hope and encouragement, and drawn us so near to you of the white race, as this opportunity offered by the Exposition; and here bending, as it were, over the altar that represents the results of the struggles of your race and mine, both starting practically empty-handed three decades ago, I pledge that in your effort to work out the great and intricate problem which God has laid at the doors of the South, you shall have at all times the patient, sympathetic help of my race; only let this be constantly in mind, that, while from representations in these buildings of the product of field, of forest, of mine, of factory, letters, and art, much good will come, yet far above and beyond material benefits will be that higher good, that, let us pray God, will come, in a blotting out of sectional differences and racial animosities and suspicions, in a determination to administer absolute justice, in a willing obedience among all classes to the mandates of law. This, this, coupled with our material prosperity, will bring into our beloved South a new heaven and a new earth.

The first thing that I remember, after I had finished speaking, was that Governor Bullock rushed across the platform and took me by the hand, and that others did the same. I received so many and such hearty congratulations that I found it difficult to get out of the building. I did not appreciate to any degree, however, the impression which my address seemed to have made, until the next morning, when I went into the business part of the city. As soon as I was recognized, I was surprised to find myself pointed out and surrounded by a crowd of men who wished to shake hands with me. This was kept up on every street on to which I went, to an extent which embarrassed me so much that I went back to my boarding-place. The next morning I returned to Tuskegee. At the station in Atlanta, and at almost all of the stations at which the train stopped between that city and Tuskegee, I found a crowd of people anxious to shake hands with me.

The papers in all parts of the United States published the address in full, and for months afterward there were complimentary editorial references to it. Mr. Clark Howell, the editor of the Atlanta *Constitution*, telegraphed to a New York paper, among other words, the following, "I do not exaggerate when I say that Professor Booker T. Washington's address yesterday was one of the most notable speeches, both as to character and as to the warmth of its reception, ever delivered to a Southern audience. The address was a revelation. The whole speech is a platform upon which blacks and whites can stand with full justice to each other."[11]

The Boston *Transcript* said editorially: "The speech of Booker T. Washington at the Atlanta Exposition, this week, seems to have dwarfed all the other proceedings and the Exposition itself. The sensation that it has caused in the press has never been equalled."

I very soon began receiving all kinds of propositions from lecture bureaus, and editors of magazines and papers, to take the lecture platform, and to write articles. One lecture bureau offered me fifty thousand dollars, or two hundred dollars a night and expenses, if I would place my services at its disposal for a given period. To all these communications I replied that my life-work was at Tuskegee; and that whenever I spoke it must be in the interests of the Tuskegee school and my race, and that I would enter into no arrangements that seemed to place a mere commercial value upon my services.

Some days after its delivery I sent a copy of my address to the President of the United States, the Hon. Grover Cleveland. I received from him the following autograph reply:—

GRAY GABLES, BUZZARD'S BAY, MASS.,
October 6, 1895

BOOKER T. WASHINGTON, ESQ.:

MY DEAR SIR: I thank you for sending me a copy of your address delivered at the Atlanta Exposition.

I thank you with much enthusiasm for making the address. I have read it with intense interest, and I think the Exposition would be fully justified if it did not do more than furnish the opportunity for its delivery. Your words cannot fail to delight and encourage all who wish well for your race; and if our coloured fellow-citizens do not from your utterances gather new hope and form new determinations to gain every valuable advantage offered them by their citizenship, it will be strange indeed.

Yours very truly,
GROVER CLEVELAND.

Later I met Mr. Cleveland, for the first time, when, as President, he visited the Atlanta Exposition. At the request of myself and others he consented to spend an hour in the Negro Building, for the purpose of inspecting the Negro exhibit and of giving the coloured people in attendance an opportunity to shake hands with him. As soon as I met Mr. Cleveland I became impressed with his simplicity, greatness, and rugged honesty. I have met him many times since then, both at public functions and at his private residence in Princeton, and the more I see of him the more I admire him. When he visited the Negro Building in Atlanta he seemed to give himself up wholly, for that hour, to the coloured people. He seemed to be as careful to shake hands with some old coloured "auntie" clad partially in rags, and to take as much pleasure in doing so, as if he were greeting some millionaire. Many of the coloured people took advantage of the occasion to get him to write his name in a book or on a slip of paper. He was as careful and patient in doing this as if he were putting his signature to some great state document.

Mr. Cleveland has not only shown his friendship for me in many personal ways, but has always consented to do anything I have asked of him for our school. This he has done, whether it was to make a personal donation or to use his influence in securing the donations of others. Judging from my personal acquaintance with Mr. Cleveland, I do not believe that he is conscious of possessing any colour prejudice. He is too great for that. In my contact with people I find that, as a rule, it is only the little, narrow people who live for themselves, who never read good books, who do not travel, who never open up their souls in a way to permit them to come into contact with other souls—with the great outside world. No man whose vision is bounded by colour can come into contact with what is highest and best in the world. In meeting men, in many places, I have found that the happiest people are those who do the most for others; the most miserable are those who do the least. I have also found that few things, if any, are capable of making one so blind and narrow as race prejudice. I often say to our students, in the course of my talks to them on Sunday evenings in the chapel, that the longer I live and the more experience I have of the world, the more I am convinced that, after all, the one thing that is most worth living for—and dying for, if need be—is the opportunity of making some one else more happy and more useful.

The coloured people and the coloured newspapers at first seemed to be greatly pleased with the character of my Atlanta address, as well as with its reception. But after the first burst of enthusiasm began to die away, and the coloured people began reading the speech in cold type, some of them seemed to feel that they had been hypnotized. They seemed to feel that I had been too liberal in my remarks toward the Southern whites, and that I had not spoken out strongly enough for what they termed the "rights" of the race. For a while there was a reaction, so far as a certain element of my own race was concerned, but later these reactionary ones seemed to have been won over to my way of believing and acting.

While speaking of changes in public sentiment, I recall that about ten years after the school at Tuskegee was established, I had an experience that I shall never forget. Dr. Lyman Abbott, then the pastor of Plymouth Church, and also editor of the *Outlook* (then the *Christian Union*), asked me to write a letter for his paper giving my opinion of the exact condition, mental and moral, of the coloured ministers in the South, as based upon my observations.[12] I wrote the letter, giving the exact facts as I conceived them to be. The picture painted was a rather black one—or, since I am black, shall I say "white"? It could not be otherwise with a race but a few years out of slavery, a race which had not had time or opportunity to produce a competent ministry.

What I said soon reached every Negro minister in the country, I think, and the letters of condemnation which I received from them were not few. I think that for a year after the publication of this article every association and every conference or religious body of any kind, of my race, that met, did not fail before adjourning to pass a resolution condemning me, or calling upon me to retract or modify what I had said. Many of these organizations went so far in their resolutions as to advise parents to cease sending their children to Tuskegee. One association even appointed a "missionary" whose duty it was to warn the people against sending their children to Tuskegee. This missionary had a son in the school, and I noticed that, whatever the "missionary" might have said or done with regard to others, he was careful not to take his son away from the institution. Many or the coloured papers, especially those that were the organs of religious bodies, joined in the general chorus of condemnation or demands for retraction.

During the whole time of the excitement, and through all the criticism, I did not utter a word of explanation or retraction. I knew that I was right, and that time and the sober second thought of the people would vindicate me. It was not long before the bishops and other church leaders began to make a careful investigation of the conditions of the ministry, and they found out that I was right. In fact, the oldest and most influential bishop in one branch of the Methodist Church said that my words were far too mild. Very soon public sentiment began making itself felt, in demanding a purifying of the ministry. While this is not yet complete by any means, I think I may say, without egotism, and I have been told by many of our most influential ministers, that my words had much to do with starting a demand for the placing of a higher type of men in the pulpit. I have had the satisfaction of having many who once condemned me thank me heartily for my frank words . . .

My own belief is, although I have never before said so in so many words, that the time will come when the Negro in the South will be accorded all the political rights which his ability, character, and material possessions entitle him to. I think, though, that the opportunity to freely exercise such political rights will not come in any large degree through outside or artificial forcing, but will be accorded to the Negro by the Southern white people themselves, and that they will protect him in the exercise of those rights. Just as soon as the South gets over the old feeling that it is being forced by "foreigners," or "aliens," to do something which it does not want to do, I believe that the change in the direction that I have indicated is going to begin. In fact, there are indications that it is already beginning in a slight degree.

Let me illustrate my meaning. Suppose that some months before the opening of the Atlanta Exposition there had been a general demand from the press and public platform outside the South that a Negro be given a place on the opening programme, and that a Negro be placed upon the board of jurors of award. Would any such recognition of the race have taken place? I do not think so. The Atlanta officials went as far as they did because they felt it to be a pleasure, as well as a duty, to reward what they considered merit in the Negro race. Say what we will, there is something in human nature which we cannot blot out, which makes one man, in the end, recognize and reward merit in another, regardless of colour or race.

I believe it is the duty of the Negro—as the greater part of the race is already doing—to deport himself modestly in regard to political claims, depending upon the slow but sure influences that proceed from the possession of property, intelligence, and high character for the full recognition of his political rights. I think that the according of the full exercise of political rights is going to be a matter of natural, slow growth, not an over-night, gourd-vine affair. I do not believe that the Negro should cease voting, for a man cannot learn the exercise of self-government by ceasing to vote any more than a boy can learn to swim by keeping out of the water, but I do believe that in his voting he should more and more be influenced by those of intelligence and character who are his next-door neighbours.

I know coloured men who, through the encouragement, help, and advice of Southern white people, have accumulated thousands of dollars' worth of property, but who, at the same time, would never think of going to those same persons for advice concerning the casting of their ballots. This, it seems to me, is unwise and unreasonable, and should cease. In saying this I do not mean that the Negro should buckle, or not vote from principle, for the instant he ceases to vote from principle he loses the confidence and respect of the Southern white man even.

I do not believe that any state should make a law that permits an ignorant and poverty-stricken white man to vote, and prevents a black man in the same condition from voting. Such a law is not only unjust, but it will react, as all unjust laws do, in time; for the effect of such a law is to encourage the Negro to secure education and property, and at the same time it encourages the white man to remain in ignorance and poverty. I believe that in time, through the operation of intelligence and friendly race relations, all cheating at the ballot-box in the South will cease. It will become apparent that the white man who begins by cheating a Negro out of his ballot soon learns to cheat a white man out of his, and that the man who does this ends his career of dishonesty by the theft of property or by some equally serious crime. In my opinion, the time will come when the South will encourage all of its citizens to vote. It will see that it pays better, from every standpoint, to have healthy, vigorous life than to have that political stagnation which always results when one-half of the population has no share and no interest in the Government.

As a rule, I believe in universal, free suffrage, but I believe that in the South we are confronted with peculiar conditions that justify the protection of the ballot in many of the states, for a while at least, either by an educational test, a property test, or by both combined; but whatever tests are required, they should be made to apply with equal and exact justice to both races.[13]

Louis Harlan, Booker T. Washington's most accomplished biographer, described Washington's Atlanta speech—far from being a vast reversal from the activism of Douglass—as endemic of a trend in black thought since the end of Reconstruction toward economic thinking as the dominant road to equality. David Levering Lewis called the Cotton States International Exposition speech in Atlanta "one of the most consequential pronouncements in American history. Neither black people nor white people were ever quite the same again." The Atlanta Constitution's *editor Clark Howell yelled from the floor, "That man's speech is the beginning of a moral revolution in America." As Washington mentions, President Grover Cleveland arrived in Atlanta a few days later and shook the Tuskegee leader's hand. Many black southerners saw a former slave receiving enthusiastic support for black education from otherwise racist whites, whereas many racist whites saw a way to appear progressive while maintaining white superiority and segregation. Regardless, the speech was, if nothing else, a revelation, and some saw it as a true bridge between the races. Among them was a young Du Bois.*[14]

W.E.B. DU BOIS

Wilberforce, 24 Sept., '95

My Dear Mr Washington: Let me heartily congratulate you upon your phenomenal success at Atlanta—it was a word fitly spoken.

Sincerely Yours,
W.E.B. Du Bois[15]

In 1895, when Du Bois wrote to Washington to congratulate him on the Atlanta Exposition Address, he also wrote to the New York Age, *commenting that "here might be the basis of a real settlement between whites and blacks in the South, if the South opened to the Negroes the doors of economic opportunity and the Negroes co-operated with the white South in political sympathy." If black America got economic concessions in return for political concessions, perhaps there could be a legitimate détente between the races.*[16]

Even though Du Bois early supported the Washingtonian plan, there was early opposition. W. Calvin Chase, editor of the Washington Bee, *for example, wrote in November 1895 that Washington "said something that was death to the Afro-American and elevating to the white people. What fool wouldn't applaud the downfall of his aspiring competitor?" A George N. Smith editorial in* Voice of Missions *thought that supporters comparing Washington to Douglass were "as unseemly as comparing a pigmy to a giant—a mountain brook leaping over a boulder, to a great, only Niagara." Francis Grimke, more considered and sedate, wrote to Washington that "there were a few who thought you were playing into the hands of the Southern Whites."*[17]

BOOKER T. WASHINGTON

As to how my address at Atlanta was received by the audience in the Exposition building, I think I prefer to let Mr. James Creelman, the noted war correspondent, tell.[18] Mr. Creelman was present, and telegraphed the following account to the New York *World:*—

ATLANTA, SEPTEMBER 18.
   While President Cleveland was waiting at Gray Gables to-day, to send the electric spark that started the machinery of the Atlanta

Exposition, a Negro Moses stood before a great audience of white people and delivered an oration that marks a new epoch in the history of the South; and body of Negro troops marched in a procession with the citizen soldiery of Georgia and Louisiana. The whole city is thrilling to-night with a realization of the extraordinary significance of these two unprecedented events. Nothing has happened since Henry Grady's immortal speech before the New England society in New York that indicates so profoundly the spirit of the New South, except, perhaps, the opening of the Exposition itself.

When Professor Booker T. Washington, Principal of an industrial school for coloured people in Tuskegee, Ala. stood on the platform of the Auditorium, with the sun shining over the heads of his auditors into his eyes, and with his whole face lit up with the fire of prophecy, Clark Howell, the successor of Henry Grady, said to me, "That man's speech is the beginning of a moral revolution in America."

It is the first time that a Negro has made a speech in the South on any important occasion before an audience composed of white men and women. It electrified the audience, and the response was as if it had come from the throat of a whirlwind.

Mrs. Thompson had hardly taken her seat when all eyes were turned on a tall tawny Negro sitting in the front row of the platform. It was Professor Booker T. Washington, President of the Tuskegee (Alabama) Normal and Industrial Institute, who must rank from this time forth as the foremost man of his race in America. Gilmore's Band played the "Star-Spangled Banner," and the audience cheered. The tune changed to "Dixie" and the audience roared with shrill "hi-yis." Again the music changed, this time to "Yankee Doodle," and the clamour lessened.

All this time the eyes of the thousands present looked straight at the Negro orator. A strange thing was to happen. A black man was to speak for his people, with none to interrupt him. As Professor Washington strode to the edge of the stage, the low, descending sun shot fiery rays through the windows into his face. A great shout greeted him. He turned his head to avoid the blinding light, and moved about the platform for relief. Then he turned his wonderful countenance to the sun without a blink of the eyelids, and began to talk.

There was a remarkable figure; tall, bony, straight as a Sioux chief, high forehead, straight nose, heavy jaws, and strong, determined mouth, with big white teeth, piercing eyes, and a commanding manner. The sinews stood out on his bronzed neck, and his muscular right arm swung high in the air, with a lead-pencil grasped in the clinched brown fist. His big feet were planted squarely, with the heels together and the toes turned out. His voice rang out clear and true, and he paused impressively as he made each point. Within ten minutes the multitude was in an uproar of enthusiasm—handkerchiefs were waved, cans were flourished, hats were tossed in the air. The fairest women of Georgia stood up and cheered. It was as if the orator had bewitched them.

And when he held his dusky hand high above his head, with the fingers stretched wide apart, and said to the white people of the South on behalf of his race, "In all things that are purely social we can be as separate as the fingers, yet one as the hand in all things essential to mutual progress," the great wave of sound dashed itself against the walls, and the whole audience was on its feet in a delirium of applause, and I thought at that moment of the night when Henry Grady stood among the curling wreaths of tobacco-smoke in Delmonico's banquet-hall and said, "I am a Cavalier among Roundheads."

I have heard the great orators of many countries, but not even Gladstone himself could have pleaded a cause with more consummate power than did this angular Negro, standing in a nimbus of sunshine, surrounded by the men who once fought to keep his race in bondage. The roar might swell ever so high, but the expression of his earnest face never changed.

A ragged, ebony giant, squatted on the floor in one of the aisles, watched the orator with burning eyes and tremulous face until the supreme burst of applause came, and then the tears ran down his face. Most of the Negroes in the audience were crying, perhaps without knowing just why.

At the close of the speech Governor Bullock rushed across the stage and seized the orator's hand. Another shout greeted this demonstration, and for a few minutes the two men stood facing each other, hand in hand.

So far as I could spare the time from the immediate work at Tuskegee, after my Atlanta address, I accepted some of the invitations to speak in public which came to me, especially those that would take me into territory where I thought it would pay to plead the cause of my race, but I always did this with the understanding that I was to be free to talk about my life-work and the needs of my people . . .

I believe that one always does himself and his audience an injustice when he speaks merely for the sake of speaking. I do not believe that one should speak unless, deep down in his heart, he feels convinced that he has a message to deliver. When one feels, from the bottom of his feet to the top of his head, that he has something to say that is going to help some individual or some cause, then let him say it; and in delivering his message I do not believe that many of the artificial rules of elocution can, under such circumstances, help him very much. Although there are certain things, such as pauses, breathing, and pitch of voice, that are very important, none of these can take the place of *soul* in an address. When I have an address to deliver, I like to forget all about the rules for the proper use of the English language, and all about rhetoric and that sort of thing, and I like to make the audience forget all about these things, too . . .

Three years ago, at the suggestion of Mr. Morris K. Jesup, of New York, and Dr. J.L.M. Curry, the general agent of the fund, the trustees of the John F. Slater Fund voted a sum of money to be used in paying the expenses of Mrs. Washington and myself while holding a series of meetings among the coloured people in the large centres of Negro population, especially in the large cities of the ex-slaveholding states.[19] Each year during the last three years we have devoted some weeks to this work. The plan that we have followed has been for me to speak in the morning to the ministers, teachers, and professional men. In the afternoon Mrs. Washington would speak to the women alone, and in the evening I spoke to a large mass-meeting. In almost every case the meetings have been attended not only by the coloured people in large numbers, but by the white people. In Chattanooga, Tenn., for example, there was present at the mass-meeting an audience of not less than three thousand persons, and I was informed that eight hundred of these were white. I have done no work that I really enjoyed more than this, or that I think has accomplished more good.

These meetings have given Mrs. Washington and myself an opportunity to get first-hand, accurate information as to the real condition of the race, by seeing the people in their homes, their churches, their Sunday-schools, and their places of work, as well as in the prisons and dens of crime. These meetings also gave us an opportunity to see the relations that exist between the races. I never feel so hopeful about the race as I do after being engaged in a series of these meetings. I know that on such occasions there is much that comes to the surface that is superficial and deceptive, but I have had experience enough not to be deceived by mere signs and fleeting enthusiasms. I have taken pains to go to the bottom of things and get facts, in a cold, business-like manner.

I have seen the statement made lately, by one who claims to know what he is talking about, that, taking the whole Negro race into account, ninety per cent of the Negro women are not virtuous. There never was a baser falsehood uttered concerning a race, or a statement made that was less capable of being proved by actual facts.

No one can come into contact with the race for twenty years, as I have done in the heart of the South, without being convinced that the

race is constantly making slow but sure progress materially, educationally, and morally. One might take up the life of the worst element in
New York City, for example, and prove almost anything he wanted to
prove concerning the white man, but all will agree that this is not a fair
test.

Early in the year 1897 I received a letter inviting me to deliver an
address at the dedication of the Robert Gould Shaw monument in
Boston . . .[20]

The exercises connected with the dedication were held in Music Hall,
in Boston, and the great hall was packed from top to bottom with one
of the most distinguished audiences that ever assembled in the city.
Among those present there were more persons representing the famous
old anti-slavery element than it is likely will ever be brought together
in the country again. The late Hon. Roger Wolcott, then Governor of
Massachusetts, was the presiding officer, and on the platform with him
were many other officials and hundreds of distinguished men.[21] A
report of the meeting which appeared in the Boston *Transcript* will
describe it better than any words of mine could do:—

The core and kernel of yesterday's great noon meeting in honour of
the Brotherhood of Man, in Music Hall, was the superb address of the
Negro President of Tuskegee. "Booker T. Washington received his Harvard A. M. last June, the first of his race," said Governor Wolcott, "to
receive an honorary degree from the oldest university in the land, and
this for the wise leadership of his people." When Mr. Washington rose
in the flag-filled, enthusiasm-warmed, patriotic, and glowing atmosphere of Music Hall, people felt keenly that here was the civic justification of the old abolition spirit of Massachusetts; in his person the
proof of her ancient and indomitable faith; in his strong thought and
rich oratory, the crown and glory of the old war days of suffering and
strife. The scene was full of historic beauty and deep significance.
"Cold" Boston was alive with the fire that is always hot in her heart for
righteousness and truth. Rows and rows of people who are seldom
seen at any public function, whole families of those who are certain to
be out of town on a holiday, crowded the place to overflowing. The city
was at her birthright *fête* in the persons of hundreds of her best citizens,
men and women whose names and lives stand for the virtues that
make for honourable civic pride . . .

One of the most encouraging signs in connection with the Tuskegee
school is found in the fact that the organization is so thorough that the
daily work of the school is not dependent upon the presence of any one
individual. The whole executive force, including instructors and clerks,
now numbers eighty-six. This force is so organized and subdivided

that the machinery of the school goes on day by day like clockwork. Most of our teachers have been connected with the institution for a number of years, and are as much interested in it as I am. In my absence, Mr. Warren Logan, the treasurer, who has been at the school seventeen years, is the executive. He is efficiently supported by Mrs. Washington, and by my faithful secretary, Mr. Emmett J. Scott, who handles the bulk of my correspondence and keeps me in daily touch with the life of the school, and who also keeps me informed of whatever takes place in the South that concerns the race. I owe more to his tact, wisdom, and hard work than I can describe.[22]

The main executive work of the school, whether I am at Tuskegee or not, centres in what we call the executive council. This council meets twice a week, and is composed of the nine persons who are at the head of the nine departments of the school. For example: Mrs. B.K. Bruce, the Lady Principal, the widow of the late ex-senator Bruce, is a member of the council, and represents in it all that pertains to the life of the girls at the school. In addition to the executive council there is a financial committee of six, that meets every week and decides upon the expenditures for the week. Once a month, and sometimes oftener, there is a general meeting of all the instructors. Aside from these there are innumerable smaller meetings, such as that of the instructors in the Phelps Hall Bible Training School, or of the instructors in the agricultural department.

In order that I may keep in constant touch with the life of the institution, I have a system of reports so arranged that a record of the school's work reaches me every day in the year, no matter in what part of the country I am. I know by these reports even what students are excused from school, and why they are excused—whether for reasons of ill health or otherwise. Through the medium of these reports I know each day what the income of the school in money is; I know how many gallons of milk and how many pounds of butter come from the dairy; what the bill of fare for the teachers and students is; whether a certain kind of meat was boiled or baked, and whether certain vegetables served in the dining room were bought from a store or procured from our own farm. Human nature I find to be very much the same the world over, and it is sometimes not hard to yield to the temptation to go to a barrel of rice that has come from the store—with the grain all prepared to go into the pot—rather than to take the time and trouble to go to the field and dig and wash one's own sweet potatoes, which might be prepared in a manner to take the place of the rice.

I am often asked how, in the midst of so much work, a large part of which is before the public, I can find time for any rest or recreation, and what kind of recreation or sports I am fond of. This is rather a difficult question to answer. I have a strong feeling that every individual owes it to himself, and to the cause which he is serving, to keep a vigorous, healthy body, with the nerves steady and strong, prepared for great efforts and prepared for disappointments and trying positions. As far as I can, I make it a rule to plan for each day's work—not merely to go through with the same routine of daily duties, but to get rid of the routine work as early in the day as possible, and then to enter upon some new or advance work. I make it a rule to clear my desk every day, before leaving my office, of all correspondence and memoranda, so that on the morrow I can begin a *new* day of work. I make it a rule never to let my work drive me, but to so master it, and keep it in such complete control, and to keep so far ahead of it, that I will be the master instead of the servant. There is a physical and mental and spiritual enjoyment that comes from a consciousness of being the absolute master of one's work, in all its details, that is very satisfactory and inspiring. My experience teaches me that, if one learns to follow this plan, he gets a freshness of body and vigour of mind out of work that goes a long way toward keeping him strong and healthy. I believe that when one can grow to the point where he loves his work, this gives him a kind of strength that is most valuable.

When I begin my work in the morning, I expect to have a successful and pleasant day of it, but at the same time I prepare myself for unpleasant and unexpected hard places. I prepare myself to hear that one of our school buildings is on fire, or has burned, or that some disagreeable accident has occurred, or that some one has abused me in a public address or printed article, for something that I have done or omitted to do, or for something that he had heard that I had said—probably something that I had never thought of saying . . .[23]

W.E.B. DU BOIS

Oh, Washington was a politician. He was a man who believed that we should get what we could get. It wasn't a matter of ideals or anything of that sort. . . . With everybody that Washington met, he evidently had the idea: 'Now, what's your racket? What are you out for?'[24]

NOTES

1. Within the relatively short span of a few months, Du Bois became the first black man to receive a PhD from Harvard, Douglass died, and

Washington gave his Cotton States address, making 1895 one of the most auspicious years for black rights in American history. Du Bois, 1972, vol. 1, 37; and Du Bois, 1968, 184.

2. Charles Cornelius Coffin Painter was a Congregationalist minister and tireless advocate of Native American rights in the second half of the 19th century. Founded in 1882 in Philadelphia, the Indian Rights Association was chartered to "bring about the complete civilization of the Indians and their admission to citizenship." After opening a corresponding office in Washington, the group became the principal lobbyist for Native rights in the United States. "President Calloway" refers to Thomas J. Calloway, president of Alcorn A&M in Mississippi. Du Bois, 1973, 37; Mathes and Brigandi, 2009, 89–118; and "Indian Rights Association Records," Collection 1523, Historical Society of Pennsylvania, Philadelphia, Pennsylvania.

3. Du Bois, 1974, 459–460.

4. Washington, 1972, vol. 2, 514–515.

5. Du Bois, 1973, 38.

6. Du Bois, 1968, 185; and Du Bois, 1973, 38.

7. Green and Driver, 1978, 9.

8. *New York Times*, 21 February 1895, 1.

9. The president of the Exposition was Charles A. Collier, an exposition veteran, the vice president and director of Capitol City Bank, and a local alderman. Rufus Brown Bullock had served as governor of Georgia during Reconstruction from 1868 to 1871, the first Republican governor in the state's history. Considered by many to be a carpetbagger, he was eventually forced from office by Ku Klux Klan threats because he unwaveringly supported the black right to vote. His reputation had revived enough by 1895, however, that he had become president of the Atlanta Chamber of Commerce. Cleland Kinloch Nelson was the first bishop of the Episcopal Diocese of Atlanta. Albert Howell, Jr., was the president of the *Atlanta Constitution* and member of its board of directors. He was the brother of Clark Howell, the paper's editor. Finally, Emma Mimms Thompson was the second wife of Joseph Thompson, a clothing merchant and member of the exposition's board of directors. *The Atlanta Exposition and South Illustrated*, 1895, 7, 73; Duncan, 1994; Malone, 1960; and *Moody's Manual of Railroads and Corporation Securities*, 1922, 231–232.

10. See Chapter 1. Washington no longer attributes the story to Hugh Brown, instead claiming it as his own.

11. Clark Howell was the brother of Albert Howell, who made a presentation before Washington's speech. He became managing editor of the paper in 1889 and would become editor-in-chief two years after the Cotton States speech in 1897. The Howell family owned and controlled the paper. Perry, 2014.

12. Lyman Abbot was a Congregationalist minister and theologian, one of the most influential religious thinkers of the 19th century. He co-edited the *Christian Union* with Henry Ward Beecher until 1881, when he became

editor-in-chief, advocating all manners of social reform. As Washington's account mentions, the magazine's name changed to *The Outlook* in 1893. See Brown, 1953.

13. Washington, 1901, 217–240. For more on the Cotton States and Washington's speech, see Perdue, 2010.

14. Harlan, 1972, 225; and Lewis, 1993, 174–175.

15. Washington, 1975, 26; and Du Bois, 1973, 39.

16. Du Bois, 1940, 55; Washington, 1975, vol. 4, 26; and Harlan, 1972, 225.

17. William Calvin Chase was a Howard trained lawyer who founded the *Washington Bee* in 1822 and edited the paper until his death in 1921. The *Bee* became one of the most influential black newspapers in the country, fighting against the rising tide of Jim Crow during the period. Harlan, 1972, 225–226; *Washington Bee*, 2 November 1895, 1. *Voice of Missions* quote from Foner, 1970, 344–347. Grimke quote from Blight, 2001, 330.

18. Creelman worked for several papers and periodicals in New York and Paris. He made his name covering the Sino-Japanese War for Joseph Pulitzer's *New York World* in 1894. Following this episode with Washington, Creelman would go on to cover the Spanish American War for William Randolph Hearst's *New York Journal*. See Milton, 1989.

19. Note that this is the same fund that financed the young Du Bois's study abroad in Germany. See Chapter 1, notes 18 and 19. See Chapter 2, note 1.

20. Robert Gould Shaw was the white Union Army officer who commanded the all-black 54th Massachusetts Infantry Regiment during the Civil War, beginning in 1863. He died in combat later that year. See Duncan, 1999.

21. Roger Wolcott was elected lieutenant governor of Massachusetts in 1893, and was serving in that post until 1896, when Governor Frederic T. Greenhalge died in office, moving Wolcott to the post. Later in the year of Washington's Boston speech, 1897, Wolcott would run for governor and win his own term, serving until 1900. See Lawrence, 1902.

22. Washington, indeed, owed him much. Emmett Jay Scott was a Houston native who cofounded the city's first black newspaper, the *Texas Freeman*, in 1893. He began working for Booker Washington in 1897 and would work for him as secretary, aide, and sometimes ghostwriter until Washington's death in 1915. Two years later, he would go to work in Woodrow Wilson's War Department, becoming the highest ranking black official in the administration. Dailey, 2003, 57–68.

23. Washington, 1901, 241–266.

24. Harlan, 1972, 254.

3

The Job Hunt

In 1896 and 1897, Washington was working with T. Thomas Fortune to fend off the first sustained challenges to his leadership in the wake of his Atlanta Compromise. Du Bois was far more interested in leaving Wilberforce for better surrounds, and that desire ultimately gave the academic his first real contact with Washington as he inquired about potential job openings at Tuskegee. He was also building an early body of work demonstrating opposition to the Tuskegee ideology. In 1897, he published a paper for the American Negro Academy, an organization that took a decidedly antagonistic stance against Washington's industrial education. Also that year, Du Bois published an essay in Atlantic Monthly, *"Strivings of the Negro People," which, although not antagonistic to Washington, did express his first public doubts about the Atlanta Compromise and the Tuskegee educational model.*

Du Bois was incredibly frustrated at Wilberforce. The school's rigid hierarchy was stifling, all centered on a board of trustees concerned principally with order and discipline. "Here grand inquisitors, there enlightened despots, these dynasts presided over Afro-America's other institutional pillar, the school," explains Du Bois biographer David Levering Lewis, "with all the trappings of royalty but seldom royalty's true noblesse." When combined with the religious fervor of the region, Du Bois soon realized he needed to go elsewhere. He was frustrated, and his mentor Albert Bushnell Hart was frustrated at his frustration. In late 1895 he convinced Du Bois to write to Washington about the possibility of a job at Tuskegee.[1]

WILLIAM EDWARD BURGHARDT DU BOIS

Wilberforce University, Ohio. 3 January 1896

Special

My Dear Mr Washington: Professor Hart[2] of Harvard on writing me recently asked me to communicate with you—I do not know that he had anything definite in mind, but I nevertheless follow his suggestion. This is my second year at Wilberforce, and although the field here is a good one, yet I am not wholly satisfied and am continually on the lookout for another position. There is a little too much church politics in the management and too little real interest and devotion to the work of real education. Then again I have no chance to teach my spec[i]alty of History and Sociology at all. I have had the good fortune to have a monograph of mine accepted at Harvard and it will be published in the spring as the first of a series of historical studies. It is on the suppression of the slave trade.

I am thinking somewhat of trying to organize a summer School of Sociology here next summer—it is a delightful and cheap place to spend the summer and I might be able to do some good.

If you hear of any opening which you think I am fitted to fill, kindly let me know. I trust you[r] work is prospering as it deserves to. My best regards to yourself and Mrs. Washington. Sincerely Yours,

W.E.B Du Bois[3]

W.E.B. DU BOIS

Wilberforce, O. Wednesday, 1 April 96

Dear Mr Washington: I have been for some time seeking a leisure hour in which to answer you[r] kind letter of the 17th January—but leisure hours are scarce here. I feel that I should like the work at Tuskegee if I could be of service to you. My idea has been that there might gradually be developed there a school of Negro History and social investigation which might serve to help place, more and more, the

Negro problem on a basis of sober fact. I think that in time various northern colleges like Harvard, Chicago, Johns Hopkins, and the U. of Penn. would join in supporting such a movement. What do you think of it?

At present I do not know just how I could be of service. I can teach most primary and secondary branches—preferring of course, History, Economics, Social Problems, &c. It seems to me that some elementary courses in these lines would be needed at Tuskeegee. I have had an indication that I may possibly expect an offer from the Univ. of Pennsylvania to conduct an investigation as to the condition of the Colored people of Philadelphia, for a year. This, it might be, would [be] a good introductory year's work after which if needed I could come to Tuskeegee and perhaps have the active aid of a great college like the Univ. of Penn. In any case I am willing and eager to entertain any proposition for giving my services to your school. As to salary I know the embarrassment of all southern schools: at the same time I shall, in the future, have to care for two i.e. I expect to marry this spring.

Hoping to hear from you at your convenience, I remain Sincerely Yours,

W.E.B. Du Bois[4]

That correspondence led Du Bois to offer a meeting between himself and Washington when Tuskegee's leader visited Wilberforce in June 1896. It is unknown whether the two actually met during that visit, but it would have been their first meeting. Hart certainly encouraged that meeting. He was loyal to Du Bois and was also an ardent advocate of Tuskegee. He felt that they should be in some kind of intellectual or educational alliance.[5]

W.E.B. DU BOIS

Wilberforce, 6 April, '96

Dear Mr. Washington: I have been wanting to have you as my guest when you visit the University in June but living in the building as I do I had no place. My friend however, Lieutenant Young[6] of the US Army, and mother, cordially unite in inviting you thro' me to be their and my guest at their residence. Answer at your convenience and let us know when you arrive that we may meet you. Sincerely,

W.E.B. Du Bois[7]

SAMUEL McCUNE LINDSAY *(Lindsay was a University of Pennsylvania sociology professor beginning in 1896. He appointed a young Du Bois to study black life in Philadelphia's Seventh Ward and sought Washington's help with the draft. The project would ultimately become Du Bois's* The Philadelphia Negro *(1899).)*

Philadelphia, Nov. 28th 1896

Dear Sir [Washington]: Enclosed please find the proof-sheets of the schedules which have been adopted for the Investigation into the Condition of the Negroes in Ward Seven of the City of Philadelphia. We desire to make this investigation as thorough as possible and to have the results in such shape as to be comparable with similar work undertaken in other cities. The work is being done by Mr. W.E.B. Du Bois, Ph.D. (Harvard) and Miss Isabel Eaton, B.L.[8] (Smith), under the direction of this department of the University which will print all results worthy of publication.

Will you kindly examine the enclosed proofs and return them at once with any corrections or suggestions which in your judgment will add to the value of the investigation?

. . . Samuel McCune Lindsay[9]

T. Thomas Fortune was a pioneering journalist and civil rights leader who nevertheless remained Booker Washington's devoted acolyte at best, sycophant at worst. Originally from Florida, Fortune arrived in New York in 1881, hoping to become a journalist but without a college degree after leaving Howard University early. Still, he worked as a printer and in 1884 founded the New York Freeman, *which, in 1888, would change its name to the* New York Age. *It became one of the most influential black newspapers in the country, and Fortune's editorship of the* New York Age, *combined with his wholehearted belief in the Tuskegee ideal, made the paper an organ for the Washington message throughout his fight with Du Bois.*[10]

TIMOTHY THOMAS FORTUNE

Jacksonville, Fla., Dec. 18, 1896

My Dear Friend: I have your favor of the 15th instant and appreciate very highly the sentiments you express concerning myself and the incoming administration . . .

I am real glad to learn that Mrs. Washington improves daily and I hope she may soon be entirely well. My father's condition remains unchanged. I have sent an editorial to The Age give Chase of the Washington *Bee*[11] a ripping up the back for his foolish and ungenerous attacks on you. With kind regards, Yours truly

T. Thomas Fortune[12]

ALBERT BUSHNELL HART *(Hart was a renowned U.S. historian who served as Du Bois's mentor and dissertation director at Harvard. An academic who did his undergraduate work at Harvard before earning his doctorate in Germany, he obviously had a profound influence on Du Bois's early academic life and career.)*

Cambridge, Mass. June 14, 1897

Dear Sir [Washington]: I was very sorry not to have seen you when you were in Boston. I hope you will give me quite an early notice of any contemplated visit—for I am quite anxious to see you, with especial reference to Professor Du Bois, who it seems to me ought naturally to find his field of labor associated with you. Sincerely yours,

Albert Bushnell Hart[13]

ALBERT BUSHNELL HART

Boston, Aug. 10, 1897

Dear President Washington: Owing to absence from the city today is the first time that I have been able to call at the Crawford House: and I find that you have left. I will with pleasure send you a contribution in a few days.

Have you no place for the best educated colored man available for college work? Prof Du Bois is a man in whom I have much confidence, based on long acquaintance. His book on the slave trade is very scholarly and able. He is a man of character. One reason why I have for years been interested in him is that I expect him to be a force in the uplifting of his race.

He has had an appointment from the University of Pennsylvania, fellowship from Harvard, and study abroad from the Slater Fund.[14] It seems as though the time has come for his own race to give him an opportunity. I feel sure that you yourself will find in him a competent aid in your great work.

Will you not let me know as soon as you come to Boston next time? I want to know you, and to have you acquainted with some of my friends. Sincerely yours,

Albert Bushnell Hart[15]

In 1897, Du Bois wrote a paper for the American Negro Academy. Founded by Alexander Crummell to foster black arts and scholarship, the 40 members of the American Negro Academy sought not only to counter Washington's industrial education and the materialism it represented, but also to clearly estab-lish a black agenda through the publication of papers and other academic work.[16] In its second published paper, the Academy's introduction argued that it "believes that upon those of the race who have had the advantage of higher education and culture, rests the responsibility of taking concerted steps for the employment of these agencies to uplift the race to higher planes of thought and action.

"Two great obstacles to this consummation are apparent: (a) The lack of unity, want of harmony, absence of a self-sacrificing spirit, and no well-defined line of policy seeking definite aims; and (b) The persistent, relentless, at times covert opposition employed to thwart the Negro at every step of his upward struggles to establish the justness of his claim to the highest physical, intel-lectual and moral possibilities." What followed that introduction was Du Bois's early manifesto, "The Conservation of the Races."[17]

W.E.B. DU BOIS

The American Negro has always felt an intense personal interest in discussions as to the origins and destinies of races: primarily because back of most discussions of race with which he is familiar, have lurked certain assumptions as to his natural abilities, as to his political, intellec-tual and moral status, which he felt were wrong. He has, consequently, been led to deprecate and minimize race distinctions, to believe intensely that out of one blood God created all nations, and to speak of human brotherhood as though it were the possibility of an already dawning tomorrow.

Nevertheless, in our calmer moments we must acknowledge that human beings are divided into races; that in this country the two most extreme types of the world's races have met, and the resulting problem as to the future relations of these types is not only of intense and living interest to us, but forms an epoch in the history of mankind.

It is necessary, therefore, in planning our movements, in guiding our future development, that at times we rise above the pressing, but smaller questions of separate schools and cars, wage-discrimination and lynch law, to survey the whole questions of race in human philosophy and to lay, on a basis of broad knowledge and careful insight, those large lines of policy and higher ideals which may form our guiding lines and boundaries in the practical difficulties of every day. For it is certain that all human striving must recognize the hard limits of natural law, and that any striving, no matter how intense and earnest, which is against the constitution of the world, is vain. The question, then, which we must seriously consider is this: What is the real meaning of Race; what has, in the past, been the law of race development, and what lessons has the past history of race development to teach the rising Negro people?

When we thus come to inquire into the essential difference of races we find it hard to come at once to any definite conclusion. Many criteria of race differences have in the past been proposed, as color, hair, cranial measurements and language. And manifestly, in each of these respects, human beings differ widely. They vary in color, for instance, from the marble-like pallor of the Scandinavian to the rich, dark brown of the Zulu, passing by the creamy Slav, the yellow Chinese, the light brown Sicilian and the brown Egyptian. Men vary, too, in the texture of hair from the obstinately straight hair of the Chinese to the obstinately tufted and frizzled hair of the Bushman. In measurement of heads, again, men vary; from the broad-headed Tartar to the medium-headed European and the narrow-headed Hottentot; or, again in language, from the highly-inflected Roman tongue to the monosyllabic Chinese. All these physical characteristics are patent enough, and if they agreed with each other it would be very easy to classify mankind. Unfortunately for scientists, however, these criteria of race are most exasperatingly intermingled. Color does not agree with texture of hair, for many of the dark races have straight hair; nor does color agree with the breadth of the head, for the yellow Tartar has a broader head than the German; nor, again, has the science of language as yet succeeded in clearing up the relative authority of these various and contradictory criteria. The final word of science, so far, is that we have at least two, perhaps three, great families of human beings—the whites and Negroes, possibly the yellow race. That other races have arisen from the intermingling of the blood of these two. This broad division of the world's races which men like Huxley and Raetzel have introduced as more nearly true than the old five-race scheme of Blumenbach, is nothing more than an acknowledgment that, so far as purely physical characteristics are concerned, the differences between men do not explain all the differences of their history. It declares, as Darwin himself said, that great as is the physical unlikeness of the various races of men their likenesses are greater, and upon this rests the whole scientific doctrine of Human Brotherhood.[18]

Although the wonderful developments of human history teach that the grosser physical differences of color, hair and bone go but a short way toward explaining the different roles which groups of men have played in Human Progress, yet there are differences—subtle, delicate and elusive, though they may be—which have silently but definitely separated men into groups. While these subtle forces have generally followed the natural cleavage of common blood, descent and physical peculiarities, they have at other times swept across and ignored these. At all times, however, they have divided human beings into races, which, while they perhaps transcend scientific definition, nevertheless, are clearly defined to the eye of the Historian and Sociologist.

If this be true, then the history of the world is the history, not of individuals, but of groups, not of nations, but of races, and he who ignores or seeks to override the race idea in human history ignores and overrides the central thought of all history. What, then, is a race? It is a vast family of human beings, generally of common blood and language, always of common history, traditions and impulses, who are both voluntarily and involuntarily striving together for the accomplishment of certain more or less vividly conceived ideals of life . . .

Manifestly some of the great races of today—particularly the Negro race—have not as yet given to civilization the full spiritual message which they are capable of giving. I will not say that the Negro-race has yet given no message to the world, for it is still a mooted question among scientists as to just how far Egyptian civilization was Negro in its origin; if it was not wholly Negro, it was certainly very closely allied. Be that as it may, however, the fact still remains that the full, complete Negro message of the whole Negro race has not as yet been given to the world: that the messages and ideal of the yellow race have not been completed, and that the striving of the mighty Slavs has but begun. The question is, then: How shall this message be delivered; how shall these various ideals be realized? The answer is plain: By the development of these race groups, not as individuals, but as races . . . For the development of Negro genius, of Negro literature and art, of Negro spirit, only Negroes bound and welded together, Negroes inspired by one vast ideal, can work out in its fullness that great message we have for humanity. We cannot reverse history; we are subject to the same natural laws as other races, and if the Negro is ever to be a factor in the world's history—if among the gaily-colored banners that deck the broad ramparts of civilizations is to hang one uncompromising black, then it must be placed there by black hands, fashioned by black heads and hallowed by the travail of 200,000,000 black hearts beating in one glad song of jubilee.

For this reason, the advance guard of the Negro people—the 8,000,000 people of Negro blood in the United States of America—must soon come to realize that if they are to take their just place in the van of Pan-Negroism, then their destiny is *not* absorption by the white Americans. That if in America it is to be proven for the first time in the modern world that not only Negroes are capable of evolving individual men like Toussaint, the Saviour, but are a nation stored with wonderful possibilities of culture, then their destiny is not a servile imitation of Anglo-Saxon culture, but a stalwart originality which shall unswervingly follow Negro ideals.

It may, however, be objected here that the situation of our race in America renders this attitude impossible; that our sole hope of salvation lies in our being able to lose our race identity in the commingled blood of the nation; and that any other course would merely increase the friction of races which we call race prejudice, and against which we have so long and so earnestly fought.

Here, then, is the dilemma, and it is a puzzling one, I admit. No Negro who has given earnest thought to the situation of his people in America has failed, at some time in life, to find himself at these crossroads; has failed to ask himself at some time: What, after all, am I? Am I an American or am I a Negro? Can I be both? Or is it my duty to cease to be a Negro as soon as possible and be an American? If I strive as a Negro, am I not perpetuating the very cleft that threatens and separates Black and White America? Is not my only possible practical aim the subduction of all that is Negro in me to the American? Does my black blood place upon me any more obligation to assert my nationality than German, or Irish or Italian blood would?

It is such incessant self-questioning and the hesitation that arises from it, that is making the present period a time of vacillation and contradiction for the American Negro; combined race action is stifled, race responsibility is shirked, race enterprises languish, and the best blood, the best talent, the best energy of the Negro people cannot be marshalled to do the bidding of the race. They stand back to make room for every rascal and demagogue who chooses to cloak his selfish deviltry under the veil of race pride.

Is this right? Is it rational? Is it good policy? Have we in America a distinct mission as a race—a distinct sphere of action and an opportunity for race development, or is self-obliteration the highest end to which Negro blood dare aspire?

If we carefully consider what race prejudice really is, we find it, historically, to be nothing but the friction between different groups of people; it is the difference in aim, in feeling, in ideals of two different races; if, now, this difference exists touching territory, laws, language, or even religion, it is manifest that these people cannot live in the same territory without fatal collision; but if, on the other hand, there is substantial agreement in laws, language and religion; if there is a satisfactory adjustment of economic life, then there is no reason why, in the same country and on the same street, two or three great national ideals might not thrive and develop, that men of different races might not strive together for their race ideals as well, perhaps even better, than in isolation. Here, it seems to me, is the reading of the riddle that puzzles so many of us. We are Americans, not only by birth and by citizenship, but by our political ideals, our language, our religion. Farther than that, our Americanism does not go. At that point, we are Negroes, members of a vast historic race that from the very dawn of creation has slept, but half awakening in the dark forests of its African fatherland. We are the first fruits of this new nation, the harbinger of that black to-morrow which is yet destined to soften the whiteness of the Teutonic to-day. We are that people whose subtle sense of song has given America its only American music, its only American fairy tales, its only touch of pathos and humor amid its mad money-getting plutocracy. As such, it is our duty to conserve our physical powers, our intellectual endowments, our spiritual ideals; as a race we must strive by race organization, by race solidarity, by race unity to the realization of that broader humanity which freely recognizes differences in men, but sternly deprecates inequality in their opportunities of development.

For the accomplishment of these ends we need race organizations: Negro colleges, Negro newspapers, Negro business organizations, a Negro school of literature and art, and an intellectual clearing house, for all these products of the Negro mind, which we may call a Negro Academy. Not only is all this necessary for positive advance, it is absolutely imperative for negative defense. Let us not deceive ourselves at our situation in this country. Weighted with a heritage of moral iniquity from our past history, hard pressed in the economic world by foreign immigrants and native prejudice, hated here, despised there and pitied everywhere; our one haven of refuge is ourselves, and but one means of advance, our own belief in our great destiny, our own implicit trust in our ability and worth. There is no power under God's high heaven that can stop the advance of eight thousand thousand honest, earnest, inspired and united people. But—and here is the rub—they *must* be honest, fearlessly criticising their own faults, zealously correcting them; they must be *earnest*. No people that laughs at itself, and ridicules itself, and wishes to God it was anything but itself ever wrote its name in history; it *must* be inspired with the Divine faith of our black mothers, that out of the blood and dust of battle will march a victorious host, a mighty nation, a peculiar people, to speak to the nations of earth a Divine truth that shall make them free. And such a people must be united; not merely united for the organized theft of political spoils, not united to disgrace religion with whoremongers and ward-heelers; not united merely to protest and pass resolutions, but united to stop the ravages of consumption among the Negro people, united to keep black boys from loafing, gambling and crime; united to guard the purity of black women and to reduce the vast army of black prostitutes that is today marching to hell; and united in serious organizations, to determine by careful conference and thoughtful interchange of opinion the broad lines of policy and action for the American Negro.

This, is the reason for being which the American Negro Academy has. It aims at once to be the epitome and expression of the intellect of the black-blooded people of America, the exponent of the race ideals of one of the world's great races . . .

The American Negro Academy must point out a practical path of advance to the Negro people; there lie before every Negro today hundreds of questions of policy and right which must be settled and which each one settles now, not in accordance with any rule, but by impulse or individual preference; for instance: What should be the attitude of Negroes toward the educational qualification for voters? What should be our attitude toward separate schools? How should we meet discriminations on railways and in hotels? Such questions need not so much specific answers for each part as a general expression of policy, and nobody should be better fitted to announce such a policy than a representative honest Negro Academy . . .

Finally, in practical policy, I wish to suggest the following *Academy Creed:*

1. We believe that the Negro people, as a race, have a contribution to make to civilization and humanity, which no other race can make.
2. We believe it the duty of the Americans of Negro descent, as a body, to maintain their race identity until this mission of the Negro people is accomplished, and the ideal of human brotherhood has become a practical possibility.
3. We believe that, unless modern civilization is a failure, it is entirely feasible and practicable for two races in such essential political, economic and religious harmony as the white and colored people in

America, to develop side by side in peace and mutual happiness, the peculiar contribution which each has to make to the culture of their common country.

4. As a means to this end we advocate, not such social equality between these races as would disregard human likes and dislikes, but such a social equilibrium as would, throughout all the complicated relations of life, give due and just consideration to culture, ability, and moral worth, whether they be found under white or black skins.

5. We believe that the first and greatest step toward the settlement of the present friction between the races—commonly called the Negro Problem—lies in the correction of the immorality, crime and laziness among the Negroes themselves, which still remains as a heritage from slavery. We believe that only earnest and long continued efforts on our own part can cure these social ills.

6. We believe that the second great step toward a better adjustment of the relations between races, should be a more impartial selection of ability in the economic and intellectual world, and a greater respect for personal liberty and worth, regardless of race. We believe that only earnest efforts on the part of the white people of this country will bring much needed reform in these matters.

7. On the basis of the foregoing declaration, and firmly believing in our high destiny, we, as American Negroes, are resolved to strive in every honorable way for the realization of the best and highest aims, for the development of strong manhood and pure womanhood, and for the rearing of a race ideal in America and Africa, to the glory of God and the uplifting of the Negro people.[19]

It was a powerful statement of Du Bois's changing philosophy, but it was directed largely toward a black audience. That same year, he would publish a more universal and public statement of his thought. In his August 1897 Atlantic Monthly *essay "Strivings of the Negro People," Du Bois expressed his first real doubts about the Compromise and Washington's leadership. When it was republished as "Of Our Spiritual Strivings" in* Souls of Black Folk *in 1903, it opened the book and established the leader's firm stand against Tuskegee, but its first appearance, and one of Du Bois's first national appearances, came in 1897.*[20]

W.E.B. DU BOIS

. . . The history of the American Negro is the history of this strife,— this longing to attain self-conscious manhood, to merge his double self into a better and truer self. In this merging he wishes neither of the older selves to be lost. He does not wish to Africanize America, for America has too much to teach the world and Africa; he does not wish to bleach his Negro blood in a flood of white Americanism, for he believes— foolishly, perhaps, but fervently—that Negro blood has yet a message for the world. He simply wishes to make it possible for a man to be both a Negro and an American without being cursed and spit upon by his fellows, without losing the opportunity of self-development.

This is the end of his striving: to be a co-worker in the kingdom of culture, to escape both death and isolation, and to husband and use his best powers. These powers, of body and of mind, have in the past been so wasted and dispersed as to lose all effectiveness, and to seem like absence of all power, like weakness. The double-aimed struggle of the black artisan, on the one hand to escape white contempt for a nation of mere hewers of wood and drawers of water, and on the other hand to plough and nail and dig for a poverty-stricken horde, could only result in making him a poor craftsman, for he had but half a heart in either cause. By the poverty and ignorance of his people the Negro lawyer or doctor was pushed toward quackery and demagogism, and by the criticism of the other world toward an elaborate preparation that overfitted him for his lowly tasks. The would-be black-savant was confronted by the paradox that the knowledge his people needed was a twice-told tale to his white neighbors, while the knowledge which would teach the white world was Greek to his own flesh and blood. The innate love of harmony and beauty that set the ruder souls of his people a-dancing, a-singing, and a-laughing raised but confusion and doubt in the soul of the black artist; for the beauty revealed to him was the soul-beauty of a race which his larger audience despised, and he could not articulate the message of another people.

This waste of double aims, this seeking to satisfy two unreconciled ideals, has wrought sad havoc with the courage and faith and deeds of eight thousand people, has sent them often wooing false gods and invoking false means of salvation, and has even at times seemed destined to make them ashamed of themselves. In the days of bondage they thought to see in one divine event the end of all doubt and disappointment; eighteenth-century Rousseauism never worshiped freedom with half the unquestioning faith that the American Negro did for two centuries. To him slavery was, indeed, the sum of all villainies, the cause of all sorrow, the root of all prejudice; emancipation was the key to a promised land of sweeter beauty than ever stretched before the eyes of wearied Israelites. In his songs and exhortations swelled one refrain, liberty; in his tears and curses the god he implored had freedom in his right hand. At last it came,—suddenly, fearfully, like a dream. With one wild carnival of blood and passion came the message in his own plaintive cadences:—

> Shout, O children!
> Shout, you're free!
> The Lord has bought your liberty!

Years have passed away, ten, twenty, thirty. Thirty years of national life, thirty years of renewal and development, and yet the swarthy ghost of Banquo sits in its old place at the national feast. In vain does the nation cry to its vastest problem,—

> Take any shape but that, and my firm nerves
> Shall never tremble!

The freedman has not yet found in freedom his promised land. Whatever of lesser good may have come in these years of change, the shadow of a deep disappointment rests upon the Negro people,—a disappointment all the more bitter because the unattained ideal was unbounded save by the simple ignorance of a lowly folk . . .

Up the new path the advance guard toiled, slowly, heavily, doggedly; only those who have watched and guided the faltering feet, the misty minds, the dull understandings, of the dark pupils of these schools know how faithfully, how piteously, this people strove to learn. It was weary work. The cold statistician wrote down the inches of progress here and there, noted also where here and there a foot had slipped or some one had fallen. To the tired climbers, the horizon was ever dark, the mists were often cold, the Canaan was always dim and far away. If, however, the vistas disclosed as yet no goal, no resting-place, little but flattery and criticism, the journey at least gave leisure for reflection and self-examination; it changed the child of emancipation to the youth with dawning self-consciousness, self-realization, self-respect. In those sombre forests of his striving his own soul rose before him, and he saw himself,—darkly as through a veil; and yet he saw in himself some faint revelation of his power, of his mission. He began to have a dim feeling that, to attain his place in the world, he must be himself, and not another. For the first time he sought to analyze the burden he bore upon his back, that dead-weight of social degradation partially masked behind a half-named Negro problem. He felt his poverty; without a cent, without a home, without land, tools, or savings, he had entered into competition with rich landed, skilled neighbors.

To be a poor man is hard, but to be a poor race in a land of dollars is the very bottom of hardships. He felt the weight of his ignorance,—not simply of letters, but of life, of business, of the humanities; the accumulated sloth and shirking and awkwardness of decades and centuries shackled his hands and feet. Nor was his burden all poverty and ignorance. The red stain of bastardy, which two centuries of systematic legal defilement of Negro women had stamped upon his race, meant not only the loss of ancient African chastity, but also the hereditary weight of a mass of filth from white whoremongers and adulterers, threatening almost the obliteration of the Negro home.

A people thus handicapped ought not to be asked to race with the world, but rather allowed to give all its time and thought to its own social problems. But alas! while sociologists gleefully count his bastards and his prostitutes, the very soul of the toiling, sweating black man is darkened by the shadow of a vast despair. Men call the shadow prejudice, and learnedly explain it as the natural defense of culture against barbarism, learning against ignorance, purity against crime, the "higher" against the "lower" races. To which the Negro cries Amen! and swears that to so much this strange prejudice as is founded on just homage to civilization, culture, righteousness, and progress he humbly bows and meekly does obeisance. But before that nameless prejudice that leaps beyond all this he stands helpless, dismayed, and well-nigh speechless; before that personal disrespect and mockery, the ridicule and systematic humiliation, the distortion of fact and wanton license of fancy, the cynical ignoring of the better and boisterous welcoming of the worse, the all-pervading desire to inculcated disdain for everything black, from Toussaint to the devil,—before this there rises a sickening despair that would disarm and discourage any nation save that black host to whom "discouragement" is an unwritten word . . .

The training of the schools we need to-day more than ever,—the training of deft hands, quick eyes and ears, and the broader, deeper, higher culture of gifted minds. The power of the ballot we need in sheer self-defense, and as a guarantee of good faith. We may misuse it, but we can scarce do worse in this respect than our whilom masters. Freedom, too, the long-sought, we still seek,—the freedom of life and limb, the freedom to work and think. Work, culture, and liberty—all these we need, not singly, but together; for to-day these ideals among the Negro people are gradually coalescing, and finding a higher meaning in the unifying ideal of race,—the ideal of fostering the traits and talents of the Negro, not in opposition to, but in conformity with, the greater ideals of the American republic, in order that some day, on American soil, two world races may give each to each those characteristics which both so sadly lack. Already we come not altogether empty-handed: there is to-day no true American music but the sweet wild melodies of the Negro slave; the American fairy tales are Indian and African; we are the sole oasis of simple faith and reverence in a dusty desert of dollars and smartness. Will America be poorer if she replace her brutal, dyspeptic blundering with the light-hearted but determined Negro humility; or her coarse, cruel wit with loving, jovial good humor; or her Annie Rooney with Steal Away?[21]

Merely a stern concrete test of the underlying principles of the great republic is the Negro problem, and the spiritual striving of the freedmen's sons is the travail of souls whose burden is almost beyond the measure of their strength, but who bear it in the name of an historic race, in the name of this the land of their fathers' fathers, and in the name of human opportunity.[22]

NOTES

1. Lewis, 1993, 110–114, 176–177.
2. Du Bois here refers to the Harvard historian Albert Bushnell Hart, who served from 1883 to 1926 and directed Du Bois's dissertation. Hart would remain friends with both Du Bois and Washington, and never really understood the rift that developed between them. He argued in 1901 that Washington was "a valuable factor in the future of American progress." Hart, 1901, 663.
3. Washington, 1975, 98–99.
4. Ibid., 152–153.
5. Lewis, 1993, 177.
6. Charles Young, a friend of Du Bois and one of the most successful early black graduates of West Point. He would have a long and distinguished military career. At the time of this letter (and from 1894 to 1898 in total) he was a colleague of Du Bois at Wilberforce, teaching military science, math, and French. Washington, 1975, vol. 4, 158.
7. Washington, 1975, 158.
8. Isabel Eaton, who obviously attended Smith College, was part of a wave of female sociologists like Jane Addams, Florence Kelley, and Katherine Bement Davis. She was Du Bois's collaborator and coauthor on *The Philadelphia Negro*. Deegan, 1988, 301–311.
9. Lindsay would ultimately go on to become professor of social legislation at Columbia University from 1907 to 1939. Washington, 1975, 240–241. See Samuel McCune Lindsay Papers, 1877–1957, MS #0785, Rare Book and Manuscript Library, Columbia University, New York.
10. See Thornbrough, 1972.
11. William Calvin Chase was one of Washington's earliest critics following the Atlanta Compromise. He never really had a defining philosophy

and vacillated often, but as editor of the *Washington Argus*, followed by the *Washington Bee*, he wielded considerable influence. He would criticize Washington from the Compromise until 1900, when he changed course and supported Tuskegee's leader. In 1901, he turned against him again, and stayed against him for the next five years. In 1906, however, Washington placed a spy in the *Bee*'s offices who was ultimately able to convince Chase to support Washington and Tuskegee in print, in return for financial concessions. He would remain a kept man until Washington's death, although often he was disgruntled about it. Ibid., 247; and Harlan, 1971, 410–411.

12. Washington, 1975, 246–247.

13. Ibid., 299. See Albert Bushnell Hart Papers, HUG 4448, Harvard University Archives, Cambridge, Massachusetts.

14. Again, this is a fund of which both Du Bois and Washington took advantage. See Chapter 2, note 19.

15. Washington, 1975, 320.

16. Ibid., 256. Crummell was a pan-Africanist Episcopal minister who spent 20 years in Liberia before returning to a pulpit in Washington, D.C. His work at St. Luke's Church would combine both political and religious advocacy, ending on December 9, 1894, when he retired at age 75. Even in retirement, however, Crummell stayed active in race politics. His chief frustration on that count came with the influence of Booker Washington. "The American people care for nought save the material outcome of the Negro problem," he wrote in 1898. "The ideals of the Negro brain, life, character are a triviality! They say to themselves—'we will do the thinking, philosophizing, the scientific work of the nation:—but you Negroes must work. That is your destiny & that will be your gain & advantage.' And there is a lot of Negro leaders who catch at this bait, & are carried away by the delusion." At the head of those Negro leaders was Washington. "Letters, literature, science and philosophy," for Crummell, had to be a central part of the development of black America, "not at some distant day, but now and all along the development of the race. And no temporary fad of doubting or purblind philanthropy is to be allowed to make 'industrial training' a substitute for it." Such was not a call "that every Negro shall be made a scholar," he wrote. "No one can make a thimble hold the contents of a bucket! But what it does mean is this, that the whole world of scholarship shall be opened to the Negro mind; and that it is not to be fastened, temporarily or permanently to the truck-patch or to the hoe, to the anvil or to the plane; that the Negro shall be allowed to do his own thinking in any and every sphere, and not to have that thinking relegated to others." Ordfield, "Introduction," in 1995, 7–11; Reddick, "Biography," 1–2; Adeleke, 1998, 70–71; and "Alexander Crummell to Frazier Miller," 20 June 1898, Box 1, Crummell Letters, Folder 6, Alexander Crummell Papers, Schomberg Center for Research in Black Culture, New York Public Library. "The Prime Need of the Negro Race," from which this excerpt comes, originally appeared in the *Independent*, 19 August 1897. It is republished in Ordfield, 1995, 200–203.

17. Du Bois, 1897, 1.

18. Thomas Henry Huxley was one of the most accomplished comparative anatomists of the late 19th century, earning the nickname "Darwin's Bulldog" for his defense of the Darwinian conception of evolution. Darwin's seminal work, of course, *On the Origin of Species*, was published in 1859, and was often dragged into phrenological discussions of racial superiority and difference, often by Huxley himself. Friedrich Raetzel was a German ethnographer who was an early exponent of what would later come to be called "cultural geography." Among his work was a study of the cities of the United States. Like Huxley, he was a vigorous social Darwinist who developed the concept of lebensraum that would later become so significant to the Nazis. Finally, Johann Friedrich Blumenbach died in 1840, well before Darwin's major publications. Still, he was a German anthropologist based in Gottingen who used skulls to develop theories about racial divisions. Du Bois alludes to the five races into which he divided humanity in 1779: Caucasians (whites), Mongolians (east Asians), Malayans (south Asians), Ethiopians (blacks), and Americans (natives). For Huxley, see Desmond 1994; and Desmond, 1998. For Raetzel, see Wanklyn, 1961. For Blumenbach, Raetzel, and Huxley, see Harris, 2001, 80–216. For Blumenbach and Raetzel, see Smith, 1991.

19. Du Bois, 1897.

20. Lewis, 1993, 200–201.

21. "Little Annie Rooney" was an incredibly popular song written by Michael Nolan. Performed at least as early as 1885, the sheet music was finally published in 1889. It was so ingrained in the culture that it spawned two movies and a long-running comic strip. "Steal Away" was a well-known Negro spiritual. The metaphor refers to replacing a relatively vacuous white popular song with a more meaningful, historical, and reverent black one. "Little Annie Rooney," www.fresnostate.edu/folklore/ballads/R774.html, accessed 23 June 2013.

22. Du Bois, 1897, 194–198; and Du Bois, 1903, 1–9.

4

The First Fissure

Boston early established itself as the home of Washington criticism, led by editor William Monroe Trotter. In 1898, Washington and T. Thomas Fortune met with critics of Tuskegee in Boston and were loudly castigated. Later that year, in September, Du Bois took over as president of the ostensibly anti-Washington American Negro Academy. In November, Washington resigned from the board of the Kowaliga Academic and Industrial Institute. It was an Alabama school founded by William E. Benson, a friend of Du Bois. Washington's friends tried to convince him to change his mind, assuring him that the school was built on the Tuskegee model, but he refused.

The nascent onset of the dispute between Du Bois and Washington generally appears in most accounts as beginning in 1900, in what Du Bois saw as a betrayal by Washington in a recommendation dispute over a school superintendency position in Washington, D.C. That first sign of weakness in the relationship was then exacerbated by the formation of the National Negro Business League, Du Bois's review of Up From Slavery, *the Boston Riot of 1903, and the publication of* The Souls of Black Folk. *The relationship between Du Bois and Washington, however, was problematic even before the Washington School District problems of 1900. A relationship that was for all practical intents cordial between 1894 and 1897 felt its first strain two years before Washington, D.C.*

Also in 1898, Washington and editor T. Thomas Fortune met with a group of Boston critics of his program at Young's Hotel. Each of them castigated Washington and Washingtonian thought, the concluding speech given by William H. Lewis, a lawyer and football coach at Harvard. The Tuskegee leader responded patiently with prepared remarks that addressed none of the angry concerns, but it was clear that the rift between Tuskegee and Boston had calcified into something virtually permanent. And Du Bois, although uninvolved in the Young's Hotel incident, was Boston to his core. It would not be Washington's last problem with the city's race advocates.[1]

WILLIAM EDWARD BURGHARDT DU BOIS

Philadelphia 22 Sept 98

My Dear Sir [Washington]: Your letter of the 18th has just reached me. I think it very probable that I can be in Boston early in December on the occasion you suggest. The final decision must of course come from the authorities at Atlanta but I've little doubt of their willingness to grant me leave of absence for the time. Awaiting further details, I remain Very Sincerely Yours,

W.E.B. Du Bois[2]

W.E.B. DU BOIS

Atlanta, Ga., 17 Oct. 1898

My Dear Mr. Washington: I laid your letter before Dr. Bumstead and he returned the enclosed reply. So that I shall be at your service. For the sake of preparing myself I should like to know how many persons & who will take part, & how long I shall be expected to speak—and whether on any particular subject &c &c. Kindly write me at your convenience. Please too return Dr Bumstead's letter.[3] Very sincerely

W.E.B. Du Bois[4]

Alexander Crummell, the founder of the somewhat anti-Washington American Negro Academy, with whom Du Bois published "The Conservation of the Races" in 1897, died on September 10, 1898. His death left a power vacuum that would be filled in the interim by John Cromwell. Ultimately, although Du Bois

would be absent from the December annual meeting because of his Atlanta University schedule, the board would elect him president "by acclimation," wounding would-be candidate Cromwell and placing Du Bois squarely in opposition to Washington. It was the first sign of fissure between Washington and Du Bois, and its consequences would be felt almost immediately.[5]

William E. Benson, a graduate of Howard, created a new school in his hometown of Kowaliga, Alabama in 1896. William had returned to Alabama with his degree in 1895, that auspicious year that witnessed the death of Douglass and the ascent of Washington. For those in Elmore County, Alabama, however, 1895 was far more notable for the racial violence practiced against the black population. John Benson, William's father, even wrote to Booker Washington in April explaining the racial turmoil that gripped the region.[6] Most immediately, the violence convinced William to devote himself to bettering the lives of local black children. John donated 10 acres and lumber for a new, two-story school building. William formed a glee club and traveled the area giving performances for donations. It was a long process. In 1896, for example, arsonists set Benson's store on fire. Benson was, however, in contact with Washington, who gave the young upstart his endorsement. Within two years, the Kowaliga Academic and Industrial Institute was completed.[7]

Among the Board of Trustees were Washington, Oswald Garrison Villard, Emily Howland, Hollis Burke Frissell, and Francis J. Garrison. It was an impressive roster for the small school in central Alabama, but it was a group in a transitional phase. Villard, of course, would, toward the end of the next decade, help found the NAACP. Another trustee, Isabel Hayes Chapin Barrows supported Booker T. Washington and helped finance Kowaliga. She led a life of diverse interests, but served for a time as part of the medical school faculty at Howard University.[8] It was, in other words, a group—for the most part—that respected Washington as a leader and supported black education when it could, but did not necessarily believe that the Hampton–Tuskegee model was superior to all others. Washington realized this even before they did. The differences in educational models would not become part of the public discourse until Du Bois made it such in the early 20th century. For most white activists, black education was black education. But Washington knew the difference between a Hampton and Howard degree. He knew that Benson was a friend of Du Bois. The nuance of such relationships was far more important to Tuskegee's leader than it was to others with an interest in Kowaliga.

"The school at Kowaliga has made good progress," Washington reported to Howland, "but one of the troubles is that these young people don't want to wait for things to grow in a natural way." For Howland, Benson was "the child of wealth, for his environment, so we cannot expect practical work-a-day wisdom from him."[9] Benson, of course, was indeed an impatient rich kid, but

the likeness to Du Bois cannot be avoided. Washington also saw Du Bois as an impatient rich kid. He too had no desire to "wait for things to grow in a natural way." Although Du Bois was not directly involved in Kowaliga, its creation by his friend Benson and the collection of personalities it brought together inadvertently created a tangible divide between him and Washington and ultimately set the educational agenda for the next two decades.

There was a steady devolution in Washington's thinking from that point forward. "One thing that makes me a little doubtful about Kowaliga is that Mr. Benson is not inclined to take advice, and for this reason he does not secure the hearty co-operation of the people in the vicinity of Kowaliga, to say nothing of those who have had opportunity of a larger experience than he has," he wrote in June 1898. "Mr. Benson likes to travel about from place to place, and I am sure a good portion of what the school receives is spent in this way."[10] He was painting a portrait of a wealthy, entitled know-it-all who would not accept the bridle of Tuskegee leadership. It was a portrait he would paint of Du Bois until Washington's death in 1915.

When Benson went to New York and visited T. Thomas Fortune, whom he assumed to be an ally, the editor was unimpressed. "Young Benson stopped a moment yesterday," he reported to Washington, "with his face turned towards Boston."[11] Boston, the intellectual home of Du Bois and the actual home of his more radical ally William Monroe Trotter, a place that had already proven itself to be against the Tuskegee ethic.

On November 8, 1898, Washington resigned from the Kowaliga board of trustees. Howland and others urged him to stay aboard, assuming that having his name attached to the school would help it survive. But Washington would not budge. Benson was not "inclined to treat a trustee with that delicate courtesy which is required to keep a trustee interested." He was "whimsical, spasmodic and rather superficial."[12] In other words, he had an educational philosophy more in line with the American Negro Academy than with Tuskegee, and because of that he failed to show Washington the proper deference. Emily Howland, Hollis Burke Frissell, and Francis J. Garrison all tried to convince Washington that Benson was an adherent of the Tuskegee philosophy, but to no avail.[13]

TIMOTHY THOMAS FORTUNE

Washington D.C., December 14, 1898

My Dear Mr Washington: Your letter of the 10th instant was received and I thank you for writing to Dr Shaw about the article for the January Review.[14] I shall do the work if he gives me the order . . .

Col Pledger writes me that he is to be at Tuskegee tomorrow.[15] The President's visit ought to be worth a great deal to you and your work. I hope much in that regard. The President is a thoroughly despicable character and I despise him, but I am glad that he went to Tuskegee, where he ought to learn something.

The idea of Dr [William Hayes] Ward comparing you and your work with that of Crogman, Du Bois and such! It is awful. It is discouraging, coming from that source.[16]

I do not feel very hopeful today; indeed I am blue. Your friend

T. Thomas Fortune[17]

EDWARD HENRY CLEMENT (*Edward Henry Clement was editor-in-chief of the* Boston Transcript *from 1881 to 1906. He was more radical than Washington, but consistently defended him in a city where many criticized.*)

[Boston, Mass.] January 2, 1898 [1899]

My Dear Mr. Washington: I am going to print the letter sent me regarding your position on the political troubles of the blacks, by Mr. Emmett J. Scott, but I wish I could have a signed article by you on the whole question, both general and going into particulars.[18] I should not ask you to contribute it free, but would pay you our best rates for contributions. Any time soon for an article of, say, 2,000 words.

I was shocked the other night to hear a reference to your policy in a meeting of colored men, hissed. Turning to my next neighbor in the pew I asked, "Is he not hitting at Washington?" and the answer was, "Yes; there is much and growing opposition to his counsels among blacks." In any candid editorial comment on the situation this surely cannot be ignored with safety.

I confess that I wonder at, and admire, your reserve and am not at all sure that yours is not the course of wisdom in the thickening difficulties which beset the upward path of your race. I am much impressed with the protests of such men as Du Bois and Dunbar against the new outburst of intolerance in the South.[19] The indifference in the North that is settling down over the whole problem is one of the most serious phenomena and it seems to me that it must be rudely shaken up once in a while to prevent the crust forming from hardening into solid substance. I wish you would write us an article. That would mark an epoch in the new year for the development of the question. Very truly yours,

E H Clement[20]

In March 1899, Washington returned to Boston to raise money for Tuske-gee and included Du Bois and Paul Laurence Dunbar on stage with him at the Hollis Street Theater. As Clement's letter suggests, the division between Du Bois still seemed salvageable, and this kind of contact did occur. The presence of Du Bois and Dunbar was largely to eliminate them as competition for his audience, but both Du Bois and Dunbar bested Washington in oratory and reception. Washington's supporters were not pleased with Tuskegee's leader being outdone by oppositional forces—or, at the very least, known allies of oppositional forces. It was after this meeting that Washington's handlers decided to send him to Europe for a vacation.[21]

BOOKER TALIAFERRO WASHINGTON

In the spring of 1899 a rather notable meeting was held in Boston, in the afternoon, at the Hollis Street Theatre. This meeting was gotten up in the interest of the Tuskegee Institute, by friends of the institution, in Boston for the purpose of raising money for the school. It was presided over by Bishop Lawrence, bishop of Massachusetts.[22] I invited to speak with me at this meeting Dr. W.E.B. Du Bois and Mr. Paul Laurence Dunbar. Dr. Du Bois read an original story and Mr. Dunbar recited from his own poems. The theatre was filled with representatives of the most cultured and wealthy men and women in Boston, and was said to be the most successful meeting of the kind that had been held for a good while. An admission was charged at the door and a generous sum was raised for the school. This was the first time that Mr. Dunbar had appeared in Boston and his readings produced a most favorable effect. The same was true of Dr. Du Bois.[23]

BOOKER T. WASHINGTON

In the spring of 1899 there came to me what I might describe as almost the greatest surprise of my life. Some good ladies in Boston arranged a public meeting in the interests of Tuskegee, to be held in the Hollis Street Theatre. This meeting was attended by large numbers of the best people of Boston, of both races. Bishop Lawrence presided. In addition to an address made by myself, Mr. Paul Lawrence Dunbar read from his poems, and Dr. W.E.B. Du Bois read an original sketch.

Some of those who attended this meeting noticed that I seemed unusually tired, and some little time after the close of the meeting, one of the ladies who had been interested in it asked me in a casual way if

I had ever been to Europe. I replied that I never had. She asked me if I had ever thought of going, and I told her no; that it was something entirely beyond me. This conversation soon passed out of my mind, but a few days afterward I was informed that some friends in Boston, including Mr. Francis J. Garrison, had raised a sum of money sufficient to pay all the expenses of Mrs. Washington and myself during a three or four months' trip to Europe. It was added with emphasis that we must go.[24]

Still, despite the post-meeting emphasis on Washington's health and vigor, and even though he was bested in oratory by Du Bois and Dunbar, the Tuskegee leader's speech was telling in its enunciation of a position that was in its conception ultimately pragmatic and distinctly southern.

BOOKER T. WASHINGTON

. . . A missionary traveling in the heart of Africa was surprised to find an African chief who was living the Christian life. When the missionary asked the African where and when he had heard of the Christian religion, the old chief replied that he had not heard of it but he had seen it for two years by daily contact with a man who had lived the Christ life. Object lessons that shall bring the Southern white man into daily, visible, tangible contact with the benefits of Negro education will go much further towards the solution of present problems than all the mere abstract argument and theories that can be evolved from the human brain. In proportion as the Negro learns to do something as well or better than a white man he will find his place in our economic and political life and his place, like that of every being possessing real worth, will be that of a man, "a man for a' that and a' that." It is not our duty to set metes and bounds upon the aspirations and ambitions of any individual or race, but it is our duty to see that the foundation is wisely and firmly laid. A race that plants itself in the ownership of the soil, the industries, the domestic arts of a country, in intelligence and religion and in the confidence of the people among whom it lives, is the race that will win regardless of all temporary makeshifts, obstacles and discouragements. Man may ruffle the surface but the permanent flow of the river can he not stop.

We of this generation in the South must lay the foundation for those that are to come. I would not advocate that the end of every Negro's education should be to excel in the ownership of property, skill in agriculture, mechanic and industrial arts, but I would with all the emphasis of my soul, remind my race over and over again that if we of this generation lay the foundation well in these, our children and children's children will find through them the surest way to recognition and success in letters, arts and statesmanship. Then will the sacred story repeat itself: "The rain descended, and the floods came, and the winds blew, and beat upon that house; and it fell not; for it was founded upon a rock."[25]

As early as 1899, Washington employed "advance agents" of Tuskegee whose job was not only to promote Washingtonian ideas but also to damage Boston Guardian *editor William Monroe Trotter and other Washington critics.*[26] *Peter Jefferson Smith, for example, founded both the* Boston Advocate *and* Boston Colored Citizen *to compete with Trotter's* Guardian, *although both publications failed. He was one of the Tuskegee Machine's chief operatives.*[27]

PETER JEFFERSON SMITH, JR.

Boston, Apr 28th 1899

My dear Mr. Washington I have seen both Mr Clement and Mr Plummer. I found Mr Clement as sound and solid as they come and expressed his disgust in the most positive manner for George W. Forbes and has promised to give me his speech on that occasion that I may send it to you after reading it for myself, he said Col. Hallowell was like himself simply disgusted, he also said that he expected an interview with Fortune on Monday afternoon. Plummer is just wild and until this time he says he did not know the friends you have in Boston and when you return from your trip abroad he will see to it that your friends extend you such a welcome as no colored man ever had given him in this city or country he denounced Forbes at the League as did I.D. Barnett.[28] I will tell you all about it when I see you. Plummer says he will try and be in New York so as to see you off. I send you the papers having matter of interest. Faithfully Yours

P.J. Smith Jr[29]

On April 24, 1899, a group of black Boston activists met at Young's Hotel to commemorate the 48th anniversary of Charles Sumner's Senate election. It soon became an anti-Washington and anti-lynching rally, with William H. Lewis arguing that "the gospel of industrial education has been declared to be the negro's only salvation. If it is meant by this that through some mysterious process a trade will give to the negro all his rights as a man and citizen, it is a sufficient refutation of the theory to say that the South would not stand for it a single moment." Lewis would eventually move to the Washington position. Du Bois was not present. He and Hart were still more concerned about the immediate exigencies of employment.[30]

ALBERT BUSHNELL HART

Cambridge, Mass. June 5, 1899

My dear Sir [Washington]: Yours of the 12th relative to Professor Du Bois is at hand. Du Bois seems to me to occupy a very unusual situation. Practically no member of his race in America has had so thorough and so well qualified opportunities for the highest education. There are no better advantages in the world than those of any first class American University, combined with foreign study, and with opportunities for investigation. It is worth a great deal for your cause to have such an example of a man of excellent abilities, thoroughly trained and at the same time modest and sensible. He is a standing refutation of some of the hardest things said about the negro race.

I write with renewed interest because of the very excellent appearance which Du Bois made here in Cambridge a few weeks ago when you were present. His address seemed to me just right; eloquent, witty and suggestive. I felt that the man had justified the expectations of his friends.

Now I do not feel sufficiently well acquainted with the conditions of the educational work in the South to say where Du Bois can render greatest service, but wherever that is he ought to be. Tuskegee of course fills a great arc in popular attention both North and South, and probably the same effort applied there will have a wider range than if put into a smaller and less famous institution. My natural interest would be to see him associated with you. I will write him in that sense.

I hope, Mr. Washington, that when you next come to Boston, you will do me the favor to let me know beforehand. I want to know more about your work; if I can help it on in any way, I want to do it. I shall feel honored to have the opportunity to make your better acquaintance. Sincerely yours,

Albert Bushnell Hart[31]

W.E.B. DU BOIS

Atlanta, Ga., 12 July 1899

My Dear Sir [Washington]: I have taken time to think over carefully your kind offer of May 12th. I assure you I appreciate the honor. For the coming year I shall as you suggest feel under obligations to remain at Atlanta University. I shall however consider your offer for the year 1900–01 and shall decide during the winter as to whether I think a change

best for all interests. Meantime I should like to hear from you more definitely as to the work you would expect & the salary. You have as you
know my best sympathy for the Tuskeegee work and whether or not I
see my way clear to join you in it my interest will be the same & I shall
be ready to help by word or deed.

I shall try during the summer & fall to think out a plan of work that
I might accomplish at Tuskeegee & when I have I shall submit it to you.
I trust you will write me freely & frankly as to any plans you may have,
that we may understand each other thoroughly.

I hope you & Mrs. W. are enjoying your outing as I know you must
be. My regards to you both. Very Sincerely,

W.E.B. Du Bois[32]

*On the final day of the first major meeting of the newly formed Afro-American
Council, held in Chicago in August 1899, a group of leaders—led by Chicago's
Reverdy C. Ransom and Indianapolis's B.T. Thornton—denounced Booker T.
Washington for not attending, although he and his wife were in Chicago at
the time. The organization was founded the year prior by T. Thomas Fortune,
Washington's great ally, and he was expected to support it. Bishop Alexander
Walters defended him, however, arguing that his position "made it impracticable for him to connect himself with the discussion of an organization which
might be radical in its utterances to the destruction of his usefulness in connection with many causes." It was, again, that pragmatism of Washington that
drove him from any appearance of radicalism so that he would be able to court
white donors to his university. He was still, however, the intellectual lodestar
for a group founded by Fortune, and the Council officially endorsed the efforts
of Washington later that day.[33]*

PETER JEFFERSON SMITH, JR.

Palmer House, Chicago. Aug 19th 1899

My dear Mr Washington You have probably seen by the morning
papers a lot of newspaper rot about your being denounced by the
Council this morning. Well now there is not one word of truth in it. It
happened in this way. Mrs Washington asked that her name be left off
the program and when her request was presented to the Council it was
made to appear as if she had expressed considerable indignation about
it, this coupled with your absence from the meeting was like shaking
the red flag in the bulls face so one or two of those crazy hot heads
whose only mission on earth is to talk and do nothing, ranted round

and blew off a lot of silly gas against you. No action was taken by the Council except to accept Mrs Washington's declination. Some crazy chump of a reporter anxious for sensation, rushes the rot you may have read into print. As soon as we saw it everything else was suspended and resolutions deprecating the action of the sensational reporter and heartily endorsing you and the great work you are doing were passed unanimously amid cheers and applause.

Prof Du Boise, Henderson of Indiana Bishop Walters Maj Buckner and all those who could get a word in were loud in there endorsement. Dr Bendy was at the meeting and helped in every way that he could to disabuse the public's mind of any such thing.[34] You will doubtless see the subsequent action of the Cou[n]cil in the later editions. I shall tell you more when I see you in Boston.

With best wishes for a successful meeting I am faithfully yours

P.J. Smith Jr.[35]

Thomas Wellington Henderson, an AME minister from Greensboro, North Carolina, and John C. Bruckner, a Chicago politician and Civil War veteran, seem likely Washington allies, per Smith's letter. Du Bois and Charles Edwin Bentley, however, would become two of Tuskegee's chief critics. Bentley was a Chicago dentist and leading political activist. In 1903, he would help create the Equal Opportunity League, which protested school segregation and housed the bulk of Chicago's anti-Washington sentiment. He would also be present at the founding of both Niagara and NAACP. The idea that he and Du Bois would defend Washington, even at this comparatively early date, seems to be a stretch. Still, Emmett Jay Scott would validate Smith's account.[36]

SCOTT C. BURRELL *(Burrell was a minister and general secretary of the Richmond Colored YMCA.)*

Richmond, Va., Aug. 22, 1899

Dear Sir & Friend [Washington]; In one of the daily papers of our city I read where there was an effort made to denounce you as a traitor, at the Afro-American Convention which was held in Chicago. I wish to say that there is one if no other in the person of myself who do not agree with such. A man who has done so much and who is still doing all that is in his power to lift up his people, as you have done, can never have such herald [hurled] at him without stirring up his friends. I am with you in all your moves especially knowing you as I do. First you have God with you, and second, Right. So you need not fear but press

on in your good work. May God give you the strength to do so . . .
Yours in the work,

S.C. Burrell[37]

EMMETT JAY SCOTT

Tuskegee, Ala., August 23, 1899

Dear Mr Washington: The Ransom attack at the closing of the Afro-
American Council was unwarranted, and failed completely of its purpose. It only served to give you another opportunity to emphasize your
views and the object of your work as you did at Saratoga. Your reply
was sent out by the Associated Press & will do good. Du Bois and
others sustain you well in the Chicago Record.[38]

It is well you never get disgusted at the smallness of some of these
little hypocritical fellows. Your composure only shows them up in
painful, envious contrast. You certainly have my sincere congratulations upon the way you met this silly attack. Yours Faithfully—

Emmett J. Scott[39]

*The incident also provides evidence of one of Washington's first attempts to
pay journalists to provide him favorable coverage. His money, through Fortune,
to John Edward Bruce for favorable editorials supporting Tuskegee against
Chicago critics would be one of many payouts over the years.[40]*

T. THOMAS FORTUNE

Saratoga, N.Y. Aug. 25–1899

Dear Mr. Washington, I have your telegram of even date. I will explain
that after talking over the extent and scope of the work cut out for Bruce
he very candidly stated his position and felt that the consideration I
offered him was inadequate for the work and for the necessity he would
be under in the future to defend, his position as an ally of ours; hence
my telegram changing the figure, which I consider a reasonable compensation under the circumstances. He has to day submitted to me the
drafts of two of the proposed letters—and corrected them together.
They are the ones for the Springfield Republican and the New York
Press. We shall have the one for the colored papers ready tomorrow. As
to the one to the Constitution I am balancing in my mind the wisdom

and the expediency of sending it any thing. It is a very ticklish force with which to deal.

The Independent and the Outlook current both have references to you in the Chicago matter but rather in your favor than otherwise. Both references appear to bear modification along the lines of my letter . . .

T. Thomas Fortune[41]

In his editorial to the Springfield Republican, *Bruce provided a typical defense. "The real friends of the negro will applaud Mr. Washington for his good sense and wise judgment in avoiding entangling political alliances, which would result only in bringing upon himself and the particular work in which he is engaged infinite confusion. An effort to combine industrial education and politics could not result otherwise." The article also, however, lauded Du Bois and Bishop Henry M. Turner (also a longtime critic of Washington) for defending Washington at the meeting.*[42]

T. THOMAS FORTUNE

New York, Sept 25, 1899

My dear Mr. Washington: I have your letter of the 22nd inst. You may be right in the reason of Dr. Mossell's antagonize, as I am sure the lady does not like you, but the doctor himself has a mule's propensity to kick in all directions. But when he comes my way I can manage things from my point of view. He is much like Ida Wells Barnett, who has just written me a sassy letter complaining about the cutting out of her disparaging reference to you in her Chicago letter. [Jerome Bowers] Peterson however did the cutting.[43] She is a sort of bull in a China Shop like Mossell . . .

T. Thomas Fortune[44]

BOOKER T. WASHINGTON

[Tuskegee, Ala.] Oct. 26, 1899

Dear Sir [Du Bois]: I have delayed writing you a little longer than I intended to do, but this has been an exceedingly busy fall with me.

I write to renew the proposition that you connect yourself permanently with this institution. What I wish you to do is to make your home here and to conduct sociological studies that will prove helpful to our people, especially in the gulf states, including both the country districts, smaller towns and cities. I am especially anxious that some systematic and painstaking work be done with the country districts in the Black Belt. Our printing office will be wholly at your service and you could use it in a way that would scatter your writings all through the country.

I should like, if possible, for you to teach at least one class in our institution, this would result in keeping the students in close touch with the line of work which you would be pursuing.

All the work of course would be done in your own name and over your own signature. I should like, of course, for the name of the institution to be in some way attached to whatever publications you should make. I repeat that it would be the policy of the school to leave you free to use your time as you decide would be most desirable.

I would have made you this offer several years ago but I did not feel it would be doing you justice to ask you to come here and tie your hands with routine work. For this work we can pay you a salary of fourteen hundred dollars ($1400.) per year and furnish you a comfortable and convenient house. If any portion of this proposition is not satisfactory to you I shall be glad to make any reasonable changes in it.

I had a letter a few days ago from Prof. Hart asking whether or not we had come to any definite decision. Yours truly,

[Booker T. Washington][45]

Meanwhile, the Georgia legislature just miles from Du Bois's Atlanta University spent much of 1899 debating a bill offered by Thomas William Hardwick involving a literacy requirement for voting eligibility with a constituent grandfather clause to protect illiterate whites. The law did not pass. Much of the white press opposed it, as did representatives from predominately black counties who feared a Populist takeover. Georgia would accomplish disfranchisement in 1908 through constitutional amendment, but narrowly avoided accomplishing the task 10 years prior.[46]

BOOKER T. WASHINGTON

Tuskegee, Ala., Nov. 7, 1899

Personal

My dear Mr. Fortune: There is another exasperating condition of things in Georgia. Certain parties are making a desperate effort through the state legislature to pass a disfranchising bill. I am almost disgusted with the colored people in Georgia. I have been corresponding with leading people in the state but cannot stir up a single colored man to take the lead in trying to head off this movement. I cannot see that they are doing a thing through the press. I am tempted to put a strong article in the Atlanta Constitution. I am writing it now but do not know whether I will publish it. It is a question how far I can go and how far I ought to go in fighting these measures in other states when the colored people themselves sit down and will do nothing to help themselves. They will not even answer my letters. Yours truly,

Booker T. Washington[47]

Even as Washington bemoaned black Georgia's inactivity in response to disfranchisement efforts, Du Bois and 23 other leading black figures signed a petition stating that "any law which proposes discrimination against 850,000 souls, and which openly clears the way for dishonesty in popular elections, is contrary to the genius of our Christian civilization and a menace to free democratic institutions." The interests of the two were at the very least close enough that Washington quoted Du Bois in his 1899 work, The Future of the American Negro.[48]

BOOKER T. WASHINGTON

. . . Frederick Douglass, of sainted memory, once in addressing his race, used these words: "We are to prove that we can better our own condition. One way to do this is to accumulate property. This may sound to you like a new gospel. You have been accustomed to hear that money is the root of all evil, etc. On the other hand, property—money, if you please—will purchase for us the only condition by which any people can rise to the dignity of genuine manhood; for without property there can be no leisure, without leisure there can be no thought, without thought there can be no invention, without invention there can be no progress."

The Negro should be taught that material development is not an end, but simply a means to an end. As Professor W.E.B. Du Bois puts it, "The idea should not be simply to make men carpenters, but to make carpenters men." The Negro has a highly religious temperament; but what he needs more and more is to be convinced of the importance of weaving his religion and morality into the practical affairs of daily life. Equally as much does he need to be taught to put so much intelligence into his labour that he will see dignity and beauty in the occupation, and love it for its own sake. The Negro needs to be taught that more of the religion that manifests itself in this happiness in the prayer-meeting should be made practical in the performance of his daily task. The man who owns a home and is in the possession of the elements by which he is sure of making a daily living has a great aid to a moral and religious life. What bearing will all this have upon the Negro's place in the South as a citizen and in the enjoyment of the privileges which our government confers?[49]

NOTES

1. Washington, 1977, vol. 5, 50.
2. Washington, 1975, vol. 4, 474.
3. Horace Bumstead was Atlanta University's second president and a Congregational minister. He was Du Bois's boss and advocate, although there would be tension between the two, as Du Bois's increasing public activism made it harder and harder for Bumstead to raise money. See Towns, 1948, 109–114.
4. Washington, 1975, vol. 4, 493.
5. Moss, 1981, 62–64. For more on this particular conflict, see Moses, 2004.
6. Sznajderman and Atkins, 2005, 24–25. See also Cox, 2007, 42–43; and Villard, 1902, 711–714.
7. Kowaliga was one of several such schools in the region. Snow Hill Normal and Industrial Institute was in Society Hill, Alabama, Mt. Meig's Institute was in Cotton Valley, and Calhoun Colored School was in Calhoun. All were ostensibly modeled on Hampton and Tuskegee. Washington, 1975, vol. 4, 243–244, 359–360; Sznajderman and Atkins, 2005, 25; and Luker, 1991, 135.
8. Washington, 1975, vol. 3, 395; and Sznajderman and Atkins, 2005, 25. Emily Howland was a noted rights activist and philanthropist. Francis J. Garrison was the youngest son of abolitionist William Lloyd Garrison. Hollis Burke Frissell was the second president of Hampton Institute, taking over for Samuel Chapman Armstrong in 1893. Oswald Garrison Villard was an activist and journalist who would have a long and intimate history with both Washington and Du Bois. For Emily Howland, see Breault, 1982. For Francis J. Garrison, see McPhereson, 1975. For Villard, see Sullivan, 2010.
9. Washington, 1975, vol. 4, 409–410; and Washington, 1975, vol. 3, 79.
10. Washington, 1975, vol. 4, 425–426.
11. Washington, 1975, vol. 4, 478–479.
12. Washington, 1975, vol. 4, 506, 512, 516–517; and Sznajderman and Atkins, 2005, 25.

13. Washington, 1975, vol. 4, 244–245.

14. Fortune here refers to Albert Shaw, founder of the American edition of *Review of Reviews*, serving as its editor from 1891 to 1937. See Graybar, 1974.

15. William A. Pledger was the first black attorney in Atlanta. He was also a newspaper editor. He earned an appointment from Chester Arthur as the city's surveyor of customs. He was a Republican and staunch activist for black rights. The term "colonel" was given to black lawyers who, prohibited from attending southern law schools, apprenticed themselves to white lawyers to learn the trade. The title "colonel" prevented white people from having to refer to black lawyers as "mister." Mason, 2000, 56.

16. William Hayes Ward was both a clergyman and a newspaper editor, his longest stint coming from 1896 to 1913, when he was editor of the New York *Independent*. It is an editorial in the *Independent* to which Fortune refers. William H. Crogman was, in 1898, a professor at Clark College, where he had served since the 1870s. In 1903, he would become the school's first black president. See Jastro, 1916, 233–241; and Crogman, 1971.

17. Ibid., 530–531.

18. Scott was the secretary and sometimes ghostwriter for Washington. Later he would become the treasurer of Tuskegee. Scott's letters for Washington were common. See Chapter 2, note 22.

19. Paul Laurence Dunbar was a poet, playwright, and novelist, one of the first black writers to gain mainstream popularity and acclaim. He was also an activist for black rights and an ally of Du Bois. That activism would not last as long, as Dunbar died of tuberculosis in 1906 at only 33 years old. See Alexander, 2001.

20. Washington, 1975, vol. 5, 5.

21. Ibid., 58; and Du Bois, 1968, 237.

22. William Lawrence, a member of the Boston Brahmin Lawrence family that included American revolutionary Samuel Lawrence and later philanthropist Amos Lawrence, was the Seventh Bishop of the Episcopal Diocese of Massachusetts, beginning in 1893. *New York Times*, 12 December 1915, 1.

23. From *The Story of My Life and Work*, Chapter 18, paragraph 1, found in Washington, 1972, vol. 1, 144.

24. Washington, 1972, vol. 1, 358–359, excerpted from *Up From Slavery*.

25. Washington, 1977, vol. 5, 54, 57–58.

26. William Monroe Trotter, educated at Harvard, founded his *Boston Guardian* in 1901. He was a loud activist for black rights and an ally of Du Bois that served as one of the founders of the Niagara Movement and the NAACP. He was one of the loudest critics of Washington. He was, however, far more radical and outspoken than Du Bois. To Trotter, Washington was "the Great Traitor" and "the Benedict Arnold of the Negro Race." See Fox, 1970.

27. Washington, 1977, vol. 5, 93.

28. George W. Forbes worked with Trotter to found and edit the *Boston Guardian*, which is why Smith is so appreciative of disgust for him. His critics in Smith's report were different. Edward Henry Clement was the white editor of the *Boston Evening Transcript*. Richard Price Hallowell was the son of abolitionist Quakers whose house was a stop on the Underground Railroad during slavery. He helped recruit black soldiers in Massachusetts during the Civil War, and supported black rights after it, becoming a staunch ally of Washington until his death in 1904. Clifford H. Plummer was a Boston lawyer and black Democrat who waffled on his support from Washington to Trotter. Plummer, like Isaiah D. Barnett, was a member of the Colored National League, where these supposed denunciations occurred. Harlan, 1983, 36; Wolters, 2003, 266; *New York Times*, 9 February 1920, 1; and Greenwood, 2009, 162.

29. Washington, 1977, vol. 5, 93.

30. Ibid., 94; *Boston Transcript*, 25 April 1899, 7; and *Boston Morning Journal*, 25 April 1899, 10.

31. Washington, 1977, vol. 5, 126–127.

32. Ibid., 152–153.

33. Reverdy Cassius Ransom was an AME minister and Christian socialist. He and Thornton were not opposed to the ideology of Washington (although Ransom would be a part of Niagara in the next decade), nor was Alexander Walters, another AME minister who helped found the Council and served as its president. Instead, their frustration was with Washington's willingness to attend. Washington, 1977, vol. 5, 175; *Chicago Tribune*, 20 August 1899, 4; and Thornbrough, 1961, 494–512.

34. Thomas Wellington Henderson was an AME minister from Greensboro, North Carolina. John C. Bruckner was a Chicago politician and Civil War veteran. "Dr Bendy" refers to Charles Edwin Bentley, a Chicago dentist and leading political activist. See note 36 hereunder.

35. Washington, 1977, vol. 5, 175.

36. So too would historian Louis Harlan. Harlan, 1972, 265; and Washington, 1977, vol. 5, 176, 181.

37. Washington, 1977, vol. 5, 181.

38. The *Record* was one of many white dailies in Chicago at the turn of the century, owned by Victor F. Lawson. It was a companion paper to Lawson's *Chicago Daily News*. *New York Times*, 27 March 1901.

39. Washington, 1977, vol. 5, 181–182.

40. Bruce, a historian and activist originally based in Washington DC, was also a journalist who contributed to many black weeklies, writing a column under the name "Bruce Grit." Crowder, 2004.

41. Washington, 1977, vol. 5, 182.

42. *Springfield Republican*, 11 September 1899, 4. AME Bishop Henry McNeal Turner was far more radical than Washington. In 1883, after the Supreme Court declared the 1875 Civil Rights Act unconstitutional, Turner called the Constitution, "a dirty rag, a cheat, a libel and ought to be spit

upon by every Negro in the land." Following Washington's Cotton States speech, Turner argued that he "will have to live a long time to undo the harm he has done our race." Angell, 1992.

43. Dr. Nathan Francis Mossell was a Philadelphia-based ally of Du Bois. Ida B. Wells-Barnett will continue to play a role in this narrative. As explained in greater depth in later chapters, Wells-Barnett was a journalist and activist against lynching and other racial issues, one of the first and most important leaders to tie race and gender concerns. Jerome Bowers Peterson, contrarily, helped found the *New York Age* with Fortune and was clearly in the Washington camp. "Letter from W. E. B. Du Bois to N. F. Mossell, November 18, 1926," MS 312, Special Collections and University Archives, University of Massachusetts Amherst; Davidson, 2009; and Bernard, 2012.

44. Washington, 1977, vol. 5, 220–221.

45. Ibid., 245.

46. Ibid., 257.

47. Ibid., 256–257. Washington often engaged in secret rights activism against his broader speech. Louisiana's constitutional convention of 1898, for example, was convened specifically to cauterize Jim Crow segregation and voting restrictions into the fabric of the state's legal system. Booker T. Washington very publicly responded to Louisiana's attempts by writing an open letter to the convention. He did not denounce voting restrictions in general, but instead argued for fairness in application. He had made much the same public protest following the state's *Plessy v. Ferguson* decision two years prior. It was a contest he would lose, but one he would revive the following year, when he worked with others in the state to challenge the principal barrier to the fairness of those restrictions, the grandfather clause. *State* ex rel. *Ryanes v. Cleason* would ultimately be the victim of strategic infighting and drop without appeal in 1903, but Washington's initiation of the case was even more significant than another loss to Louisiana's Bourbons. When donating time or money to *Ryanes*, Washington would always do so in secret, never publicly admitting his participation. The Louisiana action was Washington's entree into clandestine activities. It would breed his interest in a similar Alabama voting rights case, as well as similar fights across the South. It would also, however, lead him into a different kind of clandestine activity, one that would send Tuskegee agents to spy on black competitors like W.E.B. Du Bois. Harlan, 1971, 393–416.

48. Washington, 1977, vol. 5, 257; and *Atlanta Constitution*, 10 November 1899, 7.

49. Selection from *The Future of the American Negro*, Chapter 8 (1899), in Washington, 1977, vol. 5, 386–387.

5

The Washington School District

In 1900, a superintendency position for the African American schools of Washington, D.C. opened, and Du Bois wanted the job. Washington vacillated on a recommendation, telling Du Bois that he encouraged his hiring while simultaneously stumping for someone else. It was yet another wedge in the fracturing relationship. After the indignity of losing the chance for that job, Du Bois suffered an even greater indignity when Southern Railway officials relegated him to the segregated railroad car on a trip from Atlanta to Savannah. An incensed Du Bois wanted a high-profile lawsuit in response and sought the support of Washington for the move. That support was not forthcoming, only further growing the divide between the two.

Regardless, Du Bois sometimes claimed he was not interested in the Superintendent of Negro Schools for Washington, DC, job and was never offered the position, but Washington still recommended him anyway—or claimed to have recommended him—in a letter written to Du Bois. The reality of Washington's actions and Du Bois's interest in the position, however, were far more complicated.[1]

WILLIAM EDWARD BURGHARDT DU BOIS

Atlanta, Ga., Feb 17 1900

Confidential.

My Dear Mr. Washington: I have taken a rather unreasonable amount of time to consider your kind offer to come to Tuskeegee, and I have not yet fully decided. I want however to lay some considerations before you & then when I come to the Conference as I now think I shall, we can talk further. Since your offer was made I have had two other chances— tho' not formal offers: one to stand for a professorship in Howard University and the other to enter the race for the position of Superintendant of the Washington colored schools. Then of course there are the claims of the work here.

Now the question that really puzzles me in these cases is the one as to where I would really be most useful. Howard I cut from the list without hesitation—I'm sure I shouldn't get on well there for it's a poorly conducted establishment. On the other hand I really question as to how much I am really needed at Tuskeegee. I think to be sure I could be of use there but after all would it not be a rather ornamental use than a fundamental necessity? Would not my department be regarded by the public as a sort of superfluous addition not quite in consonance with the fundamental Tuskeegee idea? On the other hand there is no doubt that I am needed at Atlanta and that in the future as much closer cooperation between Tuskeegee Atlanta & Hampton is possible in the future than in the past. Well this is the line along which I had been thinking some months, when there came letters urging me to seek the position of superintendent of the Washington D.C. schools. It seems that Mr. Cook[2] who has held the position over 20 years has some thoughts of resigning. Now the question comes: Is not this the most useful place of the three & could I not serve both your cause & the general cause of the Negro at the National capital better than elsewhere? I wish you'd think this matter over seriously & give me your best advice. Boiled down the questions are: 1st Am I really needed at Tuskeegee. 2nd Considering the assured success of the Tuskeegee Institute already are there not weaker places where pioneer work is necessary. 3rd Is not the Washington position—provided always I could get it—such a place?

Of course if I should apply for the W. place your indorsement would go further probably than anyone's else. Could you conscientiously give it?

I write you thus frankly & hope you will consider the matter from my point of view & give me the results of your wisdom. Very Sincerely

W.E.B. Du Bois[3]

W.E.B. DU BOIS

Atlanta, Ga., Feb 26 190[0]

My Dear Mr Washington: On reaching here yesterday I found several urgent letters asking me to apply for the Washington position before it was too late. I thought therefore that application would do no harm even if on later personal investigation I found the place not to my liking. Therefore I wired you asking for your endorsement. I do not of course want you to do anything which would compromise you or make you appear to be "in politics" but if without prejudice to your position & the school's you could endorse me I shall appreciate it. I repeat that I have not definitely decided to accept the Washington place nor am I certain of not coming to Tuskegee. My present leaning however is toward Washington for I seem to see there a chance for a great work. However I shall go there next month & investigate. I want to thank you again for your hospitality during my very pleasant stay at Tuskegee. Yours &c

W.E.B. Du Bois[4]

JOHN WESLEY ROSS *(John Wesley Ross was Washington D.C.'s Commissioner of Education from 1890 to 1900.)*

Washington March 6, 1900

Dear Sir [Washington]: Knowing your intelligent interest in the cause of education, I take the liberty of addressing you with regard to a possible vacancy at the end of the current school year in the position of Superintendent of Colored Schools in the District of Columbia.

The present incumbent, Mr. Cook, is a man whom everybody respects for his personal qualities; but the entire Board of School Trustees has recommended a change. There are many ambitious applicants in the District; but, in view of the division in the ranks of the people here and the many cases of those who are prominent having relatives in the schools as teachers, it would seem to be advisable to find if possible some one thoroughly educated, of first class executive ability and of incorruptible integrity who would be available.

If you will kindly give me your views on this important matter, I assure you that they will receive due consideration by the Board of Commissioners, and that no publicity will be given to the same without your consent. Some names which have been suggested are: W.S. Scarborough, of Wilberforce; W.E.B. Du Bois, of Atlanta; and Prof. Brown, of Hampton.[5] Very truly yours,

John W. Ross
Commissioner[6]

BOOKER TALIAFERRO WASHINGTON

Grand Union Hotel, New York. Mar. 11, 1900

Dear Dr. Du Bois: Please consider the contents of this letter strictly private. If you have not done so, I think it not best for you to use the letter of recommendation which I have sent you. I have just received a letter direct from one of the Commissioners in the District asking me to recommend some one for the vacancy there and I have recommended you as strongly as I could. Under the circumstances it would make your case stronger for you not to present the letter which I have given you for the reason that it would tend to put you in the position of seeking the position. It is pretty well settled, judging by the Commissioner's letter, that some one outside of the District is going to be appointed. This will be my address for the next week. Yours truly,

Booker T. Washington[7]

According to David Levering Lewis, Washington's solution to the superintendency problem was to hide Du Bois in plain sight—to offer him Tuskegee instead of the District of Columbia public school system. On March 11, Washington told Du Bois not to make use of his recommendation. The next day, Commissioner John Ross solicited Washington's advice about the assistant superintendent position. It was not pro-Du Bois advice, and ultimately Ross went with Winfield Montgomery, the Dartmouth-trained professor of classics at Alcorn.

Washington's desire to put Du Bois at Tuskegee was understandable. The influence of Albert Bushnell Hart and the like was real, as was Du Bois's rising influence, which could only bolster the university's academic reputation. At the same time, he would be much easier to control in Alabama.

Meanwhile, Du Bois was disappointed. He wanted the job, and part of that desire was a desire to leave Atlanta. In Spring 1899, his two-year-old son Burghardt died of diphtheria. His wife Nina was unsurprisingly devastated, even while undergoing another pregnancy. She would have the couple's second child, Yolanda, in 1900.[8]

RICHARD W. THOMPSON *(Thompson was the managing editor of the* Colored American *magazine and a clerk with the Census Bureau.)*

Washington, D.C., Mar. 14, 1900

Confidential

Dear Mr. Washington: Luck is rather against my seeing you of late when you pass through Washington. I was called home to Indianapolis Feb. 27, to bury my mother. This was the day you wrote me, and I received it at office when I reported Monday morning the 12th. I feel grateful for your kindly consideration, and shall try to deserve the favors you repeatedly show me . . .

As to the school superintendency, I am inclined to believe that the most popular appointment would be a man long identified with District interests—Terrell, for instance.[9] He is young, full of originality, ambitious, clean, thoroughly educated and a "good mixer." If a squabble arises and the plum goes outside, Du Bois, of Atlanta would be the most acceptable man in the country—acceptable from a scholarly standpoint. Du Bois would command respect because of his attainments, but not popularity. It looks to people here that the fight is between Terrell and Du Bois against a minor field, and for reasons which cannot be given here, with the rank and file, the victory of either would be an "even break."

Personally, I would prefer Terrell, as against Du Bois, and the young men in the schools and departments stand with him. But, like all progressive spirits, he has bitter enemies, and he must also shoulder the enemies of his wife. These would favor Du Bois—or any outsider. Your name is mentioned, and it is conceded that you could have it by a nod of assent, and everybody of moment would be satisfied and the town would feel honored. The feeling is that you probably could not afford to locate here, but some say the acceptance of this post would enable you to happily combine the industrial and the higher education, with the result of silencing in three months all of the croakers who have been trying to corner you for the last four years. This is the situation candidly stated. A "tip" from you would put some ginger into the fight, and give it a national coloring. Suppose you are asked if you would accept the superintendency, would it not be a good idea to give me half-a-column interview to use as I see fit? *If you think so*, send to me at Census Office. I have undertaken the Washington correspondence of The Freeman, The World, Baltimore Afro-American Ledger, and Atlanta Age, and can, of course, put it in The American. More anon. Your friend,

R.W. Thompson[10]

WILLIAM A. PLEDGER

Washington, D.C. March-16-00

Dear Washington: I am sorry that you endorsed Du Bois for the Supt Negro schools here. He is not of your people. Your friends almost to a man are against him.[11] We want Terrell and you. I hope [you] can find a way to so modify your endorsement that you will not be actively against him. It might be that you could [see] commissioner Ross and go over the case. I know you make no mistake in considering the matter. We fight to make you and you must sometimes listen to us. Come over as soon as you can. I shall be here for several days. Your fr[ien]d,

W A Pledger[12]

On the night of February 19 (either 1899 or 1900), Du Bois took an Atlanta train to Savannah for a meeting of exhibition commissioners for the United States' entries to the Paris Exhibition of 1900. He was working on southern exhibits for the "Negro Section," under the direction of his friend Thomas J. Calloway. After boarding the train, Southern Railway officials refused Du Bois an overnight berth. Although he argued vehemently, he was ultimately forced to sit in the colored car at the rear of the train. He filed a formal protest and sent a copy to Washington, who would be, despite Pledger's assertion that Du Bois was "not of your people," initially receptive. His frustration, as he would later describe in his autobiography, was not only with the denigration and indignity of being segregated, but also with the lack of class distinctions afforded to black passengers. Du Bois did not like having to travel with the rabble of any race, including his own. He later made an effort to convince the Southern Railway to make its race policy clear before passengers bought tickets and boarded trains.[13]

W.E.B. DU BOIS

Atlanta, Ga., Mch 16 1900

My Dear Mr Washington: I called on Mr. Hardwick yesterday.[14] He was pleasant but cautious. He admitted that conductors of the S.R. had been given orders as to sleeping cars, but said this did not apply to inter-state travel. He *thought* a journey from here to Washington would be considered inter-state & that sleepers could be taken. He asked me to state my case in writing & he would lay it before the legal department of the R.R. & give me an early reply. I sent the enclosed letter to him today. Yours &c

W.E.B. Du Bois[15]

Du Bois wanted a high-profile response to the indignity, a lawsuit that would better clarify black rights in the age of segregation. The train he boarded was traveling from Cincinnati to Jacksonville, and it was Du Bois's position— one he claimed that some officials at the Southern Railway actually agreed with—that Plessy *did not apply to interstate travel. Considering his negotiations with Washington, Du Bois wrote to him about the incident, and Washington at first seemed encouraging. But railroad magnate and Tuskegee patron William H. Baldwin, a former vice president of the Southern Railway, convinced the Tuskegee leader otherwise, arguing that railroad presidents "feel that if the colored people should raise an issue it would cause nothing but bitterness." Calm acceptance would do as much as anything to change hearts and minds. Although Washington did not seem to buy this condescending response, he never helped finance a lawsuit against the railroad (although the sound and fury aiming to signify lasted four years before Washington finally reneged).*[16]

W.E.B. DU BOIS

Atlanta, Ga., April 10 1900

My Dear Mr. Washington: I am sorry to say that I have been unable to lay my hands upon the data mentioned and consequently could not forward it. I am sorry.

I think I ought not keep you any longer in uncertainty as to my coming to Tuskegee. I have given the matter long and earnest thought and have finally decided not to accept your very generous offer. I see many opportunities for usefulness and work at Tuskegee, but I have been unable to persuade myself that the opportunities there are enough larger than those here at Atlanta University to justify my changing at present. The only opening that would attract me now would be one that brought me nearer the centres of culture & learning and thus gave me larger literary activity. I thank you very much for the offer and for other kindnesses and I need not assure [you] that you will always have in your work my sympathy & cooperation. Very Sincerely,

W.E.B. Du Bois[17]

This was the kind of thing that convinced Du Bois that Tuskegee was not the place for him to work. David Levering Lewis described this area of the divide as a clash of temperaments, the decisiveness of Du Bois unable to mesh with "the mandarin style of Booker Washington." According to Lewis, Du Bois "would almost surely have entertained doubts about the Tuskegeean's good faith," even as he worked on a legal response to the Southern Railway. When combined with the Washington school district fiasco, his decision became relatively simple. On April 10, 1900, he turned down Washington's Tuskegee job offer. "Everything," argues Lewis, "instinct, personality, location, and politics—militated against his going to Tuskegee." Du Bois was not going to be able to achieve his goals in that environment, and the ideological and personal divide between him and Washington was already clearly set. Still, he could not yet afford to alienate the powerful southerner.[18]

NOTES

1. Du Bois, 1973, 44; and Aptheker, 1971, 119.
2. George Frederick Thompson Cook was superintendent of black schools in Washington, DC. Washington, 1977, vol. 5, 444.
3. Washington, 1977, vol. 5, 443–444.
4. Ibid., 450.
5. William Sanders Scarborough was a professor of classics from Wilberforce and would go on to become the school's president in 1908. Hampton, of course, was an obvious pool of talent being located so near Washington. See Scarborough, 2005.
6. Washington, 1977, vol. 5, 452.
7. Du Bois, 1973, 44; and Washington, 1977, vol. 5, 459.
8. Lewis, 1993, 242.
9. Thompson here refers to Robert H. Terrell, Harvard graduate and principal of Washington's M Street High School, who also held a law degree from Howard. Moore, 1999, 11.
10. Washington, 1977, vol. 5, 461–463. Thompson was the former editor of the *Indianapolis Recorder* before moving to Washington. He would, in 1903, lead the National Negro Press Bureau. He would use his position as

a leading newspaper man in Washington to advocate for the Tuskegee Machine. *Baltimore Afro-American*, 20 February 1920, 1; Moore, 1999, 68.

11. This was not necessarily true. The Washington doctor John R. Francis wrote to Washington urging him to support Du Bois. Washington, 1977, vol. 5, 466.

12. Ibid.

13. Lewis, 1993, 242–243; Du Bois, 1968, 235; and Washington, 1977, vol. 5, 464.

14. S.H. Hardwick was an attorney with the Southern Railway, serving also as "passenger traffic manager." Hearings of the Committee on Interstate and Foreign Commerce of the House of Representatives on HR 20153, 21572, and 22133, on the Subject of Railroad Passenger Fares and Mileage Tickets, 1907, 157–161.

15. Washington, 1977, vol. 5, 464.

16. Lewis, 1993, 244.

17. Washington, 1977, vol. 5, 480.

18. Lewis, 1993, 244–245.

6

The National Negro Business League

The rift between Du Bois and Washington continued in the early century with the creation of Washington's National Negro Business League (NNBL), bringing together merchants, retailers, bankers, funeral directors, and other middle-class business owners to exchange information and to promote black business. It was, on its face, a good idea. Unfortunately, it was Du Bois's idea, established during an Atlanta University conference on "The Negro in Business." Du Bois also directed the Negro Business Bureau of the Afro-American Council, which was meeting in Chicago in 1900 while Washington was in town. But Washington did not attend. The assumption from those who mistrusted him was that he was uninterested in any organization (no matter how well intentioned) that he could not control. Still, the controversy would not stop the two from meeting at a conference at Tuskegee in 1901, hoping to keep the relationship as superficially cordial as possible.

Booker Washington's NNBL, founded in 1900 to bring together merchants, retailers, bankers, funeral directors, and other middle-class business owners to exchange information and to promote black business, actually resulted from the work of Du Bois and his colleagues at Atlanta University during their 1899 "The Negro in Business" conference. Du Bois was the director of the

Afro-American Council's Negro Business Bureau, organizing local business leagues around the country. Washington and T. Thomas Fortune stopped all appropriations for postage funds, leaving Du Bois unable to complete his task. Washington then solicited Du Bois's list of names, which he used to build the NNBL. Then, in August 1900, Emmett J. Scott became director of the Afro-American Council's Negro Business Bureau, assuring that both it and the NNBL would control all black business organizing activities.[1]

WILLIAM EDWARD BURGHARDT DU BOIS

Atlanta, Ga., May 16 1900

My Dear Mr Washington: I shall try & get the list of business men [from the Negro Business Bureau of the Afro-American Council] to you in a week or two. I have been very busy. Yours,

W.E.B. Du Bois[2]

In July 1900, Ida Wells published an editorial in the Chicago Conservator *attacking Washington for forming the NNBL when the Afro-American Council already existed. Washington had not attended a single meeting of the Council when it met in Chicago, even though he was in Chicago at the time.[3]*

IDA B. WELLS-BARNETT

Here he had ample opportunity to suggest plans along business lines and Prof. Du Bois, the most scholarly and one of [the] most conservative members of the Council, who is chairman of the Business Bureau would have been glad to receive Mr. Washington's cooperation.[4]

He did not, however, because he wanted an organization where he could dictate all policy without question, so Wells suggested. Although Wells maintained her stance, the Conservator *softened toward the NNBL, praising it later that year.[5]*

BOOKER TALIAFERRO WASHINGTON

Roslindale, Mass., July 21st, 1900

Dear Mr. Scott; I have received the Conservator and also a copy of your letter sent to the Editor. The Editorial in the Conservator is written by Miss Wells. The Editorial has really I think helped the League Meeting, as I have found that several of the colored papers have taken up the matter strongly in my defence.

Miss Wells is fast making herself so ridiculous that every body is getting tired of her. Yours truly,

Booker T. Washington[6]

Although Washington's essential theft of the NNBL is often reported, biographer Louis Harlan points out that the controversy could not have taken place had not the ideas and interests of Washington and Du Bois been closely aligned. It was opportunism to be sure, but opportunism based on a sincere belief that corporate boosterism would help foster black southern economic growth, and thus move them toward full citizenship. Although the theft might be telling of Washington's personality, it also demonstrates that even through their dispute, Washington and Du Bois were essentially on the same page when it came to the concept of the NNBL. That common ground created significant conflict, but it was also a missed opportunity at reconciliation.[7]

EMMETT JAY SCOTT AND LYMAN BEECHER STOWE

(Lyman Beecher Stowe was the grandson of Harriet Beecher Stowe and the author of a biography of his grandmother, along with this work with Scott on Washington. He was an author, lecturer, and editor.)[8]

In 1900 Booker Washington founded the National Negro Business League. He was president of this league from its foundation until his death.

During the winter of 1900, after reviewing the situation at length with his friend T. Thomas Fortune, the nestor of Negro journalism, and at that time the dominant influence in the New York *Age*, who was spending the winter at Tuskegee, with Mr. Scott and others of his friends, he came to the conclusion that the time had come to bring the business men and women of his race together in a great national organization, with local branches throughout the country. He decided that such an organization might be a powerful agency in creating the race consciousness and race pride for which he was ever striving. All the then-existing organizations, other than the sick and death benefit societies and the purely social organizations, had as their main purpose the assertion of the civil and political rights of the Negro. There was no organization calculated to focus the attention of the Negroes on what they were doing and could do for themselves in distinction from what was being done for them and to them. All the existing associations laid their chief emphasis upon the rights of the Negro rather than his duties. Mr. Washington held that without in any degree sacrificing their just demands for civil and political rights a more wholesome and constructive attitude could be developed by stressing the duties and the opportunities of the race. He believed it would be helpful to emphasize in an organized way what they had done and could do in the way of business achievement in spite of race prejudice rather than what they had not done and could not do because of racial discrimination. He believed they needed to have brought home to them not how many of them had been held down, but how many of them had come up and surmounted obstacles and difficulties. He believed that they should have it impressed upon them that the application of business methods would bring rewards to a black man just as to a white man.

The first meeting of the National Negro Business League was held in Boston, August 23 and 24, 1900.[9]

BOOKER T. WASHINGTON

As I have travelled through the country from time to time I have been constantly surprised to note the number of colored men and women, often in small towns and remote districts, who are engaged in various lines of business. In many cases the business was very humble, but nevertheless it was sufficient to indicate the opportunities of the race in this direction. My observation in this regard led me to believe that the time had come for the bringing together of the leading and most successful colored men and women throughout the country who are engaged in business. After consultation with men and women in various parts of the country it was determined to call a meeting in the city of Boston to organize the National Negro Business League. This meeting was held during the 23d and 24th of August, and it was generally believed that it was one of the most successful and helpful meetings that has ever been held among our people. The meeting was called with two objects in view: first, to bring the men and women engaged in business together, in order that they might get acquainted with each other and get information and inspiration from each other; secondly, to form plans for an annual meeting and the organization of local business leagues that should extend throughout the country. Both of these objects, I think, have been admirably accomplished. I think there has never been a time in the history of the race when all feel so much encouraged in relation to their business opportunities as now. The promoters of this organization appreciate very keenly that the race cannot depend upon mere material growth alone for its ultimate success, but they do feel that material prosperity will greatly hasten their recognition in other directions.[10]

BOSTON HERALD

The national convention of colored business men began its sessions in this city yesterday in a businesslike and hopeful manner. This is not a political gathering. It is not a race gathering in the sense of one met to air sentimental grievances that spring from race oppositions . . . President Washington believes that the security and progress of the colored people in this land depend upon their development of a moral worth commanding respect and an industrial capacity that will make them both useful and independent. He apprehends that these qualities cannot be bestowed as a gift of benevolence, but must be acquired by individual energy and struggle. 'As I have noted,' he says, 'the condition of our people in nearly every part of our country, I have always been encouraged by the fact that almost without exception, whether in the North or in the South, wherever I have seen a black man who was succeeding in his business, who was a taxpayer, and who possessed intelligence and high character, that individual was treated with the highest respect by the members of the white race. In proportion as we can multiply those examples, North and South, will our problem be solved.' That is the great lesson that the members of the colored race have to learn. It will aid in extending this knowledge for those colored business men who have attained a measurable degree of success in life to meet for mutual encouragement and helpfulness.[11]

As early as 1900, Washington was planning a meeting between influential black leaders to set an agenda for the race. He postponed that meeting several times before finally soliciting funds from Andrew Carnegie and William H. Baldwin to have a private conference at Carnegie Hall in January 1904.[12] The steel magnate Andrew Carnegie became enamored with Booker T. Washington after providing Tuskegee a $20,000 grant to build a campus library in 1900. The school was able to build a building well beyond the scope of what most schools could accomplish with similar funds, owing to student labor and supplies. From there, the donations to both Tuskegee and Washington himself only continued in greater sums. He subsidized both the NNBL and the Committee of Twelve for the Advancement of the Negro Race (see Chapter 11), and his money allowed Tuskegee to flourish more than it otherwise would.

"History is to tell of two Washingtons[,] one white, the other Black, both Fathers of their people," he once said.[13]

BOOKER T. WASHINGTON

Tuskegee, Ala., Sept. 11, 1900

Dear Mr. Fortune: I presume this letter will find you in New York. I hope you had a conference with Mr. Hanna[14] and that something good came out of it . . .

I think before long that we ought to get twelve or fifteen of the strongest and most influential Negroes in the country and have a private conference lasting two or three days if necessary and in that way get hold of the whole situation and determine what are the proper efforts to be put forth to help and improve conditions as they now exist. Matters have got to get better or worse soon. Yours truly,

Booker T. Washington[15]

BOOKER T. WASHINGTON

. . . Some time ago, I sent letters to about four hundred white men scattered throughout the southern states in which these three questions were asked:

1. Has education made the Negro a more useful citizen?
2. Has it made him more economical and more inclined to acquire wealth?
3. Has it made him a more valuable workman, especially where thought and skill are required?

Answers came from three hundred of my correspondents, and nine tenths of them answered the three questions emphatically in the affirmative. A few expressed doubts, but only one answered the questions with an unmodified "No."

In each case, I was careful to ask my correspondents to base their correspondence upon the conditions existing in their own neighborhood.

The Negro is gradually branching out in nearly all lines of business. To illustrate this remark, I give a few statistics representing typical cases in different portions of the South. These statistics were gathered by Dr. Du Bois of the University. [A list of business-owners from various southern cities follows, complied by Du Bois. See below.]

From all the foregoing facts, I think we may safely find ground for the greatest hopefulness, not only for the Negro himself, but for the white man in his treatment of the Negro. In the South, especially, the prosperity of the one race enriches the other, the poverty of one race retards the progress of the other.

The greatest thing that can be done for the Negro at the present time is to make him the most useful and indispensable man in his community. This can be done by thorough education of the hand, head, and heart, and especially, by the constant instilling into every fibre of his being the thought that labor is ennobling and that idleness is a disgrace.[16]

W.E.B. DU BOIS

Atlanta, Ga., Feb 11, 1901

Dear Mr. Washington: I shall probably attend the Tuskegee conference this year again.[17] I have been thinking that perhaps I could do a service there in taking a personal census of all the visitors, especially the farmers &c.—number, property owned, age, history, crops, improvements, &c., &c. If you could furnish me 3 or 4 or 5 reliable clerks I could probably do the work & present results to the final meeting. This plan occurred to me, and I mention it to you. Very Sincerely,

W.E.B. Du Bois[18]

IDA B. WELLS-BARNETT

. . . The Afro-American Council convened at the close of that same week, and invitations were extended to the representative women of the National Association to be guests of the council at a banquet given to our own presiding officers at the Sherman Hotel. It was the first time in the history of Chicago that colored women had partaken of a dinner in one of the Loop hotels. The men had been given dinner from time immemorial in the Palmer House and other places when they entertained Douglass, B.K. Bruce during those days when he was senator, and other leading men.[19]

Mr. Pierce, the proprietor of the hotel, not only helped in every way possible to provide for our comfort and pleasure, but he expressed his disappointment to me afterward because I did not invite him to speak. I was presiding officer of the occasion and presented our president, Bishop Walters, Bishop H.M. Turner, W.E.B. Du Bois, and other representative men who had come to Chicago to attend the meeting of the Afro-American Council.[20]

Mrs. Terrell, as president of the National Association of Colored Women's Clubs, Mrs. Booker T. Washington, and other notable officers were also our guests.[21] When Mrs. Washington was called on to make a talk, she surprised us all by saying that although she was glad to be present at a dinner of the Afro-American Council, she could not say that she had approved of the attack that had been made upon her husband in our meeting, as reported by the daily press the day before.

The Afro-American Council had not made any attack upon Booker T. Washington, but a statement had been made in the meeting referred to that Bishop Walters, our president, had gone from the meeting to the Palmer House to confer with Mr. Washington. Some delegate then rose and asked why the president of our meeting had to go to Mr. Washington for a secret conference and why Mr. Washington would not appear in our meeting. The speaker went on to state that he had been informed that Mr. Washington had been sent to Chicago to hold the Afro-American Council in check so that no expression against the president of the United States would emanate therefrom, as it had done in Washington the winter before.

No one could answer that question and the incident passed. But a reporter who happened to be present rushed to an after noon paper and in big headlines announced to the public that the Afro-American Council had condemned Booker T. Washington.[22] Bishop Walters rose at once at the banquet and assured Mrs. Washington and those present of the facts as I have stated them.

Dr. Du Bois, who had worked very earnestly with us at this meeting of the council, had been placed on our program because as a coming young man just back from his studies in Germany, we thought we should encourage him and give him the opportunity to take hold in the work.[23] He rendered splendid service and we felt amply repaid for the fight we had made in the executive committee to have him with us . . .

When the Afro-American Council met in Indianapolis in the summer of 1900, we were met with the information that Mr. Booker T. Washington had called a meeting of the businessmen of the country to be held in Boston, Massachusetts, at the same time the council was meeting in Indianapolis. This was the birth of what is now known as the Business Men's League.

It seems that, having gotten the idea of what it would mean to have a national organization of his own people at his back, he had taken a leaf out of our book to organize what would be a nonpolitical body and yet would give him the moral support that he had begun to feel he needed in his school work. In his many visits to the North soliciting funds for the aid of Tuskeegee, the white people had begun to ask what interest colored people were showing in the work, and what support he was getting from them. Of course he had nothing that he could show until the idea of establishing the business league was born. Some of us felt it was unfortunate that he chose the same time as our meeting, and as a matter of course, drew from our members.

However, we made the best of the matter, since Mr. Washington himself had hitherto given us the impression that he could not ally himself with us because we were too radical. Our policy was to denounce the wrongs and injustices which were heaped upon our people, and to use whatever influence we had to help right them. Especially strong was our condemnation of lynch law and those who practiced it.

Mr. Washington's theory had been that we ought not to spend our time agitating for our rights; that we had better give attention to trying to be first-class people in a jim crow car than insisting that the jim crow car should be abolished; that we should spend more time practicing industrial pursuits and getting education to fit us for this work than in going to college and striving for a college education. And of course, fighting for political rights had no place whatsoever in his plans.

Naturally it was the best policy for him, so he thought, to steer as far as possible away from the radical group. This he felt he ought to do in the interest of his school work, and thus prevent antagonism from the white people by whom he was surrounded in Tuskeegee.

President McKinley was reelected and Mr. Theodore Roosevelt came in as vice-president. When later on President McKinley was assassinated in 1901, Theodore Roosevelt became president in his stead. It is a matter of history that Booker T. Washington became his political adviser so far as the colored people of this country were concerned. There were those of us who felt that a man who had no political strength in his own state and who could do nothing whatsoever to help elect a president of the United States was not the man to be the adviser as to the political appointment of colored men from states which not only could, but did cast votes by which the Republican president had been placed in office.

The following summer the Afro-American Council was called to its annual session in Philadelphia, Pennsylvania [1901]. On account of an anticipated visit from the stork, it was impossible for me to be present. Mr. Barnett, who had not been East, went in my place to make a report for the work which had been done during the year. When he returned home my daughter, Ida, was born.[24] The National Business League was also in session in Chicago and I was not able to be present at its deliberations. However, one particular incident of that session was brought to my bedside, and the consequences of it were indeed far-reaching.

It seems that during the session of the Business League a human being was being burned alive in Alabama. Mr. I.F. Bradley, a delegate from Kansas, offered a resolution of condemnation and that resolution was referred to the committee on resolutions.[25] Mr. Washington went into the committee and forbade the committee's reporting it back to the national body. He gave as his reason that it might endanger his school if he, as president of the Business League, permitted such a resolution to be passed.[26]

Whereupon Mr. T. Thomas Fortune, who had become an ardent convert to Mr. Washington's views, violently disagreed with him in the committee room and left the meeting. Both he and Judge Bradley came to my home and narrated the above incident. Both of them were very indignant, but there was nothing they could do about it, since Mr. Washington controlled the Business League absolutely. The *Chicago Tribune* the next morning stated that Mr. Washington gave as his reasons for not permitting the resolution's passage that he did so out of consideration for his school.

Very soon thereafter came the Atlanta, Georgia, riot [1906] in which three innocent Negroes were lynched by the frenzied mob which disgraced that city. It was lashed to fury because some white woman had made the same charge of being assaulted by some unknown Negro. The *Atlanta Journal*, edited by John Temple Graves, issued bulletins which fanned the flame of race prejudice to such heights that not only were three innocent Negroes lynched and much property destroyed, but the heads of schools, lawyers, and doctors were humiliated and made to march like criminals up the streets at the behest of the mob.[27] Again attention was directed to the fact that in all this country we had no organization which was really national in character, and which was numerically and financially strong enough to do the work which was so badly needed for making an organized fight upon this growing calamity . . .[28]

Although the rift between Du Bois and Washington was real, their relationship was superficially cordial. Du Bois did attend the Tuskegee Conference in February 1901. The next month Washington cited Du Bois heavily in a Gunton's Magazine *article on "The Negro In Business." Du Bois even agreed to a well-publicized West Virginia camping trip with Washington, Fortune, and others (although he cancelled just before the event).[29] Washington had even tried to arrange a meeting with Pullman lawyer Robert Todd Lincoln for the West Virginia trip to discuss the Du Bois segregation case.*[30]

BOOKER T. WASHINGTON

The Negro in Business

The conference of the National Negro Business League, which assembled in Boston in August of 1900, was unique. For the first time since the negroes were freed an attempt was made to bring together, from all over the United States, a company of representative business men and women of the race. Over three hundred delegates were present. They came from thirty states, and from an area which extended from Nebraska to Florida and from Texas to Maine . . .

This meeting not only showed to the country what the colored people are doing, but it gave the delegates, especially those who came from the South, an opportunity to see something of the business methods employed by northern people. I think it will have something of the same good effect on them that the bringing of the Cuban teachers to the United States may be expected to have on the Cubans.

If a record of the business enterprises operated by colored men and women in the United States were available it would be interesting and instructive, but such information has not yet been very generally reported.

From the published reports of the valuable studies of Professor W.E.B. Du Bois I make a few extracts bearing on the subject. In his book, "The Philadelphia Negro," Dr. Du Bois deals chiefly with the colored people of the seventh ward of that city. The author says that this particular ward is selected because it "is an historic center of the negro population and contains one-fifth of all the negroes in the city." The negro population of Philadelphia in 1890 was 40,000, and over 8,000 lived in this ward. Both these numbers will undoubtedly show an increase when the figures of the census recently taken are available. In this ward Dr. Du Bois found the following-named business establishments operated by negroes: 39 restaurants, 24 barber shops, 11 groceries, 11 cigar stores, 2 candy and notion stores, 4 upholsterers, 2 liquor saloons, 4 undertakers (two of these were women), 1 newspaper, 1 drug store, 2 patent-medicine stores, 4 printing offices.

There were 83 caterers in the ward, but some of these Dr. Du Bois reports as doing a small business, and others as engaged in the business only a part of the year, being otherwise employed the rest of the time. The business of catering by negroes in Philadelphia has always been remarkable for the ability and success with which it has been conducted. Several men of the race in that city have been famous for their work in this line. Dr. Du Bois, in writing of the caterer, reports "about ten who do a business of from $3,000 to $5,000 a year."

In addition to these there were at the same time in other parts of the city, among the negro business establishments, 49 barber shops, 8 grocery stores, 27 restaurants, 8 coal and wood dealers. There was a successful florist, a large crockery store, and successful real-estate dealers.

From the reports of other studies of Dr. Du Bois, in the South, I make some extracts. I do not quote his lists in full, but give only a few of the leading enterprises reported:

Birmingham, Ala.—8 grocers, 6 barbers, 4 druggists, 4 tailors. Montgomery, Ala.—6 grocers, 2 undertakers, 2 drug-store keepers, 1 butcher. Vicksburg, Miss.—2 jewelers, 2 tailors, 2 drug-store keepers, 2 newspapers, 2 dry-goods dealers, 1 undertaker. Nashville, Tenn.—9 contractors, 6 grocers, 2 undertakers, 2 saloon keepers, 2 drug stores. Houston, Tex.—11 grocers, 10 real-estate dealers, 5 contractors, 6 barbers. Richmond, Va.—2 banking and insurance men, 2 undertakers, 2 fish dealers. Tallahassee, Fla.—3 groceries, 2 meat markets. Americus, Ga.—12 groceries, 1 drug store, 1 wood yard . . .

Despite these evidences of progress, it has been said, sometimes, that negroes cannot come together and successfully unite in holding such meetings as that of the National Negro Business League, and that this is a proof of their business incapacity. I think such a meeting as that of last August disproves that theory. What gave me the most encouragement was the manly and straightforward tone used in all the papers and discussions. There were no complaints. At the next session I believe that there will be still larger numbers and stronger support. I believe that as a race we shall succeed and grow, and be a people, with our due representation in business life, right here in America. We must not be discouraged, and we must watch our opportunities and take advantage of them. There is no force on earth that can keep back a brave people that is determined to get education and property and Christian character. They never can be defeated in their progress.[31]

NOTES

1. Harlan, 1972, 266–268; Washington, 1977, vol. 5, 526; and Lewis, 1993, 245.

2. Washington, 1977, vol. 5, 526.

3. See Chapter 5.

4. Washington, 1977, vol. 5, 589; and Harlan, 1988, 99. See also *Chicago Conservator*, 7 July 1900, 8 September 1900.

5. The *Conservator* was founded by Ferdinand Barnett, who sold the paper to Wells in 1895. That year, he also married her. See Suggs, 1996.

6. Washington, 1977, vol. 5, 589.

7. Lewis, 1993, 240; and Harlan, 1983, 266–267.

8. "Lyman Beecher Stowe: Author, Editor, Lecturer," Traveling Culture: Circuit Chautauqua in the Twentieth Century, MSC0150, Special Collections Department, University of Iowa, Des Moines, Iowa.

9. Scott and Stowe, 1916, 185–186.

10. Ibid., 186–187.

11. Ibid., 188–189. See also *Boston Herald*, 24 August 1900.

12. Washington, 1977, vol. 5, 637.

13. Ibid., vol. 6, 6.

14. Mark Hanna was a Republican senator from Ohio, the head of the Republican National Committee, and, in September 1900, the campaign manager for William McKinley's reelection campaign. See Horner, 2010.

15. Washington, 1977, vol. 5, 637.

16. Washington, December 1900, 672–86; and Washington, 1977, vol. 5, 696–709.

17. He did, in fact, attend, arriving at Tuskegee on February 19, 1901. Washington, 1977, vol. 6, 33.

18. Ibid.

19. Wells here refers to Frederick Douglass and Blanche K. Bruce, a Republican politician from Mississippi who served as one of the state's senators during Reconstruction, the first black man to serve a full term in the United States Senate. See Graham, 2006.

20. Wells here refers to Henry McNeal Turner, see Chapter 5, and Bishop Alexander Walters, an AME Zion bishop who obviously served as the president of the Afro-American Council. See Walters, 1917.

21. Mary Church Terrell was a civil and women's rights advocate and the first president of the National Association of Colored Women beginning in 1896. Her career would continue for more than half a century after this meeting. For more on Booker Washington's wife, see Chapter 2. Nash, 2004, 122–136.

22. The headlines were: Colored Leader Is Denounced. Booker T. Washington and Wife Scored by the Council. Radical Report. *Chicago Journal*, 19 August 1899, 1.

23. Du Bois had studied and traveled in Europe from 1892 to 1894 on a grant from the Slater Fund. Rudwick, 1961, 26, 27.

24. Wells married Ferdinand Barnett in 1895. Ida was one of the couple's four children.

25. Bradley was a judge and businessman in the Kansas City area. The program for the League's Chicago meeting listed Bradley as representing the Kansas City Coal and Feed Company and the Wyandotte Drug

Company. That program is listed in Chapter 20 of Washington's *An Auto-biography: The Story of My Life and Work*, 1901.

26. *Chicago Daily News*, 23 August 1901, 11.

27. The defense and encouragement of lynching was not rare for Graves. The *Journal*'s editor made news in 1903, for example, for an address in Chautauqua, New York, wherein he argued, "The problem of the hour is not how to prevent lynching in the South, but the larger question: How shall we destroy the crime which always has and always will provoke lynching? The answer which the mob returns to this vital question is already known. The mob answers it with the rope, the bullet, and sometimes, God save us! with the torch. And the mob is practical; its theory is effective to a large degree. The mob is today the sternest, the strongest, and the most effective restraint that the age holds for the control of rape." *New York Times*, 12 August 1903, 1.

28. Wells, 1970, 261–267.

29. See Chapter 8.

30. Lewis, 1993, 245–246. Robert Todd Lincoln was Abraham Lincoln's first son, the former Secretary of War who had become general counsel for the Pullman Company. In 1897, he became the company's president. In 1911, he would become chairman of the board. See Emerson, 2012.

31. Washington is touting the NNBL, arguing that it has never been done, after he essentially killed the Afro-American Council to do it. Then he is using Du Bois's data to help state his case. Washington, March 1901, 209–219; and Washington, 1977, vol. 6, 76–83.

7

Up From Slavery

1901 was a big year for Booker Washington. In that year, he published his famed autobiography Up From Slavery *and ate dinner at the White House with President Theodore Roosevelt. Neither action met the approval of Du Bois. The Democrat was no supporter of Roosevelt and saw Washington's dinner as a failed power play more than anything else. And* Up From Slavery *explicated a position on education that Du Bois and his growing number of allies simply did not buy. He would make that fact very public in a critical review of the work in* The Dial. *Still, the two did plan a very public camping trip to West Virginia in each other's company, although plans eventually fell through. The two kept in correspondence and there was, despite the ideological opposition, a tenuous willingness to engage in whatever contact might be mutually beneficial to either themselves or the race.*

WILLIAM EDWARD BURGHARDT DU BOIS

Atlanta, Ga., April 17 1901

Dear Mr. Washington: Mr. [Edward Augustus] Mosely of the Inter-State Commerce Commission has advised me to retain Mr. W[illiam] C. Martin, a colored lawyer of 503 1/3 D St. N.W., Washington, for my interstate commerce case & to bring it thus to a regular trial with sworn witnesses &c.[1] What do you think of this? Do you know Martin? I shall write for his charges—I do not want to get too deeply involved financially. Very Sincerely,

W.E.B. Du Bois[2]

W.E.B. DU BOIS

Atlanta, Ga., July 3 1901

Dear Mr. Washington: I shall be delighted to accept your kind invitation of the 26th ult. to camp in West Va. My summer address is Sea Isle City, N.J. I enclose a letter from [William C.] Martin. Very Sincerely,

W.E.B. Du Bois[3]

BOOKER TALIAFERRO WASHINGTON

This volume [*Up From Slavery*] is the outgrowth of a series of articles, dealing with incidents in my life, which were published consecutively in the *Outlook*. While they were appearing in that magazine I was constantly surprised at the number of requests which came to me from all parts of the country, asking that the articles be permanently preserved in book form. I am most grateful to the *Outlook* for permission to gratify these requests.

I have tried to tell a simple, straightforward story, with no attempt at embellishment. My regret is that what I have attempted to do has been done so imperfectly. The greater part of my time and strength is required for the executive work connected with the Tuskegee Normal and Industrial Institute, and in securing the money necessary for the support of the institution. Much of what I have said has been written on board trains, or at hotels or railroad stations while I have been waiting for trains, or during the moments that I could spare from my work while at Tuskegee . . .[4]

W.E.B. DU BOIS

The Evolution of Negro Leadership
In every generation of our national life, from Phillis Wheatley to Booker Washington, the Negro race in America has succeeded in

bringing forth men whom the country, at times spontaneously, at times in spite of itself, has been impelled to honor and respect. Mr. Washington is one of the most striking of these cases, and his autobiography is a partial history of the steps which made him a group leader, and the one man who in the eyes of the nation typifies at present more nearly than all others the work and worth of his nine million fellows.

The way in which groups of human beings are led to choose certain of their number as their spokesmen and leaders is at once the most elementary and the nicest problem of social growth. History is but the record of this group leadership; and yet how infinitely changeful is its type and history! And of all types and kinds, what can be more instructive than the leadership of a group within a group—that curious double movement where real progress may be negative and actual advance be relative retrogression? All this is the social student's inspiration and despair.

When sticks and stones and beasts form the sole environment of a people, their attitude is ever one of determined opposition to, and conquest of, natural forces. But when to earth and brute is added an environment of men and ideas, then the attitude of the imprisoned group may take three main forms: a feeling of revolt and revenge; an attempt to adjust all thought and action to the will of the greater group; or, finally, a determined attempt at self-development, self-realization, in spite of environing discouragements and prejudice. The influence of all three of these attitudes is plainly to be traced in the evolution of race leaders among American Negroes. Before 1750 there was but the one motive of revolt and revenge which animated the terrible Maroons and veiled all the Americas in fear of insurrection. But the liberalizing tendencies of the latter half of the eighteenth century brought the first thought of adjustment and assimilation in the crude and earnest songs of Phillis and the martyrdom of Attucks and Salem.

The cotton-gin changed all this, and men then, as the Lyman Abbotts of to-day, found a new meaning in human blackness. A season of hesitation and stress settled on the black world as the hope of emancipation receded. Forten and the free Negroes of the North still hoped for eventual assimilation with the nation; Allen, the founder of the great African Methodist Church, strove for unbending self-development, and the Southern freedmen followed him; while among the black slaves at the South arose the avenging Nat Turner, fired by the memory of Toussaint the Savior. So far, Negro leadership had been local and spasmodic; but now, about 1840, arose a national leadership—a dynasty not to be broken. Frederick Douglass and the moral revolt against slavery dominated Negro thought and effort until after the war. Then, with the sole weapon of self-defense in perilous times, the ballot, which the nation gave the freedmen, men like Langston and Bruce sought to guide the political fortunes of the blacks, while Payne and Price still clung to the old ideal of self-development.

Then came the reaction. War memories and ideals rapidly passed, and a period of astonishing commercial development and expansion ensued. A time of doubt and hesitation, of storm and stress, overtook the freedmen's sons; and then it was that Booker Washington's leadership began. Mr. Washington came with a clear simple programme, at the psychological moment; at a time when the nation was a little ashamed of having bestowed so much sentiment on Negroes and was concentrating its energies on Dollars. The industrial training of Negro youth was not an idea originating with Mr. Washington, nor was the policy of conciliating the white South wholly his. But he first put life, unlimited energy, and perfect faith into this programme; he changed it from an article of belief into a whole creed; he broadened it from a by-path into a veritable Way of Life. And the method by which he accomplished this is an interesting study of human life.

Mr. Washington's narrative [*Up from Slavery*] gives but glimpses of the real struggle which he has had for leadership. First of all, he strove to gain the sympathy and cooperation of the white South, and gained it after that epoch-making sentence spoken at Atlanta: "In all things that are purely social we can be as separate as the fingers, yet one as the hand in all things essential to mutual progress" (p. 221). This conquest of the South is by all odds the most notable thing in Mr. Washington's career. Next to this comes his achievement in gaining place and consideration in the North. Many others less shrewd and tactful would have fallen between these two stools; but as Mr. Washington knew the heart of the South from birth and training, so by singular insight he intuitively grasped the spirit of the age that was dominating the North. He learned so thoroughly the speech and thought of triumphant commercialism and the ideals of material prosperity that he pictures as the height of absurdity a black boy studying a French grammar in the midst of weeds and dirt. One wonders how Socrates or St. Francis of Assisi would receive this!

And yet this very singleness of vision and thorough oneness with his age is a mark of the successful man. It is as though Nature must needs make men a little narrow to give them force. At the same time, Mr. Washington's success, North and South, with his gospel of Work and Money, raised opposition to him from widely divergent sources. The spiritual sons of the Abolitionists were not prepared to acknowledge that the schools founded before Tuskegee, by men of broad ideals and self-sacrificing souls, were wholly failures, or worthy of ridicule. On the other hand, among his own people Mr. Washington found deep suspicion and dislike for a man on such good terms with Southern whites.

Such opposition has only been silenced by Mr. Washington's very evident sincerity of purpose. We forgive much to honest purpose which is accomplishing something. We may not agree with the man at all points, but we admire him and cooperate with him so far as we conscientiously can. It is no ordinary tribute to this man's tact and power, that, steering as he must amid so many diverse interests and opinions, he to-day commands not simply the applause of those who believe in his theories, but also the respect of those who do not.

Among the Negroes, Mr. Washington is still far from a popular leader. Educated and thoughtful Negroes everywhere are glad to honor him and aid him, but all cannot agree with him. He represents in Negro thought the old attitude of adjustment to environment, emphasizing the economic phase; but the two other strong currents of feeling, descended from the past, still oppose him. One is the thought of a small but not unimportant group, unfortunate in their choice of spokesman, but nevertheless of much weight, who represent the old ideas of revolt and revenge, and see in migration alone an outlet for the Negro people. The second attitude is that of the large and important group represented by Dunbar, Tanner, Chesnutt, Miller, and the Grimkes, who, without any single definite programme, and with complex aims, seek nevertheless that self-development and self-realization in all lines of human endeavor which they believe will eventually place the Negro beside the other races.[5] While these men respect the Hampton-Tuskegee idea to a degree, they believe it falls far short of a complete programme. They believe, therefore, also in the higher education of Fisk and Atlanta Universities; they believe in self-assertion and ambition; and they believe in the right of suffrage for blacks on the same terms with whites.

Such is the complicated world of thought and action in which Mr. Booker Washington has been called of God and man to lead, and in which he has gained so rare a meed of success.[6]

WASHINGTON COLORED AMERICAN

Camps in West Va.

Charleston is soon to be visited by a company of representative Negroes, perhaps the most intelligent, the most cultured and the wealthiest in the United States.

The occasion is a proposed outing under the guidance of Professor Booker T. Washington, President of the Tuskegee Institute, of Alabama. He has invited and expects to have accompany him T. Thomas Fortune, author and associate editor of the New York Sun, Lloyd G. Wheeler and J.W. [Charles H.] Smiley, business men of Chicago, reputed to be the wealthiest colored men in this country, Prof. W.S. [W.E.B.] Du Bois, of Atlanta University, J.W. [John Stephens] Durham, statesman and diplomat, of Philadelphia, E.E. Cooper, of Washington, D.C. and a number of others.[7]

Here the party will be joined by Dr. H.F. Gamble, Phil Waters, B. Prillerman and others and a trip will be first made up the Elk to test the fishing spot of that stream and later the party will go to Gauley for a longer stay.[8]

For the trip up the Elk river over the C.C. & S. railroad Superintendent McDermitt has placed a private car at the disposal of the gentlemen of the party and they will no doubt enjoy the novelty of the outing very much.[9]

During his stay in this city Professor Washington has kindly consented to deliver an address on some appropriate subject at the opera house and an effort will be made to secure a large attendance of all classes.

This being Mr. Washington's home he is always ready and willing to address an audience of home folks and Charleston people are certain of a rare treat when they hear him.[10]

EMMETT JAY SCOTT AND LYMAN BEECHER STOWE

There were two particularly notable occasions upon which Mr. Washington unwittingly stirred the prejudices of the South. The first was when in [October] 1901 he dined with President Roosevelt and his family at the White House; the second, when four years later he dined with Mr. John Wanamaker and his daughter at a hotel in Saratoga, New York.[11]

The truth of his dining at the White House, of which so many imaginary versions have been given, was this: having received so many expressions of approval from all sections of the country on his appointment of ex-Governor Jones to a Federal judgeship in Alabama, which appointment was made, as described in a previous chapter, on the recommendation of Booker Washington and Grover Cleveland, President Roosevelt asked him to come to the White House and discuss with him some further appointments and other matters of mutual interest.

On arriving in Washington he went to the home of his friend, White-field McKinlay, a colored man with whom he usually stopped when in the Capital.[12] The next morning he went to the White House by appointment for an interview with the President. Since they did not have time to finish their discussion, the President, in accordance with the course he had often followed with others under similar circumstances, invited Washington to come to dinner so that they might finish their discussion in the evening without loss of time.

In response to this oral invitation he went to the White House at the appointed time, dined with the President and his family and two other guests, and after dinner discussed with the President chiefly the character of individual colored office holders or applicants for office and, as says Colonel Roosevelt, "the desirability in specific cases, notably in all offices having to do with the administration of justice, of getting high-minded and fearless white men into office—men whom we could be sure would affirmatively protect the law-abiding Negro's right to life, liberty, and property just exactly as they protected the rights of law-abiding white men." Also they discussed the public service of the South so far as the representatives of the Federal Administration were concerned—the subject upon which President Roosevelt had wished to consult him. The next day the bare fact that he had dined with the President was obscurely announced by the Washington papers as a routine item of White House news. Some days later, however, an enterprising correspondent for a Southern paper lifted this unpretentious item from oblivion and sent it to his paper to be blazoned forth in a front-page headline. For days and weeks thereafter the Southern press fairly shrieked with the news of this quiet dinner. The very papers which had most loudly praised the President for his appointment of a Southern Democrat to a Federal judgeship now execrated him for inviting to dine with him the man upon whose recommendation he had made this appointment.

Mr. Washington was also roundly abused for his "presumption" in daring to dine at the White House. This was a little illogical in view of the well-known fact that an invitation to the White House is a summons rather than an invitation in the ordinary sense. Neither President Roosevelt nor Mr. Washington issued any statements by way of explanation or apology. While it was, of course, farthest from the wishes of either to offend the sensibilities of the South, neither one—the many statements to the contrary, notwithstanding—ever indicated subsequently any regret or admitted that the incident was a mistake.

During the furore over this incident both the President and Mr. Washington received many threats against their lives. The President had the

Secret Service to protect him, while Mr. Washington had no such reliance. His coworkers surrounded him with such precautions as they could, and his secretary accumulated during this period enough threatening letters to fill a desk drawer. It was not discovered until some years after that one of these threats had been followed by the visit to Tuskegee of a hired assassin. A strange Negro was hurt in jumping off the train before it reached the Tuskegee Institute station. There being no hospital for Negroes in the town of Tuskegee he was taken to the hospital of the Institute, where he was cared for and nursed for several weeks before he was able to leave. Mr. Washington was absent in the North during all of this time. Many months later this Negro confessed that he had come to Tuskegee in the pay of a group of white men in Louisiana for the purpose of assassinating Booker Washington. He said that he became so ashamed of himself while being cared for by the doctors and nurses employed by the very man he had come to murder that he left as soon as he was able to do so instead of waiting to carry out his purpose on the return of his victim, as he had originally planned to do.

Booker Washington, with all his philosophy and capacity for rising above the personal, was probably more deeply pained by this affair than any other in his whole career. His pain was, however, almost solely on Mr. Roosevelt's account. He felt keenly hurt and chagrined that Mr. Roosevelt, whom he so intensely admired, and who was doing so much, not only for his own race but for the whole South as he believed, should suffer all this abuse and even vilification on his account. President Roosevelt evidently realized something of how he felt, for in a letter to him written at this time he added this postscript: "By the way, don't worry about *me*; it will all come right in time, and if I have helped by ever so little 'the ascent of man' I am more than satisfied."[13]

W.E.B. DU BOIS

Atlanta, Ga., Mch 4 1902

My Dear Mr. Washington: I am sorry that I was detained so long in the North with lectures that it was impossible for me to attend your conference, much as I would have liked to.

I write now to invite and urge you to attend our conference May 27, Tuesday. Our subject for this Seventh Conference is *The Negro Artisan*, we are collecting data on the history of trades among Negroes, the number & distribution of artisans in the United States; the increase & decrease in various communities, the influence of trade schools, the influence of colleges. We expect Hampton, Fisk & other schools to be represented & are particularly anxious to have you.

I think you will grant that I have sought in every way to minimize the breach between colleges & industrial schools & have in all possible ways tried to cooperate with Tuskegee in its work. I have not been so successful in getting you to cooperate with ours, altho' this is of course largely due to the fact that you are a busy man. This time, however, I hope you can serve us & will accept this invitation to speak to us on that occasion. Very Sincerely Yours,

W.E.B. Du Bois[14]

Beginning in the late 1890s, Du Bois published often in national reviews about the state of black education. It was one of several turn-of-the-century points of contact between the two, like the publication of Up From Slavery, *even though the relationship had already frayed. After Du Bois published an editorial in* Outlook *on the conditions of black public education in the South, for example, Washington wrote to him to praise the article.[15]*

BOOKER T. WASHINGTON

Tuskegee, Ala., July 15, 1902

My dear Dr. Du Bois:—

I have just read the editorial in the last number of The Outlook based upon your investigation of the condition of the public schools in the South, and I want to thank you most heartily and earnestly for the investigation of the subject referred to and also for the work which you are doing, through your conference and through your writings.[16] This editorial shows the value of such investigation. I know it is hard work and you may feel often that you are not very much encouraged in your efforts, but such an editorial ought to prove of great comfort to you. Constantly putting such facts before the public cannot but help our cause greatly in the long run.

Yours truly,
Booker T. Washington[17]

It was a kind of temporary détente between the two, but, at the same time, Washington was able to damn with faint praise, as he made it clear that his sympathy with the sentiment was made all the more poignant by the fact that Du Bois was unable to influence any sort of systemic change in the educational system. That system's policy was set by the Southern Education Board,

*wholly racist in its application, and whose leaders, principally Robert C. Ogden
and William Baldwin, appointed Washington as field secretary.*

*Baldwin, an influential railroad magnate and philanthropist, was a pater-
nalistic Tuskegee trustee who governed the university's finances. Baldwin
believed in black inferiority, and that the only way to solve the race question
was to use the Washington doctrine of work against the idealism of northerners like Du Bois. The South needed harmony, he believed, and race agitators
only killed those possibilities. Despite his unfortunate public jokes, Washington was not an advocate of black inferiority, but the public paternalism of
trustees like Baldwin only drove the rift further and emphasized differences
between the two camps that were not necessarily there. Baldwin and others
like him (many on the Tuskegee board of trustees) saw the two principal threats
to his own version of progressive reform as southern racists and black intellectuals like Du Bois. Those intellectuals, particularly black graduates of Harvard, just wanted to be white, and their elitism was misguided and problematic.
In this sense, Washington (who agreed with this analysis) became the effective
middle ground between two problematic poles.*

*Of course, Ogden and Baldwin viewed much of their educational policy
as pragmatic in a racist region, but the many northern reformers who opposed
them were easily able to class Washington as one of their own. It was, they
assumed, a continuation of his capitulation on the fight for black equality.*[18]
*In other areas, however, like Du Bois's railroad case, Washington was less will-
ing to capitulate.*

W.E.B. DU BOIS

Atlanta, Ga., November 22, 1902

My Dear Mr. Washington: We have at last got a permanent committee
formed here and our first work is to push the sleeping car matter before
the inter-state commission. I think that we had better get Smith of New
York to take it up.[19] We are going to raise money here and are going to
do three things:

1. Present personally a signed petition to Lincoln of the Pullman Co.
2. Push case before the Inter-state Commission.
3. Go to courts.

Are you still disposed to stand part of the expense, and if so, what
part? What is Smith's address? Sincerely yours,

W.E.B. Du Bois[20]

BOOKER T. WASHINGTON

Crawford House, Boston, Mass. November 28, 1902

Personal and Confidential.

My dear Dr. Du Bois: I have your letter of recent date, and if you will let me know what the total expense will be I shall be willing to bear a portion of it provided I can hand it to you personally and not have any connection with your committee. I do not want my name to go before the committee in any shape or to be used publicly in connection with this matter. I am very glad indeed to hear that you are moving in such a sensible way. Smith is a fine and able man. Yours truly,

Booker T. Washington[21]

W.E.B. DU BOIS

Atlanta, Ga., December 4, 1902

Dear Mr. Washington: Mr. W.H. Smith wrote me December the First in part as follows: "I have examined that law, and am of the opinion that it is absolutely void in its application to passengers taken up in the state and destined for points out side of the state, or passengers coming into the state from points out side of the state. I am also inclined to the belief that the law is void for all purposes." "I have not examined the extent of the jurisdiction of the Inter-State Commission where the sleeping car companies claim to act under a statute such as this. But, my idea would be to make a case before the United States Circuit Court, and have it come directly to Washington, so as to test the validity of that law." "I could not afford to give the time required from my business for less than $2,500 and I pay my own expenses, or $2,000 and the committee pay all my expenses. I mean either proposition that the committee will take care of the court costs."

I am replying to Mr. Smith asking what he thinks of a preliminary case simply before the Inter-State Commerce Commission.

I presume that he is right in preparing for the courts from the very first. What do you think of the fee charged? It's very high and I am not sure how much we can raise. Sincerely yours,

W.E.B. Du Bois[22]

Early in 1903, Du Bois attended a New York conference led by William H. Baldwin designed to address the needs of black New York. Robert Ogden,

George Foster Peabody, and others attended. After the conference, however, Baldwin took Du Bois to his home on Long Island and tried to recruit him to teach at Tuskegee. "Both he and his wife insisted that Tuskegee was not yet a good school, and needed the kind of development that I had been trained to promote." Du Bois would interview with Washington twice after his meeting with Baldwin, but decided to stay at Atlanta. (See a few pages prior for Du Bois's philosophical problems with Baldwin.) Despite the inherent deprecation of Tuskegee present in the request, however, Baldwin seems to have been coordinating the headhunting operation with Washington.[23]

WILLIAM HENRY BALDWIN, JR.

Brooklyn, N.Y. Friday Jan 23. [1903]

Dear Mr Washington, I have watched your Western trip with great interest. Your letter today is full of encouragement, and inspiration. I have taken the liberty of sending copies (of your reference to your trip) to our close friends.

It is very important.

I have spent the evening on Genl. Edn. work. Getting ready for our annual meeting tomorrow.

On Thursday next we have our first meeting under our National incorporation at Washn. D.C. and also we meet the Peabody Board.

They have asked us to help them decide important questions, and to cooperate with them. My hopes are being realized. General Education, Slater & Peabody.

It scares Mr Murphy, but I am not afraid of the results of concentration.

There are lots of things to talk over. Our meeting of the Southern Board, the Ogden dinner, the Armstrong meeting (poor) the meeting in Phila. with the Academy of Political Science (good) My New York local Negro Conference, (2nd meeting next Monday), My talk with Du Bois, etc.

Let me know soon when you expect to come North, so I can plan time for you. I am not going out much, as Mrs Baldwin is not at all well.

I want to talk with you about Tillmanism, and the Prest. And Southern (mis)representation! My regards to all. Faithfully

W H Baldwin Jr.[24]

Du Bois claimed to have two meetings with Washington in late 1902 and early 1903, the first in which Washington did not seem to know Du Bois, and

the second in which the two sat virtually in silence. The re-creation, according to Lewis, seems to be either a mistake or a lie. The two had already had significant contact. They had already survived the Washington, D.C. superintendent controversy. Baldwin had clearly coordinated the effort with Tuskegee's leader from the start. Instead, this depiction represents Du Bois's feelings of victimization and the hands of Washington, "of mental and moral estrangement that was almost molecular."[25]

But during this time, Du Bois had still not reached "absolute opposition to the things that Mr. Washington was advocating." He was not yet fully allied with Trotter or Ida Wells or others who attacked Washington's Atlanta Compromise at every turn. But there was almost a direct correlation to the worsening of the black situation, the number of lynchings, the denials of black rights, and the growing amount of power assumed by Washington. And Washington's exercise of power seemed to trump legitimate efforts to change systemic racial problems.[26]

W.E.B. DU BOIS

Things had come to such a pass that when any Negro complained or advocated a course of action, he was silenced with the remark that Mr. Washington did not agree with this.[27]

NOTES

1. Martin was obviously a black lawyer based in Washington, D.C. Mosely, originally from Massachusetts, was actually the secretary of the Interstate Commerce Commission and had been so since 1887, the only secretary the commission ever had. His principal interest was on railroads and railroad safety. Goodman, 1987, 12.

2. Washington, 1977, vol. 6, 91–92.

3. Ibid., 165.

4. Washington, *Up From Slavery*, 1901, vii–viii.

5. Henry Ossawa Tanner was the first genuinely famous black painter, studying under Thomas Eakins and Robert Henri in Philadelphia. Charles Chesnutt was a novelist from Ohio who used his success for activism. Kelly Miller was a sociology professor at Howard University and one of the most prominent black intellectuals in the country. Archibald and Francis Grimke were a lawyer and minister, respectively, who fought actively for rights and would ultimately take part in both of Du Bois's major rights ventures, Niagara and the NAACP. For Dunbar, see Chapter 4. See Mathews, 1995; Andrews, 1980; Jones, 2011; and Bruce, 1993.

6. Du Bois, 16 July 1901, 53–55; and Washington, 1977, vol. 6, 175–178.

7. Durham had been Charge d'Affairs to the Dominican Republic and Minister Resident and Consul General to Haiti from 1891 to 1893. Cooper was the editor of the *Washington Colored American*, in which this article originally appeared. "John Stephens Durham (1861–1919)," U.S. Department of State; and *Washington Colored American*, 14 September 1901, 1.

8. Dr. H.F. Gamble was a Charleston, West Virginia doctor and surgeon. Phil Waters was a Charleston, West Virginia lawyer who would eventually become chief deputy clerk of the West Virginia Supreme Court of Appeals. Byrd Prillerman was the founder and president of West Virginia State College. The trio were among the absolute leaders of black West Virginia. "Dr. H.F. Gamble Passes," 1932, 24; Washington, 1977, vol. 6, 210; and *Charleston Daily Mail*, 26 April 1929, 1.

9. C.K. McDermott was superintendent of the Charleston Clendennin & Sutton Railroad. "The Work in Progress," 7 April 1890, 258.

10. "Camps in West Va.," *Washington Colored American*, 14 September 1901, 9; and Washington, 1977, vol. 6, 209–210.

11. John Wanamaker was the famed founder of Wanamaker's Department Store in Philadelphia and postmaster general of the United States, an entrepreneur who stood as a signpost of the changing demographics of shopping in the American Gilded Age. See Fox, 1984.

12. McKinlay was a Washington, D.C. realtor and Republican operative who would eventually become collector of the Port of Georgetown. He was also one of Washington's principal contacts in the capital city. Williamson, 1984, 351, 358.

13. Scott and Stowe, 1916, 115–121.

14. Washington, 1977, vol. 6, 412–413.

15. Du Bois, 1973, 46; and Lewis, 1993, 265.

16. Du Bois's relationship with *The Outlook* varied. The popular national-circulation magazine published Washington's *Up From Slavery* in 1901. Edited by Lyman Abbott, who was devoted to Washington, *The Outlook* would be attacking Du Bois by 1906. Washington refers here to the Sixth Annual Conference of Atlanta University, which took as its theme "The Negro Common School." Washington did not attend, but the proceedings were published in 1901. The "writings" on education to which Washington refers were published in *Atlantic Monthly* (January 1899), the *Independent* (18 July 1901), and the *New York Times Magazine* (17 November–15 December 1901). Du Bois, 1973, 46. See also, Du Bois, January 1899, 99–105, for a representative example of such writings.

17. Du Bois, 1973, 46.

18. Lewis, 1993, 241, 265–273.

19. Wilford H. Smith was a black civil rights lawyer from New York who also wrote essays about the law in relation to African Americans. Perhaps his most famous works were "The Negro's Right to Jury Representation" and "The Negro and the Law," an essay that was published in the

1903 collection, *The Negro Problem*, headlined by essays from both Washington and Du Bois. *The Negro Problem*, 1903, 125–160; and Smith, 1910.

20. Washington, 1977, vol. 6, 590.
21. Ibid., 598.
22. Ibid., 605.
23. Du Bois, *Dusk of Dawn*, 1940, 78; and Washington, 1977, vol. 7, 7–10.
24. Washington, 1977, vol. 7, 9–10.
25. Du Bois, 1968, 243; Lewis, 1993, 274; Aptheker, "Introduction," in *The Souls of Black Folk*, 1973, 6; and Du Bois, 1940, 6. Much of this, and what follows hereafter for the remainder of this chapter, was repeated by Du Bois in much the same language as in his interview with Columbia University. "Reminiscences of W.E.B. Du Bois," NXCP89-A80, Columbia University Oral History Collection, Butler Library, Columbia University, New York, New York.
26. Du Bois, 1968, 243, 241; and Lewis, 1993, 274–275.
27. Du Bois, 1968, 241.

8

The First Attempt
at a Summit

As the ideological and personal positions of both Washington and Du Bois drifted farther and farther apart, Washington saw in the younger Du Bois a legitimate threat to his power. It was an untenable proposition for someone who craved control as much as Washington. And so in early 1903, he proposed a conference between various race leaders, including himself and Du Bois, to come to some sort of understanding about ideological and strategic considerations when it came to race politics. Early attempts at creating such a summit, however, ultimately fell to wrangling over control of the meeting's agenda. Meanwhile, the relationship was further strained by Du Bois's assumption that Washington was actively lobbying Atlanta University officials and threatening the loss of patronage from his white philanthropic friends to block the school's support for his sociological work. As Washington engaged in coordinating events, Du Bois was realizing—because of his suspicion of Washington and his frustration with Atlanta—that only direct action was going to change race relations, a position that would necessarily drive him farther and farther from any potential reconciliation with the leader of Tuskegee.

Washington believed that Du Bois was only interested in the advancement of a small group of black elites—based largely on his emphasis on higher education and his doctrine of the "Talented Tenth" (see Chapter 10). Although Du Bois did agree with Washingtonian concepts of black nationalism and black self-help, it is understandable why Washington might make such an assumption. People like Du Bois, Henry L. Morehouse, and AME Bishop Henry M. Turner believed that education should be more than just industrial training. It involved intellectual growth and development, the confrontation of racial problems, and the creation of wise men. Perhaps more than anything else, "it must seek the social regeneration of the Negro, and it must help in the solution of problems of race contact and cooperation. And finally, beyond all this, it must develop men." To that end, Du Bois hoped to develop an intellectual elite to lead everyone else forward. In fairness to Washington, of course, he did not deny the importance of liberal arts, he just saw industry as the foundation of progress. One hoped to show white leaders a vanguard of black intellectuals, the other a vanguard of black businessmen. Regardless, as strategic political calculations continued to shape the policy of each in relation to one another, their positions became further and further irreconcilable. Both understood, however, that such a rift might not be in the best interests of the race and thus considered the possibility of a meeting of leading black activists, a conference of black leaders normally in opposition to one another.[1]

BOOKER TALIAFERRO WASHINGTON

Tuskegee, Ala., February 12, 1903

Dear Dr. Du Bois: I am sorry that a tremendous pressure of work has delayed my sending out the letters sooner, but I am sending to you copy of such a letter as I have sent out. I shall keep you in formed as to the answers.[2] I find that I did not mention to you when you were here the name of Mr. Fortune as he is out of the country, but I find that it is probable he will return within a few weeks, and in that case, I should feel that it is proper to invite him to be present at this time. I understand that you and he do not agree on many matters. I have known Mr. Fortune for a number of years and while he has his weak points he also has his strong ones, and I think his counsel in such a meeting would be of great value. I am very anxious that the meeting be not confined to those who may agree with my own views regarding education and the position which the race shall assume in public affairs, but that it shall in every way represent all the interests of the race. Very truly yours,

Booker T. Washington

P.S. I rather think it would be better for you to write Mr. Morgan yourself.[3] I do not know him very well and then besides I rather have the idea that he has some feeling against me and would not perhaps under the circumstances be inclined to consider favorably anything that I might say. Please let me know if you will write him.

B.T.W.[4]

In 1902, Tuskegee made a major push to recruit Du Bois to campus, offering him a substantial pay raise to leave Atlanta University for the Alabama plains. In the effort, Washington enlisted some of his most influential backers, including Jacob Schiff, Robert C. Ogden, J.G. Phelps Stokes, George Foster Peabody, and, as mentioned in Chapter 7, William H. Baldwin. Du Bois even interviewed with Washington two times, but never received any specific explanation of his role in the university and grew suspicious about Washington's intentions.[5]

WILLIAM EDWARD BURGHARDT DU BOIS
(Confidential)

Atlanta, Ga. February 25, 1903.

Dear [Kelly] Miller:—

I was asked to go to Tuskegee some time ago and at that time the Conference you have been invited [to] was cooked up. A little judicious pressure and insistence lead [sp] to your invitation and that of [Clement G.] Morgan of Cambridge. I do not recall all the names but it includes [J.W.] Lyons, Bishop [Abraham] Grant, John Trower of Philadelphia, Rev. [C.T.] Walker of New York, [F.L.] McGhee of St. Paul, etc.[6]

I think this will be a chance for a heart to heart talk with Mr. Washington. I propose to stand on the following platform:

1. Full political rights on the same terms as other Americans.
2. Higher education of selected Negro youth.
3. Industrial education for the masses.
4. Common school training for every Negro child.
5. A stoppage to the campaign of self-depreciation.
6. A careful study of the real condition of the Negro.
7. A National Negro periodical.
8. A thorough and efficient federation of Negro societies and activities.
9. The raising of a defense fund.
10. A judicious fight in the courts for Civil rights.

Finally the general watch word must be, not to put further dependence on the help of the whites but to organize for self help, encouraging "manliness without defiance, conciliation without servility."

This program is hardly thought out—what is your opinion?

By the by, Washington wants to invite [T. Thomas] Fortune to the conference. I wrote him that I thought it would be a very unwise thing. I've not had an answer yet.

Please send me when you write Mrs. Mollie Keelan's address.[7]

Sincerely yours,
W.E.B. Du Bois[8]

By early 1903, the rift between Du Bois and Washington was certainly real, if not yet irreconcilable. To that end, Washington proposed a closed-door conference of race leaders for the purpose "of considering quietly all the weighty matters that now confront us as a race." This touched off a series of negotiations and strategizing among the potential attendees, each shoring up his own position as the potential meeting was planned. After months of work encompassing most of 1903, the conference was set for January 6–8, 1904, at Carnegie Hall in New York. Andrew Carnegie himself would bankroll the event. Although the meeting would be held, however, and the leaders would debate many issues related to the state of black America, any hope of a truce between Washington and Du Bois was lost in the negotiations before the meeting even started.[9]

BOOKER T. WASHINGTON

Tuskegee, Ala., March 4, 1903

Dear Dr. Du Bois: I send you herewith [a] list of persons who have been invited to the proposed conference. All of them have been written to with the exception of Mr. Clement G. Morgan. Very truly yours,

Booker T. Washington[10]

BOOKER T. WASHINGTON

New York City. March 27, 1903

Dear Dr. Du Bois: I am in receipt of your letter of March 20th. The definite date for the meeting has not been fixed. It is a very difficult matter to set a date where so large a number of busy people are concerned that will bring together the majority of the people we want, for that reason the matter has dragged. All the people invited, however, are willing to attend. I have been working at the matter ever since we had our meeting at Tuskegee. I am very much afraid however, that it will be impossible to have the meeting in any month except April unless we defer it until June. Yours truly,

Booker T. Washington[11]

BOOKER T. WASHINGTON

Hotel Manhattan, New York. April 21, 1903

Dear Mr. [Roscoe Conkling] Bruce:[12] Under all the circumstances I think it will be well to pay Dr. Du Bois' traveling expenses to Tuskegee and return for the sake of his lectures. If he chooses to be little we must teach him a lesson by bearing greater and broader than he is. Yours truly,

[Booker T. Washington][13]

OUTLOOK

Two Typical Leaders

Professor W.E.B. Du Bois; Booker T. Washington: they represent different types of character, different conceptions of the race problem, different methods for its solution, and they deal with it in a widely different spirit. These differences are strikingly illustrated in two volumes—one by Professor Du Bois, just published, "The Souls of the Black Folk," the other by Dr. Washington, published four years ago, "The Future of the American Negro."

To Professor Du Bois the negro and the American are ever separate, though in the same personality. The American negro is "two souls, two thoughts, two unreconciled strivings"; he is ever the subject of a "double consciousness"; dominated by a "sense of always looking at oneself through the eyes of others, of measuring one's soul by the tape of a world that looks on in amused contempt and pity." To Dr. Washington the negro race is a great race; during the Civil War the negro exhibited a remarkable "self-control," and was "to the last faithful to the trust that had been reposed upon him" by his master, yet was always "an uncompromising friend of the Union," and never, either in freedom or slavery, under a suspicion of being a traitor to his country; and since emancipation has he given abundant evidence that he can "make himself a useful, honorable, and desirable citizen." To Professor Du Bois

the negro is a problem, and the question is ever present in his consciousness, and from it he confesses himself unable to escape, "How does it
feel to be a problem?" To Dr. Washington America is the problem, and
the white race is as much a part of it as the black: "The problem is
how to make these millions of negroes self-supporting, intelligent,
economical, and valuable citizens, as well as how to bring about proper
relations between them and the white citizens among whom they live."
Professor Du Bois is half ashamed of being a negro, and he gives expression to his own bitterness of soul in the cry which he puts into the
mouth of his race, "Why did God make me an outcast and a stranger
in mine own home?" Dr. Washington rejoices in the honorable record of
his race; in his address at Hampton's last Commencement he cries out
to his white auditors, "We are as proud of our race as you are of yours";
and his negro auditors applauded his declaration with great enthusiasm. The sense of amused contempt and pity for his own race, caught
from the white people, is reflected in the title of Professor Du Bois's
book, "The Souls of the Black Folk"; the spirit of race pride, of national
patriotism, and of hope for the future of his race is reflected in the title
of Dr. Washington's book, "The Future of the American Negro."

We shall speak hereafter more fully of Professor Du Bois's interesting and valuable book, as we have heretofore spoken of Dr. Washington's; here we take the contrast between the two as a text for some
reflections on two parties or tendencies or influences in the negro race,
which the two respectively represent. One of these parties is ashamed
of the race, the other is proud of it; one makes the white man the standard, the other seeks the standard in its own race ideals; one demands
social equality, or at least resents social inequality, the other is too self-
respecting to do either; one seeks to push the negro into a higher place,
the other to make him a larger man; one demands for him the right to
ride in the white man's car, the other seeks to make the black man's car
clean and respectable; one demands the ballot for ignorant black men
because ignorant white men have the ballot, the other asks opportunity
to make the black man competent for the duties of citizenship, and
wishes no man to vote, white or colored, who is not competent; one
would build the educational system for the race on the university, the
other would build it on the common school and the industrial school;
one wishes to teach the negro to read the Ten Commandments in
Hebrew, the other wishes first to teach him to obey them in English; to
one labor is barely more honorable than idleness and the education
which makes "laborers and nothing more" is regarded with ill-concealed
contempt, to the other industry is the basic virtue, and the education
which makes industry intelligent is the foundation of civilization. The

first view has frequently crude representation in negro journals and by negro orators—political and religious; but the ablest and most cultivated expression of it which we have ever seen is afforded by the volume of Professor Du Bois, albeit presented with qualifications which in this brief summary it is impossible to represent; of the second view the pre-eminent representative is Dr. Washington. The Outlook heartily accepts the second view. Something like this is what it would say to its Afro-American readers:

I. Have faith in yourselves. Cultivate the spirit of self-respect; only he who respects himself will be respected by his neighbors. Decline to look at yourselves through your white neighbor's eyes; look at yourselves through your own eyes. Do not take the white man as a standard; make your own standards. Be not imitators. There is no more reason why you should imitate the white man than why the white man should imitate you. No man can make himself into another man; no race can make itself into another race. The missionary makes a mistake who tries to convert the negro into an Anglo-Saxon; the negro makes a greater mistake who desires for himself any such conversion. The Anglo-Saxon was once a subject race; it did not win its present position by trying to be Norman. Do not try to be an Anglo-Saxon; be an Afro-American, and be proud that you are one.

II. Do not push yourself forward; do not allow would-be leaders to push you forward. Do not be ambitious for social equality, or industrial equality, or political equality, or any kind of equality. Be ambitious to be men, and trust that in time the manhood will make for itself a place; it always does. The whole power of the Federal Government did not suffice to give you political power; it failed because you had not the necessary preparation for the exercise of political power. The United States Supreme Court has decided that it cannot give you political power by a judicial device. The slower way is the quicker way. Get political competence, and trust that political power will follow in due time. In most if not all the Southern States the possession of about three hundred dollars' worth of taxable property entitles you, under the amended constitutions, to a ballot. Set yourselves, by honest and intelligent industry, to get the property; then ask for the ballot. If registrars deny it to you, when you go before them with your tax receipt, appeal to the State courts to enforce the State law. If ignorant, shiftless white men vote, so much the worse for the State. It is neither for your interest nor for that of the State that you should be represented by an ignorant and shiftless negro vote. Nothing is for your interest that is not for the State's interest.

So also in the industrial and the social world. Acquire intelligence and virtue, and what usually accompanies them in this country, a moderate property, and the doors of industry and the respect of your fellow-men will follow. What Dr. Washington said at Atlanta, what Professor Du Bois calls the "Atlanta Compromise," is no compromise; it is a principle of universal application, just as true and just as applicable in the Northern factory as the Southern plantation: "In all things purely social we can be as separate as the five fingers, and yet one as the hand in all things essential to mutual progress." Never forget this principle; never demand social recognition; social recognition is never given on demand. Always work for mutual progress. What member of your race has risen to the position of social respect, won the opportunity of useful industry, and acquired the political influence of Dr. Washington? Follow in the path he has blazed for you, and you will arrive, sooner or later, at the same destination.

III. Therefore seek education—first, last, and all the time. But do not fall into the notion that education means ability to read and understand Homer and Dante. Do not let Professor Du Bois's picture of Socrates and Francis of Assisi deceive you. There are already enough "brothers of the poor" of your race in America; you do not need to add to their number. The first duty of every man is to earn his living; after that comes the duty of adding to the life of others. Seek for yourself, seek for your race, first the ability to earn a living. Is this materialism? Very well! materialism is the basis of life. What not only your race, what the great mass of the American people, need to-day is a broader education rather than a higher education. No education for any race, or for any individual of any race, is adequate which does not include manual training; and no education is worthy of the name which leaves its recipient helplessly dependent on his neighbors for his livelihood. Are you a teacher, or a preacher, or a doctor, or a lawyer, or a merchant? Can you read Greek? Can you enjoy Homer and Dante, Raphael and Titian, Beethoven and Brahms? Very well; but do not content yourself by the endeavor to pass your knowledge along to your race; use it to make them first of all self-respecting and self-supporting citizens; second, practical contributors to the welfare of the community in which they live. It is not true that Dr. Washington asks "that black people give up, at least for the present, three things—first, political power; second, insistence on civil rights; third, higher education of negro youth." It requires all our charity to think that Professor Du Bois really believes that Dr. Washington has ever asked anything of the sort. He asks his fellows to get political power by proving their capacity to exercise it; civil rights by obedience to law; and higher education by building it on a foundation of a broad industrial and ethical education. In this he is absolutely right. Political power without previously acquired capacity to use it is always dangerous to others and generally dangerous to the possessor; the civil rights of a freeman the lawless are not entitled to; and higher education without a foundation laid in elementary education is a castle in the air, which collapses at the first rude awakening of the ill-bred scholar to the exigencies of actual life.

IV. Do not think about yourself. Do not think about your woes or your wrongs. Meditate, not on "the souls of black folk," but on "the future of the American negro." Look out, not in; forward, not backward. Put your thought on your work, not on your soul; and take council of your hopes, not of your discouragements. Do not look too long on the one-roomed cabins, or on the mortgaged farms, or on the usurious rates of interest, or on the Jim Crow cars, or on the short-term schools. Remember that forty years ago few negroes in Virginia owned themselves, and that now they own seventeen and a half million dollars' worth of taxable property; that forty years ago it was a penal offense to teach a negro to read, and that now there are public schools for him, supported at public cost, in every Southern State; that forty years ago no negro could vote, and now that negroes are registering and voting and having their votes counted in every State and in nearly every county in the South.

The negro still suffers injustice; he is still subject to a sometimes cruel prejudice. The Outlook does not condone the first nor apologize for the second. But what is the remedy? Not Federal Force Bills; not Supreme Court decisions enforcing political equality; not a veneer of culture on a nature ill developed in the essentials of practical life; not self-assertiveness and clamorous demand for political rights or social equality. Character. Character—developed by broad systems of education in the negro and not less in the white race. Character—wrought in the individual and extending by a gradual process throughout the community. Character—the foundations of which are truth, honesty, chastity, temperance, industry, intelligence; the superstructure of which is material property, mutual respect, personal culture, political freedom, and social peace.[14]

Du Bois was also frustrated while at Atlanta University because, in his opinion, too much time was devoted to idealistic theoretical work instead of empirical sociological research that could find real-world answers to actual problems affecting the race. He felt that his work was never adequately funded while at Atlanta—work, he argued, that "would have thrived if Booker T. Washington had not blocked support for the project." Of course, Washington had nothing to do with Atlanta University, making such statements seem like unjustified paranoia. But the support Du Bois hoped to find most likely would have come not from his school but from white philanthropy, over which Washington had considerable influence. Still, Du Bois was able, despite obstacles, to create the university's sociology program.[15]

W.E.B. DU BOIS

There is some ground for suspicion when a small institution of learning offers courses in sociology. Very often such work means simply
prolonged discussions of society and social units, which degenerate
into bad metaphysics and false psychology, or it may take a statistical
turn and the student become so immersed in mere figures as to forget,
or be entirely unacquainted with, the concrete facts standing back of
the counting.

On the other hand every one feels how necessary social study is,—
how widespread in modern times is our ignorance of social facts and
processes. In such matters we still linger in a Middle Age of credulity
and superstition. We print in the opening chapters of our children's
histories theories of the origin and destiny of races over which the
gravest of us must smile; we assume, for instance, elaborate theories of
an "Aryan" type of political institution, and then discover in the pitso
of the South African Basutos as perfect an agora or tungemot as ever
existed among Greeks or Germans. At the same time all of us feel the
rhythm in human action; we are sure that the element of chance is at
least not supreme, and no generation has taken to the study of social
phenomena more energetically or successfully than ours. Have we, however, accomplished enough or settled the matter of scope and method
sufficiently to introduce the subject of sociology successfully into the
small college or the high school?

I am not sure that our experience at Atlanta University contributes
much toward answering this question, for our position is somewhat
exceptional, and yet I think it throws light on it. Atlanta University is
situated within a few miles of the geographical centre of the negro population of the nation, and is, therefore, near the centre of that congeries
of human problems which cluster round the black American. This institution, which forms in itself a "negro problem," and which prepares
students whose lives must of necessity be further factors in this same
problem, cannot logically escape the study and teaching of some things
connected with that mass of social questions. Nor can these things all
be reduced to history and ethics—the mass of them fall logically under
sociology.

We have arranged, therefore, what amounts to about two years of
sociological work for the junior and senior college students, and we
carry on in our conferences postgraduate work in original research.
The undergraduate courses in sociology are simply an attempt to study
systematically conditions of living right around the university and
to compare these conditions with conditions elsewhere about which
we are able to learn. For this purpose one of the two years is taken up

principally with a course in economics. Here the methods of study are largely inductive, going from field work and personal knowledge to the establishment of the main principles. There is no text-book, but a class-room reference library with from five to ten duplicate copies of well-known works.

In the next year the study comes nearer what is understood by sociology. Here again, after much experiment, we have discarded the text-book, not because a book of a certain sort would not be valuable in the hands of students, but rather because available text-books are distinctly and glaringly unsuitable. The book most constantly referred to is Mayo-Smith's "Statistics and Sociology," and after that the United States censuses. Our main object in this year of work is to find out what characteristics of human life can be known, classified and compared. Students are expected to know what the average death-rate of American negroes is, how it varies, and what it means when compared with the death-rates of other peoples and classes. When they learn by search in the census and their own mathematical calculations that 30 per cent of the negroes of New York City are twenty to thirty years of age, they immediately set to work to explain this anomaly, and so on. A large part of their work consists of special reports, in which the results of first-hand study of some locality or some characteristic of negro life are compared with general conditions in the United States and Europe. Thus in a way we measure the negro problem . . .[16]

It was that first decade of the 20th century when Du Bois realized that more than academic pursuits would be required to help fix the problems of black America. "One could not be a calm, cool, and detached scientist while Negroes were lynched," he later argued. It was, in the mind of one commentator, the natural response of an educated mulatto activist. Whatever Du Bois achieved, whatever Washington achieved, argued Alfred Holt Stone, was the result of the pair's white blood. The conflict surrounding the bizarre conflation of the two leaders would lead Stone to try to curry favor with Washington and Du Bois to challenge the entire premise. It demonstrated the kind of misinterpretation of Washington's ideas that could exist among the white population.[17]

ALFRED HOLT STONE *(Stone was a Mississippi planter, lawyer, politician, and notorious race-baiter.)*

The Mulatto Factor in the Race Problem

It is a matter of regret that in organizing the twelfth census it was determined to attempt no separate enumeration of the mulatto element of our population,—using the term in its popular sense, as denoting all persons having any admixture of white and negro blood. It will not do to say that the failure to do this will in any wise affect the solution of our race problem, for to do so would be to regard it as admitting of a sort of blackboard treatment,—the only essentials to success being an array of statistics and their proper handling. But any one who endeavors to go beyond the superficialities of the problem—to do something more than academically consider, from his particular standpoint, its external symptoms—must feel that such data would at least be of value, whatever ideas he may entertain as to its ultimate solution.

Any consideration which fails to reckon this mulatto element as an independent factor ignores what is possibly the most important feature of the problem, and is faulty in its premises, whatever the theoretical conclusion arrived at. Yet we see this constantly done, and of the hundreds of such discussions annually engaged in, it is safe to say that scarcely one is entirely free from this blunder. There appears in them but a single "problem," and every panacea proposed—education, voting, industrial training, or what not—is made to fit the same Procrustean bed. It is a primal postulate of these discussions that the negro is an undeveloped, not an inferior, race, and to this basic error may be attributed much of the confusion which surrounds the entire subject.

We have too long been guilty of the folly of trying to legislate the negro into a white man, and a pyramid of failures has apparently not yet convinced us of the futility of the undertaking. We have ignored the scientific truth of the ethnic differences among the human family, and have blindly disregarded the fact that the negro, in common with all other races, possesses certain persistent, ineradicable distinguishing characteristics. Foolishly attempting to evade the stubborn fact that the negro in Africa is to-day just what we know him to have been since he first appeared on that continent, we have sought in slavery an excuse for the natural and inevitable resemblance between the native and transplanted branches of the family, and have proceeded toward the American negro as though heredity could be overridden by constitutions and laws. Probably nothing has contributed more toward the persistence of this effort at creating an artificial being than the absolute elimination of the mulatto equation from all our considerations of the subject. It is this that has enabled those who have so long ignored the laws and operations of heredity to point, in proof of the correctness of their theory of race-problem treatment, to the achievements of men loosely accredited to the negro race. Unless through discussion the American people be able to reach a common ground, a century of polemical strife will accomplish no tangible good; and I know of no surer means of reaching a working agreement than by the frank acknowledgment of the mulatto factor in the race problem. I would not be guilty of complicating a situation already sufficiently complex through the introduction of a new factor; I rather hold to the hopeful belief that the consideration of one which already exists, though commonly ignored, may at least serve to simplify discussion, even though it fail to at once point a way out of existing difficulties. When we recognize the very simple and very patent fact that the intermixture of white and black races has given us a hybrid that is neither the one nor the other; when we get far enough along to separate this type from the negro masses in our efforts at determining what may be best for the latter; when the South is willing to lay at the white man's door many of the failings of this mulatto type and much of the meanness which he too frequently exhibits, and Northern opinion is sufficiently candid and honest to persist no longer in ascribing all his virtues and accomplishments to the negro,—I think we shall have made a distinct gain in race-problem discussion . . .

A year ago a movement was inaugurated in Congress looking to the investigation of the suffrage laws of the various states. No attempt was made to conceal the real purpose of the movement, and even though we go so far as to credit the proponent of the measure with honesty of opinion as to its necessity, what must be thought of his wisdom, and of the point of view from which he would have the so-called "investigation" made, when he himself, in the face of the facts of history and the experiences of recent years, calmly affirms that "there is no doubt that the negro is capable of unlimited development," and declares his belief in the virtue of "participation in politics" as a means of "uplifting the race"? Yet such is our looseness of expression in discussing this question, that to challenge either the wisdom or correctness of such views is to hear, as their sole support, a recital of the achievements of "famous men of the negro race,"—while, as a matter of fact, the names brought forward are merely those of well-known mulattoes,—from Murillo's favorite pupil, down to Crispus Attucks, Benjamin Banneker, Douglass, Bruce, Lynch, the late Sir Conrad Reeves, Du Bois, Washington, Chesnutt, and others . . .

If we will but study the true sources of the agitation over "negro disfranchisement," "negro cars," the deprivation of "the negro's rights," etc., it will be found that in it all the negro takes but an insignificant if any part. The cry that goes up over the "lack of opportunities under which the negro labors," and the "injustice of race distinctions," does not proceed from the negro. It is the voice of the mulatto, or that of the white politician, that is heard. If the statutes of those states which have been charged with discriminating against the negro were not in any wise enforceable against the mulatto, I strongly suspect that America's race problem would speedily resolve itself into exceedingly small and simple proportions.

Through the medium of race papers, and magazines, the pulpit, industrial and political gatherings and associations, the mulatto wields a tremendous influence over the negro. It is here that his importance as a factor in whatever problems may arise from the negro's presence in this country becomes manifest,—and the working out of such problems may be advanced or retarded, just as he wisely or unwisely plays the part which fate—or Providence—has assigned him. The negro, like the white man, responds more readily to bad influences than to good, and the example and precepts of an hundred men like Washington and Du Bois may be easily counteracted by the advice and influence of men of whom the mulatto type unfortunately furnishes too many examples. Booker Washington may in all sincerity preach the gospel of labor; he may teach his people, as a fundamental lesson, the cultivation of the friendship and esteem of the white man; he may point out the truth that for the negro the privilege of earning a dollar is of much greater importance than that of spending it at the white man's theatre or hotel; yet all these lessons must fail of their fullest and best results so long as the negro's mind is being constantly poisoned with the radical teachings and destructive doctrines of the mulatto of the other school.

The most prominent mulatto editor of the country is credited by the Washington Post with having declared that he was "tired of hearing about good niggers,—that what he wanted was to see bad niggers, with guns in their hands." One of the leading race papers in the country, published at the national capital, in enumerating certain things which it would like to see occur, as being beneficial to the negro, included "the death of a few more men like Charles Dudley Warner," and this merely because that good man and true friend of the negro had, shortly before his death, reached and expressed conclusions concerning negro higher education at variance with opinions he had formerly entertained. With Booker Washington crying from the housetops, "Peace! peace!" and the most widely read and influential of race magazines silently furnishing to the private precincts of the home and chimney corner stories revolving around themes of race prejudice, and appealing to passion and hate, together with articles which would inculcate lessons dangerous to even a stronger people,—which voice is in the end likely to prove most potent in its influence upon this childish race?

The varied tragedy of human life furnishes few more pathetic spectacles than that of the educated mulatto who is honestly seeking the welfare of a race with which a baleful commingling of blood has inexorably identified him,—who is striving to uplift to his own level a people between whose ideals and ambitions and capabilities and his own a great gulf has been fixed by nature's laws. Frequently inheriting from the superior race talents and aspirations the full play of which is denied him by his kinship to the inferior,—through no fault of his own he is doomed to be an anachronism in American political and social life. A generous mind should not too sweepingly condemn his occasional outbursts of bitterness, but rather wonder that they are not more frequent than they are. Just in proportion as their numbers diminish or increase, and their great influence be potential for good or for evil, will the problem of the future become the problem of the color line. But that of the present, whatever it may be adjudged to be, is still the problem of the negro. While it so remains, let us treat it as such, by considering it in its simplest terms; and in seeking the real good of the real negro let us invoke the aid of the best and wisest of that class with which he has so long, and to so little purpose, been confused.[18]

RAYMOND PATTERSON

Mulatto and Negro

Few contributions to the current literature of the race question have attracted so much attention among the negroes themselves as an article in a recent number of the *Atlantic Monthly*, which attempted to show that the mulattoes, or mixed-blood negroes, were chiefly responsible for the recent unrest so noticeable among the colored people. I have heard of this article in all directions among the colored people, and on that account I endeavored to see the author, Mr. Alfred H. Stone, while I was in Mississippi. He was absent from home, but I dug him up at last in his own particular alcove at the Congressional Library, where he is engaged upon an elaborate history of the thirteenth, fourteenth, and fifteenth amendments to the Constitution.

Mr. Stone is a cotton planter, and his family live in Greenville, Miss., his plantation being outside of the city, between Greenville and Indianola. I improved the opportunity while in Washington, before going back South to make a personal study of the plantation life of the negroes, to get Mr. Stone's views on the race question as a Southern man who has had personal experience with the negroes, but who, as a careful student of the race problem, I found to be singularly free from prejudice. In truth, Mr. Stone discusses the negro in his economic and industrial relations more dispassionately than almost any other Southern man I have yet talked to.

As a result of his personal experience, which is fortified by the deep study he is giving to the question, Mr. Stone is more and more convinced that it is the mulattoes who must be dealt with by the white man, and not the pure negro, who is, he asserts, blindly following the lead of his hybrid brother . . .

"The mulatto is not a degenerate," said this literary student of the race question. "On the contrary, the mixed-blood is far superior to the negro. The mulatto will solve the race question for us some day. The time is coming, and it is not so very far off, when there will be a breaking up of old associations and the mulatto and the negro will forever separate. This is the condition now in many of the West India islands, and my observation is that we are drifting into the same condition of affairs. The mulatto is all powerful in the negro community to-day. His influence is dominant either for good or for evil. I am quite aware of the fact that well-known mulatto leaders like Booker Washington and Prof. Du Bois constantly declare in public that there is no difference between the pure negro and the man of mixed blood. I believe, however, that they make these statements more as a matter of policy and to unite the race, although in their heart of hearts they know and believe that the white strain does tell, and that practically all the men of so-called negro blood who have done anything in the world are of the mulatto type . . ."

"I note Mr. Washington's reference in one of your recent interviews to my article on the mulatto and wish he could find time to reply to it. I should be very glad to make a distinct issue along the line of such a test case as he suggests. In the shape of a list of the so-called negroes who have been sent to Congress, Mr. Blaine was a pretty good judge of ability in men, and if Mr. Washington will take the pains to turn to volume 2 of 'Twenty Years in Congress' he will find facing page 304 engravings of the five men selected by the author of that great political history to represent what he considered the best type of negro Congressmen. These were all mulattoes. In fact, if my memory is not greatly at fault, we have had, Mr. Washington to the contrary notwithstanding, but two pure negroes in Congress, Robert Small[s] and Robert Elliott, both of South Carolina.[19] I am perfectly familiar with the personal history of these two men and they reflected no great credit upon the State they represented or the House in which they sat."

Warming up to his subject, Mr. Stone continued on the same tack:

"As far as concerns the truth of my contention that it is the mulatto who is the cause of dissension and unrest among the negroes, I am willing to leave that to the judgment of any fair man who will take the trouble to go over the files of representative 'negro' journals and magazines. If he does not reach the conclusion that these 'mulatto' papers and periodicals—for that is all on earth they are—are a source of great danger and a positive menace to anything like permanent good relations between the races, then I am no judge of the effect upon the human mind of constant appeals to passion and hate, of the constant parading and exaggerating of grievances and wrongs. The editor of one paper which is probably most guilty in this regard is called a negro, but in reality a combination of Indian, negro, and white man. As a factor for strife and ill feeling and discord I will match him as a mulatto against any two dozen pure negroes Mr. Washington can produce in America today."[20]

ALFRED HOLT STONE

Washington, D.C. July 2, 1903

Personal

Dear Sir [Washington]: It is, and has always been, my opinion that a man should hold his peace, rather than, in attempting to discuss any phase of our "race question," give utterance to any expression in the least calculated to mar kindly relations, or beget feelings of harsh[n]ess or distrust between men who have the good of both races at heart.

I have faithfully tried to live up to this idea, and it is because in one instance I am placed in the attitude of departing from it that I write you this letter. I allude to an "interview" appearing in the Post this morning, by Mr. Raymond Patterson.[21]

I shall not attempt to go into particulars, nor enumerate the instances wherein I have been misquoted, or my meaning utterly misinterpreted: I shall only say that I have never heard, nor claimed to hear, any mulatto "boast of his white ancestry," nor give any indication of feeling "degraded" by any "negro blood" he might possess. That I have never for a moment questioned the honesty of any views entertained by you, Dr. Du Bois, or any other man, in regard to the comparative capacities of the negro and mulatto, or any other subject, nor held to any such notion as that you were "dissembling" as to this, or any other question.

Mr. Patterson called on me a few nights since, and we had a lengthy conversation on the general subject of the so-called race question. It is in attempting to translate my ideas into his own words, and in confusing many of them in the process, that Mr. Patterson has done me the entirely unintentional injustice of misquoting me.

Mr. Patterson made no notes of our conversation, and I did not see the "interview" until its publication. The two paragraphs under the caption "Mulatto & Black Contrasted" are correctly quoted, being taken from a letter written after the appearance of your interview, though with no view to its publication.

I am writing this to place myself in the proper attitude as regards this interview, in so far as this may be possible through letters to two or three people, as against the circulation of a newspaper. In doing this I do not wish to be understood as charging Mr. Patterson with having intentionally misquoted me, though the wrong done my ideas, in numerous instances, is none the less great. Very truly yours,

Alfred H. Stone[22]

W.E.B. DU BOIS

Possibilities of the Negro:
The Advance Guard of the Race

It is usually considered that Negroes are today contributing practically nothing of importance to American civilization; that only one or two individuals of Negro blood have so risen above the average of the nation as rightly to be judged men of mark. Nor is this assumption to be wondered at for in the world of work men are not labeled by color. When, then, the average American rushes to his telephone there is nothing in the look of the transmitter to tell him that it is part product of a Negro brain; when the whizz of the engine weaves cloth, drags trains, and does other deeds of magic, it does not tell the public that the oil which smooths its turning is the composition of a black man; if the medical student reads in DaCosta of the skilled surgeon who recently sewed up a hole in a living man's heart he will not read that the surgeon was colored; the wanderer amid the beauties of the Luxemburg is not apt to know from the dark hues of the Raising of Lazarus the still darker hues of its painter; and it was a Texas girl who naively remarked: "I used to read Dunbar a good deal until I found out that he was a nigger."

Such ignorance of the work of black men is natural. A man works with his hands and not with his complexion, with his brains and not with his facial angle; and the result of his work is human achievement and not necessarily a "social problem." Thus his work becomes gathered up and lost in the sum of American deeds, and men know little of the individual. Consequently the average American, accustomed to regarding black men as the outer edge of humanity, not only easily misses seeing the colored men who have accomplished something in the world common to both races, but also misses entirely the work of the men who are developing the dark and isolated world of the black man.

So here I am seeking to bring to mind something of what men of African blood are today doing in America, by selecting as types ten living Negroes who in ability and quite regardless of their black blood have raised themselves to a place distinctively above the average of mankind . . . Of the fields of endeavor conspicuously open to Americans there are four chief groups: the field of commerce and industry, in which this land has gained worldwide preeminence; the field of political life, in the governing of a continent and seventy millions under republican forms; the field of the learned professions—law, medicine, preaching, and teaching; and, finally, the paths of literature and art, as expressive of the mighty life of a new world. In these four lines of striving the men I notice work . . .

Turning now to the field of political and social activity we may note a long line of Negroes conspicuous in the past, beginning with Toussaint L'Ouverture, American by influence if not by birth, and going past Alexander Hamilton, whose drop of African fire quite recently sent Mrs. Atherton into hysterics, down to Purvis, Nell, Douglass, and Bruce. All these are dead, and today, strange as the assertion may seem, the leading Negro political leader is Booker T. Washington. Mr. Washington is not a teacher; he has spent little time in the classroom; he is not the originator or chief exponent of the educational system which he so fervently defends. He is primarily the political leader of the New Commercial South, and the greatest of such leaders since Appomattox. His ability has been shown not so much in his educational campaign, nor in his moral earnestness, as in the marvelous facility by which he has so manipulated the forces of a strained political and social situation as to bring about among the factors the greatest consensus of opinion in this country since the Missouri Compromise. He has done this by applying American political and business methods to an attempted solution of the Negro problem. Realizing the great truth that the solution of this vexed question demands above all that somehow, sometime, the southern whites and blacks must agree and sympathize with each other, Mr. Washington started to advertise broadly his proposed basis of agreement so that men might understand it. With this justification, he advertised with a thoroughness that astonished the nation. At the same time he kept his hand on the pulse of North and South, advancing with every sign of good will and generosity, and skillfully retreating to silence or shrewd disclaimer at any sign of impatience or turmoil. The playing of this game has been simply wonderful, the success phenomenal. To be sure not all men like the outcome, not all men fail to see the terrible dangers of this effort at compromise. Some have felt it their duty to speak strongly against Mr. Washington's narrow educational program, and against the danger of his apparent surrender of certain manhood rights which seem to be absolutely essential to race development and national weal; and above all, against his failure to speak a strong, true note for justice and right; but all this is beside the object of this paper. Of Mr. Washington's great ability as a politic leader of men there can scarce be two opinions. He is manifestly one of the greatest living southerners, and one of the most remarkable of Americans.

It must not be thought that with this new political leadership the old political activity has stopped. The Negro is not eliminated from politics and never will be; he is simply passing through a new phase of the exercise of his political power. Here and there in the legislation of the land his work and influence may still be felt . . .

These are the men. But already you are impatient with a question, "How much Negro blood have they?" The attitude of the American mind toward the mulatto is infinitely funny. Mixture of blood is dire damnation, cry the men who did the mixing, and then if a prophet arise within the Veil or a man of any talent—"That is due to his mixed blood," cry the same men. If, however, we study cases of ability and goodness and talent among the American Negroes, we shall have difficulty in laying down any clear thesis as to the effect of amalgamation. As a matter of historic fact the colored people of America have produced as many remarkable black men as mulattoes. Of the men I have named, three are black, two are brown, two are half white, and three are three-fourths white. Many of those with white blood had one or two generations' start of the others, because their parents or grandparents were natural children of rich Southerners, who sent them North and educated them while the black men toiled in the fields. Then, too, the mulatto is peculiarly the child of the city; probably two-thirds of the city colored people are of mixed blood; and it is the city that inspires and educates the lowly and opens the doors of opportunity. If we choose among these men the two of keenest intellect, one is black and the other is brown; if we choose the three of strongest character, two are yellow and one is black. If we choose three according to their esthetic sensibility, one is black, one is yellow, and one is three-fourths white. And so on. Let wise men decide from such cases the exact effect of race mixture, for I cannot . . .[23]

With such racist conflations and the need for the kind of response Du Bois provided to Stone, it was clear to the race leaders that there was still a pragmatic benefit in maintaining a relationship with one another. The country, after all, was full of Alfred Holt Stones.

BOOKER T. WASHINGTON

Tuskegee, July 6, 1903

Mr. Booker T. Washington will be pleased to have you [Du Bois] take dinner with him at his home, "The Oaks, ["] at 6:30 o'clock this evening.[24]

KITTREDGE WHEELER *(Wheeler was a graduate of Wheaton College and a Baptist minister from Chicago's Fourth Baptist Church.)*

Chicago, Ill., July 20, 1903.

Prof. W.E. Burghardt Du Bois
Dear Sir:

I am very greatly interested in everything of a public character which concerns the Negro race. My father belonged to the Underground Railway in an early day, when to be a black abolitionist took nerve and courage and conscience. Some five or six years ago, at my own charges and as a private individual, I visited our schools in the South, including schools at Jackson, Miss., Selma, Montgomery, New Orleans, Nashville, Tuskegee, Atlanta and others. Now to commit myself, and not to commit you, without your knowledge, while I believe in Mr. Washington and Tuskegee, so far as it goes, yet I believe most emphatically that the battle-cry "Manual training for the Negro" is fundamentally false, and harmful, and pernicious.

The South and the North both like it. Why? Because they are willing to meet the negro on the fairest, broadest and unrestricted ground before God and man or because on its very face, it assumes and asserts a limitation in connection with the negro, and is a discrimination against him. I deplore this fact more than I can tell you; and I know, perhaps better than you, if you have been living some time in the South, how this catchword is eagerly, gladly, selfishly, accepted here. It relieves us in the North of any great responsibility! The education of the hands is easy, simple, a short cut, and if neglected well, what of it? The body perishes—dust to dust. The education of the heart and mind, and soul, the lifting up of a man—this is difficult and long and painstaking. This means—in a word—the giving of one's self to that man who is to be lifted, or to be helped! This is the way of Calvary! Not an easy road.

This catch-word has filled the minds of the people—North and South! It is misleading! It has done incalculable harm, it will take a generation and more to dislodge it. Now, the only reason why I mention Mr. Washington's name here is this: he, more than any other one man is responsible for this idea, and because he is the confessed representative of it. "Booker Washington says so: he knows. He is the foremost man of his race." And this is an answer to every objection. This is the only reply the people of the North deem it necessary to make. Indeed this is such a finality in the consideration of this race problem (I do not like this expression) that few men here in the North stop to give it a careful consideration. Now if Mr. Washington would say "I believe in Education for all men alike but manual training, or industrial education for the Negro of the South seems for the present, to be most needed, or expedient," I would not have anything to say.

Or if Mr. Washington would say: "There are many schools of higher education in the South for the negro, and my work in Tuskegee I am best adapted to give manual training." Very good! But you know that is not his attitude; not his position before the public; Mr. Washington of course says in public that Tuskegee gives academic training, and is engaged in fitting many of the students there, to become *School teachers*; but that is kept in the background, that is not his message to the people.

His name, his work, his school, all are used here in the North, even as an argument against the education of the Negro. Why is it that the ignorant, illiterate, low, profane white man of the north catches at the word—"Industrial education; Manual training for the Negro." He is not interested in any moral or educational question under heaven. How is it that such a man is so sure and clear on the best and only thing, for the Negro. I wish Mr. Washington might be persuaded to define his position more sharply; and if he believes in the education of the negro, without limitations or discriminations, or differentiations, that he would speedily say so. The sentiment "Industrial Education for the Negro" is the shackle—not removed from his hands but in addition, put upon head and heart—upon the whole man—the whole race. Let us fear him, who casts body and soul into hell! Jesus said.

This sentiment inculcated, re-enslaves the negro race. When the iron manacle was on the slave's limbs, that iron visibly marked the degree or extent of his abject condition. Physical slavery had not yet dared to invade the realm of the soul. And the implication of his subjection or inferiority did not go beyond the iron band, or the physical body.

But now this sentiment is a manacle upon the intellectual, moral, spiritual, upon the higher, nature: upon the whole man.

I think someone should endeavor to make Mr. Washington see his position; or if it be not his position, then for the sake of the Negro, and the Caucasian, the North and the South, that he should come out publicly and clear the air of this damaging and damnable misrepresentation on his part, and misapprehension on the part of the country. The position is untenable. If he do not hold it, he should say; If he does hold it, he should be driven from it.

Are you to be in Chicago within the next six weeks or in the East later? I wish very much to see you. I would be pleased to hear from you. I have no controversial spirit in this matter. It goes far deeper than that.

May I ask if any of your relatives of the preceding generation lived with Wheelers in New Brunswick in the vicinity of Fredericton?

I have been pastor of the Fourth Baptist Church here in the city for nine years.

Very fraternally,
Kittredge Wheeler[25]

NOTES

1. Green and Driver, "Introduction," 1978, 14. See also Morris, 2015.

2. This was one of Washington's first attempts at a conference of black leaders normally in opposition to one another. He would finally see it come to fruition in January 1904. Washington, 1977, vol. 7, 72.

3. Clement G. Morgan was a classmate of Du Bois at Harvard, graduating from both the college and later from Harvard Law. A Boston lawyer and politician, Morgan remained a close ally of Du Bois and an activist for black rights. He would become one of the founding members of Niagara in 1905. Sollors, Titcomb, and Underwood, 1993, 59.

4. Washington, 1977, vol. 7, 71–72.

5. Schiff and Peabody were millionaire bankers and philanthropists. Stokes was the child of a wealthy merchant family who turned his full attention to the impoverished, joining the Socialist Party and contributing to many progressive charities. Du Bois, 1973, 52. See also Cohen, 1999; Zipser and Zipser, 1989; and Orr, 1950.

6. J.W. Lyons served as Register of the Treasury in Washington, D.C., first appointed by William McKinley and continuing under Roosevelt. Bishop Abraham Grant was an AME minister from Florida. John Trower was a Philadelphia real estate magnate who owned a catering business. Reverend C.T. Walker was a famed Baptist preacher from Augusta, Georgia, who also served in New York and founded the black branch of the YMCA. Frederick L. McGhee was a lawyer and civil rights activist originally from Mississippi. Morris, 1901, 256; "Men of the Month: John S. Trower," May 1911, 10; *New York Times*, 30 July 1921; and Nelson, 2002.

7. Mollie Keelan was an influential reformer and society woman in Washington, D.C. *Colored American*, 18 January 1902, 1.

8. Du Bois, 1973, 53.

9. Aptheker, 1949, 345–351; and Du Bois, 1973, 52.

10. Washington, 1977, vol. 7, 105.

11. Ibid., 108–109.

12. Roscoe Conkling Bruce was the son of former Mississippi senator Blanche K. Bruce. Although he was educated at Ivy League schools, he served as the supervisor of Tuskegee's Academic Department from 1902 to 1906 and advocated the industrial training model of Washington. Ingram, 2009, 84–86.

13. Ibid., 124.

14. "Two Typical Leaders," 23 May 1903, 214–216; and Washington, 1977, vol. 7, 149–154.

15. Green and Driver, "Introduction," 1978, 14; and Morris, 2015.

16. Du Bois, May 1903, 503–505.

17. Green and Driver, "Introduction," 1978, 19.

18. Stone, 1903, 658–652. Alfred Holt Stone was a Mississippi lawyer and scholar who would, in 1908, publish *Studies in the American Race Problem*, in which he claimed black inferiority necessitated white control, and that successful black examples were the result of the white blood coming from race mixing. For more on Stone, see Stone, 1908; and Hollandsworth, 2008.

19. Robert Smalls (not Small) served in the U.S. House of Representatives from 1875 to 1879, 1882 to 1883, and again from 1884 to 1887. Robert B. Elliott served as the speaker of the South Carolina House of Representatives from 1874 to 1876. He served in the U.S. House from 1871 to 1874. See Rabinowitz, 1982.

20. Patterson, "Mulatto and Negro," *Washington Post*, 2 July 1903, 3.

21. The article claimed that Stone believed mixed-race leaders like Washington and Du Bois, even though they denied it made any difference in their success, really believed "that the white strain does tell, and that practically all of the men of so-called negro blood who have done anything in the world are of the mulatto type." Patterson, "Mulatto and Negro," 3; and Washington, 1977, vol. 7, 192–193.

22. Washington, 1977, vol. 7, 193.

23. Du Bois, July 1903, 3–15.

24. Washington, 1977, vol. 7, 194.

25. Du Bois, 1973, 58–59.

9

The Boston Riot

In April 1903, Du Bois published The Souls of Black Folk, *a collection of essays that included "Of Mr. Booker T. Washington and Others," which publicly established his criticisms of Washington's program of racial compromise. He attacked Washington for failing to stand up for political and civil rights and higher education for black Americans. He was even more angry that Washington was willing to compromise with the white South and that he agreed with white southerners that black people were not their equals. "Mr. Washington represents in Negro thought the old attitude of adjustment and submission," argued Du Bois, "and Mr. Washington's programme practically accepts the alleged inferiority of the Negro races."*

The Chicago publisher A.C. McClurg and Co. approached Du Bois in 1900 for a book for a broad, nonacademic audience. He ultimately gave them a collection of previously published essays with a new addition included to create The Souls of Black Folk. *The essay he wrote specifically for the book was "Of Mr. Booker T. Washington and Others." Industrial training and its accoutrements were not bad things, he argued. Quite the contrary. But devoting all energies to that at the expense of demanding further political power or higher education for black America was a damaging philosophy.[1] In April 1903, McClurg published the first edition of Du Bois's* The Souls of Black Folk.

The book was a massive success and was in its sixth edition by 1905, owing largely to the provocative essay criticizing Washington's ideology and leadership. Not everyone, however, was pleased.[2]

Five months after the publication of Souls, *William Monroe Trotter would bring the Du Bois–Washington feud to a head when he orchestrated an interruption of Washington's address to the Boston chapter of the National Negro Business League. He was questioned hostilely by those who disagreed with him, the fiasco leading to verbal and physical fights throughout the crowd. It would become known as the Boston Riot, and it served, in Washington's mind, to validate his paranoia about the efforts of his enemies and ultimately take that paranoia to new heights in the years to come.*

THE OUTLOOK

"The Souls of Black Folk" is defective, valuable, pathetic: defective because it is so characteristically personal, racial, and controversial; valuable, because it gives with absolute frankness a view of the race problem, and still more a feeling concerning the race problem, which are doubtless entertained by thousands of our fellow citizens; and pathetic, because the situation of a cultivated Afro-American in this country is one of indescribable pathos.

Mr. Du Bois was, we judge, born in New England. His earliest portrayed recollection is as a school-boy in a New England school-house; his first remembered experience one of bitter protest against a God who had made him an outcast and a stranger in his own land. This is the key to the volume. It is a cry, and a bitter cry, not against human wrong merely, but against what, in his feeling if not in his thought, is an irreparable injustice of life. The cry is Greek rather than American, pagan rather than Christian, a protest against fate. It is not easy to read without tears the extraordinary self-revelation afforded by the chapter on the birth and death of his boy, the irrepressible revolt against the tragedy of the child's prospective life, and the commingled grief and consolation in his death—a consolation more pathetic than the grief. "She who in simple clearness of vision sees beyond the stars, said, when he had flown, 'He will be happy There; he ever loved beautiful things.' And I, far more ignorant, and blind by the web of mine own weaving, sit alone winding words and muttering, 'If still he be, and he be There, and there be a There, let him be happy, O Fate'!" . . .

It must be said, however, that this is not a true portrayal of the "Souls of Black Folk;" it is a portrayal only of the souls of a few black folk. We believe that only thirty-five per cent of the negroes in the South can read and write; and of these thirty-five per cent, probably only a small minority could be called in any sense educated and cultivated. The souls of some of these educated and cultivated black folk Mr. Du Bois portrays; specifically of a certain class of mulattoes. He writes in singular ignorance of the great mass of careless, idle, happy-go-lucky negroes. It may be said that their condition is even more tragic: but it is a different kind of tragedy. And yet we can not doubt that in them there is also a potentiality of the bitterness in Mr. Du Bois's soul; that they also feel, though in a dumb, inarticulate, hardly conscious, fashion, the sense of isolation, separation, social excommunication, which is so intolerable a wrong to him.

This is the pathos and the partialism of the book; but this is also its value. The Anglo-Saxon, to understand the race problem, must understand how it appears to the exceptionally educated members of the subordinate race. He must understand that the problem is one that cannot be solved by education. Education, in the ordinary sense of that term, meaning thereby the education that gives literary and scientific culture, does but complicate the problem. There are probably very few negroes in the South who are more highly educated than Professor Du Bois. And he is and avows himself to be even to himself a problem. The most that he can say for his education is that it enables him at times to forget the problem. "I sit with Shakespeare and he winces not . . . So wed with Truth, I dwell above the Veil." This is fine; but it is no solution of the problem of nine millions of negroes, for whom and for whose children there is but little possibility of even such temporary flights from the twentieth-century realities into a land of imaginings. It is no solution even for the few; for from the land of imaginings even they must return to the twentieth century. They cannot dwell above the Veil; they can at best only make excursions thither.

And this brings us to the grave defect in this volume: its failure to point to any solution of the problem. It describes present conditions with great dramatic vividness, too partially and pessimistically to be altogether truthful, and yet conditions of inward experience which we Anglo-Saxons ought to know, and have known too little. We wish that the volume might be read sympathetically by many white Americans and by no negro; for it ought to stir and broaden the sympathy of the one, and we fear it would only excite the bitterness of the other. But, vivid as it is in description, it offers no remedy, and can hardly be said even to suggest any. It attacks the remedy proposed by Dr. Washington, in a chapter which seems to us singularly unjust. Mr. Du Bois implies that since Dr. Washington came into leadership the negro has lost his political rights. He surely ought to know that long before Dr. Washington was recognized as a leader every Southern State had been taken out of negro control, and negro suffrage had been practically eliminated as a political factor in the Nation. Mr. Du Bois affirms that Dr. Washington's doctrine "has tended to make the whites, North and South, shift the burden of the negro problem to the negro's shoulders, and stand aside as critical and pessimistic spectators." He surely ought to know that no one man, black or white, has done more than Mr. Washington to arouse Southern interest in the negro's education, and no one man, white or black, excepting only General Armstrong, has done so much as he has to interpret the negro's need to Northern audiences and win from Northern givers aid in supplying it. Mr. Du Bois affirms that "Mr. Washington distinctly asks that black people give up . . . higher education of negro youth." We venture to say that he cannot point out a single utterance of Dr. Washington to justify this accusation. Mr. Du Bois charges Dr. Washington with preaching a "gospel of work and money." He ought to know that Mr. Washington's gospel is character. It would hardly be too much to say that Mr. Du Bois urges the negro to self-assertion, Dr. Washington to self-respect. The whole of the latter's doctrine has been summed up by himself in the four words, "Property, economy, education, and Christian character."

It would seem almost axiomatic that for a race sixty-five per cent of whom are illiterate, and probably seventy-five per cent of whom are industrially dependent, first in order of importance, if not in order of time, should come primary and industrial education. But were it otherwise, were it true that Dr. Washington over-emphasizes that phase of education which many of us think pre-eminently needs emphasis just now for both black and white, it would seem that the lover of Shakespeare and Balzac and Dumas, of Aristotle and Aurelius, might emphasize the other phase of education without attacking his fellow laborer. The development of the negro race of this country in "property, economy, education, and Christian character" needs to be pushed forward by every means and in every department; and the work is so great and the corps of laborers is so small that there is no time or energy to be spared from the common work, no surplus time or energy for one wing to expend in criticising the work of the other.[3]

HARRY THACKER BURLEIGH (*Burleigh was an influential African American musician, composer, and singer.*)[4]

[New York City] July 18th 1903

Dear Mr. Washington: I have just finished reading "The Outlook's" review of Du Bois' book; and it is so strong and true an article that I can

[not] refrain from writing you, because it states your position so clearly that a blind man can see that Du Bois' work is purely personal whereas your work is general; you are for the masses while he pleads for the classes. It is obvious who has the greater and higher field. The article is a truthful justification of your methods and is timely, for many others of the (highly educated and cultivated class)? may be influenced by what Du Bois says . . .

H.T. Burleigh[5]

WILLIAM EDWARD BURGHARDT DU BOIS

Of Mr. Booker T. Washington and Others
. . . Easily the most striking thing in the history of the American Negro since 1876 is the ascendancy of Mr. Booker T. Washington. It began at the time when war memories and ideals were rapidly passing; a day of astonishing commercial development was dawning; a sense of doubt and hesitation overtook the freedmen's sons,—then it was that his leading began. Mr. Washington came, with a single definite programme, at the psychological moment when the nation was a little ashamed of having bestowed so much sentiment on Negroes, and was concentrating its energies on Dollars. His programme of industrial education, conciliation of the South, and submission and silence as to civil and political rights, was not wholly original; the Free Negroes from 1830 up to wartime had striven to build industrial schools, and the American Missionary Association had from the first taught various trades; and Price and others had sought a way of honorable alliance with the best of the Southerners.[6] But Mr. Washington first indissolubly linked these things; he put enthusiasm, unlimited energy, and perfect faith into this programme, and changed it from a by-path into a veritable Way of Life. And the tale of the methods by which he did this is a fascinating study of human life.

It startled the nation to hear a Negro advocating such a programme after many decades of bitter complaint; it startled and won the applause of the South, it interested and won the admiration of the North; and after a confused murmur of protest, it silenced if it did not convert the Negroes themselves.

To gain the sympathy and cooperation of the various elements comprising the white South was Mr. Washington's first task; and this, at the time Tuskegee was founded, seemed, for a black man, well-nigh impossible. And yet ten years later it was done in the word spoken at Atlanta:

"In all things purely social we can be as separate as the five fingers, and yet one as the hand in all things essential to mutual progress." This "Atlanta Compromise" is by all odds the most notable thing in Mr. Washington's career. The South interpreted it in different ways: the radicals received it as a complete surrender of the demand for civil and political equality; the conservatives, as a generously conceived working basis for mutual understanding. So both approved it, and today its author is certainly the most distinguished Southerner since Jefferson Davis, and the one with the largest personal following.

Next to this achievement comes Mr. Washington's work in gaining place and consideration in the North. Others less shrewd and tactful had formerly essayed to sit on these two stools and had fallen between them; but as Mr. Washington knew the heart of the South from birth and training, so by singular insight he intuitively grasped the spirit of the age which was dominating the North. And so thoroughly did he learn the speech and thought of triumphant commercialism, and the ideals of material prosperity that the picture of a lone black boy poring over a French grammar amid the weeds and dirt of a neglected home soon seemed to him the acme of absurdities. One wonders what Socrates and St. Francis of Assisi would say to this.

And yet this very singleness of vision and thorough oneness with his age is a mark of the successful man. It is as though Nature must needs make men narrow in order to give them force. So Mr. Washington's cult has gained unquestioning followers, his work has wonderfully prospered, his friends are legion, and his enemies are confounded. To-day he stands as the one recognized spokesman of his ten million fellows, and one of the most notable figures in a nation of seventy millions. One hesitates, therefore, to criticise a life which, beginning with so little has done so much. And yet the time is come when one may speak in all sincerity and utter courtesy of the mistakes and shortcomings of Mr. Washington's career, as well as of his triumphs, without being thought captious or envious, and without forgetting that it is easier to do ill than well in the world.

The criticism that has hitherto met Mr. Washington has not always been of this broad character. In the South especially has he had to walk warily to avoid the harshest judgments,—and naturally so, for he is dealing with the one subject of deepest sensitiveness to that section. Twice—once when at the Chicago celebration of the Spanish-American War he alluded to the color-prejudice that is "eating away the vitals of the South," and once when he dined with President Roosevelt—has the resulting Southern criticism been violent enough to threaten seriously his popularity. In the North the feeling has several times forced itself into words, that Mr. Washington's counsels of submission overlooked certain elements of true manhood, and that his educational programme was unnecessarily narrow. Usually, however, such criticism has not found open expression, although, too, the spiritual sons of the Abolitionists have not been prepared to acknowledge that the schools founded before Tuskegee, by men of broad ideals and self-sacrificing spirit, were wholly failures or worthy of ridicule. While, then, criticism has not failed to follow Mr. Washington, yet the prevailing public opinion of the land has been but too willing to deliver the solution of a wearisome problem into his hands, and say, "If that is all you and your race ask, take it."

Among his own people, however, Mr. Washington has encountered the strongest and most lasting opposition, amounting at times to bitterness, and even to-day continuing strong and insistent even though largely silenced in outward expression by the public opinion of the nation. Some of this opposition is, of course, mere envy; the disappointment of displaced demagogues and the spite of narrow minds. But aside from this, there is among educated and thoughtful colored men in all parts of the land a feeling of deep regret, sorrow, and apprehension at the wide currency and ascendancy which some of Mr. Washington's theories have gained. These same men admire his sincerity of purpose, and are willing to forgive much to honest endeavor which is doing something worth the doing. They cooperate with Mr. Washington as far as they conscientiously can; and, indeed, it is no ordinary tribute to this man's tact and power that, steering as he must between so many diverse interests and opinions, he so largely retains the respect of all . . .

Douglass, in his old age, still bravely stood for the ideals of his early manhood,—ultimate assimilation through self-assertion, and no other terms. For a time Price arose as a new leader, destined, it seemed, not to give up, but to re-state the old ideals in a form less repugnant to the white South. But he passed away in his prime. Then came the new leader. Nearly all the former ones had become leaders by the silent suffrage of their fellows, had sought to lead their own people alone, and were usually, save Douglass, little known outside their race. But Booker T. Washington arose as essentially the leader not of one race but of two,—a compromiser between the South, the North, and the Negro. Naturally the Negroes resented, at first bitterly, signs of compromise which surrendered their civil and political rights, even though this was to be exchanged for larger chances of economic development. The rich and dominating North, however, was not only weary of the race problem, but was investing largely in Southern enterprises, and welcomed

any method of peaceful cooperation. Thus, by national opinion, the
Negroes began to recognize Mr. Washington's leadership; and the voice
of criticism was hushed.

Mr. Washington represents in Negro thought the old attitude of
adjustment and submission; but adjustment at such a peculiar time as
to make his programme unique. This is an age of unusual economic
development, and Mr. Washington's programme naturally takes an
economic cast, becoming a gospel of Work and Money to such an extent
as apparently almost completely to overshadow the higher aims of life.
Moreover, this is an age when the more advanced races are coming in
closer contact with the less developed races, and the race-feeling is
therefore intensified; and Mr. Washington's programme practically
accepts the alleged inferiority of the Negro races. Again, in our own
land, the reaction from the sentiment of war time has given impetus to
race-prejudice against Negroes, and Mr. Washington withdraws many
of the high demands of Negroes as men and American citizens. In other
periods of intensified prejudice all the Negro's tendency to self-
assertion has been called forth; at this period a policy of submission is
advocated. In the history of nearly all other races and peoples the doctrine preached at such crises has been that manly self-respect is worth
more than lands and houses, and that a people who voluntarily surrender such respect, or cease striving for it, are not worth civilizing.

In answer to this, it has been claimed that the Negro can survive only
through submission. Mr. Washington distinctly asks that black people
give up, at least for the present, three things,—

First, political power,

Second, insistence on civil rights,

Third, higher education of Negro youth,

—and concentrate all their energies on industrial education, the accumulation of wealth, and the conciliation of the South. This policy has
been courageously and insistently advocated for over fifteen years, and
has been triumphant for perhaps ten years. As a result of this tender of
the palm-branch, what has been the return? In these years there have
occurred:

1. The disfranchisement of the Negro.

2. The legal creation of a distinct status of civil inferiority for the
Negro.

3. The steady withdrawal of aid from institutions for the higher
training of the Negro.

These movements are not, to be sure, direct results of Mr. Washington's teachings; but his propaganda has, without a shadow of doubt,
helped their speedier accomplishment. The question then comes: Is it

possible, and probable, that nine millions of men can make effective progress in economic lines if they are deprived of political rights, made a servile caste, and allowed only the most meagre chance for developing their exceptional men? If history and reason give any distinct answer to these questions, it is an emphatic No. And Mr. Washington thus faces the triple paradox of his career:

1. He is striving nobly to make Negro artisans business men and property-owners; but it is utterly impossible, under modern competitive methods, for workingmen and property-owners to defend their rights and exist without the right of suffrage.

2. He insists on thrift and self-respect, but at the same time counsels a silent submission to civic inferiority such as is bound to sap the manhood of any race in the long run.

3. He advocates common-school and industrial training, and depreciates institutions of higher learning; but neither the Negro common-schools, nor Tuskegee itself, could remain open a day were it not for teachers trained in Negro colleges, or trained by their graduates.

This triple paradox in Mr. Washington's position is the object of criticism by two classes of colored Americans. One class is spiritually descended from Toussaint the Savior, through Gabriel, Vesey, and Turner, and they represent the attitude of revolt and revenge; they hate the white South blindly and distrust the white race generally, and so far as they agree on definite action, think that the Negro's only hope lies in emigration beyond the borders of the United States. And yet, by the irony of fate, nothing has more effectually made this programme seem hopeless than the recent course of the United States toward weaker and darker peoples in the West Indies, Hawaii, and the Philippines,—for where in the world may we go and be safe from lying and brute Force?

The other class of Negroes who cannot agree with Mr. Washington has hitherto said little aloud. They deprecate the sight of scattered counsels, of internal disagreement; and especially they dislike making their just criticism of a useful and earnest man an excuse for a general discharge of venom from small-minded opponents. Nevertheless, the questions involved are so fundamental and serious that it is difficult to see how men like the Grimkes, Kelly Miller, J.W.E. Bowen, and other representatives of this group, can much longer be silent.[7] Such men feel in conscience bound to ask of this nation three things.

1. The right to vote.
2. Civic equality.
3. The education of youth according to ability.

They acknowledge Mr. Washington's invaluable service in counselling patience and courtesy in such demands; they do not ask that ignorant black men vote when ignorant whites are debarred, or that any reasonable restrictions in the suffrage should not be applied; they know that the low social level or the mass of the race is responsible for much discrimination against it, but they also know, and the nation knows, that relentless color-prejudice is more often a cause than a result of the Negro's degradation; they seek the abatement of this relic of barbarism, and not its systematic encouragement and pampering by all agencies of social power from the Associated Press to the Church of Christ. They advocate, with Mr. Washington, a broad system of Negro common schools supplemented by thorough industrial training; but they are surprised that a man of Mr. Washington's insight cannot see that no such educational system ever has rested or can rest on any other basis than that of the well-equipped college and university, and they insist that there is a demand for a few such institutions throughout the South to train the best of the Negro youth as teachers, professional men, and leaders.

This group of men honor Mr. Washington for his attitude of conciliation toward the white South; they accept the "Atlanta Compromise" in its broadest interpretation; they recognize, with him, many signs of promise, many men of high purpose and fair judgment, in this section; they know that no easy task has been laid upon a region already tottering under heavy burdens. But, nevertheless, they insist that the way to truth and right lies in straightforward honesty, not in indiscriminate flattery; in praising those of the South who do well and criticising uncompromisingly those who do ill; in taking advantage of the opportunities at hand and urging their fellows to do the same, but at the same time in remembering that only a firm adherence to their higher ideals and aspirations will ever keep those ideals within the realm of possibility. They do not expect that the free right to vote, to enjoy civic rights, and to be educated, will come in a moment; they do not expect to see the bias and prejudices of years disappear at the blast of a trumpet; but they are absolutely certain that the way for a people to gain their reasonable rights is not by voluntarily throwing them away and insisting that they do not want them; that the way for a people to gain respect is not by continually belittling and ridiculing themselves; that, on the contrary, Negroes must insist continually, in season and out of season, that voting is necessary to modern manhood, that color discrimination is barbarism, and that black boys need education as well as white boys.

In failing thus to state plainly and unequivocally the legitimate demands of their people, even at the cost of opposing an honored leader, the thinking classes of American Negroes would shirk a heavy responsibility,—a responsibility to themselves, a responsibility to the struggling masses, a responsibility to the darker races of men whose future depends so largely on this American experiment, but especially a responsibility to this nation,—this common Fatherland. It is wrong to encourage a man or a people in evil-doing; it is wrong to aid and abet a national crime simply because it is unpopular not to do so. The growing spirit of kindliness and reconciliation between the North and South after the frightful difference of a generation ago ought to be a source of deep congratulation to all, and especially to those whose mistreatment caused the war; but if that reconciliation is to be marked by the industrial slavery and civic death of those same black men, with permanent legislation into a position of inferiority, then those black men, if they are really men, are called upon by every consideration of patriotism and loyalty to oppose such a course by all civilized methods, even though such opposition involves disagreement with Mr. Booker T. Washington. We have no right to sit silently by while the inevitable seeds are sown for a harvest of disaster to our children, black and white . . .

First, it is the duty of black men to judge the South discriminatingly . . . To-day even the attitude of the Southern whites toward the blacks is not, as so many assume, in all cases the same; the ignorant Southerner hates the Negro, the workingmen fear his competition, the money-makers wish to use him as a laborer, some of the educated see a menace in his upward development, while others— usually the sons of the masters—wish to help him to rise . . .

It would be unjust to Mr. Washington not to acknowledge that in several instances he has opposed movements in the South which were unjust to the Negro; he sent memorials to the Louisiana and Alabama constitutional conventions, he has spoken against lynching, and in other ways has openly or silently set his influence against sinister schemes and unfortunate happenings. Notwithstanding this, it is equally true to assert that on the whole the distinct impression left by Mr. Washington's propaganda is, first, that the South is justified in its present attitude toward the Negro because of the Negro's degradation; secondly, that the prime cause of the Negro's failure to rise more quickly is his wrong education in the past; and, thirdly, that his future rise depends primarily on his own efforts. Each of these propositions is a dangerous half-truth. The supplementary truths must never be lost sight of: first, slavery and race-prejudice are potent if not sufficient causes of the Negro's position; second, industrial and common-school training were necessarily slow in planting because they had to await the black teachers trained by higher institutions,—it being extremely doubtful if any essentially different development was possible, and certainly a Tuskegee was unthinkable before 1880; and, third, while it is a great truth to say that the Negro must strive and strive mightily to help himself, it is equally true that unless his striving be not simply seconded, but rather aroused and encouraged, by the initiative of the richer and wiser environing group, he cannot hope for great success.

In his failure to realize and impress this last point, Mr. Washington is especially to be criticised. His doctrine has tended to make the whites, North and South, shift the burden of the Negro problem to the Negro's shoulders and stand aside as critical and rather pessimistic spectators; when in fact the burden belongs to the nation, and the hands of none of us are clean if we bend not our energies to righting these great wrongs.

The South ought to be led, by candid and honest criticism, to assert her better self and do her full duty to the race she has cruelly wronged and is still wronging. The North—her co-partner in guilt—cannot salve her conscience by plastering it with gold. We cannot settle this problem by diplomacy and suaveness, by "policy" alone. If worse comes to worst, can the moral fibre of this country survive the slow throttling and murder of nine millions of men?

The black men of America have a duty to perform, a duty stern and delicate,—a forward movement to oppose a part of the work of their greatest leader. So far as Mr. Washington preaches Thrift, Patience, and Industrial Training for the masses, we must hold up his hands and strive with him, rejoicing in his honors and glorying in the strength of this Joshua called of God and of man to lead the headless host. But so far as Mr. Washington apologizes for injustice, North or South, does not rightly value the privilege and duty of voting, belittles the emasculating effects of caste distinctions, and opposes the higher training and ambition of our brighter minds,—so far as he, the South, or the Nation, does this,—we must unceasingly and firmly oppose them. By every civilized and peaceful method we must strive for the rights which the world accords to men, clinging unwaveringly to those great words which the sons of the Fathers would fain forget: "We hold these truths to be self-evident: That all men are created equal; that they are endowed by their Creater with certain unalienable rights; that among these are life, liberty, and the pursuit of happiness."[8]

Du Bois's relationship with the novelist Jessie Fauset began as she was finishing her collegiate career at Cornell University in 1903, as she and Walter F. Willcox, dean of Cornell's College of Arts and Sciences, sought his help in getting Fauset a teaching job. With the similar educational backgrounds of both Du Bois and Fauset, they would remain close, and Fauset would remain a significant ally of Du Bois in his conversation with Washington.[9]

JESSIE FAUSET

Ithaca, N.Y., December 26, 1903.

My dear Professor Du Bois,

Last year Professor Willcox wrote to you about my desire to do summer-school work. In your answer you were kind enough to say that my name was not unfamiliar to you (it is Jessie Fauset of Philadelphia, Pa.) and you also gave me permission to use your name in making application. Let me thank you now for that kindness . . .

Professor Du Bois I am going to thank you, as though it had been a personal favor, for your book "The Souls of Black Folk." I am glad, glad you wrote it—we have needed someone to voice the intricacies of the blind maze of thought and action along which the modern, educated colored man or woman struggles. It hurt you to write that book, didn't it? The man of fine sensibilities has to suffer exquisitely, just simply because his feeling is so fine . . .

Most sincerely,
Jessie Fauset[10]

As noted by David Levering Lewis, the rift between Du Bois and Washington was professional and personal before it was ideological. Smaller cracks in any supposed unity grew into chasms as the two slowly began defining each other in opposition to one another. And then the split became permanent with the publication of The Souls of Black Folk *in 1903. The Tuskegee Machine kept notice of* Souls *out of much of the black press, but white northern newspapers tended to laud the work. White southern newspapers either pretended not to notice, or cautioned of its abject danger. Oswald Garrison Villard's* New York Evening Post *and* The Nation, *meanwhile, ran their owner's review that praised* Souls *while simultaneously worrying that its criticism of Washington may have stepped across a line.[11]*

IDA B. WELLS-BARNETT

. . . I called together a group of our women . . . We raised $150 simply by subscription among the women themselves. We were very glad to turn this over to Mrs. Wooley and show that we proposed to have some of our money in every one of the payments on the building.[12]

About this time there appeared W.E.B. Du Bois's book *The Souls of Black Folk.* Mrs. Wooley had a gathering of the literati at her home near the university to discuss it. Again there were only six colored persons present whom she knew. And we were given the privilege of opening the discussion. Most of it centered around that chapter which arraigns Mr. Booker T. Washington's methods.[13]

Most of those present, including four of the six colored persons, united in condemning Mr. Du Bois's views. The Barnetts stood almost alone in approving them and proceeded to show why. We saw, as perhaps never before, that Mr. Washington's views on industrial education had become an obsession with the white people of this country. We thought it was up to us to show them the sophistry of the reasoning that any one system of education could fit the needs of an entire race; that to sneer at and discourage higher education would mean to rob the race of leaders which it so badly needed; and that all the industrial education in the world could not take the place of manhood. We had a warm session but came away feeling that we had given them an entirely new view of the situation . . .[14]

IDA B. WELLS-BARNETT

Chicago, Ill., May 30th, 1903.

Dear Prof. Du Bois:—

Your note of April 23rd did not especially call for a reply so I did not send one. I meant though to write you about a Conference which we had over your book at the home of Mrs. Celia Parker Woolley, a very good friend of the race. She had a company of some of the most literary folks here among white folks, at her home one Sunday evening about three weeks ago, and then she had Dr. and Mrs. Bentley; Mr. Lloyd Wheeler, Prof. [Monroe] Work, Mr. and Mrs. Laing-Williams, your humble servant and her better half, all there to do the discussing.[15]

Mrs. Bentley had a fine review about which she had doubtless told you. Most of the others, save my husband and myself, confined their reviews solely to your criticisms of Booker T. and thought the book was weak because of them. Of course you know our sentiments. There was not much time for the white side of the audience to present its view but they too took the same view. Of one thing I am very certain, the discussion stimulated a curiosity to read the book.

But I feel sure you have heard about all this. . . .

Yours truly,
I.B.W.-B.[16]

CHARLES W. CHESNUTT

Cleveland, June 27, 1903.

My dear Doctor Du Bois:—

I beg to acknowledge receipt of the clipping which you return to me; it was not important but I thank you just the same.

Potts have accepted my article on the disfranchisement of the Negro.[17] I take a firm stand for manhood suffrage and the enforcement of the constitutional amendments. I take no stock whatever in these disfranchisement constitutions. The South is suffering a great deal more from malignity of the whites than the ignorance of the Negro. I have wondered whether your book on the "Souls of Black Folk" had any direct effect in stirring up the peonage investigation in Alabama; it might well have done so.

I have not forgotten what you say about a national Negro journal. It is a matter concerning which one would like to think and consult before committing himself. There are already many "colored" papers; how they support themselves may be guessed at from the contents—most of them are mediums for hair straightening advertisements and the personal laudation of "self-made men," most of whom are not so well made that they really ought to brag much about it. The question of support would be the vital one for such a journal. What the Negro needs more than anything else is a medium through which he can present his case to thinking white people, who after all are the arbiters of our destiny. How helpless the Negro is in the South your own writings give ample proof; while in the North he is so vastly in the minority in numbers, to say nothing of his average humble condition, that his influence alone would be inconsiderable. I fear few white people except the occasional exchange editors, read the present newspapers published by colored people. Whether you could reach that class of readers and at the same time get a sufficient subscription list from all sources to support the paper is the thing which I would advise you to consider carefully before you risk much money. The editing of a newspaper is the next vital consideration. To do it properly would require all the time of a good man—he ought to be as good a man as yourself. I wish I could talk with you. Where will you spend the summer? Let me know your movements and it is possible that I might find it convenient to be at the same place some time before the fall . . .

Sincerely yours,
Chas. W. Chesnutt.[18]

JENKIN LLOYD JONES *(Jones was the editor of a Chicago magazine called* Unity *and was present at the Ida Wells meeting about* Souls of Black Folk.*)*

"The Souls OF Black Folk."

A "Sunday Evening" in private parlors is apt to take on very many of the characteristics of a "social function." Of course it is expected that somebody will make a speech or read a paper, and that there will be comment and comparison from the company. But it is not expected that anyone should take the other very seriously or that decorum should be menaced by too much earnestness on such an occasion.

But the "evening" at the home of Dr. J.H. and Mrs. Celia Parker Woolley last Sunday night was not of that kind. Mrs. Woolley ventured upon a hot subject, and the discussion was lifted at once above the conventional and the commonplace . . . Last Sunday night no less than eight people had a chance to put in their word from the dusky side of that ominous color line which is supposed to be fraught with such social dangers. Mr. S. Laing Williams opened the discussion in words as wise as they were ringing; he was followed by Mrs. Bentley, who gave a short but very clear and sympathetic review of the last literary contribution to this discussion,—Prof. Du Bois's book bearing the above title. She was followed by Lloyd G. Wheeler, Mr. Wirt, a student of the University of Chicago, Mrs. Ida Wells Barnett, Dr. Bentley, Mr. Barnett and Mrs. Fannie Barrier Williams. Mr. Williams and Mr. Barnett are well known colored lawyers in the city of Chicago. Mr. Wheeler is not only a recognized leader of the colored people, but a well known and active public-spirited citizen of Chicago. He has two sons at Tuskegee,—one a professor and the other a senior in that institution; and a daughter who is a teacher in a high school (colored) in St. Louis . . .

The discussion largely turned upon the relative merits of the programs prescribed by Booker T. Washington and Prof. Du Bois, and it showed how easily there might spring up schism and factional antagonisms among the colored people themselves. And this would be a great pity, because the essential antagonisms between these two great men have in them no color significance. They represent the pedagogical perplexities of our day. Technical education or classic discipline; will our schools fit young men and young women to earn a living or to enjoy life at its maximum? This represents the unfortunate phrasing. The true pedagogue refuses to recognize the antagonism and will insist upon both, as doubtless these leaders of the colored people will insist.

There was an impressive holding of breath when one of the speakers claimed that the two greatest men in the south today are colored men. Perhaps it is too early yet to justify that claim for Mr. Du Bois, but there can be little doubt as to the fitness of the remark as applied to Mr. Washington.

Mr. Du Bois's book is a timely one. It is well to remember that colored folk have souls as well as white folk; that the ultimate needs are soul-needs, and the ultimate efficiency must be soul-efficiency. Hands must forever be subordinated to brains, and ideas are always more precious and more necessary than things. Prof. Du Bois is a poet; he knows the value of words and is able to exhibit them at their full value . . .

Notwithstanding all this, there are, as it seems to us, two sad, if not fatal, errors in this book. The first is the undertone of melancholy ever haunting the brinks of despair. There is a wail where there ought to be a song; a groan where there might be a cheer. Things are bad. The handicap of color is pathetic, but not withstanding all this, the rise of the black man since his emancipation is one of the most brilliant chapters in human progress. His achievements thus far warrant not only heroic effort to cure the ills that remain, but religious fortitude to endure the ills that for the present cannot be cured! . . .

But the more serious charge to be made against this book is that the author assumes as permanent what we have already characterized as an uncertain and movable line. The tendency of scholarship is to minimize race differences and to render uncertain race lines. Already the later books talk about the "mythical Aryan races." The old race maps, whether in time or space, have been discarded and defaced by the latest scholarship. The truth is, in the long reaches of time the races are fluid, not solid. Life is ever in a state of flux and never stationary. The distinctive features that have characterized the races are found to be not physical or even psychical in the individual sense. Rather are they manifestations of social psychology. They represent a corporate continuity of thought and feeling. Ideas and languages are more persistent than physical characteristics. In the world of science, culture, economics and statutory enactments, even in the south, there is no race question today. The race problem is purely a social one. Even the late constitutional amendments of the southern states, conceived in dishonor, brought forth in the interest of iniquity, do not, dare not, recognize a color line. They are related to the line of illiteracy, which is entirely permissible and consistent if righteously, enforced. Let the fools be disfranchised, but the line is never a color one . . .[19]

Four months after the publication of The Souls of Black Folk, *on July 6, 1903, Du Bois had dinner with the Washingtons at Tuskegee. He was lecturing at the Tuskegee summer school. Plans for a summit between the two forces had waffled, and the* Souls *publication surely rankled, but the dinner still continued without incident. The week before the dinner, pro-Washington forces had dominated the Afro-American Council, much to the frustration of William Monroe Trotter. Trotter was a Harvard graduate and founder of the* Boston Guardian *in 1901. He was a friend of Du Bois and Washington's most radical and vehement critic. Trotter had criticized Du Bois for not being more forceful in his opposition to Washington. For his part, since its creation in November 1901, Trotter had used the* Guardian *to attack the accommodationism of Washington, but he was outmaneuvered in 1902 and 1903.*[20]

Trotter was so angry at Washington that his attacks often drifted from actual substance.

WILLIAM MONROE TROTTER

His features were harsh in the extreme. His vast leonine jaws into which vast mastiff-like rows of teeth were set clinched together like a vice. His forehead shot up to a great cone; his chin was massive and square; his eyes were dull and absolutely characterless, and with a glance would leave you uneasy and restless during the night if you had failed to report to the police such a man around before you went to bed."[21]

Less than a month after the Tuskegee dinner, on July 30, Trotter would bring the Du Bois–Washington feud to a head when he orchestrated an interruption of Washington's address to the Boston chapter of the National Negro Business League, leading to arguments, fistfights, and high acrimony. It would become known as the Boston Riot, although it was not an actual riot. The meeting continued after William Monroe Trotter interrupted Washington's speech, for example. The Boston faction of Washingtonians would ultimately help get Trotter placed into jail for a month. The Riot was the moment that Washington's paranoia—and thus the intensity of the rivalries between he and, for example, Du Bois—went to new levels, where they would stay until he died. From this point there were more spies, more harassment, and more attempted sabotage.[22]

BOSTON *GLOBE*

Negroes Make Riotous Scene

- - - - -

Booker T. Washington Was Speaking to Them

- - - - -

His Opponents Sought to Have Him Answer Certain Questions

- - - - -

Large Force of Policemen Called to Zion A.M.E. Church—One Man
Stabbed and Had to be Sent to the Hospital—Three Persons
Arrested, One of Them William M. Trotter

- - - - -

Surrounded by a struggling mass of angry people of his own race, in the confusion of fainting women and fighting men, unable to address his audience or to persuade them into a state of sanity, Booker T. Washington met his first really hostile demonstration in Boston last evening at the Zion A.M.E. church, corner of Columbus ave. and Northampton st.

What at first promised to be an episode in a program which often breeds disquiet among a people quick in anger, developed into a condition of riot. At one time it seemed as if nothing could prevent the wholesale shedding of blood, and in consequence of this every available police officer in division 5 and many of division 16 were hurried to the church, prepared for harsh measures.

The Zion church was packed to its doors with colored people. They fairly swarmed inside, and there was not an inch of standing room to spare. A program had been prepared which embraced all the speakers who have locally made themselves heard among the negro race. They seemed peaceful enough at first, yet there was an ominous hush in the big auditorium when William H. Lewis, the presiding officer, arose to introduce the speakers. A wave of anti-Washington sentiment was unmistakably abroad.

Washington's Name Hissed

Mr. Lewis is assistant U.S. district attorney, of football fame at Harvard, calm and generally respected by his people. Ordinarily there would have been an immense outburst of enthusiasm to greet him as presiding officer at the welcome to Booker T. Washington. When he arose to speak, there was only a faint clapping of hands from men and women who were frightened at the sound of their own welcome.

Mr. Lewis started to speak. When he mentioned the name of the great leader, when he pronounced the name "Washington," there were hisses from every part of the hall. Mr. Lewis called for silence, and some one volunteered that the hissers should be ejected. A movement to do this met with such decided failure that the attempt died, and the disturbers remained within the walls . . .

Mr. Lewis again attempted to address his people, and succeeded in introducing T. Thomas Fortune of the New York Age, an appointee by President Roosevelt to investigate the labor problems of the Philippines. He opened his address with a loyal and eloquent support of Booker Washington, in which he arraigned his people for some of their faults in a manner that plainly did not take well with the audience. He had not proceeded far with his speech when he began to cough violently. He reached for the accustomed water bottle, only to find that some one had emptied it in the heat of the first conflict.

His coughing became so marked, and sneezing among the other speakers who occupied the platform so prevalent, that it was evident that something was decidedly wrong. It proved that the "opposition" had sprinkled the platform carefully with cayenne pepper. This necessitated another pause until Mr. Fortune could catch his breath. He finally got through with his address, and was paying a final tribute to the honored guest, when Martin, who had come back into the hall at the very first opportunity, again made himself heard. He hissed and stamped his feet. The chairman told two patrolmen, who had come into the church, to preserve peace and quiet, to put the man out. This they did.

William M. Trotter of Boston, editor of the Guardian, jumped to his feet, and cried vociferously, "Put me out; arrest me!" He was forced into his seat, and told by the patrolmen to keep quiet or his defiance would be challenged by the whole police force. Trotter sat down.

Riotous Scene

Harry Burleigh, a New York singer of some repute, arose and opportunely sang "King of Kings." The song had a quieting effect. Encouraged by the lull in the proceedings, Edward Everett Brown, a Boston lawyer, was called upon by chairman Lewis to say something to insure further peace among the people. Mr. Brown scored them heavily for making a disturbance in the house of God. He warned them that the police would be called in to quell the next disturbance that took place. Then Lewis himself arose and said:

"This is a disgrace to every individual in Boston. Those who wish to be free should know how to govern themselves. Their first duty is to preserve order in the church of God."

Mr. Fortune arose and said: "You don't indorse such vulgarity in a public meeting. (Applause.) Your duties as citizens should make you rebuke all riot and disorder." At the words "riot and disorder" the trouble commenced anew. Disregarding all the good words of the speakers, the people began to move suspiciously toward the doors to be ready at any time to take to flight. Those nearest the platform got as far back as possible and jammed against the wall in a solid mass. Some had already begun to depart.

To depart, and to attempt to depart were two very different things, under the condition of affairs existing. The stairways and lower hall were jammed full of people who could not move in any direction, and refused to leave the building.

At the point where Mr. Trotter had to be ejected, which was immediately following the arraignment of Fortune and Lewis, officer Underhill attempted to push through the crowd and get upstairs. He got up a little way and was forced back. Then reinforced by two patrolmen of the squad that was pouring from all parts of the district to the scene, he got up to the first landing of the stairway.

There someone ripped Underhill's coat up the back. "Pat" Malley, another patrolman, who had hurried down to make peace among men, was jabbed in the side with a hatpin by some woman who sympathized with Trotter in his great humiliation. Then, without warning, the whole crowd swayed a moment, and literally fell downstairs. Women fainted in the crush, and had to be taken out in the air and later sent home in carriages, and it was here that Bernard Charles, 20 years old, of 111 Bow St., Everett, was stabbed with some sharp instrument, and taken away to the station house and booked, and later carried to the City hospital.

Martin and Trotter Arrested

Martin and Trotter were also locked up at the East Dedham st. station for disturbing the peace. Maude Trotter, a sister of the editor, was later taken to the station, but no charge was made against her and she was set free. Mrs. Trotter, mother of the editor, went bail for Martin and Trotter, and both went back in the church and tried to gain admittance, but were halted at the door.

Booker Washington, throughout the struggle that was going on about him, remained calm, and succeeded in going through his address, with the aid of a few periods when the noise was too terrific. He said in part:[23]

BOOKER TALIAFERRO WASHINGTON

You here in Boston are favored with many advantages, compared with the people of the south; and I am frank to say that you are hampered by some disadvantages. One of the problems that more and more confronts our people in the northern cities is that of finding employment of such a nature as will give opportunity for progress and constant promotion. In the south, very largely, the field of labor is open to us with few restrictions. The young colored man in the north is surrounded on every hand by temptations, which will drag him down, unless he fortifies himself with the best education, and with a strong moral and religious sense of responsibility, and with the earnest cultivation of habits of industry and thrift.

You will find it easier to enter a college in Boston than to enter a shoe factory or a counting room. In other words, it is easier to secure an education in the north than to find opportunity to use it after it is secured. This leads me to emphasize a point which we, as a race, I fear, especially those men and women of us who are educated, have overlooked in too large a measure. We have attained to the place where we should no longer depend upon the good nature of other people to give us employment, but where we should so educate our heads and hands that we can create positions for ourselves . . .

I should like to see our young colored men graduate from the high school or college, and then go out and start, for example, a dairy farm, that will grow and improve until it is one of the best farms in Massachusetts. No white man will refuse to buy milk and butter because their producer is a negro college graduate. I would not in any sense limit the education of the negro, north or south, but would encourage him most emphatically to lay the foundations of future prosperity in these primary, original, and wealth-producing occupations . . .[24]

BOSTON *GLOBE*

Questions for Washington

Here follows the letter that was prepared for use when Booker Washington arose to speak at the meeting in the Zion A.M.E. church. It was constructed in parts, each one to be separately launched at Washington by some one in the opposition. The list of questions includes all those that the trouble of last evening hinged on:

1. "In your letter to the Montgomery Advertiser, Nov. 27, you said, 'Every revised constitution throughout the southern states has put a

premium upon intelligence, ownership of property, thrift and character.' Did you not thereby indorse the disfranchising of our race?

2. "In your speech before the Century club here, in March, you said, 'Those are most truly free who have passed the most discipline.' Are you not actually upholding oppressing our race as a good thing for us, advocating peonage?

3. "Again you say, 'Black men must distinguish between the freedom that is forced and the freedom that is the result of struggle and self-sacrifice.' Do you mean that the negro should expect less from his freedom than the white man from his?

4. "When you said, 'It is not so important whether the negro was in the inferior cars, as whether there was in that car a superior man, not a beast,' did you not minimize the outrage of the insulting jim-crow car discrimination and justify it by the bestiality of the negro?

5. "In an interview with the Washington Post, June 25, as to whether the negro should insist on his ballot, you are quoted as saying, 'As is well known I hold that no people in the same economic and educational condition, as the masses of the black people of the South, should make politics a matter of the first importance in connection with their development.' Do you not know that the ballot is the only self-protection for any class of people in this country?

6. "In view of the fact that you are understood to be [un]willing to insist upon the negro's having his every right (both civic and political), would it not be a calamity at this juncture to make you our leader?

7. "Don't you know you would help the race more by exposing the new form of slavery just outside the gates of Tuskegee than by preaching submission?

8. "Can a man make a successful educator and politician at the same time?

9. "Is the rope and the torch all the race is to get under your leadership?"[25]

WILLIAM MONROE TROTTER

The cause of the riot at the colored Methodist church was due to the absurd ruling of the chairman, W.H. Lewis, when he said that any one who hissed or manifested objection to the speaker of the evening, or who demanded the right to ask him to explain some of his previous statements favoring disfranchisement, and discriminating in Jim Crow cars, would be subject to arrest.

The dissatisfaction was at once manifested by those who opposed Mr. Washington, and, to add to it all, Mr. T.T. Fortune, who had been brought over from New York to make a political speech, made an attack on the New England representatives to the recent Afro-American council which was called to protest against disfranchisement, but was turned into a republican rally.

This naturally brought objection to Mr. Fortune's remarks. This hissing was increased when Mr. Washington attempted to speak and when he refused to entertain any questions.[26]

REVEREND J. HENRY DUCKERY *(Duckery was an AME Zion minister based in Cambridge, Massachusetts.)*[27]

Some of us preachers learned at 1:30 today that there was a deeply laid plot in operation to prevent Dr. Washington from speaking in Boston tonight. I have frequently warned Mr. Trotter relative to his tirade upon Mr. Washington and other persons. We understood this afternoon that Messrs. Forbes and Trotter had arranged and had placed men in different places of the church to hiss and to spread cayenne pepper around.

What makes us look with greater horror upon the proceedings of that mob is that the leaders are men who have graduated from Harvard and Amherst colleges, and others who are in some way connected with the local and national government as employees. As for the Guardian it represents nothing more or less than yellow journalism, and will soon put the race in a very bad light in the east. I was pleased with the way the great majority of the people in spite of the persistent efforts of the disturbers conducted themselves, and I think that Dr. Washington tonight is stronger with the colored people in Boston than ever before. When he had finished his address he was given a grand ovation. Boston colored people like fair play.[28]

WILLIAM HENRY LEWIS

Two or three men made an abortive attempt to break up a meeting by a hostile demonstration against Mr. Washington. The disturbers were promptly ejected by the police and the meeting went on as scheduled. The address of Mr. Washington was the most eloquent I ever listened to, and he was heartily applauded throughout by the great audience.[29]

NAPOLEON B. MARSHALL *(Marshall was a lawyer and deputy collector for the city of Boston.)*

The movement against Mr. Washington, was started by the colored people in Boston, who have been much displeased of late at the method that he has taken of trying to uplift the race. He has advocated the jim-crow car, and shows up unnecessarily the failings of the people. Thus the people took this opportunity of showing to the country their disapproval of Mr. Washington and his methods.[30]

BOOKER T. WASHINGTON

Just as a few flies are able to impair the purity of a jar of cream, so three or four ill-mannered young colored men were able to disturb an otherwise successful meeting of the colored citizens of Boston tonight.

I have rarely seen a greater triumph of the masses in favor of decency and order than I saw tonight after the police removed the three or four disturbers. I have rarely received a more hearty and welcome reception on the part of the masses than I received tonight, as was shown by their hearty applause and approval of my remarks and position.

The colored citizens of Boston as a whole should not be held responsible for the unwise acts of a few rioters. Nine-tenths of the colored people in Boston have stood by and supported me in my work, and they were never more hearty in their approval than they are today. The men who disturbed the meeting have found this an easy way to get their names into the daily newspapers and to secure a little notoriety, which they otherwise could not obtain.[31]

The riot would not just exacerbate existing rifts. It would cause new ones. Judson Whitlocke Lyons, for example, was a Howard-trained lawyer who practiced in Augusta, Georgia. He was a light-skinned southern elite, but one of the few in that category who opposed Booker Washington. Washington actually supported Lyons in his 1901 reappointment as register of the Treasury, but turned against him after Lyons was sympathetic to Trotter after the 1903 Boston Riot.[32]

EMMETT J. SCOTT

Last night, at the A.M.E. Zion Church, on Columbus Avenue, at a public meeting of the Boston branch of the National Negro Business

League, one of the most disgraceful and riotous scenes in the history of Boston was precipitated by five men, under the leadership of William Monroe Trotter, editor of the Boston Guardian, who has become insane in his opposition to Dr. Booker T. Washington, and his methods of leadership. The plan to break up the meeting was deliberately premeditated, and was of the coarsest, most vulgar sort, such as is employed everywhere by the hoodlum, rowdy elements to create riot and confusion. Trotter was backed up in his rowdyism by a half-dozen women of the street, whose vulgar services were obviously purchased. Martin, the man who began the interruption, and was most persistent in rowdyism, insisting that Mr. Washington is opposed to social equality, is a butler in a white family, and appeared at the meeting in his waiter's jacket.

But behind Trotter are the following men, who have more brains, if no more character, than he: Archibald H. Grimke, brother to Rev. Francis J. Grimke, of Washington, and recently appointed consul to San Domingo, as a democrat, by President Cleveland, Clement G. Morgan, George W. Forbes, W.H. Ferris, all college-bred men, and Jno. W.A. Shaw, a democratic soldier of fortune, who has always been down at the heels.[33] By their action these men have lost character with the white and colored people of Boston, not because they are democrats at heart, but because they have shown a rowdy and vulgar disposition in their opposition to Mr. Washington, which places them among the hoodlums of the population.

There were seen two thousand people in and about the church, drawn there by a laudable desire to see and hear Dr. Washington speak. They were honest and intelligent people, among them being many of the distinguished and respected colored people of Boston, people proud of their city, and zealous for its high reputation for intelligence, sobriety, and for law and order. Scattered among these two thousand people, were Trotter and his henchmen, who had contrived to throw red pepper about the altar before the meeting was called to order, for the purpose of confusing the speakers. As soon as the chairman, Hon. W.H. Lewis, called the meeting to order, the disturbance was begun by one Martin, with hissing by his associates. When T. Thos. Fortune, of New York, was announced as the first speaker, the man Martin became so boisterous in his talk and action that the audience was thrown into confusion, and the police had to be called in to eject him. Just before Mr. Fortune concluded his remarks, the man was allowed to return to his seat on promise of good behavior; but the interruptions continued through the address of Mr. Edward Everett Brown.[34]

When Mr. Washington was introduced, the five men created so much disorder and confusion that the audience became panicky and riotous in temper. The managers of the meeting then decided to have Trotter and all of his fellow conspirators ejected from the church. A squad of policemen, commanded by a sergeant, was called in, and in the confusion that ensued both inside and outside of the church, arrested Trotter and his sister, and two of his henchmen, and, with handcuffs on their wrists, marched them off to the station house. One was badly cut with a razor, and two policemen were injured, one of them stabbed with a hat pin in the hands, it is alleged, of Miss Maude Trotter.[35] When the rioters were removed, after two hours of confusion, the meeting proceeded in an orderly and decorous manner. At the close of the meeting, Mr. Washington was given an ovation, and was overwhelmed by the crush of people who desired to shake his hand, and assure him personally of their hearty good will and sympathy . . . It is high time that the race frown down such crazy, desperate characters as Trotter, and place the seal of their disapproval upon them in such an unmistakable way that he who runs may read.

It is worth while to emphasize the fact that Dr. Washington has during the past six months spoken a dozen or more times in white churches in Boston, but Trotter and his gang made no disturbance in any of them; they waited until Dr. Washington was to speak at a church of his own race, crowded by the flower of the race's womanhood and manhood of Boston, to carry out their program of riot and confusion. Why did they not carry it out at some one of the white churches in Boston, where Dr. Washington has spoken during the last six months?[36]

EMMETT JAY SCOTT

[Tuskegee, Ala., July 31, 1903]

My Dear Mr. Washington: I sympathise greatly with you because of the nasty mess last night—that Forbes, Trotter & the rest of that gang sh'd have made the "muss" they did. It all only shows their impotent fury that 2M[2000], people sh'd come out to hear you—in the face of all their dirty attacks. It must have exasperated them. I shall be greatly surprised if they do not receive the condemnation of all decent people—& if the end of their dirt is not in sight. Hudson had resolutions as per his draft herewith passed by the Convention.[37] He gave his consent for any changes I desired & I have sent to Advertiser, Constitution & Associated Press the report copy of which I also attach. I hope the report will go out & that you will have seen it even before this letter reaches you. It will break the force of their attack & will do good—great good! Yours Sincerely Ever,

Emmett J. Scott[38]

BURWELL TOWNS HARVEY (*Harvey was a devoted acolyte of Washington, the father of the later famous science teacher and football coach from Morehouse College.*)

Peru, Ind. July 31–1903

Dear Prof. Washington: I just read in the evening paper an associated press dispatch from Boston, Mass., where you were interrupted by some of your opposers in attempting to ask questions during the delivery of your speech at the Zion church there. It is reported as almost precipitating a riot. One policeman was stabbed with a hat pin and one of your opposers was badly cut with a razor. I pray God that nothing will happen to you in such meetings. Such self-constituted leaders are disgracing the race. To-day, while the Negro race is passing through the crucial test of its worthiness to be engrafted into the civilized life of the American people; and when God has favored the race with such a modern "Moses" as you are; having manfully worked your way up the ladder of fame and now has the ear of the American nation and the civilized world, for that matter; and is at present exerting an incalculable influence in behalf of the poor ignorant and dependent race to which you belong; the Negro who would intentionally oppose or try to reflect or detract one iota of honor from you is an enemy to the race! Any one that will envy or oppose another because he persists in magnifying his work is a crank, pure and simple. The prayers of thousands of loyal supporters, black and white, go out to you in this your trying hour of opposition from the ranks of your own race. Shame! Shame!! With best wishes I remain your humble friend and student.

B.T. Harvey[39]

Washington's principal strategy to battle the forces in Boston arrayed against him was to finance three rival black newspapers in the city to overthrow the Guardian. *It was a strategy that Washington would revert to time and time again, manipulating the press to his own ends. It often worked, but this early effort did not. All three of the* Guardian's *rivals collapsed. Still, that did not stop Washington's agents from early optimism concerning the prospect.*[40]

JAMES H. MCMULLEN (*McMullen was the pastor of the Columbus Avenue AME Zion Church, where the Boston Riot took place.*)[41]

Boston, Mass. [July 31, 1903]

Dear Dr. Washington: I am not yet over the excitement of last evening. But our victory is complete. You will never be troubled in Boston again.

The Guardian is "done for" and its thick headed Editor will be prosecuted to the fullest extent of the law. White and black are with you now as never before. A leading white citizen whose name I cant just recall but will name later said to me yesterday in the Court House, "Mr. Washington can get any kind of money he needs to carry on his work from me." I regret more than I have words to express the riotous proceedings of those individuals Thursday evening, but the end had to come and let us hope this is the end. The trial will come off next Tuesday and every effort on the part of my church will be made to punish the offenders of decency, law and order. You have won a signal victory and the colored people to a man appreciate your wise leadership and great statesmanship as displayed in all of your public utterances. I sincerely regret the disgrace which may, by unthinking ones, be charged to my church, but I am glad that I had a part in the ending of these *hoodlum leaders* and *scandel-mongers* who constantly speak disrespectfully of you. God bless you and your family. I am sorry that I did not get the opportunity to be presented to Mrs. Washington and your daughter and to have them meet Mrs. McMullen. Hope the opportunity will come again.

Count us in the future among your admirers and friends. You shall have my earnest support the remainder of my days. I am yours etc,

J.H. McMullen[42]

PETER JEFFERSON SMITH, JR.

Boston Mass July 31 1903

Case continued to Aug 4 Lewis counsel for church. Church determined to push case to the end.

P J Smith[43]

Wilford H. Smith was a Mississippi native who became Booker T. Washington's personal lawyer. In that capacity, he also acted as one of Washington's chief saboteurs. He tried to wrest control of the Boston Guardian *from Trotter, and when Trotter was in jail following the Boston Riot, Smith attempted to bankrupt the paper and buy its stock.*[44]

WILFORD H. SMITH

New York City, July 31st 1903

Dear Dr. Washington: I have read with much shame for the people of Boston, the account of the disgraceful affair at your meeting there last night. It will be used to reflect on the race, to prove its want of appreciation, and criminal instincts, by our enemies.

By all means Trotter and Forbes must be muzzled, and at once. Just as early as possible I shall go to New Haven and exert my best endeavors to bring it about through the matter there. Very truly yours,

Wilford H. Smith[45]

JAMES CARROLL NAPIER *(Napier was a Nashville lawyer and businessman and ardent devotee of Washingtonian theories.)*[46]

Nashville, Tenn., August 1st 1903

My Dear Mr. Washington: I see that the crowd of malcontents with whom we had to deal at Louisville have again been trying to give trouble—this time in Boston. They are indeed a hard and troublesome set. They are themselves continually in hot water and it is their purpose and aim to draw every one else into it with them. At Louisville they thoroughly convinced me that they are utterly unfit to govern or control themselves and therefore entirely unfit to champion the rights of others. They deserve to be severely sat down upon. I trust that the courts will mete out to each one of them his just des[s]erts.

I wish very much I could have been present at this meeting to tell them what I think of them. No self respecting colored man in the South desires to have his cause championed by any such horde of loud-mouthed, blatant blatherskites. Their course brings no good to themselves or others. Their course is severely condemned on every hand. You will not meet men of this class or make up when you come to Nashville.

Every thing looks well for the League. Be sure to leave no stone unturned to secure a large attendance. I am sure that every delegate will receive the same general courteous treatment in Nashville that he would get in Boston . . .

J.C. Napier[47]

BOOKER T. WASHINGTON

South Weymouth, Mass., 3d August, 1903

Dear Mr. [Whitefield] McKinlay: Enclosed I send you two letters from Gov. Pinchback[48] . . . You will be glad to know that Trotter, Forbes,

Grimke, and two or three others, have by their actions completely killed themselves among all classes both white and colored, in Boston. Trotter was taken out of the church in handcuffs, yelling like a baby. They are to be tried in Court tomorrow, and every effort is being exerted by the citizens of Boston to secure their conviction. Very truly yours,

Booker T. Washington[49]

BOOKER T. WASHINGTON

South Weymouth, Mass. Aug. 3. '03

My dear Mr. [Francis Jackson] Garrison, I thank you very much for your letter of August first. While the experience in Boston, Thursday evening, was painful and disagreeable, it was one of the things that had to come to a head. It was like a severe surgical operation. During the past few months I have been asked to deliver an address before the colored people of Boston. I refused to accept, chiefly because I feared that trouble might occur. When I refrained from speaking, Trotter and others began to circulate the report that I would not speak before a colored audience.

Throughout the episode and the present agitation, the thing that gives me the greatest satisfaction is to note the sane sensible view that the rank and file of our people take with reference to conditions and to note how loyally and faithfully they support any policy that has in view the actual improvement of our people.

I do not become angry with Mr. Trotter and his clientelle, but I do pity them. If he had deliberately planned to kill himself and his influence with the colored people of Boston, he could not have done it in a more successful manner. Very truly yours,

Booker T. Washington[50]

EMMETT JAY SCOTT

Tuskegee, Alabama. August 3, 1903

Dear Mr. Washington: No doubt you have noticed that four of my editorials appeared in the Colored American last week. I was especially desirous of placing Kelly Miller in direct opposition to Du Bois which I think I succeeded in doing. Cooper got out a splendid issue of the paper last week from all points of view, although he may have emphasised too much Tuskegee and its interests.[51] This is a thing I have especially asked him to guard against.

I hope that my telegram has had attention and that the Herald and Transcript were sent out promptly to various Negro newspapers. A report from them will weigh greatly I think with the Negro press and they should have first hand information upon which to base any comments they may make. I wonder if it is not possible now to reach Forbes in this matter for his part in this disgraceful riot and also the man put down as Assistant City Prosecutor, Marshall I believe his name is. Yours truly,

Emmett J. Scott[52]

BOOKER T. WASHINGTON

South Weymouth, Mass, Aug. 4 '03

My dear Mr. Scott, I thank you very much for your letter regarding the Boston episode and for the resolutions. They have appeared in all of the Boston papers and in the Associated press.

The whole affair was painful and regret[t]able from every point [of] view and it has resulted in killing Trotter and his element in the minds of both races. Even the colored people who before sympathized with him, have withdrawn. They are to be prosecuted in the courts tomorrow and they are putting up most humble pleas begging not to be punished. I have never seen the colored people of Boston so stirred up as they now are. We have certainly won a signal and far-reaching victory! Very sincerely yours,

Booker T. Washington[53]

AMOS JOY (*"Amos Joy" was a pseudonym of Washington and Scott, as they sought to feign public support for their cause.*)[54]

The colored people of Boston feel that they have won a great and far-reaching victory in the direction of decency, law, and order, in securing the conviction and punishment of three of the leaders, including Wm. Monroe Trotter, in the disorder at a recent meeting where Booker Washington spoke here. Trotter has been sentenced to spend thirty days in the work house. The ignorant waiter, who was filled with whiskey, and was carefully groomed to do the bidding of Trotter and others, received a like sentence; and the man Charles was fined. It is very likely that

Trotter's stay in the public jail will give him an opportunity to review his foolish life. From Harvard College to the gaol—the distance is great; but Trotter has travelled it in short order.

It is well known, however, by the colored people of Boston that the men who were sentenced were not the most guilty. Behind them, and urging them on, it is currently reported, are George Forbes, A.H. Grimke, and C.G. Morgan,[55] who were not so brave as those who were arrested, but in the most cowardly manner stood in the dark, urging them on, without showing their own hands.

The most interesting and encouraging thing in connection with the whole matter is to note that almost unanimously the colored people of Boston condemn the riotous acts, and are determined to see the guilty ones punished. An example made in this case will have a good effect for a long time.

Examination into the plot reveals the further information, practically reliable, that several women from the streets were hired, and drugged with whiskey, to go into the church, and do the hissing. The colored people are especially incensed over the acts of these rowdies, because it is well known that while Mr. Washington has spoken many times recently in the white churches of Boston, he has not been interrupted by Trotter, Forbes, or any of their followers. They waited until they could get the opportunity to insult a colored audience, in a colored church, filled with colored ladies & gentlemen.[56]

EMMETT JAY SCOTT

Tuskegee, Alabama. August 13, 1903

Dear Mr. Washington: I have this morning very carefully gone through all the clippings that have come to us in re the Boston outrage, and I send the most significant ones representing every section of the country. Trotter and his gang can find no comfort in the reception which their nastiness has received. I hope you will have the time before going to Nashville to read them over. I think it will be cheering for you to do so, in that evidence is revealed that the sober thought of the people of this entire country is with you and your efforts to uplift this people. I have myself received much benefit from reading the various clippings. I have not been surprised at the general attitude at all because I have been convinced, as you doubtless have been, that the sanest men and women of the country are entirely in accord with your methods. Yours truly,

Emmett J. Scott[57]

BOOKER T. WASHINGTON

[Tuskegee, Ala.] Sept. 10, 1903

My dear Mr. [T. Thomas] Fortune: I was very sorry indeed that I did not have the privilege of seeing you before I left New York. There are several important matters that I want to take up with you . . .

I am most anxious that the last dastardly attempt on the part of that Boston crowd to disgrace the race be made public in some way. Of course we have the facts that will support our side, but we want to avoid the opportunity of a libel suit if possible. I wonder if you would not be willing to use the enclosed matter editorially in your paper, making such changes as you may deem best. In case you decide to use it, I think it well for you to let our friend, Wilford H. Smith, go over it with you so as to be sure that there is no basis for a libel suit. In case you do use it I hope it will be very soon and that you will put at my disposal 500 extra copies. I will let you know where to send them. If you care to you can have a talk with Chisum and after that perhaps you can better decide what changes to make in the statement. Yours truly,

[Booker T. Washington][58]

BOOKER T. WASHINGTON

Tuskegee, Ala., Sept. 12, 1903

Mr. Scott: I wish whenever you can you would get a short note in the colored papers about the late arrest of Forbes and Trotter.

B.T.W.[59]

TIMOTHY THOMAS FORTUNE

Red Bank, N.J., September 14, 1903

My dear Mr. Washington: I thought it best and safest, after all, to have a talk with Mr. Peterson about the Boston conspiracy article, and we reached the conclusion that (1.) the article is too discursive and full of epithets and expletives, which weaken rather than strengthen a statement of facts; (2.) that the facts as stated are not based upon sufficient evidence in our possession, to protect us, in the event of their being questioned; (3.) that a libel is uttered when the facts and circumstances indicated would incriminate certain parties in the public estimation, and that an action would stand and we should in that event have to defend it. When criminal matters or actions have been contemplated and not executed and when judicial cognizance of the same has not been taken, publication or other utterance constitutes a libel.

There is grounds for regret that the conspiracy was not allowed to materialize to the extent of incriminating those concerned in it, when a sufficient police in civilian dress could have taken the parties into custody, as the facts of the conspiracy were in their possession.

We do not think it wise to make the publication in the present status of the case. Yours truly,

T. Thos. Fortune[60]

BOOKER T. WASHINGTON

My determination to stand by the programme which I had worked out during the years that I had been at Tuskegee and which I had expressed in my Atlanta speech, soon brought me into conflict with a small group of coloured people who sometimes styled themselves "The Intellectuals," at other times "The Talented Tenth." As most of these men were graduates of Northern colleges and made their homes for the most part in the North, it was natural enough, I suppose, that they should feel that leadership in all race matters should remain, as heretofore, in the North. At any rate, they were opposed to any change from the policy of uncompromising and relentless antagonism to the South so long as there seemed to them to be anything in Southern conditions wrong or unjust to the Negro.

My life in the South and years of study and effort in connection with actual and concrete problems of Southern life had given me a different notion, and I believed that I had gained some knowledge and some insight which they were not able to obtain in the same degree at a distance and from the study of books.

The first thing to which they objected was my plan for the industrial education of the Negro. It seemed to them that in teaching coloured people to work with the hands I was making too great a concession to public opinion in the South. Some of them thought, probably, that I did not really believe in industrial education myself; but in any case they were opposed to any "concession," no matter whether industrial education was good or bad.

According to their way of looking at the matter, the Southern white man was the natural enemy of the Negro, and any attempt, no matter for what purpose, to gain his sympathy or support must be regarded as a kind of treason to the race.

All these matters furnished fruitful subjects for controversy, in all of which the college graduates that I have referred to were naturally the leaders. The first thing that such a young man was tempted to do after leaving college was, it seems, to start out on a lecturing tour, travelling about from one town to another for the purpose of discussing what are known as "race" subjects.

I remember one young man in particular who graduated from Yale University and afterward took a post-graduate course at Harvard, and who began his career by delivering a series of lectures on "The Mistakes of Booker T. Washington." It was not long, however, before he found that he could not live continuously on my mistakes. Then he discovered that in all his long schooling he had not fitted himself to perform any kind of useful and productive labour. After he had failed in several other directions he appealed to me, and I tried to find something for him to do. It is pretty hard, however, to help a young man who has started wrong. Once he gets the idea that—because he has crammed his head full with mere book knowledge—the world owes him a living, it is hard for him to change. The last I heard of the young man in question, he was trying to eke out a miserable existence as a book agent while he was looking about for a position somewhere with the Government as a janitor or for some other equally humble occupation.

When I meet cases, as I frequently do, of such unfortunate and misguided young men as I have described, I cannot but feel the most profound sympathy for them, because I know that they are not wholly to blame for their condition. I know that, in nine cases out of ten, they have gained the idea at some point in their career that, because they are Negroes, they are entitled to the special sympathy of the world, and they have thus got into the habit of relying on this sympathy rather than on their own efforts to make their way . . .

My experience is that people who call themselves "The Intellectuals" understand theories, but they do not understand things. I have long been convinced that, if these men could have gone into the South and taken up and become interested in some practical work which would have brought them in touch with people and things, the whole world would have looked very different to them. Bad as conditions might have seemed at first, when they saw that actual progress was being made, they would have taken a more hopeful view of the situation.

But the environment in which they were raised had cast them in another world. For them there was nothing to do but insist on the application of the abstract principles of protest. Indignation meetings in Faneuil Hall, Boston, became at one time so frequent as to be a nuisance. It would not have been so bad if the meetings had been confined to the subjects for which they were proposed; but when "The Intellectuals" found that the Southern people rarely, if ever, heard of their protests and, if they did hear of them, paid no attention to them, they began to attack the persons nearer home. They began to attack the people of Boston because they said that the people of Boston had lost interest in the cause of the Negro. After attacking the friends of the Negro elsewhere, particularly all those who happened to disagree with them as to the exact method of aiding the Negro, they made me a frequent and favourite object of attack—not merely for the reasons which I have already stated, but because they felt that if they attacked me in some particularly violent way it would surprise people and attract attention. There is no satisfaction in holding meetings and formulating protests unless you can get them into the newspapers. I do not really believe that these people think as badly of the person whom they have attacked at different times as their words would indicate. They are merely using them as a sort of sounding-board or megaphone to make their own voices carry farther. The persistence and success with which these men sought this kind of advertising has led the general public to believe the number of my opponents among the Negro masses to be much larger than it actually is . . .

Inspired by their ambition to "make themselves heard," and, as they said, compel the public to pay attention to their grievances, this little group kept up their agitation in various forms and at different places, until their plans culminated one night in Boston in 1903. To convince the public how deep and sincere they were in their peculiar views, and how profoundly opposed they were to every one who had a different opinion, they determined to do something desperate. The coloured citizens of Boston had asked me to deliver an address before them in one of their largest churches. The meeting was widely advertised, and there was a large audience present. Unknown to any of my coloured friends in Boston, this group, who, as I have stated, were mostly graduates of New England colleges, organized a mob to disturb the meeting and to break it up if possible. The presiding officer at the meeting was the Hon. William H. Lewis, a graduate of Amherst College and of the Harvard Law School. Various members of the group were scattered in different parts of the church. In addition to themselves there were present in the audience—and this, better than anything else, shows how far they had been carried in their fanaticism—some of the lowest men and women from vile dens in Boston, whom they had in some way or other induced to come in and help them disturb the meeting.

As soon as I began speaking, the leaders, stationed in various parts of the house, began asking questions. In this and in a number of other ways they tried to make it impossible for me to speak. Naturally the rest of the audience resented this, and eventually it was necessary to call in the police and arrest the disturbers.

Of course, as soon as the disturbance was over, most of those who had participated in it were ashamed of what they had done. Many of those who had classed themselves with "The Intellectuals" before, hastened to disavow any sympathy with the methods of the men who had organized the disturbance. Many who had before been lukewarm in their friendship became my closest friends. Of course the two leaders, who were afterward convicted and compelled to serve a sentence in the Charles Street Jail, remained unrepentant. They tried to convince themselves that they had been made martyrs in a great cause, but they did not get much encouragement in this notion from other coloured people, because it was not possible for them to make clear just what the cause was for which they had suffered.

The masses of coloured people in Boston and in the United States indorsed me by resolution and condemned the disturbers of the meeting. The Negro newspapers as a whole were scathing in their criticism of them. For weeks afterward my mail was filled with letters from coloured people, asking me to visit various sections and speak to the people.

I was intensely interested in observing the results of this disturbance. For one thing I wanted to find out whether a principle in human nature that I had frequently observed elsewhere would prove true in this case.

I have found in my dealings with the Negro race—and I believe that the same is true of all races that the only way to hold people together is by means of a constructive, progressive programme. It is not argument, nor criticism, nor hatred, but work in constructive effort, that gets hold of men and binds them together in a way to make them rally to the support of a common cause.

Before many weeks had passed, these leaders began to disagree among themselves. Then they began to quarrel, and one by one they began to drop away. The result is that, at the present time, the group has been almost completely dispersed and scattered. Many of "The Intellectuals" today do not speak to one another.

The most surprising thing about this disturbance, I confess, is the fact that it was organized by the very people who have been loudest in condemning the Southern white people because they had suppressed the expression of opinion on public questions and denied the Negro the right of free speech.

As a matter of fact, I have talked to audiences in every part of this country; I have talked to coloured audiences in the North and to white audiences in the South; I have talked to audiences of both races in all parts of the South; everywhere I have spoken frankly and, I believe, sincerely on everything that I had in my mind and heart to say. When I had something to say about the white people I said it to the white people; when I had something to say about coloured people I said it to coloured people. In all these years—that is the curious thing about it— no effort has been made, so far as I can remember, to interrupt or to break up a meeting at which I was present until it was attempted by "The Intellectuals" of my own race in Boston.

I have gone to some length to describe this incident because it seems to me to show clearly the defects of that type of mind which the so-called "Intellectuals" of the race represent.

I do not wish to give the impression by what I have said that, behind all the intemperance and extravagance of these men, there is not a vein of genuine feeling and even at times of something like real heroism. The trouble is that all this fervour and intensity is wasted on side issues and trivial matters. It does not connect itself with anything that is helpful and constructive. These crusaders, as nearly as I can see, are fighting windmills.

The truth is, I suspect, as I have already suggested, that "The Intellectuals" live too much in the past. They know books but they do not know men. They know a great deal about the slavery controversy, for example, but they know almost nothing about the Negro. Especially are they ignorant in regard to the actual needs of the masses of the coloured people in the South to-day . . .[61]

BOOKER T. WASHINGTON

Tuskegee, Alabama. September 15, 1903

Personal.

My dear Mr. President [Theodore Roosevelt]: I note what you say regarding the attitude of some of the Boston colored men. I am sorry that the matter has caused you any concern. The occurrence is very much exaggerated, however, as such matters always are by the newspapers. I do not suffer myself to become very much vexed with these people, but I do pity them. I have taken a little time in which to study them from I think a purely unselfish and disinterested point of view.

First: I find that the rank and file of our people in Boston, as is true all over the country, agree with me and support my policy. The opposition in Boston is kept alive and engineered by about a half dozen colored men, most of whom, I am sorry to say, are graduates of New England colleges. At the bottom of their opposition, there is a feeling of jealousy over what they consider my success.

Second: These men, in most cases, have not had to work their way up from the bottom through natural and gradual processes. Their growth has been artificial rather than natural. They have not paid the price for what they have gotten. Hence they feel that I can take the whole colored race and place it in the same artificial position that they themselves are in.

In most cases, someone has taken these men up and coddled them by paying their way through college. At Tuskegee a man works for everything that he gets, hence we turn out real men instead of artificial ones.

Third: When a people are smarting under wrongs and injustices inflicted from many quarters, it is but natural that they should look about for some individual on whom to lay the blame for their seeming misfortunes, and in this case I seem to be the one. It is a responsibility which I have not sought, but since it has come to me, I am willing to do my duty as best I can.

Fourth: As I see the colored people throughout the country, I am convinced that I am safe in saying that no President since Lincoln has ever had their support and love to the extent that you now possess it.

Forgive me for burdening you with so long a letter. Yours very sincerely,

Booker T. Washington[62]

BOOKER T. WASHINGTON

[Tuskegee, Ala.] October 20, 1903

Dear Mr. [Robert Curtis] Ogden: In connection with our conversation when I last saw you, I think I ought to say to you that I have evidence which is indisputable showing that Dr. Du Bois is very largely behind the mean and underhanded attacks that have been made upon me during the last six months.[63] This, of course, is for your own personal information. Very truly yours,

[Booker T. Washington][64]

The Boston Riot forced Du Bois to one side or another. Trotter was far more radical than Du Bois, and Washington was far more conservative. But Du Bois, who stayed with Trotter in Boston, could not afford to be silent. Ultimately, on his return from Tuskegee, he wrote in sympathy with Trotter, arguing that he had been jailed for exercising his right to free speech. Washington's accusation that Du Bois was behind the riot is odd. At the time of the riot, Du Bois was returning to Boston from Tuskegee, where he had taught summer school. He did stay at Trotter's house (by previous arrangement) after returning to Boston and sympathized with him as a victim of Washington's dirty tricks, but Du Bois made it clear that he did not approve of Trotter's methods. He was not behind the Boston Riot. Du Bois's attacks were very public. But it is significant that Washington continued to make such charges even as he and Du Bois discussed his Pullman discrimination case by telephone. The pressure exerted by the "Tuskegee Machine" on Atlanta University over the Boston Riot was in fact so great that the board of trustees voted formal apologies to Washington because of the supposed participation of Du Bois and the overt sympathies of George Towns, another faculty member. Du Bois interpreted the board's vote as a massive betrayal and wrote a long letter explaining the impossibility of his involvement. He argued that he saw Trotter as being far closer to correct than Washington, although the Guardian's *publisher needed more restraint.[65]*

Restraint or no, however, it was clear to Du Bois that:

W.E.B. DU BOIS

Mr. Washington is leading the way backward.[66]

NOTES

1. Green and Driver, "Introduction," 1978, 17.
2. Du Bois, 1973, 54.
3. Du Bois, 11 July 1903, 669–671.
4. See Simpson, 1990.
5. Washington, 1977, vol. 7, 213.
6. Joseph C. Price, a graduate of Lincoln University and professor at Livingstone College, was an educator and orator of international acclaim during the Gilded Age, but he died young at age 39 the year before Frederick Douglass, only exacerbating the power vacuum that existed in 1895. See Meier, 1963.

7. John Wesley Edward Bowen, although born into slavery, rose to become one of the first black PhDs in the country (from Boston University in 1887). He was also a Methodist minister and activist for black rights. Van Pelt, 1934, 217–221.

8. Du Bois, 2006, 35–47.

9. Fauset would later become one of the most important authors of the Harlem Renaissance, publishing poems and essays, along with novels such as *There Is Confusion* (1924) and *Plum Bun* (1931). She would also, beginning in 1918, become literary editor of Du Bois's *Crisis*. Du Bois, 1973, 65–66. See also Sylvander, 1981.

10. Ibid., 66.

11. Villard was a journalist who owned the *New York Evening Post* and *The Nation*. He would use his wealth and pulpit for activism throughout his life, particularly championing the causes of anti-imperialism and black rights. See Chapter 4, note 8. Lewis, 1993, 286–287, 292–293, 295–296.

12. Celia Parker Woolley was a novelist, social worker, and Unitarian minister based in Chicago. See Schweninger, 1998.

13. Chapter 3 of *Souls*. See above.

14. Jenkin Lloyd Jones was the editor of a Chicago magazine called *Unity*. He was at the Ida Wells meeting about *Souls of Black Folk* and wrote about it and the book in *Unity*, 7 May 1903, 148–149. See below. Wells, 1970, 280–281; and Du Bois, 1973, 55.

15. Dr. Charles E. Bentley was an influential Chicago dentist, the leading black dentist in Illinois. Lloyd Wheeler had been a close associate of Frederick Douglass, the first black man to be admitted to the Illinois bar. Monroe Nathan Work was a sociologist teaching at Georgia State Industrial College in Savannah. He would later go on to found the Department of Records and Research at Tuskegee. Samuel Laing Williams was a Chicago lawyer, and his wife Fannie Barrier Williams was a teacher. Both were also activists for black rights. "Men of the Month: Dr. Charles E. Bentley," May 1911, 10–11; McClish, 2012, 37–73; *Chicago Tribune*, 6 May 2005; McMurry, 1985; and Reed, 1997.

16. Ida B. Wells-Barnett was a black newspaper editor from Memphis, Tennessee, until whites decided that her paper, the *Free Press*, had become too militant and drove her from town. She made lynching her principal cause, and as chair of the Anti-Lynching League she fought tirelessly for a federal anti-lynch law. Her husband, Ferdinand Barnett, was also an activist and journalist, the first black assistant state's attorney in Illinois. Du Bois, 1973, 54–56. See also Schechter, 2001.

17. Chesnutt here refers to *The Negro Problem: A Series of Articles by Representative American Negroes of Today*, a collection published by James Pott Company in 1903, which also included Du Bois's "The Talented Tenth" essay and Washington's "Industrial Education for the Negro." *The Negro Problem*, 1903.

18. Du Bois, 1973, 56–57.

19. Jones, 7 May 1903, 148–149.

20. Lewis, 1993, 297–299.

21. Fox, 1971, 39; and Lewis, 1993, 299.

22. Lewis, 1993, 299–301; and Washington, 1977, vol. 7, 239.

23. "Negroes Make Riotous Scene," *Boston Globe*, 31 July 1903, 1, 3; and Washington, 1977, vol. 7, 229–239.

24. Ibid.

25. Ibid.

26. Ibid.

27. Powell, 1918, 27.

28. *Boston Globe*, 31 July 1903, 1, 3.

29. Ibid.

30. Ibid.

31. Washington's statement appeared in the *Boston Globe*. Washington, 1977, vol. 7, 240–241.

32. Washington, 1975, vol. 4, 394.

33. John W.A. Shaw was an immigrant from Antigua who attended Howard and later became deputy tax commissioner of Queens County, New York. Jones, 2006, 216.

34. Edward Everett Brown was a black attorney based in Boston and an ally of Washington, an increasing rarity in that city. Schneider, 1997, 119, 125.

35. Maude Trotter was William's sister. Jones, 2011, 38–39.

36. Washington, 1977, vol. 7, 241–243.

37. Scott is referring to a group of Alabama black Baptists, who, meeting at a Tuskegee church, condemned the attempt of "a few irresponsible men at Boston last night to insult and humiliate Dr. Booker T. Washington of the Tuskegee Institute." Ibid., 244.

38. Ibid., 244.

39. Ibid., 244–245.

40. Lewis, 1993, 301.

41. Cromwell, 2007, 107.

42. Washington, 1977, vol. 7, 245–246.

43. Ibid., 249.

44. Ibid., vol. 5, 487.

45. Ibid., vol. 7, 246–247.

46. Clark, Winter 1990, 243–252.

47. Washington, 1977, vol. 7, 247–248.

48. P.B.S. Pinchback was elected lieutenant governor of Louisiana during Reconstruction and briefly served as governor of the state for just over a month in 1872–1873, after the sitting governor, Henry C. Warmoth, was impeached. He later served in the state legislature. In the 1890s, however, Pinchback moved to Washington, D.C., and lived as one of the black elite in the city for the remainder of his life, although obviously people still referred to him as "Governor." Grosz, 1944, 527–612.

49. Washington, 1977, vol. 7, 252.

50. Ibid., 252–253.

51. Scott here refers to Edward Elder Cooper, the paper's founder and owner.

52. Washington, 1977, vol. 7, 253.

53. Ibid., 254.

54. Harlan, 1972, 49.

55. Clement Garnett Morgan, born in Georgia, was a graduate of Harvard Law and a radical opposed to Booker T. Washington. He served as William Monroe Trotter's lawyer in his Boston Riot trial. He would also represent Boston at the January 1904 Carnegie Hall Conference and would help to found Niagara in 1905. Washington, 1975, vol. 4, 294.

56. Washington, 1977, vol. 7, 246–258.

57. Ibid., 268.

58. Ibid., 280.

59. Ibid., 283.

60. Ibid., 283–284.

61. Washington, *My Larger Education*, 1911, 102–127.

62. Washington, 1977, vol. 7, 284–285.

63. This evidence probably does not exist. Ibid., 298. Robert Curtis Ogden was a white philanthropist who served as president of the Hampton Institute Board of Trustees from 1894 to 1913. See *A Life Well Lived*, 1914.

64. Ibid.

65. Lewis, 1993, 302–304.

66. Ibid., 304.

10

The New York Summit

Washington's accomodationist stance endeared him to many white philan-
thropic leaders. William H. Baldwin, vice president of the Southern Railroad,
served as chairman of Tuskegee's board of directors. Andrew Carnegie built
29 buildings on the campuses of historically black colleges because of Wash-
ington. Julius Rosenwald, the head of Sears, Roebuck, built a series of more than
5,300 black secondary schools across the South, with Washington's guidance,
at a cost of more than 28 million dollars. Carnegie, meanwhile, also built a new
library at Tuskegee and became one of Washington's principal benefactors.

In 1904, Carnegie would bankroll the conference between the Washington
and Du Bois factions that Tuskegee's leader had always wanted, and he would
host it at Carnegie Hall. Negotiations for the meeting were tense and tenuous,
but they eventually resulted in a summit. Du Bois prepared his faction for
deviousness by the Washington faction, which essentially made the meeting a
clash between two mistrustful groups. Washington was not devious, but the
conference was controlled by his people and it would not solve the problems
between the factions.

WILLIAM EDWARD BURGHARDT DU BOIS

The Negro race, like all races, is going to be saved by its exceptional men. The problem of education, then, among Negroes must first of all deal with the Talented Tenth; it is the problem of developing the Best of this race that they may guide the Mass away from the contamination and death of the Worst, in their own and other races. Now the training of men is a difficult and intricate task. Its technique is a matter for educational experts, but its object is for the vision of seers. If we make money the object of man-training, we shall develop money-makers but not necessarily men; if we make technical skill the object of education, we may possess artisans but not, in nature, men. Men we shall have only as we make manhood the object of the work of the schools—intelligence, broad sympathy, knowledge of the world that was and is, and of the relation of men to it—this is the curriculum of that Higher Education which must underlie true life. On this foundation we may build bread winning, skill of hand and quickness of brain, with never a fear lest the child and man mistake the means of living for the object of life . . .

And so we come to the present—a day of cowardice and vacillation, of strident wide-voiced wrong and faint hearted compromise; of double-faced dallying with Truth and Right. Who are to-day guiding the work of the Negro people? The "exceptions" of course. And yet so sure as this Talented Tenth is pointed out, the blind worshippers of the Average cry out in alarm: "These are exceptions, look here at death, disease and crime—these are the happy rule." Of course they are the rule, because a silly nation made them the rule: Because for three long centuries this people lynched Negroes who dared to be brave, raped black women who dared to be virtuous, crushed dark-hued youth who dared to be ambitious, and encouraged and made to flourish servility and lewdness and apathy. But nor even this was able to crush all manhood and chastity and aspiration from black folk. A saving remnant continually survives and persists, continually aspires, continually shows itself in thrift and ability and character. Exceptional it is to be sure, but this is its chiefest promise; it shows the capability of Negro blood, the promise of black men. Do Americans ever stop to reflect that there are in this land a million men of Negro blood, well-educated, owners of homes, against the honor of whose womanhood no breath was ever raised, whose men occupy positions of trust and usefulness, and who, judged by any standard, have reached the full measure of the best type of modern European culture? Is it fair, is it decent, is it Christian to ignore these facts of the Negro problem, to belittle such aspiration, to nullify such leadership and seek to crush these people back into the mass out of which by toil and travail, they and their fathers have raised themselves?

Can the masses of the Negro people be in any possible way more quickly raised than by the effort and example of this aristocracy of talent and character? Was there ever a nation on God's fair earth civilized from the bottom upward? Never; it is, ever was and ever will be from the top downward that culture filters. The Talented Tenth rises and pulls all that are worth the saving up to their vantage ground. This is the history of human progress; and the two historic mistakes which have hindered that progress were the thinking first that no more could ever rise save the few already risen; or second, that it would better the uprisen to pull the risen down.

How then shall the leaders of a struggling people be trained and the hands of the risen few strengthened? There can be but one answer: The best and most capable of their youth must be schooled in the colleges and universities of the land. We will not quarrel as to just what the university of the Negro should teach or how it should teach it—I willingly admit that each soul and each race-soul needs its own peculiar curriculum. But this is true: A university is a human invention for the transmission of knowledge and culture from generation to generation, through the training of quick minds and pure hearts, and for this work no other human invention will suffice, not even trade and industrial schools.

All men cannot go to college but some men must; every isolated group or nation must have its yeast, must have for the talented few centers of training where men are not so mystified and befuddled by the hard and necessary toil of earning a living, as to have no aims higher than their bellies, and no God greater than Gold. This is true training, and thus in the beginning were the favored sons of the freedmen trained . . .

The total number of Negro college graduates up to 1899, (several of the graduates of that year not being reported), was as follows:

	Negro Colleges	White Colleges
Before '76	137	75
'75–80	143	22
'80–85	250	31
'85–90	413	43
'90–95	465	66
'95–99	475	88
Class Unknown	57	64
Total	1,914	390

Of these graduates 2,079 were men and 252 were women; 50 percent of Northern-born college men come South to work among the masses of their people, at a sacrifice which few people realize; nearly 90 per cent. of the Southern-born graduates instead of seeking that personal freedom and broader intellectual atmosphere which their training has led them, in some degree, to conceive, stay and labor and wait in the midst of their black neighbors and relatives.

The most interesting question, and in many respects the crucial question, to be asked concerning college-bred Negroes, is: Do they earn a living? It has been intimated more than once that the higher training of Negroes has resulted in sending into the world of work, men who could find nothing to do suitable to their talents. Now and then there comes a rumor of a colored college man working at menial service, etc. Fortunately, returns as to occupations of college-bred Negroes, gathered by the Atlanta conference, are quite full—nearly sixty per cent of the total number of graduates.

This enables us to reach fairly certain conclusions as to the occupations of all college-bred Negroes. Of 1,312 persons reported, there were:

Teachers, 53.4%
Clergymen, 16.8%
Physicians, etc., 6.3%
Students, 5.6%
Lawyers, 4.7%
In Govt. Service, 4.0%
In Business, 3.6%
Farmers and Artisans, 2.7%
Editors, Secretaries and Clerks, 2.4%
Miscellaneous, .5%

Over half are teachers, a sixth are preachers, another sixth are students and professional men; over 6 per cent. are farmers, artisans and merchants, and 4 per cent. are in government service. In detail the occupations are as follows . . .

These figures illustrate vividly the function of the college-bred Negro. He is, as he ought to be, the group leader, the man who sets the ideals of the community where he lives, directs its thoughts and heads its social movements. It need hardly be argued that the Negro people need social leadership more than most groups; that they have no traditions to fall back upon, no long established customs, no strong family ties, no well defined social classes. All these things must be slowly and painfully evolved . . .

There must be teachers, and teachers of teachers, and to attempt to establish any sort of a system of common and industrial school training, without *first* (and I say *first* advisedly) without *first* providing for the higher training of the very best teachers, is simply throwing your money to the winds. School houses do not teach themselves—piles of brick and mortar and machinery do not send out *men*. It is the trained, living human soul, cultivated and strengthened by long study and thought, that breathes the real breath of life into boys and girls and makes them human, whether they be black or white, Greek, Russian or American. Nothing, in these latter days, has so dampened the faith of thinking Negroes in recent educational movements, as the fact that such movements have been accompanied by ridicule and denouncement and decrying of those very institutions of higher training which made the Negro public school possible, and make Negro industrial schools thinkable. It was: Fisk, Atlanta, Howard and Straight, those colleges born of the faith and sacrifice of the abolitionists, that placed in the black schools of the South the 30,000 teachers and more, which some, who depreciate the work of these higher schools, are using to teach their own new experiments. If Hampton, Tuskegee and the hundred other industrial schools prove in the future to be as successful as they deserve to be, then their success in training black artisans for the South, will be due primarily to the white colleges of the North and the black colleges of the South, which trained the teachers who to-day conduct these institutions . . .

I would not deny, or for a moment seem to deny, the paramount necessity of teaching the Negro to work, and to work steadily and skillfully; or seem to depreciate in the slightest degree the important part industrial schools must play in the accomplishment of these ends, but I *do* say, and insist upon it, that it is industrialism drunk with its vision of success, to imagine that its own work can be accomplished without providing for the training of broadly cultured men and women to teach its own teachers, and to teach the teachers of the public schools . . .

I am an earnest advocate of manual training and trade teaching for black boys, and for white boys, too. I believe that next to the founding of Negro colleges the most valuable addition to Negro education since the war, has been industrial training for black boys. Nevertheless, I insist that the object of all true education is not to make men carpenters, it is to make carpenters men; there are two means of making the carpenter a man, each equally important: the first is to give the group and community in which he works, liberally trained teachers and leaders to teach him and his family what life means; the second is to give him sufficient intelligence and technical skill to make him an efficient workman; the first object demands the Negro college and college-bred men—not a quantity of such colleges, but a few of excellent quality; not too many college-bred men, but enough to leaven the lump, to inspire the masses, to raise the Talented Tenth to leadership; the second object demands a good system of common schools, well-taught, conveniently located and properly equipped . . .

The teaching of trades is no longer a simple matter. Machinery and long processes of work have greatly changed the work of the carpenter, the ironworker and the shoemaker. A really efficient workman must be to-day an intelligent man who has had good technical training in addition to thorough common school, and perhaps even higher training. To meet this situation the industrial schools began a further development; they established distinct Trade Schools for the thorough training of better class artisans, and at the same time they sought to preserve for the purposes of general education, such of the simpler processes of elementary trade learning as were best suited therefor. In this differentiation of the Trade School and manual training, the best of the industrial schools simply followed the plain trend of the present educational epoch . . .

Thus, again, in the manning of trade schools and manual training schools we are thrown back upon the higher training as its source and chief support. There was a time when any aged and wornout carpenter could teach in a trade school. But not so to-day. Indeed the demand for college-bred men by a school like Tuskegee, ought to make Mr. Booker T. Washington the firmest friend of higher training. Here he has as helpers the son of a Negro senator, trained in Greek and the humanities, and graduated at Harvard; the son of a Negro congressman and lawyer, trained in Latin and mathematics, and graduated at Oberlin; he has as his wife, a woman who read Virgil and Homer in the same class room with me; he has as college chaplain, a classical graduate of Atlanta University; as teacher of science, a graduate of Fisk; as teacher of history, a graduate of Smith,—indeed some thirty of his chief teachers are college graduates, and instead of studying French grammars in the midst of weeds, or buying pianos for dirty cabins, they are at Mr. Washington's right hand helping him in a noble work. And yet one of the effects of Mr. Washington's propaganda has been to throw doubt upon the expediency of such training for Negroes, as these persons have had.

Men of America, the problem is plain before you. Here is a race transplanted through the criminal foolishness of your fathers. Whether you like it or not the millions are here, and here they will remain. If you do not lift them up, they will pull you down. Education and work are the levers to uplift a people. Work alone will not do it unless inspired by the right ideals and guided by intelligence. Education must not simply teach work—it must teach Life. The Talented Tenth of the Negro race must be made leaders of thought and missionaries of culture among their people. No others can do this work and Negro colleges must train men for it. The Negro race, like all other races, is going to be saved by its exceptional men.[1]

BOOKER TALIAFERRO WASHINGTON

Tuskegee, Alabama. October 28, 1903

Dear Dr. Du Bois: The enclosed is a copy of a letter which I have sent out to all the parties mentioned in our previous conference, and I hope very much it will have your approval. If for any reason you think any changes should be made in the personnel of those invited, I wish very much that you would say so. Yours truly,

Booker T. Washington[2]

Washington had long sought a summit between the various factions of black leadership and had the money from white backers to make it happen. Although negotiations for the meeting were tense and tenuous, they eventually came about, and the meeting was held at Carnegie Hall in January 1904, even as Du Bois was publishing essays about his "Talented Tenth" that served as functional critiques of every available Washingtonian education model. Du Bois prepared his faction for deviousness by the Washington faction, which essentially made the meeting a clash between two mistrustful groups.[3]

BOOKER T. WASHINGTON

[Tuskegee, Ala.] Nov. 2,1903

My dear Mr. [James Carroll] Napier: We had a meeting of about twenty gentlemen in Atlanta night before last and took up fully the recent developments in regard to sleeping cars. One of the results of the meeting was the appointing of a committee including Mr. Rucker, Mr. Proctor,[4] Dr. Du Bois and myself to go to Chicago and have an interview with Robert T. Lincoln. The meeting also instructed me to invite you to accompany the committee to Chicago, and this I very much hope you can consent to do. Our present plan is to be in Chicago on the 12th or 13th of November. I have today telegraphed to Chicago to see if we can have an interview with Mr. Lincoln on these dates either in Chicago or New York, wherever he should happen to be . . .[5]

KELLY MILLER

Washington, D.C. Nov 4 1903

Dear Du Bois: Yours received this day—Of course Prof Booker T. has notified you of the date for the New York Conference (Jan. 6th, 7th, 8th). Our local conference I fear is almost a matter of "help me Cassius or I sink." I am glad that Mr. W. will be present. It will give weight and currency to the movement. I do not think that the conference can be stampeded by his presence. I shall stand uncompromisingly opposed to the endorsement of any individual or his platform.

Roscoe [Conkling Bruce] will also be here. You should come by all means. Will you come if free transportation can be procured?

I was both glad and sorry to see your Guardian letter—glad for the sympathy expressed for as sincere a man as there is in the race; but sorry in that I feel sure your expression will be misjudged.

I am sending you a list of my fugitive articles—also list topics suggested for conference. Yours truly,

Kelly Miller[6]

BOOKER T. WASHINGTON

Tuskegee, Alabama. November 5, 1903

Dear Dr. Du Bois: Replying in part to yours of November 3d, I want to get your opinion on the question as to whether or not either Bishop Turner or Bishop Holsey[7] should not properly be included in our New York conference. Both of these men represent in a way the John Temple Graves idea and that is an element which I wonder if it is safe for us to ignore if we wish to have all sides of the question fairly and honestly considered.[8]

I will write you later about the other suggestion raised in your letter.

In looking over the list I find that we have no representative from the state of Texas. Texas is so large within itself that I have been wondering if that section of the country should not be represented, in that case have you any one to suggest? I think you know R.L. Smith, a graduate from Atlanta University, and a man who has done excellent work in many directions in Texas.[9] In case you decide to have some one from that state I can think of no one who is more representative in his character. Perhaps you know some other person.

I have been telegraphing trying to make arrangements for our reception in Chicago ever since I reached home, but up to the present time nothing is very satisfactory. Mr. Lincoln is evidently waiting for some developments in the South or trying to hedge. The last telegram wanted to know the names of the committee and parts of the country that they represented and the object to be covered by the conference. This information I telegraphed day before yesterday, but still no answer. Yours truly,

[Booker T. Washington]

It may be, however, that the company is holding out in our favor and is trying to avoid seeing committees in order to not attract attention and thus not stir up the South to any great extent.[10]

BOOKER T. WASHINGTON

[Tuskegee, Ala.] November 6, 1903

Dear Mr. [Henry Hugh] Proctor: On reaching home on Monday, I telegraphed to Chicago with a view of having a time set when our committee would be received by Mr. Lincoln. I stated that either the 12th or 13th would be convenient. The next day I received a telegram in reply asking the names of the committee, the parts of the country they represented, and the object to be covered by our conference. I immediately telegraphed in reply this information. Up to the present time I have received no answer to my last telegram.

In the meantime I have received a letter from Mr. S. Laing Williams, a copy of which I enclose. I rather think that this letter throws a great deal of light on the whole subject, and I doubt very much whether our committee will secure a hearing. As individuals none of us I think, would have any trouble in being received by Mr. Lincoln, but it is evident for some reason he means to avoid receiving any committee. I do not think that Mr. Lincoln's action in this regard is to be taken as unfriendly or unfavorable; I rather think that he is trying to avoid stirring up the question as much as possible, and that he fears if it were known that we are pressing the matter in Chicago that a back fire might be started by the Southern people. Neither do I think that any decision has been reached by the company, otherwise I think Mr. Williams' committee would have been so informed. It is evident that the many letters and telegrams which have been sent to Chicago on the subject have done good, and I advise that in every way possible this agitation be kept up. I have talked with Dr. Du Bois through the telephone this morning, and both he and I are of the opinion that under the present circumstances it would be useless to go to Chicago unless we get a definite reply as to an audience.

Will you be kind enough to show a copy of this letter to the other members of the committee? I have sent a copy direct to Dr. Du Bois.

Enclosed I return the petition or letter addressed to Mr. Lincoln which I have signed. You and the other members of the committee can do as you think best about forwarding this if it is not taken by the committee . . .[11]

BOOKER T. WASHINGTON

Tuskegee, Alabama. Nov. 8, 1903

Dear Dr. Du Bois: Please be kind enough to let me have your opinion of the following matters just as early as possible as time is pressing: Of course the main object of our New York Conference is to try to agree upon certain fundamental principles and to see in what way we understand or misunderstand each other and correct mistakes as far as possible. I agree with your suggestion that in Chicago, for example, we ought to have as far as possible, all shades of opinion represented. I have no objection to inviting either Dr. Bentley or Mr. Morris.[12] Which one do you prefer? Of course we could not invite them both. In this same connection I think that we ought to have W.H. Lewis from Boston as we could only get at both sides of New England thought by having him or some such man, as well as Mr. [Clement G.] Morgan. The more I think of it, the more I feel convinced that Dr. J.W.E. Bowen ought to be present.[13] He represents a very large constituency and I have found him on all questions a pretty sane man. I have already written you as to your opinion about either Bishop Turner or Bishop Holsey. Of course we must avoid having the conference too large and too expensive. Do you really think that Dr. Grimke would represent some idea or element that would not be represented by somebody else already invited? Please think of this and write me. As to Fortune; we may or may not agree with a great many things that he does, but I think there is no question but that he influences public opinion in a very large degree. We must make an especial effort to drop out of consideration all personal feelings, otherwise the conference will be a failure from the beginning.

So far in making up the conference, I fear it has one especially weak point which should be strengthened if possible. We should bear in mind that the bulk of our people are in the South and that the problems relating to their future very largely surround the Southern colored people, and we should be very sure that there is a large element in the conference who actually know Southern conditions by experience and who can speak with authority, and we should not have to depend too much on mere theory and untried schemes of Northern colored people. Yours truly

Booker T. Washington[14]

W.E.B. DU BOIS

[undated]

Dear Mr. Washington:

I do not think it will be profitable for me to give further advice which will not be followed. The conference is yours and you will naturally constitute it as you choose. I must of course reserve the right to see the final list of those invited and to decide then whether my own presence is worth while.

W.E.B. Du Bois[15]

The fraught conference negotiations, however, were not the only point of contention between the two. Although Du Bois published a biography of John Brown in historian Ellis Paxson Oberholtzer's "American Crisis Biographies" series for George W. Jacobs and Co., for example, such was not the original plan. Du Bois first agreed to write a biography of Frederick Douglass, but Oberholtzer had to rescind the invitation after Booker T. Washington, whom Oberholtzer had originally asked, finally agreed to do the work. It was an embarrassing situation for the editor, but also only fueled the resentment between the two black leaders. Du Bois wanted to substitute the would-be Douglass biography with one on Nat Turner, but at Oberholtzer's urging, he finally agreed to write a biography of John Brown. Washington's Douglass

biography appeared in 1907, Du Bois's work on Brown in 1909, but the nego-
tiations for the books happened as the two would-be authors plotted their
Carnegie Hall summit.[16]

ELLIS P. OBERHOLTZER *(Oberholtzer was the editor of the "American*
Crisis Biographies" series, the literary editor for Philadelphia's Public
Ledger, *and an author of historical biographies.)*

Philadelphia, November 11, 1903.

Prof. W.E. Burghardt Du Bois
Dear Sir:

I have projected with Mr. Jacobs, the publisher of this city, a series of
biographies which we shall call "The American Crisis Biographies." It
is our object in this Series to give an impartial view of the causes, the
course, and the consequences of the Civil War . . .

Of the twenty-five volumes about ten will be of Southern men, including Calhoun, Jefferson Davis, Alexander Stephens, Robert Toombs,
General Lee, "Stonewall" Jackson, and perhaps one or two others yet
to be chosen. It is intended that the lives of the Southern men shall be
written by Southern writers as a guaranty of greater impartiality.

In a recent conversation with Professor MacMaster it was suggested
that you, if you were willing, might give us a life of Frederick Douglass. With that would be included the history of the Fugitive Slave
Law, some account of the African Slave Trade, and a description of
the operations of the underground railroad. I have never seen anything in print which could be considered for a moment as an adequate history of the underground railroad to Canada.

Hoping to hear from you, I am,

Very truly yours,
Ellis P. Oberholtzer.[17]

W.E.B. DU BOIS

Atlanta, Ga., Nov. 18, 1903

My Dear Sir [Ellis Oberholtzer]:

I think I should like to write a life of Douglass on the lines laid down
in your favor of November eleventh. Something would depend of

course on the time when you would want the ms. and the general terms. There are as you know I presume several lives of Douglass—his autobiographies, one in the American Reformer series & one in the Beacon Biographies. I presume too you know of [W.H.] Siebert's Underground Railroad.[18] I shall be glad to hear from you further on the subject.

Very Respectfully,
W.E.B. Du Bois[19]

ELLIS P. OBERHOLTZER

Philadelphia November 21, 1903.

Professor W.E.B. Du Bois
My dear Sir:

I was pleased to have your letter of the 18th inst. with its expression of willingness to contribute a life of Frederick Douglass to our "American Crisis Series." I know that Mr. Douglass has had several biographies, but I do not think that anyone has done the work quite as you and I would have it done. Certainly in such a series as the one we have projected it would be necessary to bring out other phases of his life, that it might form a chapter in the general history of the struggle between the northern and southern states . . .

I know of your own good work in the historical field from the time when you were in Philadelphia, and I shall be very glad if I can arrange to have your cooperation in an enterprise which interests me personally very much.

Very truly yours,
Ellis Paxson Oberholtzer[20]

ELLIS P. OBERHOLTZER

Philadelphia January 25, 1904.

Dr. W.E. Burghardt Du Bois
My dear Sir:

I have delayed forwarding you the contract for the life of Frederick Douglass for our *American Crisis Series* because of a letter received from Booker T. Washington, concerning the same subject. I had written him first, but not having heard from him for a considerable time and desiring, personally, that you should do the volume because of your superior historical training, I had rather too eagerly sought to secure your cooperation for this volume. I regret to tell you that I must give it to him. The publishers are very desirous of adding Mr. Washington's name to the list of authors for the Series, and it was in vain that I endeavored to have him take an assignment to some character illustrating a later period in the negro's development, some freedman, a period he knows very well, and one that calls for less historical learning. I had from the first planned to have two volumes on colored men.

Now can you suggest any other name which you would be willing to take instead of Douglass? The name while it must be worthy of a place beside the others in the series of twenty-five, will be only a rallying point for a great deal of historical knowledge of the time which I know you can glean, and for a point of view which I know you will give the reader in any study that you undertake.

I hope that you will understand this matter as it is, and can suggest a way by which I can bring you into the Series, as I particularly desire your aid, and that in any case you will forgive me for what is apparently a very great discourtesy.

Believe me,

Very truly yours,
Ellis P. Oberholtzer[21]

W.E.B. DU BOIS

Atlanta, Ga., Jan. 30, 1904

My dear Sir [Oberholtzer]:

I have your favor of the 25th. If it falls within your scheme the best subject for me would be Nat Turner—around him would center the slave trade, foreign & internal, Negro insurrections from Toussaint down to John Brown, the beginnings of the Underground railroad, the beginning of abolitionism, the movements of the free Negroes of the North & the whole plantation economy which was changing critically in the thirties, and the general subjective Negro point of view of the system of slavery. Another suggestion would be B.K. Bruce & reconstruction but this does not attract me as much.

W.E.B. Du Bois[22]

ELLIS P. OBERHOLTZER

Philadelphia February 3, 1904.

Prof. W.E.B. Du Bois
Dear Sir:

I am very much obliged to you for your favor of January 30th, and the suggestion which it contains. Perhaps it might be possible to make Nat Turner the central point for a description of the conditions prevailing in the South in the early part of the Century. I confess, however, that I am a little ignorant about the life of Turner and the importance of the movement which he led. If his insurrection had any permanent influence upon the development of the American Crisis, as for instance, in making the Black Laws more stringent, and in altering relations between masters and slaves, as I presume it may have done, I think there would be a good deal of propriety in a biography of the man. Is there sufficient material for such a purpose, and could he be made to appear as anything more than a deluded prophet who led a little band of men armed with scythes and broad axes?

I know your studies will enable you to answer these questions satisfactorily, and awaiting your early reply, I am

Very truly yours,
Ellis P. Oberholtzer[23]

W.E.B. DU BOIS

[undated]

Dear Sir [Ellis P. Oberholtzer]:

In my opinion no single man before 1850 had a greater influence on Southern legislation & feeling than Nat Turner and in the North it disfranchised the Negroes of Penn. & strengthened the black laws. There is abundant material for his life & times. I should however not be satisfied to have you depend entirely on my opinion in this matter, but would be glad to have you to get the opinion of men like Professor McMaster & Professor Hart.[24]

W.E.B. Du Bois[25]

ELLIS P. OBERHOLTZER

Philadelphia, February 16, 1904

Dear Dr. Du Bois:

I am very much interested in what you have told me in regard to Nat Turner and his times. I had already spoken to Professor MacMaster regarding the subject, and have had another talk with him since receiving your note. He is very anxious that someone should make a study of the condition of the free negro before the War, although I scarcely see how a name can be found as a rallying point for such an investigation as important as it must be considered to be. I fear you will think me very hard to suit, but I should prefer, if you can see your way clear to do it, that you should make John Brown the centre for your volume. That, I think, will enable you to give such an account as you outline of the Southampton and other insurrections, and the changing economic system in the South which may have been the result of that affair. It will also give us an opportunity for a chapter or two about the troubles in Kansas, which I am fearful may not elsewhere find a place in the Series. Although Brown has been done by Professor Von Holtz, F.B. Sanborn, and others, your view of him, and the events which led up to the Harpers Ferry Movement would entertain me very much, and I am certain many others too.[26]

I enclose a partial list of authors already assigned to subjects in the Series, and I hope that the arrangement herein indicated may be satisfactory to you. I do not think that of necessity it will greatly change the subject matter of the study, while at the same time giving us a central figure which can be placed beside the other figures we have selected for this Series.

Hoping to hear from you, I am

Sincerely yours,
Ellis P. Oberholtzer[27]

EDWARD ELDER COOPER (*Cooper was a black newspaper magnate who founded the* Indianapolis World, *the* Indianapolis Freeman, *and the* Colored American, *based in Washington, D.C.*)[28]

Washington, D.C, Nov. 25, 1903

Dear Mr. Washington: I presume you are very busy, too much so to be annoyed with a letter from me, and yet

"A little nonsense now and then
Is relished by the wisest men."

I am publishing in this week's Colored American a letter from my Memphis correspondent, a Mr. Turner.[29] He is a good agent, but is inclined to be cranky, is down on the mulattoes, although he has a mulatto wife, is a letter carrier by profession, and a fourth edition of Ida B. Wells. He is a clever fellow for he has obtained a weekly circulation of about five hundred copies each week for Memphis, for The Colored American. He is a great admirer of Prof. Du Bois and in an article which I have printed this week, I can see the fine Italian hand of Du Bois all the way through it. They made several thrusts at you and to have published the letter, as it was written would have kept it from going through the mails, under the rule of obscene literature.

I have cut all of the poison out of the article, and will send you an extra copy tomorrow night. The point I want to make is that a great many people are over rating Du Bois. He is a small fellow, and will do a little trick. He is soon to start a paper from Atlanta to be known as "The Black American." In this he hopes to array the full blooded Negroes, as he terms them against the mulattoes. It will please a certain class of whites and a certain class of Negroes no doubt; but like the Irish agitators in Ireland they could not write down just what they wanted, if they were given paper and pen and ink. I will send you the manuscript if you would like to see it. It is typewritten and you will see what I have cut out . . .

E E Cooper[30]

BOOKER T. WASHINGTON

[Tuskegee, Ala.] December 5th, 1903

Dear Dr. [Francis James] Grimke: I have your letter of recent date. I very much hope that you, yourself, will attend the conference as I do not think any one taking your place can be of the service that you would.

In regard to your brother; there are one or two considerations which I wish to call to your attention. First; you will note that he resides in Boston, and we have already invited two persons from that city; this, it seems to me, would give Boston an undue representation. Second; in politics I understand that he is a Democrat, and you will note that we have already invited one prominent Democrat from the West. Of course we have had to keep in mind two things; first, not to make the conference too expensive, second, not to have it too large to be so unwieldy that it will be a mere forum of discussion rather than a quiet[,] confidential, serious, heart to heart talk.

I will take up with Dr. Du Bois the name of the other persons that you suggest. All of them are good men and I wish there might be no hesitation in inviting them. Yours very truly,

[Booker T. Washington][31]

BOOKER T. WASHINGTON

Hotel Manhattan, New York City. December 14th, 1903

Dear Dr. Du Bois: Enclosed I am sending you a copy of the opinion of Mr. [Paul D.] Cravath upon the Pullman Car question.[32] Another step in this direction will soon be taken. I wish that you would be kind enough to let all the Atlanta members of the Committee see the opinion. I have sent a copy direct to Rev. Proctor. Very truly yours,

[Booker T. Washington][33]

W.E.B. DU BOIS

December 28, [190]3

My dear Mr. [George Foster] Peabody[34]:—

Some time ago Mr. [Edward T.] Ware, our Chaplain, spoke to me of a letter received from you in which you spoke of certain rumors as to my connection with the disturbances over Mr. Washington in Boston last summer. Later Dr. Bumstead[35] wrote me of a similar letter not mentioning from whom he had received it, but I took it that it was probably from you.

I want therefore to write you frankly of my position in this matter that there may be no misapprehension, and I want you to feel at liberty to use the letter as you may wish.

Mrs. Trotter the wife of the editor of the Guardian is an old friend of mine of school days. Mr. Trotter I have not known so long or so well but met him in college. I had then and afterward disagreed with him rather sharply over many questions of policy and particularly over Mr. Washington. But nevertheless both then and now I saw in him a clean-hearted utterly unselfish man whom I admired despite his dogged and unreasoning prejudices. Last summer while Mrs. Du Bois and I were looking for a boarding place, Mrs. Trotter offered to share her home with us and we gladly accepted. I went first to Tuskegee and then made a trip on a coast steamer. I did not arrive in Boston until after the Zion Church disturbance.[36] Before seeing the account in the morning papers, I had had no inkling or suspicion in any way of the matter. I did not know Mr. Washington was in Boston or intending to go there as I had just left him at Tuskegee. I had had no correspondence with Mr. Trotter for six months save in regard to a boarding place. When I arrived in Boston and heard of the meeting I told Mr. Trotter and Mr. Forbes in plain terms my decided disapproval of the unfortunate occurrence and my conviction that it would do harm. Although I was unable at that time to defend Mr. Washington's position as I once had, I nevertheless took occasion to address a meeting of men at Mr. Trotter's home and remind them of the vast difference between criticizing Mr. Washington's policy and attacking him personally.

Nevertheless, brought into close contact with Mr. Trotter for the first time my admiration for his unselfishness, pureness of heart and indomitable energy even when misguided, grew. And, too, I saw how local jealousies were working to make mountains out of mole hills. So far as I could learn had it not been for Mr. Lewis, the chairman of the Washington meeting, there would have been no riot—the disturbance could have easily and quickly [been] quelled and the dignity of the occasion saved. This same Mr. Lewis a few years ago was a rabid anti-Washington man and wanted to "burn down Tuskegee." I labored with him and Trotter and Forbes in past years was instrumental in getting Mr. Washington and Mr. Lewis together at a small luncheon so that they might understand each other. They evidently came to understand each other so well that Mr. Lewis got a political appointment and turning around proceeded to abuse his former comrades—a conversion in which I had as little faith as I had in his former radical stand.[37]

There were a great many other things not generally known that made me pity and admire Mr. Trotter as well as condemn his lack of judgment and there were also things that made me have less and less faith in Mr. Washington. Nevertheless I steadfastly condemned Mr. Trotter's action from that day to this—a fact which he will frankly testify to. When the matter was pushed to the extent of actual imprisonment I felt this was too much in view of all the facts and still feel so and I wrote an open letter to the "Guardian" expressing my disagreement on many points with him but my admiration for his honesty of purpose.

While then I had absolutely no knowledge of the Washington meeting before hand and no part, active or passive, in the disturbance and while I did then and do now condemn the disturbance, I nevertheless admire Mr. Trotter as a man and agree with him in his main contentions. When I think him in the right I shall help him, when his methods or opinions go beyond law and right, I shall condemn them.

As between him and Mr. Washington I unhesitatingly believe Mr. Trotter to be far nearer the right in his contentions and I only pray for such restraint and judgment on Mr. Trotter's part as will save to our cause his sincerity and unpurchasable soul in these days when every energy is being used to put black men back into slavery and when Mr. Washington is leading the way backward.

I am sorry that I was not at the University when you called to welcome your party.

Very sincerely yours,
W.E.B. Du Bois[38]

GEORGE FOSTER PEABODY

Brooklyn, New York, Jan 9th 1904

My Dear Doctor Du Bois

I am sorry that several relatives present at my house today (I have no family but myself) have prevented my going to Manhattan and also have been unable to make a time when I could ask you to be here with certainty that I could see you—I wanted to have a chance for a careful and frank talk with you—expressing my sympathy with your feeling as shown in many of your remarkable writings and as well asking you to let me tell you of how I thought you were leading people to false views of yourself and so injuring your work and your future reputation that you leave to your family and to your people—I also wanted to tell you of the many strong expressions of sympathy with your position as taken in your book on many points from prominent and pronounced Southerners—Especially on my recent visit South—I was grateful for the frank expressions in your letter but I was deeply sorry to note the unfrank and vague words of depreciation of others and think you too largely endowed and in too important a relation to your race to indulge them—When you are next to be out I should be glad to know in advance if you would care for a frank talk with sympathy even where I may not agree.

Very Truly Yours
George Foster Peabody[39]

Du Bois and Washington rode together to Carnegie's house before the opening of the conference. Washington asked Du Bois whether he had read Carnegie's The Gospel of Wealth, *to which Du Bois replied that he had not. "You ought to read it," he said. "He likes it." And, indeed, Washington seemed almost reverentially deferential to Carnegie. And Carnegie, in turn, opened the conference by praising Washington and his policies, as did all of the whites in attendance. "It was," Du Bois thought, "a wrong note to strike in a conference of conciliation."*[40]

KELLY MILLER

New York City January 6th, 7th and 8th, 1904

It is the sense of this conference

1. That the bulk of the Negro race should be encouraged to remain in the South, and especially in those sections where the present physical domination must ultimately bring political and civic equality; and that every effort should be made to uplift and develop them in their present domicile.

At the same time, under favorable circumstances, individuals may properly be encouraged to take advantage of the more liberal conditions of the North and West.

2. That in a democratic republic the right to vote is of paramount importance to every class of citizens and is preservative of all other rights and interests. The Fourteenth and Fifteenth Amendments were justifiable, and should be upheld and enforced by national authority. We should stand at all times for full, free and equal suffrage for colored men, upon the same terms that apply to white men, and should put forth every legal effort in our power to maintain the right of suffrage.

That for the furtherance of our political rights, we urge the organization of colored voters in the North and West by congressional districts for the sole purpose of electing to Congress and to the State Legislatures men who, at all times, will vote for measures promotive of the rights of the Negro race.

In the South, both in those states which have revised their constitutions and in those which have not, we urge each eligible Negro voter to qualify and to vote at every election.

3. That we are opposed to all restrictions of our civil rights in matters of travel and public accommodations, and we urge the institution of suits against common carriers in cases of discrimination and that efforts be made to secure absolutely equal accommodations on all public

conveyances. We stand for no compromise, or equivocal statement, respecting our civil rights, but insist on the equality of all men before the law.

4. That the education of the Negro race should consist of:

(1) Thorough training of leaders and teachers in the higher institutions of learning;

(2) Thorough elementary training for every Negro child;

(3) Industrial training of the masses in trades and handicrafts.

5. That we vigorously denounce lynching and all modes of punishment without due process of law; and, while we condemn rape and every other crime, we are certain that skillfully exaggerated reports of rapeful assaults by Negroes have been and are being used to discredit the race and blacken its reputation. Means should be devised of carefully investigating and publishing the truth of all such accusations.

6. That Negroes should cooperate with the fair-minded and progressive element of the Southern white people, in so far as they can do so without compromise of manhood.

7. That the Northern white man, the Southern white man and the Negro are the three constituent factors of the race problem, and that there should be a conference of representatives of these three elements to consider methods of solution.

8. That effort should be made to disseminate a knowledge of the truth in regard to all matters affecting our race, so that the North, the South and the Negro himself may be adequately informed as to race data and conditions.

RESOLUTION 1. It is the sense of this conference that there should be appointed by this body

A Committee of Safety

1. That this committee should be composed of twelve (12) men;
2. That the duties of this committee be as follows:
   (a) To be a bureau of information on all subjects relating to the race;
   (b) To seek to unify and bring into cooperation the action of the various organizations;
   (c) To be a central bureau of communication between all parts and sections of the country.
3. That this committee meet several times a year, at the discretion of the chairman.

This resolution was signed by:

Booker T. Washington, W.E.B. Du Bois, A. Grant, Charles W. Anderson, Archibald H. Grimke, Robert Russa Moton, H.T. Kealing, T.

Thomas Fortune, S. Laing Williams, Fredrick L. McGhee, E.H. [Elias Camp] Morris, Samuel E. Courtney, J.C. Napier, G.L. Knox, I.B. Scott, Clement G. Morgan, E.C. Morris, A. Walters, R.L. Smith, P.B.S. Pinchback, John S. Trower, William H. Steward, James H. Hayes, Judson W. Lyons, Kelly Miller, C.T. [Charles Thomas] Walker, Whitefield McKinlay, Emmett J. Scott, Hugh M. Browne, and was formally passed unanimously by the conference.[41]

Booker T. Washington, W.E.B. Du Bois and Hugh M. Browne were made members of the Committee of Safety and authorized to select the other 9 members.[42]

RESOLUTION 2. That the conference request of the publishers of McClure's Magazine the privilege of reprinting the article by Hon. Carl Schurz in the January issue.[43]

RESOLUTION 3. That we extend to Hon. C.W. Anderson, of New York, our sincere appreciation of his generous services in furnishing the conference with the conveniences and comforts that have made the proceedings pleasant and agreeable.[44]

RESOLUTION 4. That, in consideration of the thoughtful initiative of Dr. Booker T. Washington in calling the conference, we express our gratitude to him for taking the lead in this movement, and also we extend to him our thanks for his helpful address delivered before the closing session of the conference.

Kelly Miller, *Secretary*.[45]

HORACE BUMSTEAD

New York, Jan. 26, 1904.

My dear Dr. Du Bois:

Your letter to me and the copy of Mr. Peabody's letter to you were very interesting and brought me much encouragement. You seem to have had remarkable success in securing from the conference some of the things that we most desire.[46] Yesterday I saw Dr. [William Hayes] Ward and he gave me some of the results in detail as he had learned them from Bishop [Alexander] Walters.[47] I congratulate you most heartily. It seems to me that, whatever doubts we may have as to the sincerity of what has been done, or as to the backing which the action may receive from the white leaders here in New York, we should credit all hands with entire sincerity and proceed as if we had not the slightest doubt on that point.

Especially important does it seem to me that we should do every-thing in our power to conciliate Mr. Peabody and make a good friend of him. This last letter of his is certainly admirable in tone and shows a spirit of conciliation that ought to be met at least half way. From what I had heard indirectly, I had supposed that he was very much dis-pleased with your letter to him, and so this reply of his is all the more of a surprise to me, especially the extent to which he gives voice to the sympathy of himself and other southern men with some, at least, of the phases of your book. I think he is a man who is willing to work with us and with whom we can work amicably without necessarily holding the same views, if we only can avoid giving him needless irritation. And just here I am going to be frank and say that I think your letter to him would have been very much more effective if you had left out some of the last sentences referring to Mr. Washington. I do not think that they were "unfrank," as Mr. Peabody called them, because you could not well go into details in such a letter, and you were doubtless ready to substantiate your statements if requested to do so. But the legitimate purpose of this letter was accomplished, it seems to me, when you had cleared yourself of any complicity with the Trotter dis-turbance and expressed your attitude toward him as a man and toward his principles. If you had stopped there, I do not see how anybody could take any exception to the letter. I read the letter the other day to a meeting of our Executive and Finance Committees, all the members being present and also Dr. Hall of New York, and Mr. Twichell of Hart-ford.[48] When I had finished, there was quite an outburst of dissent from fully half of those present—all based, I judged, on the closing portion. I think I added considerably to their horror by then telling them that I had written to you that I thought it a frank and manly letter and that I was glad that you had written it. I did not think it best just then to qualify my endorsement of the letter by any dissent from the last part of it, as I have expressed it above to you, but I went on to explain your position and to justify your liberty of opinion and utterance on matters of vital interest to your race, especially as you were one of the very few men of your race who were able to defend its rights with ability, dig-nity, and courtesy. I do not know how much effect my words may have had. But I came away from the meeting with a fresh sense of the difficulty of being honest with ourselves and at the same time being judicious in dealing with those who do not agree with us. Sometime I will talk this over with you more fully . . .

Yours very sincerely,
Horace Bumstead.[49]

W.E.B. DU BOIS

The Parting of the Ways

The points upon which American Negroes differ as to their course of action are the following: First, the scope of education; second, the necessity of the right of suffrage; third, the importance of civil rights; fourth, the conciliation of the South; fifth, the future of the race in this country.

The older opinion as built up under the leadership of our great dead, Payne, Crumell, Forten and Douglass, was that the broadest field of education should be opened to black children; that no free citizen of a republic could exist in peace and prosperity without the ballot; that self-respect and proper development of character can only take place under a system of equal civil rights; that every effort should be made to live in peace and harmony with all men, but that even for this great boon no people must willingly or passively surrender their essential rights of manhood; that in future the Negro is destined to become an American citizen with full political and civil rights, and that he must never rest contented until he has achieved this.

Since the death of the leaders of the past there have come mighty changes in the nation. The gospel of money has risen triumphant in church and state and university. The great question which Americans ask to-day is, "What is he worth?" or "What is it worth?" The ideals of human rights are obscured, and the nation has begun to swagger about the world in its useless battleships looking for helpless peoples whom it can force to buy its goods at high prices. This wave of materialism is temporary; it will pass and leave us all ashamed and surprised; but while it is here it strangely maddens and blinds us . . .

Meantime an awakening race, seeing American civilization as it is, is strongly moved and naturally misled. They whisper: What is the greatness of the country? Is it not money? Well then, the one end of our education and striving should be moneymaking. The trimmings of life, smattering of Latin and music and such stuff—let that wait till we are rich. Then as to voting, what is the good of it after all? Politics does not pay as well as the grocery business, and breeds trouble. Therefore get out of politics and let the ballot go. When we are rich we can dabble in politics along with the president of Yale. Then, again the thought arises: What is personal humiliation and the denial of ordinary civil rights compared with a chance to earn a living? Why quarrel with your bread and butter simply because of filthy Jim Crow cars? Earn a living: get rich, and all these things shall be added unto you. Moreover, conciliate your neighbors, because they are more powerful and wealthier, and the price you must pay to earn a living in America is that of humiliation and inferiority.

No one, of course, has voiced this argument quite so flatly and bluntly as I have indicated. It has been expressed rather by the emphasis given industrial and trade teaching, the decrying of suffrage as a manhood right or even necessity, the insistence on great advance among Negroes before there is any recognition of their aspirations, and a tendency to minimize the shortcomings of the South and to emphasize the mistakes and failures of black men. Now, in this there has been just that degree of truth and right which serves to make men forget its untruths. That the shiftless and poor need thrift and skill, that ignorance can not vote intelligently, that duties and rights go hand in hand, and that sympathy and understanding among neighbors is prerequisite to peace and concord, all this is true. Who has ever denied it, or ever will? But from all this does it follow that Negro colleges are not needed, that the right of suffrage is not essential for black men, that equality of civil rights is not the first of rights and that no self-respecting man can agree with the person who insists that he is a dog? Certainly not, all answer.

Yet the plain result of the attitude of mind of those who, in their advocacy of industrial schools, the unimportance of suffrage and civil rights and conciliation, have been significantly silent or evasive as to higher training and the great principle of free self-respecting manhood for black folk—the plain result of this propaganda has been to help the cutting down of educational opportunity for Negro children, the legal disfranchisement of nearly 5,000,000 of Negroes and a state of public opinion which apologizes for lynching, listens complacently to any insult or detraction directed against an eighth of the population of the land, and silently allows a new slavery to rise and clutch the South and paralyze the moral sense of a great nation.

What do Negroes say to this? I speak advisedly when I say that the overwhelming majority of them declare that the tendencies to-day are wrong and that the propaganda that encouraged them was wrong. They say that industrial and trade teaching is needed among Negroes, sadly needed; but they unhesitatingly affirm that it is not needed as much as thorough common school training and the careful education of the gifted in higher institutions; that only in this way can a people rise by intelligence and social leadership to a plane of permanent efficiency and morality. To be sure, there are shorter and quicker methods of making paying workingmen out of a people. Slavery under another name may increase the output of the Transvaal mines, and a caste system coupled with manual training may relieve the South from the domination of labor unions. But has the nation counted the cost of this?

Has the Negro agreed to the price, and ought he to agree? Economic efficiency is a means and not an end; this every nation that cares for its salvation must remember.

Moreover, notwithstanding speeches and the editorials of a subsidized Negro press, black men in this land know that when they lose the ballot they lose all. They are no fools. They know it is impossible for free workingmen without a ballot to compete with free workingmen who have the ballot; they know there is no set of people so good and true as to be worth trusting with the political destiny of their fellows, and they know that it is just as true to-day as it was a century and a quarter ago that "Taxation without representation is tyranny."

Finally, the Negro knows perfectly what freedom and equality mean—opportunity to make the best of oneself, unhandicapped by wanton restraint and unreasoning prejudice. For this the most of us propose to strive. We will not, by word or deed, for a moment admit the right of any man to discriminate against us simply on account of race or color. Whenever we submit to humiliation and oppression it is because of superior brute force; and even when bending to the inevitable we bend with unabated protest and declare flatly and unswervingly that any man or section or nation who wantonly shuts the doors of opportunity and self-defense in the faces of the weak is a coward and knave. We refuse to kiss the hands that smite us, but rather insist on striving by all civilized methods to keep wide educational opportunity, to keep the right to vote, to insist on equal civil rights and to gain every right and privilege open to a free American citizen.

But, answer some, you can not accomplish this. America will never spell opportunity for black men; it spelled slavery for them in 1619 and it will spell the same thing in other letters in 1919. To this I answer simply: I do not believe it. I believe that black men will become free American citizens if they have the courage and persistence to demand the rights and treatment of men, and cease to toady and apologize and belittle themselves. The rights of humanity are worth fighting for. Those that deserve them in the long run get them. The way for black men to-day to make these rights the heritage of their children is to struggle for them unceasingly, and if they fail, die trying.[50]

NOTES

1. Du Bois, "The Talented Tenth," 1903, 33–75.
2. This letter Washington sent to Du Bois just one week after accusing him of treachery. Washington, 1977, vol. 7, 315.
3. Lewis, 1993, 305–306.

4. H.A. Rucker was the black collector of customs for the port of Atlanta. Henry Hugh Proctor was a graduate of Fisk and Yale Divinity, the pastor of Atlanta's First Congregational Church and a race activist with ties to both Du Bois and Washington. See Blight, 2001; and Lewis, 1993.

5. Lincoln rejected the proposed meeting. Washington, 1977, vol. 7, 324.

6. Washington, 1977, vol. 7, 330–331.

7. Lucius Henry Holsey was a bishop of the Colored Methodist Episcopal Church based in Atlanta. He was also a race activist who built several industrial schools across Georgia. Eskew, 2009, 106–140.

8. See Chapter 6, note 27.

9. Smith's "excellent work in many directions" included leading the Oakland, Texas, Normal School for Negroes, founding the Farmers' Improvement Society of Texas, speaking around the country for black rights, and serving in the Texas state legislature. Du Bois, 1898, 34; and Marable, 1997, 163.

10. Washington, 1977, vol. 7, 331–332.

11. Ibid., 335–336.

12. Edward H. Morris was a prominent Chicago lawyer and activist for black rights. For Bentley, see Chapter 4. "Personal: Edward H. Morris," April 1943, 258–259.

13. See Chapter 9, note 7.

14. Washington, 1977, vol. 7, 339–340; and Du Bois, 1973, 53–54.

15. Du Bois, 1973, 54.

16. Ibid., 60–61, 63.

17. Ibid., 61–62.

18. Siebert, 1899.

19. Du Bois, 1973, 62.

20. Ibid., 62–63.

21. Ibid., 63–64.

22. Ibid., 64.

23. Ibid.

24. Du Bois here refers to his advisor, Albert Bushnell Hart, and John Bach McMaster, professor of U.S. history at the University of Pennsylvania.

25. Du Bois, 1973, 64–65.

26. Oberholtzer refers to von Holst, 1888; and Sanborn, 1885.

27. Du Bois, 1973, 65.

28. Baltimore *Afro-American*, 18 July 1908, 1.

29. William M. Turner, a Memphis postman, wrote under the pseudonym Brom Bones. Washington, 1977, vol. 7, 353. See also, *Washington Colored American*, 28 November 1903, 1–3.

30. Washington, 1977, vol. 7, 352.

31. Ibid., 359.

32. Cravath was a prominent Manhattan corporate lawyer. Roberts, 2005, 194–215.

33. Washington, 1977, vol. 7, 369.

34. George Foster Peabody, a white businessman and philanthropist, was a Tuskegee trustee and benefactor for many other colleges and universities. He was also a powerful figure in the Democratic Party. Du Bois, 1973, 56–67.

35. Horace Bumstead served as president of Atlanta University from 1886–1907. His attempts at fundraising in the North were often hindered by the militancy of Du Bois, and thus the two maintained a relatively strained relationship. Problems stemming from that relationship would ultimately contribute to Du Bois's exit from the university in 1910. Du Bois, 1973, 67; and Towns, 1948, 109–114.

36. Du Bois here refers to the Boston Riot.

37. William Henry Lewis did become the first black assistant attorney general of the United States, appointed by William Howard Taft due largely to the influence of Booker T. Washington. He also, among other things, served as a football coach at Harvard. Du Bois, 1973, 68.

38. Du Bois, 1973, 67–69.

39. Ibid., 69.

40. Lewis, 1993, 306–307; Du Bois, 1968, 247; Du Bois, 1940, 81; and "Reminiscences of W.E.B. Du Bois," NXCP89-A80, Columbia University Oral History Collection, Butler Library, Columbia University, New York.

41. William H. Lewis and Henry H. Proctor did not sign, Lewis leaving early. Washington, 1977, vol. 7, 387.

42. Hugh Mason Browne was the principal of the Institute for Colored Youth in Pennsylvania, the institution that would later become Cheyney University. "The Horizon," February 1924, 180–181.

43. Schurz, 1904, 259–275.

44. Charles W. Anderson was one of Washington's chief agents in New York. He was the Collector of Internal Revenue for the Wall Street district of New York, appointed by Roosevelt thanks largely to Washington's support. Moore, 2003, 165.

45. Washington, 1977, vol. 7, 384–387.

46. Bumstead here refers to the Carnegie summit.

47. See Chapter 4, note 33.

48. Joseph H. Twichell and C. Cuthbert Hall were ministers from Hartford, Connecticut and New York, New York, respectively, who were also members of Atlanta University's Board of Trustees. *Catalogue of the Officers and Students of Atlanta University, 1903–1904*, 1904, 3.

49. Du Bois, 1973, 69–70.

50. Du Bois, April 1904, 521–523.

11

The Committee of Twelve

On the surface, the Carnegie summit went well. Washington reportedly acknowledged that he supported civil and political rights for African Americans and that he wanted full equality. He lauded higher education for those with the money and capacity for it. Du Bois admitted that most of black America would and should stay in the South, and that industrial education was necessary for most of them. Both sides would support lawsuits to provide access to public facilities and voting rights, and they would work together to form a Committee of Twelve to coordinate leadership.

Such niceties were without real depth of feeling at best, or calculated strategies for gaining position on opponents at worst. No one left the Carnegie summit confident of real unity. Du Bois, particularly wary of the Committee of Twelve, tried to make it an executive board for a larger representative congress of black leaders across the country. Predictably, although Washington praised the proposal's ambition, he argued that they should wait on such plans until after seeing how the Committee functioned alone. Then he excluded Du Bois from meeting preparations.[1] Du Bois responded, predictably, by resigning from the Committee in 1905. "The Parting of the Ways" had made it all but a formality. It was a move that worried tenuous allies such as Kelly Miller and Archibald Grimke.[2]

RICHARD LLOYD JONES *(Jones was a writer and associate editor of*
Collier's Weekly.*)*

New York, January 7, 1904.

Prof. W.E.B. Du Bois
My dear sir:

I wish very much you could find it possible to appropriate from your
busy time five or ten minutes in which to write for me an editorial comment or opinion of not more than 500 words in length, on what you
may conceive to be the most direct solution of the negro problem. This
of course is a subject on which volumes have been written, and might
still be written, but if I am not mistaken, your views and those of my
friend, Mr. Washington, are diametrically opposed, or at least in that
you feel that his program in all particulars is not in harmony with the
modern spirit.

I would appreciate it very much if you would state your own thought
in this short editorial fashion, with directness and frankness, for our
use and send it to me at this time.

Very truly yours,
Richard Lloyd Jones[3]

RICHARD LLOYD JONES

New York, January 18, 1904.

My dear sir [Du Bois]:

I am very much obliged to you for the very excellent editorial statement which you have sent to me. I shall be glad to receive at all
times your editorial thought on the race problem, or anything else that
appeals to you and upon which you would like to address the American public.

I am sorry to note that you seem to feel that Collier's Weekly has
treated the negro with injustice. We certainly have no editorial policy
of this kind, and I do not know just what particular article or statement has appeared in our paper to cause this offense.

At all times believe me to be

Very heartily yours,
Richard Lloyd Jones[4]

WILLIAM EDWARD BURGHARDT DU BOIS

Atlanta, Ga., Jan. 30, 1904

Dear Mr. Jones:

I have been thinking over the invitation you gave in your letter to me of the 18 of Jan. to send you my "editorial thought." Have you ever thought of this: the color line is belting the world today; about it world interests are centering. Would it not be an interesting experiment to start in Colliers a column—or half a column—called "Along the Color Line" or the "Voice of the Darker Millions" and put therein from week to week or month to month note & comment on the darker races in America, Africa, Asia &c, from their standpoint & the standpoint of the serious student & observer—the spirit of it being rather informing & interpretive than controversial. Would it pay? Would the public stand it? I think I could edit such a column.

W.E.B. Du Bois[5]

RICHARD LLOYD JONES

New York, February 3, 1904

Dear Dr. Du Bois:

I appreciate very much the courtesy of your letter of January 30th. I am afraid it will not be possible, with the wide demands that press for space in our pages, to conduct a regular column or half column on "Along the Color Line," or "Voices of the Darker Millions." I wish very much indeed, however, that you would try to make it possible to give me an editorial thought of about 500 words in length on the idea you suggest—the color line belting the world today and the growing interests that are centering therein . . .

Very cordially yours,
Richard Lloyd Jones[6]

BOOKER TALIAFERRO WASHINGTON

[Tuskegee, Ala.] Jan. 22, 1904

Personal

My dear Major [Robert Russa] Moton:[7] Perhaps I had better write you what I had in mind about not inviting Dr. Du Bois to Hampton. Some months ago Mr. Baldwin invited him to his house for a frank conference, and I learn from two or three sources that Dr. Du Bois afterwards said that it was the purpose of Mr. Baldwin to try to bribe him or change his opinion regarding Hampton and Tuskegee and myself.[8] I was wondering if he was invited to Hampton at this time if he would not place some such interpretation upon the invitation? You remember in his opening address that he said to the effect that persons had attempted to bribe him in order to pull him off from his course. Of course later on, after we get our committee of twelve selected we can perhaps thrash out all these matters and come to a full understanding. Yours truly,

[Booker T. Washington][9]

BOOKER T. WASHINGTON

[Tuskegee, Ala.] January 22, 1904

My dear Mr. [William Henry] Baldwin: I have your good letter of January 18th for which I thank you. Except what you tell me from time to time I find that I have little knowledge of what is being done by the two boards and friends of Southern education. The fact is, that either consciously or unconsciously, I very much fear it is the policy of those in charge to drift out of touch with the colored people engaged in education in the South. I can remember six or seven years ago when almost every important step bearing upon education in the South some colored man was consulted. Now such consultation is becoming more and more rare, and if matters go on as they now are, within a few years no attention will be paid to the colored people at all, I mean so far as conferences are concerned. I meet Southern people here in the South constantly in business conferences, and as you know, such men as Mr. Hare, Mr. Campbell and Mr. Simpson meet with our colored trustees both here in the South and in New York and think nothing of it.[10] There is no earthly reason why a Southern man whose opinion and influence are worth a pinch of salt should refuse to sit in a business conference in New York City with one or two colored people present. The social feature, the dinners, etc., is entirely another matter, and no colored man with any self-respect would seek to obtrude himself in a dinner party where he is not wanted. There is one difficulty in my speaking so plainly to others as I am to you, and that is the minute I should make these suggestions one would get the idea that I was urging myself for recognition. That is far from being true. I have all the responsibilities at present that I care for, but when these meetings take place from time to time, as they do in New York and in the Southern States, as for example at Richmond last year, with out even the presence, to say nothing of the voice, of a single invited colored man however important his work in education in the South, and the colored people learn gradually, I fear, to distrust the whole effort and become critical and cold when they should be warm and sympathetic. This attitude is taken largely because of ignorance and neglect and oversight on the part of those in control. Now I understand perfectly well that it is easier to make such criticisms and to find fault than it is to find a way out of the difficulty. I realize some of the difficulties, but at the same time I think that some way can be found gradually to improve present conditions. In one way or another, and perhaps more than you or any member of the board can realize, the colored people blame me for their not getting such representation as I have suggested . . .

Now in regard to our conference I . . . say that after threshing out matters pretty fully for three days and we reached this decision, that a central committee of twelve should be appointed who should as far as possible, take charge of the race's interest during the year, and this committee was to meet at the call of myself. The members of this committee have not been appointed as yet, but are to be appointed by Prof. Hugh M. Browne,[11] Dr. Du Bois and myself at a meeting which we shall perhaps hold in New York sometime in February or March. I am quite sure that several of the members, perhaps the majority of them who have been in opposition, are either silenced or won over to see the error of their way. There were others of whom this cannot be said, but will have to be watched in the future in order to determine how they should be classed. All of them, however, I am sure, were overwhelmed by the general sentiment of the conference and by the high character of the men present. I feel that it was a very helpful meeting from every point of view and among the most important efforts that I have ever had part in.

I am very anxious for a long conference with you . . .[12]

W.E.B. DU BOIS

Philadelphia, 24 Jan., 1904

Dear Sir [Washington]: I might possibly get to the Conference if I could be of any particular use. Had you anything especial in mind? I am here at present lecturing for the University Extension and shall return just about the time of your conference.

As to the sleeping-car matter I did nothing more. [William C.] Martin's fee seemed to me too high.[13] I have additional complaint now. I wanted to come north on the regular express & was refused even a ticket on the ground that the train was all Pullman's now & they could not accommodate me on account of the law. This is a clear case. I can not afford to spend as much as Martin wanted, but I am willing to push the matter if the cost is lowered. Yours sincerely,

W.E.B. Du Bois[14]

BOOKER T. WASHINGTON

[Tuskegee, Ala.] January 27, 1904

Dear Dr. Du Bois: Even before our committee is formed, I think there are one or two matters that we might attend to effectively. First. I presume you have seen something of the recent decision handed down by the U.S. Supreme Court bearing upon the question of colored men serving upon juries. So far as I can get hold of the facts, this is a clear, clean cut decision in our favor, and I think it will be a good idea for you, Mr. Browne and myself to arrange to have Mr. Wilford H. Smith, the lawyer who had charge of the case, make up a letter of instruction that might serve as a guide to colored people throughout the South and have this circular printed as far as possible in the colored papers and distributed also separately as far as possible. If the facts and proper instruction as to methods of procedure are put before the colored people and they do not secure representation upon the juries they will have no one to blame but themselves. Please let me have your idea as soon as possible upon the advisability of taking this course.

Second. Either before or soon after the committee of twelve has been formed, I think it well to get Mr. Smith, or some competent authority, to make a digest of the various requirements for voting in the various Southern States and put it in pamphlet form for large circulation among the colored people throughout the South. I find that in many cases the people do not vote simply because they are careless or ignorant of the law. For example, as the law now stands in Alabama, a very large number of colored people could vote if they were aware of the fact that they must pay their poll tax between now and February 1st. Unless some individual however, takes it upon himself to keep the poll tax matter constantly before them between now and February, comparatively few of them will pay this tax. It seems to me that our committee might have for one of its objects the keeping of such matters constantly before the people.

I do not mind saying for your private information that I think I could get Mr. Smith to compile the circular bearing on the jury system without charge since I employed him to take the case through the Supreme Court. Yours very truly,

[Booker T. Washington][15]

BOOKER T. WASHINGTON

[Tuskegee, Ala.] January 28, 1904

My dear Sir [Allerton D. Hitch]: I am very glad to receive your kind letter of January 25th and to be reminded that we met at the home of your grandfather some years ago . . .

I would state in a word, that I think the main difference between Dr. Du Bois' position and that of my own is, that he believes that what the race is entitled to can be secured mainly through making "demands" and asserting "grievances."[16] My belief is that we will secure more quickly and have in our possession more permanently the rights which we should possess through the more slow but sure channel of development along all commercial and industrial lines in connection with education, morality and religion. I believe that one successful Negro operating a bank is more potent in securing respect and justice for the race than a hundred men making mere abstract speeches or abstract demands for justice; but to make a long story short, I send you by this mail a copy of my book, "Up from Slavery," which will show you clearly my position. If I can send you further information please be kind enough to let me know. Yours truly,

[Booker T. Washington][17]

BOOKER T. WASHINGTON

[Tuskegee, Ala.] February 23, 1904

Dear Dr. Du Bois: Enclosed I send you manuscript for a circular on the question of the Negro and the Jury. This was compiled by Lawyer Wilford H. Smith, the gentleman who secured the favorable decision from the Supreme Court, and he says that it answers all purposes. I would suggest that some explanatory acts be added.

What do you think of the wisdom of having this put in pamphlet form and getting the colored newspapers to republish it and get it before the masses of the colored people in every possible way? This might be done at once. Yours truly,

Booker T. Washington[18]

BOOKER T. WASHINGTON

Tuskegee, Alabama. February 25, 1904

Dear Dr. Du Bois: I have not answered your letter in which you enclose suggestions as to "The Committee of Safety," for the reason that I want to have some days in which to think the matter over.

The more I think of it, the more I am inclined to believe that while the plan outlined by you in many respects would prove helpful and wise, I am inclined to the feeling rather strongly that for a year at least, the Committee would better consist of twelve only. If we can make that a success, it may prove the basis for a larger and more thorough organization. Very truly yours,

Booker T. Washington[19]

BOOKER T. WASHINGTON

[Tuskegee, Ala.] February 27, 1904

Dear Dr. Du Bois: In regard to the decision of the conference to institute a suit against the Pullman Car Co., I would state that I have done everything I could to get such a suit started, but the people in Nashville for some reason have not thought it wise to begin the suit. In the first place, Mr. Baldwin wanted us to wait until he could have opportunity to have a conference with Robert T. Lincoln himself, but as this conference was delayed I wrote urging Mr. Napier to start the suit in accordance with our agreement at New York, but there is failure to act so far.[20] I rather think that this delay or failure comes about by reason of the fact that our people in Nashville find themselves not so much inconvenienced by the recent action of the State Railroad Commission as they thought they were going to be, still the fact is that no action has been taken. Yours truly,

Booker T. Washington[21]

BOOKER T. WASHINGTON

[Tuskegee, Ala.] March 4, 1904

My dear Mr. [Hugh Mason] Browne: I am glad to have your letter of March 1st. I note what you say about the composition of the committee of twelve.[22] In my opinion, I do not think the fact that a man is an office-holder should weigh very much against him, or very much in his favor. My general feeling is that each man ought to be taken at his real worth . . .

I presume you have already received copies of the jury article. I did not put anything on it to indicate from whom it was because I thought it better that our committee should make a decision on that point before any definite label was put upon our publications. Of course, the general preface should also be in a large measure uniform, and I did not know what was the wish of the committee in that regard either.

I think the plan of Dr. Du Bois has some good points in it toward which we should work, but I have the feeling that it is rather large and complicated for our present purposes.[23] I do not know how much experience you have had in dealing with large numbers of colored people, but my own experience leads me strongly to the feeling that the smaller the number, the more effectively one can work. I have written Dr. Du Bois that my thought is that if we can make a success of a committee of twelve for a year or two, we will then be in a position to take on a larger number. Then, too, since a good portion of our work will be confidential, I think we should go slowly in revealing ourselves to men unless we are very sure that they can be thoroughly trusted . . .

By this mail I send you a dozen copies of a circular which I have just printed on lynching. Very truly yours,

Booker T. Washington[24]

BOOKER T. WASHINGTON

Hotel Manhattan, New York City. March 27th, 1904

Dear Mr. Scott: Perhaps you can take up and arrange in a private manner with Mr. [Arthur D.] Langston of St. Louis the program for Negro Day.[25] I prefer to let Du Bois draw his own crowd, and I will draw mine. I understand that there will be two or three sessions. Very truly,

B.T.W.[26]

IDA B. WELLS-BARNETT

Booker T. Washington and His Critics

Industrial education for the Negro is Booker T. Washington's hobby. He believes that for the masses of the Negro race an elementary education of the brain and a continuation of the education of the hand is not only the best kind, but he knows it is the most popular with the white South. He knows also that the Negro is the butt of ridicule with the average white American, and that the aforesaid American enjoys nothing so much as a joke which portrays the Negro as illiterate and improvident; a petty thief or a happy-go-lucky inferior . . .

There is a Negro faculty at Tuskegee, some of whom came from the masses, yet have crossed lances with the best intellect of the dominant race at their best colleges. Mr. Washington knows intimately the ablest members of the race in all sections of the country and could bear testimony as to what they accomplished before the rage for industrial schools began. The Business League, of which he is founder and president, is composed of some men who were master tradesmen and business men before Tuskegee was born. He therefore knows better than any man before the public to-day that the prevailing idea of the typical Negro is false.

But some will say Mr. Washington represents the masses and seeks only to depict the life and needs of the black belt. There is a feeling that he does not do that when he will tell a cultured body of women like the Chicago Woman's Club the following story:

"Well, John, I am glad to see you are raising your own hogs." "Yes, Mr. Washington, ebber sence you done tole us bout raisin our own hogs, we niggers round here hab resolved to quit stealing hogs and gwinter raise our own." The inference is that the Negroes of the black belt as a rule were hog thieves until the coming of Tuskegee.

There are those who resent this picture as false and misleading, in the name of the hundreds of Negroes who bought land, raised hogs and accumulated those millions of which they were defrauded by the Freedmen's Savings Bank, long before Booker Washington was out of school. The men and women of to-day who are what they are by grace of the honest toil on the part of such parents, in the black belt and out, and who are following in their footsteps, resent also the criticism of Mr. Washington on the sort of education they received and on those who gave it.

They cherish most tender memories of the northern teachers who endured know that the leaders of the race, including Mr. Washington himself, are the direct product of schools of the Freedmen's Aid Society, the American Missionary Association and other such agencies which gave the Negro his first and only opportunity to secure any kind of education which his intellect and ambition craved. Without these schools our case would have been more hopeless indeed than it is; with their aid the race has made more remarkable intellectual and material progress in forty years than any other race in history . . .

That one of the most noted of their own race should join with the enemies to their highest progress in condemning the education they had received, has been to them a bitter pill. And so for a long while they keenly, though silently, resented the gibes against the college-bred youth which punctuate Mr. Washington's speeches. He proceeds to draw a moral therefrom for his entire race. The result is that the world which listens to him and which largely supports his educational institution, has almost unanimously decided that college education is a mistake for the Negro. They hail with acclaim the man who has made popular the unspoken thought of that part of the North which believes in the inherent inferiority of the Negro, and the always out spoken southern view to the same effect.

This gospel of work is no new one for the Negro. It is the South's old slavery practice in a new dress. It was the only education the South gave the Negro for two and a half centuries she had absolute control of his body and soul . . .

No human agency can tell how many black diamonds lie buried in the black belt of the South, and the opportunities for discovering them become rarer every day as the schools for thorough training become more cramped and no more are being established. The presidents of Atlanta University and other such schools remain in the North the year round, using their personal influence to secure funds to keep these institutions running. Many are like the late Collis P. Huntington, who had given large amounts to Livingston[e] College, Salisbury, North Carolina.[27] Several years before his death he told the president of that institution that as he believed Booker Washington was educating Negroes in the only sensible way, henceforth his money for that purpose would go to Tuskegee. All the schools in the South have suffered as a consequence of this general attitude, and many of the oldest and best which have regarded themselves as fixtures now find it a struggle to maintain existence. As another result of this attitude of the philanthropic public, and this general acceptance of special educational standards for the Negro, Tuskegee is the only endowed institution for the Negro in the South.

Admitting for argument's sake that its system is the best, Tuskegee could not accommodate one-hundredth part of the Negro youth who need education. The Board of Education of New Orleans cut the curriculum in the public schools for Negro children down to the fifth grade, giving Mr. Washington's theory as an inspiration for so doing. Mr. Washington denied in a letter that he had ever advocated such a thing, but the main point is that this is the deduction the New Orleans school board made from his frequent statement that previous systems of education were a mistake and that the Negro should be taught to work. Governor Vardaman, of Mississippi, the other day in his inaugural address, after urging the legislature to abolish the Negro public school and substitute manual training therefor, concluded that address by saying that all other education was a curse to the Negro race.[28]

This is the gospel Mr. Washington has preached for the past decade. The results from this teaching then would seem to be, first, a growing prejudice in northern institutions of learning against the admission of Negro students; second, a contracting of the number and influence of the schools of higher learning so judiciously scattered through all the southern states by the missionary associations, for the Negro's benefit; third, lack of a corresponding growth of industrial schools to take their places; and fourth, a cutting down of the curriculum for the Negro in the public schools of the large cities of the South, few of which ever have provided high schools for the race.

Mr. Washington's reply to his critics is that he does not oppose the higher education, and offers in proof of this statement his Negro faculty. But the critics observe that nowhere does he speak for it, and they can remember dozens of instances when he has condemned every system of education save that which teaches the Negro how to work . . .

Does some one ask a solution of the lynching evil? Mr. Washington says in substance: Give me money to educate the Negro and when he is taught how to work, he will not commit the crime for which lynching is done. Mr. Washington knows when he says this that lynching is not invoked to punish crime but color, and not even industrial education will change that.

Again he sets up the dogma that when the race becomes taxpayers, producers of something the white man wants, land owners, business, etc., the Anglo-Saxon will forget all about color and respect that race's manhood . . . It is indeed a bitter pill to feel that much of the unanimity with which the nation today agrees to Negro disfranchisement comes from the general acceptance of Mr. Washington's theories.

Does this mean that the Negro objects to industrial education? By no means. It simply means that he knows by sad experience that industrial education will not stand him in place of political, civil and intellectual liberty, and he objects to being deprived of fundamental rights of American citizenship to the end that one school for industrial training shall flourish. To him it seems like selling a race's birthright for a mess of pottage.

They believe it is possible for Mr. Washington to make Tuskegee all it should become without sacrificing or advocating the sacrifice of race manhood to do it. They know he has the ear of the American nation as no other Negro of our day has, and he is therefore molding public sentiment and securing funds for his educational theories as no other can . . .

The demand from this class of Negroes is growing that if Mr. Washington can not use his great abilities and influence to speak in defense of and demand for the rights withheld when discussing the Negro question, for fear of injury to his school by those who are intolerant of Negro manhood, then he should be just as unwilling to injure his race for the benefit of his school. They demand that he refrain from assuming to solve a problem which is too big to be settled within the narrow confines of a single system of education.[29]

EMMETT JAY SCOTT

Tuskegee, Alabama. July 13, 1904

Dear Mr. Washington: In a recent editorial which appears in the Guardian July 2nd, is the following sentence: "We do not wish to misrepresent the views of any one, much less of so good a friend as Register Lyons, whose repugnance to our being jailed by the *Tuskegeean*, we shall ever appreciate."

Little by little, the names of the persons who have stood behind Trotter, are being revealed. I have marked this editorial and shall keep it for future use. Very truly,

Emmett J. Scott[30]

W.E.B. DU BOIS

Credo

I BELIEVE in God who made of one blood all races that dwell on earth. I believe that all men, black and brown and white, are brothers, varying, through Time and Opportunity, in form and gift and feature, but differing in no essential particular, and alike in soul and in the possibility of infinite development.

Especially do I believe in the Negro Race; in the beauty of its genius, the sweetness of its soul, and its strength in that meekness which shall yet inherit this turbulent earth.

I believe in pride of race and lineage and self; in pride of self so deep as to scorn injustice to other selves; in pride of lineage so great as to despise no man's father; in pride of race so chivalrous as neither to offer bastardy to the weak nor beg wedlock of the strong, knowing that men may be brothers in Christ, even tho they be not brothers-in-law.

I believe in Service—humble reverent service, from the blackening of boots to the whitening of souls; for Work is Heaven, Idleness Hell, and Wage is the "Well done!" of the Master who summoned all them that labor and are heavy laden, making no distinction between the black sweating cotton-hands of Georgia and the First Families of Virginia, since all distinction not based on deed is devilish and not divine.

I believe in the Devil and his angels, who wantonly work to narrow the opportunity of struggling human beings, especially if they be black; who spit in the faces of the fallen, strike them that cannot strike again, believe the worst and work to prove it, hating the image which their Maker stamped on a brother's soul.

I believe in the Prince of Peace. I believe that War is Murder. I believe that armies and navies are at bottom the tinsel and braggadocio of oppression and wrong; and I believe that the wicked conquest of weaker and darker nations by nations whiter and stronger but foreshadows the death of that strength.

I believe in Liberty for all men; the space to stretch their arms and their souls; the right to breathe and the right to vote, the freedom to choose their friends, enjoy the sunshine and ride on the railroads, uncursed by color; thinking, dreaming, working as they will in a king-dom of God and love.

I believe in the training of children black even as white; the leading out of little souls into the green pastures and beside the still waters, not for pelf or peace, but for Life lit by some large vision of beauty and goodness and truth; lest we forget, and the sons of the fathers, like Esau, for mere meat barter their birthright in a mighty nation.

Finally, I believe in Patience—patience with the weakness of the Weak and the strength of the Strong, the prejudice of the Ignorant and the ignorance of the Blind; patience with the tardy triumph of Joy and the mad chastening of Sorrow—patience with God . . .[31]

After Du Bois's "Credo" was published in October 1904, he was inundated with letters of support and desires to reprint it as a poster. One came from the registrar at Tuskegee, another from the offices of the Boston Guardian. *The "Credo," then, might have been one of the only statements on which both insti-tutions could agree, particularly as the fractures between the two camps were growing in the wake of the Carnegie summit. Still, it was designed to lift the pride of many who needed a formal ideology of hope explained to them, but also to provide a specific explanation of his ideology, to give people a clear idea of his beliefs to counter their already clear idea of Washington's.*[32]

JESSIE FAUSET

. . . I saw your article "Credo" sometime ago . . . I meant to write you to tell you how glad I was to realize that that was your belief, and to ask you if you did not believe it to be worth while to teach our colored men and women *race* pride, *self*-pride, self-sufficiency (the right kind) and the necessity of living our lives as nearly as possible, *absolutely*, instead of comparing them always with white standards. Don't you believe that we should lead them to understand that the reason we adopt such and such criteria which are also adopted by the Anglo-Saxon, is because these criteria are the best, and not essentially because they are white? This kind of distinction would in the end breed self-dependence and self-respect, and subjective respect means always sooner or later an outcome of objective respect. You, I should say, are in an excellent position to inculcate this doctrine, and to illustrate it by your splendid example. I am so proud, you know, to claim you on our side.

Living as I have nearly all my life in a distinctly white neighbor-hood, and for the past four years as the only colored girl in a college community [Cornell] of over 3,000 students, I have *had* to let people know that we too possess some of the best—or else allow my own personality to be submerged. It has been with much pleasure that I have pointed to you as an example of the heights to which it is possible for some of us to climb. It is with the same pleasure and sincerity that I tell you this now—in the desire that in the hour when your work—always arduous—grows irksome through apparent lack of appreciation, you may take heart by remembering that somewhere afar off, some one or other is "rendering unto Caesar the things which are Caesar's."[33]

BOOKER T. WASHINGTON

That the distinctive feature of Tuskegee Institute—ample provision for industrial training—has received in the public prints almost exclusive attention is not strange. But it is well to remember that Tuskegee Institute stands for education as well as for training, for men and women as well as for bricks and mortar.

Of course, the distinction involved in the words, "education" and "training," is largely theoretical. My experience convinces me that training to some productive trade, be it wagon-building or farming, educates. For example, one of our students is foreman on the large and beautifully planned Collis P. Huntington Memorial Building, now in process of construction; that young man is notable for a simple honesty, an unobtrusive confidence and self-reliance, that abundantly testify to his manliness. That this manliness is in large degree directly traceable to his skill and his experience in bearing industrial responsibility—in short, to his training—is beyond peradventure. Indeed, in running over the long list of students who, for one reason or another—lack of money or lack of taste for books—have left Tuskegee without completing the prescribed course in the Academic Department, I have been forcibly impressed with the fact that training to productive industry directly tends to develop sound judgment and manly independence—those qualities of the mind and heart that collectively constitute the character of the educated man.

Another example of the effect of the training given at the Tuskegee Institute on the mind of the student occurs to me. A few weeks ago it was decided to modify the Day School system. To make any change in a great organisation like ours requires great discriminating judgment and care. The faculty discussed the change in its every phase, and I finally called the students of the four upper classes together, presented to them our plans, and explained to them the reasons for the proposed change.

Their response was not a negative acquiescence, but a series of direct and searching questions. They were alert and quick to see minor defects, and to give direct and constructive criticism in regard to many details. Their work in the shops and on the farm had brought them into touch with real issues and real things—their daily work in constructing and equipping our buildings and in helping to build the institute had brought with it an intelligent interest in the school and an enlightened appreciation of values; in other words, it had taught them to think.

It is obvious that a man cannot build wagons or run a farm with continuous success who is unable to read, write, and cipher. But, far deeper than the mere commercial advantage of academic studies, is the fact that they afford incentives to good conduct and high thinking. To make a boy an efficient mechanic is good, for it enables him to earn a living and to add his mite to the productiveness of society; but a school must do more—must create in him abiding interests in the intellectual achievements of mankind in art and literature, and must stimulate his spiritual nature. And so Tuskegee has always maintained an Academic Department, at present housed mainly in four buildings . . .

The practical usefulness of the Academic Department lies in the aid which the study of physics and chemistry and mathematics and drawing offers to the blacksmith, the carpenter, the nurse, and the housewife—an aid that does much to transform listlessness and drudgery into vivacity and gratifying efficiency.[34]

SAMUEL H. COMINGS (*Comings was a white Southern author who championed a version of industrial education that appeared similar to that of Booker T. Washington.*)

Fairhope Ala. Nov'5th, 1904

Prof' DuBoies
My dear Sir,

I am quite disappointed in getting the letter I sent you back with no word of comment from you.[35] I sincerely hope you will not be personally offended at what you may feel is very severe criticism of your words in your able book. I have taken pains to heartily thank all the severest critics I have had and quote one who widely differs with me.

The study of this problem for both races is of too much importance to us all to warrant any personal feeling to blind our anxious eyes, if we can possibly avoid it. It seems to me you ought to see in my severe criticism of our own arrogant and silly race pride, that I am trying to be fair and even in my criticisms, and that I am as much alarmed for the future of all the Anglo Saxon civilization, as you can be for your own race.

In your book I noted with intense interest and pain your able description of the pathetic situation of so many of the "renters" on the old plantation and your picture is well and correctly drawn; but do you know that in Mo'[,] Kansas, Arkansas, Ill, and all the So'West, the white "renters" are almost if not quite as badly off, and drifting into a "Serf class" and a serf condition, as pitiable, and undemocratic, as your picture of your own people in the cotton belts. Single men coming to own whole counties, or towns and their "Rack-rents" eating all the products except the barest subsistence for their tenants, of their own race.

However we may differ now as to details, let us work together for the one common end and aim, the uplift of a true *Democracy*, a higher idea of *Human Brotherhood*. We may be either of us mistaken as to details, but let us agree on the general effort at the same end, and we will come to unity as to means in time in essentials.

Cordially Yours
S.H. Comings.[36]

W.E.B. DU BOIS

Nov. 18, 1904

My Dear Mr. Comings:

Do not for a moment think that I was offended by your criticism. I am quite used to being differed with as all thinking beings must be. I confess however that some of your errors seem to be so obvious that they make me impatient of even attempting reply. The chief of these are:

1. Your assumption that educated Negroes are idle & vicious

2. Your assumption that industrial schools can be made self supporting

3. Your assumption that present methods of study are simply memorizing

4. Your assumption that mental labor is not creative work

5. Your failure to see that the making of good "hands" out of Negroes, with little mental culture & no enlightened leaders will but educate a docile mass of workmen who can be used as [a] club to beat union white labor into submission.

I cannot argue these points at length but will simply assert that (1) is absolutely false—not that no educated Negro is idle or vicious but that certainly the overwhelming majority of those educated by present methods are good & useful citizens. As proof of this in the case of a single institution I enclose a leaflet on the work of our graduates. Similar data is available from nearly every Negro college. If you want to test these facts write to the towns where these people work & find out. That the history of Hampton, Tuskegee, Talladega & some dozen other industrial schools has long since proven the falsity of; in proof of this I enclose a paper. (2) That every modern course of study recognizes the value of manual training & laboratory methods. Certainly we also at A.U. [believe that] of all creative labor that of the mind is the highest & best; and the mass of men who preach exclusive industrial education for Negroes are simply welding new shackles for workingmen white & black.

On the other hand I agree with you on the following points:

1. The importance of well-trained handicraftsmen
2. The value of physical labor for brain workers
3. The value of manual training for children
4. The danger of despising manual toil.

I trust this will make my position clearer. I still stick to the thesis "Teach workers to work & thinkers to think" but I do not mean by this that workers should not think, nor that thinkers should despise manual toil. I mean merely that in the limited time given us to live we must specialize and that with all his thinking the mason must bend his chief energy to laying bricks & that with all his chopping trees, Gladstone must first of all guide empires.

With all this I still agree with you that there is far too much thoughtless toil & far too little knowledge of the material world among thinkers.

W.E.B. Du Bois[37]

ISAAC MAX RUBINOW (*Rubinow was a statistician and socialist economist who helped pioneer state and federal social security and health insurance plans.*)[38]

Washington Nov. 10 1904

Dear Professor Du Bois,

Some time ago I came across an item in the Washington Post quoting your address before an Iowa meeting, as saying that you considered the Negro question a part of the general social problem of distribution of wealth. There were other things ascribed to you which I am quite sure you could not have said—as for instance that the colored student was a menace to the white race—and similar things characteristic of the careless writing of our newspapers. I am sorry that I have lost the clipping—you would probably find it amusing. But your main point of view—as to the identity in the final analysis of the race problem with the whole social or labor problem—if you have been quoted correctly—is what made me write to you. It is a point of view that I have always held and that you will find widespread among the more educated socialists of this country—that the actual foundation of the race prejudice is the desire of the stronger to exploit the weaker, though of course historical causes have contributed to the survival of these prejudices—and that the present tendencies in regard to the treatment of the Negro are also largely explained by the same desire of exploitation—that only through emancipation of the whole working class can the emancipation of the negro be brought about. Now this is no desire to instruct you, but merely an effort to find whether there are any points of contact between your point of view and the Socialist doctrine, to which I adhere . . . I must say that even among certain groups of socialists the Negro problem is not fully understood, and the new Southern members of the movement have not altogether succeeded in freeing themselves from the prejudices that arose in chattel slavery, and persist in wage slavery. But I imagine you will agree that the Socialist party is the only organization in the country that moves in the right direction. It always appeared to me extremely naive to point to acquisition of private capital and bank accounts as a solution of the problem—for the mass of negroes can no more expect to become all capitalists, than the mass of white men can. Mr. B. Washington's is a remedy for the *few*, while what is necessary is relief for the *many*.

I should be happy to have the opportunity to discuss that matter with you . . .

Sincerely yours,
I.M. Rubinow[39]

WALTER FRANCIS WILLCOX (*Willcox was a statistician who taught at Cornell University.*)

Ithaca, New York, Nov. 14, 1904

Dear Mr. Washington: Thank you for your letter of November 9th about the amount of property accumulated by negroes. I am inclined to think that the figures of the last Census make it safe to venture a very rough estimate on the subject and am pleased to find that your general conclusion derived independently and from different data is in fair agreement with mine. I am disposed at present to set it down at about 300,000,000, and probably neither less than two hundred and fifty or more than three hundred and fifty. I have submitted my argument in manuscript to Professor Du Bois of Atlanta, who is a member with me of a committee of the American Economic Association on this subject, and he thinks my figures should be raised fifty million dollars. I have submitted them also to Mr. L.G. Powers of the Census Office and he agrees with them.[40] At present I am not disposed to agree with Professor Du Bois that they are too small, but shall carry on a discussion with him by correspondence in the hopes that we may eventually reach an agreement and so unanimously report. With renewed thanks for your full reply I remain, Yours sincerely,

W.F. Willcox[41]

BOOKER T. WASHINGTON

Crawford House, Boston, Mass. November 23, 1904

My Dear Mr. [Hugh Mason] Browne: Your letter received; would it not be a good plan to print under the words, "Committee of Twelve," on your letter heads, "For the advancement of the interests of the Negro race?"

I have asked Mr. Scott to send you from Tuskegee, the list of names I think it would be well to send the "Grimke Article." Dr. Du Bois' letter[42] is very interesting and instructive as well. I very much fear you will be in danger of ass[ass]ination if you write him again. Very truly yours,

Booker T. Washington[43]

ROSCOE CONKLING SIMMONS (Simmons was a black journalist, devoted Republican, and acolyte of Washington.)[44]

New York, N.Y., December 13, 1904

My dear Uncle Booker: I want to call your attention to several things about the December number of "The Voice of the Negro," which are so directly flings at you, that if you cannot answer them, which no one would have you do, certainly you can refrain from contributing to its circulation, and adding dignity to its columns.

In an editorial on "What is a Good Negro," the two first paragraphs are as follows:[45]

"A 'good Negro' is one who says he does not want the ballot. He orates before his people and advises them against going into politics. He says to them 'Keep out of politics.' Go to the farms; keep quiet and let the whites handle the government." The next hits hard:

"'A good Negro' is one who says that his race does not need the higher learning; that what they need is industrial education, pure and simple. He stands up before his people and murders the truth and the Kings English in trying to enforce upon them the evils of a College Education and the beauties of a plow."

Now, sir, this is so clearly a thrust at you, that I can hardly reconcile the announcement that you are to contribute to the columns during the coming year.

In the announcements for 1905, after naming and presenting the photographs of about half dozen unknown characters, as some of those engaged, your cut accompanied by nine lines of three letters each, appears. I have seen your name first in the Atlantic Monthly announcement. And so bent are these people on having Dr. Du Bois, who is known not beyond the clique of academic theorists that infest the country, appear as great, if not greater, than you in the eyes of its readers, that on page 629, in the announcement of the January issue of their paper, they tell us "Dr. W.E. Burghardt Du Bois and Dr. Booker T. Washington" will contribute, and further, that "each man is known and respected among both races the country over," when there are millions of people who do not know Du Bois lives, and would not know if he should die; and on the other hand, your fame rests throughout the world. The plan is to have you and Du Bois contemporaneous. I object, and every body else objects, and the world has long ago registered its objection. If you cannot see through all of this, then like Ajax you are blind because you want to be. There are magazines that pay large sums of money to have things written about you; here is a little sheet seeking to humiliate you, and has always sought to do so, and announces in the same breath, that you have not only acquiesced in the humiliation, but will actually contribute to the spreading of the gospel among its readers.

Who is Du Bois? Who knows him? Who cares anything about him, or what he writes? What does he lead?

The world has long ago placed the laurel wreath of leadership, not only of a race, but of a thought, on your brow, and as long as I can see to write, none shall disturb it. And I intend to make you see these marplotic thrusts, even if you do not care to see them. The Colored American Magazine, by far the largest and best of these two publications, has a magnificent article on your worth and work in the last edition. It espouses the cause, and agrees with the world that you have no compeer in the world's estimate. And will you write for the one, and ignore, in your writings, the other? Nay, Nay. If there is any writing to be done, it should and must come this way.

Let me see you when you are here again. Most affectionately your nephew,

Roscoe

This case is something like one of your New York friends whom you have recently placed here. He writes alright, but how he does curse you in conversation. You and your friends![46]

Early in 1905, a delegation of leading anti-Washington leaders proposed a meeting with Theodore Roosevelt, a meeting that never happened largely because of Roosevelt's pro-Washington position. Most in that delegation would become part of the Niagara Movement later in 1905.[47]

ALEXANDER WALTERS AND KELLY MILLER

Boston, January 13, 1905-

Prof. W.E.B. Du Bois
Dear Sir:

At conference held at Mr. Trotter's office today it was agreed that a committee of representative men should visit the President and present broad lines of policy which we desire him to pursue concerning the colored race.

Three definite propositions have been suggested:

First: That the facilities of the Attorney General's office be utilized to uphold the Fifteenth Amendment in connection with cases that may be brought in the Supreme Court, testing the constitutionality of the revised Constitutions of the South.

Second: To wield the influence of the administration to carry out the Interstate Commerce Clause of the Constitution affecting Interstate traffic including the passenger service.

Third: To encourage national aid to education in the most needy States . . .

It is thought best not to include any known office seeker or office holder on the Committee . . .

If you approve of this will you serve with the following gentlemen as a committee on arrangements . . .

> Yours truly,
> A. Walters
> Kelly Miller[48]

W.E.B. DU BOIS

[undated]

Dear Bishop Walters:

I shall be glad to act with the committee suggested in your letter of the 13th. I suggest as additional members to the committee:
W.M. Morris of Minneapolis, Minn.
A.H. Grimke of Boston, Mass.
C.E. Bentley of Chicago

> W.E.B. Du Bois[49]

The end of Du Bois's participation in the Committee of Twelve, which would continue without him until 1908, would, to David Levering Lewis, make the strained relationship finally and fully irreparable. "There was no turning back now for Du Bois," wrote Lewis, "no more socially correct sojourns at Tuskegee, no further charades of compromise and cooperation." If the split began with the Kowaliga school controversy in 1898 and it became official with the publication of The Souls of Black Folk, *it became a chasm too wide to cross with Du Bois's resignation from the Committee.*[50]

W.E.B. DU BOIS

Atlanta, Ga., March 21, 1905

My dear Messrs. Grimke and Miller:

You will remember that at the first suggestions of a meeting with Mr. Washington my determination communicated to both of you was to enter into no organization controlled by Mr. Washington where he would have me at his mercy by simply having his men outvote me. This position I have always maintained. There was at the New York meeting no obligation expressed or implied that I intended to enter into any permanent organization. I was asked to make some suggestion to keep the meeting from being an utter failure and I suggested the committee of 12. Moreover I went further than this and outlined the possible work and organization of such a committee. This plan I sent to Mr. Washington and Mr. Browne and it was essentially ignored. It was my unalterable decision from the first that unless the committee was so organized as to allow real work by individual members that I would not be a member of it. I was going to St. Louis with the ultimatum: if this committee is to be delivered into the power of Mr. Washington and his followers, I will not serve.

Meantime I was taken ill and cancelled all engagements. The next thing I heard, about the middle of July [1904], was that a meeting had been called in New York "to meet my convenience" and that the meeting had done precisely what I had expected: namely, turned the whole organization into Mr. Washington's hands. I had received absolutely no intimation that the meeting was to be held in New York. I was at the time in Des Moines, Iowa and could not have attended if I had received notice, as I was still unwell.

There was one course left to me and that was to resign. That I did and that resignation stands today. Under no circumstances will I withdraw it.

I am of course sorry to lose the cooperation of you two gentlemen. I count it a great misfortune to the Negro race when two clear headed and honest men like you can see their way to put themselves under the dictation of a man with the record of Mr. Washington. I am sorry, very sorry to see it. Yet it will not alter my determination one jot or tittle. I refuse to wear Mr. Washington's livery, or to put on his collar. I have worked this long without having my work countersigned by Booker Washington or laid out by Robert Ogden, and I think I'll peg along to the end in the same way.[51]

I beg however that neither of you feel at any time or under any circumstances obliged to defend the sincerity of my beliefs or the good faith of my actions. That I trust future history will attend to, and if not it is a small thing anyhow and so let it go. At present I propose to fight the battle to the last ditch if I fight it stark alone.

Very respectfully yours,
W.E.B. Du Bois[52]

BOOKER T. WASHINGTON

Tuskegee Institute, Alabama. January 23, 1905

Personal

My dear Mr. [Hugh Mason] Browne: I take for granted that the enclosed letter is a copy of one sent to all the members of the Committee including Mr. Grimke and Prof. Du Bois; I am very anxious that they see that their resignations are not affecting our work.

Now as to future work, I am wondering if we could not get up some little newspaper squibs bearing upon the decrease in lynching during the last three or four months. This would tend, I think, to encourage the white and colored people. If I have the facts correctly in my mind, I think you will find that there was no lynching in November, only two in December, and so far none have occurred in January. These figures will have to be verified, however, by direct information from the Chicago Tribune.

I have been much on the train lately and have not been able to keep in touch with you, but I shall hope to do so hereafter. I am to be in Philadelphia during the first week in February and perhaps we can have a conference. Yours truly,

Booker T. Washington[53]

NOTES

1. Lewis, 1993, 307–309.

2. Aptheker, 1971, 118–126; Lewis, 1993, 309–311; and Du Bois, 1973, 104.

3. Jones is writing on behalf of *Collier's Weekly*, edited by Robert T. Collier. Du Bois's first reply has not been saved. Du Bois, 1973, 72–73.

4. Du Bois, 1973, 73.

5. Ibid.

6. Ibid., 73–74.

7. Robert Russa Moton was the commandant of cadets at Hampton Institute, a position similar to dean of students. He was a close ally of Washington, president of his National Negro Business League. In 1915, after Washington's death, Moton would take over Tuskegee. See Moton, 1921.

8. Washington here refers to William Henry Baldwin, railroad magnate and Tuskegee trustee. See Du Bois, 1940, 78.

9. Washington, 1977, vol. 7, 407.

10. Charles W. Hare was a white local from Tuskegee, as was George W. Campbell. R.O. Simpson was from Furman, Alabama. All were on Tuskegee's board of trustees, and Campbell was its president. See *Twenty-Fourth*

Annual Catalogue of the Tuskegee Normal and Industrial Institute, 1904–1905, 1905.

11. Educator Hugh Mason Browne was a longtime Washington ally. Washington gave him credit as the source for his "cast down your bucket" metaphor during his Atlanta Exposition speech. He attended the January 1904 Washington–Du Bois New York conference. Browne, Washington, and Du Bois were designated to be selected what would become the Committee of Twelve for the Advancement of the Negro Race. Du Bois, "The Problem of the Twentieth Century Is the Problem of the Color Line," *Pittsburgh Courier*, 14 January 1950.

12. Washington, 1977, vol. 7, 409–411.

13. See Chapter 7, note 1.

14. Washington, 1977, vol. 7, 412.

15. Ibid., 414–415.

16. Coal contractor Allerton D. Hitch wrote to Washington after reading the critique of him in *The Souls of Black Folk*. Ibid., 417.

17. Ibid., 416–417.

18. Ibid., 449.

19. Ibid., 451–452.

20. See Chapter 9, note 46.

21. Washington, 1977, vol. 7, 453.

22. Hugh Mason Browne had argued that no appointed government official should be eligible to serve on the Committee of Twelve. Ibid., 460.

23. Du Bois proposed a large general committee divided into six subcommittees for political action, legal redress, social reform, defense and information, economic cooperation, and finance. Ibid.

24. Ibid., 459.

25. Arthur D. Langston was an Oberlin-educated teacher in the St. Louis public school system. For the bulk of his career, he served as principal of Dessalines School in the city. Wright, 2002, 80.

26. Washington, 1977, vol. 7, 478.

27. Collis Potter Huntington was one of the most influential railroad magnates of the 19th century. Along with Livingstone, Huntington also gave large sums to Hampton. See Lavender, 1998.

28. James K. Vardaman served as governor of Mississippi from 1904 to 1908. He was an unabashed racist who even advocated lynching as a remedy to black militancy. Wells's point was repeated by many of Washington's critics, namely that his stance on black education gave racists like Vardaman an excuse to deny funding to liberal arts education. See Holmes, 1970.

29. Wells-Barnett, April 1904, 518–521.

30. Washington, 1979, vol. 8, 17.

31. Du Bois, 6 October 1904, 787.

32. Du Bois, 1973, 81; Lewis, 1993, 312; and "Reminiscences of W.E.B. Du Bois," NXCP89-A80, Columbia University Oral History Collection, Butler Library, Columbia University, New York, 159.

33. Aptheker, 1969, 900.

34. Washington, *Working With the Hands*, 1904, 82–97.

35. Samuel Huntington Comings's 1904 book *Pagan Versus Christian Civilizations* criticized Du Bois based on a misunderstanding of his *Souls of Black Folk*, claiming a radical democracy but belying an obvious racism. Du Bois, 1973, 78–79. See also, Comings, 2011.

36. Du Bois, 1973, 78–79.

37. Ibid., 80–81.

38. Brown and Fee, 2002, 1224–1225.

39. Du Bois, 1973, 81–82.

40. Le Grand Powers was chief statistician for the United States Bureau of the Census in charge of agriculture. Powers, 1902, 764.

41. Washington, 1979, vol. 8, 131.

42. Du Bois wrote to Browne that "under no circumstances whatsoever is my name to be used in connection with the so-called 'Committee of Twelve,' nor do I wish any further communication concerning it." Ibid., 146.

43. Ibid.

44. Simmons, born in 1881, was in his early twenties in 1904, but would later make his name at the *Chicago Defender* and with Republican presidential administrations like that of Herbert Hoover. Kaye, 2003, 79–98.

45. Simmons is citing "What Is a Good Negro," December 1904, 618.

46. Washington, 1979, vol. 8, 154–156.

47. Du Bois, 1973, 92.

48. Ibid., 92–93.

49. Ibid., 93.

50. Lewis, 1993, 311.

51. For Ogden, see Chapter 7, and Chapter 9, note 63.

52. Du Bois, 1973, 105–106.

53. Washington, 1979, vol. 8, 179.

12

The Machine

Booker T. Washington, for all of his better qualities, lorded power over black political appointments, the black press, and white philanthropy to black causes, and his sensitivity to criticism (such as that in The Souls of Black Folk*) often made him vindictive, bringing the full force of what became known as the "Tuskegee Machine" to bear on his opponents.*

Du Bois, for his part, was perhaps frustrated most by Washington's control of the black press, and made his frustrations clear in a 1905 editorial in Voice of the Negro, *in which he accused Washington of bribing newspapers to control their content. The charges were vague, seemed to many like sour grapes, and earned Du Bois a significant backlash. Privately, however, he systematically demonstrated the reasons for his public accusations.*[1]

BRADLEY GILMAN *(Gilman was a Unitarian clergyman, a Harvard graduate, and a close ally of Washington.)*[2]

Boston Mass. Jan 25/1905

My dear Mr Washington, I had a long talk last week with Mr Alexander editor of the "Colored Citizen," of this city.[3] He presented the work of his paper mainly. He also went over the situation here in Boston and New England, so far as it is being affected by the "Guardian."

Later, after a talk with Rev. Edward Cummings, of the South Congl. Church,[4] it was agreed by us two that I should write you this letter to ask advice.

I think that you believe that the best and only wise way in which the Guardian's evil work can be met is by making the "Colored Citizen" as good a competing paper as possible.

To do this, money is needed. Now what do you think of the plan of Cummings and myself taking from you a list of a dozen or more generous white men of Boston, and trying to get them interested in backing the "Citizen"? . . .

I suggested to Mr Dole, president of the Twentieth Century Club, that we have Prof. Du Bois speak before that club, when he is in Boston. Some of us would like to ask him some questions.[5]

I have heard it asserted strongly that Atlanta University gives money to the "Guardian," thinking that by aiding it to cripple your work, more attention and aid will be given it. Do you suppose that can be true? Very truly yours

Bradley Gilman[6]

CHARLES ALEXANDER (*Alexander was the editor of the* Colored Citizen, *one of the papers backed by Washington in order to drive William Trotter's* Boston Guardian *out of business in Boston.*)

Boston, Mass., February 6th, 1905

My Dear Doctor Washington: I have hesitated for sometime to write you this letter for many reasons. I did not like the idea of calling to your attention matters that would have a tendency to make you feel uncomfortable, and for this reason I have delayed writing about a very important matter which I have discovered here in Boston. I think you ought to know that a certain element of Bostonians, the so-called four hundred, have organized very strongly to kill the influence of the Boston Colored Citizen. They have circulated all sorts of reports concerning the paper and have made it impossible in many instances for us to secure news items that would be of real value to the paper . . . I hope you will see the necessity of helping in this matter. We cannot win out unless we have funds with which to win out. I am doing a very good business at this time but the money which I earn in my printing business is consumed in the paper. The paper is paying now about 25% of its actual cost. It is increasing steadily in circulation and in efficiency as a news medium, but the advertising patronage has not increased and is not likely to increase except I can find someone who will work steadily on that particular department, and no one is willing to do that unless I offer good pay at the very start. I need immediately about two hundred and fifty dollars ($250) to fight this fellow to a finish. I am sure that if I can tell my lawyer that I have funds at my command to meet the demands of the court, that there will be no trouble of swamping him. I have not purchased the cylinder press which I proposed for the reason that I could not do so owing to the obligations which must be promptly met in order to save my honor and name among people who are known to and by this fellow Trotter.

You probably know that they are getting up a great banquet here in honor of Professor Du Bois of Atlanta. I thought at first that I would accept their invitation and subscribe two dollars and attend the thing in order to see just what would be said, but upon second thought I decided not to go and have held up the letter which I wrote this morning. I do not think that I can advance our interest by subscribing even five cents to the other fellow's scheme. Professor Du Bois wrote me a very ugly letter recently which showed a spirit not at all becoming a man of his great experience and large scholarship. Again, I very much fear that if I attended the affair I would come in contact with Trotter and he would say something to insult me, and if he insulted me, I am very sure that I could not refrain from striking back as is my nature, and in thus I would bring disgrace upon myself and upon those who might be associated with me. I do not want to be the cause of any commotion or sensation in Boston and will not be unless circumstances arise over which I can have absolutely no control . . .

I have had many complimentary letters lately from some very distinguished white men in this community concerning my recent editorial regarding your visit to the West. Not a few have said that it is one of the best estimates of a great man that they had ever read. I received a beautiful letter from Elbert Hubbard, the editor of the Philistine in which he also commends the Citizen and agrees that my estimate of you is about as accurate as anything he had read.

I hope that you will give this letter your personal attention and will let me hear from you promptly. If you are in New York soon let me know. I must see you and talk it all over. I very much fear that vigorous protests are not being made here in Boston against the workings of Trotter and his element which means harm for us. I could explain more if I could see you, but long letters are not read and rarely digested. Sincerely yours,

Charles Alexander

Send what money you can to help in this matter. I am working hard to hold up the dignity and honor of the cause.[7]

EMMETT JAY SCOTT

[Tuskegee, Ala.] February 20, 1905

Personal

Dear Friend [Charles William Anderson]:[8] You were sent a wire today advising you to be in Washington during the inauguration so as to keep your eyes on the enemy.

The particular point is that Du Bois, Kelly Miller, Trotter, Grimke, and some of that crowd are to have special meetings during the inauguration, and are planning among other things, to call upon the President.

[Lafayette] Hershaw is arranging to resuscitate the Pen and Pencil Club for a banquet during inaugural week, and of course will be very anxious to feature your little Atlanta friend [Du Bois] as a big attraction.[9] The Wizard believes that it would be well for you to be on hand and if possible, as you easily can, secure an invitation to the Pen and Pencil Club banquet so as to meet the enemy on any ground that may be offered.

I have no word yet that I am to be there with you, as I should like to be. Perhaps however, the Doctor may decide in the end to have me go, but on this point I have no word yet . . .

Emmett J. Scott[10]

WHITEFIELD MCKINLAY (*McKinlay was a Washington, D.C., realtor and Republican operative who would, with Washington's help, eventually become Collector of the Port of Georgetown.*)[11]

Washington, D.C, Feby 22/05

Dr Mr Washington Yr telegram at hand. Kelly Miller called at my office today & remained some time & during the conversation I got the following names without [his] suspecting my object. He said that Bishop Grant will probably attend the Conference at his home tho he did not sign the memorial which has been sent to the Presdt. Neither Pinchback, Lyons, Dancy nor Terrell have been invited to the Conference, but I shall do all in my power to have Pinchback there to aid me in suppressing those ambitious only for notoriety.[12]

J W E Bowen; W E B Du Bois; Bishop A Walters; D.A. Straker; Rev Proctor, Atlanta; S.L. Corrodiers;[13] Kelly Miller; Archie Grimke; M. Trotter . . .

W McKinlay[14]

In January 1905, Du Bois published an editorial titled "Debit and Credit" in Voice of the Negro *accusing portions of the black press of conspiring to prop up Washington and the Tuskegee ideal against their better judgment because of blatant bribery. The magazine, published in Atlanta by Du Bois's friend Jesse Max Barber, soon began to lose advertisers, and Du Bois received many angry responses. (Among them were letters from allies like William Hayes Ward and Oswald Garrison Villard, see hereunder.) In February 1905, the* Colored American *magazine also expressed its displeasure and called for Du Bois to be more specific about his accusations and show his sources. The cause of so much offense was "Debit 5," which charged that the Tuskegee Machine had paid $3,000 to bribe black newspaper editors and silence critics of Washington. The reaction was less a defense of Washington and more a retrenchment around the ethics of the black press, but that did not make the controversy any less heated.[15]*

WILLIAM EDWARD BURGHARDT DU BOIS

Debit and Credit
The American Negro In Account With . . .
The Year of Grace Nineteen Hundred and Four

DEBIT

1. To persistent disfranchisement of Negro voters in the South.
2. To the spread of "Jim Crow" car legislation to Maryland together with attempts in Missouri and in various cities.
3. To the lynching and burning of 100 or more unconvicted black men suspected of crime.
4. To a still threatening residuum of crime, poverty and ignorance among ourselves.
5. To $3000 of "hush money" used to subsidize the Negro press in five leading cities.

CREDIT

1. By a declaration of the Republican party against "special discrimination" in the elective franchise, emphasized by a plurality of two million votes.
2. By a defense of Negro womanhood at Indianola and Negro manhood at Charleston, ratified by the votes of the greatest majority ever given a president.
3. By the possession of over 12,000,000 acres of farm land.
4. By the accumulation of at least $350,000,000 worth of property.
5. By the elimination of 58 per cent, of our illiteracy since 1860.
6. By a reduction of our death rate in cities by 12 per cent, during the last decade, and a general reduction throughout the land.
7. By increased economic prosperity as shown by the
   (a) increase of housewives and decrease of women working in the fields.
   (b) decrease of farm laborers and increase of farmers.
   (c) increase of professional men, teachers, merchants, artisans, miners, salesmen and draymen.
8. By an aroused race consciousness, in the face of which it is no longer possible for any Negro to dare tell an American audience that Negroes ought not to vote until they are perfect, ought not to complain of "Jim Crow" cars until they own railroads, or that they ought not to go to college until they are rich.

To balance this account
we need
more courage, more patience
less cowardice and venality
and always
Work,
Work,
Work.[16]

EMMETT JAY SCOTT

[Tuskegee, Ala., ca. February 1905]

Personal

Dear Mr. [Frederick Randolph] Moore:[17] Dr. Washington has suggested that I write you rather freely as I am sure you would like to have me do, in regard to the February number of the Colored American Magazine. He does not feel that the treatment of the Du Bois matter, page 67, is dignified, and in fact thinks there is altogether too much of Tuskegee in this number, giving vindication to the impression that a great many enemies of the magazine have endeavored to foist on the general public.

Tuskegee appreciates most sincerely all that you and your magazine have done toward helping our work, but we would not for one minute have the magazine interfered with by any too general impression that it is a Tuskegee publication . . .

Emmett J. Scott[18]

WILLIAM HAYES WARD *(Ward was the publisher of the* Independent, *which often published Du Bois's work.)*

New York, Feb. 18, 1905.

My dear Professor Du Bois:—

I see a number of the colored papers are taking up your statement pretty vigorously about the five newspapers that sold out so cheap, and are asking you to give their names. Have you anything to say on the subject? What is the meaning of it? I am a little concerned in the matter. It is unpleasant to find that one whom we so heartily respect as you should be losing the sympathy of the colored people, as if you had been guilty of a slander. It is not at all incredible that what you said was true.

Very truly yours,
William Hayes Ward[19]

W.E.B. DU BOIS
(Personal & Confidential)

March 10, 1905

My Dear Dr. [William Hayes] Ward:

The only Negro papers that are taking vigorous exception to my plain statement are the ones who have sold out to the "Syndicate," viz: the N.Y. Age, the Chicago Conservator, the Boston Citizen, the Washington Colored American, the Colored American Magazine, & the Indianapolis Freeman. Two of these papers have recently died & one is sick seriously. Of course I do not propose to wash our dirty linen in public & consequently I shall say nothing further in print on the subject until I think a further warning necessary. What I have already said is absolutely true & is well known to leading colored men & provable by documentary evidence: viz that in order to forestall criticism of certain persons & measures money has been freely furnished a set of Negro newspapers in the principal cities; partly this has come as a direct bonus, part in advertising & all of it has been given on condition that these papers print certain matter & refrain from other matter. This movement has been going on now for 3 or 4 years until it is notorious among well-informed Negroes & a subject of frequent comment. You must not be at all worried at my losing the confidence of Negroes—I never had the confidence of those who are aroused over my declaration and never expect it.

W.E.B. Du Bois[20]

BOOKER TALIAFERRO WASHINGTON

New York, N.Y. March 11, 1905

Dear Mr. Scott: Enclosed I send you an editorial,[21] kindly pass it on to Davis of the Independent.[22]

I have urged Mr. Fortune to stop giving attention to Du Bois and The Voice, and I think this ought to be observed in all the rest of the Afro-American papers excepting the local papers in Atlanta.

By paying attention to them only advertises them all the more. Very truly yours,

B.T.W.[23]

BOOKER T. WASHINGTON

A Base Slander of the Afro-American Press (Draft)

In a recent issue of a magazine, published in Atlanta, Ga., one of the Professors of the Atlanta University makes the statement that $3000 of "Hush Money" had been used to subsidize the Afro-American Press in five of the leading cities.

This is a statement which calls for proof, explanation or retraction. No institution, for the uplifting of the Afro-American has stood out more strongly for forty years, than the Afro-American Press. Many of the Editors and publishers have almost pauperized themselves in standing for the rights of the race. The Afro-American press has held their columns open in defence of the Negro and has advocated his advancement and education in Industrial schools, Colleges and Universities.

From the inception to the present, the Afro-American press has stood loyally by the Atlanta University in all its struggles and its triumphs. At the present time, when there is existing a spirit of peace, harmony and unity, among our people all over the United States, such as has never existed before, for a Professor in the Atlanta University to make the bold bare statement that a large proportion of the Afro-American press has been bribed, is an insult to the race and to our Negro press, unless such a statement can be proven. We want the Professor to name the five leading cities and name the five newspapers. If he cannot do this, or does not, the race will decide to [that] in making this statement, the Professor had no other idea than to stir up strife, or to slander the Afro-American press.

As the matter now stands, every Negro paper and every city, according to the Professor, is now under suspicion. We know individuals and organizations that have and are spending money in order to enable a Negro paper to speak out in defence of the race, but we repeat we want the names of the papers who have received $3000 to prevent them speaking out their sentiments.[24]

Oswald Garrison Villard was the grandson of William Lloyd Garrison and the son of Henry Villard, founder of General Electric and owner of the New York Evening Post. *Villard took over the paper after his father's death. He also owned magazines such as the* Nation. *Villard donated much to Tuskegee and was a devout advocate of Washington until 1910, when he broke with Tuskegee to support Du Bois and to help found the NAACP. Still, his relationship with Du Bois would remain tense, if not strained, throughout.*[25]

OSWALD GARRISON VILLARD

New York City, February 7, 1905.

Professor W.E.B. Du Bois
My dear Sir:—

I notice in a recent publication over your name a statement that $3,000 was used in the year 1904 to purchase the influence of the colored press. As I take it for granted that you have not made so grave a charge without positive proof I write to ask you to kindly let us have the facts for publication in the Even Post.

Yours truly,
Oswald Garrison Villard[26]

W.E.B. DU BOIS

March 9 [1905]

My Dear Mr. [Oswald Garrison] Villard:

I thank you for your kind offer of the 7th inst. but beg leave to say that I have at present no further matter to publish on the subject.

You are quite right in taking it for granted that the grave charge was not made without positive proof and I should be glad, if you should wish, to furnish for your personal information the nature of the proof.

W.E.B. Du Bois[27]

OSWALD GARRISON VILLARD

New York, March 13, 1905.

Dear Dr. Du Bois,

In reply to your letter of the 9th, if you cannot submit your proof for publication I shall be glad to have it for my personal information. I cannot understand, however, your making such a charge without having proofs which you are willing to put into print. If we were to run our newspaper on this basis we should not get very far.

Your very truly,
Oswald Garrison Villard.[28]

W.E.B. DU BOIS

Atlanta, Ga., March 15 1905

Dear Trotter:

Please send me by return mail every scrap of evidence you have going to prove Washington's bribery of newspapers. Send me as many documents as possible, references to documents, illustrative facts & sources for further knowledge & information. I want this for the private conversion of an influential man and you can assure contributors that there will be no public use of their names without their consent. Give me facts & hurry them to me. Send a part at a time if necessary.

W.E.B. Du Bois[29]

WILLIAM MONROE TROTTER

Boston, Mass. March 18. '05

Dear Du Bois

I have sent one or two things more to-night. To-morrow I shall send you all the evidence I can find. It is necessarily of a circumstantial nature. Much depends upon the reasonableness of your prospective convert. Would to God I had the direct evidence. But we may get that yet. [E. E.] Cooper has it and I have written a man at D.C. to see him. [D.R.] Wilkins has the thing and I have written him to divulge to you.[30] Please return to me everything I send you.

Yours for the cause,
W.M. Trotter[31]

W.E.B. DU BOIS

Atlanta, Ga., March 24, 1905

(confidential.)

My dear Mr. [Oswald Garrison] Villard: In reply to your letter of the 13th inst, I am going to burden you with considerable matter. I do this reluctantly because it seems like imposing on a busy man. At the same time I want to say frankly that I have been sorry to feel in your two letters a note of impatience and disbelief which seems to me unfortunate and calling for a clear, even, if long, statement.

In the *Voice of the Negro* for January, I made the charge that $3000 of hush money had been used to subsidize the Negro press in five leading cities. The bases upon which that charge was made were in part as follows:

The offer of $3000 to the editor of the Chicago *Conservator* on 2 separate occasions to change its editorial policy, and the final ousting of the editor by the board of management, and the installing of an editor with the required policy; with the understanding that financial benefit would result. (Exhibit A.) The statement of the former editor of the Washington *Record* that he was given to understand that the *Record* received $40 a month from the outside to maintain its policy. (Exhibit B.)

The statement of one of the assistant editors of the Washington *Colored American* that it was worth to them $500 a year to maintain its policy. (Exhibit C.) There is similar testimony in regard to papers in other cities particularly the *Freeman* of Indianapolis, the *Age* of New York and the *Citizen* of Boston. All these papers follow the same editorial policy, print the same syndicated news, praise the same persons and attack the same persons. Besides the more definite testimony there is a mass (Exhibit D) of corrob[or]ative circumstantial evidence, and all this leads me to estimate that $3000 is certainly the lowest possible estimate of the sums given these 6 papers in the year 1904; I firmly believe that the real sum expended was nearer $5000 and perhaps more than that.

The object of this distribution of money and other favors was, I believe, to stop the attacks being made on the policy of Mr. B.T. Washington. The reason for this belief is as follows:

1. The fact that these papers praise all that Mr. Washington does with suspicious unanimity.

2. The existence of a literary bureau at Tuskegee under Mr. Washington's private secretary, Emmett Scott, (cf. Exhibit B and F. No. 2.)

3. The sending out of syndicated matter from the bureau to appear simultaneously in the above mentioned papers and several others. This appears often in the form of editorials. (Exhibit E.)

4. The change of policy toward Mr. Washington of such papers as the *Age*, which formerly bitterly opposed his policy.

5. The creation of new papers and buying up of old papers by Mr. Washington's friends or former employees. (Exhibit F.)

6. The rewarding of favorable newspapers by Mr. Washington. (Exhibit G.)

7. The abuse and warning of enemies through the syndicated papers, sending out of cartoons, etc. (Exhibit H.)

8. The use of political patronage to reward and punish.

Finally I was not the first to make this charge. It was common property among colored people, spoken and laughed about and repeatedly charged in the newspapers. (Exhibit J.)

What now ought to be the attitude of thinking Negroes toward this situation, assuming the facts alleged to be substantially true? Two things seem certain:

1. There was some time ago a strong opposition to Mr. Washington's policy developed among Negroes. In many cases this opposition became violent and abusive and in one case even riotous.

2. Since that time by the methods above described and also as the result of conference and statements by Mr. Washington, this opposition has been partially stopped.

Now personally I strongly oppose Mr. Washington's positions: those positions have been considerably modified for the better since the time of my first public dissent from them; but they are still in my mind dangerous and unsatisfactory in many particulars.

At the same time I have been very sorry to see the extremes to which criticism has gone. I anticipated this mud-slinging in my book and deprecated it, although I knew it would come. My rule of criticism has been, (a) to impute no bad motives (b) to make no purely personal attack. This has I think been adhered to in every single public utterance of mine on the subject hitherto. And when others have not adhered to it I have not hesitated to criticise them.

Moreover most of the criticism of Mr. Washington by Negro papers has not been violent. The *Conservator* was insistent but courteous; the *Record* under Cromwell was always moderate and saw things both to praise and condemn; The *Freeman* and *American* were open to the highest bidder on either side; the *Guardian* was at times violent although more moderate now than formerly, and has gained in standing as it has become less bitter. All this was a good sign. The air was clearing itself, the demand of the people known, and a healthy democratic out-come of the controversy seemed possible. It seemed at one time indeed possible that even the *Guardian* would see the situation in a better light. Then gradually a change came in. Criticism suddenly stopped in many quarters and fulsome adulation succeeded. Violent attacks on all opposers were printed in a certain set of papers. National organizations of Negroes were "captured" by indefensible methods. (Exhibit K.)

It thus became clearer and clearer to me and to others that the methods of Mr. Washington and his friends to stop violent attack had become a policy for wholesale hushing of all criticism and the crushing out of men who dared to criticise in any way. I felt it time to speak at least a word of warning.

I could not however make this warning as definite as I would have liked for three reasons.

1st. I did not want to drag Atlanta University into the controversy since the proceeding was altogether of my own initiative.

2nd. I did not want to ask those who privately gave me information to do so publicly. They are poor men and if, for instance, Mr. Cromwell, a teacher in the Washington Colored schools, were to testify as to the facts in public he might lose his position.[32]

3rd. I uttered the warning to a Negro audience and it was addressed particularly to them; so far as possible I want to keep the internal struggles of the race in its own ranks. Our dirty linen ought not be exhibited too much in public.

For this latter reason many of my friends do not agree with me in the policy of speaking out. Kelly Miller, A.H. Grimke and others have repeatedly expressed to me that they are perfectly satisfied that Mr. Washington is furnishing money to Negro newspapers in return for their [the newspapers'] support. But they say: What are you going to do about it? He has the support of the nation, he has the political patronage of the administration, he has apparently unlimited cash, he has the ear of the white press and he is following exactly the methods of that press; and moreover his attitude on the race question is changing for the better. These are powerful arguments, but they do not satisfy me. I am however constrained by such representations to take up the matter cautiously and to see what warnings and aroused conscience in the race will do toward stopping this shameful condition of affairs.

On the other hand when I am convinced that the time has come, that bribery is still going on and gag law manifest, and political bossism saddled on a people advised to let politics alone, I will speak again in no uncertain words and I will prove every statement I make.

I regret to say that honest endeavors on my part in the past to understand and cooperate with Mr. Washington have not been successful. 'I recognize as clearly as anyone the necessity of race unity against a common enemy—but it must be unity against the enemy and not veiled surrender to them.' My attitude is not actuated by my sympathy with Mr. Trotter, editor of the Guardian. There was once a rumor that I was acting jointly with him. My reply to that was made in a letter to George F. Peabody, which I venture to enclose as Exhibit L.[33] I went into conference last winter with Mr. Washington and his friends. Mr. Washington selected the personnel of the conference and it did not altogether please me but I attended and urged such of my friends as were invited to come also. In that conference I did not beat around the bush but told Mr. Washington plainly and frankly the causes of our differences of opinion with him.

Mr. Washington replied in a very satisfactory speech and his friends asked me to draw up a plan of a central committee of 12. This I did. The resulting committee which I helped select was good save in two cases where I was overruled by Mr. Washington and his friend. I was taken ill during the summer and the meeting of the committee was postponed; finally the committee was organized at a meeting to which I was not invited, and of which I knew nothing till 2 weeks afterward. Whether this was by accident or design I do not know. At any rate the committee was so organized as to put the whole power virtually in the hands of an executive committee and the appointment of that committee was left to Mr. Washington. Upon hearing this some two weeks after, I resigned my membership. I could not conscientiously deliver my freedom of thought and action into the hands of Mr. Washington and his special abettors like Fortune.

I am still uncertain as to how Mr. Washington himself ought to be judged in the bribery matter. I especially condemn the bribe-takers and despise men like Fortune, Cooper, Alexander, Manly and Knox who are selling their papers.[34] If they agree with Mr. Washington and he wishes to help them, the contributions ought to be open and above board; and if the contrary is the case and it is, to my unwavering belief, in 3 or 4 of the above instances, these men are scamps. Mr. Washington probably would defend himself by saying that he is unifying the Negro press, that his contributions are investments not bribes, and that the Tuskegee press bureau is a sort of Associated Negro Press. The reply to this is that the transactions do not appear to be thus honorable, that the character of the matter sent out is fulsome in praise of every deed of Mr. Washington's and abusive toward every critic, and that the men who are conducting the enterprises are not the better type of Negroes but in many cases the worst, as in the case of Fortune, Cooper, Knox and Thompson.[35] (Exhibit M.)

In the trying situation in which we Negroes find ourselves today we especially need the aid and countenance of men like you. This may look to outsiders as a petty squabble of thoughtless self-seekers. It is in fact the life and death struggle of nine million men. It is easy of course to dismiss my contentions as the result of petty jealousy or short-sighted criticism—but the ease of the charge does not prove its truth. I know something of the Negro race and its condition and dangers, and while I am sure, and am glad to say, that Mr. Washington has done and is doing much to help the Negro, I just as firmly believe that he represents today in much of his work and policy the greatest of the hindering forces in the line of our true development and uplift. I beg to remain Very respectfully yours,

W.E.B. Du Bois

Exhibits A, B, C, D, E, F, G, H, J, K, L, M.

Please return.

Nota Bene. No attempt is made in the following exhibits to present all the evidence obtainable—I am simply giving typical examples of the sort of proof upon which I rely.

W.E.B.D . . .

Exhibit A (2).

Copy of a part of a letter to W.E.B.D. from Dr. Bentley.[36]

Chicago, March 18, 05.

. . . He was approached by a gentleman and his wife of this city who are upon intimate terms with B.T.W. They also have the respect of the community. They submitted the proposition: if he—[D.R.] Wilkins— would use the columns of the Conservator in support of the work done at Tuskegee and cease to criticise Washington as a leader, that the sum of $3000 per year would be paid quarterly to him in advance. He took the matter under advisement, he says; that receiving no answer they came a second time and repeated the proposition adding that if he did not agree in all Mr. Washington said he need not stultify himself; but to give unqualified support to his work at Tuskegee, and that they would trust to time for his conversion upon all things else as represented by Mr. Washington.

Later on Mr. W. came to Chicago to lecture at Quinn Chapel. After he had gone Mr. Allison Sweeney—late editor of the *Conservator*— approached Wilkins and said there was $3000 per year, in advance for him—Wilkins—if he would change the policy of the paper as regards B.T.W. Wilkins says you are at liberty to use this data as you see fit. He would not divulge the names of the man and wife—altho that would not be hard guessing—but had no hesitancy in calling Sweeney's name. He also says that Sweeney became editor largely upon the representation made by him to the stockholders—that certain substantial contributions could be had from B.T.W. if he were made editor.

The *Conservator*, as you may know has gone under through the mismanagement of Sweeney—and the Charter, good will and mailing list are now matters of litigation between its owners and Wilkins. He has no doubt of finally securing the paper. Some of us are helping him in the fight . . .

Hastily yours,
(Signed) C. E. Bentley . . .

Exhibit B.
Washington, D.C. March 18, 1905.

. . . While I was with the *Record* I got definite information that there was a literary bureau at Tuskegee. In the month of September 1903, Mr. Frank Manly one of the owners of that paper, almost immediately after the adjournment of the Business Men's Convention held at Richmond, left this city to take a place at Tuskegee.[37] Shortly after this items respecting Tuskegee and Mr. Washington appeared quite regularly. It was rare that this copy passed through my hands . . .

Very truly yours,
(Signed) J. W. Cromwell.
From the Washington *Bee*, March 11, 1905 . . .

Exhibit D.
Some of this proof is as follows:

1. The well known fact that the New York *Age* was in financial difficulties until its editor's intimate association with Mr. Washington began. The policy of the *Age* has in recent years been quite different than earlier.

2. The venality of the *Freeman* is proverbial. Its columns are for sale and have been offered to me indirectly, but plainly.

3. Mr. Charles Alexander, editor of the *Citizen* of Boston was quite without capital according to his statement to me in 1902, and is running his paper at a loss according to his sworn testimony in court.[38]

4. The printers of the Boston *Citizen* speak of it as B.T. Washington's paper.

5. The purchase of the *Colored American* magazine by representatives of Mr. Washington and its removal from Boston to New York. The present editor [Roscoe Conkling Simmons] a relative of Mrs. Washington and the business manager is Mr. Washington's assistant private secretary, Mr. [Richard Le Roy] Stokes. Mr. Stokes also acts as business manager of the *Age*. The former business manager of the Age [Jerome Bowers Peterson][39] was appointed to a consulship in South America on recommendation of Mr. Washington . . .

Exhibit F.

1. After the Boston "riot" against Mr. Washington, the Boston *Citizen* was started by P.J. Smith a former collecting agent employed in the North by Tuskegee.[40] He was succeeded in management by J. Will Cole, assistant editor of the *Colored American* of Washington D.C. Later Charles Alexander, formerly head of the printing department

of Tuskegee took charge. None of these men had ever before given evidence of having any capital themselves.

2. In that paper, notes like the following have appeared. "If Washington would notice this toad he would be satisfied, and, as a friend of that good man, I would suggest you mentioning to Washington that if he will invite this creature to dinner, or show him any courtesy whatever, he will cease his continued meanness, and sell himself for 'recognition.'"

• • •

This led to a libel suit and a cross suit.

Under cross examination of Mr. Alexander by Attorney Benjamin the following was brought out, in regard to the above article.

Question. To whom did you refer in your article?
Answer. The editor of the *Guardian*.
Q. By whom was it written?
A. I assume the responsibility of its authorship.
Q. By whom was it written?
A. I assume the responsibility of it. I could not tell who wrote it. In fact I wrote some of it.
Q. How did you get it?
A. Through the mail.
Q. Do you know who sent it?
A. Yes.
Q. Who sent it?
A. Mr. Emmett J. Scott.
Q. Where does he reside?
A. In Tuskegee, Alabama.

3. Mr. Wilford Smith who has formerly acted as Mr. Washington's lawyer in various cases and has spent considerable time at Tuskegee, came from New York, and offered the publishers of the Boston *Guardian* $500 for the outstanding notes of that paper which represented their full value.[41] He stated to the firm: "We have plenty of money behind us as you, of course, know . . ."

Exhibit J.
These charges have been made by several papers and very generally in private conversation for 2 or 3 years back. Recent instances are:

The Boston Guardian, July 30, 1904.

"We submit that in the evidence we have brought forth that there is a strong odor of corruption. Is it not corrupt for a man who is begging money for a philanthropic institution to be offering money for the notes of a Colored paper that is supposed to be in trouble? Can such a man legitimately secure the chief space in ten or a dozen weekly papers to boom himself? Can he legitimately hire a man to write for him in several papers each week? Is not corruption apparent when a newspaper arises from nobody knows what source, but espoused by men notoriously without money, who have been the employees or agents of a Negro educator, supposed to be, and which paper on some occasions has ten out of thirteen editorials in praise of said educator and whose columns are ever open for any attack on a paper that opposes him? Is a man corrupt who recommends corrupt men for political appointment, and who depends upon men of bad reputation to do his work for him?"

From the Washington Bee, March 11, 1905.

. . . We supported him loyally from the day he was nominated at Chicago, and we are willing to have the matter which appeared in our columns for the period covering the Presidential canvass compared with the matter which appeared in the columns of the known subsidized organs, and leave it to any just person to judge if our support was not as thorough and whole hearted as the support of the subsidized organs.

It is discouraging to say the least, to see those charged with the formation of the minds and characters of those who are to greatly influence the race resorting to the methods which have made Tweedism, Crokerism and Tammanyism synonyms for corruption and graft.

Exhibit K.

The Afro-American Council when it met in St. Paul in 1902 was 6 or 7 years old and in shape to do good honorable work. Its president was Bishop A. Walters of the Zion Church. His logical successor was Bishop Scott, a man of sterling honesty, recently sent by the white M.E. Church as bishop to Africa.[42] Mr. Washington and his private secretary appeared on the scene and to my astonishment announced his preference for T.T. Fortune as president. I pled with him because I knew the selection would kill the organization among decent Negroes. Mr. Washington was non-committal; Then by a scheme engineered by Mr. Washington's private secretary and Bill Pledger the chairman, the election was sprung on the body at the noon hour when a majority of the members were at dinner, and the proceeding was veiled under the guise of "accepting the report of the nominating committee." This the chairman ruled was equal to an election and installed Mr. Fortune over the protest of the majority of the body.

In 1903 the council met at Louisville. I refused to attend and went to Tuskegee to lecture to the summer school. Only last week a prominent lawyer in St. Paul, F.L. McGhee, explained the outcome there to me.[43] He said "We had them easily beaten and would have elected Bishop Scott president, when a lot of new voters qualified by paying their fees of $5 and beat us by re-electing Fortune. *It must have cost Washington over $300 to carry the organization!*" Fortune however was unable to do anything with the council and soon resigned the presidency. The organization is now practically dead . . .[44]

FRANCIS JACKSON GARRISON *(Garrison was the son of abolitionist William Lloyd Garrison and Oswald Garrison Villard's uncle.)*

The Cedars, [Lexington, Mass.] April 9, 1905

Dear Oswald [Garrison Villard]: I return the Du Bois letter & documents herewith, after showing them to Uncle William, who sympathizes with my view of the matter as expressed in my hasty letter of Friday to you. I do not know that I have much to add to what I then wrote. It will take a great deal more than what Du Bois has written or presented to shake my faith in Washington's purity of purpose & absolute freedom from selfishness & personal ambition. In spite of all the praise & honors & laudation that he is constantly receiving, I do not believe that he has any thought or purpose but the uplifting of his race, & I am sure that whatever he does is with that single object in view. Nor have I ever seen the slightest trace of personal jealousy, bitterness or resentment in him towards those who have been so despiteful towards him. His spirit & temper have been wonderfully calm & patient & enduring. Certainly the same cannot be said of Trotter & his sympathizers, & I cannot take any such stock in him as Du Bois does. I believe there is a vast deal of petty jealousy & spite in all this criticism of Washington, & I have never liked the bitterness betrayed by my friends the [Butler Roland] Wilsons, (Mrs. W. especially) & by Mrs. Bumstead, when B.T.W. was mentioned.[45] Their spirit seemed to me far, far below his, & their "atmosphere" was as unpleasant as his was inspiring. Trotter's behavior & speech at the mob meeting were that of a blackguard, & his purpose to wreck the meeting was deliberate.

Now as to the charges of subsidizing the negro press, the evidence offered by Du Bois is circumstantial & plausible, & I do not doubt that B.T.W. is doing all he can to influence the colored papers & secure unity rather than contention & discord, & this not because he cares for the attacks on himself, but because he knows that some of his assailants would gladly see Tuskegee wrecked if necessary to discredit & pull him down. He does show bad taste, or careless supervision of Scott, in allowing the latter to send fulsome praise of himself as syndicate matter. Theresa [Holmes Garrison] suggests that he may draw on his personal income ($7500) from the Carnegie gift for this press business.[46]

As for the men he influences, those mentioned by Du Bois are for the most part poor sticks, & like the mass of white politicians ready to sell their principles for an office or an income. I dare say Lewis would, though I have never heard before that B.T.W. had anything to do with his appointment, which was Roosevelt's reply to the taunt that he made colored appointments at the South only, & R. of course knew Lewis through his Harvard athletic career, which was sufficient without any prompting from W. I must close abruptly for the mail, but shall be glad to respond to any points which you may wish to ask specifically about. In haste, affecty

Uncle Frank

I see B.T.W. quotes you in the April Southern Workman (p.200) without naming you.[47]

OSWALD GARRISON VILLARD

[New York City] April 18th, 1905

Dear Dr. Du Bois, I found your long letter with its enclosures on my return from the South. I must say frankly that it will take a great deal more than the evidence you have presented to shake my faith in Mr. Washington's purity of purpose, and absolute freedom from selfishness and personal ambition. At the same time, the evidence would seem to show that the literary bureau at Tuskegee under Mr. Scott has been extremely injudicious. It also looks as if money aid had been given; but you have failed to substantiate your positive statement in the Voice of the Negro that three thousand dollars was the sum used, since you say the testimony "leads me to estimate." Several of your counts I do not think you substantiate at all, notably the use of political patronage. So far as your witnesses are concerned, I am unable to judge of their reliability . . .

I shall certainly speak to Mr. Washington about Scott's ac[tivities] and I think it would be a very good thing if you would let me submit the whole correspondence the next time he comes to New York. I want particularly to take him to task for your connection with the council, and ask him whether the apparent slight to you was not really due to accident. I think you made a great mistake in resigning from it.

I hold no brief for Mr. Washington. As my writings show, I am a sincere believer in the higher education of the negro, and I am doing what I can to help Atlanta and similar institutions. I may also lay claim to being a devoted friend to the race, to whose interests I am giving a very large share of my time. You will perhaps permit me therefore to say frankly that I greatly regret your position and your attitude towards Mr. Washington. I do not think that there are any essential differences between your positions. I do believe that for the masses of the negro race industrialism is the all-important question of the hour. It goes without saying that to have proper industrial schools we must have such institutions as Atlanta and Fisk to furnish proper instructors.

As for Trotter, he was under me at Harvard, and his father was a sergeant in my uncle's company in the 55th Massachusetts. I consider young Trotter a very dangerous, almost irresponsible, young man, whose conduct at the Boston riot should make it impossible for anyone to consider seriously his opinions upon any subject relating to his race.

In the hope that you will grant me the permission I desire, Yours very truly,

[Oswald Garrison Villard][48]

W.E.B. DU BOIS

Atlanta, Ga., April 20, 1905

Confidential

My dear Sir [Oswald Garrison Villard]: Good faith to my correspondents will not allow the proposed use of the matter sent you.

I trust you will not misinterpret my position: your attitude toward the Negro has been commendable; I am not seeking to change your opinions, I am merely showing you, at your own request, the reasons why my faith in Mr. Washington has been shaken.

It happens that in the same mail with your letter are two other letters. One is from a man who has edited a Negro newspaper 22 years; he says:

"But for the assistance Booker T. Washington has and is rendering the Cleveland O. *Journal* it would have been dead many weeks ago. The same is true of the Boston *Colored Citizen*. That he has subsidized the New York *Age* and Indianapolis *Freeman*, and owns the *Colored American*

Magazine as well as assisting other alleged race papers, you are doubtless aware."

Another is from one of the most intelligent young Negro physicians in New England, who serves some of the best white families:

"He told me a story which firmly convinces me that Mr. Washington heads an organization in every large city whose purpose it is to ruin any man who openly criticises his methods in any particular. And I am now of the opinion that it is time that the decent element of the race take a stand for the things which are necessary for our further progress."

Such actions are not "injudicious," Mr. Villard, they are now *wrong*. I do not believe you can make Mr. Scott, the scape goat for them—it is scarcely conceivable that he has acted without Mr. Washington's full knowledge and consent.

As I have intimated, I am not submitting to you all the evidence obtainable, nor am I submitting it to a court of law. I am merely showing you the sort of testimony that has moved me to speak and act, and naturally its weight with me depends on the character of the witnesses whom I know and you do not.

Contrary to your opinion there was to my mind no alternative left me but to resign from Mr. Washington's committee: I thoroughly believed that by means of downright bribery and intimidation he was influencing men to do his will and had obtained a majority of such men on his committee; that he was seeking not the welfare of the Negro race but personal power; under such circumstances with the additional slight of not being invited to the most important meeting of the Committee, could I continue to cooperate with him?

You have attacked Mr. Roosevelt harshly. Does that mean that he is a rascal? No, but it does mean that you think he loans himself to indefensible deeds and measures, and that the general tendency of his policies is dangerous; if you believe this you have a right to proclaim it and act accordingly, and people must respect your intentions even if they doubt your judgment. So in this case: I am convinced of Mr. Washington's wrong course. You are not. Very well, I only ask for my convictions the same charity that you ask for yours. Respectfully yours,

W.E.B. Du Bois[49]

Whereas Du Bois debunked Washington's ideas in The Souls of Black Folk, *he would after "The Parting of the Ways" begin an attempt to debunk the man himself. Ideas, he realized (and realized that Washington had known for years), were meaningless without the ruthless politics required to see them succeed. And so he would have to respond with a similar ruthlessness. At the same time, those politics would require a new organization.*[50] *Du Bois discussed his desire to create a new black rights group with Jacob Henry Schiff in early 1905. Schiff was a banker and philanthropist, and Du Bois sought monetary aid. "Nothing ever came of this, because, as I might have known, most of Mr. Schiff's friends were strong and sincere advocates of Tuskegee." Still, Schiff would be a generous financial supporter of the later NAACP from its founding.[51]*

W.E.B. DU BOIS
(Confidential)

April 14 [1905]

Mr. Jacob Schiff
Sir:

You will probably remember having met me at Bar Harbor in 1903. I spoke at an Atlanta Univ. meeting then, was at your home & you were kind enough to ask me to call on you in N.Y. which I have not yet had the opportunity to do.

I want to lay before you a plan which I have and ask you if it is of sufficient interest to you for you to be willing to hear more of it & possibly to assist in its realization.

The Negro race in America is today in a critical condition. Only united concerted effort will save us from being crushed. This union must come as a matter of education & long continued effort. To this end there is needed a high class journal to circulate among the intelligent Negroes, tell them of the deeds of themselves & their neighbors, interpret the news of the world to them & inspire them toward definite ideals.

Now we have many small weekly papers & one or two monthlies but none of them fill the great need I have outlined. I want to establish therefore for the 9 million American Negroes & eventually for the whole Negro world a Monthly Journal . . .

W.E.B. Du Bois[52]

ALBERT BUSHNELL HART

Cambridge, Mass., April 24, 1905.

My dear Du Bois:—

. . . Of course in the heat of the discussion I hear of you everywhere. I am rather troubled to find that a great many people suppose that you head a kind of opposition to Booker Washington's ideas; so far as I understand, there is no innate lack of harmony between your purpose in life and his. You take a certain thing which must be done, viz. the higher education of those who can profit by it; he takes another end of the same problem; naturally each of you thinks that his interest is the more important; if you did not, you would exchange activities. But I do not see how either excludes the other. Our bumptious friend Trotter has made a great deal of unnecessary trouble by his assaults on Mr. Washington, in season and out of season, and I have actually found people who seemed to suppose that you and Trotter were working together.

Sincerely yours,
Albert Bushnell Hart[53]

W.E.B. DU BOIS

[undated]

Dear Professor [Albert Bushnell] Hart

. . . As to Mr. Washington, the people who think that I am one of those who oppose many of his ideas are perfectly correct. I have no personal opposition to him—I honor much of his work. But his platform has done the race infinite harm & I'm working against it with all my might. Mr. W. is today chief instrument in the hands of a N.Y. clique who are seeking to syndicate the Negro & settle the problem on the trust basis. They have bought & bribed newspapers & men.

W.E.B. Du Bois[54]

BOOKER T. WASHINGTON

I have learned much from reporters and newspapers. Seldom do I go into any city, or even step out on the platform between trains, but that it seems to me some newspaper reporter finds me. I used to be surprised at the unexpected places in which these representatives of the press would turn up, and still more surprised and sometimes embarrassed by the questions they would ask me. It seemed to me that, if there was any particular thing that I happened to know and did not feel at liberty to talk about, that would be the precise thing that the reporter who met me wanted to question me about. In such cases, too, the reporter usually got the information he wanted, or, if he didn't, I was sorry afterward, because if the actual facts had been published they would have done less damage than the half truths which he did get hold of.

I confess that when I was less experienced I used to dread reporters. For a long time I used to look upon a reporter as a kind of professional pry, a sort of social mischief-maker, who was constantly trying to find out something that would make trouble. The consequence was that when I met reporters I was likely to find myself laying plans to circumvent them and keep them in the dark in regard to my purposes and business.

A wide acquaintance with newspapers and newspaper men has completely changed my attitude toward them. In the first place I have discovered that reporters usually ask just the questions that the average man in the community in which the newspapers are located would ask if he had the courage to do so. The only difference is that the reporter comes out squarely and plumply and asks you the question that another person would ask indirectly of some one else.

For my part, I have found it both interesting and important to know what sort of questions the average man in the community was asking, for example about the progress of the Negro, or about my work. The sort of questions the reporters in the different parts of the country ask indicate pretty clearly, not only what the people in the community know about my work, but they tell me a great deal, also, about the feeling of the average man toward the members of my race in that community and toward the Negro generally. Not only do the newspaper reporters keep me informed, in the way I have described, in regard to a great many things I want to know, but frequently, by the questions that they ask, they enable me to correct false impressions and to give information which it seems important the public should have, in regard to the condition and progress of the Negro.

One other consideration has changed my attitude toward the reporters. As I have become better acquainted with newspapers I have come to understand the manner and extent to which they represent the interests and habits of thought of the people who read and support them. Any man who is engaged in any sort of work that makes constant demands upon the good-will and confidence of the public knows that it is important that he should have an opportunity to reach this public directly and to answer just the sort of questions the newspapers ask of him. As I have said, these inquiries represent the natural inquiries of the average man. If the newspaper did not ask and answer these questions, they would remain unanswered, or the public would get the information it wanted from some more indirect and less reliable source.

Several times, during the years that I have been at Tuskegee, a representative from some Southern paper or magazine has come to me to inquire in regard to some rumour or report that has got abroad in regard to conditions inside our school. In such cases I have simply told the reporter to take as much time as he chose and make as thorough an examination of the school and everything about it as he cared to. At the same time, I have assured him that he was perfectly free to ask any questions on any subject, of any person that he met on the grounds. In other words, I have given him every opportunity to go as far as he wanted, and to make his investigation as thorough as he desired.

Of course, in every institution as large as ours, there is abundant opportunity for a malicious or ill-disposed person to make injurious criticism, or to interpret what he learns in a way that would injure the institution. But in every such case, instead of printing anything derogatory to the school, the newspaper investigation has proved the most valuable sort of advertisement, and the rumours that had been floating about have been silenced. There is no means so effectual in putting an end to gossip as a newspaper investigation and report. On the other hand, I have found that there is no way of so quickly securing the goodwill of a newspaper reporter as by showing him that you have nothing to conceal. . . .

It seems to me, also, that there has been a noticeable improvement, in recent years, in the method of getting and preparing newspaper reports. I am not sure whether this is due more to the improvement in the class of men who represent the papers or whether it is due to a better understanding on the part of the public as to the methods of dealing with reporters; to a more definite recognition on the part of both the public and the newspapers of the responsible position which the modern newspaper occupies in the complex organization of modern social life. Both private individuals and public men seem to have recognized the fact that, in a country where the life of every individual touches so closely the life of every other, it is in the interest of all that each should work, as it were, in the open, where all the world may know and understand what he is doing.

On the other hand, newspapers have discovered that the only justification for putting any fact in a newspaper is that publication will serve some sort of public interest, and that, in the long run, the value of a piece of news and the reputation of a newspaper that prints it depend upon the absolute accuracy and trustworthiness of its reports . . .

Of course it is just as true that a man who has become well known and gained the confidence of the public through the medium of the press can use that power for purely selfish purposes, if he chooses, as that he can use it for the public welfare. I have no doubt that nearly every man who has in any way gained the confidence of the public has every year many opportunities for turning his popularity to private account.

Several times in the course of a year, for example, some one makes me a present of shares of stock in some new concern, and, on several occasions, I have had deeds of lots in some land scheme or new town presented to me. I have made it a rule to promptly return every gift of that kind, first of all for the good business reason that it would not pay me to have my name connected with any enterprise, no matter how legitimate it might be, for which I could not be personally responsible, and the use of my name, under such circumstances, so far as it influenced any one to invest in the scheme, would be a fraud.

A second reason is my desire to keep faith with the public, if I may so express it. In order to do that, I have never been able to see how I could afford to give any of my time or attention to any enterprise or any kind of work that did not have to do specifically and directly with the work of Negro education, in the broad spirit in which I have interpreted it.

I have already said that, in my early experience with newspaper reporters, I used to think it was necessary to be very careful in letting them know what my ambitions and aims in regard to my work were. But I have learned that it is pretty hard to keep anything from the newspapers that the newspapers think the public wants to know. As a result of what I have learned I try to be perfectly frank with newspaper men. For some years I have made it my custom to talk with them concerning all my plans and everything of a public nature in which I am interested. I talk with them just the same as I would with one of my friends or business acquaintances. When a reporter comes to interview me I tell him what I wish he might publish, and what I wish he would not publish. Frequently I have discovered that the newspaper man understood better than I how to state things in a way that should give the right impression to the public. This seems to be especially true of the Washington correspondents of the great dailies, who, considering the many important matters which they have to handle, exercise, it seems to me, a remarkable discretion as to what should, and should not, be printed . . .

One of the questions which I suppose, every man who deals with the public has to meet sooner or later is how to deal with a false newspaper report. I have made it a rule never to deny a false report, except under very exceptional circumstances. In nine cases out of ten the denying of the report simply calls attention to the original statement in a way to magnify it. Many people who did not see the original false report will see the denial and will then begin to search for the original report to find out what it was. And then, unfortunately, there are always some newspapers that will spread a report that is not justified by facts, for the purpose of securing a denial or of exciting a discussion. My experience is that it always gives a certain dignity and standing to a slander or a falsehood to deny it. Every one likes a fight, and a controversy will frequently lend a fictitious interest and importance to comparatively trivial circumstances . . .

The important thing, it seems to me, about the newspaper is that it represents the interest and reflects the opinions and intelligence of the average man in the community where the paper is published. The local press reflects the local prejudice. Its failings are the common human failings. Its faults are the faults of the average man in the community, and on the whole it seems to me best that it should be so. If the newspapers were not a reflex of the minds of their readers, they would not be as interesting or as valuable as they are. We should not know the people about us as well as we do. As long as the newspaper exists we not only have a means of understanding how the average man thinks and feels, but we have a medium for reaching and influencing him. People who profess to have no respect for the newspapers as a rule, I fear, have very little understanding or respect for the average man.

The real trouble with the newspapers is that while they frequently exhibit the average man at his worst, they rarely show him at his best. In order to read the best about the average man we must still go to books or to magazines. The newspaper has the advantage that it touches real things and real persons, but it touches them only on the surface. For that reason I have found it safe never to give too much weight to what a newspaper says about a man either good or bad.

Nevertheless I have learned more from newspapers than I have from books. In fact, aside from what I have learned from actual contact with men and with things, I believe I have gained the greatest part of my education from newspapers. I am sure this is so if I include among the newspapers those magazines which deal with current topics. Certainly I have been stimulated in all my thinking more by news than I have by the general statements I have met in books. In this, as in other matters, I like to deal at first-hand with the raw material and this I find in the newspapers more than in books.

Frequently I have heard persons speak of the newspaper as if its only purpose in making its reports was to tear down rather than build up. It is certainly true that newspapers are rather ruthless in the way in which they seem to bring every man, particularly every public man, to the bar of public opinion and make him explain and justify his work.

Nevertheless it is important that every man who is in any way engaged, directly or indirectly, in performing any kind of public service should never be permitted to forget that the only title to place or privilege that any man enjoys in the community is ultimately based on the service that he performs. I believe that any man, public or private, who meets newspaper men and deals with the newspaper in that spirit will find himself helped immensely in his work by the press rather than injured.

For my own part I feel sure that I owe much of such success as I have been able to achieve to the sympathy and interest which the newspaper press, North and South, has shown in the work that I have been trying to do. Largely through the medium of the newspapers I have been able to come into contact with the larger public outside of my community and the circle of my immediate friends and, by this means, to make the school at Tuskegee, not merely a private philanthropy, but in the truest sense of that word a public institution, supported by the public and conducted not in the interest of any one race or section, merely, but in the interest of the whole country.[55]

Washington also owed much of his success to the influence of political leaders like president Theodore Roosevelt. Du Bois was no supporter of Roosevelt, largely because he acted as a public advocate for Washington and Tuskegee. Still, Du Bois would put his differences with the president aside for the betterment of his cause.[56]

W.E.B. DU BOIS

May 22, 1905

Mr. Theodore Roosevelt
Sir:

I learn that you are expecting to visit Atlanta this fall and I want to ask you to visit Atlanta University. This is asking a good deal, but I am not making the request lightly. Atlanta University has stood for nearly forty years as an institution peculiarly devoted to the high aspirations of the American Negro. We have suffered for this—we are suffering for it but we are sticking to our ideals. At the same time we think we deserve something of the American people and therefore of you as their Chief representative. We were glad to have President McKinley come to Atlanta even though he did not visit us, and we were glad when he visited a sister institution where many of our graduates teach.[57] Yet when we face the prospect of your doing the same thing we feel differently. You are yourself a college man and have enunciated the highest ideals fearlessly. This institution is the child of Harvard & Yale. It has sent into the world 500 black men & women who mean something. You are coming to our very threshold—will you not step in a moment and tell us and the world that you have the same faith in the right sort of college-bred black men that you have in the right sort of artisans and workingmen? I sincerely hope you can. A.U. is right in the city—a mile from the post office so that a call will take but a little time.[58] I beg to remain, Sir,

W.E.B. Du Bois[59]

WILLIAM LOEB, JR. *(Loeb was Roosevelt's presidential secretary.)*

Washington, May 25, 1905

My dear Sir [Du Bois]:

Your letter of the 22nd instant has been received and the President thanks you for the kind invitation extended to him to visit Atlanta University on the occasion of his proposed trip through the South. Your wishes will be borne in mind and given consideration when the details of the trip are taken up.

Very truly yours,
Wm. Loeb Jr.
Secretary to the President.[60]

Roosevelt never came.

NOTES

1. Meier, 1953, 67–90; Harlan, 1979, 45–62; and Green and Driver, "Introduction," 1978, 18.

2. "News from the Classes: 1880," 1912, 153; and Holtzclaw, 1915, 185.

3. Charles Alexander was the editor of the *Colored Citizen*, one of the papers backed by Washington in order to drive William Trotter's *Boston Guardian* out of business. The paper would fail, but Washington would fund it unto the death. Pendergast, 2000, 85; and Brown, 2008, 551.

4. Cummings, pastor of the South Congregational Church in Boston, previously taught sociology at Harvard and even had Trotter as a student. Washington, 1979, vol. 8, 183.

5. Charles Fletcher Dole was an influential peace activist and Unitarian minister from Boston. The Twentieth Century Club was founded in January 1894 by many of the city's leading social leaders to promote public service. See Dole, 1914, 572–577.

6. Washington, 1979, vol. 8, 182–183.

7. Ibid., 189–192.

8. Charles William Anderson was a New York Republican and ally of Washington. The relationship expressed in Scott's letter, wherein Anderson is really an agent for Tuskegee's dirty tricks, paid off for Anderson, as later in 1905 Washington would use his influence with Roosevelt to have Anderson appointed internal revenue collector for the lower half of Manhattan. See Meier, 1963.

9. Lafayette McKeen Hershaw was a graduate of Atlanta University, a clerk in the land office of the Interior Department, a charter member of Niagara, and a critic of Washington. He worked with Du Bois on publication of the *Horizon*. Washington, 1977, vol. 6, 345.

10. Washington, 1979, vol. 8, 195.

11. See Chapter 7, note 12.

12. J.W. Lyons served as Register of the Treasury in Washington, D.C., first appointed by William McKinley and continuing under Roosevelt (see Chapter 8, note 6). Robert H. Terrell, Harvard graduate and principal of Washington's M Street High School (see Chapter 5, note 9). John C. Dancy was the recorder of deeds in Washington. Harlan, 1983, 101–102.

13. The two names on McKinlay's list not yet mentioned are D. Augustus Straker, a Detroit lawyer and the first black attorney to appear before the Michigan Supreme Court, and S.L. Corrodiers, who does not appear in the historical record.

14. Washington, 1979, vol. 8, 198–199.

15. Du Bois, 1973, 95; and Washington, 1979, vol. 8, 206–207.

16. Du Bois, January 1905, 677.

17. Frederick Randolph Moore was the editor of the *Colored American Magazine*, placed there and financed by Washington, and therefore he also served as one of Tuskegee's agents in Boston. Hurwitt, 2004, 807–808.

18. Washington, 1979, vol. 8, 206–207.

19. Du Bois, 1973, 95–96.

20. Aptheker, 1969, 850–851; and Du Bois, 1973, 96.

21. See "A Base Slander of the Afro-American Press," below.

22. Benjamin Jefferson Davis was a journalist and southern political figure. He founded the *Atlanta Independent* in 1903. Washington, 1979, vol. 8, 213.

23. Ibid., 212–213.

24. Ibid., 213–214.

25. Du Bois, 1973, 96–97. See Chapter 9, note 11 for more on Villard.

26. Ibid., 97.

27. Ibid.

28. Ibid.

29. Ibid., 97–98.

30. E.E. Cooper was the editor of Washington, D.C.'s *Colored American*. D.R. Wilkins was the editor of the *Chicago Conservator*. *The Broad Ax*, 13 July 1907, 1; and *Colored American*, 27 April 1901, 10.

31. Du Bois, 1973, 98.

32. John Wesley Cromwell was a teacher and principal at several Washington, D.C. public schools. Prior to his teaching service, he was both a lawyer and editor in and around the city. "Notes," July 1927, 563–566.

33. Peabody was a banker and philanthropist who was, more than most, interested in social activism related to black rights. See Chapter 8, note 5.

34. Alex Manly was the editor of the *Wilmington Daily Record*. George L. Knox was editor of the *Indianapolis Freeman*. See Knox, 1979; and Litwack, 1999.

35. John L. Thompson was the editor of the *Iowa State Bystander*, headquartered in Des Moines. *Iowa State Bystander*, 24 October 1913, 1.

36. Charles Edwin Bentley was a Chicago dentist. See Chapter 4, note 36.

37. Frank Manly was Alex Manly's brother, co-owner of the *Wilmington Daily Record*.

38. See note 3.

39. Stokes did work for Washington. He also served as vice president of the National Afro-American Council. Justesen, 2008, 179. For Peterson, see Chapter 4, note 43.

40. See Chapter 4, note 27.

41. See Chapter 9, note 44.

42. For Bishop Alexander Walters, see Chapter 4, note 33. Isaiah Benjamin Scott was a Methodist Episcopal bishop and the first black president of Wiley College in Marshall, Texas. He also served in a bishopric in Liberia. See Lyght and Keaton, 2012.

43. Frederick L. McGhee was born a slave in Mississippi, but settled in Minnesota, where he was the first black lawyer in the state. See Nelson, 2002.

44. Ibid., 98–102; and Washington, 1979, vol. 8, 224–242.

45. Butler Roland Wilson and his wife Mary Evans Wilson were cofounders founders of the Boston NAACP, along with Garrison and others, and were the principal black leaders of the organization in the city. Schneider, 1997, 136. For the Bumsteads, see Chapter 10, note 35.

46. Theresa was the wife of Francis.

47. Washington, 1979, vol. 8, 251–252.

48. Ibid., 261–263; and Du Bois, 1973, 102–103.

49. Washington, 1979, vol. 8, 265–267; and Du Bois, 1973, 103–104.

50. Lewis, 1993, 311.

51. Du Bois, 1940, 83; and Du Bois, 1973, 108.

52. Du Bois, 1973, 108.

53. Ibid., 110.

54. Ibid., 111.

55. Washington, *My Larger Education*, 1911, 81–101.

56. Du Bois, 1973, 111.

57. McKinley attended a Peace Jubilee in Atlanta in 1899 and went to Tuskegee while in the South. Du Bois, 1973, 111. See Washington, *Up From Slavery*, 1901, 301–310.

58. Roosevelt, a supporter of Washington and Tuskegee, did not come to Atlanta University. Du Bois, 1973, 111.

59. Ibid., 111–112.

60. Ibid., 112.

13

Niagara

The creation of the Niagara Movement was one of the most decisive early moments in the 20th-century fight for black rights and is often used as the genesis point for what historians call the long civil rights movement. Its goal was to set an agenda for rights activism over and against the agenda of the Tuskegee Machine. "We repudiate the monstrous doctrine that the oppressor should be the sole authority as to the rights of the oppressed," the movement announced. It was a group that was organized against bigotry, but its makeup also made it clear that it was also organized against the ideology of Booker Washington.

Niagara lasted for several years, but it was no match for the Tuskegee Machine. Washington used every means at his disposal to undermine the movement, paying editors to attack Du Bois in print and sending spies to Niagara meetings to report on the group's activities. By the end of the decade, the Niagara Movement had collapsed.

WILLIAM EDWARD BURGHARDT DU BOIS

The time seems more than ripe for organized, determined and aggressive action on the part of men who believe in Negro freedom and growth. Movements are on foot threatening individual freedom and our self respect. I write you to propose a conference during the coming summer for the following purposes:

1. To oppose firmly the present methods of strangling honest criticism, manipulating public opinion and centralizing political power by means of the improper and corrupt use of money and influence.

2. To organize thoroughly the intelligent and honest Negroes throughout the United States for the purpose of insisting on manhood rights, industrial opportunity and spiritual freedom.

3. To establish and support proper organs of news and public opinion.

If you are in accord with the above objects will you kindly write me at your earliest opportunity as to whether or not you can join the movement indicated in the enclosed circular? Are there any other reliable men in your section, who do their own thinking, whom we could invite to join us?[1]

The year following the failed New York summit, Du Bois called his own meeting, inviting a select group of 29 delegates to a meeting at Niagara Falls to create a political agenda in his own image. The group famously met on the Canadian side of the falls, as no New York hotels would allow their stay. The group argued for the right to vote, an end to segregation, better schools, health care, and housing. They protested against employment discrimination and against the unchristian racism of churches. The constitution of what would come to be known as the Niagara Movement was, in fact, based heavily on Du Bois's unsuccessful Committee of Twelve proposal and emphasized that protest to change the nation's fundamental inequalities would need to be paramount to the black cause.[2]

W.E.B. DU BOIS

Declaration of Principles

Progress: The members of the conference, known as the Niagara Movement, assembled in annual meeting at Buffalo, July 11th, 12th and 13th, 1905, congratulate the Negro-Americans on certain undoubted evidences of progress in the last decade, particularly the increase of intelligence, the buying of property, the checking of crime, the uplift in home life, the advance in literature and art, and the demonstration of constructive and executive ability in the conduct of great religious, economic and educational institutions.

Suffrage: At the same time, we believe that this class of American citizens should protest emphatically and continually against the curtailment of their political rights. We believe in manhood suffrage; we believe that no man is so good, intelligent or wealthy as to be entrusted wholly with the welfare of his neighbor.

Civil Liberty: We believe also in protest against the curtailment of our civil rights. All American citizens have the right to equal treatment in places of public entertainment according to their behavior and deserts.

Economic Opportunity: We especially complain against the denial of equal opportunities to us in economic life; in the rural districts of the South this amounts to peonage and virtual slavery; all over the South it tends to crush labor and small business enterprises; and everywhere American prejudice, helped often by iniquitous laws, is making it more difficult for Negro-Americans to earn a decent living.

Education: Common school education should be free to all American children and compulsory. High school training should be adequately provided for all, and college training should be the monopoly of no class or race in any section of our common country. We believe that, in defense of our own institutions, the United States should aid common school education, particularly in the South, and we especially recommend concerted agitation to this end. We urge an increase in public high school facilities in the South, where the Negro-Americans are almost wholly without such provisions. We favor well-equipped trade and technical schools for the training of artisans, and the need of adequate and liberal endowment for a few institutions of higher education must be patent to sincere well-wishers of the race.

Courts: We demand upright judges in courts, juries selected without discrimination on account of color and the same measure of punishment and the same efforts at reformation for black as for white offenders. We need orphanages and farm schools for dependent children, juvenile reformatories for delinquents, and the abolition of the dehumanizing convict-lease system.

Public Opinion: We note with alarm the evident retrogression in this land of sound public opinion on the subject of manhood rights, republican government and human brotherhood, and we pray God that this nation will not degenerate into a mob of boasters and oppressors, but rather will return to the faith of the fathers, that all men were created free and equal, with certain unalienable rights ...

Protest: We refuse to allow the impression to remain that the Negro-American assents to inferiority, is submissive under oppression and apologetic before insults. Through helplessness we may submit, but the voice of protest of ten million Americans must never cease to assail the ears of their fellows, so long as America is unjust.

Color-Line: Any discrimination based simply on race or color is barbarous, we care not how hallowed it be by custom, expediency or prejudice. Differences made on account of ignorance, immorality, or disease are legitimate methods of fighting evil, and against them we have no word of protest; but discriminations based simply and solely on physical peculiarities, place of birth, color of skin, are relics of that unreasoning human savagery of which the world is and ought to be thoroughly ashamed.

"Jim Crow" Cars: We protest against the "Jim Crow" car, since its effect is and must be to make us pay first-class fare for third-class accommodations, render us open to insults and discomfort and to crucify wantonly our man hood, womanhood and self-respect . . .

Oppression: We repudiate the monstrous doctrine that the oppressor should be the sole authority as to the rights of the oppressed. The Negro race in America stolen, ravished and degraded, struggling up through difficulties and oppression, needs sympathy and receives criticism; needs help and is given hindrance, needs protection and is given mob-violence, needs justice and is given charity, needs leadership and is given cowardice and apology, needs bread and is given a stone. This nation will never stand justified before God until these things are changed . . .

Agitation: Of the above grievances we do not hesitate to complain, and to complain loudly and insistently. To ignore, overlook, or apologize for these wrongs is to prove ourselves unworthy of freedom. Persistent manly agitation is the way to liberty, and toward this goal the Niagara Movement has started and asks the cooperation of all men of all races . . .[3]

Washington, of course, had eyes on the meeting, hoping to learn what he could in aid of ensuring that the group would have no impact. The Niagara meeting would serve as the inauguration of the first significant civil rights group of the 20th century, but it would exacerbate the activities of the Tuskegee Machine.

BOOKER TALIAFERRO WASHINGTON

[Tuskegee, Ala.] July 8, 1905

[To Margaret James Murray Washington] Write Mrs. Talbert[4] to keep you closely informed about proceedings and names of people connected with the Buffalo meeting next week . . .[5]

BOOKER T. WASHINGTON

[Tuskegee, Ala.] July 8, 1905

[To Charles William Anderson] Tell Crosby[6] look after Buffalo meeting sharply. It is to be held next week. Inside data can be gotten from Talbert.[7] Keep me closely informed [at] my expense. Think they are making effort to rope Crosby in . . .[8]

BOOKER T. WASHINGTON

Tuskegee Ala July 10 1905

[To Julius Robert Cox] See [Clifford] Plummer[9] at once give him fifty dollars tell him go to Buffalo tonight or tomorrow morning ostensibly to attend Elks convention but to report fully what goes on at meeting to be held there Wednesday and Thursday. Get into meeting if possible but be sure name of all who attend and what they do answer when you have completed this matter . . .[10]

SAMUEL LAING WILLIAMS

Chicago, July 10—1905

My Dear Mr [Emmett Jay] Scott: . . . I got a telegram from Dr. Washington yesterday asking for some data concerning the Buffalo Conference to be held Wednesday and Thursday of this week. I did my best to get hold of some facts about the matter, but those who have knowledge are very secretive. What I said in my reply telegram represents the extent of my knowledge. Invitations were sent to the following Chicago people, Morris, Bentley, Wilson[,] Wesley[,] E.H. [Edward H.] Wright, Oscar De Priest Dr Wesley Col Marshall and James S Madden.[11] Of these Madden and Bentley have gone, and I understand Wilkins is going. I have not heard for certain of any others going. Magee [Fredrick L. McGhee] of St. Paul, [George H.] Woodson of Iowa, and [Brown Sylvester] Smith of Kansas City—all lawyers have passed through the City on their way to Buffalo.[12]

As an evidence of the meanness of some of these people, Smith of Kansas City Kans. said to a friend of mine that Mr Washington's visit to Kansas recently was responsible for a law recently enacted providing Separate High Schools for Colored Students! Smith admits that

Mr Washington said nothing in his addresses in that State to justify such action, but such was the "impression" of Mr Washington's presence that the law providing for separation followed as a matter of course!

It occurred to me that it might be a good thing for you to write to Mr Ira Guy of Topeka, Secretary of the Topeka Negro Business League and get from him the facts in the case.[13] Guy is a strong friend of Mr Washing[ton] and I know if there is any gossip or general impression that in the least justifies Smith's extravagant assertion he would know it.

Referring to League matters there is prospect for a large delegation from the West . . .

S. Laing Williams[14]

CHARLES WILLIAM ANDERSON[15]

New York, N.Y., July 14, 1905

Personal.

My dear Doctor [Washington]: Enclosed you will find clippings from the Buffalo papers relative to the Du Bois conference, together with a letter from Crosby. As you will note, they failed to interest Crosby in the movement, and as you will also notice, Crosby in his note to me, makes the point that the true measure of their influence and their honesty of purpose is revealed in the fact that they had to seek a meeting place outside of the United States.[16] The meeting seems to have been held at the Fort Erie Beach Hotel, Fort Erie, Canada. Concerning the list of names printed in the enclosed clipping, you are doubtless aware that not one tenth of them were present. I know the men too well to believe that they would spend one dollar to support the holiest cause ever devised by the wit of man. The printed list of names was undoubtedly prepared by Professor Du Bois or some other enterprising citizen, and handed to the newspaper. I think perhaps you ought to make an effort to have that man Hershaw removed.[17] Can that not be done in some way? Can you in any way find out just how many of these men really attended the conference? Of course the movement will never be dangerous, because there is not a man in it who would be willing to finance it over, or contribute anything towards that end. They are a lot of "unmoneyed" patriots, and you know better than almost any other man living, how much an unmoneyed patriot can accomplish . . .

Charles W. Anderson[18]

CLIFFORD H. PLUMMER *(Plummer was a Boston lawyer and Democrat who defended William Monroe Trotter after the Boston Riot.)*[19]

Boston, Mass., July 16, 1905

My dear Dr. Washington: I arrived home this morning and called you up first thing; but Mrs. Washington informed me that you left home last evening. Dr. Courtney gave me your address. He also showed me the article in the Transcript;[20] he was not aware that I was anywhere near the scene. And therefore he could not imagine my thoughts in the matter. I have not had such a feeling of indignation for a long time as I had when I saw it. Knowing as I did that the report was not true; in fact there really was no conference in Buffalo where delegates were in attendance. The names of the delegates might have been communicated to a certain gentleman and they were carried to Buffalo; but the gentlemen themselves were not there. I was located near 521 Michigan Avenue from Wednesday morning until Friday and I can state positively that none of the men named in the report were present except Du Bois. Notwithstanding the fact that the conference amounted to nothing, the local editors informed me that some colored man did bring in a report such as appeared in the Boston papers; but no reporter was assigned to the seat of the conference . . .[21]

BOOKER T. WASHINGTON

New York 7–17 190[5]

[To Emmett Jay Scott] Telegraph Thompson and other newspaper men that you can absolutely trust to ignore Niag[a]ra movement Fortune, Anderson and I think this best white papers in the north leave [have] practically ignored it all together . . .[22]

EMMETT JAY SCOTT

Tuskegee Institute, Alabama. July 18, 1905

Dear Mr. Washington: I send you herewith a copy of Du Bois' suggestions for the Committee of Twelve. Perhaps you will want to go over them with some of the friends. They seem to indicate, I should say, some of the plans he will try to follow in the work of his Niagara Movement committee . . .[23]

EMMETT JAY SCOTT

Tuskegee Institute, Alabama. July 18, 1905

Dear Mr. Washington: I have taken measures, in accordance with your telegram, to have Thompson ignore the Niagara Movement.[24] He will be willing to abide by your suggestion. I have asked him on his own initiative to influence other of our friends similarly.

The Boston Transcript of Saturday, July 15th, has an extended telegram from Buffalo bearing upon this movement. You must have seen it. Their purpose most likely will be to secure issues of the Transcript or Buffalo papers if any of them carried the report, and send marked copies to all of our newspapers.

I am very glad that you have been in conference with Mr. Fortune and Mr. Anderson.

I fear nothing from it beyond the ordinary ripple which a new movement of any character usually creates. Yours truly,

Emmett J Scott

I hope you sent, or will send, Mr. Laird[25] of Montgomery Journal last Saturday's Transcript Editorial.[26]

EMMETT JAY SCOTT

[Tuskegee, Ala.] July 18, 1905

Personal

Dear [Richard W.] Thompson: I have just wired you today to the effect that a conference of our friends thinks it wisest to in every way ignore absolutely the Niagara Movement. I am sure you can trust their judgment in this matter. The best of the white newspapers in the North have absolutely ignored it and have taken no account of its meetings or its protestations. I think, then, as I have intimated, if we shall consistently refuse to take the slightest notice of them that the whole thing will die a-borning. With kindest regards ever, I am, Yours truly,

Emmett J. Scott

P.S. Of course anything you may do in the direction of influencing others to ignore them, as I have intimated, will be a good thing. By all means try to influence the Freeman people and the Charleston Advocate accordingly.[27]

EMMETT JAY SCOTT

Tuskegee Institute, Alabama. July 24, 1905

Dear Mr. Washington: I am sending you with papers today a number with the item sent out from here bearing upon the coming meeting of the Business League. They represent a wide strip of territory and show that we have been able to reach the papers pretty well. We sent it out to the complete list of all that we have, and I feel reasonably sure that the notice will appear in 90 per cent of them any way. They are running the notice with extended head lines and in other ways are stirring up interest in the meeting.

I also include a number of papers that have references to the Niagara movement. I do not believe that aside from the Atlanta Age, and it straddles, that any papers that have been heretofore favorable will be deflected from support of the great principles for which you have been laboring. I shall be very greatly surprised if it does not turn out in the end that the whole effort of these brethren is to secure a little notoriety. Yours truly,

Emmett J. Scott[28]

BOOKER T. WASHINGTON

South Weymouth, Mass., July 27, 1905

Dear Mr. Scott: On your way North I wish that you would stop and have a conference with the Atlanta Age man, I forget his name, and show him the true inwardness of Du Bois. Perhaps it would be better to have him come to Tuskegee, at our expense, for a conference, without you letting him know the exact reason. I am very anxious that we lose not one of our friends on the account of this new movement . . .[29]

EMMETT JAY SCOTT

[Tuskegee, Ala.] July 27, 1905

Personal

Dear Mr. [W. Allison] Sweeney:[30] I have your kind letter of July 25th asking "a thought" as to the Niagara Movement. I have only to say that a number of my newspaper friends have written me that it is not their purpose to take the slightest notice of the organization since Du Bois was, as is well known, a member of another committee at work along the same lines, but because he could not be, as he wanted, the central figure in the movement and at the expense of others, he has gone out to duplicate that movement . . .[31]

BOOKER T. WASHINGTON

[South Weymouth, Mass.] August 7,1905

Dear Mr. Scott: I am quite sure it will interest you to know that Kelly Miller and Grimke have broken off completely from Du Bois and his crowd.

It seems that Du Bois has insulted both of them. Grimke had a long talk with me and went over many of the details covering the devilment of the whole gang. He seems more than anxious now to line up with us.

Kelly Miller feels the insult very keenly and resents it in very strong language, but he is mushy and cannot be depended upon for a straight out fight. Very truly yours,

Booker T. Washington[32]

BOOKER T. WASHINGTON

South Weymouth, Mass., August 7, 1905

Dear Mr. Scott: I am returning Cable's letter to you the one written to Thompson.[33]

Mr. Cable's views are all right when dealing with gentlemen, but not scoundrels, whose purposes are wholly known.

Some of our friends of the colored press have taken for granted that those connected with the Niagara Movement are honest and from that point of view have discussed the declarations, which makes it a rather puzzling condition to deal with, but in the end, I am sure they will find out their ultimate purpose. Very truly yours,

Booker T. Washington[34]

BOOKER T. WASHINGTON

[South Weymouth, Mass.] August 7, 1905

Dear Mr. Scott: I am of the opinion it would be well to stop in Washington, on your way North, and see Terrell and Dancy; let them understand that I do not feel exactly comfortable over the fact that the three papers, in or near Washington, are continually knocking me and there is nothing to indicate an action on the part of my friends, or supposed friends.

You can use your own judgment in this matter . . .[35]

BOOKER T. WASHINGTON

South Weymouth, Mass., August 7, 1905

Personal & Confidential.

My dear Mr. [John A.] Hertel:[36] The enclosed clipping from a Buffalo paper, where the meeting was held, will give you the true aim of the persons in it. I have found out definitely that not over 12 or 15 persons were in the meeting, and as I said to you, you will find that they will attempt to use your magazine as a propaganda, and if permitted, you will find that [Jesse Max] Barbour will show his hand more fully in the September number.[37] Very truly yours,

[Booker T. Washington][38]

Washington's blatant opposition to Niagara, his insistent attacks on its members and ideas, and the corresponding attacks of his representatives did not win him any new converts and actually played a significant role of turning many toward Du Bois. His behavior turned many white philanthropists, the bedrock of Washington's power, away from him, as well. Those white philanthropists would ultimately form the core support for the NAACP.[39]

Thus, Niagara was the turning point in the relationship between Du Bois and Washington. From that point, Washington's influence began to wane, whereas Du Bois's continued to rise. Their dynamic would never be the same. From 1906 forward, Du Bois would have the upper hand. This is significant because it would be this condition that would define the bulk of the relationship. Through much of the 1890s, the two were on fairly good terms. Things grew problematic from 1898 to 1903. The conflict began in earnest after that date, but Du Bois was able to gain leverage with his Credo and with Niagara. And so, even though Du Bois is usually depicted as the victim of Washingtonian treachery, beset by a leader more powerful than himself, and thus heroic by default, he was actually in possession of the figurative upper hand for the bulk of the conflict, spanning the last 10 years of Washington's life. When combined with his long life following the passing of Washington, Du Bois worked from a position of strength for the vast majority of the two's feud. Viewed in that light, Washington's machinations seem more like acts of

*desperation from someone trying to maintain influence, rather than the cruel
power plays of a king trying to suppress a particularly radical and ambitious
subject.*

EMMETT JAY SCOTT

Tuskegee Institute, Alabama. August 7, 1905

Dear Mr. Washington: A letter received from Thompson assures me of
his willingness to work with us in good spirit and heartily in connection with the coming meeting of the League. I think that he and Mr. Simmons will help us out very materially. Mr. [Ernest Ten Eyck] Attwell is
planning to be there, and I can utilize both him and Mr. Cox should it
become necessary and your approval is given.[40]

Thompson tells me in his letter that the Bishop [Alexander Walters]
writes him that the new Council matter is to kill off the Niagara movement and that he, the Bishop, is with you now till death. The Bishop is
quite mercurial in temperament, but I feel sure he will be disposed to
stick since he was crowded out of recognition by the other fellows.
Yours truly,

Emmett J. Scott[41]

*After the founding of Niagara in July 1905, Du Bois went to Massachu-
setts for Atlanta University and Niagara business. There he wrote to Kelly
Miller and Archibald Grimke, who had not been at the July meeting, asking
for their support. They would ultimately decide not to join the group, influenced, in part, by the strained relationships brought by Du Bois's resignation
from the Committee of Twelve earlier that year.*[42]

W.E.B. DU BOIS

Williamstown, Mass., August 13, 1905

Messrs Archibald Grimke and Kelly Miller
Gentlemen:

Sometime ago you urged me to a step which I declined to take. As it
seemed to me at the time the strongest argument you put forward was
the fact that Mr. Washington's committee was practically the only efficient active force in the field, so that it was that or nothing. I determined that this should not long be the case and the result has been the

successful launching of the Niagara Movement. I did not ask you two gentlemen to join me in this movement, first because you both belonged to Mr. Washington's committee & membership in both organizations seemed to me inconsistent; and secondly I was not sure that I would find 50 men who had not bowed the knee to Baal.

Today we have a growing enthusiastic organization of nearly 75 members, educated, determined & unpurchasable men. I am writing to ask you men to join us as charter members. The platform is I am sure essentially agreeable to you. The members want you & regretted your absence at Buffalo. We are invited for active work, not against persons but for principles. Will you not join us? I shall send you a copy of the constitution & declaration if you desire them. Meantime I await your decision with interest.

Very sincerely yours,
W.E.B. Du Bois[43]

BOOKER T. WASHINGTON

[Tuskegee, Ala.] September 13, 1905

Personal

Dear Mr. [George H.] Woodson:[44] When we had our last conference you were in some doubt as to the policy of the organization that you are connected with [Niagara]. You stated that you were not fully convinced that their object was a personal one.

I wonder if you have been reading the chief organ of that organization during the last three weeks, and if you are still convinced that the leaders have an unselfish and patriotic ambition, or if their only object is to try to accomplish the downfall of one individual? I am sure you are too broad and sensible a man to be deceived. You know that incident which is made the basis of the most vile attacks on me is simply another way certain people in the South say to the Negro that he must go so high and no higher, and that the South wants to control the Negro not only in the South but out of the South. When they attack me, it is not B.T. Washington who is attacked, but the race. If these men had an iota of manhood in them and were not controlled by petty spite, now is the time when they would come out and stand up for the race, but you know what they are doing. I should like very much to hear from you on this subject. Yours very truly,

Booker T. Washington[45]

WHITEFIELD MCKINLAY

Washington, D.C, Sept. 20/05

Dr Mr Washington I have delayed thus long answering your letter of this week in order to learn from several of our friends who are in close touch with the "Antis" what are their comments etc. They tell me what I naturally conclude, that it has done the Guardian more harm than good. One of the Antis frankly told me that he didnt approve of their methods.

In my neighborhood a sample copy was left at each house and I presume the same thing was done thro out the City. Aside from a few narrow minded people who have no decided views or convictions on any subject, I feel certain that the bulk of the people who read the issue sympathize with you in the Wannamaker affair. In fact I think for every friend you may lose you gain two from them. Only this week one of their most intelligent followers told me that the more he has studied you, the more he realized that he had misunderstood you.

I am about to praise A. Grimke on his last letter but he will find as I constantly pointed out to him that there [are] a number of would be leaders that were formerly associated with him that are beyond reason & cant be brought into any movement that has your name attached thereto—hence I waste but very little efforts on them. Never the less the article is very timely & I think will do much good. I always told him & his brother Frank that they would rue the day that their names were associated [with] the Guardian, because he is downright crazy. Du Bois is the Iago.

Yr hold on the colored people of this City is such that in order for that gang to weaken it they would have to prove to their satisfaction that you are a criminal. Very truly

W McKinlay[46]

John Elmer Milholland was a white liberal writer for the New York Tribune *who became a successful businessman in the pneumatic tube industry. He was a consistent champion of black rights who, like Oswald Garrison Villard, supported Washington in the 1890s but broke with him because of his conservatism. Milholland was scheduled to speak at a meeting of Washington's National Negro Business League (NNBL) in 1905, when Washington pulled him aside and asked him not to talk about disfranchisement. From that point, Milholland turned away from him. He would become a founder of the*

NAACP and its first treasurer and would also support the more radical Trotter.[47]

CHARLES WILLIAM ANDERSON[48]

New York, N.Y., September 26, 1905

Private.

My dear Doctor: This, in strictest confidence. Moore called upon me today, and advised me of an interview which he had with Mr. [John Elmer] Milholland;[49] and strange to say, Moore seemed to agree with him on many points. The tale is entirely too long to relate in detail, but the sum total of it was, that Milholland has some property in Brooklyn which he desires to place in the hands of the Realty Company to be sold to coloured tenants, on the easy payment plan. Moore evidently sees a dollar or two in it, and appears to be quite impressed with the importance of Milholland. After discussing the Realty proposition, they fell to discussing you. Brother Milholland maintained that you had been standing in the way of the suffrage movement, and would have to stop it. He said that he was your friend, but he felt that you ought to talk straight, and not attempt to play with him. He also said that Du Bois was a very strong character, and that he had been told that he would be a very useful man to the suffrage movement. He further stated that the Southern people were not your friends, and if you did not look out, you would get into trouble. He reflected in many ways upon you, and made some rather sharp comment on your attitude on the race question. The upshot of it all was that it is plain that he is very mad at you, and is starting another one of his "bluff" games. His threat to take up Du Bois and thereby furnish the Niagara movement with funds, is, in my judgment, only hot air. It would not be worth repeating except for the fact that in some mysterious way he seems to have half way convinced Moore. Privately, I am afraid that Fred thinks that there is a little money in sight, and is ready and willing to cultivate Milholland on that account. I told Moore that he was a very dangerous man to tie up with, and that I would advise caution. I am going to see Milholland myself this afternoon and find out just what it all means. In the meantime, please keep this strictly confidential, and do not let Moore know that I have mentioned the matter to you. How quickly these fellows will run after strange Gods when there is a little "graft" in sight. I have always felt that Moore's one redeeming quality was his loyalty, but I am afraid

I had my faith shaken in him today. Of course he did not take sides against you, but he assumed the familiar attitude of feeling that there was much to be said on both sides of the proposition . . .

C.W.A.

P.S. Humphreys has just been in & he too intimated that you were unsound on the suffrage question—I gave him to understand that you were my friend. He then said "so am I, Dr Washington's friend." He has been over "hobnobbing" with Trotter in Boston.[50]

FREDERICK RANDOLPH MOORE

New York, September 28th, 1905

My dear Mr. Washington: Mr. John E. Milholland telephoned me to call on him Monday last, which I did, ostensibly to talk about some lots he owns in East New York, Brooklyn, but really to talk over the matter of the suffrage question. He did the talking and I did the listening, and he is very emphatic in his determination to bring that question to an issue this fall, and says that your stand is the only hindrance, but intimated that they were determined to take the "bull by the horns," and force the issue.

I suggested that he see you when next you come to the city, and talk over the matter with you before deciding on a definite plan of operation. I mentioned the fact that I had noted Mr. Humphrey's visit to Boston and his agitation there, and he replied, that they were sending Mr. Humphrey about to focus attention on the question, and that they had secured Mr. Du Bois, whom he had been told was a strong man and would be most helpful to the cause.[51]

If Du Bois and those with him get an idea that they are regarded as helpful agents by Mr. Milholland and those with him, and realize that funds are at hand to wage a battle, it seems to me that they can make a deal of trouble, and it will be just what they are looking for, "the necessary implements of war."

I told Charlie Anderson of my conversation, and he has called on Mr. Milholland, and has perhaps advised you of his conversation. I have not seen him since, but would say, that while Mr. Milholland is very very friendly to you, he thinks that you should stand "from under" or talk frankly with him over the matter. I told him that I would talk with you and arrange to have you see him when next you are in the city, and that Anderson and I would come with you if agreeable . . .[52]

BOOKER T. WASHINGTON

[Tuskegee, Ala.] Sept. 29, 1905

Personal

My dear Mr. [Charles William] Anderson: I have your letter of September 26th, and of course shall treat the whole matter in the strictest confidence. I am not at all surprised to hear of the attitude of Milholland and Humphrey, in fact, I have been expecting it. I noted that Humphrey attended some suffrage meeting in Boston some days ago. The more experience I have, the more I think of your remarks to the effect that a professional friend of the Negro is a man to be watched. Both of those parties have it in for me because, in the first place, they hold me responsible for defeating their plans with the President. I have been perfectly frank with Milholland all along. I told him in the first place that while I had my views on the matter of cutting down Southern representation I should not give them to the public or any one else unless compelled to. Immediately after President Roosevelt was reelected he sent for me to come to the White House and give him my views concerning the policy of cutting down Southern representation, and that was a command which I could not dodge. I had to tell him frankly that I could see no good to come from the move to the colored people. I wrote Milholland and told him frankly as the enclosed copy of letter will show my attitude so that he could see personally that I was not trying to tote water on two shoulders. Very soon after I had seen the President, Milholland, Harry Cummings and ex-Senator Warner Miller called to see him, and the President gave them the cold shoulder, telling them I was opposed to the movement.[53] Ever since then, they have had it in for me. Milholland and Humphrey have in turn taken up Hayes and Cummings, and I suppose they will in turn take up Trotter and Du Bois. They have already dropped Hayes, and I suppose they will drop the other fellows in turn.

It is rather strange as well as interesting to note that these people have just become alarmed on account of my unpopularity with the Southern white people and also fear that I am likely to get into trouble with this same element. Heretofore their complaint was to the effect that I was too popular with the Southern white people and was seeking to cultivate their friendship at the expense of the race.

It is very interesting to note that Vardaman, of Mississippi, has just come out in favor of cutting down Southern representation; in fact, he stands exactly on the same platform as Milholland and Humphrey.

I shall hope to see you soon and talk the whole matter over with you. When it comes to expending money, I really do not think that

Milholland or Humphrey have much to spend on any movement. I know the principal sources from which they get their money and can come pretty near closing up these sources at any time. We must not fail, however, to let men like Humphrey and Milholland understand that if they are to take up such scoundrels as Trotter and Du Bois that we can have nothing to do with them. Yours truly,

Booker T. Washington[54]

Although the Niagara Movement was struggling to maintain its solvency from 1905 to 1910, it remained important because of its unequivocal stand for civil rights, and thus its opposition to Washington's ideology. It gave those disagreeing with Washington a place to go, and it became the seedbed for more successful groups like the NAACP.[55]

BOOKER T. WASHINGTON

Trotter and Trotterism

The New York Age has, up to this time, been silent concerning the so-called Niagara Movement, for the reason that we did not want to prejudge the movement, nor seek to influence the utterances of other journals upon this subject. From the first we have had our suspicions about the original objects of the organization, but we wanted to wait to have these suspicions confirmed, as we knew they would be, by the main mover in the organization. The head and front of this organization has now revealed himself and his objects, and the move, which he has now made, shows that he has not wisdom enough to protect his friends, when such wisdom might help his cause. The mainspring and moving spirit in this organization is none other than Monroe Trotter of Boston, Mass. In a recent issue of his paper he reveals the plot and plan of "The Niagara Movement." Since this meeting was held on foreign shores, in Canada, Monroe Trotter has celebrated the anniversary of the famous Boston Church Riot. Two years ago the editor of *The Age* happened to be present at the meeting which it was attempted to be broken up by the mob tactics directed by Trotter and his gang. In connection with the celebration of this riot he comes out boldly and frankly says that the "Church Riot Movement" and the "Niagara Movement" are one and the same thing, he says that the Niagara Movement is the outgrowth of the Church riot. That is, he claims the two are one and inseparable, and on this basis he asks for the support and confidence of the race. Further, in a recent magazine article, Dr. Du Bois himself says that Trotter is the "backbone," whatever that means, of the Niagara Movement.

In order that our readers and the members of the race generally may not now lose sight of the connection of the two movements we must remind them that a meeting was planned to take place in the Columbus Avenue Zion Church, Boston, in 1903, and a regular program had been planned. A few hours before the meeting was to be held (1) Monroe Trotter, or some of his fellow-conspirators, went into the church and scattered pepper in and around the sacred chancel; (2) Monroe Trotter and his gang of fellow-conspirators were instrumental in bringing into the church a gang of dissolute and drunken women from the streets; (3) they then stationed others of their conspirators in various parts of the church so that they might create a disturbance and drown the speakers' voices; (4) not withstanding the presence of refined women and many children, a deliberate crime and insult to the race was planned and partly carried out (if Trotter had been truly brave he would have selected a white church to perpetrate this crime); (5) after Trotter and his main followers were arrested they tried, in the courts and in every conceivable manner and by all kinds of falsehoods to get out of the difficulty, but he and his ignorant followers were compelled to serve time in jail.

In order to show that the real object of the Niagara Movement is not to help the race but to break down the helpful influence of one member of the race, we have but to mention one or two facts.

First, there is not a plank in their address to the country but what has been sent out in almost the identical words time and again during the last thirty years.

Second, throughout the platform they say they are in existence mainly to bring about free discussion of all subjects, and yet Trotter was not invited to the Columbus Avenue Church meeting, he was not on the program to speak, and it was not presumed that he would speak. And then, besides, the meeting in Zion Church was called for the very purpose of hearing free speech and the main mover in the opposition to prevent free speech and free discussion, through the medium of a mob, was Monroe Trotter. One of the professed objects of the new "movement" was to secure personal liberty, freedom of action. In accepting the invitation to dine with a distinguished merchant outside of the South, in the way he has been doing for fifteen years, Dr. Washington was doing the very thing which the Niagara Movement professes to be in favor of; but Trotter, the real leader of this movement, was so narrow and evil-minded that he could not even keep silent and could not refrain from putting all of his friends in an awkward position because of his personal malice.

But this is not all: we give to the public now, what we should never have divulged, and what has not been published before, had not Monroe Trotter boldly said the Church riot and the Niagara Movement are one and the same thing . . . It was whispered by many and believed at the time by not a few that Du Bois had a hand in these Church riots, and now lo and behold Trotter, himself, has boldly declared that the church riots and the Niagara Movement are connected.

Now, according to Trotter, the Niagara Movement sympathizes with and expects to pursue the same policy adopted by him as regards these two meetings. Still more recently, and still more to the point in the direction of proving that the men connected with this "movement" have nothing in view but to exhibit their personal dislike and jealousy toward one individual of the race, we call attention of the Afro-American public to the recent disgraceful alliance of Mr. Trotter through his paper with the vilest character of Southern newspapers in trying to breed a spirit among the Southern white people in the South that would result in the intimidation or assassination of Dr. Washington himself or in the burning of the property of the Tuskegee school. No Southern paper, however vile, has gone further than Trotter in this respect; in fact, no one could read Trotter's vile sheet without seeing that he has seconded every move and every suggestion that the lowest type of Southern white papers have made. Not a single one of the Southern papers which abused Dr. Washington for accepting Mr. Wanamaker's invitation at Saratoga printed as much abusive matter, or put it in such disgusting form, as did Trotter's paper, the organ of the Niagara Movement.

Another disgraceful feature, in connection with this recent outbreak of Trotter in connection with the vile portion of the Southern press, consists in the fact that Dr. Du Bois himself, has been in Boston during the greater part of the summer, and that he and Trotter have worked hand in glove in connection with the carrying out of all of these plans. The race, as we know it, is not yet ready to follow the criminal and inciter to riots in churches nor to follow the vilest portion of the press of the South in abetting assassination and destruction of school property . . .

We have said their program is insincere and that petty spite against one individual of the race actuates them. We repeat it. In this editorial we do not, in proof of this assertion, elaborate the fact that Trotter's chief aide is Dr. Du Bois, who does not vote anywhere in this country and who plays no part in the politics of the race. They consider themselves, for the most part, too high to break down the influence of one individual of the race . . .

There is hardly a person connected with the Niagara Movement who can be pointed to as having taken the lead in a single movement for the betterment of the race. The only service they perform in behalf of the race is the making of speeches and the passing of resolutions. They are rarely seen in Negro churches or Sunday Schools where they could be of service to the race and community. We repeat, the race will not follow such leadership, it will not exalt or follow criminal characters . . .[56]

BOOKER T. WASHINGTON

[Tuskegee, Ala.] October 2, 1905

Personal and Confidential

My dear Mr. [John C.] Asbury:[57] . . . I have never felt that we could gain a great deal by being put upon the defensive, that, it seems to me, is an element of weakness. I want to write an article that will show constructive, progressive effort . . . The work here has stood for twenty-five years and is its own defense . . .

No other white man has ever attempted to damage and discredit the work of this institution and my own efforts more than Du Bois has done, and you will note that during the past summer that Du Bois and Trotter have been in Boston editing the Guardian, and they have outdone even the South in their attempts to villify me for exercising my rights in dining with Mr. Wanamaker. They have joined hands with the vilest element of the South and have scattered more broadcast than any Southern paper has done the vilest language used about me. Under the circumstances, I repeat, it would be interesting to note what kind of reply Du Bois could make . . .[58]

BOOKER T. WASHINGTON

[Tuskegee, Ala.] October 5,1905

My dear Mr. [Francis Jackson] Garrison:

. . . I am very sorry that you got the impression that my Business League address was meant as a rejoinder or reply to the Niagara

Movement. I went over that address carefully with several colored people of different temperaments, some radical and some conservative, with a view of letting nothing appear in it that might give the impression of being a reply to anything that was said by the Niagara people. I think you misunderstood the meaning and spirit of what I said in regard to people who are at work in the South. I meant to condemn any effort on the part of people living out of the South who condemned those who are working in the South doing the best they could. I do not believe that your father would have condemned any man who, while living in the South, was working in the best manner that he could to bring about the same results that he was seeking to bring about yet by different methods. I do not claim that it would be proper for all persons who are working for the elevation of our race to live or work in the South, but I do think it an error for those who do not work in the South to condemn the men and women who are trying to do the best they can in the field . . .[59]

JESSE MAX BARBER[60]

Atlanta, Ga. November 29, 1905

Dear Dr. Washington:

. . . I regret very much that you cannot find time to prepare an article for the January issue of our Magazine . . . Dr. W.E.B. Du Bois is to write on the Niagara Movement. He will recommend that the united support of the race be given to this Movement. We are very anxious to have a consensus of opinion from the leading thinkers of the race on the proper attitude the Negro should exercise towards educational questions, towards property getting, towards political affairs and towards national racial organizations. We want to give all sides free scope in our Magazine to discuss the questions we have just named. It is not our desire—and never has been—to appear one-sided and narrow. Of course, if the press of business is so great that you will not have time to prepare the article, we will have to state to the public that you were invited, but were not able to give us the article because of pressing duties, but we very much prefer that you give us an article, although it be ever so brief. Yours very truly,

J. Max Barber[61]

BOOKER T. WASHINGTON

[Tuskegee, Ala.] Dec. 1, 1905

Dear Mr. [Jesse Max] Barber: Your letter has been received . . . The fact is that I must fulfill some of my back promises in the way of articles before I attempt to make new pledges. I am under obligation for articles long since promised to several magazines, and besides, am under promise to write one or two books which have not been finished. Aside from all this, I have to raise money each month to pay the salaries of 151 officers and teachers. Aside from looking after the executive work of this institution, I have to raise over $200,000 each year. This, with the numerous calls to serve the public in any number of ways, makes it almost impossible for me to do all that my heart would lead me to do in the way of furnishing contributions to such publications as yours. Yours truly,

Booker T. Washington

P.S. You speak of making some statements regarding my not writing an article; this, it seems to me is unusual for a magazine of your character. It is perfectly right to discuss an article that I have written but quite unusual to discuss an article that I have not written.[62]

BOOKER T. WASHINGTON

[Tuskegee, Ala.] Dec. 2,1905

Dear Mr. [Francis Jackson] Garrison:

. . . In regard to Mr. Trotter, I would say that his case is almost a pathetic one . . . Trotter's case, however, is not the saddest; I am more and more convinced that Du Bois is behind him and using him as a tool to keep up this dirty work . . .[63]

EMMETT JAY SCOTT

[Tuskegee, Ala.] Dec. 4, 1905

Dear Dr. [James Griswold] Merrill:[64] Mr. Washington is on the eve of going North, and asks me to take care of the correspondence that he has been having with you with reference to his speaking at your coming anniversary . . .

Your recent letter states that you are planning to have Dr. Du Bois also speak. Mr. Washington is of the opinion that since Dr. Du Bois is an alumnus of Fisk that he would perhaps give a much more satisfactory address for the university than he could give. He also asks me to state that since the point of view of himself and Dr. Du Bois might differ, he does not think that it will be wise to have anything in the way of a seeming controversy, that more good would be accomplished by having one distinct impression left. With these facts in view, it would seem wiser for him to defer going to Fisk until some other occasion . . .[65]

P.B.S. PINCHBACK

Washington Dec 10—05

Dear Doctor [Washington],

. . . Went to Grimke's Church to hear him on Garrison. He dwelt on the necessity of organization and unity and spoke of Du Bois as a fighter etc. Nothing objectionable in his paper from our point of view.

Will attend another meeting at Grimke's Church this afternoon and hear Miss Cooper Mr. Cooke & Tunnell & Miller.[66] Yours very truly,

Pinchback . . .[67]

CHARLES WILLIAM ANDERSON

New York, N.Y., January 8, 1906

Confidential.
My dear Doctor [Washington]:

. . . I have just been advised that Du Bois' speech here last night, in Charlie Morris' church, was a failure. My Deputy, Harry Middleton, was on the ground to take notes, as was also Fred Moore.[68] Morris announced himself as being heart and soul with the Niagara movement, and called upon his friends to stand by him. He asked all those who were willing to follow him in this direction, to stand up, and, while quite a few stood up, they were composed almost entirely of women and boys. Middleton informs me that not more than twenty men were in the audience. Gilchrist Stewart was one of these . . .[69]

Charles W. Anderson[70]

T. Thomas Fortune's Afro-American League, founded in the late 1880s, was defunct by 1893. It was designed to fight for civil rights and black southern voting rights, but was not able to draw enough members. He revived the group in 1898 as the National Afro-American Council. Dominated by Fortune and AME Zion bishop Alexander Walters, the organization was too conservative for most inclined to join such organizations. Fortune and Walters were closely associated with Washington, who also had a hand in the organization, and the Council became a hub of the conciliatory approach. Du Bois's call for a new, more radical organization in 1905 was spurred, in part, by the ineffectiveness of the Council. The Council, in turn, made one last push at effectiveness after the founding of Niagara, holding a 1906 New York meeting in which white leaders like Oswald Garrison Villard participated. Still, the organization would not last, and along with Niagara would be replaced by the NAACP.[71]

W.E.B. DU BOIS

The Growth of the Niagara Movement

Any organization that pretends, however imperfectly, to represent something of the upward strivings of a great people, owes to that people periodically, a report of what it is doing to fulfill its promise and what its further program is. The numerical growth of the Niagara Movement has been as follows:

July, 1905—29 members from 14 states.

September, 1905—54 members from 18 states.

December, 1905—150 members from 30 states.

In addition to these there are about 50 affiliated members, making a total strength of about 200 men . . .

This growth has been perfectly normal and gained without any spectacular methods. No attempt whatever has been made to drum up a membership, to force in men for the sake of numbers, or to do anything inconsistent with a thoughtful, dignified attempt to unite in one National organization men who think alike . . .

The principles of the Niagara Movement are well known and yet for fear of misunderstanding, let us put them in bold print once more:

(a) FREEDOM OF SPEECH AND CRITICISM.

(b) AN UNFETTERED AND UNSUBSIDIZED PRESS.

(c) MANHOOD SUFFRAGE.

(d) THE ABOLITION OF ALL CASTE DISTINCTIONS BASED SIMPLY ON RACE AND COLOR.

(e) THE RECOGNITION OF THE PRINCIPLE OF HUMAN BROTHERHOOD AS A PRACTICAL PRESENT CREED.

(f) THE RECOGNITION OF THE HIGHEST AND BEST TRAINING AS THE MONOPOLY OF NO CLASS OR RACE.

(g) A BELIEF IN THE DIGNITY OF LABOR.

(h) UNITED EFFORT TO REALIZE THESE IDEALS UNDER WISE AND COURAGEOUS LEADERSHIP.

Who are the men back of these principles? We can say in all modesty that no organization in the United States, white or black, represents to-day in its membership a higher grade of character and efficiency. We have on our rolls ministers, lawyers, journalists, physicians, teachers, merchants, artisans and servants.

Moreover these men are standing for something in a day when it costs something to come out in the open, hold up your head and dare to say,

Yes, I belong to the Niagara Movement.

I believe in voting.

I believe in a free press.

I believe that I am just as good as any other man and

I bow to no Boss.

What has the Niagara Movement done thus far? It has done five things.

1. It has established strong local organizations in 17 of the thirty states in which it is represented and is rapidly organizing the other 13.

2. It has inaugurated an annual and simultaneous celebration, throughout the nation, of the work of the great abolitionists.

3. It has joined in the celebration of Garrison's 100th anniversary.

4. It has encouraged the free unsubsidized Negro Press.

5. It has aroused and focused public opinion throughout the nation and put new life into all the older Negro organizations . . .

In the Niagara Movement to-day are some of the founders and most prominent workers of the Afro-American Council. Why did they leave that organization? Because its leaders stooped to methods of election and control which were unfair and disgraceful, and because in six years of life it accomplished so little in the way of tangible results.

The Negro Business League was founded and started on the basis of an investigation which I carried out at Atlanta University and gave to the world gratis. I tried to get the Afro-American Council to form an organization on the basis of this information and they refused. I was glad afterward to hand the mass of data to the founders of the present League and it was on this basis that the League was formed. On the other hand I have never taken any part in the League, because I am not a businessman; I am a teacher. I have never seen, and do not now see, how teachers, politicians and editors can tell merchants how to run a business man's organization.

The mysterious "Committee of Twelve" was begun on a plan which I myself drafted. A conference was called in New York for uniting Negro forces. In that conference I expressed myself frankly in good, plain, unmistakable English. I was finally asked to draft a plan of co-operation. I proposed a Committee of Twelve representing various interests. I proposed in addition that each member of this committee form a local organization back of himself, so that the committee would represent an organization of about 1200 persons, would pay its own expenses, meet regularly and be divided into departments of work and investigation. The committee was selected so as to include men of whom I could not approve as representative; it was organized in my absence so as to make it a close corporation, irresponsible to anybody; its whole effective power was put into the hands of an executive committee of five, and that committee was to be appointed by one man. Moreover, that same man was to pay the expenses of the committee from some unknown secret fund in his possession. On hearing the details of this organization, three-members, including myself, promptly resigned . . .

I mention these things to show that I and all the men in the Niagara Movement have always done all we could to help Negro organizations. Not only this, we are still ready to help. We welcome the renewed activity of the Afro-American Council. We welcome the excellent literature of the Committee of Twelve. We welcome all the good done by the Business League. All these organizations can at all times count on the co-operation of the Niagara Movement in any work they wish to do for the real uplift of the Negro race . . . The Niagara Movement has grown and will grow. And we welcome to it intelligent, manly men who are not afraid to stand up and be counted.[72]

ARCHIBALD HENRY GRIMKE (*Grimke was a lawyer, journalist, and activist for black rights based in Boston and Washington, D.C.*)[73]

Washington, Jan. 10/06

Dear Mr. Washington: Your letter of the 4th inst. was duly rec'd. Since its receipt I have read Du Bois' article in The Voice,[74] & agree with you that it is full of false statements touching The Committee of Twelve & his relations to it. I have seen Kelly Miller & asked him to reply to it in

The Voice. He had not at the time seen the article, & so could not say that he would comply with my request. It seems to me that Kelly is the best member of the Committee to make the answer . . . That is of course if you think a reply is called for on the part of our Committee. Du Bois & The Guardian people would like to involve us in a controversy, at least they would like nothing better than to involve you & me, for against us they are especially bitter. With best regards, I am Cordially yours,

Archibald H. Grimke[75]

MELVIN JACK CHISUM (writing as codename Nine) *(Chisum was a spy hired by Washington to help infiltrate the Niagara Movement.)*[76]

[New York City] Sunday night Feb 11th, 06

Dear Dr. Washington: As result of a bit of getting about, it is my good fortune to be in possession of a couple of facts that are I believe, worth while.

Mr. Hump[h]rey was sent to Phil., on Wednesday and is back—informs me that the Philadelphia meeting was about to fall through—the League has "staked" them (the Philadelphians) and the meet will take place Feb 21st.

The Niagara people will attend tomorrow night, but not in a body or as an organization.

You will find me waiting at the Stevens House at 1 p.m. tomorrow (Monday). Will wait there until 2:30, later if necessary. I am, Your obedient humble servant.

Nine

P.S. I got copy of program from—Dr Gilbert today and will get same printed tomorrow by all means.[77]

LEWIS GARNETT JORDAN *(Jordan was a Baptist minister from Mississippi and a lifetime member of the NNBL.)*

Louisville, Ky. Feb. 12, 1906

My dear Sir & Bro [Emmett Jay Scott]: This comes to you strictly private. I want your advice and if you think well of it suggest it to Mr. Washington. It is this—"The Moon" now being published by Mr. Du Bois is the supposed mouthpiece of the Niagara Movement and will in time doubtless become very readable. As you know the Niagara Movement is chiefly to overthrow what they call the Booker Washington idea. The only charge that has been made against the Afro-American Council is, that it was domineered by Booker T. Washington. A little semi-monthly paper in the interest of the Council is almost a necessity . . .[78]

MELVIN JACK CHISUM

Washington, D.C. Feb 20th, 06

Dear Dr. Washington:

. . . It was my good fortune to attend The Metropolitan Literary Society's meeting tonight. Miss Nan[n]ie Burroughs,[79] spoke and in her speech she raked you mercilessly, before she got through she raked also Bishop Turner, Prof Du Bois, Mr Kelly Miller and "all" the colored men in Washington D.C. This gave me a chance and I brought the house down by flaying her in a nice sort of a way and closing with the statement that while we were at a loss we would be glad to have her find us, especially so, since we were informed (by her) that she had more brains than Profs. Washington, Kelly Miller, Du Bois, Bishop Turner and all the men in Washington rolled into one.

She is a dangerous little tramp, as is also that Rev Jordan—the missionary man, who also spoke . . .[80]

BOOKER T. WASHINGTON

[Tuskegee, Ala.] February 21, 1906

Dear Mr. [Timothy Thomas] Fortune: . . . Du Bois in his new role of an agitator is fast making a fool of himself through his little paper. When he stuck to the business of scientific investigation he was a success, but he is going to prove a failure as an agitator following in the wake of a crazy man like Trotter. I have refrained from mentioning his name in the editorial and hope you will not put it in the paper as I do not want to give him any free advertising . . .[81]

BOOKER T. WASHINGTON

[Tuskegee, Ala.] March 20, 1906

Confidential

My dear Mr. [Henry A.] Rucker:[82] Without letting any one know who wants the information, will you be kind enough to find out for me, if it is not too much trouble, who of the persons on the enclosed list voted at the last Presidential election, and indicate also which of them have met the conditions for voting in the way of paying poll taxes, etc. Yours truly,

Booker T. Washington

Bishop Turner
Bishop Gaines[83]
Dr. Bowen
Mr. I. Garland Penn
Prof. [John] Hope[84]
Prof. Towns[85]
Dr. Du Bois
Prof. [William H.] Crogman
Dr. [Joseph Simeon] Flipper[86]
J. Max Barber
Mr. Herndon[87]

JESSE MAX BARBER[88]

Southern Representation

The Constitution League has committed itself to the proposition to reduce Southern representation in Congress. A division of opinion arises here even among the friends of the League. There is room for a diversity of opinion. The writer was once of the opinion that the reduction program was not the course of wisdom. He has been converted and gives to our readers the reasons for his present position. It is granted by all except intellectually stranded bigots that the Negroes, generally speaking, have been boldly disfranchised in the South, and that this class legislation has worked harm to the political health of the whole section. The South has perpetrated on the country a kind of tyranny that literally kills our free institutions and destroys constitutional and representative government. The supreme law of the land has been made the scorn of its constituents. Something must be done. The

South must not be granted unchecked liberty to annul the Federal Constitution at its sovereign whim and caprice. The time has come when laxity must cease, when the government must be asked to hold a whip over a section of the country in order to compel it to respect its authority . . .[89]

TIMOTHY THOMAS FORTUNE

New York, April 5, 1906

Dear Mr. [Jesse Max] Barber, After reading the April number of the Voice of the Negro and being shocked by the brutal coarseness and vulgarity of your treatment of the question of those who think differently from you on the question of the reduction of Southern representation, with the very coarse cartoon accompanying the editorial I decided at the last moment not to use the enclosed article and cut. If Dr. Washington's mouth is padlocked on the question of Southern Representation, it was padlocked by me, as he came over to my view of the matter reluctantly after I had shown him the danger which lurked in that proposition.[90]

I have come to the conclusion that we can do nothing with you Niagara people because you appear to me naturally to run to coarseness and vulgarity in your treatment of men who differ from you, and in criminal practices, as in the case of Trotter, and in underhand throat cutting as in the case of a great many of those who write for the press but don't sign their names from this territory . . .[91]

W.E.B. DU BOIS

May 22, 1906

Mr. Andrew Carnegie
Sir:

You will possibly remember me as being presented to you and Mr. Carl Schurz at Carnegie Hall some years ago.[92]

I beg leave to bring to your attention the work of the Atlanta Conference with a view to securing if possible your financial support for this work.

I enclose herewith a report on Negro Crime, which is the ninth annual report published by the Conference. The object of this Conference is the systematic and exhaustive study of the American Negro, in order that in the future philanthropists and others who seek to solve this serious set of problems may have before them a carefully gathered body of scientifically arranged facts to guide them . . .

So far this work has been carried on by small voluntary contributions. As it begins its second decade it finds a growing field of investigation before it, and it needs to enlarge its scope and improve its methods of research. This work is of such a nature that it cannot be carried on by ordinary scientific agencies—it would naturally be hampered by strong local feelings and prejudices, if, for instance, its work was essayed by the Carnegie Institution.

I have made bold therefore to appeal directly to you and to ask if you would be enough interested to look into the merits & needs of this work. If you are I should be glad to lay before you (a) a complete set of our publications (b) our programs of future study & (c) Press notices & commendations of our work . . . I am well aware that you are overwhelmed with communications of this sort, but I know of no other way by which to bring to your attention a work which seems to me one of the worthiest and neediest in the land.

I beg to remain, Sir,

Very Respectfully Yours,
W.E.B. Du Bois[93]

MELVIN JACK CHISUM

New York, N.Y. June 11th, 1906

Dear Dr. Washington: . . . I beg to advise that I was in Brooklyn yesterday (Sunday) with a crowd of Niagara Movement men. They do not know the date as yet. As soon as they do, I will also.

They are working like beavers to get up a crowd to go to the convention and are complaining because Mr Du Bois will not decide the date. I thank you very much for the check. Yours faithfully,

Chisum

P.S. Rev. Miller:[94] Has a list to be signed by all who intend going to the Convention. I was requested to sign it yesterday, but did not. Do you wish me to go? Is it best?[95]

MELVIN JACK CHISUM

New York, N.Y. June 16th 1906

Dear Dr. Washington: The Niagara Movement people have about-faced. Their convention will be at Harpers Ferry, W.Va. and will begin Wednesday morning August 15th and adjourn Saturday night Aug 18th.

I attended a meeting last night in Brooklyn where I learned this. That much and that much only is settled. Another meeting Wednesday night next. The enclosed blanks are being sent to all who have registered their names with them and their various local secretaries.

I am almost sure I will be able to attend the secret conferences at the Convention, if you desire me to go please notify me. Your obedient servant,

Chisum[96]

MELVIN JACK CHISUM

New York, N.Y. July 27 [1906]

Dear Doctor [Washington]: It is 2 in the morning, I have just returned from Brooklyn, where I have been visiting with the N. M. [Niagara Movement] friends.

Aug 2d meeting has fallen through—Du Bois has informed Rev Miller that Morgan has a case in the Boston court that will preclude the possibility of his attending, while he himself (Du Bois) finds the trip will entail an extra expense, not justified by the returns up to date, which have fallen about $400.00 short of his (Du Bois) expectations.

I am nursing and encouraging the Morris situation as dexterously as I can . . .[97]

RICHARD THEODORE GREENER (Greener was the first black graduate of Harvard and Dean of Howard's law school.)[98]

Storer College, Harper's Ferry, [W.Va.] July 31st, 1906

Private and Confidential

My dear friend [Washington]: . . . Since, I am here, I learn of the approaching "Niagara" convention, to be held here. My intent has been to return here in any event. Now, I seem to see a chance to be present, as a spectator, and perchance have an opportunity to say a word, in reconcilement of apparently conflicting elements, which at the present time, of all others, ought to be completely in harmony, to be effective. Will you be north again before this Niagara meeting? If so, can you not let me know, in advance, so that we can have a private talk over the situation . . .[99]

William Henry Flemming was an Augusta lawyer and former member of the House of Representatives. On June 19, 1906, he gave a speech in Athens that became the pamphlet, Slavery and the Race Problem in the South, with Special Reference to the State of Georgia *(Boston: Dana Estes & Co., 1906). In the pamphlet, Flemming towed a fine line. Both North and South were responsible for slavery. The Reconstruction amendments turned out to be good, although they were harsh at the time. "The white people of the South, and especially the state of Georgia, can now proceed to work out their racial problem on lines of justice to the negro, without imperiling white supremacy," which was still absolutely necessary. He argued against disfranchisement, but approved of the party primary and the poll tax. Booker T. Washington loved it.*[100]

BOOKER T. WASHINGTON

[Omaha, Neb.] August 8, 1906

My dear Mr. [Francis Jackson] Garrison: . . . Have you read the speech of the Hon. Walter H. Fleming, which he delivered before the University of Georgia? It is, in my judgement, one of the finest expressions, from a Southern white man, that I have ever read. Very truly yours,

Booker T. Washington[101]

EMMETT JAY SCOTT

[Tuskegee, Ala.] August 8, '06

Dear Mr. Washington: I send you herewith summary of the first meeting—the Conference—out of which grew the Committee of Twelve. In it you will find the statement signed by all of those who were present, including, of course, Du Bois. The original must be in the hands of Mr. H.M. Brown[e] or Kelly Miller who was the first Secretary. In addition also I am sending you the recommendations submitted by Du Bois for the government of the body, & a newspaper report of the organization of the Niagara Movement. *These are the only copies of each of these documents*, & I hope they will come back in good shape for our records. I send the things not asked for with the thought that you may find them useful.

E J Scott[102]

BOOKER T. WASHINGTON

August 11, 1906

Personal
My dear Prof. [Richard Theodore] Greener:

. . . You will find, in the last analysis, that the whole object of the Niagara Movement is to defeat and oppose every thing I do. I have done all I could to work in harmony with Du Bois, but he has permitted Trotter and others to fool him into the idea that he was some sort of a leader, consequently he has fritt[er]ed away his time in agitation when he could succeed as a scientist or sociologist . . .[103]

SAMUEL LAING WILLIAMS

Chicago 8/12/1906

My Dear Dr Washington . . . It requires no ordinary soul in these times to stand erect and look straight ahead with confidence that right must come through error and wrong doings. I would regard it as a calamaty to our progress if you and others with you became discouraged by the seeming increase of criticism and lying by our own people. You are everlastingly right, and what you stand and contend for is bound to prevail unless the world and everything good in it comes to an end. I am satisfied that there is no use in attempting to conciliate this crowd of indignation-people. I met Bently on the cars last night and he began on me at once about the great harm you are doing to the cause of negro advancement. He became quite impatient with me because I showed him specific instances in which he and his kind had grossly misrepresented you in doing and saying certain things which you never did and never said. They are disappointed and fume just as soon as you show them that the things that they have been taking as true are false. They are like a criminal lawyer who is paid to make out a case. I doubt if there can be found in the country an organization of men at the foundation of which there is so much false assumption untruth and disappointed hopes as in these Niagara folks. . . .[104]

Du Bois downplayed his desire, but he wanted the Washington, D.C., superintendent job, and continued to want it for the next six years since his first failure. He had his own allies in Washington who stumped for his consideration over the incumbent Montgomery. The fight would explode again in August 1906, but Washington's forces—most notably Mary Church Terrell—outmaneuvered him. Washington instead helped his chosen candidate, Roscoe Conkling Bruce, into the position. He would take over in 1907, and from that point, there was no chance that Du Bois would get the job, and his pursuit functionally ended.[105]

BOOKER T. WASHINGTON

[Tuskegee, Ala.] August 20, 1906

Personal

My dear Sir [William Estabrook Chancellor]:[106] I am doing that which I very rarely consent to do and that is, without solicitation from you, writing a letter of endorsement of one of our workers. Mr. Roscoe Conkling Bruce is, I understand, desirous of obtaining a position of responsibility in the city of Washington in the colored Public Schools. Mr. Bruce has been at the head of the Academic Department of this institution for four years and has rendered high and efficient service. It will be a matter of regret and loss to have him leave us but he naturally looks upon such a change as being a promotion and we feel, in view of this, that we cannot consistently oppose his making the change.

I can give you no better idea of the efficiency of Mr. Bruce's work than to enclose a pamphlet containing copies of letters from Superintendents of Education who visited us some years ago inspecting the work done under Mr. Bruce . . .[107]

Booker T. Washington[108]

BOOKER T. WASHINGTON

[Tuskegee, Ala.] August 27, 1906

Dear Mr. [Richard Le Roy] Stokes: I think the policy that the Age has pursued during the last three or four months has driven the Niagara people to the point where they see that they cannot afford any more to let the public understand that their organization is opposing me. This is shown by the fact that none of the speakers made reference to me and there was less direct reference in their resolutions. Since we have accomplished this much, the next policy to pursue is to ignore the whole organization as much as possible. Without the use of my name, it is impossible for them to keep themselves before the public very long. Yours very truly,

Booker T. Washington[109]

THE OUTLOOK

The Platform of the Niagara Movement

The second annual meeting of the so-called Niagara Movement was held recently at Harper's Ferry. This is a movement of negroes for negro rights. It represents the more political and the more assertive spirit in the negro race, under the leadership of Dr. Du Bois, as the Tuskegee Movement under the leadership of Dr. Washington represents the more industrial and the more pacific spirit. It is probably not unjust to say that something of the quality of the Niagara Movement is indicated by the fact that its leaders chose this year Harper's Ferry for its place of assemblage, and in its closing utterance the assembly declared, "Here, on the scene of John Brown's Martyrdom, we reconsecrate ourselves, our honor, our property, to the final emancipation of the race which John Brown died to make free." Its adopted platform comprises five principles: (1) The right to vote: "We want full manhood suffrage, and we want it now, henceforth, and forever." (2) Condemnation of all race discrimination in public accommodations: "Separation in railway and street cars, based simply on race and color, is un-American, undemocratic and silly." (3) Freedom of social intercourse: "We claim the right of freemen to walk, talk, and be with them that wish to be with us. No man has a right to choose another man's friends, and to attempt to do so is an impudent interference with the most fundamental human privilege." (4) Equality in the enforcement of laws: "Justice even for criminals and outlaws;" "Congress to take charge of

Congressional elections;" "the Fourteenth and Fifteenth Amendments enforced." (5) "The National Government to step in and wipe out illiteracy in the South;" an undying hostility to "any proposal to educate black boys and girls simply as servants and underlings, or simply for the use of other people."

The Platform of the Outlook

We can best state our views respecting these demands by putting with them what appear to us to be the just and reasonable bases for the settlement of the so-called race issue. Those bases we should state somewhat as follows: (1) Manhood suffrage, provided the manhood comes first and the suffrage afterwards. The ballot is not a natural right, like the right to the protection of person and property; it is a prerogative to be given only to those, black or white, who have furnished some evidence that they possess the intellectual and moral qualifications to use the ballot for the benefit of the community. But it should be based on personal qualifications, not on race or color. (2) It is better for both races that they have their separate schools and separate churches. It is no more an injustice to the black race than to the white race to provide separate cars for them, if the accommodations are equally good for both races. (3) Social fellowship cannot be restrained by law, neither can it be claimed as a right. In general, the way to secure social recognition is not to demand it. (4) The demand for the equality of law enforcement is wholly just. The demand for Congressional charge of Congressional elections is wholly unnecessary. Congress has already charge of Congressional elections. It has the right to reject any Representative on evidence that his election has been accomplished by corruption, fraud, violence, or threatening of any description, and it ought to exercise this right far more vigorously than it has been accustomed to do. (5) We want the National Government to "wipe out illiteracy in the South," and we protest against any "proposal to educate black boys and girls simply as servants and underlings;" but we also affirm as a truth of universal applicability that the end of all education should be to fit the pupil for the work which it is probable he will have to do, for the service which he will probably have to render. We add the demand for the open door of industrial opportunity to all men, black and white, and insistence upon the principle that every man shall fit himself, as his first duty to the community, to render the best service of which, taking account of his training and his inheritance, he is capable. On the whole, we think the Niagara Movement would be more useful if it demanded more of the negro race and put less emphasis on its demands for the negro race.[110]

BOOKER T. WASHINGTON

[Tuskegee, Ala.] Sept. 2, 1906

Personal
My dear Dr. [Lyman] Abbott:[111]

. . . In the last issue of the Outlook I fear you gave too much serious attention to Dr. Du Bois and his movement.[112] I have watched it
closely from the beginning. All told I do not believe there are more
than two or three hundred colored people of any prominence or influence who are inclined to follow such folly as he is the leader of. The
actual attendance at the Harpers Ferry meeting was less than 50.
There were at least 600 delegates present at our Atlanta meeting. Yours
truly,

Booker T. Washington[113]

JAMES A. COBB *(Cobb was a young Washington, D.C. lawyer and an
ally of Washington.)*[114]

Washington, D.C. September 3, 1906

Dear Mr. [Emmett Jay] Scott: The school question is warmer now than
ever, Du Bois is turning heaven and earth to be appointed assistant
superintendent. I suppose you have seen some of the Washington
papers, if so, you have seen where [W.S.] Montgomery's position is
very precarious at present; the friends of Du Bois are trying to oust him
and place Du Bois in his place.[115] Mrs. Terrell came home Saturday
night and hasn't slept any since. Judge and I have been at work on the
matter. Will write you later. Very sincerely yours,

James A. Cobb[116]

BOOKER T. WASHINGTON

(Tuskegee, Ala.] September 4 [1906]

Dear Dr. [William Estabrook] Chancellor: I shall be very glad indeed if
you decide to appoint Mr. Bruce to a Supervisorship. I feel quite sure
that he will perform the service well and satisfactorily as he has ability
of a high order.

I hope at some time to have the privilege of meeting you in a personal way. Yours truly,

Booker T. Washington[117]

BOOKER T. WASHINGTON

[Tuskegee, Ala.] September 5, 1906

Personal

My dear Mr. [Richard] Carroll:[118] I have your kind letter of September 1st and you do not know how very grateful [I am] indeed for your kind and generous expressions regarding me. I am glad you see the conditions in their true light.

The little crowd who are opposing me are seeking, in the first place, notoriety, and in the second place they are very largely actuated by motives of jealousy. They seem to want to do something but hardly know what to do nor how to do it. The effect of the resolutions passed at Harper's Ferry was most hurtful, and practically every newspaper in the country has condemned them. As your own letter suggests this crowd is hurting the race instead of helping it . . .[119]

BOOKER T. WASHINGTON

Tuskegee Institute, Alabama, September 6, 1906

Personal

My dear Mr. [Oswald Garrison] Villard: I am taking the first opportunity I can seize to thank you for permitting Miss [Mary White] Ovington to report our proceedings in Atlanta for your paper.[120] Aside from accomplishing good, in my opinion, for the whole race, I am quite sure it was very fortunate that we went to Atlanta at the special time that we did. When I got there I found the feeling between the races intensely strong, almost to the breaking point . . . One of the afternoon papers was advocating openly the formation of a Ku Klux Klan, another had offered a thousand dollars for the lynching of a colored man guilty of one of these crimes. My first action was to go directly to the managing editor of each of the four newspapers in Atlanta and talk the situation over frankly with them, and in every case I was received with cordiality, and all expressed the feeling that they needed help. The result was that under the circumstances I think the papers gave us reasonably good attention, but the good that we did was not evidenced so much in the local newspaper reports as by the expression of individuals which we heard from many quarters. The result was that one of the bitterest afternoon newspapers gave us [more] space than any other Atlanta newspaper, and had several editorials of an encouraging character. The last day that we were in Atlanta, the protest contained in the Journal against the formation of a Ku Klux Klan was circulated and printed. I have had numerous letters from colored people since the meeting was over, thanking us for coming to Atlanta, and expressing the feeling of relief because of the changed situation. Yours very truly,

Booker T. Washington[121]

SAMUEL LAING WILLIAMS

Chicago, Ill. 22/10/1906

My Dear [Emmett Jay] Scott,

. . . There is something devilish about the way Dr. Washington is being misrepresented by the Conservator. This thing seems to have been intensified by the presence of the "fleeing editor," I have not had a chance to have any talk with him . . . I was at a meeting yesterday where the Niagara people gave a report of the Harpers Ferry meeting. The speakers were Bentley, Barber, Madden and [Edward E.] Wilson.[122] They all protested that the aim of the "Movement" was in no way in opposition to Dr. Washington! Mrs. Wool[l]ey told me that she had become thoroughly sick of Du Bois. She calls his "litany"[123] was simply "sickening" . . .[124]

BOOKER T. WASHINGTON

[Tuskegee, Ala.] October 25, 1906

My dear Mr. [Samuel Laing] Williams: I really have been so busy lately that I have not kept up with the correspondence which I hear is appearing in one or two of the Niagara Movement papers. I understand that they are stating with continual emphasis that my speech at the League was prepared or suggested very largely by the white people in Atlanta.

The fact is, my speech was sent out to the Associated Press before I even went to Atlanta, and it was not altered in a single line or sentence after I got there. I always prepare my speeches at least a week ahead, and not only that, but I go carefully over them with friends of the race with different points of view . . .

Booker T. Washington[125]

RAYMOND ALBERT PATTERSON *(Patterson was the Washington bureau chief of the* Chicago Tribune.*)*[126]

Washington, D.C. Nov. 18, 1906

Confidential

My dear Mr. Washington: I was very glad to get your letter regarding my rather hastily written article on the ever recurring negro problem. I may possibly say to you confidentially that I had chiefly in view a situation right here in the District of Columbia. The new Superintendent of Schools here is not the kind of man who ought to be in such a position. He is quite in sympathy with the colored representatives on the school board. Their point of view is exactly that to which I called attention. So true is this that they had under consideration the calling to Washington as Assistant Superintendent of Professor Du Bois. I have great regard for him and I think he is many generations ahead of his race, some what unfortunately for him and for the race. He is a wonderful man in his way, but I do not think his theories are good for the colored people. I know they are diametrically opposed to those you hold.

Of course it is quite true that only a few of the colored people are in the north while the many millions of them are in the south. Yet I think you will agree with me that the great bulk of the whites are in the north, and in the future some day it must be those whites who after all will solve this race problem for the country. The agitators, the politicians, the mere talkers among the colored people are those who make themselves known most commonly in the north. The colored man in the southern states today is not much of a free agent, as you have cause to know. He is surrounded by a distinctly unfriendly white population, for whatever they say of themselves, they fear the negro and they hate him in about equal proportions.

If anything is to be done in the future by the national administration for the uplifting of the negro, it will be done, in my judgment, by the sober pressure of public opinion in the wealthy and populous northern states. I believe as you do that the negro in the south as a race needs first of all an elementary education and then a knowledge of how to use his physical strength and his dawning mental strength to the best advantage. I believe you are going about it in the right way, and I am hoping that in the future the conscience of the nation will be aroused so that it will undertake to build not universities nor post graduate schools for the negro, but sensible manual training institutions, and enterprises such as that you have by your own great genius so skillfully organized and conducted . . .

In what I have written hitherto I have been deeply impressed by your work. I am entirely in sympathy with it, and I shall always testify everywhere to the great benefit I believe you have been to the negro race and almost equally, of course, to the white race, to which you also belong. From time to time I have been disturbed by the apparent success of the people who are not in sympathy with your work. Just at present here in Washington they are, in my judgment, influencing the colored people of this city in the wrong direction. What I have written thus far has been designed, so far as haste would permit of any design, to discourage the growth of this dangerous sentiment and to promote respect among whites and blacks for the utilitarian ideas with which your name has been associated in such an honorable manner . . .[127]

NOTES

1. Aptheker, 1969, 900–901.
2. Lewis, 1993, 322.
3. Aptheker, 1969, 901–904.
4. Mary Burnett Talbert was a Buffalo high school teacher and race leader who was loyal to Washington. Washington, 1979, vol. 8, 321.
5. Ibid., 321.
6. Crosby is most likely a pseudonym for either Melvin J. Chisum or Clifford H. Plummer, two of Washington's spies. Ibid.
7. William Henry Talbert, a black leader in Buffalo devoted to Washington. Ibid.
8. Ibid.
9. Clifford H. Plummer was a far more successful Washington saboteur. He served as an attorney for one of the Boston Riot defendants in 1903 while maintaining secret contact with Tuskegee. He then infiltrated Trotter's New England Suffrage League. He also attended the first Niagara meeting as a spy for Washington. Washington, 1977, vol. 5, 93–94.
10. Washington, 1979, vol. 8, 322.
11. For Morris, see Chapter 10. For Bentley, see Chapter 9. For Butler Roland Wilson, see Chapter 12. Wesley was a Chicago physician. Edward Herbert Wright was a Chicago lawyer and Republican politician. Oscar

Stanton De Priest was a member of the Cook County board of commissioners, and would go on to become a member of the United States House of Representatives. James S. Madden was a Chicago bookkeeper. John R. Marshall was the first black colonel in command during the Spanish American War. Sweeny, 2010, 84; "Some Chicagoans of Note," September 1915, 37–38; and Day, 1980, 6–17.

12. For McGhee, see Chapter 12, note 43. George Henry Woodson was a lawyer and Republican activist in Des Moines, Iowa, one of the founders of the Iowa chapter of the Afro-American Council and the Iowa Negro Bar Association. Brown Sylvester Smith was a Kansas City lawyer and member of the city council. See Silag, Koch-Bridgford, and Chase, 2001; and Shutter, 1923, 735.

13. Ira Guy was a successful barber in Topeka, and along with serving as secretary of the Topeka branch of the NNBL, he also served as the first vice president of the national organization. Cox, 1982, 175.

14. Washington, 1979, vol. 8, 324–325.

15. See Chapter 12, note 8.

16. Edward W. Crosby was a close friend of Du Bois, who was functionally serving as a double agent, reporting to Washington (through Anderson) on events at Niagara. Forth, 1987, 45–56.

17. Lafayette M. Hershaw was a lawyer and an employee with the Department of the Interior, a scion of black Washington, D.C., and a founding member of the Niagara Movement. Carle, 2013, 183–184; and Moore, 2003, 81–82.

18. Washington, 1979, vol. 8, 327.

19. Greenwood, 2009, 160–161.

20. Washington's agents prevented the Associated Press and most newspapers from reporting on the Niagara meeting. Trotter, however, printed an account in the *Transcript* upon his return to Boston. Dr. Samuel E. Courtney was one of Washington's Boston allies and his former student. Washington, 1979, vol. 8, 329; and Harlan, 1983, 46, 103.

21. Washington, 1979, vol. 8, 328–329.

22. Ibid., 329.

23. Ibid., 329–330.

24. Richard W. Thompson was one of Washington's agents in Washington, D.C., a civil servant and columnist for various black newspapers. Harlan, *1983*, 87, 94–95.

25. Hervey W. Laird edited the Montgomery *Times* and served as correspondent for the Birmingham *Age-Herald*. Washington, 1979, vol. 8, 330.

26. Ibid.

27. Ibid., 331.

28. Ibid., 332.

29. Washington, 1979, vol. 8, 332.

30. W. Allison Sweeney was the editor of the *Chicago Conservator*, a paper supported by Washington. Kreiling, 1993, 176–203.

31. Washington, 1979, vol. 8, 332–333.

32. Ibid., 337.

33. George Washington Cable was a white novelist of Creole Louisiana, one of the most accomplished of the Gilded Age "local color" writers, an opponent of Jim Crow, and an associate of Booker T. Washington. Butcher, 1948, 462–468.

34. Washington, 1979, vol. 8, 337–338.

35. Ibid., 338.

36. John A. Hertel owned a publishing company that began by publishing bibles, but expanded to publish a variety of materials. It was based both in Toronto and in Chicago. Rowe, 1921.

37. Jesse Max Barber was the editor of the *Voice of the Negro*, a monthly literary magazine published in Atlanta, an ally of Du Bois and thus an enemy of Washington. See Chapter 12.

38. Washington, 1979, vol. 8, 338–339.

39. Lewis, 1993, 322–323.

40. For Roscoe Conkling Simmons, see Chapter 11. Ernest Ten Eyck Attwell was Tuskegee's football coach. Julius R. Cox was a member of Tuskegee's secretarial staff. Harlan, 1983, 86, 250.

41. Washington, 1979, vol. 8, 339.

42. Du Bois, 1973, 112; and Aptheker, 1969, 900–915.

43. Du Bois, 1973, 112–113.

44. See note 12.

45. Washington, 1979, vol. 8, 357–358.

46. Ibid., 363–364.

47. Washington, 1977, vol. 5, 477.

48. See Chapter 12, note 8.

49. For Frederick Randolph Moore, see Chapter 12, note 17. John Elmer Milholland began as a newspaper reporter, then moved into government service in New York City. He was a devoted Republican, but he eventually left politics for business, running the Batchelier Pneumatic Tube Company. Although he was a wealthy white man, he was devoted to black rights and would eventually become one of the founders of the NAACP. Riser, 2010, 170–171.

50. Washington, 1979, vol. 8, 374–375.

51. Andrew B. Humphrey was an ally of both Milholland and Washington, the secretary of the Constitution League, based in New York. Alexander, 2012, 232.

52. Washington, 1979, vol. 8, 378–379.

53. Harry S. Cummings was a black Baltimore politician, the first African American elected to the city council. Warner Miller had served as a Republican U.S. Senator from New York in the 1880s. By this time, he was serving as a state tax commissioner, but, of course, was still known as "senator." See Greene, 1979, 203–222; and "Miller, Warner, (1838–1918)," *Biographical Dictionary of the United States Congress*.

54. Washington, 1979, vol. 8, 380–381.

55. Green and Driver, "Introduction," 1978, 18.

56. Washington, 1979, vol. 8, 382–387.

57. John Cornelius Asbury was a black lawyer and devoted Republican from Philadelphia. Smith, 1996, 169–203.

58. Washington, 1979, vol. 8, 387–388.

59. Ibid., 394–396.

60. See note 38.

61. Washington, 1979, vol. 8, 453–454.

62. Ibid., 454–455.

63. Ibid., 455–456.

64. James Griswold Merrill was president of Fisk University, serving from 1901 to 1909. See the Merrill, James G. Collection 1899–1919, Fisk University Library, Special Collections and Archives, Nashville, Tennessee.

65. Merrill informed Scott that Du Bois was not coming, so Washington agreed to speak. Washington, 1979, vol. 8, 460.

66. Pinchback here refers to Anna Julia Cooper, Charles C. Cook, William V. Tunnell, and Kelly Miller. Moore, 1999, 97.

67. Washington, 1979, vol. 8, 463.

68. Reverend Charles Morris was a minister in Wilmington, North Carolina. Harry Middleton and Frederick Randolph Moore were Tuskegee agents. Noll and Nystrom, 2011, 41. For Frederick Randolph Moore, see note 50.

69. Gilchrist Stewart was a New York lawyer, businessman, and Republican activist. He would later become an official with the New York branch of the NAACP. "Men of the Month: Gilchrist Stewart," August 1911, 147; and Johnson, 2003, 83–85.

70. Washington, 1979, vol. 8, 488–489.

71. Washington, 1972, vol. 2, 357–358.

72. Du Bois, January 1906, 43–45.

73. Grimke, born into slavery in South Carolina, rose to power after graduating from Harvard. He would go on to become vice president of the NAACP. He was the nephew of Sarah and Angelina Grimke and the brother of Francis Grimke. See Perry, 2001.

74. In "The Growth of the Niagara Movement," published in *Voice of the Negro* in January 1906, Du Bois claimed to be the NNBL's founder, that his plan led to the establishment of the Committee of Twelve, but that he resigned because of the dictatorial power and secret money that controlled its activities. See above. Washington, 1979, vol. 8, 495.

75. Ibid.

76. Jones, 2011, 35.

77. Washington, 1979, vol. 8, 520. Dr. Matthew W. Gilbert was minister of the Mt. Olivet Baptist Church and a founding member of Niagara. He was a member of the group's Committee of Organization. Alexander, 2012, 279; and Niagara Movement, Committee of Organization, "Report on the

Committee of Organization," December 1907, University of Massachusetts Amherst, Special Collections and University Archives.

78. Washington, 1979, vol. 8, 520–521.

79. Nannie Helen Burroughs was a leader of the black women's club movement and a lifetime member of the NNBL. Ibid., 530.

80. Ibid.

81. Ibid., 531.

82. Rucker was the collector of Internal Revenue in Atlanta and one of the most powerful black politicians in the city. Mixon, 2005, 485–504.

83. A bishop in the AME church since 1885, Wesley John Gaines served at various churches throughout Georgia and helped to found Atlanta's Morris Brown College. Sewell, 1981, 133–136.

84. John Hope was a professor at Morehouse College and would become the institution's president in 1906. He was one of the seminal black leaders in Atlanta and the nation and would be part of both Niagara and the NAACP. See Davis, 1998.

85. George Alexander Towns was a graduate of Atlanta and Harvard and professor at Atlanta during the early 20th century. He sided clearly with Trotter in the Boston Riot incident and was a thorn in the side of an Atlanta administration who dealt with many who supported Washington. Washington, 1977, vol. 7, 296.

86. Joseph Simeon Flipper was president of Morris Brown College in Atlanta. "Joseph Simeon Flipper," January 1945, 109–111.

87. Washington, 1979, vol. 8, 552–553.

88. See Chapter 12.

89. Barber, 1906, 242–243.

90. See above.

91. Washington, 1979, vol. 8, 568–569.

92. Schurz was a former Republican Secretary of the Interior who had switched parties in the 1890s because of his anti-imperialist stance, which put him into contact with Andrew Carnegie, who was also an anti-imperialist. See Trefousse, 1982.

93. Du Bois, 1973, 121–122.

94. George Frazier Miller was a member of Niagara and president of the National Equal Rights League. He would be a part of NAACP when it was founded. Washington, 1980, vol. 9, 30.

95. Ibid.

96. Ibid., 31–32.

97. Ibid., 47.

98. See Mounter, 2002.

99. Emmett Jay Scott wrote on the letter, "Here is a good chance to get a good friend into the inner portals of the Niagara meeting. He gives his Washington address in case you want to write him. He writes in grateful & sincere terms. E J Scott 8/2." Du Bois, 1973, 48.

100. Flemming, 1906; and Washington, 1980, vol. 9, 52.

101. Washington, 1980, vol. 9, 51–52.

102. Ibid., 52–53.

103. Ibid., 55–56.

104. Ibid., 57–58.

105. Lewis, 1993, 246.

106. William Estabrook Chancellor was Washington, D.C.'s superintendent of schools. Washington, 1980, vol. 9, 60.

107. Washington's recommendation came after Bruce asked for a letter and told Washington that he heard Du Bois was a candidate. Ibid.

108. Ibid., 59–60.

109. Ibid., 62.

110. "The Platform of the Niagara Movement," 1 September 1906, 3–4.

111. See Chapter 2, note 12.

112. The magazine described Niagara as "the more assertive spirit of the negro race, under the leadership of Dr. Du Bois," while still claiming to prefer "the more industrial and more pacific spirit" of Washington. See above. Washington, 1980, vol. 9, 67.

113. Ibid.

114. A graduate of Howard Law, Cobb would go on to teach at the university in 1917. He would be appointed municipal court judge under the administration of Calvin Coolidge. But in 1906, he had only been a member of the bar for four years and had yet to achieve the level of success he would later accomplish. Pitre, 1979, 101–102.

115. For more on Winfield Montgomery, see Chapter 5.

116. Washington, 1980, vol. 9, 68.

117. Ibid.

118. Richard Carroll was a Baptist minister headquartered in Columbia, South Carolina, a believer in industrial education, and a staunch supporter of Washington. Newby, 1973, 168–169; and Washington, 1980, vol. 9, 69.

119. Washington, 1980, vol. 9, 68–69.

120. Mary White Ovington was a liberal reformer and race rights activist who would, along with Villard, help found the NAACP. She would eventually develop an incredibly close relationship with W.E.B. Du Bois. She will obviously become more prominent in the conversation as time passes. See Ovington, 1947.

121. Washington, 1980, vol. 9, 69–70.

122. Wilson was a Chicago lawyer and activist, opposed to Washingtonian accomodationism. Ibid., 193.

123. "Litany of Atlanta," a protest poem by Du Bois originally published in the *Independent* 51 (11 October 1906): 856–858.

124. Washington, 1980, vol. 9, 102.

125. Ibid., 103–104.

126. Richmond *Times Dispatch*, 14 November 1909, 1.

127. Washington, 1980, vol. 9, 135–137.

14

The Spies and the Radicals

The Tuskegee Machine remained active well after Niagara's founding, continuing to work against the group until its collapse and simultaneously working to counter the increasingly public persona of Du Bois. At the same time, the public activism of both leaders led the white mainstream to begin understanding the reality of a feud between the two and the existence of two distinct poles of black political leadership. Many, if not most, whites supported Washington's theories, partially because they demanded less of white people and partially because they seemed more pragmatic in the face of southern intransigence. Washington and Du Bois interpreted black rights debates for them whenever possible between 1907 and 1909 while continuing to stump for their own positions and causes.

CHARLES WILLIAM ANDERSON

New York, N.Y., February 25, 1907

(Personal)
Private.

My dear Mr. [Emmett Jay] Scott: Replying to your favor of the 22nd instant, permit me to say that from a source which I do not care to

mention on paper, of which the Doctor will advise you, I learned that
Du Bois, Wetmore and Owen Waller met in Wetmore's room at the
Hotel Marshall, during Du Bois's recent visit to this city.[1] At this conference, or interview, Du Bois took occasion to criticise the Doctor and
myself as frauds, and to say that you were a very mean and rascally
person. He paid you the very high compliment of being the man who
inspired all the mischief that is hatched out at Tuskegee. As for myself,
he found no colors black enough in which to paint my picture. The
same was true with reference to his estimate of the Doctor. The Doctor
will tell you that I have a way of finding out what goes on in the office
or the apartment of Brother Wetmore . . .

Please pardon me for wasting so much paper on such cattle. Please
let the Doctor read this letter . . .[2]

*J. Douglas Wetmore, a Jacksonville lawyer, was a Washington supporter
and member of the National Negro Business League, but he also maintained
connections with Du Bois and other Washington critics. Washington, who
knew about this, worked against him in retribution at every turn.[3] Meanwhile,
Mary White Ovington had been disappointed in Washington since she chaired
a New York dinner for him and heard him speak. On the other hand, she was
taken with Du Bois and maintained a long correspondence with him.[4]*

MARY WHITE OVINGTON

Brooklyn, N.Y., April 13, 1907.

My dear Dr. Du Bois:—

I have heard of your visiting New York, and I know that you did
splendid work here.

Isn't it good that Dr. Boas is writing at last?[5] I have not yet read his
article in Van Norden's, but I know it must be an excellent antidote to
much of the nonsense that is about today. . . .

Always sincerely,
Mary W. Ovington

Mr. Alexander Irvine, a socialist & preacher who went South for three
months disguised as a laborer and worked in turpentine fields &
coal mines besides visiting convict camps will write on peonage for
Appleton. I met him the other night & he said: "I started South full of
admiration for Washington, but after I had been in Alabama among

the laborers for a time I could not go to Tuskegee. I knew that he was wrong." Then he spoke in highest praise of you. I wish he might be invited to speak on Socialism at next Summer's Niagara Meetings. Get him to tell of the Socialist party in the South.[6]

Du Bois, Freeman Henry Morris Murray, and Lafayette M. Hershaw published the Horizon *from 1907 to 1910. Known as "A Journal of the Color Line,"* Horizon *served as the official publication of the Niagara Movement. Lafayette Hershaw was a lawyer and educator who moved back and forth between Atlanta and Washington, D.C. Murray was also a clerk in the War Department, and his affiliation with Du Bois led Charles W. Anderson to continually try to get him fired from his job.[7]*

BOOKER TALIAFERRO WASHINGTON

[Tuskegee, Ala.] May 27, 1907

Personal and Confidential

My dear Mr. [James Rudolph] Garfield:[8] I write to second most heartily what Mr. Charles W. Anderson, of New York, said to you lately regarding the bad influence of a colored man by the name of Hershaw. I perhaps understand how difficult it is to deal with such cases and how much you dislike to even notice such people, but it is a fact which I could easily make you understand if I should have opportunity to talk with you, that this man, and others in Washington, is doing much to injure not only the colored people but to the administration by constantly misrepresenting the President and his officials and by keeping the colored people stirred up, especially in such matters as the Brownsville affair.[9] He is so sly and deceitful in his methods that it is very difficult for a man who has not known him for years not to be deceived by him. If he cannot be removed, if some change were made in his work or his salary lowered or something done to indicate that the administration had its eye upon him it would have a far-reaching effect. He, together with Du Bois and one other man in the War Department, publishes a monthly paper called The Horizon, and it is full each month of matter abusing the President and at the same time putting wrong and false ideas into the heads of the colored people. Yours truly,

Booker T. Washington[10]

JAMES A. COBB[11]

Boston, Aug. 26 1907

Dear Dr. Washington: I am here in the City where the Niagara Movement is expected to hold forth, and expect to attend sessions, if I can find out where it will meet. There seems to be no Esprit de Corps—everybody is up in the air—in fact there is no definite program as yet. The leaders seem to be disgruntled among themselves. However, I shall remain and see the outcome . . .[12]

JAMES A. COBB

Washington, D.C. Sept. 5, 1907

Dear Bro. [Emmett Jay] Scott: I have just returned home after a three weeks visit out East. Found your two several communications waiting me upon desk on my arrival. Thank you very much for badge and receipt and glad to know that you had such a good meeting of the Business League; sorry that I can't say as much for the N.M. [Niagara Movement], which met in Boston, and of which I was in attendance, it seemed to have been beset with misgivings and discord. Only one public meeting and no well arranged program at that, the others were committee meetings where Trotter and [Clement G.] Morgan wrangled.

I think the Movement has about met its "watermellon-lou" as would be said by Bob Cole in the Shoo-fly Regiment,[13] when some thing is about to be smashed up . . .[14]

ROSCOE CONKLING SIMMONS

New York Oct. 2, 1907

Personal

Dear Uncle Booker: I have not before written you on the [Constitution League] "Conference" because I wanted to get my editorial matter out of the way for the current week . . .

Now, the Conference specifically considered the advisability of holding a "huge" demonstration in Cooper Union; and definitely decided to "pack the house" on the evening of Nov. 14th; aiming to attract the attention of the country towards the Senate investigation of the Brownsville riot, which, you will remember, resumes its hearings on

Nov. 18th. This meeting is to immediately follow a Conference to be held in Philadelphia for several days during the same week . . .

By the way, it is possible that Du Bois will speak at the Cooper Union meeting. I tried to get a place for Ben Davis, and had his name recorded, when this Martin of the Guardian, sprung this editorial of Ben's on Roosevelt and the Soldiers, which appeared a week or so ago.[15] I knew if Ben could have been placed he would have rung true, and most likely attacked the spirit of the meeting. This, I believe, is a full and faithful report of the word and spirit of the "Conference" . . .[16]

BOOKER T. WASHINGTON

[Tuskegee, Ala.] November 4, 1907

My dear Mr. [Roscoe Conkling] Simmons: Mr. W.H. Ferris, of Boston, whom I think you know, has some very interesting stuff that I happen to know he is trying to get published.[17] If you could drop him a line indicating you would like to see the matter and would perhaps publish it, without letting him know how you got the information, I think it might result in your getting the matter. It exposes the inside work of the entire Niagara movement. It is a pretty long letter and you might publish it in sections from week to week. I think it would create great interest and result in the increased circulation of your paper. Yours truly,

Booker T. Washington[18]

EMMETT JAY SCOTT

Tuskegee Institute, Alabama, November 20, 1907

My dear Mr. Washington: Dr. Williams came down from Nashville to Atlanta and on to Tuskegee, without any charge whatever, to perform two very difficult operations . . .[19]

I had opportunity to talk quite at length with him with reference to our friend, who has recently gone to Chicago. In him, Dr. W. you have a real jewel of a friend. He is into the situation and knows what is transpiring all the time. It has been rather industriously circulated in Chicago that Fortune is out of The Age by reason of your action, despite the evidence to the contrary, which Fortune has placed in our hands, namely, his letter notifying me of transferring his interest to Moore.[20] He thinks that Mr. F. is almost irresponsible and that he is undoubtedly suffering even now from softening of the brain. He has pretended to the Chicago people that he has a great deal more money than is anywhere in sight . . .

While in Atlanta, he took an hour off and went up to call on Du Bois. He tells me that Du Bois confessed to him that he, too, has an interest with Fortune and the rest of them in the publication to be launched in Chicago. He says that Du Bois insists that what they really need is the Conservator and that he, Du Bois, is urging them to that effect. Dr. W. will watch the case, however, and thinks he can altogether thwart their efforts to secure it. I told him the beginning and the ending of F's negotiations with Moore for his interest, showed him a copy of [the] letter that F wrote me and told him just how much money he was receiving from Moore and how often. Dr. W. thinks that he is now altogether or practically out of money and hopes that you will not be too swift to send any money from yourself, as it would only go into the hands of the wolves . . .[21]

WILLIAM EDWARD BURGHARDT DU BOIS

Atlanta, Ga., Dec. 10, 1907.

Mr. Samuel May, Jr.
My Dear Sir:—

I am very sorry to see in your circular, with regard to the school at Eatonville, Fla., two propositions made which are extremely dangerous, and unnecessary to your cause.[22] The first is: that segregation of the black is a good thing. Segregation of any set of human beings, be they black, white or of any color or race is a bad thing, since human contact is the thing that makes for civilization, and human contact is a thing for which all of us are striving to-day. Of course, some segregation must come, but we do not advocate it; we do not advertise it, and we do not think it is in its self a good thing. The second thing is the peculiar idea expressed that industrial education is the only education worthy of consideration for the Negro to-day. How are your Industrial schools going to be taught? Can they teach themselves? From whence are the teachers coming? Is it a good thing to dry up the very sources, which make Industrial schools, and common schools possible? Can you have teachers of Industrial and Common schools without having higher schools? It seems to me that people who argue in this way, surely have forgotten that the College is the foundation of every system of education. And that in this respect the black men are no exception to the universal rule. I have so much sympathy with Industrial education and with common school education that I am sorry to see the foundation of their success ignored or attacked.

Very sincerely yours,
W.E.B. Du Bois[23]

SAMUEL MAY, JR.

Boston, Dec. 14, 1907

Prof. W.E.B. Du Bois
Dear Sir,

I am in receipt of your favor of Dec 10th. It seems to me that you cannot be familiar with the feelings of our Northern folk who contribute most largely to the education of the colored people in the South. I think that the feeling quite generally is that it is best to bring to the front more prominently the industrial side of negro education and make the so-called higher education the next step forward.

Of course there must be opportunities provided for the education of teachers; but it is impolitic to ask contributions for courses of education which are in advance of those which are open to the poor whites of the South, or even of the North. Our Northern citizens are contributing large amounts of money each year for colored schools, and they certainly have a right to express an opinion of the manner in which it shall be used. As the lowest classes of men must be civilized before they can be Christianized, so the next grades must be taught the use of their hands before their brains receive a higher polish.

There has been, I think, too much discussion of the subject of higher education; it has certainly turned away a good many from giving on the theory that good artisans are being sacrificed to make way for preachers, lawyers, physicians &c. &c.

I am very busy or I would go into the matter more fully with you, but let me quote from a letter which I have received this month from a prominent lady of this City. She writes as follows:

"In reply to yours I must tell you that I no longer give to the *blacks* of the South. I think great trouble is in store for the "*poor whites*" from overdoing the education of negros. They treat the poor whites so badly that *in a few* years the matter *will* have to be taken up. I give when I can to the education of the White Mountain boys and other whites. It is absolutely necessary to keep them up to the blacks. And the material is better to work on—they do not come to be so indolent as the colored. I therefore decline to send to your appeal."

We are laboring in a good cause and little differences must be put aside to make the cause successful; and in order to make it successful we must get money; and those who give the money are they who believe in advertising more eminently the industrial side of education. Referring to your remarks about segregation of the blacks, I would ask you if you have seen any of the reports of speeches recently made in various places by friends of the blacks; I cannot lay my hand on any at the moment else I would send you copies.

> Yours, very truly (in haste)
> Saml May Jr.[24]

W.E.B. DU BOIS

> Atlanta, Ga., Dec. 24, 1907.

Mr. Samuel May, Jr.
My Dear Sir:—

I thank you for your letter of December 14th, but I am still convinced that you do not realize the full import of what your appeal means. It is not a matter of offering exceptional opportunities for colored boys when the whites have no such opportunities. It is matter of present necessity for present common and Industrial schools. Schools like Tuskegee and hundreds of other schools of the Industrial type, together with thousands of the public schools, would have to close their doors today, if it were not for Institutions like Atlanta University. It is utterly impossible to carry on the work of the common schools and the Industrial schools unless teachers are properly taught. Moreover, teachers can not be taught except by those who have had some higher training. Therefore in the teaching of teachers, and in the teaching of those who are to prepare teachers, there must be, not by and by, but now, higher institutions of learning. This has been proven again and again in the history of civilization. When those beneath are to be civilized it is not a matter of gradually raising them from beneath; it is a matter of putting ahead of them a group who can lift them up. The college is the foundation stone of the school system and not its cap-stone.

> Very sincerely yours,
> W.E.B. Du Bois[25]

WILLIAM HENRY FERRIS *(Ferris was a journalist, educator, and AME Zion minister who had allied with Trotter and Du Bois, and was thus anathema to the Tuskegee Machine.)*[26]

Cambridge, Mass. Nov. 26th, 1907

My Dear Sir [Washington] . . .

While I do not always agree with everything you say, I believe that the greatness of your work & grandeur of your achievement, & your grasp of the industrial conditions in the South entitles you to rank with the great constructive geniuses of the century. I remain Very truly yours,

W.H. Ferris

P.S. Our friend Trotter like the cat in the story seems to have nine editorial lives. But I believe that he is almost at the end of his tether. The fight in the Niagara Movement means that the conservative wing has cut loose from Trotter . . .[27]

WILLIAM HENRY FERRIS

Cambridge, Mass. Dec. 16th, 1907

Dear Dr. Washington . . .

I listened to you with a great deal of interest yesterday. On the whole, it was the most inspiring & most optimistic address that I have ever heard you deliver . . .

As to the content of your address, I have this to say, I met some of the most prominent members of the Niagara Movement to day. They think that you have sympathy for the higher aspirations of the Negro; but think the vulnerable part of your address is that a man must have a bank account or own a brick house before he can be regarded as a full fledged, full orbed man. For myself, I haven't reached final & definite conclusions upon the debated points of your address . . .[28]

WILLIAM HENRY FERRIS

New Haven, Conn. Jan. 9th, 1908

My Dear Dr. Washington . . . I am now putting the finishing touches upon My History of the Negro Race. I will entitle it "The Negro in

American Civilization." The book now numbers nearly one thousand typewritten pages & I expect to finish it next week . . .

One white man wrote me yesterday "I have lost hope for your people. I do not see how their condition can be bettered—indeed I am convinced that their condition will grow worse & worse instead of better—for reason inhereing in themselves as well as those outside of them. All the powerful forces of our civilization are coming more & more to be exerted against them—they are doomed."

I think this is a rather gloomy picture. I believe that if the Negro will absorb & assimilate & appropriate the Anglo Saxon's civilization, he will ultimately come to his own in this country. The race problem will solve itself or rather time the alleviator of all wrongs, the righter of all grievances will solve the delicate & complicated problem caused by two races differing in hair, feature & complexion dwelling side by side in the same country. Meanwhile we need leaders like yourself, who will tell the Negro to get money & land & become an industrial & financial factor in this country. And we also need leaders like Du Bois who will tell the white people, "The Black Man is not only a Physical Organism of the *Genus Homo*; but a *Moral Personality of the Genus Vir*.["]

This is the conclusion that I finally arrive at in my prospective book . . .[29]

WILLIAM HENRY FERRIS

New Haven, Conn. Jan. 24th, 1908

My Dear Dr. Washington,

. . . When I began to write my History of the Negro race two years ago, I soon discovered that you were an unusual Negro. I saw that while our race had produced many scholars, theologians, philosophers, artists, painters, poets, writers, orators & politicians, it had produced few men of constructive & creative genius. Then I saw that you were a masterful strategist, a resourceful tactician & an astute diplomat . . .

III. I believe that it is recognized at present that the masses of the Negro race need Industrial Education, while the Talented Tenth need the Higher Education.

IV. The difference of opinion between you & my Niagara Movement friends comes in with regard to the delicate situation caused by the Negro desiring the manhood rights guaranteed by the Constitution of the U.S. I have no solution of the race problem to offer; but here are five axiomatic truths, five facts of human nature.

First. The world never puts a higher estimate upon a race or individual than that race or individual puts upon himself or itself. *Secondly.* The world as a rule does not give a race or individual more than he or it asks & claims for. *Thirdly.* Men tolerate but do not respect the race or individual, who will be kicked & cuffed without an audible protest. *Fourthly.* The world only respects the individual, who regards himself as a man. Fifthly. A completely disfranchised & segregaded race will lose the respect of mankind.

But on the other hand, the South says "Go back to the farm & leave the government in the hands of white men." There is the dilemma. I believe that ultimately an adjustment will be reached in the South satisfactory to both races. Faithfully yours,

W.H. Ferris

P.S. Some of my friends say that if I adopt the Kelly Miller role of taking a middle ground between you & Trotter, I cannot logically & consistently ask any favors of you or any aid from you.

The Niagara Movement fight last summer convinced me that with Trotter, you must go the whole distance or not go at all. That is what caused the split? We were willing to go half the way with Trotter but not all the distance. Trotter has written to his friends that I have sold out to you . . .[30]

KANSAS CITY STAR

. . . The appeal for the Booker T. Washington work at Tuskegee calls attention to the two distinct tendencies for race elevation that have developed among negroes. One is represented before the country by Booker Washington and the Tuskegee institute, the other by Prof. W.E. Burghardt Du Bois and the so-called Niagara movement.

Prof. Du Bois in his pathetic study, "The Souls of Black Folk," cries out against the social discrimination to which his black skin subjects him. The leaders of the Niagara movement meet yearly to protest against exclusion from the ballot and the running of Jim Crow cars. They have no pride of race. Their policy implies a constant lament that they are not white. The movement is a standing appeal for sympathy and for their "rights."

In striking contrast is the attitude of Booker Washington and the negroes for whom he speaks.

In effect Washington says to his people: "Ours is a race to be proud of. Considering the few generations we have been out of barbarism we have made splendid progress. Let us be thankful for our opportunities and make the most of them. Let us not waste our time whining over difficulties. Let us set to work to make ourselves such desirable citizens that the white race will be glad to have our cooperation in conducting the government. The Jim Crow cars may not be up to the standard. Very well. We will improve our economic condition until the railroads will be glad to furnish us cars as good as the best. In other words, let us not lament that we aren't white. Let us not try to be hangers-on to another race. Let us take pride in our own and build it up."

It is between the two policies here outlined that the progressive negro of today is compelled to choose. The outsider cannot doubt that the way of progress is that indicated by Booker Washington.[31]

W.E.B. DU BOIS

To The Star: In your editorial columns of January 18 there is an argument which is so unusual that I would like to say a word with regard to it, since I take it you want to express the truth about certain strivings among colored people. It seems to me very extraordinary that you should regard the man who stands up for his rights as being ashamed of himself. If a man strikes me or insults me or insults those who belong to me, does it show that I am ashamed of my race or of my family or of myself, if in a decent and civilized way, I resent such insult? Is it an indication of no pride of race when a man resents having his wife and children degraded by a Jim Crow car? Did the Revolutionary fathers (and my great-great grandfather who was one of them) show no pride in America and in themselves when they refused to be taxed without representation? Are the people to-day in America who resent being fleeced by insurance societies and corporations proving thereby that they are ashamed of themselves?

It seems to me that in all these cases we have exactly parallel examples to the thing that is happening among the colored people to-day; those who wish to be treated as men are the ones who really show pride of race. Moreover, you assume that so long as some negroes are not deserving of treatment as men, no negro should complain of mistreatment; that there is no one among the negro people who deserves to-day to be treated as a man. You would at least admit, I presume, that Mr. Washington ought to be treated as an American citizen, and yet you say in effect that so long as any black man is not worthy of decent treatment, that it is perfectly right for people to insult and degrade Mr. Washington.

On the other hand, it seems to us who are Niagara movement men that whenever a man, be he white or black or yellow, acts as a man and deserves to be treated as a man he ought to be so treated, and that to insult a man because his father was not an earl, or because his father was an Irishman, or because he is of a certain color is barbarism; and that any nation or part of a nation or editor of a newspaper who stands up for that sort of thing does not stand up for civilization. Nor is it sufficient in this case to answer, This is but "human nature" or these men are "exceptions." Let the negro be as bad as his most bitter detractors allege and the more tremendous is the argument for treating decent black men decently and refusing to sneer at those of them who not for lack of race pride, but for race pride's very self, demand absolute equality of treatment with other men according to individual des[s]ert. I am, sir, very sincerely yours.

> W.E.B. Du Bois
> Atlanta University, Atlanta, Ga., Feb 3[32]

W.E.B. DU BOIS

There lives in Chicago a young man whom I know. This knowing is hardly personal, for I have clasped his hand but once, I believe. Our knowing is but a knowing of soul for he is a Brother of Mine; he is a brother of mine in song—his soul within him sings, not freely yet nor powerfully but with promise; he aspires, he knows pain, he has passed through the Valley of the Shadow.

Now, once God in his goodness gave this brother of mine his Chance—made him editor of the *Conservator* on the day he clouded poor [D.R.] Wilkins' mind. I rejoiced. Why? Did I want personal praise in his columns? No, thank God I am not yet quite so small as that. Was it because I wanted him to tear and scold and curse, at some real or fancied Enemy? O, little Brother of Mine have I so narrowly revealed my life and purpose that such foul end seems its true interpreting? God forbid! No, I welcomed James Edgar French to his editing because I said: Now we shall have stalwart, clear, honest writing; a poem here and there, a fine bit quoted, and ever the lofty atmosphere of high and striving ideals.

And what did I see? Halting ambiguous phrases; hesitating assertions, as of one feeling his way cautiously and afraid to talk; neglected columns, carless space-filling rambles; till I came to lift my once stalwart *Conservator* and lay it aside with a sigh. Why? Because it said things that I disagreed with? Because it bestowed praise where I thought no praise due? No, Little Brother of Mine, no; but because it lacked Conviction, Faith, Determination. Just so with the *Age*. Did I agree with Fortune's *Age*? Hardly. But Fortune was at bottom honest. At bottom there was Conviction, Faith and Determination, even though half-buried in Subsidy. When then Fortune went and a bag of mush was dumped into his chair, I recorded the loss to the Race.

And now: Did I blame *you*, Brother of Mine for this emasculated *Conservator*? No indeed. I know who owns the *Conservator* stock. I know what narrow bounds and commands were probably laid upon you. I might blame you for accepting the limitations—for not standing up straight and saying: "By God, Sir, I'll be Editor or Nothing." But perhaps this was impracticable. I placed no blame therefore—I simply said: *Lost*. Was I far wrong, Little Brother of Mine?[33]

BOOKER T. WASHINGTON

Hotel Manhattan, New York March 2, 1908

Dear Mr. Scott: Mr. [Ray Stannard] Baker was kind enough to let me see the proof of the article which he has written concerning Du Bois and myself.[34] I have read it very carefully. It is a fine article, clear and clean-cut, and I am satisfied with his treatment of the subject. He certainly has a way of getting at the truth. When Du Bois, Trotter and his crowd read what Baker has written I think they will squirm . . .[35]

Ray Stannard Baker's article would appear in American Magazine *two months later in the May 1908 issue, and clearly demonstrated a pro-Washington position, even uncritically quoting the* New York Age *without explaining its Tuskegeean leanings. Still, Baker made it clear, as did the* Kansas City Star, *that whites were evolving in their conception of rights activism and seeing the division that existed between the two camps that dominated thinking about black activism.*

RAY STANNARD BAKER

One of the things that has interested me most of all in studying Negro communities, especially in the North, has been to find them so torn by cliques and divided by such wide differences of opinion.

No other element of our population presents a similar condition; the Italians, the Jews, the Germans, and especially the Chinese and Japanese are held together not only by a different language, but by ingrained and ancient habits. They group themselves naturally. But the Negro is an American in language and customs; he knows no other traditions and he has no other conscious history; a large proportion, indeed, possess varying degrees of white American blood (restless blood!); and yet the Negro is not accepted as an American. Instead of losing himself gradually in the dominant race, as the Germans, Irish and Italians are doing, adding those traits or qualities with which Time fashions and modifies this human mosaic called the American nation, the Negro is set apart as a peculiar people.

With every Negro, then, an essential question is: "How shall I meet this attempt to put me off by myself?"

. . . It is scarcely surprising, then, that upon such a vital question there should be wide differences of opinion among Negroes. As a matter of fact, there are almost innumerable points of view and suggested modes of conduct, but they all group themselves into two great parties which are growing more distinct in outline and purpose every day. Both parties exist in every part of the country, but it is in the North that the struggle between them is most evident . . .

Two Great Negro Parties

Now, the Negroes of the country are meeting the growing discrimination against them in two ways, out of which have grown the two great parties to which I have referred. One party has sprung, naturally, from the thought of the Northern Negro and is a product of the freedom which the Northern Negro has enjoyed; although, of course, it finds many followers in the South.

The other is the natural product of the far different conditions in the South, where the Negro cannot speak his mind, where he has never realized any large degree of free citizenship. Both are led by able men, and both are backed by newspapers and magazines. It has come, indeed, to the point where most Negroes of any intelligence at all have taken their place on one side or the other.

The second-named party, which may best, perhaps, be considered first, is made up of the great mass of the colored people both South and North; its undisputed leader is Booker T. Washington.

The Rise of Booker T. Washington

Nothing has been more remarkable in the recent history of the Negro than Washington's rise to influence as a leader, and the spread of his ideals of education and progress. It is noteworthy that he was born in the South, a slave, that he knew intimately the common struggling life of his people and the attitude of the white race toward them. He worked his way to education in Southern schools and was graduated at Hampton—a story which he tells best himself in his book, "Up From Slavery." He was and is Southern in feeling and point of view. When he began to think how he could best help his people the same question came to him that comes to every Negro:

"What shall we do about this discrimination and separation?"

And his was the type of character which answered, "Make the best of it; overcome it with self-development."

The very essence of his doctrine is this:

"Get yourself right, and the world will be all right."

His whole work and his life have said to the white man:

"You've set us apart. You don't want us. All right; we'll be apart. We can succeed as Negroes."

It is the doctrine of the opportunist and optimist: peculiarly, indeed, the doctrine of the man of the soil, who has come up fighting, dealing with the world, not as he would like to have it, but as it overtakes him. Many great leaders have been like that: Lincoln was one. They have the simplicity and patience of the soil, and the immense courage and faith . . .

Being a hopeful opportunist, Washington takes the Negro as he finds him, often ignorant, weak, timid, surrounded by hostile forces, and tells him to go to work at anything, anywhere, but go to work, learn how to work better, save money, have a better home, raise a better family . . .

It is, indeed, to the teaching of service in the highest sense that Washington's life has been devoted. While he urges every Negro to reach as high a place as he can, he believes that the great masses of the Negroes are best fitted to-day for manual labor: his doctrine is that they should be taught to do that labor better: that when the foundations have been laid in sound industry and in business enterprise, the higher callings and honors will come of themselves.

His emphasis is rather upon duties than upon rights. He does not advise the Negro to surrender a single right: on the other hand, he urges his people to use fully every right they have or can get—for example, to vote wherever possible, and vote thoughtfully. But he believes that some of the rights given the Negro have been lost because the Negro had neither the wisdom nor the strength to use them properly . . . Measured by any standard, white or black, Washington must be regarded to-day as one of the great men of this country: and in the future he will be so honored.

Dr. Du Bois and the Negro

The party led by Washington is made up of the masses of the common people; the radical party, on the other hand, represents what may be called the intellectuals. The leading exponent of its point of view is unquestionably Professor W.E.B. Du Bois of Atlanta University—though, like all minority parties, it is torn with dissension and discontent. Dr. Du Bois was born in Massachusetts of a family that had no history of Southern slavery. He has a large intermixture of white blood. Broadly educated at Harvard and in the universities of Germany, he is to-day one of the able sociologists of this country. His economic studies of the Negro made for the United States Government and for the Atlanta University conference (which he organized) are works of sound scholarship and furnish the student with the best single source of accurate information regarding the Negro at present obtainable in this country . . .

Dr. Du Bois has the temperament of the scholar and idealist—critical, sensitive, unhumorous, impatient, often covering its deep feeling with sarcasm and cynicism. When the question came to him:

"What shall the Negro do about discrimination?" his answer was the exact reverse of Washington's: it was the voice of Massachusetts:

"Do not submit! Agitate, object, fight."

Where Washington reaches the hearts of his people, Du Bois appeals to their heads. Du Bois is not a leader of men, as Washington is: he is rather a promulgator of ideas. While Washington is building a great educational institution and organizing the practical activities of the race, Du Bois is the lonely critic holding up distant ideals. Where Washington cultivates friendly human relationships with the white people among whom the lot of the Negro is cast, Du Bois, sensitive to rebuffs, draws more and more away from white people.

A Negro Declaration of Independence

Several years ago Du Bois organized the Niagara movement for the purpose of protesting against the drawing of the color line. It is important, not so much for the extent of its membership, which is small, but because it represents, genuinely, a more or less prevalent point of view among many colored people.

Its declaration of principles says:

"We refuse to allow the impression to remain that the Negro-American assents to inferiority, is submissive under oppression and apologetic before insults . . ."

The object of the movement is to protest against disfranchisement and Jim Crow laws and to demand equal rights of education, equal civil rights, equal economic opportunities, and justice in the courts. Taking the ballot from the Negro they declare to be only a step to economic slavery; that it leaves the Negro defenseless before his competitor—that the disfranchisement laws in the South are being followed by all manner of other discriminations which interfere with the progress of the Negro . . .

Two Negro Parties Compared

These two points of view, of course, are not peculiar to Negroes; they divide all human thought. The opportunist and optimist on the one hand does his great work with the world as he finds it: he is resourceful, constructive, familiar. On the other hand, the idealist, the agitator, who is also a pessimist, performs the function of the critic, he sees the world as it should be and cries out to have it instantly changed.

Thus with these two great Negro parties. Each is working for essentially the same end—better conditions of life for the Negro—each contains brave and honest men, and each is sure, humanly enough, that the other side is not only wrong, but venally wrong, whereas both parties are needed and both perform a useful function . . .

One reason why the South to-day has a better development of Negro enterprise, one reason why Booker T. Washington believes that the South is a better place for the Negro than the North, and advises him to remain there, is this more advanced racial spirit. Prejudice there, being sharper, has forced the Negro back upon his own resources . . .

"Despite much talk, the Negro is not discouraged, but is going forward. The race owns to-day an acreage equal to the combined acreage of Holland and Belgium. The Negro owns more land, more houses, more stores, more banks, than has ever been true in his history. We are learning that no race can occupy a soil unless it gets as much out of it as any other race gets out of it. Soil, sunshine, rain, and the laws of trade have no regard for race or color. We are learning that we must be builders if we would succeed. As we learn this lesson we shall find help at the South and at the North. We must not be content to be tolerated in communities, we must make ourselves needed. The law that governs the universe knows no race or color. The force of nature will respond as readily to the hand of the Chinaman, the Italian, or the Negro as to any other race. Man may discriminate, but nature and the laws that control the affairs of men will not and cannot. Nature does not hide her wealth from a black hand."

. . . Out of this ferment of racial self-consciousness and readjustment has grown, as I have shown, the two great Negro parties. Between them and within them lie the destinies of the race in this country, and to no small extent also the destiny of the dominant white race. It is, therefore, of the highest importance for white men to understand the real tendencies of thought and organization among these ten million Americans. For here is vigor and ability, and whatever may be the white man's attitude toward the Negro, the contempt of mere ignorance of what the Negro is doing is not only short-sighted but positively foolish. Only by a complete understanding can the white man who has assumed the entire responsibility of government in this country meet the crises, like that of the Atlanta riot, which are constantly arising between the races.[36]

SANDY W. TRICE (*Trice owned a department store in Chicago that catered to black customers.*)[37]

Chicago, Ill., March 12, 1908

Personal and Confidential.

Dear Sir [Washington]: This will inform you that I have made a change in the editors of the Conservator and in doing so I have been made a defendant in a suit for $1000.00 five hundred against the company and five hundred against me personally and in order to defend myself and the company I have had to employ a high class lawyer in the person of Patrick H. O'Donnell.[38] This is a move I am sure on the part of the Niagara Movement people to get the paper which they have been after for some time, and now to make a long story short I want to tell you that in order to maintain the stand that I have taken I must have some immediate financial assistance as I have a hard fight on my hands.

The gentleman that you spoke with me about called on me and we have things arranged satisfactory but that does not relieve my immediate needs, so I appeal to you to help me out of this difficulty, if you can possibly do so, so that nothing will hinder the progress of the paper during the period of litigation . . .[39]

In 1906, 1908, and 1910, Washington sent agents to Atlanta to discover "whether or not Dr. D is actually a registered voter in Atlanta." There were rumors floating to the contrary, and Washington thought he could gain the rhetorical upper hand by catching Du Bois in an act that he could portray as hypocrisy.[40]

WILLIAM HAYES WARD *(Ward was the editor of the* Independent, *which often published Du Bois's work.)*[41]

New York, March 18th, 1908.

Professor W.E.B. Du Bois
My Dear Sir:—

May I ask you a personal question? Do the negroes of intelligence and position about Atlanta, and so far as you know in Georgia, pay taxes and vote? Do you pay taxes and vote? I have heard it said that you do not, and that would certainly surprise me. I have been hoping that gradually the negroes would not claim but be allowed the right to vote, and it would seem to me to be the only right policy.

Pardon me for asking the question if it seems to you impertinent.

Very truly yours,
William Hayes Ward[42]

W.E.B. DU BOIS

Atlanta, Mar. 27, 1908.

My Dear Dr. Ward:—

Replying to your letter of March 18th, let me say that practically all the Negroes of intelligence and position about Atlanta and in most of the cities of Georgia, and to a large extent in the country districts, pay taxes. A smaller percent of them vote. I, myself, pay taxes but do not vote in the minor elections; in the more important elections, I do vote. The reason for this is there are a good many of the smaller elections, and it is absolutely useless on account of the white primary system to try and vote, and it takes a great deal of valuable time. What is needed here of course is concerted effort on the part of the Negroes to have them all vote . . . I believe with you that gradually the Negro is going to get the right to vote in the South, and that one of the ways to get [it] is persistently to vote. But unless we can have the enlightened public opinion of the North back of us, we labor under very great handicap. . . .[43]

NEW YORK *AMERICAN*

WHITE GIRLS AT AN "EQUALITY FEAST" WITH NEGROES
Orators Openly Advocate the Intermarriage of Whites and Blacks

Social equality and intermarriage between the races were advocated last night at a banquet of the Cosmopolitan Society of Greater New York, where twenty white girls and women dined side by side at table with negro men and women . . .

Miss Mary White Ovington, a Brooklyn society girl, who has been prominent in settlement work, and whose father is proprietor of the Hotel St. George in Brooklyn, was the only white girl who occupied a seat at the speakers' table. Negroes were clustered all about her. On her right hand sat William H. Ferris, colored graduate of Harvard, who told later of his effort to implant his "Boston education" in the South. At this table also sat Hamilton Holt, introduced as "editor-in-chief of The Independent," and whose subsequent utterances on intermarriage stirred his auditors to enthusiastic applause.[44]

At the left of Miss Ovington was Editor Harold G. Villard, [Oswald Garrison Villard] of the New York Evening Post, and his plea for "equality and abolition of caste spirit" a few minutes later drew forth another wild outburst . . .

"I am very glad I have been asked to welcome you in behalf of the Cosmopolitan Club," said Miss Ovington. "We hope to have many of such clubs as this soon and we shall know by next season if our movement is going to be a success. Caste spirit is not simply a race question. I am in this work because it is human. The danger of this caste spirit is not a racial matter, but relates to we men and women of this republic. It means moral and physical ruin, especially in the South" . . .

About this time Dr. Ferris, the colored collegian, was called upon. He was delighted to speak, and said:

"Is it too soon to admit the negro into the brotherhood of equality in the human family? This meeting means more to the negro of the Black Belt of the South than to the negro of the North. It marks an epoch for the down south negro. It is a question of recognizing them as a man and as an equal. There is only one way to succeed—demand your equality.

"We have two leaders. Booker Washington advocating peaceful resistance, and then there is Du Bois saying, 'Exercise your rights.' Now, which shall it be?"

"Exercise our rights!" shouted a voice followed by great applause, which was joined in by white and black alike . . .[45]

RALPH WALDO TYLER *(Tyler was a black journalist, activist, and acolyte of Booker Washington.)*[46]

Washington, D.C. July 10/08

My Dear Friend [Emmett Jay] Scott:

... Well I see the negro Democrats got cold comfort from the Democratic convention. Not a line in their platform to animate the disgruntled Hamites. Understand the Democrats have ordered one million copies of the June Horizon with Du Bois article on Taft, to use as campaign matter among negroes . . .[47]

R.W. Tyler[48]

BOOKER T. WASHINGTON

Washington, D.C, Sept. 7, 1908

If we may judge by the attendance at the recent meeting of the Niagara Movement, from the District of Columbia, we can safely say that the movement is practically dead. So far as can be learned, no one went from Washington to attend this meeting except Mrs. Wm. H. Clifford, the wife of Mr. Clifford, who is an employee in the Treasury Department.[49] We understand that at the meeting of the Niagara Movement, strong resolutions were passed endorsing Mr. Bryan for President. Mrs. Clifford and Dr. Du Bois seem to have been the only people in attendance . . .[50]

OSWALD GARRISON VILLARD

[New York City] September 10, 1908

Dear Mr. Washington: I am sorry that I cannot, personally, help you in that matter, except by editorial comment in The Evening Post. I am in your same situation of having been squeezed dry, by my John Brown undertaking and other things.[51] I would suggest your writing to Mr. George Foster Peabody and see if he would not advance the money. You see, this is precisely the kind of a case for which I want my endowed "Committee for the Advancement of the Negro Race."[52] With such a body we could instantly handle any similar discrimination against the negro, and carry the case, if necessary, to the higher court. Sooner or later we must get that committee going . . .[53]

BOOKER T. WASHINGTON

New York, Nov. 12, 1908

Personal

My dear Mr. [Frederick Randolph] Moore: The Age for this week on the whole is very creditable. There are several improvements which I hope you will make at once. The main one is this: You are not giving enough space by far to local matters, especially New York and Brooklyn. You are to bear in mind that you have some 25,000 or more colored people in Brooklyn and about 40,000 or more in New York and thousands in Jersey City and nearby towns. For example, you give a column of matter on the front page to Chicago where you have very few readers, a city that is many hundreds of miles away . . .

Hereafter please suggest to the people in your office that the matter which I send in the form of editorials remain in the same form that I write them. What I wrote about the poem of James W. Johnson is of no value because of the changes that were made in what I said.[54] You only print two verses of the poem, when I said plainly in my editorial that these two verses were only given as a sample of the high character of the poetry.

There are several other little matters that need closer attention . . .

Don't you think there is a little danger of advertising Du Bois too much?[55]

Thus the conversation between the two leaders continued to appear, at times, more like an espionage novel than a substantive debate. But there was still a substantive debate. Another point of difference between Washington and Du Bois, for example, was the question of women's suffrage. Du Bois was for it, Washington not. Their beliefs about the roles of women mirrored those about the roles of black men. Washington made his position clear in a December 1908 New York Times *article.*

BOOKER T. WASHINGTON

The Woman Suffrage Movement

I am in favor of every measure that will give to woman, the opportunity to develop to the highest possible extent, her moral, intellectual, and physical nature so that she may make her life as useful to herself and to others as it is possible to make it. I do not, at the present moment, see that this involves the privilege or the duty, as you choose to look upon it, of voting.

The influence of woman is already enormous in this country. She exerts, not merely in the homes, but through the schools and in the press, a powerful and helpful influence upon affairs. It is not clear to me that she would exercise any greater or more beneficent influence upon the world than she now does, if the duty of taking an active part in politics were imposed upon her . . .[56]

Washington had as his allies in such causes women like Annie Nathan Meyer, an anti-suffrage activist who was, like Washington, still an advocate for business and educational opportunities for women. Meyer also recognized the power of education and served as a tireless advocate for collegiate courses for women. She would be the principal force behind the founding of Barnard College in New York.[57]

ANNIE NATHAN MEYER

New York. Jan. 7 [1909]

My dear Dr. Washington, I have been hoping ever since I read it to get time to thank you for the admirably expressed, calm, restrained words on the question of Woman Suffrage . . .

Of course the feeling among the Suffragists is very bitter and some may be small enough to try to make you eat your words. But perhaps you remember last summer I wrote you after reading your helpful book "Working with the Hands." I knew you could not be a suffragist— your vision is too clear. I want you to read Appleton's for Feb. "Some Problems of Enfranchisement" by me[58] in which I show how your example is needed among workers—to set about doing the work of the past more effectively—not seeking new spheres. I want you to read it as my tribute to you is most sincere. I don't know if you read the mawkish—at bottom—in sincere letter to Prof Du Bois in Jan. American.[59] I shall answer it some day—full of real sex antagonism—& a reluctance to accept the differentiations of sex . . . Cordially

Annie Nathan Meyer
(Mrs. Alfred Meyer)[60]

Meyer was particularly outraged at gender positions like those of Du Bois, whose support of women's rights mirrored his views on race (as Washington's views mirrored his own racial views, as well). Typical of Du Bois's thinking

on the matter, "The Problem of the Intellectual Woman," to which Meyer refers, appeared just after Washington's piece in the Times.

W.E.B. DU BOIS

The Problem of the Intellectual Woman
A Letter from an American Woman to the American Negro
(In Care of W.E.B. Du Bois)

In your "Souls of Black Folk," Dr. Du Bois, you have lifted the veil and revealed to the white people of the United States, the consciousness of a million and a half of people of mixed blood within our borders . . . You have touched the hearts of all your readers, but no one has been so much moved as the modern intellectual woman, whose situation is somewhat analogous to yours. It suffices neither of us to be told that we are exceptions to our kind, and that we must pay the penalty of our abnormality. It does not satisfy you that you, personally, may be admitted to the company of your peers in the North, only to be told that your race is hopeless. It does not satisfy us to be told that the great majority of women are, and prefer to remain, in tutelage . . .

You suffer under the perpetual disability of color; we under the perpetual disability of sex—from the point of view of the governing class . . .

We women have had a longer history, and in some parts of the world are as much sinned against as you. We have the perpetual physical disability caused by preparation for maternity, its actual existence, and its consequences. The little girl who must give up her freedom in sports at thirteen or fourteen years of age feels an inward rebellion not unlike yours when you first realized your darker skin. Her expansive and joyous nature is gradually restrained and turned inward to protect herself. When the sacrifices of this period have passed and she has become accustomed to this set of limitations, she enters upon the period of education, and there is the long discussion of where, and how, and why, and why not. If she takes this in her own hands, as you did, and gets all the education she can, she forms her ideals of life and chooses her profession, and then finds herself facing the great dilemma. To marry is to leave behind her all that the scientific men who have educated her have told her are the noblest aims in life. Not to marry is to cut herself off from the stream of human existence, from all the close ties that no man of her acquaintance of the same station and education would think of renouncing. Being of honorable mettle she chooses to attack the problem, and not to eliminate it. She must have the human life and the intellectual life . . .

Woman came out of her traditional place at the outset much as some of your people are trying to come out now, by asserting her abstract rights to citizenship under democracy. No one doubts nowadays that if all women wanted suffrage they would get it, just as they get their clothes, because each one would bring the necessary pressure to bear in her own family. So must the negro get the civil rights he has not, by convincing the white men next to him that he ought to have them. How has liberty been won by the oppressed since the beginning of time? By fighting, say the English Suffragists . . .

The economic pressure of the period has been such as to confine men more and more to business, while the increase of labor-saving machinery has freed wives of men of a certain status more and more from domestic cares. Therefore women have given more attention to the affairs of the community, the city and the state. It is now upon the basis of our demonstrated ability to co-operate with each other and with men that women are asking for the extension of the right of suffrage . . .

Any comparison of your race with my own sex must, at last, lead to the inclusion of any who are backward, from whatever cause. The laboring classes as a whole, have been the first to find a way to better conditions through organization. Women must always remain a part of the laboring classes more than men. By organizing themselves women have obtained the right to work, the right to higher education, and some recognition of their social service. The tangible result of their organized work may be small, but it is the only form which men really respect. Our attainments as scholars, artists or literary personages have been considered exceptions, the caprice of genius or the result of good training by some man. Women's clubs are a form of social organization which women themselves have originated. You must enter the world by the forms which you originate . . .

Is our situation much better than yours? Long we have borne the burden of physical inequality, and have considered maternity a sufficient compensation; long have we suffered vicariously for the sins of men, who may be forgiven by society while we may not. We have suffered social ostracism while our betrayers have been honored and respected; we have gone to prison for infanticide while they have gone free; we have performed for family and society what they have considered too menial; and now, after we have toiled over the long, slow path and have done about all we can by organized effort without a share in the government, we are refused the ballot on grounds that amount to sex prejudice. Just as you believe that the policy of treating all negroes alike, because they are negroes, puts a premium on inefficiency and crime, so do we believe that disfranchising us because we are women will put an end to all the best things we have been doing. We therefore join hands with you in asking that the ballot be put on another basis than color and sex . . .[61]

BOOKER T. WASHINGTON

New York. May 1, 1909

Dear Mr. [Hugh Mason] Browne:[62] Dr. Du Bois has really a very fine and sensible article in the May World's Work.[63] What would you think of having the Committee send it out? I do not know how Du Bois would take such a suggestion nor how the members of the Committee would take it. Du Bois is such a big dunce that one never knows how to take him, but I have an idea that he is learning a little sense but I am not sure of this . . .[64]

W.E.B. DU BOIS

Georgia Negroes and Their Fifty Millions of Savings

One state in the Union has kept a series of economic measurements of the freedman and his sons for a period of thirty-five consecutive years. Two other states have recent partial records, but Georgia alone has an account of Negro property from Reconstruction times to the present. To the facts and meaning of these figures I want to call attention.

Emancipation had its legal, educational, economic, and moral phases. Legal emancipation came in 1863. Educational emancipation is coming more slowly, as the record of Georgia shows.

There is a larger amount of illiteracy in Georgia to-day than there was in 1870, which shows how poorly public-school facilities have kept pace with population. But the illiterates of to-day have a body of educated black men to lead them, who have been trained chiefly in the private schools supported by philanthropy.

It is, however, in the economic phase of emancipating black men that the nation is most deeply interested to-day, because slavery was largely, if not primarily, an economic problem. And since the economic development of the United States is its greatest and most absorbing world-triumph, we are, naturally, especially attracted to the economic phases of all its social problems . . .

From the almost nothing of 1863, the Georgia Negro had come to the place, in 1907, where he was assessed at twenty-five millions of dollars.

This does not include untaxed church and school property, and, as the assessments in Georgia are very low, this amount probably is not more than 50 per cent of the market value of all property. So that we may hazard the estimate that Georgia Negroes have saved about fifty million dollars.

Turning now to the details of this saving, one is especially interested in the land. The Negroes of Georgia own to-day a twenty-fourth part of the soil of the state and nearly one-twentieth of the cultivated land. Their holdings amount to 1,420,888 acres, or 2,220 square miles—a tract of land larger than Delaware (2,050 square miles). It is assessed at $7,149,225, but it is worth nearly $15,000,000, which was the price the United States paid for the Louisiana Purchase . . .

Mere totals, however, teach but little; for a half-dozen large owners, rich by good luck, may raise the average and give a false appearance of prosperity to a poverty-stricken mass. A careful examination of typical counties indicates the following approximate division of land throughout the state.

A little less than a third of the owners have small garden spots or house lots outside the city limits, comprising about a sixtieth of the total land owned. Another portion of the population, slightly less than a third, have the traditional 40 acres, comprising an eighth of the land owned. A sixth of the owners hold a little over a sixth of the land in parcels between 50 and 100 acres, while something less than a fifth hold nearly half the land in tracts of from 100 to 300 acres. The remaining quarter of the land is held by that thirtieth part of the Negro owners who are the large landlords of the race. Comparing this with the condition seven years earlier, we find the smaller holdings growing larger, but no growth in the relative proportion of large landlords . . .

We see, then, a wide distribution of small holdings among a mass of people with little apparent tendency to concentration, but evidences of a general advance in prosperity among them all . . .

The property of the Georgia Negroes has been accumulated with difficulty. There are few encouragements or inducements for the poor to save in Georgia. Wages are low, the race problem tends to lower self-respect, happenings like the Atlanta riot decrease confidence, and the laws do not adequately protect the poor against cheating and fraud. Despite this, saving is possible . . .

One thing needs to be said in concluding. These figures are absolute proof of nothing, but they are certainly hopeful. If they teach anything, they teach that the tendency to save, here manifest, should be encouraged . . .[65]

EMMETT JAY SCOTT

Monrovia: Liberia May 15, '09

Personal:

My Dear Mr. W: There is quite a nasty situation here at the American Legation . . . Ellis, the present secretary is a very narrow & very little man, with little sense & no discretion[66] . . . He is from all accounts a strife breeder & more than that he seeks to embarras[s] every effort of the Minister so far as you are concerned. For instance: He made an outcry about your being put in charge of the Envoys last year & said *Du Bois* & the intellectuals were the proper people & that the mission w'd be a failure because you were in charge of it. *Then*: when the President & Congress at Lyon's request conferred the medal of the Order of African Redemption on you he again came out & said the Negroes of the U S w'd oppose it unless Du Bois also received one.[67] Lyons then fought openly against this proposition & when the Envoys returned & said that they c'd not have succeeded without you—& when *Du Bois* jumped on the Envoys in the *Horizon* they saw what a fool Ellis is & refused Du Bois the medal, altho' it was given out by Ellis that *Du B* also received one. I read all of this in the papers last summer but did not know who it came from. We have on file *there* in the office a letter from *Ellis* telling of the Congress act to give you & Du Bois medals. You will find same, if you care to have it looked up. *Then* he makes copies of Legation stuff & keeps *Du B* supplied & everything that Dr Sale got from *Du B* on Liberia has Ellis name written on it[68] . . . We ought to have a friend for this place & not one of the enemy . . .[69]

NOTES

1. J. Douglas Wetmore was a Jacksonville lawyer. Owen Waller was a Brooklyn doctor. Both were part of the Niagara Movement. *New York Age*, 2 December 1939, 1.
2. Washington, 1980, vol. 9, 223–225.
3. Washington, 1979, vol. 8, 189.
4. Lewis, 1993, 349. See Chapter 13, note 122.
5. Franz Boas was the leading anthropologist in the country. The year before Ovington's letter, Du Bois invited Boas to give the commencement address at Atlanta University. Lewis, 2001, 447–467.
6. Du Bois, 1973, 131–133. Alexander Irvine was a socialist preacher based at the Church of the Ascension in New York. D. Appleton & Company was a publishing house founded by Daniel Appleton in 1831. It published

books, but also a magazine called *Appleton's Magazine*. Grant, 1909, 145–157. For an example of the work Ovington is discussing, see Irvine, 1907, 3–15.

7. Washington, 1980, vol. 9, 277.

8. James Rudolph Garfield was Secretary of the Interior under the administration of Theodore Roosevelt. He was the son of the former president Garfield. See James Rudolph Garfield Papers, MS 4573, Western Reserve Historical Society, Cleveland, Ohio.

9. The Brownsville Affair was a 1906 incident in Brownsville, Texas, when a black regiment of Buffalo Soldiers were accused of responsibility for the deaths of a white bartender and police officer. The entire regiment was dishonorably discharged, despite the fact that there was no evidence of their involvement. They would be exonerated posthumously in the 1970s. See Weaver, 1992.

10. Washington, 1980, vol. 9, 278.

11. See Chapter 13, note 116.

12. Washington, 1980, vol. 9, 334.

13. *The Shoo-Fly Regiment* was an African American musical about black soldiers in the Spanish American War. Bob Cole produced and scored the show, as well as starring in it. He was perhaps the most well-known black musical composer of his day. "The Development of An African-American Musical Theatre, 1865–1910," *The Library of Congress: American Memory*.

14. Washington, 1980, vol. 9, 334.

15. Granville Martin was an associate of Trotter on the *Boston Guardian* and a coconspirator in the Boston Riot. Benjamin Davis was a powerful figure in black Atlanta, the publisher of the community's largest newspaper at the time, the *Atlanta Independent*, and a staunch Republican leader. Horne, 1994, 18, 328; and Bacote, 1955, 325. See also Fox, 1971.

16. Washington, 1980, vol. 9, 359–361.

17. William Henry Ferris was a graduate of Yale and Harvard, a journalist, educator, and AME Zion minister who had allied with Trotter and Du Bois, and was thus anathema to the Tuskegee Machine. "William Henry Ferris," October 1941, 549–550.

18. Washington, 1980, vol. 9, 394.

19. Samuel Laing Williams. See Chapter 9, note 15.

20. Frederick Randolph Moore. See Chapter 12, note 17.

21. Washington, 1980, vol. 9, 404–405.

22. Samuel May, Jr. was a Boston lawyer, the son of a prominent abolitionist. May's circular for the Robert Hungerford Industrial School in Eatonville argued that "the best form of education for the negro—and the only one worthy of consideration at the present time—is industrial education." In addition, May also advocated segregation, which would end "the eternal discord, arising from sectional differences over the negro." It was a typical white play on Washingtonian thought. Du Bois, 1973, 137–138.

23. Ibid., 138.

24. Ibid., 138–139.

25. Ibid., 139–140.

26. See note 17.

27. Washington, 1980, vol. 9, 410.

28. Ibid., 423.

29. Ibid., 437–438.

30. Ibid., 446–447.

31. *Kansas City Star*, 18 January 1908, 4.

32. Du Bois, "From a Distinguished Negro," *Kansas City Star*, 7 February 1908, 2.

33. Du Bois, February 1908, 18–20.

34. Ray Stannard Baker was, along with Lincoln Steffens and Ida Tarbell, the founder of *American Magazine*. He refers to Washington as the real leader of black America and to Du Bois as a simple critic who was incapable of leading. Washington, 1980, vol. 9, 459. See Bannister, 1966.

35. Washington, 1980, vol. 9, 459.

36. Baker, 1908, 60–70.

37. Buck, 1907, 210–211.

38. O'Donnell was a prominent Chicago lawyer, one of the founders of the law school at St. Ignatius College, which would later become Loyola University. Haney, 2010, 651–653.

39. Washington, 1980, vol. 9, 466–467.

40. Du Bois, 1973, 141; and Harlan, 1971, 409.

41. See Chapter 12.

42. Du Bois, 1973, 141.

43. Ibid.

44. Hamilton Holt was editor of the *Independent*, taking over for William Hayes Ward as Ward became honorary editor. Kuehl, 1960.

45. "White Girls At An Equality Feast With Negroes," *New York American*, 29 April 1908, 1; and Washington, 1980, vol. 9, 515–520.

46. At Washington's urging, Tyler was appointed by Roosevelt as consul to Brazil. Lorenz, 2005, 3–12.

47. See Du Bois, June 1908, 1–8.

48. Washington, 1980, vol. 9, 592–593.

49. Clair W. Clifford was a women's club leader and anti-lynching activist. She worked against segregation and disfranchisement and argued that the Afro-American Council should merge with Niagara to strengthen the left wing of civil rights activism. Ibid., 619.

50. Ibid.

51. Villard, 1910.

52. Villard would later change the name of his proposed organization to the NAACP. Washington, 1980, vol. 9, 623.

53. Ibid., 622–623.

54. James Weldon Johnson was, like so many eventual residents of Harlem, a southerner. He grew up in Jacksonville, Florida, where he created

and edited a newspaper. In 1897, he became the first black lawyer to be admitted to the Florida bar. But he was also a songwriter, and with his brother wrote hundreds of songs. In 1900, they took their comic opera *Tolosa* to New York. That did not work, but he turned his eyes toward other things, using his connections with New York's Republican party to become U.S. consul to Venezuela from 1906 to 1908, then to Nicaragua from 1909 to 1912. In 1912, he wrote *The Autobiography of an Ex-Coloured Man*. He would go on in 1916 to become field secretary for the NAACP. In 1920, he would become NAACP secretary and would stay in that post until 1930. See Levy, 1973.

55. Washington, 1980, vol. 9, 691–693.

56. Washington, "The Woman Suffrage Movement," *New York Times*, 20 December 1908, SM3.

57. See Goldenberg, 1987.

58. Meyer, 1909, 194–197; and Washington, 1981, vol. 10, 8.

59. Meyer here refers to Du Bois's article, "The Problem of the Intellectual Woman." See below.

60. Annie Nathan Meyer was a staunch opponent of women's suffrage. She did want business and educational opportunities for women, however. Washington, 1981, vol. 10, 7–8.

61. Du Bois, January 1909, 288–290.

62. See Chapter 11, note 11.

63. Washington refers to Du Bois's "Georgia Negroes and Their Fifty Millions of Savings." See below.

64. Washington, 1981, vol. 10, 93.

65. Du Bois's original included graphs. They are not included here. Du Bois, May 1909, 11550–11554.

66. George Washington Ellis was part of the American legation to Liberia. Upon his return in 1910, he would start a law practice in Chicago. Gordon, 2000, 49; and Williams, 2002, 544–550.

67. Ernest Lyon was U.S. consul general to Liberia. "Items," November 1908, 57.

68. George Sale was one of the commissioners, along with Roland Falkner and Emmet Scott, sent by the United States in March 1909 to investigate conditions in Liberia. Starr, 1913, 223.

69. Washington, 1981, vol. 10, 102–103.

15

NAACP

As white leaders began to fully comprehend the bipolar divide in the struggle for racial equality, they naturally began taking sides. For those who wanted to make the case against segregation, disfranchisement, and political murder, the battle lines were clear. Thus, after the collapse of Niagara and an initial gathering of white progressive leaders in January 1909, Oswald Garrison Villard called for another meeting in February, encouraging "all believers in democracy to join a national conference to discuss present evils, the voicing of protests, and the renewal of the struggle for civil and political liberty." Villard was a newspaper editor and the grandson of William Lloyd Garrison. And that was significant. Abolition had been largely a white movement, and there were many influential whites who wanted to revive that instinct. Jane Addams, Clarence Darrow, Moorfield Storey, Mary White Ovington, and Joel Spingarn were all involved, working to create a new interracial organization that would revive the spirit of antebellum white northern abolitionism. They combined with a handful of black leaders like Du Bois and his allies like Ida B. Wells, creating the National Association for the Advancement of Colored People. The NAACP would create its own problems among white radicals and Du Bois, but more important, it signaled Du Bois's growing influence, as many of the early members of the NAACP were once sympathetic to Washington.

OSWALD GARRISON VILLARD

New York May 26, 1909

Dear Mr. Washington: I sincerely wish that you might be present at our approaching conference on the status of the American negro, because I look for great results from it. We have an unusually fine list of speakers and the people who have promised to come, like Prof. [John] Dewey, Prof. [Burt Green] Wilder, Albert E. Pillsbury of Boston, Judge [Wendell Phillips] Stafford of the District of Columbia, Clarence Darrow and others, are tried and fast friends of the colored race.[1] There is not the slightest intention of tying up this movement with either of the two factions in the negro race. It is not to be a Washington movement, or a Du Bois movement. The idea is that there shall grow out of it, first, an annual conference similar to the Indian conference and the Arbitration meeting which take place every year at Lake Mohonk, for the discussion by men of both races of the conditions of the colored people, politically, socially, industrially and educationally. Besides this, I hope there will grow out of it a permanent organization, a sort of steering committee of the race along lines which I have indicated to you in conversations in the past; an incorporated and endowed committee which shall have a press bureau, a bureau of study and investigation to let the country know exactly the facts about the progress of the colored race; a legal bureau to take up any case of crime against the negro; a political bureau to contend against political wrongs; an educational bureau to raise funds for distinctively negro institutions, etc., etc.

Now it is intended that this committee, when duly authorized and organized—perhaps a year hence at the second annual conference— shall absorb the association for the industrial improvement of the negroes in this city, and also, perhaps, the Constitutional League. It is intended that the organization shall be an aggressive one ready to fight hard for the rights of the colored people, to strike hard blows in and out of Congress, to take up precisely such wrongs as the Brownsville incident and fight them to a finish as did the Constitutional League in this matter.

Now, while I am not writing officially for the conference, I know that I express its feeling of friendliness for you and for the work you are doing, but as I explained to you in regard to the original call, the men who have gotten up this movement do not wish to embarrass you; they do not wish to seem to ignore you, or to leave you out, or to show any disrespect whatever. On the other hand, they do not wish to tie you up with what may prove to be a radical political movement. Hence, they have not felt like urging you very hard to join the new movement, but have wanted you to know that you would be welcome at the conference, or if you decided you could not attend, the conference would least of all misinterpret your absence. I do not know of any movement which bids fair to do so much for the colored people. So far as I, myself, am concerned, if it can be carried out as I, and others, am planning it, it will realize the greatest ambition of my life, and I shall expect to concentrate my interest upon it as strongly as possible, outside of my professional duties, and I feel that we can count on your sympathetic interest and help even if, because of educational affiliations, you do not desire to become closely allied with us. Of course, I feel more keenly the delicacy of your position in regard to all movements of this kind because I am one of your warm friends who is unhappy about your political activities and is worried by the danger of your being forced against your will into the untenable position of being the political clearinghouse for the colored race, a position no one can fill in the long run with success, or without causing the most intense hostility on the part of your colored fellow-citizens . . . Always sincerely yours . . .[2]

BOOKER TALIAFERRO WASHINGTON

Tuskegee Institute, Alabama May 28, 1909

Personal and Confidential.

My dear Mr. [Oswald Garrison] Villard: I thank you very much for your kind letter of May 26th and for the invitation to be present at the forthcoming conference. Now, I know you want me to be perfectly frank.

First, let me say, as my plans stand, it will be physically impossible for me to be present, but aside from that I do not believe that it would be best for me to be present at the first session at least, as I do not think it would help the conference. I fear that my presence might restrict freedom of discussion, and might, also, tend to make the conference go in directions which it would not like to go.

Secondly, I hardly feel that in the present conditions in the South, it would be best for the cause of education, in which you and I are both so deeply interested, for me to be present.

Now, I am sure that you will not misunderstand me when I make these statements. I am not afraid of doing anything which I think is right and should be done. I have always recognized, as I have stated to you more than once, that there is a work to be done which no one placed in my position can do, which no one living in the South perhaps can do. There is a work which those of us who live here in the South can do, which persons who do not live in the South cannot do. If we recognize fairly and squarely this, then, it seems to me that we have gone a long ways.

Third, I have always recognized the value of sane agitation and criticism, but not to the extent of having our race feel that we can depend upon this to cure all the evils surrounding us . . .

I want to state, in conclusion, that in so far as I have followed the plans of the conference and noted the persons to be connected with it, you have made great progress in getting rid of an element of people who have always been a loadstone about the neck of such movements, and if this element is subdued, or kept quiet, or out of such meetings it will mean much in getting a good, strong following.

Please assure the members of the committee that I understand thoroughly their attitude toward me and their reasons for not insisting upon my presence, and that I have no feeling whatever, growing out of being left out . . .[3]

CHARLES WILLIAM ANDERSON

[New York City] Sunday May 30/09

Dear Doctor [Washington]: I "wired" you this morning about the enclosed, which was clipped from the "Sun" of this A.M.

I am doing all I can to discredit this affair. I think I have succeeded in defeating the dinner project to Du Bois, by asking all of my friends and yours not to subscribe to it. They will either have to drop it, or give him a small private dinner.

I feel confident that a big public testimonial, such as was planned, cannot be pulled off . . .[4]

CHARLES WILLIAM ANDERSON

New York, May 31st—1909

Du Bois, Waldron, Walters, Sinclair, Max Barber, Wibecan, Dr Mossell[,] Bulkley, Milholland[,] Ida Wells, and entire cosmopolitan dinner crowd in Secret conference to-day.[5] Public meeting to-night have had newspapers cover it another secret session tomorrow. Think Villard is with them . . .[6]

OSWALD GARRISON VILLARD

The celebration of the centennial of the birth of Abraham Lincoln widespread and grateful as it may be, will fail to justify itself if it takes no note and makes no recognition of the colored men and women to whom the great emancipator labored to assure freedom. Besides a day of rejoicing, Lincoln's birthday in 1909 should be one of taking stock of the nation's progress since 1865. How far has it lived up to the obligations imposed upon it by the Emancipation Proclamation? How far has it gone in assuring to each and every citizen, irrespective of color, the equality of opportunity and equality before the law, which underlie our American institutions and are guaranteed by the Constitution?

If Mr. Lincoln could revisit this country he would be disheartened by the nation's failure in this respect. He would learn that on January 1st, 1909, Georgia had rounded out a new oligarchy by disfranchising the negro after the manner of all the other Southern states. He would learn that the Supreme Court of the United States, designed to be a bulwark of American liberties, had failed to meet several opportunities to pass squarely upon this disfranchisement of millions by laws avowedly discriminatory and openly enforced in such manner that white men may vote and black men be without a vote in their government; he would discover, there, that taxation without representation is the lot of millions of wealth-producing American citizens, in whose hands rests the economic progress and welfare of an entire section of the country . . . In many States Lincoln would find justice enforced, if at all, by judges elected by one element in a community to pass upon the liberties and lives of another. He would see the black men and women, for whose freedom a hundred thousand of soldiers gave their lives, sit apart in trains, in which they pay first-class fares for third-class service, in railway stations and in places of entertainment, while State after State declines to do its elementary duty in preparing the negro through education for the best exercise of citizenship.

Added to this, the spread of lawless attacks upon the negro, North, South and West—even in the Springfield made famous by Lincoln— often accompanied by revolting brutalities, sparing neither sex, nor age nor youth, could not but shock the author of the sentiment that "government of the people, by the people, for the people shall not perish from the earth."

Silence under these conditions means tacit approval. The indifference of the North is already responsible for more than one assault upon democracy, and every such attack reacts as unfavorably upon whites as upon blacks. Discrimination once permitted cannot be bridled; recent history in the South shows that in forging chains for the negroes, the white voters are forging chains for themselves . . . This government cannot exist half slave and half free any better to-day than it could in 1861. Hence we call upon all the believers in democracy to join in a national conference for the discussion of present evils, the voicing of protests, and the renewal of the struggle for civil and political liberty.[7]

IDA B. WELLS-BARNETT

1909 was the one hundredth anniversary of the birth of Abraham Lincoln. Just before his birthday, a round robin had been sent through the country for signatures and was then given to the press. It called attention to the fact that while the country was preparing to celebrate Lincoln's one hundredth anniversary, the Negro race, whose history was inseparably linked with that of Lincoln, was still far from emancipation. It spoke of lynchings, peonage, convict lease systems, disfranchisement, and the jim crow cars of the South.

It suggested that the finest celebration of Lincoln's one hundredth anniversary would be one which put forth some concrete effort to abolish these conditions. That appeal was signed by Jane Addams and myself, representing Chicago, and by many representative thinkers in other parts of the country.

The immediate celebration of this centenary which took place in Chicago was held in Orchestra Hall on the night of 12 February, at which time an address was delivered by Dr. Du Bois, and a chorus of one hundred voices sang Negro spirituals . . .

Not long after that came a summons from New York, asking a conference of those who had signed the round robin which had been sent out in January. Following this a group of representative Negroes met in New York City in a three-day conference, deliberating on the form which our activities ought to take. It was called the National Negro Committee, although many white persons were present. There was an uneasy feeling that Mr. Booker T. Washington and his theories, which seemed for the moment to dominate the country, would prevail in the discussion as to what ought to be done.

Dr. Du Bois had written his *The Souls of Black Folk* the year following the fiasco of the Afro-American Council in Saint Paul.[8] Although the country at large seemed to be accepting and adopting Mr. Washington's theories of industrial education, a large number agreed with Dr. Du

Bois that it was impossible to limit the aspirations and endeavors of an entire race within the confines of the industrial education program.

Mr. Washington had a short time before held a conference of representative Negro men from all sections of the country, whose expenses had all been paid by some unknown person, and the feeling prevailed at our conference that an effort would be made to tie us to the chariot wheels of the industrial education program. Mr. Oswald Garrison Villard, the grandson of William Lloyd Garrison, was very active in promoting our meeting. He had been an outspoken admirer of Mr. Washington, and the feeling seemed general that an endorsement of his industrial education would be the result.

Mr. Washington himself did not appear. But this feeling, like Banquo's ghost, would not down. I was among those who tried to allay this feeling by asserting that most of those present were believers in Dr. Du Bois's ideas. It was finally decided that a committee of forty should be appointed to spend a year in devising ways and means for the establishment of an organization, and that we should come together the following year to hear its report. It was to be known as the National Negro Committee.

The subcommittee which had been appointed to recommend the names of persons to be on that committee included Dr. Du Bois, who was the only Negro on it. It was also decided that the reading of that list should be the last thing done at the last session of our conference. Excitement bubbled over . . . and I went from one to the other trying to allay the excitement, assuring them that their fears were groundless; that I had seen the list of names; that I had been elected as one, and that Mr. Washington's name was not only not on the list, but that mine was, along with others who were known to be opposed to the inclusiveness of Mr. Washington's industrial ideas.

When at last the moment arrived at which the committee was to make its report, Dr. Du Bois had been selected to read it. This was a compliment paid him by the white men who had been associated with him in the work, and I thought it gave notice of their approval of his plan and their disposition to stand by the program of those who believed that the Negro should be untrammeled in his efforts to secure higher education. Dr. Du Bois read the forty names chosen, and immediately after a motion to adopt was carried and the meeting adjourned.[9]

BOOKER T. WASHINGTON

Huntington, L.I., N.Y. August 11, 1909

My dear Mr. [Jesse Edward] Moorland:[10]

. . . In regard to the employment of Dr. Du Bois. I have had a conference with the president of the University, and he understands my position thoroughly. Personally I have no feeling in the matter one way or the other. I have told Dr. Thirkield I should agree to whatever was for the best interests of the University.[11] I should be surprised, however, if a man of Dr. Du Bois' importance can be secured at the small salary which the University is able to pay . . .[12]

BOOKER T. WASHINGTON

Huntington, L.I., N.Y. August 15, 1909

My dear President [Wilbur Patterson] Thirkield:

. . . As to the employment of Dr. Du Bois at Howard, I repeat in substance what I said to you. Personally, I do not believe that he will be of any value to the institution. On the other hand, my fear is that he would be a hindrance. Then, too, I question whether a man of his importance can be secured for the small wage which Howard University is able to pay.

Now that I have stated my personal feeling in the matter, I wish you to feel perfectly satisfied if you as President of the University nominate Dr. Du Bois to the position I shall support you with my vote. On the other hand, if you feel that he ought not to enter the service of the University, I shall stand by you. In a word, I feel that you as President of the University know more than anybody else what it needs, and it seems to me that this is a matter in which you will have to largely if not wholly decide for yourself. That would certainly be the attitude I would take if Tuskegee were placed in a similar position . . . In this case I feel all the more hesitation in expressing my views for reasons you well understand, but as a trustee of the institution I cannot shirk any duty however unpleasant it may be . . .

All that I am trying to say can be summed up in this: If you as President of the University decide that you want him, I think the trustees will follow you in carrying out that wish, but, on the other hand, if you decide you do not want him, I think the trustees will support you . . .[13]

BOOKER T. WASHINGTON

[Tuskegee, Ala.] September 4, 1909

Personal
My dear Dr. [John R.] Francis:[14]

. . . So far as Dr. Du Bois is concerned, I think it is not treating Dr. Thirkield with unfairness to send you a copy of a letter which I wrote him on the subject. This letter expresses my own feeling frankly and fully. Of course, I should not like for any one aside from yourself and Dr. Moorland to see this letter, because it would be unfair to President Thirkield to write him on the subject then pass the letter around generally to be seen by others. I very much prefer to have you return the Thirkield letter to me after you and Dr. Moorland have read it . . . .[15]

JAMES A. COBB

Washington, D.C. Dec 21, 1909

Dear Emmett [Jay Scott]: I have already mailed to you today the last two copies of the Horizon. Saw Kelly Miller and he says Prof Du Bois has made himself impossible so far as the University is concerned, by his last but veiled attack upon the Dr. . . . .[16]

John Hope, close friend of Du Bois and president of Atlanta Baptist Seminary, soon to become Morehouse College in 1913, was known for his diplomatic skills but struggled to demonstrate them when it came to Washington. Hope had been in the audience for the Atlanta Compromise and the following year, for the 1896 commencement of Nashville's Roger Williams University, he asked his audience, "If we are not striving for equality, in heaven's name for what are we striving?" John Hope was one of the most important rights and educational leaders in the country, but was also a college administrator who needed to produce pragmatic results. He opposed the Tuskegee Machine as well as he could, although he later sought to mollify Du Bois's public criticism.[17]

JOHN HOPE

Providence, R.I., January 17, 1910

My dear Du Bois:

. . . Du Bois was the one man to whom I thought I might owe an explanation. Why Du Bois? Because I have followed him; believed in him; tried even, where he was not understood, to interpret him and show that he is right; because I have been loyal to him and his propaganda—not blatantly so, but, I think, really loyal; and because, in spite of appearances, I am just as truly as ever a disciple of the teachings of Du Bois regarding Negro freedom.

It is also true that through the kindness of Mr. Booker Washington I was enabled to secure a conditional offer of ten thousand dollars from Mr. Andrew Carnegie. I may here say that I have credit for more good scheming than I deserve. Without any effort on my part a friend of the school first approached Mr. Washington and pointed a way to me which seemed, and still seems, to me perfectly honorable and so generous as to have called for selfishness on my part not to accept on behalf of a school that needed the assistance and ought to be helped rather than hampered by its president. All of this I carefully thought over and—naive as it may appear to you—prayed over. Then without any persuasion or pressure from any one I went frankly to Mr. Washington; told of what I heard; told him my purpose for the school and that larger facilities would mean better opportunity for carrying on the work of this school as it now is without any change of its educational policy and ideals. After hearing this, he was quite as willing to help and did so.

Now Du Bois, I expect to be criticized, perhaps publicly; would be surprised if so great a flop, flop as it *seems*, should go unnoticed and unknocked. I should not wonder that from your position you would have to knock quite savagely. All this and more I expect, would be surprised if I did not get, but would not lift my finger to avert.

Then why write you all this? My impression is that *friendship*—not acquaintanceship or perfunctory intercourse but real friendship—is based not so much on agreement in opinion and policies and methods but upon downright confidence, upon simple faith, no matter what the view or appearances. You and I for nearly ten years have been friends, at least I have fancied so. I write to ask, no matter whether you doubt the wisdom of or resent my action, are we friends?

You may remember that in the early and bitterly misunderstood efforts of the Niagara Movement, I was the only college president that

ventured to attend the Harper's Ferry meeting to take part in its deliberations. You may remember too, that while some may have answered
the call to that seemingly radical meeting in New York last May, I
was the only president, colored or white, of our colleges that took part
in the deliberations of that meeting. I cite this to show that I have dared
to live up to my views even when they threw me in the midst of the
most radical. Furthermore, every man on our faculty does the same
and will as long as I am head of the institution. But, Du Bois, may there
not be a *tyranny* of views? Have we not required such severe alignments that it has been sometimes as much a lack of courage as a mark
of courage to stand either with Du Bois or Washington to the absolute
exclusion of one or the other in any sort of intercourse? I confess that
it is unpleasant to be charged with apostasy even in joke when one is
not truly apostate . . .

Now, I have not known Washington long, but what I know of him in
my personal relations is perfectly pleasant and generous. If I should
find out later otherwise, I suppose I would express it as simply and
with as little vehemence as I am now writing. I am glad that as a man
interested in education I can associate properly with another man who
is interested in education yet from a different angle as Washington is.
I am primarily interested in education. Quite as heartily as ever I shall
disagree with Washington's views where they do not accord with mine,
and I would not yield a principle for the benefit of myself or my school,
obviously for such could not really benefit . . .

> Your very dear friend,
> John Hope[18]

WILLIAM EDWARD BURGHARDT DU BOIS

Atlanta, Ga., January 22, 1910

My dear Hope:

You must not think that I have not known and appreciated your friendship for me or that I ever have doubted or doubt now your loyalty to
the principles which we both so sincerely believe. If I thought even that
you were going back on those principles, my friendship is not of so
slight a texture that I would easily give you up. Of course I am sorry to
see you or anyone in Washington's net. It's a dangerous place, old man,
and you must keep your eyes open. At the same time under the circumstances I must say frankly I do not see any other course of action

before you but the one you took. In your position of responsibility your institution must stand foremost in your thought. One thing alone you must not, however, forget: Washington stands for Negro submission and slavery. Representing that, with unlimited funds, he can afford to be broad and generous and most of us must accept the generosity or starve. Having accepted it we are peculiarly placed and in a sense tongue-tied and bound. I may have to place myself in that position yet, but, by God, I'll fight hard before I do it.

I know, however, that you, my friend, are going to do the right as you see it, and I'm too sensible of my own short comings and mistakes to undertake to guide you. As I have said, so far, you have done what you had to do under the circumstances. I only trust that the pound of flesh demanded in return will not be vital . . .[19]

NEW YORK *EVENING POST*

Mr. Washington in Politics

The old issue as to what attitude the colored people should take towards their political disabilities is recalled anew by a recent speech in this city of Dr. W.E.B. Du Bois of Atlanta University and a letter from him to the Boston Transcript. Few people are yet aware, we believe, of the extent of the cleavage between him and his followers and those negroes led by Booker T. Washington, or of the bitterness that has developed. Dr. Du Bois's attitude is one of resentment toward wrong, of steadfast opposition to disfranchisement, and to the withdrawal of civil and political rights guaranteed by the Constitution of the United States. He believes that agitation and protest are necessary not only to recover lost ground, but to prevent the loss of more. He will not sit silent in the presence of wrong . . . With this attitude the Evening Post has frequently sympathized. It counsels no man to wear a padlock when his rights as a citizen are endangered.

Dr. Washington, on the other hand, subordinates everything else to the uplifting of the negro industrially and economically. His success at Tuskegee needs no affirmation, North or South. His in estimable usefulness as an interpreter of one race to the other in the South we dwelt upon at length after his recent extraordinary trip through Tennessee. To be industrious, sober, honest, and to acquire property, this is his doctrine for the colored man. He lets discussion of political rights severely alone—an attitude which is justified by most people as the right one for the head of an institution located in the South in the midst of deep racial prejudices. There is much to be said for all college heads keeping bravely aloof from political entanglements. Dr. Washington counsels his people to submit to disfranchisement. Hence he is welcome in the South wherever he goes. He arouses no prejudices; his industrial doctrine fits in well with the controlling Southern opinion that the negro should aspire to be nothing more than a hewer-of-wood and a drawer-of-water, and so he reaches the ears and broadens the minds and softens the hearts of thousands who would not listen to a word from Dr. Du Bois. Moreover, Dr. Washington is heartily supported in the North by all conservatives—those who believe that the South should be allowed to work out the problem unmolested by criticism or agitation, and are convinced that time will heal all present sores and wounds.

Now, as we have intimated, this is a defensible attitude for the principal of a school to take. It commends itself particularly to those who believe in compromises for the sake of peace and living pleasantly with their neighbors. If Dr. Washington were to keep silent altogether and immerse himself exclusively in his work at Tuskegee, no colored man would, we think, object to his silence. It is his advice to his people to submit to government and taxation without representation that has hurt, and the fact that he has at the same time assumed or been forced into the place of political boss of his race. The two positions are hopelessly inconsistent. As Dr. Du Bois puts it in his letter to the *Transcript*:

> Mr. Washington has for the last eight years allowed himself to be made the sole referee for all political action concerning 10,000,000 Americans. Few appointments of negroes to office have been made without his consent, and others' political policies have been deferred to him. Now, if Mr. Washington was consulted solely because of his knowledge of men and wide acquaintanceship, there would be less ground of criticism. But what ever the purpose, it has been inevitable that only those negroes should be put in political control of black men who agree with Mr. Washington's policy of non-resistance, giving up of agitation, and acquiescence in semiserfdom.

And he properly asserts his right as a free man to protest against the establishment of any political boss of a section of the population, white or black, Christian or Jew, Italian or German.

There is high authority for Dr. Du Bois' position. The late Carl Schurz once warned Mr. Washington that if he heard of the head of Tuskegee going into politics he would know that the waning of Mr. Washington's influence had begun.[20] But the White House has insisted on making use of Dr. Washington's rare knowledge of Southern conditions. It is hard, if not impossible, to resist requests for advice or counsel from this source. Dr. Washington naturally has the deepest interest in seeing that fit colored men only are appointed to office. Could he refuse to answer if Mr. Roosevelt asked him whether John Smith or Thomas Brown would represent his race better in an internal revenue office or as an assistant United States District Attorney? If we are correctly informed, the reason for Dr. Washington's withdrawal from the Liberian Commission to which Mr. Roosevelt appointed him a year ago was Mr. Taft's insistence that he stay within reach. At least, this was current gossip in Washington at the time, and instead, Mr. Washington's secretary went to Liberia.[21] Moreover, Mr. Washington is such a national figure that everyone turns to him for advice on matters relating to the colored people. It is not as if there were three or four men of equal rank in the public estimation.

In other words, we have here the usual conflict between the uncompromising and those who believe in progress one step at a time, with the least friction possible. Time will fight on the negro's side, in any event, and the accumulation of wealth and the possession of land, together with the increased national respect which follows material success—all these will lend power to the negro, when the time comes for the issue of political equality to be joined by all concerned. We are frank to say that if we were of the colored race we should feel that that time had come now; that every moment's failure to protest by those who can against present discriminations means the tightening of chains that must some day be broken if this is to be a republic in more than name. Eternal vigilance is the price of liberty for the negro as well as for the white man, and Dr. Du Bois is merely living up to the highest traditions of American life when he fights for the rights of his own people to a voice in their government. We must say frankly, too, that we wish tomorrow might be the day that will free Dr. Washington from his embarrassing position as political dictator. Then he would begin to win back in some measure the regard of the most intellectual portion of the colored people, of which he is now largely deprived.[22]

BOOKER T. WASHINGTON

Hotel Manhattan, New York. April 25, 1910

Personal
My dear Dr. [Daniel] Merriman:[23]

. . . I do not know why it is that Dr. Du Bois and Atlanta University take the attitude that they do. I never abuse Dr. Du Bois, never refer to him in public except in some complimentary manner. Wherever I speak, in nine cases out of ten I refer in a complimentary way to Atlanta University. In my recent book, "The Story of the Negro," I refer many times to Dr. Du Bois.[24]

The most unusual and indelicate part of the whole proceedings it seems to me is that a representative of one institution should go before the public and criticise a sister institution, but notwithstanding any attitude that Dr. Du Bois may pursue in the future, and no matter what he may say or do, I shall not be taken off my feet. I will not grow bitter, but will go on with my work hoping at some time that he and Atlanta University may see the better way of doing things.

I shall hope to talk the whole matter over with you and at length sometime when I see you.

I suppose you know that Dr. Du Bois and two of his friends publish a monthly magazine. This publication is almost filled every month with either insinuations or bitter criticisms either against Tuskegee Institute or against myself. What his object is for all this I cannot understand. Certainly no good purpose so far [as] I can see is being accomplished . . .[25]

BOOKER T. WASHINGTON

New York City. April 27, 1910

Personal and Confidential

Dear Judge [Robert Heberton] Terrell:[26] I suppose you have seen the printed program of the meeting to be held here sometime in May under the auspices of the opposition crowd.[27]

Not a few of your friends here are nonplussed as to why Mrs. Terrell's name appears among the members of the executive committee and as one of the speakers on the program.[28] This kind of thing is really embarrassing. I think it but just to your friends to let us know where you are at. This organization, as was true last year, is likely to engage in wholesale abuse of the President of the United States as well as other friends of ours. Whenever your name comes up for confirmation, your friends unhesitatingly go to the front. To have Mrs. Terrell's name appear on a program where the opposition is in charge naturally makes it harder for your friends to help you when the time comes, but makes it embarrassing from every point of view. Of course I am not seeking to control anybody's action, but I simply want to know where we stand . . .[29]

BOOKER T. WASHINGTON

[Tuskegee, Ala.] May 3, 1910

Personal

Dear Mr. [Ray Stannard] Baker: . . . As you already suggest, there are several counties in the South where they make it a habit not to register colored people, but I am glad to say that these counties so far as Alabama is concerned are the exception rather than the rule.

Sometime, perhaps, you might bring out the point that it is largely the fault of colored people themselves that they do not vote. In most cases where there is some foresight to be exercised or some money to be paid in the form of taxes in advance, the colored people cut themselves off. You would be surprised, for example, in a state like Georgia where there has been no law prohibiting the colored people from voting until recently, to see how few colored people vote. I think you will find, for example, that Dr. Du Bois of Atlanta, who tries to lead in the matter of agitation in the matter of the franchise, has never voted in Atlanta or attempted to register, and I do not believe he votes anywhere in America. His case illustrates many others. Here at Tuskegee for example, there is practically no trouble in any colored man registering and voting. Notwithstanding this is true, I find it the most difficult task to get our teachers, especially those who are graduates of colleges, to pay their taxes and vote. If you were to go into a city like Atlanta and make an individual canvass, you would be surprised at the large number of educated colored people who have never attempted to register or vote. Yours very truly,

Booker T. Washington[30]

EMMETT JAY SCOTT

New York. May 16th, 1910

Personal

Dear Mr. [Hightower T.] Kealing:[31]

. . . Your friends and the Niagara Movement are trying to resuscitate that moribund organization by the formation of a new organization to be called the National Negro Conference which is now holding a meeting here in New York City. Your name I learn, has been proposed as a member of the Executive Committee. I hope I may have the privilege of talking to you before you accept of this proffered place . . .[32]

BOOKER T. WASHINGTON

[Tuskegee, Ala.] May 24, 1910

My dear Mr. [Ray Stannard] Baker: Your letter of May 13th has been received.[33] I note what you say regarding the effect of your address on the Negro Conference. I am not surprised at the kind of reception that it was given. I happen to know the individuals who compose this conference. Nothing that has real sense in it would be received with any degree of enthusiasm. What they want is nonsense.

I would have some sympathy with this organization if I did not know that a majority, not all, of the white men who are leading in the matter are not sincere, and that a majority of the colored people in it are not sincere. I know the individuals. I have tried to work with them. I have found them in most cases either without sincerity or without stability. For the most part the white people who are in this organization are deceived as to the character of the colored people in it. There are few colored men in this organization of any real standing in their own communities. And then it is sinful in the highest degree for any set of white men to lend their influence of deceiving the colored people into the idea that they can get what they ought to have in the way of right treatment by merely making demands, passing resolutions and cursing somebody. No individual in America realizes more keenly than I do the injustices put upon our race, but at the same time I realize fully that we cannot change conditions by merely demanding that they should be changed.

Of course this organization with a certain element of our people holds out a great temptation. If a child is sick and you offer it candy in one hand and castor oil in the other, the child is more likely to ask for the candy than the castor oil, though the one may result in making him more sick and the other in curing his body; but the masses of the colored people are not deceived and are making real progress . . .[34]

RAY STANNARD BAKER

East Lansing Mich June 20 1910

Dear Mr. Washington:

. . . I had hoped for a good deal from the conference; but fear it will not be effective. They have asked me to serve on the committee, but I have refused, thinking it better not to appear to support a cause with which I find myself in disagreement at so many points . . .[35]

BOOKER T. WASHINGTON

[Tuskegee, Ala.] July 11, 1910

Personal

Dear Mr. [Charles William] Anderson: I see that our friend, Du Bois, has finally decided to locate in New York.

In order to counteract such evil tendencies as may ensue, I strongly urge that you pursue the policy of getting one representative of every strong organization in your club. To bring about this result, it may be necessary for you to broaden your club somewhat. I think your club should become in a large degree the "clearing house" for Negro organizations in New York City. That is you ought to have in it one representative from every organization, in that way you could easily control the whole situation . . . .[36]

IDA B. WELLS-BARNETT

. . . The following summer, thanks to a suggestion of mine adopted at the board meeting of the newly organized NAACP, Miss Frances Blascoes journeyed to Louisville, Kentucky, to attend the meeting of the National Association of Colored Women's Clubs. Miss Elizabeth Carter of New Bedford, Massachusetts, was president of the National Association at this time, and she had urgently insisted that I attend that meeting.[37] It was my first visit to the meeting since the one which was held in Chicago in 1899, and I was greeted with a great deal of applause.

Before the meeting adjourned, however, I again ran across that spirit which seems to dominate every organization we have. Mrs. Ione Gibbs, chairman of the executive committee, had recommended that the office of editor of the *National Notes* be an elective one[38] . . . She said it was up to the delegates, whereupon I called for the adoption of the report by sections.

It was decided to give us five minutes in which to discuss them. When we got to the section calling for the election of an editor, I led the discussion and moved its adoption. This was objected to. Then I turned to the delegates and reminded them of the complaints they had made about the irregularity of the *National Notes*, about its failure to publish matter sent, about the dissatisfaction of subscribers who had never received the paper. I reminded them that this was the time and place to change the situation by electing an editor who would be responsible to the body. I called for a rising vote, which showed that the motion prevailed. Miss Carter then ruled that the motion had been out of order because the recommendations of the executive board could not be acted upon until the next session, two years later.

An appeal from the decision of the chair was demanded on the ground that the ruling was not made until after the motion to adopt was passed. This brought down upon my head a storm of disapproval. Mrs. Lucy Thurman stepped to the front of the platform and said the delegates ought to resent action of one who challenged the decision of the chair, and came down there attempting to teach them.[39] The women hissed me from the floor. I went home and went to bed instead of appearing at the big banquet which was given to the delegates that night.

I had already been made chairman of the committee of resolutions. I went to the meeting next morning, read my resolutions, had them adopted, and withdrew from the meeting. I learned afterward that Miss Carter was very much upset, insisting that I was her special guest, and that she had never dreamed that her partisans would go to such extremes.

I also learned that Mrs. Washington's friends had construed my activity to mean that I wanted the paper to be taken away from her, and to be elected editor myself. Always the personal element. It seems disheartening to think that every single move for progress and race advancement has to be blocked in this way. Mrs. Washington had started the *Notes* on her own motion, and out of her enthusiasm, in an effort to give the National Association an organ of its own. Of course as long as she paid the expense out of her own pocket and had it printed at Tuskeegee, the women felt a delicacy in finding fault with anything about it . . .

I wended my way back to Chicago and again took up the work of the Negro Fellowship League. The effort we had made to secure jobs for the young men who frequented our reading room brought forth a demand from the state department and private employment agencies that I take out a license . . .

I tried so hard to make a good showing, because I hoped for a continuation of the help which we were receiving. An appeal was made to Mr. Julius Rosenwald to help us.[40] Mr. Rosenwald sent an investigating committee to visit the place. After looking us over, the committee was invited to be seated. Mr. [Paul J.] Sachs said that he had heard Booker T. Washington the night before at the Standard Club. He said, "He told us a very funny story about an old man who said his wife had left him; that he did not mind her going so much, but she had left the chicken coop door open and all the chickens had gone home, too."

He laughed very heartily as he told the story, but when he saw I didn't laugh he asked me if the colored people accepted Mr. Washington as their leader, and if they didn't believe in his doctrine. I said, "We have very great respect for Mr. Washington's ability to reach the influential people of this country and interest them in his theories of industrial education and secure their help for the same. We don't all agree entirely with his program.

"As to his being our leader, I will answer your question by asking one. Rabbi [Emil G.] Hirsch is your leading Jew in Chicago. He is constantly invited to appear before representative gentile audiences, and because of his wonderful eloquence is a general favorite. But I am wondering if you Jews would acclaim him so highly if every time he appeared before a gentile audience he would amuse them by telling stories about Jews burning down their stores to get their insurance?" His face turned very red, and I said, "I am sure you would not, and a great many of us cannot approve Mr. Washington's plan of telling chicken-stealing stories on his own people in order to amuse his audiences and get money for Tuskeegee." Needless to say, the conversation ended there.[41]

The 1910 Pink Franklin case was the first major case undertaken by the NAACP's Legal Redress Committee. It was also the only NAACP case that included the cooperation of Washington. Although the South Carolina Supreme Court had already ruled the law invalid, officers attempted to arrest Franklin— an illiterate farmhand—for peonage. A shootout in Franklin's bedroom ensued, injuring him and his wife and killing a policeman. Although Franklin's wife was acquitted, he was sentenced to be executed. The U.S. Supreme Court upheld the decision on appeal, so the NAACP turned to Washington to persuade President Taft to intercede. Instead, Washington suggested to South Carolina intermediaries to appeal to South Carolina Governor Martin Frederick Ansel. Eventually, the sentence was commuted to life imprisonment. Despite the successful outcome for Franklin, however, the collaboration was a missed opportunity that demonstrated that Washington was only willing to participate when absolutely necessary, and only to a very limited point.[42]

OSWALD GARRISON VILLARD

Winter Harbor, Maine, August 4, 1910

My dear Mr. Washington, I do not know if your attention has been called to the Pink Franklin case. I enclose copy of a letter just received, from Ex-Attorney General Bonaparte who takes the same view as

Mr. Pillsbury, that Franklin has been sacrificed to the stupidity and conceit of his colored counsel.[43] In any event, an innocent man who shot in self-defence, will be done to death unless prompt measures are taken.

We are endeavoring to circulate a petition through our organization. I am wondering if we could not get the President to take an interest in the case. A word from Mr. Roosevelt would help, of course. You yourself may have certain lines of action among white and colored people which could be quickly put into effect and might at least cause the commutation of the sentence. If you care to see it and have not already done so, you can obtain a copy of Mr. Bonaparte's brief on the Pink Franklin case from my office. Do help to save this victim of race prejudice![44]

BOOKER T. WASHINGTON

Huntington, N.Y. August 9, 1910

My dear Mr [Oswald Garrison] Villard: Answering your letter regarding the Pink Franklin case, I would state that in my opinion I do not believe anybody outside of South Carolina can be of much service. I would suggest one of two courses.

First, if the money is available, to employ one of the strongest white lawyers in the state of South Carolina that can be gotten to take the matter up with the Governor.

Or failing in this, I would suggest, secondly, that Rev. Richard Carroll, of Columbia, S.C., be asked to undertake to secure what is desired from the Governor.[45] Richard Carroll is a man who has many qualities that neither you nor I would admire, but at the same time there is no discounting the fact that he has tremendous influence with the white people of South Carolina . . . If you think well of the latter course you can either write directly to Carroll yourself, or I shall be glad to do so if you think it wise.

We are looking forward with interest to seeing you on the 18th . . .[46]

OSWALD GARRISON VILLARD

Winter Harbor, Me. Aug 12, 1910

Dear Mr. Washington, Many, many thanks for your prompt reply. Please do everything you can thru Carroll for this unfortunate man. We have no money to hire a prominent white lawyer. Hastily yours,

Oswald Garrison Villard[47]

W.E.B. DU BOIS

The object of this publication [the *Crisis*] is to set forth those facts and arguments which show the danger of race prejudice, particularly as manifested today toward colored people. It takes its name from the fact that the editors believe that this is a critical time in the history of the advancement of men. Catholicity and tolerance, reason and forbearance can today make the world-old dream of human brotherhood approach realization; while bigotry and prejudice, emphasized race consciousness and force can repeat the awful history of the contact of nations and groups in the past. We strive for this higher and broader vision of Peace and Good Will . . .[48]

OSWALD GARRISON VILLARD

New York September 20, 1910

Dear Mr. [Charles Dyer] Norton:[49]

. . . Permit me to call your attention to certain phases of the situation among the colored people which may, perhaps, be of service to you in elucidating some of the problems before you. You are, I think, generally aware that the colored people in the United States are split into two parts, or factions, one headed by Booker Washington and the other by Dr. Du Bois, who has reached a greater intellectual height than perhaps any other colored man. Because Dr. Du Bois, and rightly in my judgment, insists upon fighting for the rights guaranteed to the colored people by the 13th, 14th and 15th Amendments to the Constitution, he has been set down in some places as aspiring for "social equality," and as being wholly antagonistic to Booker Washington. The two schools have represented, also, in the public mind the question of higher education and manual training, though Dr. Du Bois has repeatedly endorsed the work of such schools as Tuskegee, and Dr. Washington has similarly urged the absolute necessity of more institutions of the higher kind like Atlanta, as has Mr. Taft recently, I believe. So far as Mr. Washington's position is concerned, I can assure you that the opposition to him among his own people increases steadily. The great majority of the men who have risen above the ranks consider him a traitor to the race. You would be surprised at their vehemence, but you must know about it because one reason for the opposition to Mr. Washington is that he has become, not by his own volition, but through the friendship of Mr. Taft and Mr. Roosevelt, the office broker for the race, a position into which, as I have told Mr. Washington frankly, no man ought to allow himself to be forced, however gratifying it may be, or how little he may have sought the honor. Of course, the negro office holders, like McKinlay, W.H. Lewis, and others, and many of the negro editors, are entirely on Mr. Washington's side.[50] If you consult only with them you will please only them, and you will correspondingly offend the other faction . . .[51]

Du Bois resigned from Atlanta in 1910 after realizing that the financial difficulties of the school were, at least, in part, attributable to his own radicalism and to Washington's opposition to it. His help in forming the NAACP would be his next major project, although his editorship of the Crisis *would create a rift between himself and the NAACP Board of Directors, as the magazine largely became the mouthpiece for his own philosophy, not necessarily that of the broader white NAACP membership. His position led him in 1915— following the death of Washington—to become the most important of the country's black leaders.*[52]

W.E.B. DU BOIS

Already we had formed the National Association for the Advancement of Colored People, a precarious thing without money, with some influential members, but we were never quite sure whether their influence would stay with us if we "fought" for Negro rights. We started in tiny offices at 20 Vesey Street and then took larger ones at 26. Finally on the eve of the undreamed-of World War we had moved to 70 Fifth Avenue.

There have been many versions as to how this organization was born, all of them true and yet not the full truth. In a sense William English Walling founded it a hundred years after Lincoln's birth, because of his indignation at a lynching in Lincoln's birthplace.[53] But in reality the thing was born long years before when, under the roar of Niagara Falls, there was formed the Niagara Movement by twenty-nine colored men. How they screamed at us and threatened! The *Outlook*, then at the zenith of its power, declared that we were ashamed of our race and jealous of Mr. Washington. The colored press unanimously condemned us and listed our failures. We were told that we were fighting the scars in their courses. Yet from that beginning of the Niagara Movement in 1935 down to the formation of the National Association for the Advancement of Colored People in 1909, we were welding the weapons, breasting the blows, stating the ideals, and preparing the membership for the larger, stronger organization. Seven of the twenty-nine went on the first Board of Directors of the N.A.A.C.P., and the rest became leading members.

There came six years of work. It is perhaps, hard to say definitely just what we accomplished in these six years. It was perhaps a matter of spirit and getting ready, and yet we established the *Crisis* magazine and had it by 1916 almost self-supporting. We had branches of our organization throughout the country. We had begun to move upon the courts with test cases. We had held mass meetings through the country. We had stirred up Congress and we had attacked lynching.[54]

NOTES

1. John Dewey was a famous and influential instrumentalist philosopher and educational reformer. Although he began his teaching career at the University of Chicago, by 1909 he was teaching at Columbia. Burt Green Wilder was a neurologist working at Cornell. Albert Enoch Pillsbury was a Boston lawyer, former Massachusetts attorney general, and activist for black rights who would ultimately draft the NAACP's bylaws. Wendell Phillips Stafford was a federal district court judge for the District of Columbia and a law professor at George Washington University. And Clarence Darrow was one of the most famous lawyers in the country, in 1909 working principally labor cases. See Pappas, 2008; Burt Green Wilder Papers, 1841–1925, Collection Number 14-26-95, Division of Rare and Manuscript Collections, Cornell University Library, Ithaca, New York; *New York Times*, 24 December 1930, 10; Noel and Downing, 1919, 77; and Vine, 2005.

2. Washington, 1981, vol. 10, 116–118.

3. Ibid., 118–120.

4. Ibid., 127.

5. John Milton Waldron was a Baptist minister from Alabama who, at the time, was pastor of Shiloh Baptist Church in Washington, D.C. Dr. William Albert Sinclair was an author and historian who had, in 1905, published a study of the consequences of slavery in the late 19th century titled *The Aftermath of Slavery*. George E. Wibecan was a Republican leader from Brooklyn. William Lewis Bulkley was a PhD in Latin from Syracuse and a public school principal in New York City. Moore, 1999; Sinclair, 2012; Wilder, 2000, 119; and Carle, 2013, 28–30. For Bishop Alexander Walters, see Chapter 4, note 33. For Jesse Max Barber, see Chapter 13, note 38. For Nathan Francis Mossell, see Chapter 4, note 43. For John Elmer Milholland, see Chapter 13, note 50. For Ida B. Wells, see Chapters 4, 6, 7, 9, 10, and 11.

6. Washington, 1981, vol. 10, 127.

7. "Committee on the Negro 'Call' for a National Conference, February 1909," Ray Stannard Baker Papers, Manuscript Division, Library of Congress.

8. Mrs. Barnett regarded the Saint Paul meeting as a fiasco because it was dominated by Booker T. Washington, who succeeded in having the council elect a slate of officers friendly to him. Thornbrough, 1961, 504.

9. Wells, 1970, 321–324.

10. Jesse Edward Moorland was a Congregational minister and secretary of the Washington, D.C. branch of the YMCA. He received his master's degree from Howard and was still closely associated with the university. Mjagkij, 1994, 50–52.

11. Methodist Episcopal minister Wilbur P. Thirkield was president of Howard University from 1906 to 1912. Garrett, 1967, 947.

12. Washington, 1981, vol. 10, 154–155.

13. Ibid., 156–157.

14. John Richard Francis was a prominent black Washington, D.C. physician and surgeon. Washington *Colored American*, 23 January 1904, 11.

15. Washington, 1981, vol. 10, 160–161.

16. Ibid., 248–249.

17. Lewis, 1993, 255–256. See Chapter 13, note 86.

18. Hope was a close friend and advocate of Du Bois. He served as president of Morehouse College while Du Bois was at Atlanta University. Du Bois, 1973, 164–167.

19. Ibid., 167.

20. For more on Schurz, see Chapter 13, note 94.

21. See Chapter 14.

22. Washington, 1981, vol. 10, 309–311; and "Mr. Washington In Politics," New York *Evening Post*, 1 April 1910, 8.

23. The Reverend Doctor Daniel Merriman was a graduate of Williams College and pastor of Central Church in Worcester, Massachusetts. He also served as a trustee of Atlanta University. See Merriman, Daniel, Correspondence, 1892–1893, Misc. mss. boxes "M," American Antiquarian Society Manuscript Collections, Worcester, Massachusetts.

24. Washington, *The Story of the Negro*, 1909.

25. Washington, 1981, vol. 10, 321–322.

26. Terrell was principal of Washington's M Street High School, who also held a law degree from Howard. See Chapter 5, note 9.

27. Washington here refers to the meeting of the National Negro Committee—the early NAACP—scheduled for May 12–14, 1910. Washington, 1981, vol. 10, 323.

28. Mary Church Terrell, Robert Heberton Terrell's wife, was an educator and activist for both black rights and women's rights. Jones, 1982, 20–33.

29. Washington, 1981, vol. 10, 322–323.

30. Ibid., 323–324.

31. Hightower Theodore Kealing was the editor of the *AME Church Review* and the president of Paul Quinn College in Texas. Smith, 1997, 142–143.

32. Washington, 1981, vol. 10, 331.

33. Baker wrote after attending the NAACP conference, "I delivered my address last night at the Negro Conference here, and I am afraid it did not meet with the approval of most of the radicals there. The more I see of this whole matter, the more I feel sure that you are on the right track—that it is only by patient development and growth that the evils can be met." Ibid., 334.

34. Ibid., 333–334.

35. Ibid., 342.

36. Ibid., 355.

37. Elizabeth Carter Brooks became the fourth president of the organization in 1908 and maintained that position until 1912. See Leslie, 2012.

38. Ione L. Gibbs was a prominent member of the Association from Minnesota, the first president of that state's chapter. See Leslie, 2012.

39. Lucy Thurman was a Michigan delegate, the first president of that state's chapter. See Leslie, 2012.

40. Julius Rosenwald was the head of Sears, Roebuck and a philanthropist who often donated to black causes. He built a series of black secondary schools across the South with Washington's guidance. Between 1913 and 1932, under Rosenwald's guidance, more than 5,300 schools were built, at a cost of more than 28 million dollars. See Ascoli, 2006.

41. Wells, 1970, 329–331.

42. Washington, 1981, vol. 10, 362–363; and "Pink Franklin," *Crisis* 1 (December 1910): 26.

43. Charles Joseph Bonaparte was a lawyer and progressive who served as, first, Secretary of the Navy, and, second, Attorney General under Theodore Roosevelt. See Goldman, 1943.

44. Washington, 1981, vol. 10, 362.

45. Richard Carroll was a minister and one of the leading black figures in South Carolina. He knew Theodore Roosevelt, edited a black newspaper, and founded the South Carolina Race Conference to promote racial harmony in the state. See Richard Carroll Papers, 1908–1977, University South Caroliniana Society Manuscripts Collection, University of South Carolina, Columbia, South Carolina.

46. Washington, 1981, vol. 10, 364–365.

47. Ibid., 366.

48. Du Bois, "Editorial," November 1910, 1.

49. Charles Dyer Norton was a Chicago merchant who, in September 1910, was serving as private secretary for William Howard Taft. *The Merchants Club of Chicago, 1896–1907*, 1922.

50. For Whitefield McKinlay, see Chapter 7, note 12. For William H. Lewis, see Chapter 4.

51. Washington, 1981, vol. 10, 385–387.

52. Green and Driver, "Introduction," 1978, 20–21.

53. William English Walling was a labor and peace activist. The lynching Du Bois mentions, however, occurred in Springfield, Illinois. Walling's investigation moved him to race activism and to become a cofounder of the NAACP. (Of course, although Lincoln grew up in Illinois, he was born in Hodgenville, Kentucky.) Craig, 1998, 351–376.

54. Du Bois, 1925.

16

The Milholland and
Britain Letters

*The controversy between the competing ideologies of the NAACP and Tuskegee,
Du Bois and Washington, became international in late 1910 when, on a speaking tour in England, Washington touted continually improving race relations
in the United States. The statements not only rang hollow to much of black
America but they also angered a group who believed such comments were tanta-
mount to damaging treachery, stifling the possibility of genuine foreign support
and potential diplomatic pressure to help generate change to the racial situation
in the United States. In response, both John Milholland and W.E.B. Du Bois
wrote public letters explaining the American racial situation to the people of
Britain and castigating Washington for calling an empty glass half-full.*

JOHN ELMER MILHOLLAND

Tuskegee and the American Negro:
Dr. Booker T. Washington's Industrial Education
Propaganda Dispassionately Reviewed in the
Light of Actualities by an American Citizen

Dear Sir, I must decline your Society's kind invitation to the Luncheon in honour of my fellow countryman, Dr. Booker T. Washington. I do so with regret. Dr. Washington, like myself, is a Citizen of the United States. He is also a friend of many years . . . The Sunday following his famous Luncheon at the White House with President Roosevelt, when the consequent excitement—that exhibition of barbarism—was at its height, I gave a dinner in his honour at the leading hotel of New York. Not less than $50,000 was realised for his school on that occasion. At the time I also held his view on the Tuskegee propaganda.

From this you can perhaps infer that if your Luncheon involved merely the personal equation, I would gladly come, but it involves a great deal more . . .

Dr. Washington and his institution at Tuskegee practically stand for the industrial education or material progress of the American Negro, and for that alone.

I do not. Neither do I stand for the industrial education of the Jews, the Irish, the Dutch, or any other race. It would be just as rational to say that the men of Kent or Surrey shall all be wheelwrights, every Welshman an electrician, every Scotchman a gardener, or that the young women of Yorkshire, even when qualified to go in for the Mathematical Tripos at Cambridge, shall all become Red Cross Nurses, as to lay down one course of study and development for 10,000,000 American citizens whose skins are coloured, but who differ from one another in brain and body just as much as the people of other nations.

More than a hundred years ago, when Slavery flourished in the United States, North and South, Alexander Hamilton, one of the greatest Statesmen, keenest observers, and among the most logical reasoners ever produced in America, declared, after exhaustive examination, that the Negro's "natural faculties are every bit as good as ours." A century's experience confirms this view, for even that ancient lie about certain "fundamental differences in the brain structure," has been so completely demolished in the cold processes of scientific demonstration . . . that we shall be troubled less with it in the future consideration of this subject. There are Negroes, and possibly the majority of them, as in the case of the Whites, who may or may not be fit for higher education; but to say that the hundreds of thousands who unquestionably are shall be denied the cultivation of their faculties is an outrage upon the individual and a crime against humanity.

Again, Dr. Washington stands for the inadequate education of his Race, and tacitly accepts the shameful violation of the Constitutional rights of the Afro-American. About 3,000 students of both sexes attend Tuskegee and his theory seems to be that by a gradual multiplication of his School throughout the country the entire field will be covered in time. It certainly will require a very long time even to supply industrial education, but, as I heard him declare—and in doing so strikingly illustrated Sir Harry Johnston's remark that none were more callous to the Negro's sufferings than the Negro himself—in the Manhattan Hotel, New York, that "a hundred years would be required to qualify his people for citizenship." I suppose he feels more reconciled to this deliberate procedure than are the overwhelming majority of American Citizens, whose representatives in Congress more than forty years ago wrote into our Constitution that fitness for Citizenship was no longer to be conditioned upon "race, colour or previous conditions of servitude . . ."

The authorities estimate that more than four million children, about equally divided between white and coloured, are growing up in the United States to-day without an opportunity to acquire even the rudiments of an education . . . Deplorable under any circumstances, it is doubly so in this instance because it is absolutely unnecessary. The United States, spending tens of millions for a new Navy and hundreds of millions for a Panama Canal, is abundantly able to provide for the educational needs of every boy and girl beneath the flag. It is able, and the great mass of our people are willing to do so. They were willing to do so twenty years ago, when that practical, comprehensive scheme of legislation known as the Blair Education Bill, put forth as an adequate expression of the popular desire, was passed again and again by the Senate, and only beaten finally by one of the most discreditable combinations of political selfishness, foolish leadership, misguided philanthropists and religious bigotry ever evidenced at Washington . . .[1]

Those who were responsible for the Bill's defeat—and Dr. Washington has some knowledge on this point—boasted that ample school facilities would be provided by the various States, supplemented with private philanthropy. The prediction has not been fulfilled. In one State, at least, the annual provision for popular education does not amount to a dollar a year, per capita, and all the private enterprises, the Peabody Fund, Slater Fund, Mr. Carnegie's and Mr. Rockefeller's large donations, Hampton, Fisk, Nashville, Howard and Tuskegee, all rolled together, are but a drop in the bucket, and fail to do more than ripple the surface of this sea of ignorance.

Not in their inadequacy, however, lies the gravest objection to these attempts to substitute spasmodic philanthropic enterprise for a stern, imperious Government duty. The argument rests upon deeper foundations. If popular education is, according to Burke, the bulwark of any nation, what sort of statecraft is it that would have this tower of strength dependent upon the humanitarian impulse of rich men and women, or the mendicancy of Dr. Washington and others like him? Education is not to be sought or bestowed as a charity; it is nothing if not an inherent right of every American child, sanctioned by the overwhelming majority of American taxpayers, whose will has been thwarted by misguided people in magnifying the importance of their individual efforts to the detriment of the masses, and whose experiments, after a fair trial, extending over a quarter of a century, as a solution of the Race problem, have been dismal failures. Such individual institutions as Tuskegee have grown and prospered, but the social and political condition of the Negro in the South has become steadily worse, until to women like Mrs. Terrell and men like Dr. Du Bois it is to-day simply intolerable . . .

Please understand that I do not deplore Tuskegee's prosperity. I rejoice that thanks to Mr. Carnegie and others, Dr. Washington has been able to collect such large sums of money. He would be successful in any calling. A shrewder, a more adroit man would be difficult to find in Dixie. He has the genius of persuasion and diplomacy. What I object to is his endeavour to make people here believe an untruth, as he has done to an alarming extent in America, namely, that his scheme of industrial education is a panacea, when he should know perfectly well that it is nothing of the kind. Industrial education was had by the Negro in Slavery. They were the mechanics and artisans of the South, as well as the tillers of the soil, and whatever may be said on behalf of the system, it surely will not be admitted by sane, thinking people that a man must acquire a trade at the price of his individual or political manhood. That is the crux of the situation . . .

In other words, the Negroes have proved themselves as worthy of citizenship as any other element of our population, and yet, notwithstanding this, they are to-day without a single representative in Congress, the Courts, the Cabinet, or practically in any of the State Legislatures, something that cannot be said of any other body of American citizens. The German Americans are no more numerous, but you find few Municipal or State governments in which they are not represented in accordance with their numerical strength in the electorate; their spokesmen are conspicuous in the halls of national legislation. The same is true of the Swedes, the Hungarians, the Italians, and, of course, conspicuously true of the Irish. The Indians have a United States Senator. The Jews are represented even in the Cabinet, and no sensible man thinks it should be otherwise. The Negro is excluded, not because of any personal unfitness (his representatives were always among the ablest in Congress), but for no other reason than that of his colour and

Race. He is a victim of shameless class legislation, of force, fraud, intimidation and murder . . .

To sum up, Dr. Washington stands for private, spasmodic schemes of education based upon private charity; condones the disfranchisement of the Negro, in fact if not in form, negatively if not positively; deems it unwise to denounce lynching or peonage, or protest against the numberless shameless outrages perpetrated upon his Race throughout the country. He thinks he can do more by overlooking them and by persuading everybody else he can to overlook them also. He has been tolerably successful up to the present time, but he has reached the limit. His staunchest upholders in America, such, for example, as *The Evening Post* of New York, which was foolishly led to oppose the Blair Education Bill years ago, has at last become aroused to the absurdity of the Tuskegee proposition as the salvation of the Negro, typifying in this the beclouded brain clearing and long dormant conscience awakening of the Nation.

The lynching habit has grown in America until the average during the past few months has reached one a day, or about double that which has prevailed during the last twenty years. Sixty men were massacred in Texas in July without any Government investigation or inquiry, and yet Dr. Washington comes over here and blandly assures the British public that the Races are dwelling together more amicably than in the past. He is utterly mistaken, and in refutation of what he says, I offer you this unchallenged statement made in the United States Senate by one of the most widely known of that body, a Southerner of Southerners, Senator Tillman, of North Carolina, who in a speech delivered before the Senate openly declared:[2]

> Race hatred grows day by day. There is no man who is honest, going through the South and conversing with the White People and Blacks, but will return and tell you this is true. Then I say to you of the North who are the rulers of the land, who can change this or do something to relieve conditions, what are you going to do about it? Are you going to sit quiet? If nothing else will cause you to think, I notify you, what you already know, that there are a billion dollars or more of Northern capital invested in the South in railroads, in mines, in forests, in farm lands, and self interest, which fact, if nothing else—ought to make you set about hunting some remedy for this terrible situation. As it is the South is helpless. We can do nothing. We are one-third of the population. You are two-thirds. Every year your members are being added to by a million immigrants in the North, who stay there, while none go to us. The million who came in last year represent five

Congressmen. Those who came in year before last represent five more Congressmen. There is no danger of political power ever drifting away from the North. Therefore we say to you it is your duty to do something. It is your duty to move. It is your duty to begin the discussion. For the time being the South is occupying an attitude of waiting. It is occupying an attitude of constant friction, race riot, butchery, murder of Whites by Blacks and Blacks by Whites, the inevitable, irrepressible conflict.

Thanking you again for your kind invitation, wishing your Society all prosperity, and your Guest health of body and a clearer vision, I beg to remain, Yours sincerely,

John E. Milholland[3]

BOOKER TALIAFERRO WASHINGTON

Tuskegee Institute, Alabama October 24, 1910

Personal and Confidential.

Dear Major [Robert Russa] Moton:[4] The enclosed is a circular which John E. Milholland had printed and distributed in London while I was there.

I am wondering in view of Mr. [Oswald Garrison] Villard's protests and explanations to you as we came from Bar Harbor to the effect that their movement is not in opposition to me, if you would not like to send Mr. Villard this circular and call his attention to the fact that in spite of his protests Mr. Milholland, who is the writer of this circular, is one of the main movers in company with Mr. Villard and is the principal backer of the Du Bois movement; and in view of this circular the advantage would be rather to make anybody believe that the movement has not for its principal object the discouragement of the fundamentals of Hampton and Tuskegee and everything that we stand for.

It might be well also for you to ask Mr. Villard if Mr. Milholland is authorized to make a statement to the effect that "The Evening Post" is against me . . .

Of course the circular had no effect whatever as people in London readily saw that the man had some personal end to gain and besides Milholland is as well known in London as an unbalanced agitator as he is in this country . . .[5]

BOOKER T. WASHINGTON

[Tuskegee, Ala.] October 26, 1910

Personal and Confidential
My dear Mr. [Charles William] Anderson:

. . . You have no idea how much people talk and gossip around New York. This reminds me that I ought to let you know that some little fellow in New York, a graduate of Harvard who was formerly employed on The Age, [Aubrey Bowser] is rather active in stating to his friends and therefore to the public, that you and he have a certain understanding as to certain items of news which he is to send to the Boston Guardian.[6]

One other thing. Nothing could hurt our cause worse just now than for any newspaper or any individual to get the idea that we could be moved to take certain action or refrain from taking certain action by reason of a threat to go over to a certain person if this or that is not done. In all of my experience I find that the man who expects to move you in this or that direction by a threat sooner or later will betray you, and I very much hope that our friends in New York will let it thoroughly be understood that we cannot be moved to do this or that thing by reason of a threat that somebody makes to go over to Du Bois or anybody else. Yours very truly,

Booker T. Washington . . .

I wish it thoroughly understood that I do not own or control, directly or indirectly, a single dollar in the New York Age property notwithstanding frequent statements to the contrary.[7]

In 1910, Washington gave a series of speeches in England arguing that America's race problems were in the process of resolution. The speeches seemed to many to be further examples of Washington's willingness to minimize the problems faced by African Americans in aid of serving as a booster for southern business interests. John E. Milholland, one of the NAACP's founders, who had already written his own public letter, wrote to Du Bois and convinced him to respond to what both saw as rank naïveté. "Race Relations in the United States," published in October, was addressed to the English and signed by 23 black leaders calling themselves the National Negro Committee. It would only stoke the fires of an already massive conflagration.[8]

WILLIAM EDWARD BURGHARDT DU BOIS

An Open Letter to the People of Great Britain and Europe[9]

Headquarters National Negro Committee,
20 Vesey St., New York, U.S.A. October 26, 1910

To the People of Great Britain and Europe: The undersigned Negro-Americans have heard, with great regret, the recent attempt to assure England and Europe that their condition in America is satisfactory. They sincerely wish that such were the case, but it becomes their plain duty to say that if Mr. Booker T. Washington, or any other person, is giving the impression abroad that the Negro problem in America is in process of satisfactory solution, he is giving an impression which is not true. We say this without personal bitterness toward Mr. Washington. He is a distinguished American and has a perfect right to his opinions. But we are compelled to point out that Mr. Washington's large financial responsibilities have made him dependent on the rich charitable public and that, for this reason, he has for years been compelled to tell, not the whole truth, but that part of it which certain powerful interests in America wish to appear as the whole truth. In flat contradiction, however, to the pleasant pictures thus pointed out, let us not forget that the consensus of opinion among eminent European scholars who know the race problem in America . . . is that it forms the gravest of American problems. We black men who live and suffer under present conditions, and who have no reason, and refuse to accept reasons, for silence, can substantiate this unanimous testimony. Our people were emancipated in a whirl of passion, and then left naked to the mercies of their enraged and impoverished ex-masters. As our sole means of defence we were given the ballot, and we used it so as to secure the real fruits of the war. Without it we would have returned to slavery; with it we struggled toward freedom. No sooner, however, had we rid ourselves of nearly two-thirds of our illiteracy, and accumulated $600,000,000 worth of property in a generation, than this ballot, which had become increasingly necessary to the defence of our civil and property rights, was taken from us by force and fraud. Today in eight states where the bulk of the Negroes live, black men of property and university training can be, and usually are, by law denied the ballot, while the most ignorant white man votes. This attempt to put the personal and property rights of the best of the blacks at the absolute political mercy of the worst of the whites is spreading each day. Along with this has gone a systematic attempt to curtail the education of the black race. Under a widely advertised system of "universal" education, not one black boy in three today has in the United States a chance to learn to read and write. The proportion of school funds due to black children are often spent on whites, and the burden on private charity to support education, which is a public duty, has become almost intolerable. In every walk of life we meet discrimination based solely on race and color, but continually and persistently misrepresented to the world as the natural difference due to condition. We are, for instance, usually forced to live in the worst quarters, and our consequent death-rate is noted as a race trait, and reason for further discrimination. When we seek to buy property in better quarters we are sometimes in danger of mob violence, or, as now in Baltimore, of actual legislation to prevent. We are forced to take lower wages for equal work, and our standard of living is then criticised. Fully half the labor unions refuse us admittance, and then claim that as "scabs" we lower the price of labor. A persistent caste proscription seeks to force us and confine us to menial occupations where the conditions of work are worst. Our women in the South are without protection in law and custom, and are then derided as lewd. A widespread system of deliberate public insult is customary, which makes it difficult, if not impossible, to secure decent accommodation in hotels, railway trains, restaurants and theatres, and even in the Christian Church we are in most cases given to understand that we are unwelcome unless segregated. Worse than all this is the wilful miscarriage of justice in the courts. Not only have 3,500 black men been lynched publicly by mobs in the last twenty-five years without semblance or pretense of trial, but regularly every day throughout the South the machinery of the courts is used, not to prevent crime and correct the wayward among Negroes, but to wreak public dislike and vengeance, and to raise public funds. This dealing in crime as a means of public revenue is a system well-nigh universal in the South, and while its glaring brutality through private lease has been checked, the underlying principle is still unchanged. Everywhere in the United States the old democratic doctrine of recognising fitness wherever it occurs is losing ground before a reactionary policy of denying preferment in political or industrial life to competent men if they have a trace of Negro blood, and of using the weapons of public insult and humiliation to keep such men down. It is today a universal demand in the South that on all occasions social courtesies shall be denied any person of known Negro descent . . . Against this dominant tendency strong and brave Americans, white and black are fighting, but they need, and need sadly, the moral support of England and of Europe in this crusade for the recognition of manhood, despite adventitious differences of race, and it is like a blow in the face to have one, who himself suffers daily insult and humiliation in America, give the impression that all is well. It is one thing to be optimistic, self-forgetful and forgiving, but it is quite a different thing, consciously or unconsciously, to misrepresent the truth.[10]

BOOKER T. WASHINGTON

[Tuskegee, Ala.] November 11, 1910

Personal and Confidential.
My dear Sir [Charles Lee Coon]:[11]

. . . Regarding the New York meeting: To speak frankly, I do not believe that you could accomplish any good by going there, and further, I believe that your fine influence in the South would be crippled by so doing. Mr. Villard, in my opinion, is a well-meaning, unselfish man, but he does not understand people. He has gathered about him a class of colored people, who have not succeeded, who are bitter and resentful and who, without exception, I think, live in the North. The white people who are with him, for the most part, with few exceptions, are dreamers and otherwise impractical people, who do not understand our conditions in the South . . . No one on earth knows what these people are likely to do, or likely to say at one of these meetings.

I always speak more strongly in the South when speaking to the Southern white people concerning their duties toward the Negro than I do in the North. It is one thing to speak to a people and another thing to speak about them. I think we can accomplish more good by speaking to the Southern white people than by speaking about them . . .[12]

ROBERT RUSSA MOTON

[Hampton, Va.] Nov. 15, 1910

My dear Mr. [Oswald Garrison] Villard: In view of the conversation which we had . . . regarding the National Association for the Advancement of Colored People, in which you assured me that the movement did not have for its object the attacking of Hampton, Tuskegee, or Dr. Washington, I am taking the liberty to enclose you herewith a printed circular which I got from Dr. Washington. This circular was circulated in London while Dr. Washington was there. In view of the fact that Mr. Milholland was one of the promoters of the movement and is at present an important officer in the Association, it would be difficult, in the light of this circular, to persuade any one to believe that the Association was not trying to tear down what Hampton and Tuskegee stand for. While the Association is not mentioned in the circular, a person so prominent in its development must influence its policies . . .

I am informed also that in an address, recently delivered in Washington, Dr. Du Bois devoted much time to an attack on Dr. Washington. I understand also that in a recent meeting in Chicago, much of the time was taken up with a discussion of the faults and failings of Dr. Washington. All of this leads me to doubt whether you yourself are entirely acquainted with the workings of the organization. It does look as if the effort is along the same old lines of trying to tear down what many of us have been trying to do . . .

A number of us, when we heard of the new organization, felt hopeful that it was going to accomplish a great good in working along needed lines, without antagonizing those forces that are trying to accomplish the same results through different methods . . .

What I would like to see is the uniting of the forces that are working towards the same end, and I still think there is patience enough and Christianity enough to bring it about . . .

I am sending a copy of this letter to Dr. Du Bois. Yours very truly . . .[13]

W.E.B. DU BOIS

[New York City] November 21, 1910

My Dear Mr. [Robert Russa] Moton: Enclosed is my address delivered at Washington. Will you kindly look it over and mark those passages to which you object?

The circular issued by Mr. Milholland in London was on his own personal responsibility. On the other hand, the one which I wrote for London is enclosed. It was not, however, an official publication of the Committee.

I may say with regard to Mr. Washington or you or President Taft or anybody else that whenever they do things which are, in my opinion, hurtful to the Negro race I propose to criticize them. I am going to make that criticism open and courteous, but it is going to be criticism and good plain criticism . . . On the other hand, this committee is not organized to attack or tear down, it is perfectly sympathetic with all uplift work, whether at Hampton or Tuskegee or Atlanta or Fisk, and the thing that I cannot understand about a good man like you is that your eagerness to keep Mr. Washington, for instance, from well-merited criticism is greater than your eagerness to help the Negro race . . .[14]

JOHN HOPE[15]

Atlanta, Georgia, November 21, 1910

My Dear Major [Robert Russa] Moton: . . . I believe that I am more hopeful than you as to the possible closing of the chasm between those two gentlemen, Doctors Washington and Du Bois. Each thinks that he has good grounds for opposition to the other; but I do think that they could be made to see and feel that they could and ought to work together for the good of our people. I think with you, that public utterance will do little good towards bringing the men together. I rather fear that even such friendly correspondence as you are carrying on just now will do little good. I do think, however, that a conversation between these two men would be helpful and that is what I would like to get them to consent to. Neither one of them need say of what the conversation consisted if he did not want to. The misfortune of that famous meeting in New York several years ago was that Mr. Washington and Mr. Du Bois were talking before other people and not to each other. It would be better if that convention had never occurred. If some of us could have these two gentlemen meet and then leave them to talk out their ideas for five or six hours in the freest possible way, they would know each other better and probably all of us would be better off. This, I believe, is possible and if this can not be brought to pass, I see no way of having any co-operation between Messrs Du Bois and Washington. As I have said to you, the fact that both of them are doing good service apart is not sufficient argument for their not coming together. I am sure that both can do a better work if they are more in harmony. Young Negroes especially are being greatly injured, in their point of view and in progress by the fact that these two men seem to be at such cross purposes . . .[16]

BOOKER T. WASHINGTON

[Tuskegee, Ala.] November 23, 1910

Personal.

Dear Sir [Clark Howell]:[17] . . . I appreciate, of course, your motives and deep interest in this matter, but I cannot feel at present anything would be gained by my making a statement, coming out in print, regarding the men who have signed this circular . . .

These men are well known and they represent the same old gang that has been trying to oppose me and stir up race hatred during the last twelve or fifteen years. You will notice, that with but few exceptions, these men live in the North and know little about the South and have little interest in the masses of the colored people. In most cases, they are men with no influence with our race, simply because they have proved themselves to be absolute failures. They have a grievance and they think everybody else has a grievance; because they have failed, they think the whole race has failed. If I were to write a letter calling attention to their circular, I think it would be just what they would want. They crave notoriety and they like to feel that they are stirring somebody up and I do not believe it well to accommodate them in this regard.

Their special point of grievance against me just now seems to be that I told the people of Europe that the Negro in America was succeeding, that he had friends in the South, as well as friends in the North. I also told the people wherever I spoke in Europe that there is no spot in the world where there are so many black people and white people living side by side, where the relations, all things considered, are friendly and helpful as they are in our Southern states . . .

I think it is too bad that an institution like Atlanta University has permitted Dr. Du Bois to go on from year to year stirring up racial strife in the heart of the South. While Du Bois, as I understand it, has left Atlanta for New York, he is to come back to Atlanta in the spring and summer and conduct some kind of racial conference . . .[18]

OSWALD GARRISON VILLARD

New York. November 23, 1910

Dear Major [Robert Russa] Moton: . . . The National Association for the Advancement of Colored People cannot be held responsible for the individual opinions or actions of its members. Whatever Mr. Milholland's personal opinions the fact remains that the Association is in no wise endeavoring to injure what Hampton or Tuskegee stand for. Of course, Mr. Milholland has no warrant or authority whatever for stating that the Evening Post has "At last become aroused to the absurdity of the Tuskegee proposition." At the same time, if you have read what the Evening Post has had to say about Dr. Washington during the last two years you must be aware that there is a strong similarity between Mr. Milholland's views and our own, at least to this extent: We, too, believe that Dr. Washington's political activities are most hurtful to the negro race and to his own influence, so much so, that if they are persisted in they must deprive him to a considerable extent of the high position he now holds. We have pointed out that Dr. Washington is popular in the South because he says to the Southerners what they want to hear; because they believe that he is with them in thinking that the sole destiny of the negro race is to act as hewers of wood and drawers of water. I find myself more and more opposed to Dr. Washington's entire philosophy of compromise and expediency and of saying nothing about the unquestioned wrongs of the race, politically and socially. I could justify that, if Dr. Washington confined himself absolutely to his educational duties and assumed neither to speak for his race to the nation nor to be the political broker for his people. But as long as he assumes to be the spokesman for the race I cannot but feel that his London utterances gave a totally wrong picture of the situation in America. Had I been in London, while I should not have been as extreme or as violent as Mr. Milholland, I should have unquestionably sought the opportunity to protest that in my opinion as a grandson of Garrison, this continual crying that all is well with us is nothing short of a real betrayal of the race . . .

As to Dr. Du Bois, he has sent you his speech and you can judge for yourself how far he has gone. I reiterate my statement to you that so far as I have succeeded in moulding it or putting spirit into it, the National Association is not anti-Washington or pro-Du Bois, but is just what its title makes it. If, however, Dr. Washington should go further and do something which in the opinion of that Association called for emphatic protest as being inimical to the welfare of the race, I could not, of course, personally under take to prevent the Executive Committee from making a public reply to Dr. Washington. At the same time, I have never failed in every meeting of the Committee in which Dr. Washington's name has come up to express my hope that some day we shall have him standing on our platform and speaking for us at one of our annual conferences. We ought to have his support in every way, even though it should appear to him that we are his critics along certain lines, so great is the service we can render to the race.

You must yourself be aware how the race has progressed under Dr. Washington's leadership, in many ways, but race prejudices and discrimination have progressed still faster, and he, himself has done almost nothing to stop them. You must also be aware that the great majority of the highly educated members of the race find themselves more and more in opposition to him . . .

Finally, you may rest assured that although the policy of the Association may not commend itself to you, there is not the slightest effort, and never will be an effort, to "tear down" anything that has been built up for the colored man. Our only desire is to build up in this and every other direction, but that does not mean that we shall be tongue-tied, like Dr. Washington, on the fundamental problems of negro citizenship, or that we shall even bear the appearance of acquiescing in monstrous injustice to the black man. Very truly yours,

Oswald Garrison Villard[19]

BOOKER T. WASHINGTON

New York Dec 8 [1910]

Mr E[mmet] J Scott Du Bois & crowd getting number of letters published in New York and other daily papers think these letter[s] prepared by Du Bois and signed by weak pliable colored men as usual our friends are silent think good plan for you to have three or four good strong letters sent the Sun—World & Times signed by three or four different people . . .[20]

BOOKER T. WASHINGTON

Hotel Manhattan, New York. December 11, 1910

Personal

My dear Mr. [Oswald Garrison] Villard:

. . . I have just had a long talk with Mrs. Terrell, and she tells me that your committee did not send out that circular regarding my supposed utterances when I was in Europe. This I was very glad to hear. Of course I do not question the right of your committee to send out any kind of circular that it chooses to send out, but what was contained in this circular was so far at variance with what you first wrote me regarding the purposes of the committee that I confess I was greatly surprised when I saw it as coming from your committee as I suppose. If you have not seen the circular itself, I hope you will see it, and after reading it I think you will agree with me that it was very natural that any one should feel that it was a document sent out by your committee. At the head of the circular (quoting from memory as I have not a copy of it before me) I think you will find these words: "Headquarters of the National Negro Committee, 20 Vesey St . . ."

Enclosed I send you a clipping from the New York Sun which published the appeal, and states that "The National Association for the Advancement of Colored People" issued the circular, etc.

Under these circumstances I think you will agree with me that any person would be naturally misled, and of course the majority of the people have been . . .

I have never directly or indirectly connected your committee with the sending out of this circular except in one case; I did speak to Mrs. Baldwin and told her what I honestly believed; that it was sent out by your committee. I have, however, since seeing Mrs. Terrell conveyed to Mrs. Baldwin the information which Mrs. Terrell has given me.[21]

When there is so much that is needed to be done in the way of punishing those who are guilty of lynching, of peonage, and seeing that the Negro gets an equitable share of the school fund, and that the law relating to the ballot is enforced in regard to black men and white men, it is difficult to see how people can throw away their time and strength in stirring up strife within the race instead of devoting themselves to bringing about justice to the race as a whole . . .[22]

BOOKER T. WASHINGTON

Washington, D.C. December 12, 1910

Dear Mr. [Emmett Jay] Scott: I confess that I am gradually coming around to the opinion that it is a valuable thing to have Mrs. Terrell connected with that committee. She made a speech in New York last week, and I am told by several people who heard her that she referred several times most complimentar[il]y to Tuskegee and to myself, but not to the other side at all. I had a long talk with her in New York, and she told me many things of interest. One of her values is in this direction. She gets on the inside of things and is always capable of stirring up trouble in any organization that she has a part in. Of course all this is strictly confidential, as I have told her that her name would not be used. I can keep in close touch with her if her name is not quoted. She tells me that she and Du Bois have absolutely nothing to do with each other; they scarcely speak, and she did not see him during her stay in

New York, but more important than this, she says, the European circular was an imposition on the committee, that Villard, a white woman and all the head people are disgusted and considerably torn up that such a circular should have been sent out presumably under the guise of the committee . . . At any rate they seem to be in a pretty big row among themselves, and the circular seems to have caused it. Mrs. Terrell appears to be very much disgusted with the whole affair, and I think she will make matters pretty lively from now on. Yours very truly,

Booker T. Washington[23]

OSWALD GARRISON VILLARD

New York December 13, 1910

My dear Mr. Washington: I have yours of December 11th which comes as I was on the point of writing you to tell you what Mrs. Terrell has already conveyed to you. I regret that in an unauthorized way the envelopes of the National Association were used in sending out the protest of the thirty-two colored men. This mistake I have carefully investigated and find that it was absolutely accidental as far as this office was concerned (the letters were not mailed from 20 Vesey Street). Orders were also given to erase the words "headquarters of the National Negro Committee" on every copy. If you have one on which the words are not erased it is because the stenographer to whom they were submitted did not follow instructions. That this should have happened is, of course, humiliating, but it is one of the incidents, which, I suppose, happens to most every organization which has not yet had time or means to work out an absolutely effective organization . . .

So far as the circular is concerned, I am heartily of the opinion that the protest was a desirable one. I agree with you that when there is so much to be done for the colored people it is a pity that people should have to waste time and strength in presenting different views instead of being united upon one. I have, therefore, in this organization thrown my weight wholly against taking any notice of your, to me, often mistaken speeches and attitude on public questions. Sorry as I am to say it, I cannot but feel that your speeches abroad were a misrepresentation of actual conditions in this country. Your optimism is leading you astray. It goes without saying that I respect your sincerity and know that you are endeavoring to do what is right. I would never have stated that you were influenced, even unconsciously, by those who contribute to your school, but I do feel that, from my point of view, your philosophy is wrong, that you are keeping silent about evils in regard to which you should speak out, and that you are not helping the race by portraying all the conditions as favorable. If my grandfather had gone to Europe say in 1850 and dwelt in his speeches on slavery upon certain encouraging features of it, such as the growing anger and unrest of the poor whites, and stated the number of voluntary liberations and number of escapes to Canada, as evidences that the institution was improving, he never would have accomplished what he did, and he would have hurt, not helped, the cause of freedom. It seems to me that the parallel precisely affects your case. It certainly cannot be unknown to you that a greater and greater percentage of the intellectual colored people are turning from you and becoming your opponents, and with them a number of white people as well. I can only repeat, as I wrote to Major Moton, that so long as the National Association is guided by my advice it will not take official notice of your utterances; but the time may easily come when, in the judgment of a majority of the Executive Committee, it might become necessary to oppose publicly a position of yours. As the Association is self-governing and does not belong to Mr. Milholland, or Dr. Du Bois, or myself, or anybody else, it will make up its own mind on this point. From the bottom of my heart I hope that you will make no more such speeches as those you made in Europe, for I want to see you preserve your standing and reputation, precisely as I want to see your work at Tuskegee flourish and become more and more effective . . .[24]

BOOKER T. WASHINGTON

Boston Mass Dec-17–10

[To Emmett Jay Scott] Think good policy discreetly advise our friends stop complete[ly] for considerable while giving attention to European circular and other matters bearing upon Du Bois he is getting good deal of advertisement which he likes . . .[25]

WILLIAM ARCHER (Archer was a British journalist and drama critic.)[26]

Two Leaders
"People are always laying stress on the white blood in me," said Mr. W. E. Burghardt Du Bois, "and attributing to that anything I do that is worth doing. But they never speak of the white blood in Mr. Booker Washington, who, as a matter of fact, has a larger share than I have . . ."

Principal Booker T. Washington is a negro in every lineament, and not, one would say, of the most refined type. His skin is neither black nor copper-coloured, but rather of a sort of cloudy yellow, to which the other shades are, perhaps, aesthetically preferable. His hair, his ears, his nose, his jaw, all place his race beyond dispute; only his grave, candid, forceful eyes announce a leader of men. He is above middle height, and heavily built; seated, he is apt to sprawl. He has a curious trick of drawing back the corners of his mouth, so as to reveal almost the whole of his range of teeth. At first I took this for a slow smile, heralding some humorous remark; but humour is not Mr. Washington's strong point. His grin is a nervous habit, and scarcely a pretty one. Altogether, in talking with him, you have no difficulty in remembering the race of your interlocutor, and if you make an untactful remark—if you let the irrepressible instinct of race-superiority slip out—you have all the more reason to be ashamed.

With Mr. Du Bois the case is totally different. His own demonstration notwithstanding, I cannot believe that there is more of the negro in him than in (say) Alexandre Dumas fils.[27] Meeting this quiet, cultivated, French-looking gentleman, with his pointed beard, olive complexion, and dark melancholy eyes, it is hard to believe that he is born, as he himself phrases it, "within the Veil." In appearance he reminded me a good deal of Gabriele d'Annunzio, only that d'Annunzio happens to be fair, while Mr. Du Bois has something more like the average Italian complexion.[28] In speaking to this man of fine academic culture—this typical college don, one would have said—the difficulty was to feel any difference of race and traditions, and not to assume, tactlessly, an identical standpoint.

These two men are unquestionably the leaders of their race today; but their ideals and their policy are as different as their physique. Mr. Washington leads from within; Mr. Du Bois from without. Should he read this phrase he will probably resent it; but it may be none the less true. Mr. Washington could never have been anything else than a negro; he represents all that is best in the race, but nothing that is not in the race. Mr. Du Bois is a negro only from outside pressure. I do not mean, of course, that there are no negro traits in his character, but that it is outside pressure—the tyranny of the white man—that has made him fiercely, passionately, insistently African. Had there been no colour question—had the negro had no oppression, no injustice to complain of—Mr. Du Bois would have been a cosmopolitan, and led the life of a scholar at some English, German, or perhaps even American University. As it was, he felt that to desert his race would be the basest of apostasies; but it was because he could have been disloyal that he became so vehemently—one might almost say fanatically—loyal.[29]

W.E.B. DU BOIS

The London Nation comments as follows on Mr. B.T. Washington's words in Europe:

Mr. Booker T. Washington recently gave us a glowing picture of the progress, industrial, intellectual and moral, made by his colored fellow-citizens in the United States during recent years. His policy, "Let politics alone and acquire efficiency," is, however, repudiated by a strong body of educated opinion in America, which finds expression in a remarkable letter published this week in the Press. The signatories point out that the withholding of the franchise, in the States where most Negroes live, is attended by a refusal of criminal and civil justice, a denial of equal opportunities of education, a caste proscription which practically excludes from most skilled trades and other grave disabilities . . . The doctrine of "equal rights for all civilized men" is definitely contravened by the constitutions and laws of most Southern States. Among the signatories of this powerful appeal to Europe, we find the names of many of the most influential teachers and professional men among the colored people.[30]

BOOKER T. WASHINGTON

Tuskegee Institute, Alabama January 7, 1911

Dear Mr. [Hugh Mason] Browne: Mr. Carnegie has declined to continue the money for the work of The Committee of Twelve. I have written his Cashier, Mr. Franks, however, that there is due us the final payment of $1350 promised for last year's work.

It does seem that we shall not be able to get the money for circulating Mr. Weatherford's book[31] or in fact money beyond the $1350. Yours very truly,

Booker T. Washington[32]

CHARLES WILLIAM ANDERSON

New York, N.Y., January 7, 1911

Personal

My dear Doctor [Washington]: Only a line about the Sumner meeting last night under the auspices of the N.A.A.C.P. Ahem! The small hall of the Ethical Culture rooms was about two-thirds filled—certainly no more than that. The addresses were all read from manuscript, and were intensely monotonous. There was distinctly something lacking in all of them . . . In short, the whole function lacked fire and heart and enthusiasm, and that dynamic force which goes out from a speaker and warms all hearts, and impels all hearers to care for higher things. The bugle call of the leader of a good cause, cheering men onward for their fight for larger liberty and more exact justice, was not heard. It was just such a little meeting as might have been held by the ladies of a sewing circle of a country Episcopal church . . .

You may be interested to know that the Chairman took occasion to ask for subscriptions for the movement. This is significant. I am afraid they need a little ready cash, and I shrewdly suspect that some one is getting tired of putting it up . . .[33]

BOOKER T. WASHINGTON

[Tuskegee, Ala.] January 10, 1911

Personal.
My dear Mr. [Oswald Garrison] Villard:

. . . There has been much discussion of my speeches in Europe, but no one has pointed out to me any specific utterance to which objection is made.

Mr. Milholland's first circular of protest was issued October 6th, before I had made a single speech in London. I did not speak there until October 7. Before you get through with Mr. Milholland, you will finally agree with me that he is not a man whose word can be depended upon . . .

My speeches in Europe did not differ from my speeches in this country. When I am in the South speaking to the Southern white people, anyone who hears me speak will tell you that I am frank and direct in my criticisms of the Southern white people. I cannot agree with you, or any others, however, that very much or any good is to be gained just now by going out of the South and merely speaking about the Southern white people. I grant that there are times when something can be gained in that direction, but I do mean that it should not be the main line of procedure. I think it pays to do such talking to the people who are most responsible for injustice being inflicted upon us in certain directions rather than to spend much time, as I have already stated, in talking about them.

It seems to me that there is little parallel between conditions that your grandfather had to confront and those facing us now. Your grandfather faced a great evil which was to be destroyed. Ours is a work of construction rather than a work of destruction. My effort in Europe was to show to the people that the work of your grandfather was not wasted and that the progress the Negro has made in America justified the word and work of your grandfather. It seems to me that it would be an insult to the memory of your grandfather for me to have gone to Europe and told the people there that what he did had amounted to nothing when I could sincerely and honestly state that the race was making progress as a result of its freedom.

You, of course, labor under the disadvantage of not knowing as much about the life of the Negro race as if you were a member of that race yourself. Unfortunately, too, I think you are brought into contact with that group of our people who have not succeeded in any large degree, and hence are sour, dissatisfied and unhappy. I wish you could come more constantly into contact with that group of our people who are succeeding, who have accomplished something, and are not continually sour and disappointed.

I keep pretty closely in touch with the life of my race, and I happen to know that the very same group of people who are opposing me now have done so practically ever since my name became in any way prominent, certainly ever since I spoke at the opening of the Atlanta Exposition. No matter what I would do or refrain from doing, the same group would oppose me. I think you know this . . .

I cannot agree with you that there is an increasing number of intellectual colored people who oppose me, or are opposed to me. My experience and observation convince me to the contrary. I do not see how any man could expect or hope to have to a larger extent the good will and cooperation of the members of his race of all classes than I have, and it is this consciousness that makes me feel very humble.

I confess that I cannot blame any one who resides in the North or in Europe for not taking the same hopeful view of conditions in the South that I do. The only time I ever become gloomy or despondent regarding the condition of the Negro in the South is when I am in the North. When I am in the North, I hear for the most part only of the most discouraging and disheartening things that take place in the South, but when I leave the North and get right in the South in the midst of the work and see for myself what is being done and how it is being done, and what the actual daily connection between the white man and the black man is, then it is that I become encouraged . . .[34]

BOOKER T. WASHINGTON

[Tuskegee, Ala.] January 12, 1911

Personal.

Dear Mr. [Charles William] Anderson: I thought you would like to see from a disinterested source something of an official summing up of my London speech about which so much noise was made . . .

You will also note that our friend Milholland is working over time in order to make a big man of our friend Du Bois. To do this he has got the hardest job on his hands he has ever tackled. It is rather interesting to know how he is trying to copy what I have attempted to do. Yours very truly,

Booker T. Washington[35]

CHARLES WILLIAM ANDERSON

New York, N.Y., January 19, 1911

(Personal)
My dear Doctor [Washington]:

. . . I am enclosing herewith a copy of the invitation to the Black and White dinner.[36] You will be interested to note the subjects, as well as those who are to discuss them. The last half of the title of the subject assigned to Miss M.R. [Maritcha Remond] Lyons rather discloses the moral tendencies of the movement, in my judgment.[37] One needs only to glance over this invitation, printed as it is on yellow paper, and note the names of the speakers and the long-winded topics they are to discuss, to be convinced that they are a bunch of freaks. I shall do my best to see that the movement gets a full newspaper report. I would suggest that you do something along that line also. Much good can be accomplished by having the Associated press, and other distributing news agencies send a full report of this meeting through the country. Yours very truly,

Charles W. Anderson[38]

OSWALD GARRISON VILLARD

New York January 19, 1911

Dear Mr. Washington: I beg to inform you that at the last meeting of the Executive Committee of the National Association for the Advancement of Colored People and the representatives of the Constitutional League, it was decided that the two organizations should not coalesce as had originally been planned, and that here after they would continue separate existences. Our Association is being incorporated under its own name, the National Association for the Advancement of Colored People, in the State of New York. I write this so that you may not in any way hold us liable for any actions taken by the Constitutional League.[39] Very truly yours,

Oswald Garrison Villard[40]

W.E.B. DU BOIS

On October 26 a statement and appeal was sent to Europe signed by thirty-two Negro Americans. The appeal was not sent out by the National Association for the Advancement of Colored People, nor did the association stand sponsor for it. It was sent solely on the authority of the men who signed it . . .

This appeal has provoked widespread comment all over the world. The Vienna (Austria) Die Zeit, in publishing the document, says:

"During the sojourn in Vienna of Booker T. Washington, the distinguished apostle of the Negro, there appeared in Die Zeit a report from his pen in which he defended the white race of North America against the charge of systematic race prejudice and pictured the condition of the Negro race as on the whole very favorable. This report created great excitement in America and a deep disagreement among the intelligent leaders of the American Negroes. Booker T. Washington was warmly attacked in many American papers by both white and black speakers, and finally the American Negro leaders drew up an outspoken protest against Washington's declarations . . ."

In the United States the comment has taken wide range. From the South comes some bitterness when, for instance, the Raleigh News and Courier says:

"It is hard to tell which is the worst enemy of the Negro race—the brute who invites lynching by the basest of crimes, or the social-equality-hunting fellow like Du Bois, who slanders his country. Fortunately for the peaceable and industrious Negroes in the South, the world does not judge them either by Du Bois or the animal, and helps them and is in sympathy with their efforts to better their condition."

The Richmond Leader adds:

"Efforts on the part of the Negro to give practical expression to the dream of equality may, indeed, cause temporary trouble and discomfort to the whites, but ultimately and necessarily they could not fail to provoke stern repression, and, if necessary, cruel punishment to the blacks. Fortunately, the great bulk of the Negro population in the South realizes this, and, having—at least for the time—accepted it as inevitable, they adjust themselves to the subordinate place to which their race consigns them, and in which the very existence of the superior race makes it absolutely necessary to keep them. There is little friction, therefore, between them and the white people among whom they live."

The Chattanooga Times regards the document as "treasonable incendiarism," and many papers denounce it as a demand for "social equality . . ."

The New York World says:

"Undeniably, the black population of the United States has just grievances. So also has the white population in the United States. Race prejudice is here as it is in Europe, and blacks are not the only sufferers. There is brutal tyranny in industry, but the blacks are not the only victims. There are social limitations that are cruel and inexcusable, but the blacks are not the only ones against whom the gates are shut.

"This is a world in which true men give and take. It is a world in which all must make allowances. It is a world in which, after all, men are judged not so much by race or nationality or possessions as by personal merit. Otherwise, how could a Booker Washington, born a Virginia slave, have 'stood before kings' and associated for the greater part of his life with the earth's greatest and best?

"We do not condemn the American men of color who have made this protest. We simply remonstrate with them. They are asking more than a white man's chance, and in the circumstances that is inadmissible . . ."

Finally, the Buffalo Express says emphatically:

"The memorial recites the long and familiar list of Negro wrongs— the political disfranchisement, the denial of education in some States, the discriminations in public places, the forcing into menial occupations, the hostility of trades unions, the attempts to confine Negroes to certain quarters of towns, the insults to Negro women, etc. It need not be gone over here. Readers of the Express are familiar with the shameful record. The fact that this is an appeal to the people of Europe against the people of the United States will arouse fresh antagonism to the Negro in some quarters, but, on the whole, it will do good. For shame's sake, if not for that of justice, it may arouse us to do our duty . . ."[41]

W.E.B. DU BOIS

It is unfortunate that in the recent newspaper discussion of an Appeal to Europe sent out not by this Association but by a number of colored men of influence and standing, reference was constantly made to the lowest personal motives and seldom to the arguments presented.

It is true that with all peoples, and especially with a race in the throes of birth-pain, personal likes and jealousies play a wretchedly large part. But it does not follow that they explain all the struggle and difference of opinion. It is true that the rise of a man like Mr. Booker T. Washington to a place of commanding influence has made him an object of envy to many narrow souls. But it does not follow that the thousands of intelligent people who differ with Mr. Washington are all actuated by such motives, or are unable to distinguish great and vital principles apart from personal feeling . . .[42]

NOTES

1. The Blair Education Bill, sponsored by Republican New Hampshire senator Henry W. Blair, proposed federal aid for education, which would, it was hoped, ensure that black southerners would not be deprived of education by white southern state governments, making them all the more vulnerable to other limitations like literacy tests. The principal opposition to the bill, unsurprisingly, came from the white South. See Going, 1957, 267–290; and Crofts, 1971, 41–65.

2. Milholland here mistakes North Carolina for South Carolina. Benjamin Tillman was a populist and white supremacist politician, first serving as governor of South Carolina before moving to the senate from 1895 until 1918. See Kantrowitz, 2000.

3. Washington, 1981, vol. 10, 394–400.

4. See Chapter 11, note 7.

5. Washington, 1981, vol. 10, 416–417.

6. Bowser was a New York journalist. He moved from the *Age* to the *Amsterdam News*, where he would make his reputation over the next several decades. van Notten, 1994, 163.

7. Washington, 1981, vol. 10, 421.

8. Du Bois, 1973, 172–173; and Aptheker, 1969, 884–886.

9. In *Dusk of Dawn*, Du Bois claimed sole authorship, but Washington believed Milholland was involved. Villard assumed Du Bois wrote it and

that its writing on NAACP stationery created the confusion. See Rudwick, 1968 for more. Du Bois, 1940, 229; and Washington, 1981, vol. 10, 425.

10. The letter was signed by 23 leaders, including J. Max Barber, C.E. Bentley, Du Bois, Archibald H. Grimke, Clement G. Morgan, William Sinclair, William Monroe Trotter, and Alexander Walters. Washington, 1981, vol. 10, 422–425; and Aptheker, 1969, 884–886.

11. Charles Lee Coon was a white educational reformer from North Carolina who advocated for better educational opportunities for African Americans. See Willard, 1974.

12. Washington, 1981, vol. 10, 454.

13. Ibid., 472–473.

14. Ibid., 480–481.

15. See Chapter 13, note 86; and Chapter 15, note 17.

16. Washington, 1981, vol. 10, 481–482.

17. See Chapter 2, note 11.

18. Washington, 1981, vol. 10, 483–484.

19. Ibid., 487–489.

20. Ibid., 501–502.

21. Washington here refers to Mary Church Terrell and Ruth Standish Baldwin, the wife of railroad magnate and Tuskegee trustee William Henry Baldwin. See Chapter 7.

22. Washington, 1981, vol. 10, 502–504.

23. Ibid., 504–505.

24. Ibid., 505–506.

25. Ibid., 508.

26. Woodfield, 1984, 26, 41, 46–47.

27. Alexandre Dumas, fils, was a French novelist and playwright, the son of Alexandre Dumas. His paternal grandfather was the son of a Hatian slaveowner and slave, making Dumas, fils, 1/8 black. The insinuation here is that the best parts of Dumas, fils, were his white parts, as were Du Bois's. See Maurois, 1957.

28. D'Annunzio was a prominent Italian writer who, to be fair, did bear something of a resemblance to Du Bois.

29. Archer, 1910, 45–47.

30. Du Bois, December 1910, 15.

31. Willis Duke Weatherford was a white advocate for peaceful interracial relations in the South, working mostly through the YMCA. In 1919, he would create the Commission on Interracial Relations. His book, *Negro Life in the South, Present Conditions and Needs*, however, argued that black immorality and ignorance held back the white race. Slavery was a civilizing influence. It was a book published by the YMCA Press and created to appeal to white southern college students. Still, it did support industrial education and criticized the radicalism of Du Bois. Washington, 1981, vol. 10, 535.

32. Ibid.

33. Ibid., 536–538.

34. Ibid., 540–544.

35. Ibid., 545.

36. Anderson refers to the annual dinner of the Cosmopolitan Society of America, January 24, 1911. Du Bois and John Milholland were among the speakers. Ibid., 554; and Harlan, 1971, 413–415.

37. Lyons was a Brooklyn school teacher and author, active in race activism and women's clubs in New York. "Maritcha R. Lyons (1848–1929)," 1996, 417–421.

38. Washington, 1981, vol. 10, 553–554. Washington would use the information to try to denigrate the movement. Planted articles in the *New York Press* trumpeted, "Three Races Sit at Banquet for Mixed Marriage," and "Fashionable White Women Sit at Board with Negroes, Japs and Chinamen to Promote 'Cause' of Miscegenation." Harlan, 1971, 413–415.

39. Washington forwarded this letter to Charles Anderson, adding, "This indicates one of two things, either that he and Milholland have broken, or that they have agreed between them to let the Constitutional League do the dirty work and use the other organization to inveigle our friends into believing in their sincerity." Washington, 1981, vol. 10, 555.

40. Ibid., 554–555.

41. Du Bois, January 1911, 9–11.

42. Ibid., 16.

17

Presidential Politics

The feud continued from 1911 to 1912. Washington's sojourn overseas had damaged his reputation, but he regained some sympathy after being, as he explained, "assaulted by a band of ruffians" on the streets of New York City. The fallout from Britain had yet to subside, but his image did improve after the assault. The event also allowed Washington's old friend Theodore Roosevelt to revive his defense of the leader. Meanwhile, the battle drifted into presidential politics (where it had not been since Roosevelt's presidency) over influence with current president William Howard Taft. The Republican was allied, as much as any white politician could be, with Washington, but Tuskegee's leader feared that Du Bois and the NAACP were also jockeying for influence with the White House.

BOOKER TALIAFERRO WASHINGTON

[Tuskegee, Ala.] January 20, 1911

Personal.
My dear Mr. [Timothy Thomas] Fortune:

... Du Bois did run away from Atlanta. All the time that the [Atlanta] riot [of 1906] was going on, Du Bois was hiding at the Calhoun School in Alabama—a school which I was responsible for establishing some fifteen years ago. He remained there until the riot was over and then came out and wrote a piece of poetry bearing upon those who were killed in the riot.[1]

There are some curious things going on. It seems strange that our friends Villard and John E. Milholland are attempting to run and control the destinies of the Negro race through Du Bois. I think they will have a tough time of it, as in my opinion, the Negro in New York like the Negro everywhere else is going to do his own thinking and own acting and not be second fiddle to a few white men, who feel that the Negro race belongs to them. I am glad that you went for Du Bois in the way that you did.[2]

Very confidentially, I am glad to say now that the funds for the tribute to you are coming in at an encouraging rate. Please use the enclosed in any way you may deem fitting.

It seems rather strange, too, that persons like Walling, who is a Russian and some white woman, whose name I cannot recall, who is put down as the Secretary of the new organization, whom no one has ever heard of, should come in at this late date to take charge of our race . . .[3]

William English Walling was chair of the executive committee of the NAACP, but was involved in a drawn-out breach-of-promise lawsuit from 1909 to 1911. The case resulted from the complaint of Anna Berthe Grunspan, a Russian immigrant living in Paris whom, she claimed, Walling promised to marry in 1905. He actually married another woman, fellow activist Anna Strunsky, in 1906. When Grunspan moved to the United States in 1911, however, she sued Walling for breach of promise from the claimed proposal six years prior. A jury acquitted Walling, but it was a very public scandal, and the Tuskegee Machine sought to take advantage. Frederick Randolph Moore attacked him in the New York Age *in 1909 and again in 1911 at the request of Washington. Walling resigned from active participation in the NAACP in January 1911, although he stayed on the board of directors.[4]*

TIMOTHY THOMAS FORTUNE

New York, N.Y. January 23, 1911

My dear Dr. Washington:

. . . I have put Dr. Du Bois in a ragged hole in this town. In all public places, and the Amsterdam News goes everywhere in this town, the discussion hinges on the hole I have put him [in], as to the facts and suggestions raised by him, and as to the arguments pro and con. I have discussed with our Mr. [James Henry] Anderson [Amsterdam News editor] sometime ago the point you suggest that Du Bois is allowing himself to be used to put race leadership in the hands of white men, and we agreed that I should write a series of articles on that subject.[5] But I felt that it was necessary to discredit Du Bois in the matters I have before taking up the other and more vital matter. I have done that now, and shall take up the main question in the near future. I attended a Socialist meeting at Lenox and 116th street Friday evening last to hear him speak on the race problem. It was a great meeting of long hairs and discontents and he had a glorious opportunity to present the Negro case for labor men so that it would do the most good, but he put the meeting in a fighting attitude on the race question.

I am so very much surprised that few of our newspapers have noticed the admission Du Bois was forced to make in the January Crisis that the National Association for the Advancement of Colored People was not responsible for the statement and appeal that I call your attention to it.

When we get done with Dr. Du Bois I am sure that he will have some trouble in handing over the leadership of the race to white men. Your view of that matter is entirely correct, and it is necessary to popularize it and to keep your name out of the discussion of it as much as the presentation of the case will allow of . . .

By the way, when you have anything (news) for the paper here after send it to Mr. James H. Anderson, and he and I will take care of it, as we are in accord as to the policy of the paper and as to our good will towards you. With kind regards, Yours sincerely,

T. Thos. Fortune[6]

OSWALD GARRISON VILLARD

New York February 7, 1911

Dear Mr. Washington:

. . . I realize, of course, that Mr. Milholland has his weaknesses, but he is a tried friend of human liberty and has worked unselfishly and still is working unselfishly according to his lights, to help on the race. You certainly used to find his friendship of value.

As to the analogy of the present situation with 1859, I should never have asked you to state in Europe that the race was not making progress as a result of its freedom, because we all know that it is making tremendous strides. But I do not think that bad conditions should be glossed over. I think every leader of the race for instance, ought to come out and denounce in unmitigated terms the movement towards segregation in Baltimore, now happily temporarily checked by the courts; but it has already spread to Richmond and is likely to go elsewhere. The difficulty of your presentation as I see it is that you present but half the case—the pleasant side . . . You record cases of friendliness, but are silent about the increasing prejudice and in justice and the retrogression of the public school system in the South. As I said to you in my earlier letter, it seems to me that where we differ is in the fundamental philosophy. You feel that this is the best way to aid the case; I feel that other ways are better, and that stressing the evils of the situation ought never to be neglected for a moment. I respect your position though I dissent from it.

I do resent, however, your saying that I am brought into contact with that group of your people "who have never succeeded in any large degree and hence are sour, dissatisfied and unhappy." I do not know one of this class who has seemed to you "sour, dissatisfied and unhappy." I know colored men and women who are achieving great things under very great difficulties and with very great cheerfulness . . . I think you are also under a mistaken comprehension as to what you call the opposition to yourself. The opposition is never to you personally as I have noticed it, but to the doctrines you advocate and the things you have said . . .[7]

BOOKER T. WASHINGTON

[Tuskegee, Ala.] February 17, 1911

Dear Mr. [George A.] Myers:[8]

. . . Your report of the meeting held in behalf of the N.A.A.C.P. interested me very much. It is probable that our friends will wake up to the futility of a program of obstruction and denunciation. Any cause that is based upon right principles can well withstand such opposition as that . . .[9]

WILLIAM EDWARD BURGHARDT DU BOIS

[Atlanta, Feb. 28, 1911]

Dr. E. [Ettie] Sayer[10]
My dear Madame:

I have been considerably distressed over the developments in London in regard to my visit. I had planned to come to the Races Congress in July, and then it was proposed that I come earlier in order to counteract in some degree Mr. Washington's utterances. This has of course led to much discussion as to my attitude toward Mr. W., which has been very annoying. I am not an "enemy" of Mr. W., neither do I "attack" him, nor stand for everything which he does not. I do not agree with much that Mr. Washington does and says, and that which I do not agree with I criticize frankly—but also, I trust, courteously. My object in coming to England was not to talk about or against Mr. W., but to discuss the race problem in the U.S . . .

As your kind letters came to Mr. Milholland I began to fear more & more that if I came I would come as an agitator almost forcing his way among a people who were with difficulty restraining their dislike.

I shrink from such a situation and for that reason was hesitating over going when the demands of my work here settled the question for me peremptorily. We are just getting into working shape the N.A.A.C.P. It has been far more successful than we dreamed but not successful enough to stand at the moment my prolonged absence. Especially does the rapid increase in circulation of our little magazine, the Crisis, make it imperative that I remain here for several months more . . .[11]

BOOKER T. WASHINGTON

[Tuskegee, Ala.] March 1, 1911

My dear Mr. [J.R.] Barlow:[12]

. . . I note what you say regarding Mr. Du Bois. He and I do not agree on most matters regarding the course to pursue in reference to our race in this country. In the first place, I do not think Dr. Du Bois understands conditions in the South. He was born in New England and has never been in the South among the rank and file of Southern white people and Southern colored people long enough to really understand conditions and to get hold of a true point of view. At present, he is living in New York and comes in little contact with the real problems of the

South, but the most fundamental difference between us is in the following direction: I believe that the Negro race is making progress. I believe that it is better for the race to emphasize its opportunities than to lay over-much stress on its disadvantages. He believes that the Negro race is making little progress. I believe that we should cultivate an ever manly, straightforward manner and friendly relations between white people and black people. Dr. Du Bois pursues the policy of stirring up strife between white people and black people. This would not be so bad, if after stirring up strife between white people and black people in the South, he would live in the South and be brave enough to face conditions which his unwise course has helped to bring about; but instead of doing that, he flees to the North and leaves the rank and file of colored people in the South no better off because of the unwise course which he and others like him have pursued.

We are making progress as a race—tremendous progress—and I believe it is better to hold up before the colored people the fact that they are making progress than to continually hold up a picture of gloom and despair before them.

I say all this fully conscious of the wrongs suffered by my race. I say all this not with the idea of in any degree limiting or circumscribing the progress or growth of the race in any direction, but I want to lay a sure foundation for progress. In a word, the great weakness, in my opinion, of Dr. Du Bois' position is that he fails to recognize the fact that it is a work of construction that is before us now and not a work of destruction. Mr. Garrison and his followers had to destroy a great evil. Those of us who are now at work have got to build up the physical education and moral resources of the South and besides, have got to cement friendly relations between black people and white people, rather than tear the two races asunder . . .[13]

CRISIS

CRIME.

Mr. Booker T. Washington, principal of Tuskegee Institute, while calling at an apartment house in West 63d Street, New York, was set upon by one of the tenants and several bystanders. Mr. Washington ran, but was severely beaten before the police interfered.[14]

BOOKER T. WASHINGTON

[Tuskegee, Ala.] March 28, 1911

Personal:

My dear Mr. [Charles William] Anderson: There is no need for my trying to find words with which to thank you for the fine, wise and unselfish service which you rendered me during my trying days in New York last week. I shall not try to put my thanks in words, but in the future I shall try to express them more in deeds than in words.

I have just sent our friend Moore a long telegram urging him to stop fighting people and to pursue the course of reconciliation, especially in view of the fact that practically every one of our enemies excepting Du Bois has had his heart softened and I think we can pursue a wise conciliatory course just now especially in view of the fact that Villard wants my help and we will leave Du Bois standing high and dry on a desert island . . .

You will be glad to know that the South has stood by me magnificently. I had a Pinkerton man with me on the train all the way, and he said that the only remark he heard made against me by any of the people on the train was made by a man from Boston. This illustrates the remark I have often heard you make. Yours very truly,

Booker T. Washington[15]

THEODORE ROOSEVELT

San Francisco March 28th, 1911

My dear Dr. Washington: I have been equally concerned and indignant at the account of the assault upon you. I earnestly hope that you will press the charge. Apparently, whatever may have been the previous character of the man who attacked you, the assault itself was utterly wanton; and I hope your case will be pressed and a verdict obtained. Then you can do as you think best about getting the sentence reduced. Faithfully yours,

Theodore Roosevelt[16]

GILCHRIST STEWART[17]

New York, March 28, 1911

My dear Dr. Washington; I trust you will not consider it presumptuous but will consider it in the same spirit that actuates this letter, i.e. a desire to acquaint you with average public sentiment upon the outrageous attack accorded you in this city . . .

Public opinion, as I have sized it up . . . does not seem to exactly understand your reasons for being in that locality at that number. They seem to think that there was some particular and special motive of a character not explained to the public, i.e. there is an indefinite assumption that a laxity of morals was involved in looking for something or somebody . . .

Now I merely write this confidentially so that you may have an idea of what you should lay most emphasis upon at the trial. The biggest and best men of the city do not countenance the charge or the matter at all. I am merely telling you what the lowly and the humble of public opinion . . . feels.

It is needless for me to say to you, that I am with you in this matter as in all others, while as you know I am out of all "movements," it has been a great source of pleasure for me to interject myself into the situation sufficiently to assure certain white friends of the race, such as, Villard, Milholland, Walling, and others, that you were perfectly innocent in the matter . . .

Milholland, Villard and Walling, Miss Ovington, et al. are with you in this matter in despite of the efforts of a number of people to try and convince them that there was an ulterior motive in your being around 63rd Street. Yours sincerely,

Gilchrist Stewart[18]

CHARLES WILLIAM ANDERSON

New York Men 29/1911

[To Booker T. Washington] Fear it would be unwise to decline Villard proposition let refusal to cooperate come from other side if it comes at all Would word telegram cautiously but with ring of sincerity.[19]

WILLIAM HENRY LEWIS[20]

Washington, D.C. March 29th [1911]

[To Booker T. Washington] Suggest following telegram: Knowing your life-long interest and activities in behalf of my race, I gladly welcome any suggestions coming from you looking toward a friendly co-operation of all the workers for the general advancement of the colored people. It seems to me that while we necessarily work along different lines, we may still work together in perfect harmony and sympathy and mutual understanding. It would be a happy day for my race and country, if we could unite all our forces.

William H. Lewis[21]

ROBERT RUSSA MOTON

Richmond Va 3–29–11

[To Booker T. Washington] I should by all means send Villard guarded telegram expressing willingness to co-operate . . .[22]

BOOKER T. WASHINGTON

[Tuskegee, Ala.] March 30, 1911

[To Oswald Garrison Villard] Your telegram of March twenty ninth received. Confirming the conversation we had in New York I would state that your lifelong interest and activities in behalf of my race urge me to repeat that I shall be glad to work in friendly cooperation with all the workers for the general advancement of the colored people especially in constructive directions.

It seems to me that while we necessarily may in the future as in the past work along different lines we still may work together in harmony, sympathy and mutual understanding. I am convinced that the time has come when all interested in the welfare of the Negro people should lay aside personal differences and personal bickerings and anything and everything that smacks of selfishness and keep in mind only rendering the service which will best promote and protect the whole race in all of its larger interests. In the last analysis I am sure that we all agree on more points than we disagree on. Further than this, the experience through which I have been passing convinces me that deep down in the heart of all of us there is a feeling of oneness and sympathy and unity. I am sure that all of my friends everywhere will happily cooperate with you in the directions I have mentioned. If your organization now in session can see its way clear to appoint two or more fraternal delegates to attend the next meeting of the National Business League I feel quite sure that our organization will reciprocate in kind.[23] It will be a happy day for my race when all of the forces and organizations while still remaining individually separate can sympathetically and heartily cooperate and work together for its larger good.

Booker T. Washington[24]

BOOKER T. WASHINGTON

Tuskegee Institute, Alabama [ca. Mar. 31, 1911]

My dear Mr. President [William Howard Taft]:[25] I sent you a telegram from New York expressing my deep thanks for the magnificent and generous service which you rendered me at a trying and critical hour . . .

Of course the most trying part of the experience was to be charged with a *base falsehood* which affected my character. My friends how ever have stood by me finely and more friends have come to light than I ever knew that I had.

The Southern white people I am glad to say have stood by me finely . . .[26]

OSWALD GARRISON VILLARD

Boston, Mass., March 31, 1911

[To Booker T. Washington] I am glad to tell you that the National Association For The Advancement Of Colored People at its meeting today passed the following resolution:

Resolved that we put on record our profound regret at the recent assault on Dr. Booker T. Washington in New York City in which the Association finds renewed evidence of race discrimination and increased necessity for the awakening of the public conscience.

Oswald Garrison Villard[27]

OSWALD GARRISON VILLARD

New York. April 5, 1911

My dear Major [Robert Russa] Moton:

. . . You will have noticed that the Association passed a resolution of sympathy with Dr. Washington, which we hope marks the beginning of friendly relations with him and the National Negro Business League. It is certainly time that Dr. Washington called off his papers like the Age that have been so villainous in their attacks upon us. This is no time for the colored people to be divided; they should present a solid front to the enemy. With best wishes, Very truly yours,

Oswald Garrison Villard[28]

BOOKER T. WASHINGTON

Parker House, Boston. April 19, 1911

My dear Mr. [Oswald Garrison] Villard: . . . I meant to have sent you a letter and thought I had done so, thanking the Association for the Advancement of Colored People for the fine resolution which they passed regarding myself. I regret that my word of thanks has not reached you before. It was a most generous act on the part of the Association, and I shall never fail to appreciate it. This resolution, as you say, has been widely used in both white and colored papers, and has accomplished much good. . . .

A short time ago I had a talk with Mr. Moorfield Storey, and told him that we are planning to get all the forces to work together.[29] This I am sure can be done. I have had talks recently with several important colored people and white people in the same direction, and all agree with my policy . . .

Confidentially I want to say that I have had several frank talks with the editor of the New York Age and have gotten friends to talk with him, and I think you will find in the near future that he will modify the tone of his paper regarding your organization. Insofar as I can, I am going to get other colored papers to pursue the same course . . .[30]

CRISIS

CRIME

In the case of the assault on Mr. Booker T. Washington, principal of Tuskegee Institute, the latest developments are as follows: Daniel C. Smith, auditor of Tuskegee, has said that he had no appointment with Mr. Washington. Mr. Washington's private secretary says that the mistake was his. Several Southern towns are reported to have raised money for [Henry] Ulrich's defense and one lynching has taken place on account of an argument between a white man and a colored man.[31] The colored people have held a mass meeting in New York to express confidence in Mr. Washington, and a delegation has thanked President Taft for his telegram. The Associated Press reported that Mr. Washington thought that Ulrich's attack upon him was justifiable under the circumstances. Mr. Washington denied this report and stated his determination to press the charge. The case came up April 3, but Mr. Washington was not present and it was postponed indefinitely.[32]

ROBERT RUSSA MOTON

Hampton, Virginia May 13, 1911

Very Personal.
My dear Dr. Washington:

. . . I tried to see Mr. Villard in New York but did not. One thing I am sure of that however sanguine Mr. Villard may feel there is a determined effort to do all they can to weaken your influence in this country and abroad. I have information directly from the meeting held in New York night before last or rather a reception to Dr. W.H. Sheppard under the auspices of Miss Ovington in which Milholland, Du Bois and Miss Milholland of course discussed plans by which they could "down" Booker Washington.[33] Dr. Sheppard who took breakfast with me yesterday morning at my invitation gave me the whole story. He, of course, being entirely ignorant of the feeling. I will not go further into details but I shall take up the matter with vigor. I am convinced that Dr. Du Bois, Milholland and Miss Ovington will do everything they can in London this summer to undo the good that you did last year . . .[34]

BOOKER T. WASHINGTON

[Tuskegee, Ala.] May 23, 1911

My dear Major [Robert Russa] Moton:

. . . What you say regarding the conversation between Milholland, Du Bois and Miss Ovington is very interesting, but not surprising. I do hope, however, that you will seek the very first opportunity at your command to see Mr. Villard and let him know exactly what you have heard. Mr. Villard is being deceived somewhat by these people, but he is gradually getting his eyes open, I think. It is very generous of you to look after my interests in so fine a way. I appreciate it most highly . . .[35]

BOOKER T. WASHINGTON

[Tuskegee, Ala.] May 24, 1911

Personal
My dear Mr. [Charles William] Anderson:

. . . The main thing about what I want to write is this. I think in one direction we had better not deceive ourselves. Milholland I am sure is making a desperate effort to get President Taft to recognize Du Bois in some way. He has been in Washington three or four times recently and has had Du Bois at the White House once. I hear Milholland is pushing Du Bois for the Haytian Mission. In case Vernon should be defeated and Du Bois get this place, it would be charged up against New York. Aside from that consideration, of course there are others more serious. If you were to take this matter up with the President, or I were to take it up with him, it would be misunderstood. Perhaps you could work it in this way: Explain the whole situation to Mr. Loeb and get him to write a frank letter to the President or to Mr. Hilles telling him about Du Bois' and Milholland's opposition to the President that is constant and personal.[36] It would be one of the worst things the President could do to recognize a man like Du Bois. In the first place, Du Bois has no strong following, and in the second place, if Du Bois and Milholland are recognized because of their bitter opposition to the President in the hope of placating them, it will be putting a premium on opposition in the future and every little white man and Negro will feel that the way to get recognition is to oppose the President in the way Milholland and Du Bois have been doing.

Enclosed I send you a cartoon which appeared in Du Bois's magazine a few months ago. This cartoon itself ought to settle Du Bois forever in the mind of President Taft.[37]

Of course I am writing largely on supposition, but I do not believe I am wrong in making the statement that Milholland is doing every thing he can to bring about this man's recognition. Yours very truly,

Booker T. Washington[38]

CHARLES WILLIAM ANDERSON

New York, N.Y. May 29, 1911

(Personal) Private
My dear Doctor [Washington]:

. . . Concerning the matter mentioned in yours of the 24th instant, I beg to say that I took it up with Mr. Loeb on Saturday and he promised to write "our friend" [Taft] at Washington at once and tell him all about the man Milholland is pushing [Du Bois]. I have secured several samples of the literature put out by the colored democrats last Fall, which was written by "the Atlanta man." All of it criticises, and much of it abuses, President Taft. This ought to prevent his landing. Rest assured that I will leave no stone unturned. Yours very truly,

Charles W. Anderson[39]

CHARLES WILLIAM ANDERSON

New York, N.Y., June 5, 1911

Private & confidential

My dear Dr [Washington]: Immediately on receipt of your letter about Du Bois I called on Mr. Loeb and urged him to write at once and tell "our friend" all about this man's antecedents . . . He wrote a strong letter against Du Bois, calling attention to the fact that he had opposed the President when he was a candidate, and is still criticising him with unrepentant hostility. He advised Mr. Hilles that a glance at Du Bois' paper would convince the President that nothing ought to be done for him, and ended his letter by suggesting that the arrangement with respect to Moore and myself would bring the Age into line . . . He then read me his answer to this letter, which was to the effect that the Age had opposed the last Administration (Roosevelt's), as persistently as it had this one, and that it was his understanding that it was Milholland and not yourself, that really controlled the paper.

During our conversation Mr. L. said that your opponents had been calling on "our friend" in great numbers and reminding him that he was placing the friends of a man who controlled a newspaper that was persistently criticising and misrepresenting the President and his Administration. He stated further that whenever "our friend" would say that you did not control the paper, these people would invariably say "of course he disclaims it, but everybody knows that he does control it, and most people believe that he does own this paper and that Moore would not dare make war on the Administration unless it had his sanction." I got two very distinct impressions from this interview, one was, that nothing large or small will be done for Moore, and the other was that "our friend" believes that the Age's attitude is winked at by you, and that his determination to appoint Vernon was a sort of service of notice on you, that if this paper does not mend its ways, some appointments will be made from the other group. From what Mr. L. says, the other fellows are running to the White House very frequently.

I thought it also significant that although Mr. L. devoted a large part of his first letter to the hostility of Du Bois toward the administration, nothing whatever was said about Du Bois in the answer. The answer was devoted to showing what had been done for your friends both in appointments and retentions, and what was not being done by your friends in the way of supporting the administration. I noticed also that "the Judge" was not included among your friends who were appointed or retained . . .[40]

In June 1911, Du Bois sailed to England for the First Universal Races Congress. Milholland and others wanted Du Bois to give a speaking tour similar to that of Washington, but Du Bois was wary about making such events look like a competition between the two. Instead, London's Lyceum Club held a "Races Education Dinner" in Du Bois's honor on June 26, 1911. Conservative forces in England and other logistical problems made the dinner difficult, and Du Bois suggested cancelling it. The problems were solved, however, and the dinner commenced. And whether in speeches or in his publications, Du Bois was at no loss for publicly countering the messages of Washington.[41]

W.E.B. DU BOIS

Two utterances by Mr. Booker T. Washington this week illustrate the reasons why so many thinking men, black and white, are coming to doubt Mr. Washington's statesmanship. One statement is in the current

Outlook and is to the effect that Mr. John E. Milholland and "certain members of my own race in the North have objected because they said I did not paint conditions in the South black enough . . . I have never denied that the Negro in the South frequently meets with wrong and injustice, but he does not starve." And he quotes facts to show that there is actual starvation in London.

This argument reduces itself to several propositions:

I. It is not well to tell the whole story of wrong and injustice in the South, but rather one should emphasize the better aspects . . .

The first proposition has been the keynote of Mr. Washington's propaganda for the last fifteen years. It has, however, been ineffective in practice and logically dangerous. It is ineffective in practice because under its aegis—under the silence, the absence of criticism, the kindly sentiments and widespread complacency, we have seen grow up in the South a caste system which threatens the foundations of democracy, and a lawlessness which threatens all government.

We have seen wholesale disfranchisement of colored voters, color caste carried to the point of positive cruelty, the rule of the mob and the lynching of 2,000 men without legal trial, growing discrimination in schools, travel, and public conveniences, and an openly declared determination to stop the development of millions of men at the dead line of color.

To offset this Mr. Washington has a right to point to increased accumulation of property among Negroes and increased numbers of intelligent and forceful black folk. But what has been the result of this? It has been an intensified prejudice as shown in the new Ghetto laws, the strikes against black workers, spread of civil discrimination, and the crystallization of the disfranchising sentiment. How any intelligent American can calmly and without hysteria or prejudice look on the development of the Negro problem in the United States in the last ten years and say that race and color prejudice has decreased, South or North, or shows reasonable signs of abating in the near future, passes our comprehension. And yet Mr. Washington is reported to have said at the recent Unitarian dinner that "Prejudice still exists, but it is not so bitter as it was," and that the South is an example of the overcoming of race prejudice.

Why now does Mr. Washington persist in making from time to time statements of this kind? It is, we believe, because of a dangerous logical fallacy into which Mr. Washington and his supporters fall. They assume that the truth—the real facts concerning a social situation at any particular time—is of less importance than the people's feeling concerning those facts. There could be no more dangerous social pragmatism. Its basic assumption is that the facts are in reality known, while its whole action prevents the facts from being known. It is a self-contradictory and deceptive position and it has historically led to social damnation in thousands of awful cases. Even where its complacent ignorance has accidentally evolved into good, the good came not because of it but in spite of it. Just here it is that Mr. Washington utterly fails in his English comparisons: It is not starvation that civilization need fear, if civilization faces the awful fact and calls it starvation, knows its gaunt and threatening shape and says with Lloyd-George, We will stop it if we shake the economic foundations of the empire.[42] But the starvation which the world and Mr. Washington would do well to fear is that which blinds its eyes to stalking misery in the East End and cries, "Lo! the Power of England!" So, too, in the United States: Awful as race prejudice, lawlessness and ignorance are, we can fight them if we frankly face them and dare name them and tell the truth; but if we continually dodge and cloud the issue, and say the half truth because the whole stings and shames; if we do this, we invite catastrophe. Let us then in all charity but unflinching firmness set our faces against all statesmanship that looks in such directions.[43]

W.E.B. DU BOIS

... The argument of those who uphold this discrimination is based primarily on race. They claim that the inherent characteristics of the Negro race show its essential inferiority and the impossibility of incorporating its descendants into the American nation. They admit that there are exceptions to the rule of inferiority, but claim that these but prove the rule. They say that amalgamation of the races would be fatal to civilisation and they advocate therefore a strict caste system for Negroes, segregating them by occupations and privileges, and to some extent by dwelling-place, to the end that they (a) submit permanently to an inferior position, or (b) die out, or (c) migrate.

This philosophy the thinking Negroes and a large number of white friends vigorously combat. They claim that the racial differences between white and black in the United States offer no essential barrier to the races living together on terms of mutual respect and helpfulness. They deny, on the one hand, that the large amalgamation of the races already accomplished has produced degenerates, in spite of the unhappy character of these unions; on the other hand, they deny any desire to lose the identity of either race through intermarriage. They claim that it should be possible for a civilised black man to be treated as an American citizen without harm to the republic, and that the modern world must learn to treat coloured races as equals if it expects to advance . . .

At the meeting of two such diametrically opposed arguments it was natural that councils of compromise should appear, and it was also natural that a nation, whose economic triumphs have been so noticeable as those of the United States, should seek an economic solution to the race question. More and more in the last twenty years the business men's solution of the race problem has been the development of the resources of the South. Coincident with the rise of this policy came the prominence of Mr. B.T. Washington. Mr. Washington was convinced that race prejudice in America was so strong and the economic position of the freedmen's sons so weak that the Negro must give up or postpone his ambitions for full citizenship and bend all his energies to industrial efficiency and the accumulation of wealth. Mr. Washington's idea was that eventually when the dark man was thoroughly established in the industries and had accumulated wealth, he could demand further rights and privileges. This philosophy has become very popular in the United States, both among whites and blacks.

The white South hastened to welcome this philosophy. They thought it would take the Negro out of politics, tend to stop agitation, make the Negro a satisfied labourer, and eventually convince him that he could never be recognised as the equal of the white man. The North began to give large sums for industrial training, and hoped in this way to get rid of a serious social problem.

From the beginning of this campaign, however, a large class of Negroes and many whites feared this programme. They not only regarded it as a programme which was a dangerous compromise, but they insisted that to stop fighting the essential wrong of race prejudice just at the time, was to encourage it.

This was precisely what happened. Mr. Washington's programme was announced at the Atlanta Exposition in 1896. Since that time four States have disfranchised Negroes, dozens of cities and towns have separated the races on street cars, 1,250 Negroes have been publicly lynched without trial, and serious race riots have taken place in nearly every Southern State and several Northern States, Negro public school education has suffered a set back, and many private schools have been forced to retrench severely or to close. On the whole, race prejudice has, during the last fifteen years, enormously increased.

This has been coincident with the rapid and substantial advance of Negroes in wealth, education, and morality, and the two movements of race prejudice and Negro advance have led to an anomalous and unfortunate situation. Some, white and black, seek to minimise and ignore the flaming prejudice in the land, and emphasise many acts of friendliness on the part of the white South, and the advance of the Negro. Others, on the other hand, point out that silence and sweet temper are not going to settle this dangerous social problem, and that manly protest and the publication of the whole truth is alone adequate to arouse the nation to its great danger.

Moreover, many careful thinkers insist that, under the circumstances, the "business men's" solution of the race problem is bound to make trouble: if the Negroes become good cheap labourers, warranted not to strike or complain, they will arouse all the latent prejudice of the white working men whose wages they bring down. If, on the other hand, they are to be really educated as men, and not as "hands," then they need, as a race, not only industrial training, but also a supply of well-educated, intellectual leaders and professional men for a group so largely deprived of contact with the cultural leaders of the whites. Moreover, the best thought of the nation is slowly recognising the fact that to try to educate a working man, and not to educate the man, is impossible. If the United States wants intelligent Negro labourers, it must be prepared to treat them as intelligent men.

This counter movement of intelligent men, white and black, against the purely economic solution of the race problem, has been opposed by powerful influences both North and South. The South represents it as malicious sectionalism, and the North misunderstands it as personal dislike and envy of Mr. Washington. Political pressure has been brought to bear, and this insured a body of coloured political leaders who do not agitate for Negro rights . . .[44]

ROBERT RUSSA MOTON

London, W.C. July 23 [1911]

Dear Dr. Washington: . . . I have had a frank talk with Dr Du Bois & have read his address with care. While he refers to your program as an unsatisfactory one and failing to do what you & others honestly hoped it would accomplish, he says you were perfectly *honest & sincere* in your feelings—that you thought the acquiring of *properly, education & character* were best method to get political and other rights. He says what he has said before that under your teachings things have gotten steadily worse. He puts you down as the *leading educator* of the *race* and of the *present generation*. It is on the whole a fine paper & strong & his reference to you is purely impersonal—& very dignified . . .[45]

BOOKER T. WASHINGTON

Fort Salonga, Long Island, N.Y. August 8, 1911

Dear Mr. Scott: Do not fail to remind me at Little Rock to have three fraternal delegates elected to attend the next meeting of the Association for the Advancement of Colored People. I want to get three strong men . . .[46]

ROBERT RUSSA MOTON

Hampton, Virginia Aug. 11, 1911

My dear Dr. Washington: . . . The Congress on the whole was very good and was in my opinion worthwhile. So far as the American Negro is concerned his case was very well put. Dr. Du Bois, who by the by gave me every possible consideration. I spoke frankly with him and he did the same with me. His speech was really very good. He simply made a scientific statement of the case of the Negro in general and in America with relation to other races. There was, of course, no reference made to any particular thing in the United States. He did not read his paper as there was no time for it. He really put the case very well . . . But Milholland, to my great surprise, who spoke after Prof. [William Sanders] Scarborough put things with as much emphasis and optimism as you would have put it.[47] His address was very different from the letter he wrote regarding you a year ago. Indeed he took just the opposite view. He said that we did not come to England to air any grievances about America, but that the American people black and white would settle their problems, the Negro simply asked equal chances and in his opinion would get it. Indeed some of his sentences sounded as if you had written them out for him. I gave Mr. Moore a brief report for the "Age" and I think it is very fine that he is going to give both Milholland and Du Bois credit for having shown very good judgment and sanity so far as his public utterances were concerned . . .[48]

BOOKER T. WASHINGTON

[Tuskegee, Ala.] December 1st, 1911

Personal and Confidential.

My dear Mr. [Ralph Waldo] Tyler:[49] Before you go too far in seeking the promotion of our friend, Mr. Johnson, the United States Consul in

South America, it might be well to inquire if his father-in-law is not a rabid, anti-Taft and pro-Du Bois man.[50]

I am very fond of Mr. Johnson, and did what I could to get him his present job, but I think it just as well to know the facts . . .

Please do not use my name, but I think it is time for people to stand up and show their true colors, or be openly against us. Yours very truly,

Booker T. Washington[51]

BOOKER T. WASHINGTON

Boston, March 20, 1912

Dear Mr. Scott: Du Bois and his aggregation are going to meet in Chicago the latter part of April. I wish you would ask Mr. Hosmer[52] in his own way to get into close touch with what is going on in Chicago in connection with this organization, and keep us informed . . .[53]

BOOKER T. WASHINGTON

My dear Sir [editor of the *Indianapolis Star*]: I have read with interest your recent editorial upon Dr. Du Bois' lecture in Indianapolis, also the letter which he wrote in answer to your editorial, and also your brief comment on his letter.[54]

I would state in the beginning that I have no personal animosity toward Dr. Du Bois, in fact, rather than disliking him I rather pity the man. He is puffed up with insane vanity and jealousy, and this deprives him, it seems, of common sense. He misrepresents my position on most occasions. He knows perfectly well I am not seeking to confine the Negro race to industrial education nor make them hewers of wood and drawers of water, but I am trying to do the same thing for the Negro which is done for all races of the world, and that is to make the masses of them first of all industrious, skillful, and frugal, to enable them to combine brains with hand work to the extent that their services will be wanted in the communities where they live, and thus prevent them from becoming a burden and a menace.

Dr. Du Bois is in the position of a doctor offering a sick child candy or medicine. The average child will take the candy because it pleases him for the minute and refuse the medicine which will permanently cure his ills. I am glad to say, however, that the great masses of colored people are not deceived by Dr. Du Bois' sophistry and are seeing more and more the wisdom of what I am trying to teach them . . .[55]

CORNELIUS BAILEY HOSMER *(Hosmer was a Tuskegee graduate originally from Louisiana who worked as a Midwestern field agent for Tuskegee after his graduation.)*[56]

Milwaukee, Wis. April 20—1912

Dear Mr. [Emmett Jay] Scott—in addition to what I have said elsewhere concerning the agitation carried on in Chicago preparatory to the holding of "the Conference of the Association for the Advancement of Colored People"—April 28th. to 30th.—the following may be of some interest. I learn that enemies of our cause and Dr. Washington followed him at his various meetings recently in Chicago for the purpose of criticism in the immediate future . . . I have heard Mrs. Ida-Wells-Barnette speak to her followers lately. Her talks bespeak jealousy at the influence of Dr. Washington, at the growth and importance of the Local and National Negro Business League, as well as at the success of the Chicago Negro Y.M.C.A. And so it goes . . .

Much talk centers about Chicago now concerning Prof. W.E.B. Du Bois' recent address in Indianapolis, Ind., in which he denounced "the teaching of too much industrial work" in the schools of Indianapolis. I havent been able to secure a report of his speech from the papers.

Is it desired that I attend some of the sessions of this Du Bois meeting in Chicago the 29th of April? It is impossible for me to find out just what kind of resolutions are going to be adopted now. Very Sincerely

C.B. Hosmer[57]

WILLIAM HENRY LEWIS

Washington. June 19, 1912

Dear Dr. Washington: I have received the enclosed suggesting that I become a member of the Association for the Advancement of Colored People.[58] I am inclined to do so if you see no objection. It may be that I can be of service by being on the inside . . .[59]

EMMETT JAY SCOTT

[Tuskegee, Ala.] June Twenty-Second
Nineteen Hundred and Twelve

Personal

Dear [William Henry] Lewis: In re: your letter to Dr. Washington just received:

Please pardon a word of temerity from an old friend. If that association should succeed in annexing you, I think you are likely to find yourself in association with that entire group of malcontents who opposed your appointment and at the same time, or afterward, did every thing they could to bring about the failure of your confirmation.

Their first movement always seems to be to go about "annexing" those friends of ours that they can, so as to put themselves in position to continue their underhanded, and as we are able to definitely state, malicious attacks upon the Doctor and his work, and at the same time, say they have our friends as members of their association, and therefore, are not opposing him . . .[60]

BOOKER T. WASHINGTON

[Tuskegee, Ala.] September 10, 1912

Personal

My dear Mr. [Charles Sanderson] Medbury:[61]

. . . Any person who would be guilty of the charge made against me in connection with that New York incident would not hesitate to deny if the charges were true. I would state in the first place that I visited the point where I did visit in New York upon a perfectly legitimate mission, and while there I was assaulted by a band of ruffians. After they found out who I was and after the main leader had been locked up in the station house two hours after he was locked up he induced the woman with whom he was living to make a false charge; that was made with a view of mitigating his punishment. They also got three or four persons who lived in the neighborhood to give false testimony against me. I being alone and almost without witnesses was at the mercy of a lot of perjurers. Notwithstanding my disadvantage, I was determined to see the matter through the courts and do my duty in having the man punished if it were possible. During the first week of November of last year the case was tried before the Court of Special

Sessions. Two of the judges deciding to dismiss the man and one deciding that he ought to be punished. Everybody who understood the case and the circumstances in New York was convinced that the decision of the judges was simply a Tammany plot, the two judges who voted in favor of acquitting the man were Tammany men and the one voting to sustain my side of the case was not. Of course in the court room I had the unpleasant task of hearing all this manufactured false testimony, but I was determined to go through it and do my duty in trying to have the man punished.

I might add further that there is not the slightest foundation for any charge to the effect that I was peeping through a key hole or spoke improperly to any woman. This is something I have never done in my life . . .

I ought to add that the man who assaulted me was immediately rearrested as soon as the trial which concerned me was over, and taken to New Jersey where he is now serving sentence in the penitentiary for failing to support his wife . . . .[62]

W.E.B. DU BOIS

Thirty-two years ago a brown boy was born in Carolina. He had not only ability but pluck. He was trained in the local schools, and eventually went to Virginia Union University, where he did his academic work; and also was a leader in student activities. On graduating he became editor of the *Voice of the Negro,* and immediately the name of J. Max Barber became known throughout the colored race.

Then came the severest temptation a young man can meet. A little dishonesty to his own ideals, a little truckling diplomacy, and success and a fine income awaited him. This he refused to give. Perhaps there was some arrogance of youth in the decision to hew to the line of his thought and ideal, but it was fine arrogance, and when defeat came and the *Voice* stopped publication, he simply set his teeth and started life again. Only menial employment was open to him, but he took it, faced poverty, and began to study dentistry. For four long years he studied, until last spring, when he graduated from a Philadelphia dental college, among the best in the class.[63]

That "truckling diplomacy" was a reference to Washington's attempt to manipulate the black press. Barber failed at the journalism business after refusing to cow to the Tuskegee Machine, and no contemporary reader would have misunderstood Du Bois's veiled attack. Washington's alliances with and patronage of various newspapers for various pro-Tuskegee ends were not a well-kept secret. Many of his machinations were ostensibly secret, but the bitter invective that ran through the conversation between him and Du Bois was incredibly public.

CHARLES WILLIAM ANDERSON

New York, N.Y. November 8, 1912

(Personal) *Private*

My dear Doctor [Washington]: . . . The black democrats are crowing very loudly, and have already divided the offices now held by colored republicans, among themselves. Du Bois, who prepared their literature during the campaign (for pay) is talked of for Hayti. A half dozen of them are pointed for my place, and each place in Washington is claimed by a dozen candidates. And thus the merry war goes on.

Among the many curious features of this very curious campaign, is that those Taft colored republicans, who were so bitterly opposed to the Colonel and so much devoted to the President, did not move a finger in his behalf after the nomination. In this city, such men as our old friend, "the Governor," [P.B.S. Pinchback] deputy assistant Dist. Atty. [Cornelius W.] McDougald and others, who praised the President and objurgated the Colonel, did not make a single speech during the campaign.[64] They clamored for the President's re-nomination, and then sat down and left it to the rest of us to elect him. But that's the way of the world. The man who is first to buckle on his sword in time of peace is also first to take it off in time of war . . .[65]

RALPH WALDO TYLER

Washington, D.C, Dec. 11, 1912

My dear Emmett [Jay Scott]: Here is a matter I wish you would take up with the Doctor, and see if something can be done along the line suggested.

Cannot some help be gotten from the Carnegie fund for publicity for The Bee? I am not familiar with the purposes of that fund, but thought the Doctor and yourself would be. "After the deluge," when "our crowd" are out of office and scattered, the anti-Washington crowd here will be sure to secure the influence of The Bee. In fact their lines are already laid . . . With proper help, The Bee might be made the most powerful Negro newspaper in the country for weal or woe—the most widely quoted. With some help it can be maintained as a dam— if nothing else, to the purposes of the Du Bois crowd, who are more considerable in numbers here than any place in the country—more resourceful and more aggressive . . . Some time ago I suggested the matter to the Doctor, in a general way, and he said he would look into it at some time. I presume, especially as it was not even near-urgent at that time, he forgot the suggestion. I dont want to appear as an alarmist, but knowing conditions here as I do, having kept my finger on the pulse more constantly than most of the followers, I am prepared to say that there will be something doing just as soon as we, "our crowd" here quit the game . . .[66]

NOTES

1. Washington here refers to the Atlanta Riot of 1906, wherein several dozen black residents were killed by whites as a result of tension over the availability of jobs and demands for civil rights, much of that demand stemming from Atlanta University. The notion that Du Bois had the opportunity to stay and fight during the riot but did not was a continual pet conspiracy theory of Washington. Mixon, 2005.

2. "I am after Du Bois and their business of tearing down everything and building up nothing," wrote Fortune on January 10, 1911. "He writes the Amsterdam News this week denying that he ran away from Atlanta during the riots, but as to my oilier characterizations of him he is dumb." Washington, 1981, vol. 10, 556.

3. Ibid., 555–556.

4. See Boylan, 1998.

5. James Henry Anderson founded the *New York Amsterdam News* in Harlem in December 1909. At this point, the paper had just completed its first year of existence. Weiner, 2010, 185.

6. Washington, 1981, vol. 10, 556–557.

7. Ibid., 573–575.

8. George A. Myers was a barber and a prominent black Republican from Cleveland, Ohio. Washington *Colored American*, 2 June 1900, 2. See also Garraty, 1956.

9. Washington, 1981, vol. 10, 589–590.

10. Ettie Sayer, "the lady doctor," was assistant medical officer to the London County Council Board of Education and also served the London School Board. *Queanbeyan Age*, 29 May 1908, 3; and "Bravery and Hypnotism," 4 March 1908, 254.

11. Du Bois, 1973, 173–175.

12. J.R. Barlow was a member of the most prominent family in Edgeworth, England, near Bolton. He and Washington had become acquainted during the latter's travels abroad. Washington, 1981, vol. 10, 610.

13. Washington, 1981, vol. 10, 608–609.

14. "Crime," April 1911, 11.

15. Washington, 1981, vol. 11, 46.

16. Ibid., 50.

17. See Chapter 13, note 71.

18. Washington, 1981, vol. 11, 50–51.

19. "For us to decline the olive branch," Anderson wrote in a separate letter, "would be to expose us to the charge of being narrow, and it would give the scoundrels on the other side an excuse for wielding the dirty weapons, which they know so well how to use." Ibid., 53.

20. See Chapter 4.

21. Washington, 1981, vol. 11, 53.

22. Ibid., 53.

23. Villard's response, after the NAACP passed a resolution denouncing the Ulrich incident, argued, "Our people feel that as we have taken this first move it is your move next." Ibid., 55. See below for resolution.

24. Ibid., 54–55.

25. William Howard Taft was the Republican successor to Theodore Roosevelt, serving from 1909 to 1913 and, like his predecessor, had a strong relationship with Washington. Anderson, 1973.

26. Washington, 1981, vol. 11, 64–65.

27. The NAACP debated a stronger resolution, but decided not to pass it. Ibid., 69.

28. Ibid., 83.

29. Moorfield Storey was a prominent Boston lawyer and activist who served as the first president of the NAACP until 1915. See Hixon, 1972.

30. Washington, 1981, vol. 11, 109.

31. Henry Ulrich, the assailant, was a white man who thought Washington was a burglar. It was not an attack on Washington because he was Washington, it was an attack on Washington because he was black. Thus the support from southern towns. Schroeder, 2005, 123.

32. "Crime," May 1911, 7.

33. William Henry Sheppard was a Presbyterian missionary who spent 20 years in the Congo. He was close to Mary White Ovington and others associated with the NAACP, but he also was a graduate of Hampton. Cureau, 1982, 340–352.

34. Washington, 1981, vol. 11, 155–156.

35. Ibid., 166–167.

36. William Loeb was the collector for the port of New York. Charles Hilles was Taft's secretary. *Boston Evening Transcript*, 8 November 1911, 2.

37. The cartoon featured Taft as a chef offering William H. Lewis a taste of "political pot stew" with a spoon that reached across a "color line." "Mr. Lewis gets his!" read the caption. *Crisis* 1 (April 1911): 31.

38. Washington, 1981, vol. 11, 169–170.

39. Ibid., 176.

40. Ibid., 192–193.

41. Du Bois, 1973, 172–173; and Aptheker, 1969, 884–886.

42. David Lloyd George, as fits the quote, was at the time Chancellor of the Exchequer, serving from 1908 to 1915. He would, of course, go on to be prime minister of Great Britain during the First World War. See Creiger, 1976.

43. Du Bois, June 1911, 62–64.

44. Du Bois, "The Negro Race In the United States of America," 1911, 348–363.

45. Washington, 1981, vol. 11, 273.

46. Ibid.

47. See Chapter 5, note 5.

48. Washington, 1981, vol. 11, 295–296.

49. Chapter 14, note 46.

50. Washington here refers to James Weldon Johnson. See Chapter 14, note 54.

51. Washington, 1981, vol. 11, 379–380.

52. Cornelius Bailey Hosmer was a Tuskegee graduate originally from Louisiana who worked as a Midwestern field agent for Tuskegee after his graduation. Ibid., 487.

53. Hosmer reported that "Du Bois and Villard are expected to be very bitter; and radical in their speeches" at the NAACP convention. Ibid., 486–487.

54. Du Bois spoke at Bethel AME Church in Indianapolis, arguing that higher education was more essential than industrial and technical education. The *Star* called this "a dangerously misleading doctrine." Du Bois responded that he was not criticizing workers, just that the goal of education should be "not the output of goods but the training of men." The *Star* responded, "The Star is not a Negro hater; but it looks upon the teaching of Dr. Du Bois as false and mischievous for the children of any race. Booker Washington is right and Dr. Du Bois is wrong." *Indianapolis Star*, 30 March 1912, 16; 31 March 1912, 16; 8 April 1912, 6; and Washington, 1981, vol. 11, 518.

55. Washington, 1981, vol. 11, 517–518.

56. See note 52.

57. Washington, 1981, vol. 11, 524–525.

58. Mary Childs Nerney, NAACP secretary, sent the invitation, arguing that membership would help the group support his membership to the American Bar Association. Ibid., 551.

59. Ibid.

60. Ibid., 554–555.

61. Reverend Charles Sanderson Medbury was an author, lecturer, and chaplain of Drake University in Des Moines, Iowa. "Represented at Minneapolis," *The League Bulletin*, 7 September 1917, 54.

62. Washington, 1983, vol. 12, 6–7.

63. Du Bois, November 1912, 16.

64. Cornelius W. McDouglad spent five years as an assistant district attorney for the county of New York. Hill, 1986, 286.

65. Washington, 1983, vol. 12, 49–50.

66. Ibid., 87–88.

18

Irreconcilable Differences

The existence of the NAACP ensured that the contest between Washington and Du Bois would not die. Oswald Garrison Villard, founder of the group, was a former Washington ally and still maintained a relationship with Tuskegee. That relationship, however, was obviously strained. Washington was not only hurt by the defections but also empowered to ramp up his spying and sabotage efforts as any statements in favor of a Du Bois position by anyone in the NAACP automatically made him assume that the organization was designed specifically to sabotage him. That led Du Bois to respond by defending the group, telling his readers to "ignore the mischievous intimation of venal colored editors that we are 'fighting' Booker T. Washington. We are fighting slavery, caste and cowardice in black men and white; nothing more and nothing less."

BOOKER TALIAFERRO WASHINGTON

[Tuskegee, Ala.] February Twenty-seventh, 1913

Dear Mr. [Oswald Garrison] Villard: I have your letter of recent date with enclosures, calling attention to a meeting to be held in New York

City in April.[1] I fear it is not going to be possible for me to be present at the meeting.[2]

The truth of the matter is I have been under very great and unusual pressure during the past few months, and today I am leaving Tuskegee for a somewhat extended visit to the Pacific Northwest where I am seeking new friends for Tuskegee Institute . . .

It has become necessary, because of my duty to the school here and to our Trustees, to refuse to attend the Trustees meeting of Howard University and Fisk University, the latter being an especially important meeting because they are going to elect a new president. You have no idea of the calls I have upon me in connection with other institutions . . .[3]

BOOKER T. WASHINGTON

Portland, Oregon, March 21, 1913

My dear Mr. [Oswald Garrison] Villard:

. . . As I wrote you sometime ago, I fear it would be impossible for me to attend the conference on the 17th of April for the reason that I have already been kept away from the school more than I ought to be for this year, but if you could see your way clear to have the meeting held at some place other than the headquarters of the Association for the Advancement of Colored People I should be very glad to make an effort to have Tuskegee represented even if I could not be present myself. I think it would be a mistake to confuse the work which that organization is doing with education in the South. I do not think it would help matters, and in fact I feel rather sure it would hinder matters, and it would be impossible for a meeting of the character you name to be held at the headquarters of the Association without such a meeting being associated with the work of the Association. I am not undervaluing the work of the Association, but we must face conditions as they actually are in the South . . .[4]

JAMES CARROLL NAPIER[5]

Washington April 1, 1913

My dear Mr. Washington: Enclosed I am handing you a card of invitation to three lectures delivered by Mr. Du Bois at Howard University.

I heard the two delivered at night and regret that I did not hear the midday one.

Each was of one hour's duration and was an interesting account, or rather recount, of prehistoric governments in Africa . . . He seemed not to have discovered this opportunity and during his three hours failed utterly to offer a single word of advice or counsel touching the practical side of the life which these young people will soon have to face. His paramount aim seemed to be to show that he had profound learning and had made deep research. No thought of the influence he might exert in shaping the lives or activities of his hearers seems ever to have entered his mind. He simply showed "learning."

After it was over and Mrs. Napier and I came to compare notes we agreed that there was little or no benefit to be derived from these lectures; and that one of your speeches of an hour's length would result in greater benefit to the race and to all who might hear it than a whole month of such recitals would bring.

J.C. Napier[6]

ROBERT RUSSA MOTON

Hampton, Virginia April 3, 1913

My dear Mr. [Emmett Jay] Scott: The enclosed letter from Mr. Villard[7] is interesting. All the same I think Dr. Washington was wise in suggesting a change of place for the meeting. In view of Du Bois' sayings and attitude I should certainly doubt the wisdom of Dr. Washington meeting in his office, but as he very well put it in his letter, though he did not mention Du Bois (wisely) that the meeting should be on common ground and disassociated from the National Association. Sincerely yours,

R.R. Moton

Dr Washington's letter showed courage and a great deal of it too.[8]

OSWALD GARRISON VILLARD

New York April 4, 1913

Dear Mr. Washington: . . . In the first place, you are under a complete misapprehension. From the first conference at which this organization

[NAACP] was formed, it took for its field the education of the colored race. We have, therefore, had the matter of education specifically in mind ever since we began, and have quietly been working on one or two phases of it. We are, therefore, only steering our proper course in doing what should have been done by Tuskegee or Hampton years ago in getting the rural industrial schools together in a strong organization [The Association of Negro Industrial and Secondary Schools] to standardize and systematize and weed out the unworthy, like Smallwood's.[9] It is greatly to be regretted that Tuskegee will not be represented. Major Moton expects to be present from Hampton, and most of the leading schools of this kind will be represented. Tuskegee's absence will perhaps be misunderstood, and will doubtless be regarded as hostility on your part either to our organization or to some persons in it; this will be very regrettable.

You must, of course, be your own judge of conditions in the South, but I cannot help saying to you how strongly I feel that in giving way to prejudice as much as you do in the stand you have taken in the letter before me you increase prejudice and weaken yourself . . . More than that, we have been recently called upon by the Alabama & Vicksburg Railroad, a Southern corporation, manned and officered by Southern white men, to aid them in the Supreme Court of the United States to overthrow the recent decision of the Supreme Court of Mississippi which would "Jim Crow" the Pullman cars. Does this look as though it would injure you or Tuskegee in any way to attend a meeting which, as a matter of fact, will not even be held in the rooms of the Association, but merely in a vacant space in the same building? The call, as you are aware, was not signed by me, or the Association but by six of the leading colored educators in this field who naturally look to Tuskegee for leadership, and are amazed to find it holding aloof. I have always dealt perfectly frankly with you, as you are aware, and I must say that I think your timidity is running away with you, and that, as you suggest, you are too fearful. Is it not a time for you to appeal to the undercurrent in the life of the South, to the many men and women who know that the present policies are wrong, who despise the agitators and demagogues and want to do what is right by the colored people?[10]

BOOKER T. WASHINGTON

Tuskegee Institute, Alabama April 8th, 1913

Dear Mr. [Oswald Garrison] Villard: . . . If it will do the cause any good I am willing to plead guilty to the charge of cowardice and timidity. If you feel quite sure that the cause of education will be advanced I shall see to it that our institution is represented by two of our workers, Mr. J.R.E. Lee, the Head of our Academic Department, who is in constant touch with the small schools, and Dr. Robert E. Park, whose special work is to visit the smaller schools . . .[11]

Let me add that while both in the present and in the future we may differ as to methods, I wish you, however, to understand that I never cease to feel grateful to you for your personal kindness to me and also for your generous action from time to time toward this institution. I think we can always depend upon this, that I will be frank with you and when we can cooperate I shall be glad to do so. When I cannot agree with you, I of course will say so in the most frank and kindly way. I very much hope that this letter paves the way for at least our cooperation and united effort in reference to the forthcoming conference. Yours very truly,

Booker T. Washington[12]

CHARLES WILLIAM ANDERSON

Saratoga Springs, N.Y. Aug. 19, 1913

My dear Doctor Washington:

. . . Did you see the Du Bois circular letter to President Wilson? It was undoubtedly prepared under the eye of Mr. Villard. You will notice that they complain of placing all of our folks in one bureau, whereas there has been no such action taken or contemplated. The segregation of which we complain, is, that although our people are scattered all over the buildings, they are required to go to a particular toilet room on the top floor. Again, the last paragraph of the letter states that this segregation was established by persons who desired to benefit us. This is a falsehood made out of whole cloth, and the writer of it, knew it to be one. In fact the whole communication was a piece of special pleading put out for the purpose of befogging the real issue and obscuring the real cause of complaint. Why was not something said about the number of men, holding presidential places, that have been separated from the service? On this subject the Du Bois letter is as silent as the grave. As a matter of fact, the only presidential appointee in whom Du Bois is interested, Henry Lincoln Johnson, is still in office.[13] The letter is also silent with respect to the reflex influence of the Administration's attitude towards us. This influence is more hurtful than all of the

removals, demotions, and segregation put together. It inspires our enemies all over the country to feel at liberty to run amuck at any time
without fear of punishment and it notifies the oppressor that oppression is safe and protected by the highest authorities in the land. I do
hope that some other organization will speak out soon and tell the true
and whole story . . .[14]

NETTIE J. ASBURRY *(Asburry was corresponding secretary of the
Tacoma branch of the NAACP.)*

Tacoma, Wash. Sep 15—'13

My Dear Mr Washington: You are of course aware of the Race discrimination now practiced in the Federal buildings at Washington. You
must be noting with satisfaction that the colored people all over the
United States are holding Mass Meetings protesting against this infer-
nal predjudice . . . Dont you think it is about time you lifted your voice
in defense of the American Negro? We acknowledge you as our leader
yet we take issue with you in your great fault of *Omission*. You have
accomplished a great work, your deeds will live after you have passed
away. We all love and revere you for what you have achieved but we
could love and honor you so much more if you would speak out for
your people. We are human beings with well developed senses and
keen aspirations therefore it goes without saying that we are more
than mere *money making machines. Of course* we should acquire land
holdings and learn trades but there is a birthright which every human
being is heir to. Without this natural bequest life is a Comedy, (or a
tragedy) . . .

Nettie J Asburry[15]

CHARLES WILLIAM ANDERSON

New York, N.Y. September 26, 1913

Personal

My dear Doctor [Washington]: Enclosed please find a copy of Tyler's
second attack.[16] I would especially invite your attention to his references
to Lincoln Johnson. A short time ago he contributed a signed article
to the "Evening Post" in which he gave entire credit for the removal
of the objectionable segregation signs in the Treasury Department to
Mr. Villard, Du Bois and their committee. Now he takes occasion to

praise Johnson for it. He also denies that he is the author of the article, not withstanding the fact that the proprietor of the News, Mr. Edward Warren,[17] told me without hesitation that the article was prepared by Tyler. This week's article was not inserted but was sent to my office by the Amsterdam News people, and is now in my possession . . .

The News is under the influence of Robt. Wood, James D. Carr and Prof. Du Bois[18] . . . The editor of the Amsterdam News, last week, promised after reading the article, not to print it. I learned afterwards that the Wood-Carr-Du Bois faction, who are throwing their printing to the News, ordered it in. This week's contribution would have also been inserted had it not been that a dozen or so advertisers in the paper, among them one whose ads are worth from $250 to $500 a year, threatened to withdraw their patronage if I were again assailed in the columns of that journal; this, together with the severe criticism that the editors have received for allowing a coward who fears to sign his own name, and who does not live in this city, to covertly assail a man whom some people here regard as being, at least, a useful citizen caused Warren, who really owns the paper, to immediately send his man to me with the article . . .[19]

LESTER A. WALTON *(Walton was a manager and theater editor for the* New York Age.)[20]

New York, Nov. 14–13

Dear Friend [Emmett Jay Scott]: . . . Oswald Garrison Villard wrote me a letter the other day asking me if I would call to see him. Anxious to ascertain what it was all about I made an appointment and called at noon to-day. Was cordially received and he thanked The Age for running account of his speech made in Baltimore some weeks ago. Said he thought probably it meant that there was an inclination on the part of The Age to get together with him. I told him that we ran article because we deemed it worthy of consideration and that our actions possessed no significance.

I was then asked how paper was doing, and the answer was very good, better than ever. The next question put to me was what financial position did Mr. [Fred] Moore occupy on The Age and I replied— owner.[21] Then he wanted to know what was Dr. Washington's influence with The Age. I said that the doctor was Mr. Moore's personal friend; that Mr. Moore was a warm admirer of the doctor, and as Mr. Moore was known for either being with or against you he could readily understand Mr. Moore's position.

Mr. Villard then proceeded to tell me that he admired Dr. Washington but that he disagreed with him on some points; that in the chair I was then sitting he had made known to the doctor where he had disagreed with him; such as writing optimistic letters about the Negroes being thankful, etc. I informed him that I was a warm admirer of Dr. Washington because he was doing great constructive work. On this he agreed with me, declaring that even his Tuskegee work, in his opinion, was not as great as his work in the South telling the white people of their faults on the race question—something no other person could do. Then we disagreed somewhat on the terms "cowardice" and "diplomacy."

Mr. Villard complained that when his association sent out its letter none of the strong papers favorable to the doctor published a line. This seemed to hurt him very much. The fact that The Age did not use matter particularly seemed to affect him. I told him that we were making our fight in our own way, and he admitted that we were doing much good. The fact that Dr. Washington is so influential with the colored press seems to worry him.

Then, after I kept leading up to Du Bois for sometime without any results, I told him that while I thought the doctor had the greatest admiration for him (Villard) I did not think he was so kindly disposed to the impractical methods of some of his friends. We finally brought up Du Bois. He said he admired both Dr. Washington and Du Bois; that he had criticised both and did not think there should be any ill feeling for taking issues. I told him I thought the doctor a very broad minded man and declared I did not think he could have accomplished so much had he not been broad. I then dropped the opinion that I did not think Du Bois broad. He disagreed with me, but declared that Du Bois lacked tact and he was ill-tempered. My reply was that tact and a good temper were two requisites one who aspired to be a leader should possess. Mr. Villard assured me that he thought Du Bois was a leader and acclaimed him the scholar of the race. He pointed out the Crisis as a great piece of literary work and said it had a circulation of over 33,000. I congratulated them on their effort.

I was also told that the National Association was gaining friends daily, and that even the Hampton people were being won over. I again stated that I was glad to learn of such a victory, as co-operation was necessary in our fight. . . .

Lester A Walton

P.S. I also told Mr. Villard about a conference held some years ago at which both factions agreed to work together and that a few days later Du Bois broke his word. Villard said he could not believe it.[22]

CHARLES WILLIAM ANDERSON

New York, N.Y. Nov. 17th, 1913

Personal.
My dear Doctor:

. . . Did you know that the Emancipation Commission is at logger-heads? James D. Carr and Du Bois have had a falling out. Du Bois is said to have sworn some brave Spanish oaths at Carr, and Carr is reported to have retorted in kind. Wood and Carr have also had a serious difference, but this was about campaign funds alleged to have been supplied by Tammany Hall, and appropriated by Wood to his own personal uses. It is further reported that the Governor has sent auditors to go over the accounts of the Commission. On the appearance of these auditors, I am advised, that Wood, Carr and [James Henry] Anderson took to the high brush and attempted to unload the responsibility for $1800 which is missing, on the eminent sociologist.[23] The said eminent sociologist seems to be in danger of being made the scapegoat for the rest of the Commission. Wood maintains that the editor of "The Souls of Black Folks" was in debt to him to the extent of $800, before the celebration opened, for printing "The Crisis." He seems to have put him on the Commission in order that he might be able to settle up. This gave the distinguished editor a taste of warm blood and he appears to have developed the appetite of Gargantua. Carr accuses Du Bois of having stated that he, Carr, was leading an improper private life, and has expressed his opinion of "The Educator" in terms which I dare not consign to paper. "The Educator," in turn, referred to Carr as a one-eyed something or other. The Deputy Assistant Corporation Counsel did not seem to relish the inferred similitude between himself and the cyclops, and threatened to impair the personal beauty of the professor's cephalic configuration, and so on "ad infinitum" . . .[24]

RALPH WALDO TYLER

Washington, D.C. January 4th., 1914

My dear Emmett [Jay Scott]:

. . . The N.A.A.C.P. is growing fast, and it has all but blanketed this community here. I found in my travels its influence was rapidly spreading, and wherever it was increasing in numbers I found a very noticeable decrease in proper respect and appreciation for the Doctor's work.[25] In Washington its leaders are either avowed opponents of the Doctor or indifferent friends . . . Some of "our friends" here whose past success was due almost entirely to the Doctor's influence in their desire for retention under the present administration have changed from strong Washington partizans to middle of the road men . . .

In the past two months the local branch here of the N.A.A.C.P. has collected and forwarded to Villard almost $2000. This alone tells, in a few words, of its activity and growing strength. They had practically (when the administration changed) captured Thompson who was disseminating their news while he tightened up on news in the Doctor's interest, to whom he is greatly indebted. There was only one alternative—close him up and out. And I have done this effectually. Have placed him in a jam—he can neither hurt us or help the bear.

Growing strong, the enemy now sees the need of good organs, and a good publicity man. With funds at their disposal they will secure both . . .

The fact is we have, and are losing ground, and the enemy is gaining. We cannot afford to openly oppose the N.A.A.C.P. for the reason that its fundamental principles are precisely what we all desire to see in force. With its present leaders, we cannot afford to go over to it in a body. As I see it, we must not withhold approval—we surely must not antagonize, while emphasizing, in no offensive manner the things which the Doctor is trying to do.

Now here is the situation, and here is the confronting condition. We have friends who were with us strong when we were serving their meals and washing their clothes. Now that they believe we can no longer feed or clothe they are preparing to hurdle the fence. We held them by favor then. We must hold them now by fear. Sincerely,

Ralph[26]

RALPH WALDO TYLER

Washington, D.C., Jan. 6., 1914

Dear Doctor [Washington]: Villard meeting, last evening, was a big success, in p[o]int of attendance, enthusiasm and funds raised . . .

Mr. Villard quoted you in his address, saying that "Dr. Booker Washington never said a better thing when he said that 'you cant keep a man down in the ditch without staying down there with him.' "

To date, the local branch here has raised about $2500 in cash, sending same to New York. Rosco[e] Bruce is a grand high priest now in the N.A.A.C.P. movement, hurdling from his past friends who saved him to hoped for new friends. Rosco[e] is for any port in time of storm . . .[27]

BOOKER T. WASHINGTON

Parker House, Boston. Jan. 16, 1914

Dear Mr. Scott:

. . . I find that all the old, strong forces have either been put out of Villard's organization, or have withdrawn. This is true with few exceptions. There seems to be a general spirit of unrest and dissatisfaction among them. Dr. Mossell has withdrawn or been put out.[28] The same is true of Ida Wells Barnett, and Trotter of course. The most interesting of all, I have learned from a reliable source that Villard and Du Bois do not speak to each other. They have been at daggers points for a good many weeks.

There are a good many colored people who resent the idea of a white man assuming to lead and control the colored people. One point that Bishop Walters and [I] agreed upon was that we use our influence in all the colored publications to emphasize in every way possible the matter of Negro leadership for Negroes . . .[29]

GEORGE WESLEY HARRIS *(Harris was the editor of the* New York News *and former editor of the* Amsterdam News.*)*[30]

New York Feb 20 1914

My Dear Dr Washington: I want to thank you for your letter just received with its enclosure, receipt for which you will find enclosed. It comes at a time when it is badly needed as it enabled me to finish a bill for this week. But I am, too, sorry, Doctor, that you could not help me substantially at this time. The Amsterdam News has not been able as yet to get its paper out for this week and as their printer is the same as ours I am sure of what I am telling you that if I can get the News out for the next two weeks I am saved and will have the field practically to myself . . .

Relations between the "scholar" and editor [W.E.B. Du Bois and O.G. Villard] are becoming more strained he said despite the fact that the former is siding on every vital question with the latter. Hoping that you will strain a point Doctor, and help me in a way that will be a lifesaver to The News I am As Ever Yours Very Respectfully,

George W. Harris[31]

Joel Elias Spingarn was a Columbia literature professor who helped found the NAACP and served in several positions of leadership. By 1914, he had resigned his position at Columbia in protest over a colleague's dismissal. Spingarn was a devoted progressive activist, but even without a university appointment, he continued his academic work. He was also devoted to the NAACP ideal, of course, but still supported Tuskegee through annual donations. He was one of the few leaders who could walk the line between them with relative ease.[32]

ROBERT RUSSA MOTON

[Hampton, Va.] March 5, 1914

My dear Mr. [Oswald Garrison] Villard:

. . . It would be a good thing if you and I, who have been generally frank with each other, might talk out in absolute frankness the whole situation, as man to man and friend to friend. I am in no sense lacking in appreciation of what you are doing for the Negro and the Nation I do question seriously, sometimes, the methods of the National Association. There is no doubt that there is plenty to do and the Association has a splendid opportunity.

I was a little disturbed by the report that the Chairman of your Executive Committee was rather severe in his criticisms of Dr. Washington in Chicago, but that might not be an accurate report. I feel that Mr. Spingarn is anxious to help and I want to be fair in my judgment of him . . .

I am going to make this suggestion, that you and Mr. Fred R. Moore of the "New York Age" talk the situation out. You tell him all that is in the back of your head and let him tell you all that is in the back of his. I have no doubt but that each of you will help the other; certainly you should come to a better and more sympathetic understanding. I remember once your remarking to me that the "Age" had been generally hostile to the Association, and I am sorry this is true, but I think if you two could spend an hour talking out the situation it would be a very good thing. It has always seemed to me most unfortunate that men working for the same cause should seem to be antagonistic to the other. I don't mean, of course, that we must think or act alike, but I have sincerely wished there were more harmony among the forces that are working for the good of colored folk . . .[33]

BOOKER T. WASHINGTON

Los Angeles, March 9th, 1914

Dear Mr. Scott:

. . . One thing for your private information which will interest you. I met a group of the most prominent colored men at Mr. Owens' house last night. Most of them for the main part were those who were engaged in bringing Dr. Du Bois here some months ago. Without my referring to the subject, they volunteered the information that Du Bois, notwithstanding they had been friendly to him, had practically killed himself in this vicinity, and without any hesitation they said he would not be invited here again. It seems he made a perfect fool of himself by trying to snub everybody. So far as I can judge from what they said, his address seemed a failure. I find nobody here who has a good word for him . . .[34]

ROBERT RUSSA MOTON

Hampton, Virginia March 23, 1914

My dear Mr. [Emmett Jay] Scott:

. . . Our friend, Moore is very anxious to tell Mr. Villard some things which we think he ought to know regarding Dr. Du Bois and some others. I think, however, that it is a thankless task for accomplishing anything. The trouble is, Dr. Washington is a Leader and cannot help it, he is a born Leader, and the others are leading but they have nobody following them. Yours sincerely,

R.R. Moton[35]

WILLIAM EDWARD BURGHARDT DU BOIS

The Western trip of the chairman of the board of directors [of the NAACP] was a clarion call to arms . . . Mr. Spingarn told the people, colored and white that the time had come for organization and work. The new abolitionism has come. Its workers are in the field and its voice is heard from St. Paul to New Orleans and from sea to sea.

Already the Bourbon press of the South, abetted by colored traitors in the North, is taking notice. The Richmond *Times-Dispatch* said in its leading editorial of January 12:

"Someone has sent us a special number of a Negro monthly magazine, which appears to us to be about the most incendiary document that has passed through the mails since the anarchists' literature was barred . . ."

It is the reactionary Bourbonism of the *Times-Dispatch* and its ilk that makes a great moral battle for a new abolition absolutely necessary in the land. The editor thinks that:

"This particular magazine is of limited circulation, and is probably the organ of ambitious Negroes in New York. Its remarks, therefore, are scarcely worthy of consideration and its opinions beneath notice. But were this spirit to spread among the Negroes, we can but think how disastrous would be its workings."

The Crisis sold 32,000 copies of its January number, which is a larger circulation than the *Times-Dispatch* has. And The Crisis renews the invitation to every American, black or white: Join or die. Join the National Association for the Advancement of Colored People. Support its work, advocate its principles.

Ignore the mischievous intimation of venal colored editors that we are "fighting" Booker T. Washington. We are fighting slavery, caste and cowardice in black men and white; nothing more and nothing less.[36]

ROBERT RUSSA MOTON

Hampton, Virginia April 8, 1914

My dear Dr. Washington:

. . . I think you are absolutely right regarding the attitude of Mr. Villard and the National Association. So far as I am personally concerned, and I voice the sentiment of ninety-five percent if not ninety-nine percent of the thoughtful Negroes of this country and white people as well when I say, we have absolute faith in your judgment and in your methods of work. As I said to Mr. Villard, I am absolutely on your side, not leaning towards your side, and have always been there. I have sincerely and honestly tried to help Mr. Villard and those associated with him to do better what they are trying to do. It does seem that there are possibilities in that organization, but as it is constituted at present I don't think we can accomplish anything for them or with them and I have told Mr. Villard so . . .[37]

W.E.B. DU BOIS

New York City, April 9th 1914.

My dear Miss [Mary White] Ovington:

I have received from Miss Nerney an invitation to attend a caucus of "a few friends" at 55 Liberty Street, on Monday April thirteenth.[38] I shall be out of town on that date but even if I were here I do not think I should attend.

I feel that I recognize the meaning of the meeting and I am sure that its objects will be best attained if I am not there and I can then be frankly discussed and criticized.

The Association has come to the parting of the ways. I have used every endeavor to stave off this day as long as possible so that we might face it with a sense of responsibility and with a body of work done. It is perhaps on the whole well to fight the matter out now.

The question is whether this organization is to stand on its original radical platform or is to go that way of conservative compromise which turned the Ogden movement, the Southern Education Board and the General Education Board so completely from their original purpose.[39]

What this Association should stand for I have endeavored for three and a half years to set forth clearly and unmistakably in the Crisis. I do not mean that the exposition has been perfect or that mistakes have not been made but on the whole *Crisis* principles have been those which I conceive should be the principles of the National Association for the Advancement of Colored People.

The question now is does the Association agree with this? I do not mean complete and absolute agreement in all details but substantial agreement. If the Association agrees then the proper action would be to arrange in the plan of reorganization for me to continue as the responsible editor under the same general supervision as is provided for other officers.

In the proposed measures which you are to discuss on the thirteenth the Crisis and its editor are put under the "immediate" charge of the executive committee and absolutely barred from all real initiative. No other executive officer is thus humiliated . . .

It therefore goes without saying that I should regard the adoption of the proposed provision a vote of lack of confidence and I should immediately resign my position. Meantime, while the matter is under discussion I shall oppose the adoption of the measure before the board, before the membership and before the colored people. I shall do this, however, by honorable means. I shall stoop to no secret cabals or caucuses or seek to force snap judgment at the last moment. And I shall oppose this, I hope you will believe, for no merely personal reasons or mere stubbornness of opinion. I am sorry that the impression is widespread that I do not receive or desire any advice. It is not true . . . I think you can all understand that the insults which I receive in my life may have made me reticent but it is unfair to assume that therefore I deem my thought or way self sufficient.

I realize the forces opposed to my platform and to me personally in this organization: Mr. Villard has been frank from the beginning. He opposed my coming to the position in the first place and has systematically opposed every step I have taken since. He has told me plainly that he should not rest until I and the Crisis were "absolutely" under his control or entirely outside the organization. On the other hand, there are not in the organization two persons in closer intellectual agreement on the Negro problem than Mr. Villard and myself. It is in matters of personal relation that we disagree. Mr. Villard is not democratic. He is used to advising colored men and giving them orders and he simply cannot bring himself to work with one as an equal.

This same subtle difficulty (which is one of the curious and almost unconscious developments of the race problem) has come in the Association in other ways. In most organizations of this kind the problem has frankly been given up as insoluble and usually an entire force of one race is hired. It has been my dream to make this organization an exception and I have tried desperately and have failed. Every conceivable effort, conscious, half-conscious, unconscious, has been made in the last three and a half years to force me into a position of subordination to some other official. I have resisted not out of a stubborn desire to dominate, as some think, but because I knew that there was no argument on experience or efficiency that ought in reason to force me to be the secretary's assistant or the chairman's secretary . . . This struggle has been all the more unpleasant because my associates have all the time been working so wholeheartedly and effectively for the very things which lie so near my heart. It is an enormously complicated situation and the temptation to submit to the seemingly inevitable is, I confess, strong. And yet, that very submission stands in my mind as so fundamental a part of the absolutely essential problem of the Negro in the modern world that I cannot bring myself to acquiese. If in this Association white and black folk cannot work together as equals; if this Association is unable to treat its black officials with the same lease of power as white, can we fight a successful battle against race prejudice in the world?

. . . I am writing you quite frankly, Miss Ovington, because you are one of the few persons whom I call Friend. I wish you to read this entire letter to the caucus, unless, of course, you deem it quite unnecessary . . .

Very sincerely yours,
W.E.B. Du Bois[40]

MARY WHITE OVINGTON

Brooklyn, N.Y., April 11, 1914.

My dear Dr Du Bois,

Your letter comes on the morning of my birthday and makes me feel like voicing the praise in Ecclesiastes . . .

I have thought for some time that there was something the matter with the Crisis from the viewpoint of its white readers. It seemed to me monotonous, and I proposed to you some rather foolish little things that might be introduced that would have made little difference. But while I was away, and in a country where two races of such different traditions lived together, I thought the Crisis matter out—it seemed to me somewhat more clearly. This is my conclusion: *The magazine is the organ of two races, but its psychology is the psychology of the colored race.*

Now perhaps you will get at my point more clearly if you think of the magazine as edited solely by a white man, and a man who has stood always for the things for which our Association has stood since it printed its first platform. Don't you think that such a man might sometimes offend his colored readers, and be wholly unconscious of it? He might, for instance, patronize a little, he might dictate too much, he might rub his readers the wrong way, and yet he would feel that he was only speaking the truth, and that if he said anything else he would be compromising with his conscience. He would be absolutely honorable and yet he would offend.

Now no colored man who stood squarely and unswervingly on our platform can come to the Crisis and edit it and not sometimes make what I should call psychological failures with our white readers. I believe you have made comparatively few, and I think we have usually passed them by as comparatively unimportant; but as our organization grows in power and authority, it must have increasingly careful oversight of its publications and of its speakers. And just as Mr Villard, let us say, in his writing sometimes offends the colored people by giving them orders; so sometimes you offend the white people by calling them hogs, by saying that they are reactionary heathen, by giving them the feeling that they are insulting you, when they have no insult in their heart.

I have thought about this a great deal; and wondered what made you write as you sometimes did, and I came to the conclusion that it was because you had before you a colored audience. Now no one can be more persuasive than you before a white audience, or can write more persuasively to white people. But when you edit the Crisis that white audience is sometimes forgotten and its feelings are badly hurt, or feelings of resentment are aroused. And the white audience to which I allude is the white audience which stands just as squarely on our platform as your colored audience does—sometimes, I think, more squarely.

Now what is the wisest thing for us to do?

Don't we need first to face the issue squarely? Is this a work for colored and white people to do together, or is it a work of revolution for the colored people only? Should we preach race consciousness just as the socialist preaches class consciousness, and should we teach the black man to regard every white man as his enemy except he who repudiates his race? This is a question for each one to answer personally, but unquestionably the Association, through its very organization, has answered it negatively. And if our work, then, is for white and colored, you must work out how we are to get common representation on the Crisis. After reading your letter I think it is something for you to tackle . . .

As to our being reactionary—I don't think we are nearly as reactionary as when we started. Why, think, we had to fight to keep B.T.W. off the committee in those days! We may have grown to believe that as an organization we must say the right word at the right time, that we cannot each one be a voice in the wilderness crying out what ever comes into our head without regard to what is happening. Anarchism is jolly, and we are all anarchists at heart, but when we get into an organization, whether it is a State or an N.A.A.C.P., we have to consider each the other's work . . .

It's always been difficult for me to see why you didn't want a Crisis committee that should take much of the detail off your shoulders. I am angered when ever I think of it—that the one man of genius in our company should deliberately tie himself down to a mass of detail, and from a poet become a preacher—and that most awful type of preacher, an *editor*, laying down the law every month!

. . . Yours,
Mary W. Ovington.[41]

CAMILIUS G. KIDDER *(Kidder was a New York lawyer and scholar of constitutional law.)*

Orange, New Jersey, April 9,1914.

Dear Sir:

If your engagements permit, will you not kindly tell me in what respect Robert C. Ogden fell short with regard to the colored race, as the "Crisis" article intimates.[42]

I did not know him personally, but somehow had an entirely different notion.

Yours very truly
C. [Camilius] G. Kidder[43]

W.E.B. DU BOIS

New York April 20, 1914.

My dear Sir [C.G. Kidder]:

As I said in my notice of Mr. Ogden, it is difficult to write of him and not give a false impression.

He was a good man and did good. At the same time he was a man without broad vision and without a deep knowledge of human nature. When therefore, he was almost accidentally set to the unravelling of one of the most difficult of human problems it is small wonder that he fell short, and yet he made the same mistake that most Americans make. They have made up their minds that it is impossible for colored people to be human and free in the same sense as the citizens of modern white countries. If this were simply a belief no great harm would be done, but immediately such people start out to make their belief come true. They seek to educate colored children as inferiors, they lay out inferior careers for colored men, they open up limited opportunity for colored youth and when colored folk chafe under these limitations they regard them as fighting against fate. This, in my opinion, was Mr. Ogden's essential attitude.

I knew him personally and have been treated with great kindness by him, but I have learned that he was much put out and intensely dissatisfied by my general attitude of insistence of equality of opportunity for American Negroes.

As a result of his general attitude the southern point of view on the Negro problem has become widely popular in the North and persons can at once regard themselves as friends of the Negro and yet defend laws which degrade Negro women, defend the "Jim-Crow" car laws, defend disfranchisement and caste.

I regard all this as exceedingly unfortunate and I regard Mr. Ogden as in part to blame for it.

Very sincerely yours,
W.E.B. Du Bois[44]

BOOKER T. WASHINGTON

Tuskegee Institute, Alabama April 27, 1914

Dear Sir [M. Gatewood Milligan, Jr.]:[45] . . . I do not advocate the inter-marriage of the races nor do I know of any colored man who does. I noticed recently in an article in the Survey that Dr. W.E.B. Du Bois, of the National Association for the Protection of Colored People, declared that Negroes and white persons should have the right to marry if they wanted to. But I am sure that he would never think of urging interracial marriage. He knows as does every one else who has had experience in these matters that, where such marriages have occurred the parties have generally met with ostracism from both races.

As you know we are a mixed race in this country. Whenever the black man intermingles his blood with that of any other race the result is always a Negro, never a whiteman, Indian or any other sort of man . . .[46]

MELVIN JACK CHISUM

Baltimore, Md. May 26th, 1914

My dear Dr Washington: . . . The Afro-American is a great supporter of the N.A.A.C.P., I am running a paper in Baltimore . . .

I am sending you the front and editorial pages of both the Colored Man & the Afro-American, please observe the two. If you read the Colored Man then I am satisfied for then you know how religiously I am hewing to the Tuskegee line . . .[47]

BOOKER T. WASHINGTON

[Tuskegee, Ala.] May 27th, 1914

Dear Mr. [Oswald Garrison] Villard: . . . For sometime a number of us have been trying to find an effective way to relieve the unsatisfactory condition of things as far as the schools of the South are concerned . . .

In my opinion it would be a hazardous experiment and a waste of money for such a matter to be put in the hands of anybody except people who are actually acquainted with conditions in the South by reason of actual contact with the schools and their teachers . . .

First of all . . . as a basis for any intelligent action, we must have facts, it seems to me, with reference to the character of the schools, the kind of work they are doing, their relation to the population, etc. We ought to know, for example, to what extent college work is being done, the amount of technical, industrial and agricultural work being done, etc., and such information as will afford a basis for intelligent suggestion and action.

One of the greatest needs of the South just now is more and better medical schools. It is becoming increasingly difficult for young colored men to get a medical education in the Northern institutions. We have only one school in the South that is doing anything like first-class work in the direction of training physicians . . .

Finally, I must repeat what I have said before, that I do not believe that it is the best thing for education in the South to have these smaller schools coupled up with the ideas and activities of the Association for the Advancement of Colored People. I think there is a line of work needed to be done in the South just now that can best be done separate from that organization. I also think there is a line of work needed to be done in the North and elsewhere that can best be separated from the educational work in the South for colored people. Yours very truly,

Booker T. Washington[48]

OSWALD GARRISON VILLARD

New York June 3, 1914

Dear Dr. Washington: I wrote you then [in May] that the National Association for the Advancement of Colored People had nothing to do with the new Association of Rural and Industrial Schools;[49] it is not in the slightest degree "coupled up with the ideas and activities of the

National Association for the Advancement of Colored People"—no more today than when I wrote you a year ago, in fact less so. The only connection that there has ever been was that the idea originated with me and for the first two meetings the National Association extended the hospitality of its rooms . . . Is it too much to hope that you will now dismiss this idea from your mind and take my word for it that there is absolutely no connection between the two?

Oswald Garrison Villard[50]

RALPH WALDO TYLER

Washington, D.C. June 3rd., 1914

Dear Doctor [Washington]: Just a note to advise you that "we" can expect little from The Bee, in the way of publicity, for the reason that Roscoe Bruce has it subsidized, as has also the N.A.A.C.P. people The Sun, the new publication here. All "our friends" joined and contributed financially to the N.A.A.C.P., the anti organization, although it was very hard to get them to contribute financially to any movement to conserve your interests. If any one had told me that "our" friends here would join the army of ingrates I would not have believed it . . . The Washington Negro knows neither gratitude or honor, and he quickly forgets the hand that fed him, and just as quickly burns the bridge that carried him over, and I include all "our friends" in this, with the one exception of McKinlay.[51] McK. did join and contribute to the N.A.A.C.P., but he was thoughtless as to its real purpose, and largely influenced by his relatives, the Grimke brothers.

Respectfully,
Ralph W Tyler[52]

W.E.B. DU BOIS

Professor John M. Mecklin of the University of Pittsburgh has written a book of 273 pages on "Democracy and Race Friction."[53]

So far as the race problem is concerned, the book is symptomatic of the average of our national thought and is of scientific value only as it shows how far science dares go to-day in its anti-Negro campaign . . .

"The militant race philosophy preached by a certain group of Negro writers and thinkers is not one that the sincere friend of the Negro would like to see him adopt (p. 156)."

However, all is not dark. Mr. Washington's philosophy of submission is at hand and there lies the way of salvation . . .

And, therefore, we have a chapter which revels in the various shortcomings of colored men; their lack of unity in a certain Lincoln Emancipation Celebration; their lack of pride, and particularly their sex immorality. This, the author returns to again and again with a peculiar smacking of lips . . .[54]

WILLIAM COLFAX GRAVES *(Graves was Julius Rosenwald's secretary.)*[55]

Chicago September 29, 1914

Dear Dr. Washington: Mr. Rosenwald, as a member of the Advisory Committee of the National Association for the Advancement of Colored People, has been asked to make suggestions as to the possible candidates for the first award of the Spingarn Medal. This medal, as no doubt you are aware, is offered by Dr. J.E. Spingarn annually "to be awarded for the highest or noblest achievement by an American Negro during the preceding year" upon certain terms and conditions. It is a gold medal not costing more than $100.00. Mr. Rosenwald would very much appreciate your assistance in recommendations to this Committee. Will you, at your convenience, write him what Colored man or what Colored woman, or several of them, who might be considered candidates for the award?

Thanking you, I am Very sincerely yours,
William C. Graves[56]

TIMOTHY THOMAS FORTUNE

Washington, D.C. Oct. 14, 1914

Dear Mr. [Emmett Jay] Scott:

. . . We are also using in the current issue a splendid article by Prof. Charles H. Moore backing up my editorial position as to what Dr. Washington meant in the quotation attributed to him, and enlarging on the splendid work Dr. Washington has done for the race.

I am surprised to find Washington a hot bed of Association for the Advancement of Colored People sentiment, and opposition to Dr. Washington, which is generally ascribed in large part to [William Calvin] Chase's vile and vacillating support of Dr. Washington and his policies.[57] It would serve us all better if Chase [editor of the *Washington Bee*] were an out and out opponent of Dr. Washington . . .[58]

GEORGE CLEVELAND HALL *(Hall was a prominent Chicago physician and the founder of the Cook County Physicians Association.)*[59]

Chicago Jan 6 [1915]

My Dear Dr. Washington . . .

I have had lots of fun with Mr. "Woodrow" Trotter my new name for him. He gave me this clipping and said that for once you two were agreeing upon the same thing and he wished it could continue. I told him it could if he could see his way clear to stop his bitter personal attacks upon you—I told him that I thought he was crazy upon the subject and that he was hurting not only himself, but everything he touched by his spirit of vilification. When he left me he said that he hoped that through the immigrations bill all factions might learn to stand on a common platform—He thought what a fine thing it would be for You, Du Boise & Himself to appear in Washington arm in arm, fighting against the measure, he was willing to agree to an Armistice until the fight was won, at least . . . Never saw a Man so hungry for money and cheap notoriety—

G G Hall[60]

W.E.B. DU BOIS

. . . William H. Holtzclaw's *The Black Man's Burden* is a most interesting book.[61] Its evident frankness and honesty are of the most compelling character and the reader will scarcely put it down without finishing at least the first fourteen chapters. Mr. Holtzclaw tells frankly a gripping story of poverty and effort beginning with "the windowless house in which I first saw the light,—the light that scantily streamed through the cracks in the wall. It was a little cabin fourteen feet by sixteen feet made of split pine with only dirt for a floor." He tells how the family was crushed by the landlord with charges of twenty-five to two hundred per cent on the food and clothes "advanced;" how his mother spent all her time cooking for the "white folks" and how in the morning she left a large pan on the dirt floor in the middle of the cabin with the children's breakfast . . .

Mr. Holtzclaw was trained at Tuskegee and he has a frank and beautiful worship for Mr. Washington. After graduating he and his wife founded a school in darkest Mississippi and there after many years they have built up Utica Institute.

It is a story of unselfish effort and good result which one hesitates to criticize at all. There comes, however, the shadow of a wish that the author had refrained from quoting some commendations of his work but after all there is a certain honesty in that. One other thing, however, is more important. Mr. Holtzclaw continually speaks of the almost frantic fear of the poor, ignorant rural Negroes for the "white man" and he almost intimates that he does not know just why this fear exists. This is not fair to his readers even if it does protect his institute. Mr. Holtzclaw knows perfectly well why Mississippi Negroes are afraid of Mississippi white men . . .[62]

EMMETT JAY SCOTT AND LYMAN BEECHER STOWE

Just fifteen years [after the founding of the Negro National Business League], in August, 1915, Booker Washington presided over the last session of the league held during his lifetime. This meeting also was held in Boston. There attended it seven hundred delegates from thirty different States. Mr. Washington in his annual address as president summed up what had been accomplished by the race during the fifteen-year interval and projected what they should strive for in the future. He also took occasion publicly to thank his foremost colleagues in developing the work of the league, particularly Mr. Scott, the secretary of the league. Undoubtedly he fully realized that it was his farewell meeting. He practically collapsed before the sessions were over. In less than three months he was dead.

Among other things he said in this speech:[63]

BOOKER T. WASHINGTON

With our race, as it has been and always will be with all races, without economic and business foundation, it is hardly possible to have educational and religious growth or political freedom.

We can learn some mighty serious lessons just now from conditions in Liberia and Hayti. For years, both in Liberia and Hayti, literary education and politics have been emphasized, but while doing this the people have failed to apply themselves to the development of the soil, mines, and forests. The result is that, from an economic point of view, those two republics have become dependent upon other nations and races. In both republics the control of finances is in the hands of other nations, this being true notwithstanding the fact that the two countries have natural resources greater than other countries similar in size. . . . Mere abstract, unused education means little for a race or individual. An ounce of application is worth a ton of abstraction. We must not be afraid to pay the price of success in business—the price of sleepless nights, the price of toil when others rest, the price of planning to-day for to-morrow, this year for next year. If some one else endures the hardships, does the thinking, and pays the salaries, some one else will reap the harvest and enjoy the reward . . .

No matter how poor you are, how black you are, or how obscure your present work and position, I want each one to remember that there is a chance for him, and the more difficulties he has to overcome the greater will be his success.[64]

EMMETT JAY SCOTT AND LYMAN BEECHER STOWE

Perhaps the most significant speech at this conference, next to that of Booker T. Washington, was that of William Henry Lewis who is probably the foremost lawyer of the Negro race in America. Mr. Lewis is a graduate of Harvard where he distinguished himself on the foot-ball field as well as in the classroom. After graduation from the Harvard Law School he served with distinction in the Massachusetts Legislature, was appointed Assistant United States District Attorney for the Boston district by President Roosevelt, and became Assistant Attorney-General of the United States under President Taft.

In opening his speech Mr. Lewis said:[65]

WILLIAM H. LEWIS

Booker Washington has always been from fifteen to twenty years ahead of any other leader of his race. . . . While most of us were ago-nizing over the Negro's relation to the State and his political fortunes, Booker Washington saw that there was a great economic empire that needed to be conquered. He saw an emancipated race chained to the soil by the Mortgage Crop System, and other devices, and he said, 'You must own your own land, you must own your own farms'—and forth-with there was a second emancipation. He saw the industrial trades and skilled labor pass from our race into other hands. He said, 'The hands as well as the heads must be educated,' and forthwith the educational system of America was revolutionized. He saw the money earned by the hard toil of black men passing into other men's pockets. He said, 'The only way to save this money is to go into business—sell as well as buy.' He saw that if the colored race was to become economically self-sufficient, it must engage in every form of human activity. Himself a successful business man as shown by Tuskegee's millions, he has led his race to economic freedom.[66]

EMMETT JAY SCOTT AND LYMAN BEECHER STOWE

Such a tribute from one of the most rarely and genuinely talented members of "The Talented Tenth" was indeed a triumph for Booker T. Washington and his policies. In fact, it may fairly be said that this event marked the end of the honest opposition from this element of the Negro race—the end of the honest opposition of a group or section of the race in distinction from the of course inevitable opposition of individuals here and there.[67]

NOTES

1. Villard wrote Washington enclosing an invitation to an NAACP meeting of "heads of all industrial or agricultural schools for colored youth patterned after Tuskegee and Hampton." Washington, 1983, vol. 12, 128.

2. Villard tried again in March and again was turned down.

3. Washington, 1983, vol. 12, 127.

4. Ibid., 144–145.

5. See Chapter 9, note 46.

6. In response, Washington replied, "I am not at all surprised to note what you write, because it is exactly in line with what I have heard from other sources in the general content of his lectures on 'The History of the Negro Race.'" Washington, 1983, vol. 12, 153–154.

7. Villard's letter asked Moton to attend because, "Dr. Washington has declined for the cowardly reason that the meeting is being held in the rooms of the National Association. To meet that objection we have hired a gymnasium outside of our quarters." Ibid., 158.

8. Ibid.

9. John J. Smallwood was the leader of the Temperance Industrial and Collegiate Institute in Claremond, Virginia. See Drew, 2010.

10. Washington, 1983, vol. 12, 159–160.

11. John Robert Edward Lee was Tuskegee's Director of Academics, and later served as president of Florida A&M. Neyland, 1962, 75–78. For

more on Park and his relationship with Tuskegee and Washington, see Morris, 2015.

12. Washington, 1983, vol. 12, 164–166.

13. Henry Lincoln Johnson was a Republican lawyer who served as Recorder of Deeds for Washington, D.C. He was also the husband of the poet Georgia Douglas Johnson. See Hull, 1987.

14. Washington, 1983, vol. 12, 258–259.

15. Ibid., 279.

16. Ralph Waldo Tyler. See Chapter 14, note 46.

17. Edward Warren aided James H. Anderson in founding the New York *Amsterdam News* in 1909. Washington, 1983, vol. 12, 299. See Chapter 17, note 5.

18. James Dickson Carr was the first black graduate of Rutgers University. He was a lawyer and, later, an assistant district attorney for New York City. *New York Times*, 3 October 1899, 1.

19. Washington, 1983, vol. 12, 297–299.

20. Walton would work for several papers as a journalist and would ultimately migrate to politics and serve as a diplomat to Liberia. See Lester Walton Papers, Sc MG 183, Schomburg Center for Research in Black Culture, The New York Public Library, New York, New York.

21. See Chapter 12, note 17.

22. Washington, 1983, vol. 12, 332–334.

23. See Chapter 17, note 5.

24. Washington, 1983, vol. 12, 335–336.

25. The reference to "the Doctor" here refers to Washington.

26. Washington, 1983, vol. 12, 401–403.

27. Ibid., 404–405.

28. Nathan Francis Mossell was a Philadelphia physician, the first black medical school graduate from the University of Pennsylvania. In 1895, he cofounded the Frederick Douglass Memorial Hospital and Training School. Nathan Francis Mossell Papers, 1873–1983, UPT 50 M913, University Archives and Records Center, University of Pennsylvania, Philadelphia, Pennsylvania.

29. Ibid., 417.

30. Harvard College, Class of 1907: Secretary's Fourth Report, 1917, 174.

31. Washington, 1983, vol. 12, 447–448.

32. Washington, 1981, vol. 10, 254–255. See also Ross, 1972.

33. Washington, 1983, vol. 12, 468–470.

34. Washington wrote to Scott a few days later, "I think if we wanted to get rid of Du Bois as an influence, the best way would be to send him through the country and let the people meet him." Ibid., 470–471.

35. Ibid., 486.

36. Du Bois, March 1914, 238–239.

37. Washington, 1984, vol. 13, 6–8.

38. Mary Childs Nerney was the executive secretary of the NAACP from 1912 to 1916. Stutman, 2008.

39. The Ogden Movement, named for Robert C. Ogden—a trustee of Hampton and Tuskegee—was an effort to reform Southern education that became increasingly more conservative and Washingtonian in its outlook. Du Bois, 1973, 189. See also Harlan, 1957, 189–202.

40. Du Bois, 1973, 188–191.

41. Ibid., 191–193.

42. When Robert Ogden died in August 1913, Du Bois wrote critically of his career and educational thinking, prompting this letter and Du Bois's response. Ibid., 193. See also "Men of the Month," April 1914, 274–275.

43. *New York Times,* 26 October 1894, 1; and Du Bois, 1973, 194.

44. Du Bois, 1972, vol. 1, 194.

45. M. Gatewood Milligan, Jr., was a Presbyterian minister based in Colorado. *Minutes of the General Assembly of the Presbyterian Church in the United States of America,* 1915, 516.

46. Washington, 1984, 11.

47. Ibid., 35–36.

48. Ibid., 36–38.

49. The Association of Rural and Industrial Schools was formed to guide northern philanthropists in giving to southern secondary schools, with an eye to ensuring that the education provided was a full liberal arts education. Washington rightly interpreted it as a threat to his own educational mission. *New York Times,* 26 March 1914, 20.

50. Washington, 1984, vol. 13, 41–42.

51. Chapter 7, note 12.

52. Washington, 1984, vol. 13, 43.

53. Mecklin, 1914.

54. "Another Study in Black," July 1914, 410–414.

55. "Life Memberships," May 1924, 3–4.

56. Washington, 1984, vol. 13, 137.

57. See Chapter 3, note 11.

58. Washington, 1984, vol. 13, 145–146.

59. Lawlah, 1954, 207–210.

60. Washington, 1984, vol. 13, 216–217.

61. Holtzclaw, 1915.

62. Du Bois, September 1915, 251–252.

63. Scott and Stowe, 1916, 189–190.

64. Ibid., 190–192.

65. Ibid., 192.

66. Ibid., 192–193.

67. Ibid., 194.

19

The Death of Washington

Washington's paranoia, as evinced by the work of the Tuskegee Machine, would only conclude with the leader's death in 1915. That death also put the Du Bois–Washington conversation back into mainstream white media, as pundits of all races and political positions sought to come to conclusions about the complicated life and legacy of an enigmatic leader who fought for black rights by praising the white South. Du Bois himself was flummoxed by the passing, arguing in a widely criticized obituary (of sorts) that Washington was "the greatest Negro leader since Frederick Douglass, and the most distinguished man, white or black, who has come out of the South since the Civil War." At the same time, he admitted, "there can be no doubt of Mr. Washington's mistakes and short comings." The bulk of the country was less concerned with shortcomings in the wake of the leader's passing, and thus part of the celebration of Washington became the denigration of Du Bois.

CRISIS

With simple ceremonies and the singing of Negro folk songs Booker T. Washington was buried at Tuskegee Institute. Many distinguished persons, white and black, were present. Memorial meetings for Mr. Washington have been held throughout the United States and in Canada.[1]

EMMETT JAY SCOTT AND LYMAN BEECHER STOWE

In the fully developed man of the last decade of his life we find the same traits and qualities which began to show themselves in those early years of constant struggle and frequent privation. There is the same intense mental and physical activity; the same readiness to fight against any odds in a good cause; the same modesty, frankness, open-mindedness, and passion for service.

One of the many illustrations of this intense activity was shown in a trip he made to Atlanta, Ga., three or four years before he died. Even at this time his strength had begun to wane. In accordance with his unfailing practice he got up at six o'clock in the morning, and after visiting his poultry and his beloved pigs, mounted his horse and rode over farms and grounds inspecting crops and buildings and what-not until eight o'clock, when he went to his office and attacked his huge morning's mail. After dictating for an hour or more he left his office just in time to catch a train which brought him to Atlanta at two o'clock in the afternoon. At the station he shook hands with four hundred people who had gathered to meet him. As he went along the streets to the Government Building he shook hands with many others who recognized him in passing. At the Government Building he shook hands with another large group assembled there to meet him. After the dinner tendered him by some of the leading individuals and associations among the Negroes of the city he posed for his photograph with a group of those at the dinner. He then made a tour of the city by motor, during which he visited three or four schools for Negroes and at each made a half-hour speech into which, as always, he threw all the force and energy there was in him.

After supper that evening he addressed twelve hundred people in the Auditorium Armory, speaking for an hour and a half. From the armory he went to a banquet given in his honor where he gave a twenty-minute talk. He did not get to bed until one o'clock. Four hours later he took a return train which brought him back to the school by ten-thirty. He went at once to his office and to work, working until late in the afternoon when he called for his horse and took his usual ride before supper. After supper he presided at a meeting of the Executive Council and after the Council meeting he attended the Chapel exercises. After these exercises were over at ten o'clock he made an inspection on foot of various parts of the buildings and grounds before going to bed. By just such excessive overwork did he constantly undermine and finally break down his almost superhuman strength and powers of endurance.

This he did with an obstinate persistence in spite of wise and increasingly urgent warnings from physicians, friends, and associates. Where his own health was concerned he obdurately refused to listen to reason. It would almost seem as though he had deliberately chosen to put forth herculean efforts until he dropped from sheer exhaustion rather than to work with moderation for a longer span of life.

Booker Washington was a man who thought, lived, and acted on a very high plane. He was, in other words, an idealist, but unlike too many idealists he was sternly practical. His mind worked with the rapidity of flashes of lightning, particularly when he was aroused. This led him at times to feel and show impatience in dealing with slower-minded people, particularly his subordinates. He was often stirred to righteous indignation by injustice, but always kept his temper under control. He had a lucid mind which reasoned from cause to effect with machine-like accuracy. His intuitions were amazingly keen and accurate. In other words, his subconscious reasoning powers were very highly developed. Consequently his judgments of men and events were almost infallible. Although practically devoid of personal vanity, he was a very proud and independent man, and one who could not brook dictation from any one or bear to be under obligation to any one. He had the tenacity of a bulldog. His capacity for incessant work and his unswerving pursuit of a purpose once formed, were a constant marvel to those who surrounded him. While he was without conceit or vanity he had almost unlimited self-confidence. While it cannot be said that he overrated his own abilities, neither can it be said that he underrated them. His sympathies were easily aroused and he was abnormally sensitive, but he never allowed his emotions to get the better of his judgment. He forgave easily and always tried to find excuses for people who wronged, insulted, or injured him. In repartee he could hold his own with any one and enjoyed nothing more than a duel of wits either with an individual or an audience . . .

Although apparently indifferent to the treatment he received from those about him Booker Washington was in reality, as has been said, unusually sensitive. No matter what his engagements he always insisted upon being at home with his wife and children on Thanksgiving Day and on Christmas. One Christmas, about ten years ago, it so happened that no Christmas presents were provided for him. The children gave presents to one another and to their mother and she to them, but through oversight there were no presents for Mr. Washington.

Mrs. Washington says that after the presents had been opened her husband drew her aside and said in broken tones: "Maggie, they've not given me a single Christmas present!" From then on Mrs. Washington saw to it that the children remembered their father at Christmas . . .

Mr. Washington's strength of will and determination were never better shown than in the closing hours of his life. When he was told by his doctors at St. Luke's Hospital, New York, whither he had been taken by the New York trustees of the Institute after his final collapse, that he had but a few hours to live, he insisted upon starting for home at once. His physicians expostulated and warned him that in his condition he could not reasonably expect to survive the journey. He insisted that he must go and be true to his oft-repeated assertion, "I was born in the South, I have lived and labored in the South, and I expect to die and be buried in the South." This remark, when sent out in the Associated Press dispatches announcing his death, touched the South as nothing else could have. No Negro was ever eulogized in the Southern press as he was . . .

In this condition, then, he set out upon the long journey from New York to Tuskegee . . . And when finally he reached Chehaw, the little station five miles from Tuskegee, he was fairly trembling with eager expectancy. As we have said, he reached Tuskegee apparently stronger than when he left New York and strong enough to enjoy the final triumph of his indomitable will over his overworked and weakened body. The next morning, November 14, 1915, he was dead.[2]

WILLIAM EDWARD BURGHARDT DU BOIS

The death of Mr. Washington marks an epoch in the history of America. He was the greatest Negro leader since Frederick Douglass, and the most distinguished man, white or black, who has come out of the South since the Civil War. His fame was international and his influence far-reaching. Of the good that he accomplished there can be no doubt: he directed the attention of the Negro race in America to the pressing necessity of economic development; he emphasized technical education and he did much to pave the way for an understanding between the white and darker races.

On the other hand there can be no doubt of Mr. Washington's mistakes and short comings: he never adequately grasped the growing bond of politics and industry; he did not understand the deeper foundations of human training and his basis of better understanding between white and black was founded on caste.

We may then generously and with deep earnestness lay on the grave of Booker T. Washington testimony of our thankfulness for his undoubted help in the accumulation of Negro land and property, his establishment of Tuskegee and spreading of industrial education and his compelling of the white south to at least think of the Negro as a possible man.

On the other hand, in stern justice, we must lay on the soul of this man, a heavy responsibility for the consummation of Negro disfranchisement, the decline of the Negro college and public school and the firmer establishment of color caste in this land.

What is done is done. This is no fit time for recrimination or complaint. Gravely and with bowed head let us receive what this great figure gave of good, silently rejecting all else. Firmly and unfalteringly let the Negro race in America, in bleeding Hayti and throughout the world close ranks and march steadily on, determined as never before to work and save and endure, but never to swerve from their great goal: the right to vote, the right to know, and the right to stand as men among men throughout the world.

It is rumored that Mr. Washington's successor at Tuskegee will be Robert Russa Moton, Commandant of Cadets at Hampton. If this proves true Major Moton will enter on his new duties with the sympathy and good will of his many friends both black and white.[3]

CRISIS

BOOKER T. WASHINGTON
The Northern Press

"Dr. Washington has often been called the leader and the representative of the Negro race in the Republic. He was a leader in a qualified sense, since he devoted his life to directing the Negroes in what he believed to be the path of progress. But he was far from being their acknowledged leader. On the contrary, very many of them, and these among the more intellectual, did not share his ideas or accept his policy. Besides these, there was a multitude of the more ignorant who were quite unable to understand either his motives or his methods, who thought him timid, and even treacherous, to the race, as to some of whose wrongs he was, of set purpose and deliberately silent . . ."—*Times*, New York City.

"Booker T. Washington was a great man by every account and along many lines—the leader of the Negro race throughout the world; a citizen of America, who had promoted his country's greatness by raising toward fitness for full citizenship and economic independence a people just emerged from slavery; a man whose influence was inspiring and helpful to the whole country. That a man born a slave, turned out upon the world when a child as an outcast, forced to gain his early education, a book in his hand at night while working as a boy in a coal mine, should accomplish what Washington did and reach the eminence he attained, is in itself a proof of the man's personal greatness. But the more cogent proof is found in the sum of achievement and the impulse for future progress which he has left behind. Tuskegee and its methods and ideals have affected the whole scheme and method of industrial education in this country . . .

"Booker Washington came, to some extent, into conflict with certain of the abler men of his own race, who thought that he showed too much humility—that he submitted too willingly to the suppression of the Negro vote in the southern states, and, by emphasizing the industrial side of the education that he supplied, consented to the relegation of his race to an inferior position forever. There are some colored people today who believe that Washington helped to condemn their race to a new slavery. The answer to this charge is that the race which rises from slavery can rise only by means of economic improvement or by revolution . . . Booker Washington knew that well, and proved his greatness by a life of consistent devotion to the ideal."—*Evening Transcript*, Boston, Mass.

"In Booker Washington the country loses not only a leader, but one who was in his person a real triumph of democracy . . . He was not the standard-bearer of a united race. It is a rare educational leader who does not compromise on some questions, and in his peculiarly trying position, where a single false step might mean the ruining of his work— even the burning of his school—Dr. Washington did not speak out on the things which the intellectual men of the race deemed of far greater moment than bricks and mortar, industrial education, or business leagues—the matter of their social and political liberties. He was silent by choice in the face of many a crying wrong and bitter injustice, and more and more colored men came to resent it . . ."—*Evening Post*, New York City.

"Dr. Booker T. Washington's work among the members of his race was based on the belief that the Negro would win social and political advancement only after he had achieved economic independence and stability . . . This policy brought Dr. Washington into conflict with many other leaders of the Negroes, but he maintained it from the beginning of his work in Tuskegee. He was not less concerned with the progress of the blacks in the United States than were those with whom he could not agree as to methods; their dispute was over the means to be used, not the end to be sought. His belief was supported by the intelligent judgment of thousands of citizens who saw in Tuskegee a possible instrument for the solution of a pressing problem."—*Sun*, New York City.

"The future is brighter because Booker Washington lived. It is brighter because he was able to penetrate the encircling blackness with a vision that brought him confidence and the will to conquer. His never failing optimism through forty years of contact with the least promising condition in America could not die with him. That personal conviction of final success for his race, in harmony even with the 'white man's civilization,' the more easily dominates other minds because he had held it so tenaciously . . ."—*Republican*, Springfield, Mass . . .

"Everything about the black man's past goes to show that, until the blight of slavery was put upon him by peoples who had a better running start toward power, his history was honorable, though, because of climatic conditions, it did not follow the lines of the northern races. The colored man in America, with the help of such institutions as Tuskegee, has shown himself capable of advancement, and the advancement has largely been accomplished through efforts of men like Washington, Du Bois and others of the race."—*Press*, New York, and Washington (D.C.) *Times*.

"Dr. Washington was a wiser leader than those impetuous souls who demanded for the Negro at once every political right and cultural opportunity. The Negro is on the soil. He is in the South. His surest, shortest road to an assured road is efficiency. Dr. Washington was farseeing in his desire to work in harmony with white men of his section. It is to the credit of the whites that they were so ready to work with him."—*World*, New York City.

"The death of Booker T. Washington should recall every square-toed American citizen to the fact that, sooner or later, in the North, in New England and in Massachusetts, we must face manfully, and in justice to both races and to the cause of humanity, a problem which we have been cruelly and cowardly dodging . . ."—*Traveler and Evening Herald*, Boston, Mass.

"To wage a militant campaign for the rights of the Negro, as Mr. Du Bois is doing, appeals to the sympathies. But we believe that the verdict of time will give to Dr. Washington the palm for the greater accomplishment in seeking conciliation rather than the deepening of hatreds, in bearing wrongs with infinite patience instead of breaking out in revolt against them, and in making his people intrinsically worthy of the things denied them."—*Evening Post*, Chicago, Ill.

"He held that the present duty of all Negroes is to improve their economic position by thrift and industry and build up a reputation as law-abiding citizens, leaving political problems to be settled later. For this he was bitterly attacked by the more impatient leaders of his own race; but the chances are heavy that the cool judgment of Washington will be found a better guide than the impassioned eloquence of Du Bois."—*Evening Journal*, Chicago, Ill.

"Estimated in gross, it may be that the influence of this son of a slave woman and an unknown father has been the greatest of all American forces for progress in our generation. The computation is beyond finite minds. Only the Supreme Judge can know the answer to the question. But at least we mortals can bid farewell to the departed man with deep respect and an acknowledgement of his to us unmeasurable value to our time."—*Free Press*, Detroit, Mich . . .

The Copperhead Press

". . . The temptation to those interested in benefiting the Negro was to scold the whites for their refusal to recognize him. Race pride protested against Jim Crow cars, segregation in theatres, restrictions in residence.

"This is precisely the kind of work Dr. Washington did not do. He seldom scolded the whites, and took his rebuffs with philosophy. Instead of calling upon the colored men to assert their rights, he set out to eradicate those Negro characteristics which made it impossible for Negroes to achieve rights."—*Tribune*, Chicago, Ill.

"Booker Washington was a black, thick-lipped, ungainly specimen, born in slavery without a knowledge of his father or his birth date. That is the picture of a real Negro. . . .

"He plodded along, pulling his race with him, looking after the needs of the most lowly in a moral and intellectual way, demonstrating to the Negro that he could never be anything else but a Negro, that there was really no place worthy his effort in the political life of this nation to which he could reasonably aspire as a race for generations to come."—*Record*, Long Branch, N.J.

The South

"The death of Booker T. Washington is a national misfortune, for his life was a national benefaction. He stood head and shoulders above any man of his race, and his towering figure for more than a generation was as a pillar of fire to light his people out of the darkness of ignorance, indolence and error. He was the Negro's wisest, bravest teacher and leader. He saw, as none more clearly, the black man's shortcomings and possibilities, his need and his hope. He devoted his life—every day of it, every energy of it—to bringing the descendants of the slaves to see these things as he saw them, to setting their feet upon the one path that opens their way to real freedom, material independence, respected and self-respecting citizenship . . ."—Louisville (Ky.) *Courier Journal.*

"At Tuskegee he merely taught the Negro to help himself, to be more valuable as an artisan, a servant, a laborer. To fit him for this he readily obtained funds from southern white men. That he told the less sincere sources of income in the North that he was making doctors and lawyers and great intellects in Tuskegee was thoroughly understood in the South and not criticized. Washington was practical; he knew that to reach the pocketbooks of people who were not intimately acquainted with the Negro and his problems and his tremendous needs he must appeal to their imaginations. So he did . . ."—Macon (Ga.) *Telegraph* . . .

"The North has been misrepresented by a small class of fanatical and impracticable doctrinaires. Its supposed historic attitude toward the Negro race is a lie—not a conscious lie reduced to the terms of an equation, but a lie nevertheless. This Booker Washington had the wit to perceive and he turned it handsomely to the account of his people in the South. Wealthy northerners saw, or thought they saw, the expediency of localizing the Negro problem. Washington was a handy and a willing instrument to carry out their plans . . ."—Columbia (S.C.) *State.*

"He was a great man. Not great in a comparative sense or in that narrow judgment which merely records him as one who achieved well considering the circumstances that he was a Negro, but regardless of all limitations. His career must stand as an ample answer to the theory that the Negro is not capable of high intellectual and spiritual development, because he blazed his own way to usefulness and fame. . . .

"The southern white people are ultimately to have as their neighbors many millions of black people ignorant, immoral, criminal, inefficient, filthy, diseased and hopeless or they are going to have as their neighbors a Negro race that is intelligent, virtuous, efficient, honest, patriotic, friendly. Intelligent men and women know that the South needs the latter. Washington strove for the better choice and he has blazed the way that the leaders of his race will surely follow with patience, earnestness and determination."—Houston (Tex.) *Post* . . .

"Some Negroes and some northern white men thought him too subservient to the opinion of the white South; some white men in the South thought he had too lofty ambitions for his race; some regarded him as a chameleon—proclaiming one race law South of the Potomac and another to the North. Sometimes, as in the famous Roosevelt episode, Washington gave ground for criticism; at other times and in most things, he went his way cautiously, conscious of his responsibilities and aware of the influence of his example . . ."—Richmond (Va.) *News Leader.*

"If Washington ever had any ideas of race equality, he never showed it or uttered it. He wanted his people to take help from their white neighbors and to live well the parts of humble citizens. But he wanted them to live unto themselves and he had no mistaken ideas about amalgamation of the two races, the superior and the inferior . . ."—Denton (Tex.) *Record Chronicle* . . .

". . . On the streets of Tuskegee, whether walking or driving behind his team of two beautiful bays, he represented to Tuskegee people 'a good Negro'—nothing less, nothing more."—Oklahoma City (Okla.) *Oklahoman.*[4]

CHARLES HENDERSON *(Henderson was the governor of Alabama at the time of Washington's death.)*[5]

In the death of Booker T. Washington the colored race has lost its greatest leader. He was a man of unusual force and executive ability, and in many respects rose above the environment of race. In my opinion, his efforts toward the development of his people have been of great benefit to them and to the entire South. Born a slave, living a life of earnest endeavor, and at his death the chief executive of an institution of nation-wide reputation created by his own brain and energy, demonstrates to the world the unbounded possibilities open to those whose purpose is to accomplish something, and marks him as one of the able men of his time.[6]

ISAAC FISHER *(Fisher was president of the Tuskegee Alumni Association.)*

No persons have sustained so great a loss as have the members of the Tuskegee Alumni Association; and I come to bear testimony to the depth and sincerity of their grief.

There is a story which has not yet been told, in connection with the spread of industrial education in the South and throughout the entire country. I must tell that story here before I can make clear just how great is the Alumni's loss.

In telling of the spread of industrial education, during the past twenty-five years, we seem not to know that the work has been difficult and prosecuted at great sacrifice on the part of the Tuskegee graduates who have sought to interpret Dr. Washington's theory that economic fitness was the basis of racial growth in many other directions.

The people did not take kindly to this form of education, believing that it was the same old slavery from which we have emerged under a new name; and the Tuskegee graduates have prosecuted their work in the face of the misrepresentations, prejudice, opposition, and ridicule of those of their own race who could or would not understand the spirit of industrial education—a spirit broader and finer than the phrase suggests. More than this: in the communities where they have worked it has been the fashion to permit our graduates to do the difficult tasks and carry all the burdens of leadership; but if there were any honors to be bestowed, they were given to the graduates of other schools.

Being human and denied those honors and public marks of esteem which always gladden the heart, these Tuskegee men and women have often grown discouraged and have been tempted to lay down their work. But like Daniel, when those gloomy hours came, they have turned their faces toward Jerusalem, to Tuskegee, over which the great spirit of Dr. Washington brooded and lived; and from this place he has sent back to them whenever they have called, encouragement, counsel, and help.

Sometimes they have been so depressed that they have come to Tuskegee just to see and talk with their prophet once more and to be baptized again in his sweet and noble spirit. Many times we have seen them here and wondered at their presence. They were here to receive comfort, and to hear Mr. Washington say in his own convincing manner: 'It has been my experience that if a man will do the right thing and go ahead, everything will be all right at last.' And these men and women who have sat at his feet and who trusted him have gone back to their work with new and increasing strength.

But now Dr. Washington is gone, and the graduates of the school will never again receive his counsel and encouragement, however gloomy their paths may be. That is the measure of our loss.

And yet our Principal is not buried out yonder. It is his tired body which is resting just beyond that wall; but he is not buried in that grave. The real Dr. Washington is buried in the graduates who sat at his feet and imbibed his spirit, and he lives in them . . .[7]

CLEMENT RICHARDSON (*Richardson chaired the Tuskegee English department.*)

Just as he touched the students and teachers with little thoughtful deeds so he touched the town and State, both white and black. One feature of his funeral illustrated how complete had been his triumph over narrow prejudices. He was always talking about the white man up the hollow, back in the woods. How many times have I heard him urge picturesquely upon gatherings of teachers to 'win that old fellow who, when you begin to talk Negro education and Negro schoolhouse, scratches his head, leans to one side, and looks far away. That's the man,' he would say, 'that you've got to convince that Negro education is not a farce.'

Well, that man was at Booker T. Washington's funeral. He came there on foot, on horseback, in buggies, in wagons. He was there in working clothes, in slouched hat, with no collar.

During the service I chanced to stand near the end of the platform. Pretty soon I felt a rough brushing against my elbow. As I turned I saw a small white child, poorly clad, being thrust upon the end of the flower-laden platform. Then followed an old white man, collarless, wearing a dingy blue shirt and a coat somewhat tattered. After him came two strapping fellows, apparently his sons. All grouped themselves there and listened eagerly, freely spitting their tobacco juice on the platform steps and on the floor.

How thankful would Dr. Washington have been for their presence. What a triumph! Ten years ago those men would not stop at the school. They cursed it, cursed the whole system and the man at the head of it. But quietly, persistently, he had gone on with that everlasting doctrine that service can win even the meanest heart, that an institution had the right to survive in just so far as it dovetailed its life into the life of all the people. Beautiful to behold, to remember forever; there was no race and no class in the Tuskegee chapel on Wednesday morning, November 17th; heart went out to heart that a common friend had gone . . .[8]

"The personal combat with Washington was over," writes David Levering Lewis about the state of black affairs following Washington's death, "but the competition by the two belief-systems for minds and hearts engendered by that combat now entered another phase, one in which all points of reference, every undertaking (economic, educational, political), and even the most casual relationships, were to be subordinated to the Manichean social and civil values of what succeeding generations of African-Americans called the Du Bois-Washington controversy."[9]

W.E.B. DU BOIS

A simple and feasible memorial to Booker T. Washington may be contributed by the colored people alone.

As we said in our last number the mortgage on the Frederick Douglass Home, near Washington, D.C. must be raised. Mr. Washington was interested in this project and helped raise a part of the mortgage. Could not his colored friends and admirers raise the rest and present it to the Douglass Home as a Booker Washington Memorial Fund?[10]

W.E.B. DU BOIS

The Southern white man who writes the *Outlook* editorials on the Negro said recently: "The social intimacy (or so called social equality) that some disloyal Negroes have craved and the sort of politics that created the evils of the Reconstruction era, have been the two main causes of the race complication."[11] This is as flat a falsehood as could easily be told. The cause of the difficulties in Reconstruction was the determination of the white South to re-enslave Negroes, and the determination of the Negroes to be really free.

The writer goes on to say that the late Booker T. Washington believed that "the only social intimacy the Negro required was that open to him among his own people." This is not true. No American Negro ever accepted so much social recognition as Mr. Washington. He dined with white men and women, he sat in the parlors of his white friends, he was entertained at their homes, he met and conferred with them on all possible social occasions. Why did he do this? Because he craved their company? No. He did it for the reason given by the late Justice Lamar of the United States Supreme Court, a Mississippian and a Confederate.[12] Justice Lamar, in a speech made several years before his appointment to the bench, in speaking of the Negro problem, said: "He can only be elevated by education—not the mere education of books, but the education that comes from contact with the 'superior mind'." Wherever that "superior mind" is found the Negro will be found. Sometimes it is found in a white skin; sometimes it is found in a black skin; but any social life which tries to forbid common contact of human minds is not only wrong and dangerous but in the long run it is impossible.[13]

Robert Russa Moton served as the commandant of cadets at Hampton, essentially the dean of students, in 1891 (see Chapter 11). He was a close ally of Booker Washington, perhaps the leading officer of the school that was closest in outlook and philosophy to Tuskegee. So following the death of Washington, Tuskegee's board of trustees named Moton to be his friend's successor.[14]

W.E.B. DU BOIS

AN OPEN LETTER TO ROBERT RUSSA MOTON

The Crisis hastens to extend to you on your accession to the head-ship of Tuskegee the assurances of its good will and personal respect. The *Crisis* does this all the more willingly because it has to some extent been the mouthpiece of many who have had occasion repeatedly to criticize the words and deeds of your predecessor.

It would be a matter of hope and rejoicing if your assumption of new duties could be the beginning of a new era of union and understanding among the various groups of American Negroes.

But understanding and cooperation must be based on frank confer-ence and clear knowledge. As a preliminary step to such understand-ing the *Crisis* ventures in this open letter to express to you publicly its hopes and fears.

It hopes that the aims of the colored American have become suffi-ciently clear to admit of no misunderstanding or misstatement. We desire to become American citizens with every right that pertains to citizenship:

1. The right to vote and hold office.
2. Equality before the law.
3. Equal civil rights in all public places, and in all public services.
4. A proportional share in the benefits of all public expenditures.
5. Education according to ability and aptitude.

With these rights we correlate our duties as men and citizens—the abolition of poverty, the emancipation of women, the suppression of crime and the overcoming of ignorance . . .

We assume, without demur, that following the late Booker T. Wash-ington you will place especial emphasis on vocational training, prop-erty getting and conciliation of the white South. These are necessary policies, but they have their pitfalls, and against these the *Crisis* speaks this warning word:

1. Only the higher and broader training will give any race its ulti-mate leadership. This Mr. Washington came to realize, and this you must not forget.

2. Individual accumulation of wealth must gradually and inevitably give way to methods of social accumulation and equitable distribution.

3. Finally: Conciliation is wise and proper. But how far shall it go? It is here that the *Crisis* confesses to its deepest solicitude in your case. It cannot but remember its unanswered query of you in the case of the St. Louis luncheon. It has before it the heading of a Rochester paper which gives as your opinion that "from North one gets distorted view

of South." And finally, there is the recent case of the Pullman car and your family.

The *Crisis* will assume in all of these cases that you have not been correctly reported; that you did not voluntarily give up lunching at the St. Louis City Club; that you did not assert that the South was maligned usually at the North, and above all, that you did not say that you had no sympathy with the attempt of members of your family to ride on Pullman cars in the South.

The *Crisis* knows only too well the way in which Southern newspapers put such sentiments into the mouths of colored leaders; but the point upon which we insist is this: that such atrocious statements cannot be always passed in silence . . .

We hope to see, therefore, at Tuskegee in the future a carrying out and development of the best of its past work and a continued attempt to come to terms of understanding with the best of the white South; but to these policies we hope to see added a policy of making it clearly understood to the people of this country that Tuskegee does believe in the right to vote; that it does not believe in Jim-Crow cars; that it recognizes the work of the Negro colleges, and that it agrees with Charles Sumner that "Equality of rights is the first of rights . . ."[15]

THEODORE ROOSEVELT

It is not hyperbole to say that Booker T. Washington was a great American. For twenty years before his death he had been the most useful, as well as the most distinguished, member of his race in the world, and one of the most useful, as well as one of the most distinguished, of American citizens of any race.

Eminent though his services were to the people of his own color, the white men of our Republic were almost as much indebted to him, both directly and indirectly. They were indebted to him directly, because of the work he did on behalf of industrial education for the Negro, thus giving impetus to the work for the industrial education of the White Man, which is, at least, as necessary; and, moreover, every successful effort to turn the thoughts of the natural leaders of the Negro race into the fields of business endeavor, of agricultural effort, of every species of success in private life, is not only to their advantage, but to the advantage of the White Man, as tending to remove the friction and trouble that inevitably come throughout the South at this time in any Negro district where the Negroes turn for their advancement primarily to political life.

The indirect indebtedness of the White Race to Booker T. Washington is due to the simple fact that here in America we are all in the end going up or down together; and therefore, in the long run, the man who makes a substantial contribution toward uplifting any part of the community has helped to uplift all of the community. Wherever in our land the Negro remains uneducated, and liable to criminal suggestion, it is absolutely certain that the whites will themselves tend to tread the paths of barbarism; and wherever we find the colored people as a whole engaged in successful work to better themselves, and respecting both themselves and others, there we shall also find the tone of the white community high . . .

He was never led away, as the educated Negro so often is led away, into the pursuit of fantastic visions; into the drawing up of plans fit only for a world of two dimensions. He kept his high ideals, always; but he never forgot for a moment that he was living in an actual world of three dimensions, in a world of unpleasant facts, where those unpleasant facts have to be faced; and he made the best possible out of a bad situation from which there was no ideal best to be obtained. And he walked humbly with his God . . .

While he did not believe that political activity should play an important part among Negroes as a whole, he did believe that in the interests of the White, as well as in the interests of the Colored, race, the upright, honest, intelligent Black Man or Colored Man should be given the right to cast a ballot if he possessed the qualities which, if possessed by a White Man, would make that White Man a valuable addition to the suffrage-exercising class.

No man, White or Black, was more keenly alive than Booker T. Washington to the threat of the South, and to the whole country, and especially to the Black Man himself, contained in the mass of ignorant, propertyless, semi-vicious Black voters, wholly lacking in the character which alone fits a race for self-government, who nevertheless have been given the ballot in certain Southern States . . .

In the same way, while Booker T. Washington firmly believed that the attention of the Colored race should be riveted, not on political life, but on success sought in the fields of honest business endeavor, he also felt, and I agreed with him, that it was to the interest of both races that there should be appointments to office of Black Men whose characters and abilities were such that if they were White Men their appointments would be hailed as being well above the average, and creditable from every standpoint . . .

I profited very much by my association with Booker T. Washington. I owed him much along many different lines. I valued greatly his friendship and respect; and when he died I mourned his loss as a patriot and an American.[16]

The year following Washington's death, a group of leaders, including Du Bois and at the urging of Joel Spingarn, attempted to take advantage of the absence of such a polarizing figure. The group, including Moton, Scott, and others of Washington's camp, met at Spingarn's estate in Amenia, New York, in an effort to bridge the divides that had remained over the course of the Washington–Du Bois split. It was a sincere attempt at détente between northern and southern black leaders, and it was seen by many, including Du Bois, as the official end of the era of Booker T. Washington.[17]

W.E.B. DU BOIS

. . . The wall between the Washington camp and those who had opposed his policies was still there; and it occurred to J.E. Spingarn and his friends that up in the peace and quiet of Amenia and around this beautiful lake, colored men and women of all shades of opinion might sit down and rest and talk and agree on many things if not on all.

The conference, as Mr. Spingarn conceived it, was to be "under the auspices of the N.A.A.C.P." but wholly independent of it, and the invitations definitely said this. They were issued by Mr. Spingarn personally, and the guests were assured that they would not be bound by any program of the N.A.A.C.P. Thus the conference was intended primarily to bring about as large a degree as possible of unity of purpose among Negro leaders and to do this regardless of its effect upon any organization, although, of course, many of us hoped that some central organization and preferably the N.A.A.C.P. would eventually represent this new united purpose.

One can hardly realize today how difficult and intricate a matter it was to arrange such a conference, to say who should come and who should not, to gloss over hurts and enmities . . .

About two hundred invitations to white and colored people were actually issued, and in making up this list the advice of friends of Mr. Washington, like Major Moton and Mr. Emmett Scott and Mr. Fred Moore, was sought . . .

I doubt if ever before so small a conference of American Negroes had so many colored men of distinction who represented at the same time so complete a picture of all phases of Negro thought. Its very completeness in this respect was its salvation. If it had represented one party or clique it would have been less harmonious and unanimous, because someone would surely have essayed in sheer fairness to state the opinions of men who were not there and would have stated them necessarily without compromise and without consideration. As it was, we all learned what the majority of us knew. None of us held uncompromising and unchangeable views. It was after all a matter of emphasis. We all believed in thrift, we all wanted the Negro to vote, we all wanted the laws enforced, we all wanted assertion of our essential manhood; but how to get these things,—there of course was infinite divergence of opinion.

But everybody had a chance to express this opinion, and at the same time the conference was not made up of sonorous oratory. The thing was too intimate and small . . .

The Amenia Conference in reality marked the end of an era and the beginning, as we said in our resolutions: "The Amenia Conference believes that its members have arrived at a virtual unanimity of opinion in regard to certain principles and that a more or less definite result may be expected from its deliberations. These principles and this practical result may be summarized as follows:

(1) "The conference believes that all forms of education are desirable for the Negro and that every form of education should be encouraged and advanced.

(2) "It believes that the Negro, in common with all other races, cannot achieve its highest development without complete political freedom.

(3) "It believes that this development and this freedom cannot be furthered without organization and without a practical working understanding among the leaders of the colored race.

(4) "It believes that antiquated subjects of controversy, ancient suspicions and factional alignments must be eliminated and forgotten if this organization of the race and this practical working understanding of its leaders are to be achieved.

(5) "It realizes the peculiar difficulties which surround this problem in the South and the special need of understanding between leaders of the race who live in the South and those who live in the North. It has learned to understand and respect the good faith, methods and ideals of those who are working for the solution of this problem in various sections of the country.

(6) "The conference pledges itself to the inviolable privacy of all its deliberations. These conclusions, however, and the amicable results of all the deliberations of the conference are fair subjects for discussion in the colored press and elsewhere.

(7) "The conference feels that mutual understanding would be encouraged if the leaders of the race could meet annually for private and informal discussion under conditions similar to those which have prevailed at this conference."

It is a little difficult today to realize why it was necessary to say all this. There had been bitterness and real cause for bitterness in those years after the formation of the Niagara movement and before the N.A.A.C.P. had come to the front. Men were angry and hurt. Booker Washington had been mobbed by Negroes in Boston. Monroe Trotter had been thrown in jail; the lowest motives that one can conceive had been attributed to antagonists on either side—jealousy, envy, greed, cowardice, intolerance, and the like. Newspapers and magazine articles had seethed with threat, charge, and innuendo.

Then there had been numberless attempts at understanding which had failed. There was, for instance, that conference in Carnegie Hall when Andrew Carnegie through Booker T. Washington financed a general meeting of Negro leaders. It was a much larger conference than that at Amenia but its spirit was different. It was a conference carefully manipulated. There was no confidence there and no complete revelation. It savored more of armed truce than of understanding. Those of us who represented the opposition were conscious of being forced and influenced against our will, . . . Numbers of rich and powerful whites looked in upon us and admonished us to be good, and then the opposition between the wings flamed in bitter speech and charge. Men spoke with double tongues saying one thing and meaning another. And finally there came compromise and an attempt at constructive effort which somehow no one felt was real. I had proposed a Committee of Twelve to guide the Negro race, but when the committee was finally constituted I found that it predominately represented only one wing of the controversy and that it was financed indirectly by Andrew Carnegie, and so I indignantly withdrew . . . There were other efforts, but it needed time and understanding, and when the Amenia Conference came the time was ripe . . .

It not only marked the end of the old things and the old thoughts and the old ways of attacking the race problem, but in addition to this it was the beginning of the new things. Probably on account of our meeting the Negro race was more united and more ready to meet the problems of the world than it could possibly have been without these beautiful days of understanding. It was a "Close ranks!" before the great struggle that issued in the new world . . . It was all peculiarly appropriate, and those who in the future write the history of the way in which the American Negro became a man must not forget this event and landmark in 1916.[18]

NOTES

1. "Social Uplift," January 1916, 113.
2. Scott and Stowe, 1916, 300–306, 321–322.
3. This editorial note on Booker T. Washington was reproduced and commented upon, quite critically, especially by the white press; examples are Chicago *Evening Post*, December 13, 1915, and Sioux City (Iowa) *Journal*, December 7, 1915. Several Black newspapers, friendly to Washington, also attacked Du Bois, but a spirited and lengthy defense of his estimate, by Rev. William A. Byrd of Rochester, N.Y., entitled "Be Just to the Living," appeared in the Cleveland *Gazette*, February 19, 1916. Washington, 1984, vol. 13, 492–493; and Du Bois, December 1915, 82.
4. "Booker T. Washington," January 1916, 122–128.
5. Henderson was a Democrat from Troy, Alabama. Like Washington, his two principal interests were business and education. He was a part of several enterprises, from railroads to cotton, and was instrumental in founding the school that would become Troy University. "Alabama Governors: Charles Henderson," Alabama Department of Archives and History.
6. "Booker T. Washington," January 1916, 122–128.
7. Fisher's words here came at the university's memorial service for Washington. Scott and Stowe, 1916, 322–329.
8. Ibid., 322–331.
9. Lewis, 1993, 502.
10. Du Bois, January 1916, 135.
11. The quoted passage comes from "Booker Washington and His Race," 24 November 1915, 700–703.
12. Lucius Quintus Cincinnatus Lamar was a U.S. Supreme Court justice from 1888 to 1893. *New York Times*, 25 January 1893, 8.
13. Du Bois, May 1916, 30.
14. See Chapter 11, note 7.
15. Du Bois, July 1916, 136–137.
16. Roosevelt, "Preface," 1916, ix–xv.
17. Holloway, 2002, 11.
18. Du Bois, 1925.

20

Du Bois Shapes the Legacy

Booker T. Washington was 12 years older than W.E.B. Du Bois and rose to prominence long before his counterpart. He was founding Tuskegee while Du Bois was still in grade school and thus occupied what national stage was allowed to a black southerner long before Du Bois found his voice. Washington's death in 1915, however, gave Du Bois that national stage all to himself. The Tuskegee leader's reputation waxed and waned in the years following his death, but the predominant images of him were those of a scheming overlord and a sniveling Uncle Tom. They were caricatures, and neither caricature was accurate, but they existed largely because Washington's death and Du Bois's long life allowed the latter to interpret and reinterpret the former's role in turn-of-the-century race relations and rights advocacy without allowing Washington to defend himself.

EMMETT JAY SCOTT AND LYMAN BEECHER STOWE

. . . No Negro was ever so liked, respected, admired, and eulogized by the Southern whites as Booker Washington. The day following his great speech before the Cotton States Exposition in Atlanta in 1895 when he went out upon the streets of the city he was so besieged by white citizens from the highest to the lowest, who wanted to shake his hand and congratulate him, that he was fairly driven in self-defense to remain indoors. Not many years after that it had become a commonplace for him to be an honored guest on important public occasions throughout the South. On occasions too numerous even to note in passing he was welcomed, and introduced to great audiences, by Southern Governors, Mayors, and other high officials, as well as by eminent private citizens. Such recognition came partly as a spontaneous tribute to the great work he was doing and partly because of his constantly reiterated assurance that the Negro was not seeking either political domination over the white man or social intercourse with him. He reasoned that the more Southern whites he could convince that his people were not seeking what is known as social equality or political dominance, the less race friction there would be . . .

At the opening of the first Negro agricultural fair in Albany, Georgia, in the fall of 1914, the Mayor of the city and several members of the City Council sat on the platform during the exercises and listened to his speech with most spontaneous and obvious approval . . .

It was an interesting illustration of the illogical workings of race prejudice that this man to whom the city fathers from the Mayor down gave up practically their entire day—this man to whom the city hall was thrown open and at whose feet sat the leading citizens as well as the officials of the city, could not have found shelter in any hotel in town. This man whom the officials and other leading citizens delighted to honor arrived at night on a Pullman sleeping car in violation of the law of the State; and, after all possible honor had been paid him, save allowing him to enter a hotel, departed the next night by a Pullman sleeper in violation of the law!

This constant "law-breaker" was welcomed and introduced to audiences by Governor [Newton C.] Blanchard of Louisiana at Shreveport, La.; by Governor [Allen D.] Candler at Atlanta, Ga.; by Governor [George W.] Donaghey at Little Rock, Ark.; by Governor [William A.] McCorkle of West Virginia, and successively by Governors [William D.] Jelks and O'Neil of his own State of Alabama.[1] Still other Southern Governors spoke from the same platform with him at congresses, conventions, and meetings of various descriptions . . .

In short, Booker Washington met race prejudice just as he did all other difficulties, as an obstacle to be surmounted rather than as an injustice to be railed at and denounced regardless of the consequences.[2]

Ultimately, Washington's death, combined with Du Bois's largesse and influence—to say nothing of his consistently prolific output—allowed Du Bois to set the agenda of commentators and historians and thereby place Washington in a less-than-positive light that would continue throughout much of the century. With a respected champion for race rights placing himself as the protagonist in a philosophical battle for the souls of black folk, it was all the easier for others to interpret Washington as the antagonist.[3]

WILLIAM EDWARD BURGHARDT DU BOIS

As to the resolutions of the Tuskegee conference touching the migration of Negro labor to the North . . .[4]

The southern white papers assert editorially and in their news columns that the chief burden of the Tuskegee resolutions is advice to the Negro not to migrate from the South. From this advice, it goes without saying, that the Crisis absolutely dissents . . .

As a matter of fact, the Tuskegee resolutions may be thus analyzed: out of fifteen inches of printed matter the following subjects are treated:

The Boll-Weevil and Floods, one inch; "Advice to remain in the South," five inches; "Diversified Farming," one and one-half inches; "A Plea to the South in Behalf of the Negro," two and one-half inches; "Lack of Enforcement of the Law," one-half inch; "Congratulating the South and Urging Co-operation of Races," three and one-half inches.

With the subject matter of the various resolutions we have no quarrel. In few cases do we dissent from the statements, taken by themselves; but we do solemnly believe that any system of Negro leadership that today devotes ten times as much space to the advantages of living in the South as it gives to lynching and lawlessness is inexcusably blind.[5]

W.E.B. DU BOIS

June 12th, 1923.

Memo to Mr. [Walter] White[6]:—

1. The weakness of the Booker Washington philosophy was the assumption that economic power can be won and maintained without political power. The strength of the Washington philosophy was its insistence upon the necessity of manual labor, and its inculcation of thrift and saving.

2. The past twenty years have shown that Mr. Washington was right in his encouragement of industry, saving and business enterprise among Negroes. That he was wrong in his assumption that this increase

of Negro wealth, efficiency and intelligence was going to decrease the prejudice of the whites, without any further action or power on the part of the Negroes.

3. The favorable effect of Mr. Washington's propaganda was to make the white people think about Negro problems, and make the colored people have faith in white people. The unfavorable effect was to lead the white people to mistake a temporary makeshift for an eternal solution; and on the part of the colored people it made them dream that they could get their rights by individual working and saving; and that group organization and sturdy resistance to aggression was unnecessary.

There is no reason for retaining much of Mr. Washington's philosophy except as an interesting historical fact. No Negro dreams to-day that he can protect himself in industry and business without a vote and without a fighting aggressive organization. No intelligent white man believes that the Negro is going to accept caste and peonage without a struggle; he knows that the day when white people can choose Negro leaders to tell the colored people what they want the colored people told has not passed to be sure, but is rapidly passing.

P.S. I might add that on the educational side of Mr. Washington's philosophy, he undoubtedly over-emphasized the place and value of manual training and industry as a means of education; and did not appreciate the history and meaning of college training. This was natural because of his own difficult and limited education. Moreover, this philosophy was valuable to the white world, which having already well-established colleges and universities, was undoubtedly neglecting manual training. On the other hand, for the Negro schooled in the hard experience of industrial life and almost without facilities for higher training, Mr. Washington's educational plans were almost fatal and are being rapidly overturned to-day. Already Hampton has added a college department and is trying to cut off her lower grades; while Tuskegee has become a high school and will eventually become a college.

W.E.B. Du Bois[7]

W.E.B. DU BOIS

Tuskegee and Moton

Our hats are in the air to Tuskegee and Moton. The victory at Tuskegee over the Ku Klux Klan and the Bourbons of the Southern South cannot be over estimated. First the South asked Separation. Then they demanded the right to step on our side of the color line and order us around, tell us what to think and to do. They claimed especially that State and Nation belonged to them and that anything done for us by the government was a boon to outsiders and to be supervised and directed by white Southerners. Southern Negroes led by Tuskegee yielded and yielded and yielded. They depended on the "good white folks" and the good white folks continually lied to them and betrayed them. At last they stood with backs to the wall . . . And the white cowards threatened. They promised murder and disgrace; they used every scheme to make Moton yield. And Moton wavered, hesitated—and stood. Stood firmly and calmly with his back to the wall. He and the Negro world demanded that the Government Hospital at Tuskegee be under Negro control. Today, at last, it is . . .

Moton has learned that not all rich white Northern philanthropists nor professional Southern "friends" of the Negro can be trusted. Some of them betray the most sacred trusts. The only salvation of the Negro is to stop yielding supinely to every demand of Northern bribery and Southern bluff and fight and fight and fight for right. Moton is learning this slowly and in bitter disillusion. But for every white and condescending flatterer whom he loses in his new-found manhood he will gain a hundred staunch of loyal black followers . . .[8]

W.E.B. DU BOIS

We congratulate Hampton and Tuskegee for their five million dollars of new endowment. They have earned it. They deserve it. Any set of folk who have successfully conducted good black schools in Ku Klux Alabama and in Virginia where fanatics are secretly planning the deportation of twelve million Americans to Africa, such folk deserve much.

And we are, we trust, not overfractious if we add: Now that you have adequate endowment, for God's sake stop running your schools as if they were primarily for the benefit of Southern whites and not for blacks . . .

Stand up, Hampton and Tuskegee. Your new wealth is New Freedom.[9]

W.E.B. DU BOIS

. . . One of the most interesting chapters in James E. Amos' *Theodore Roosevelt: Hero to his Valet* is the chapter on the Booker Washington dinner.[10] There have been several attempts to make people think that this invitation of Booker T. Washington to dinner at the White House was quite unpremeditated and accidental. Mr. Amos shows that it was not, but he adds to this his own characteristic point of view. A few years before he died Mr. Roosevelt asked him:

" 'Now, James, what did you think about it?'

'I think it was all a mistake,' I said.

'You do?' he said, looking up rather surprised. 'And what was the trouble with it?'

'Of course,' I replied, 'I don't mean to say that you made a mistake, Mr. Roosevelt. I criticize Washington for accepting your invitation. He knew the white people of the South and he must have known that the affair would bring you—a true friend of the colored race—into a lot of unfriendly criticism. He had plenty of time to think it over and he could easily have found an excuse not to accept the invitation.'

'So that's what you think?' he asked.

'Yes,' I answered.

'Well, by George, I don't agree with you,' he said, and that was all."

This shows that the master had considerably more sense than his valet; which is not always true.[11]

W.E.B. DU BOIS

. . . And now to Tuskegee. It is twenty-five years or more since I saw Tuskegee. Booker Washington was then at his zenith and the Tuskegee idea was triumphant. It was a combination of something insistent but suspicious that led to my invitation twenty-five years ago to talk to the Tuskegee summer school. I come back to find the school a city. One can no longer speak of a single institution, or judge this mass of buildings, roads and institutions as one thing. It is a great historic growth, and most significant of all, it has grown beautiful. It lies in curving undulating hills, with pines and trees and grass, and the happy voices of thousands of young folk.

I was interested to know about these young people, but I had only time to glimpse them. In other days, Tuskegee was a silent marching regiment. It had no soul. There is still regimentation. The silence of the chapel was uncanny. The marching is over-done, and yet, the grade of the students, their intelligence, their initiative, has greatly increased. I talked to a college of over 100 students (fancy a college at Tuskegee! and no openings of graves, no waving of cerements.) They were bright-eyed men and women. They were doing something. But, of course, Tuskegee is caught in the problem of its own making. It has its artisans and its grammar school students, its High School students, and its college, it has its teachers, who are a jumble of all kinds of culture and training. Only the unity of a great ideal can carry such an institution on to success. And there can be no doubt, it is moving on.

The National Hospital at Tuskegee is a miracle. Here black Americans have done the impossible with great buildings and beautiful grounds, and the Circle of the officers dwellings. The spirit of efficiency and discipline, is exactly the thing which even black people, a few years ago, said we were not prepared for. Of the fifty-one Veterans' Hospitals, this one stands well within the first half dozen. It has an excellent library with books that are read. It has secured experts, and it succeeded in the face of an Alabama mob, which threatened to lynch Robert R. Moton, unless he put white men in the control of the hospital, and sent "nigger nurse maids" to wait on white nurses, lest they touch black skins. One can hardly reconstruct that extraordinary outburst, even in memory . . .[12]

W.E.B. DU BOIS

Dr. Moton's *What the Negro Thinks* . . . is a book that would have been unthinkable ten years ago and would have caused something like a riot twenty years ago.[13] It is, on the whole, the best thing that has come out of Tuskegee. Even, when one remembers *Up From Slavery* and Industrial Education itself, it is best because it is frank and clear.

Up From Slavery, the biography of Booker T. Washington, was a work of art with characteristic reticences and careful arrangement. Dr. Moton's book is straight-forward and candid. He has left his old habit of merely saying something nice for the consumption of white folks; he has dropped most of his jokes, and written a straight-forward word which will receive the assent of practically every Negro reader, and cannot be gainsaid by white readers . . .

Mr. Moton considers Negro disabilities: segregation, "jim-crow" cars, schools, housing, the ballot, the courts; and in every single case, instead of the hedging and special pleading that many of us have always expected from Tuskegee, his statements are almost without exception the sort of thing that we ourselves could have said. "No phase of discrimination against the Negro touches the race more widely or intimately than segregation." There is a description of the difficulties of "jim-crow" cars and streetcars; of Pullman travel; of food while traveling; of waiting rooms and ticket offices; of treatment on the trains; of steamboat lines and bus lines; and the final declaration that all this segregation "is regarded as the most humiliating form of racial discrimination with the least substantial excuse of justification." The school situation is explained and it is shown that separate schools mean "distinctly discrimination, neglect and inferior provisions for the Negro."

"The thinking Negro refuses to accept the idea that race prejudice is natural and inevitable, that it is inherent in the child, either white or black. He insists that it is acquired and cultivated, and that the greatest single aid to its cultivation is segregation."

Mr. Moton then goes on to explain the feeble line of demarcation today between the N.A.A.C.P., on the one hand, and the Hampton and Tuskegee school of thought on the other, and he concludes fairly:

"The two groups are alike opposed to legal segregation in principle; both regard it as undemocratic and unchristian, as unfair in principle as well as in practice. In truth, they are working for the same thing in different spheres and by a different approach."

In the same way the housing difficulty is frankly set forth; the record of the Negro in Reconstruction is defended, and despite any murmurings from the grave of Booker T. Washington, the author writes:

"The thinking Negro insists that the white man's civilization is as safe with a ballot in his hands as it is with a bullet or bayonet ..."

It is extraordinary that a book like this can come out of Tuskegee, Alabama, even in 1929 ...[14]

W.E.B. DU BOIS

In May, 1881, Booker T. Washington arrived at Tuskegee to start a school for which the Legislature had appropriated $2,000 a year ... On this foundation Tuskegee was built. It has since done much for the Negro race and it is fitting that the President of the United States and other great citizens should join in its jubilee. But the success of Tuskegee is not due to a realization of the program which is usually associated with its name. Tuskegee started out to be a school and as a school it has done excellent and never-to-be-forgotten work. It is still doing that work. To this original program there was gradually added, because of its wide popularity, a proposal to train Negroes primarily as workers in Southern industry and as farmers and farm-laborers. This program has never been accomplished. The number of graduates of Tuskegee who have become farmers and artisans is small. The facts have never been, published, but it is certain that the large majority of Tuskegee graduates have become teachers and professional men with a smaller number in business. Some of the graduates and numbers of the former students have worked as farmers and artisans, but they have found in most cases that surrounding economic conditions were too much for them. The condition of affairs in the rural districts of the South has discouraged the Negro farmer. The new industrialization of the white South has pushed the Negro artisan closer and closer to the wall, particularly since in most cases he has been politically disfranchised. All this is not the fault of Tuskegee Institute. It is the fault of those persons who planned the industrial and educational program which for a time was so closely associated with the names of Hampton and Tuskegee. Today a new era has come and new economic plans must be made.[15]

LOUISA F. STRITTMATER *(Strittmater was a member of the New Jersey branch of the National Women's Party.)*[16]

Bloomfield, N.J., July 18, 1932

Dear Sir:

. . . The chapter on Washington in "The Souls of Black Folk" has so constrained me to express my views of the divergence of your respective policies with regard to conciliation, that with your indulgence I will presume upon a few moments of your valuable time and address myself to you candidly and as briefly as possible.

Quoting: "While it is a great truth to say the Negro must strive and strive mightily to help himself, it is equally true that unless his striving be not simply seconded but rather aroused and encouraged by the initiative of the richer and wiser environing group, he cannot hope for success."

Granted. But how can you expect to elicit encouragement from the richer and wiser environing group without softening at least their harshest prejudices? without conciliation?

For the present, it devolves upon Negroes as a subject class to forge their advancement along two divergent avenues of approach, namely, education and conciliation. Both of these must progress abreast; they are mutually important. Education has no function or value if those educated are restrained from using or materially profiting by their acquirement, And certainly they will be, just so long as the master class are hostile to them or their education. Education must be sustained by conciliation. Each, individually, is impotent and powerless with out support from the other, in the present status of the Negro.

Security for the Negro race depends upon acquisition of, and opportunity to exploit, means of a competent livelihood; of inner growth and expansion, moral and spiritual; and of equal protection of the law. How can any of these vital and fundamental factors of the Negroes' development advance appreciably or normally in the fact of the unconciliated prejudices of the master class? There cannot be a maximum of progress for Negroes until at least the harshest hostilities of the power in control are allayed and their aspiration for a greater measure of assimilation into American society is viewed with more tolerance, kindliness and understanding . . .

Washington secured that difficultly acquired encouragement and sponsorship from the best white people for which you plead. He did not bring the race to its ultimate maximation; he could not, nor can any other individual. The race can not be established in one person's lifetime. But among other things, he did gain much of what you would have, by methods which you disapprove, preferring for your own part, truculence and bitterness to conciliation.

Your aim, if I interpret it correctly, is not paramountly justice for the Negro, but rather vindication of the Negro, as such. In this aspiration, if I make so bold, you are reaching for the moon, centuries over the times in which you live, and oblivious to the possibilities inherent in the conditions in which both races stand today. For the present, practical men with not too long-ranged vision, for the service of the race must apply themselves to doing first things first, however unpleasant. That is, they must attend to the initial step of establishing the race in the best status obtainable as an accepted and recognized, integral part of the American commonwealth, however humble, in which position they can ensconce and entrench themselves, and as opportunity allows, peaceably and permanently extend and widen their status' horizon into eventual full citizenship. Such men are vastly more adapted to advance the well-being of the race at this early and chaotic day of its nominal independence than are they who aim to establish and direct by the tenets of promiscuous censure, blind defiance and tactless aggressiveness towards the governing class. That, in my opinion, is mistaken zeal. You cannot bully evolution, nor sentiment . . .

Respectfully,
L.F. Strittmater[17]

W.E.B. DU BOIS

August 3, 1932.

Mr. L.F. Strittmater
My dear Sir:[18]

The chapter which you have read concerning Booker T. Washington in my "Souls of Black Folk" was written nearly thirty years ago. Since then, I have written a good deal to explain and expand my philosophy, although I do not think that there has been any essential change in it . . .

Briefly, of course, conciliation must be in any social worker's program, but, on the other hand, fawning and stupid yielding to the vagaries of a master class not only secures nothing from them, but helps to submerge one's own self-respect. In the last quarter century, the colored people of the United States, following very largely my advice and the advice of others, based upon it, have made notable strides in advance, and by standing up as men instead of crawling like animals, they have forced you and your friends to yield much which you never would have yielded to the Washington program alone. Minority must always "vaunt its powers," otherwise, it will lose what little power it has, and while I should hate to be justly accused of bitterness and vindictiveness, nevertheless, if what I am writing in *The Crisis* comes under that head, you will, I regret to say, see as much of it in the future as you have in the past . . .[19]

W.E.B. DU BOIS

. . . Washington, who was a mulatto, was born a slave and educated at Hampton Institute. He grew up during the days of reconstruction and in 1881 became principal of Tuskegee Institute, then a small state school for Negroes in Alabama. American Negroes had long been trying to use their newly acquired political power in order to gain education and social advancement, but when their efforts were partially frustrated by the political developments of 1876 a period of bitter disillusion followed. In 1895 Washington at Atlanta enunciated a new economic philosophy for Negroes, urging them "to dignify and glorify common labor, and put brains and skill into the common occupations of life." In speeches made throughout the country he minimized political power and emphasized industrial education. For this purpose he collected money for Tuskegee, which he developed into a large and flourishing institution.

Difficulties arose, however, in the fulfillment of Washington's program. His truce with the whites was met in the south by a radical demand for a system of color caste instead of acceptance of the Negro as a citizen with eventual political rights. The Negro was practically disfranchised and segregated with inferior treatment and accommodations; a public stigma of inferiority was put legally on all persons of Negro blood. Many Negroes bitterly resented disfranchisement and the caste system and held Washington partly responsible for them. Negro labor was used as a non-union substitute for white labor at lower wages, which gave the unions an excuse for their already wide practise of excluding Negroes as members. Furthermore the changing techniques of industry throughout the United States led to the displacement of individual trades by machinery and mass production, so that it became increasingly difficult for industrial schools such as Tuskegee to teach current techniques. The condition of Negroes in industry did not improve therefore as rapidly as Washington's philosophy had anticipated.

Washington's net contribution was thus psychological rather than economic. He instilled into the Negroes a new respect for labor and impressed upon the whites the value of the Negro as a worker. His earnestness, shrewd common sense and statesmanlike finesse in interracial contacts mark his greatness; and Tuskegee Institute stands as his magnificent monument.[20]

W.E.B. DU BOIS

The American public is not yet used to hearing Negroes complain. They are still under the spell of the Booker T. Washington technique. They want to hear entertainment if possible from minstrelsy of the traditional Negro variety; failing that, they would listen to pleasing and encouraging stories of the rise and development of the Negro people in America, and get a pleasant glow from remembering that even such curses as slavery, lynching and "jim-crow" laws, can work for good in the Lord's time without much effort on their part.

Such folk should read Richard Wright's book, and look at its striking illustrations.[21] The book is a complaint and an indictment, made by a young American writer who has written a "best-seller" and ranks high as an author. He is bitter. He is not deceived by success stories of "good niggers":

"This text assumes that those few Negroes who have lifted themselves, through personal strength, talent, or luck, above the lives of their fellow blacks—like single fishes that leap and flash for a split-second above the surface of the sea—are but fleeting exceptions to that vast, tragic school that swims below in the depths, against the current, silently and heavily, struggling against the waves of vicissitudes that spell a common fate."

Those who dare listen to the voice of the stricken Negro masses should read this book and scan its sad pictures.[22]

W.E.B. DU BOIS

. . . Because of a past of chattel slavery, we were for the most part common laborers and servants, and a very considerable proportion were still unable to leave the plantations where they worked all their lives for next to nothing.

There were a few who were educated for the professions and we had many good artisans; that number was not increasing as it should have been, nor were new artisans being adequately trained. Industrial training was popular, but funds to implement it were too limited, and we were excluded from unions and the new mass industry.

We were housed in slums and segregated districts where crime and disease multiplied, and when we tried to move to better and healthier quarters we were met by segregation ordinance if not by mobs. We not only had no social equality, but we did not openly ask for it. It seemed a shameful thing to beg people to receive us as equals and as human beings; that was something we argued "that came and could not be fetched." And that meant not simply that we could not marry white women or legitimize mulatto bastards, but we could not stop in a decent hotel, nor eat in a public restaurant nor attend the theatre, nor accept an invitation to a private white home nor travel in a decent railway coach . . .

This was our plight in 1901. It was discouraging, but not hopeless . . . We could look back on a quarter century of struggle which had its results. We had schools; we had teachers; a few had forced themselves into the leading colleges and were tolerated if not welcomed. We voted in Northern cities, owned many decent homes and were fighting for further progress. Leaders like Booker Washington had received wide popular approval and a Negro literature had begun to appear.

But what we needed was organized effort along the whole front, based on broad lines of complete emancipation. This came with the Niagara Movement in 1906 and the NAACP in 1909. In 1910 came the Crisis magazine and the real battle was on.

What have we gained and accomplished? The advance has not been equal on all fronts, nor complete on any. We have not progressed with closed ranks like a trained army, but rather with serried and broken ranks, with wide gaps and even temporary retreats. But we have advanced. Of that there can be no atom of doubt.

First of all in education; most Negro children today are in school and most adults can read and write . . .

Secondly, in civil rights, the Negro has perhaps made his greatest advance. Mob violence and lynching have markedly decreased. Three thousand Negroes were lynched in the last half of the Nineteenth Century and five hundred in the first half of the twentieth. Today lynching is comparatively rare. Mob violence also has decreased, but is still in evidence, and summary and unjust court proceedings have taken the place of open and illegal acts . . . The Negro has established, in the courts, his legal citizenship and his right to be included in the Bill of Rights. The question still remains of "equal but separate" public accommodations, and that is being attacked. Even the institution of "jim-crow" in travel is tottering. The infraction of the marriage situation by law and custom is yet to be brought before the courts and public opinion in a forcible way.

Third, the right to vote on the part of the Negro is being gradually established under the 14th and 15th amendments. It was not really until 1915 that the Supreme Court upheld this right of Negro citizens and even today the penalties of the 14th amendment have never been enforced . . .[23]

This is the start of a tendency which will grow; we are beginning to follow the American pattern of accumulating individual wealth and of considering that this will eventually settle the race problem. On the other hand, the whole trend of the thought of our age is toward social welfare; the prevention of poverty by more equitable distribution of wealth, and business for general welfare rather than private profit. There are few signs that these ideals are guiding Negro development today. We seem to be adopting increasingly the ideal of American culture.[24]

W.E.B. DU BOIS

There is need for a careful biography of Booker T. Washington, who was certainly a notable and influential American. Unfortunately, the book under review [Samuel R. Spencer's *Booker T. Washington and the Negro's Place in America*] does not fill the need and adds nothing of importance to the biographies by Stowe and Scott, Riley, Mathews, and Shirley Graham.[25]

First of all, the title of this book is misleading, since it does not treat in any thorough way "the Negro's place in American life." Something is noted on this broader topic but this is incidental to the facts of Washington's life. Indeed, the author's concept of biography is an outline of what a man did, with little reference to his surroundings. This is interesting, but singularly misleading in the study of a life which had its chief significance in its historical and social setting. Here was a poor Negro, with small chance at education and/or experience, who became the center of the attempt to solve, after the Civil War, the problem of the future of freed slaves in a great democracy. At any time this would be a problem of huge dimensions, but during the last decade of the nineteenth and first decade of the twentieth centuries, amid economic imperialism, industrial monopoly, and mass production, it was a tremendous social situation.

Of these broader connotations of Washington's career, the author shows neither grasp nor understanding. He mentions, to be sure, American industry, but only as it touched Washington's personal life. That anyone of any race who proposed a solution of the Negro problem in the United States after emancipation would meet opposition and argument, was expected. But the author of this book treats the opposition of some Negroes to Washington's panacea as the work of envious "scoundrels" and devotes many pages to pity Washington under their criticism. In fact, when we compare the squabbles of the Irish and Italians; the Germans and even Americans over their natural and quite understandable differences of opinion about the best paths to their future, we can easily see that Booker T. Washington was treated with extraordinary respect and understanding by his fellow Negroes, even when they believed he was bartering their rights for a mess of pottage.

Mr. Spencer, being a Southern white man, liked Booker Washington, which is understandable. Washington spoke the language of the Southern whites about Negroes better than they could afford to themselves. Washington could aim shafts of criticism at lazy Negroes and black upstarts filled with "Latin and Greek," much more bitingly and effectively than became a "Southern Gentleman." But this is no proof that his program for the uplift of the Negro was flawless. Granted, as it must be, that Washington was a hard-working, sincere man, who wanted the best for his people; nevertheless, it is just as true that if the Negro, in defiance of this well-meant advice, had not fought desperately to retain the right to vote, to gain civil rights and social recognition, and more than that for the education of his gifted children, for a place among modern men, their situation today would have been disastrous.

It was not Washington's fault that he did not see this or that when he realized these truths he was afraid to voice them. This was the fault of the white South and the industrial North, which deliberately used Washington as a pawn to beat back ambitious Negroes, and to build in the South a mass of cheap black labor warranted not to strike or to imitate the white labor movement. When Washington, quite aware of the danger of a disfranchised laboring class and the fatal insult of color-caste, offered a compromise at Atlanta to the loudly applauding whites, he had a right to expect a chivalrous return offer of yielding on the part of the white South. Instead, in the years from 1895 to 1910, Negroes were disfranchised in every Southern state and color caste became frozen into law.

It was this development which frightened the Negroes, and they were further infuriated when Washington, turning from education, entered politics and built a political machine so strong that no Negro could hold national or local political office without Washington's endorsement and beyond that, few Negroes could even get good jobs as teachers, white collar workers, or as master artisans without the consent of Tuskegee. Behind this power lay the vast influence of the white leaders of the nation and a unanimous white press; but further, Washington came gradually to own or control nearly the whole Negro press, although he long lied about it.

This program had to be stopped. But it was not attacked by abuse but by organized and systematic work by the Niagara movement and the National Association for the Advancement of Colored People. Contrary to Spencer's word, the *Crisis* never carried on a feud against Washington. From the beginning we were pledged not to do this by Oswald Garrison Villard, Washington's close friend and a founder of the NAACP. But the *Crisis* did attack Washington's program and helped to supersede it by a more militant and modern one. So much so that Hampton and Tuskegee are no longer "industrial" schools but modern colleges.

Little of this could be gathered from Spencer's book by the casual reader. Rather, we have painted here a martyr appreciated mainly by Southern whites and not by his fellow Negroes. This fairy tale may suit the present rulers of Mississippi and Georgia, but to me it is not convincing.[26]

In 1930, Howard University invited Du Bois to give its commencement address. In that speech, he dealt specifically with the educational controversies of himself and Washington, comparing college and industrial schools.

Published in 1932, the speech represents an older Du Bois looking back on the feud with a decade and a half of perspective.

W.E.B. DU BOIS

Between the time that I was graduated from college and the day of my first experience at earning a living, there was arising, in this land, and more especially within the Negro group, a controversy concerning the type of education which American Negroes needed. You, who are graduating today, have heard but echoes of this controversy and more or less vague theories of its meaning and its outcome. Perhaps it has been explained away to you and interpreted as mere misunderstanding and personal bias. If so, the day of calm review and inquiry is at hand. And I suppose that, of persons living few can realize better than I just what that controversy meant and what the outcome is. I want then today in the short time allotted me, to state, as plainly as I may, the problem of college and industrial education for American Negroes, as it arose in the past; and then to restate it as it appears to me in its present aspect.

First of all, let me insist that the former controversy was no mere misunderstanding; there was real difference of opinion, rooted in deep sincerity on every side and fought out with a tenacity and depth of feeling due to its great importance and fateful meaning.

It was, in its larger aspects, a problem such as in all ages human beings of all races and nations have faced; but it was new in 1895 as all Time is new; it was concentered and made vivid and present because of the immediate and pressing question of the education of a vast group of the children of former slaves. It was the ever new and age-young problem of Youth, for there had arisen in the South a Joseph which knew not Pharoah,—a black man who was not born in slavery. What was he to become? "Whither was his face set? How should he be trained and educated? His fathers were slaves, for the most part, ignorant and poverty-stricken; emancipated in the main without land, tools, nor capital,—the sport of war, the despair of economists, the grave perplexity of Science. Their children had been born in the midst of controversy, of internecine hatred, and in all the economic dislocation that follows war and civil war. In a peculiar way and under circumstances seldom duplicated, the whole program of popular education became epitomized in the case of these young black folk.

Before men thought or greatly cared, in the midst of the very blood and dust of battle, an educational system for the freedmen had been begun; and with a logic that seemed, at first, quite natural. The night school for adults had become the day school for children. The Negro day school had called for normal teaching and the small New England college had been transplanted and perched on hill and river in Raleigh and Atlanta, Nashville and New Orleans, and half a dozen other towns. This new Negro college was conceived of as the very foundation stone of Negro training.

But, meantime, any formal education for slaves or the children of slaves not only awakened widespread and deep-seated doubt, fear and hostility in the South, but it posed, for states men and thinkers, the whole question as to what the education of Negroes was really aiming at, and indeed, what was the aim of educating any working class. If it was doubtful as to how far the social and economic classes of any modern state could be essentially transformed and changed by popular education, how much more tremendous was the problem of educating a race whose ability to assimilate modern training was in grave question and whose place in the nation and the world, even granted they could be educated, was a matter of baffling social philosophy. Was the nation making an effort to parallel white civilization in the South with a black civilization? Or was it trying to displace the dominant white master class with new black masters or was it seeking the difficult but surely more reasonable and practical effort of furnishing a trained set of free black laborers who might carry on in place of the violently disrupted slave system? Surely, most men said, this economic and industrial problem of the New South was the first—the central, the insistent problem of the day.

There can be no doubt of the real dilemma that thus faced the nation, the Northern philanthropists and the black man. The argument for the New England college, which at first seemed to need no apology, grew and developed. The matter of man's earning a living, said the college, is and must be important, but surely it can never be so important as the man himself. Thus the economic adaptation of the Negro to the South must in education be subordinated to the great necessity of teaching life and culture. The South, and more especially the Negro, needed and must have trained and educated leadership if civilization was to survive. More than most, here was land and people who needed to learn the meaning of life. They needed the preparation of gifted persons for the profession of teaching, and for other professions which would in time grow. The object of education was not to make men carpenters, but to make carpenters men.

On the other hand, those practical men who looked at the South after the war said: this is an industrial and business age. We are on the threshold of an economic expansion such as the world never saw before. Whatever human civilization has been or may become, today it is industry. The South because of slavery has lagged behind the world. It must catch up. Its prime necessity after the hate and holocaust of war is a trained reliable laboring class. Assume if you will that Negroes are men with every human capacity, nevertheless, as a flat fact, no rising group of peasants can begin at the top. If poverty and starvation are to be warded off, the children of the freedmen must not be taught to despise the humble work, which the mass of the Negro race must for untold years pursue. The transition period between slavery and freedom is a dangerous and critical one. Fill the heads of these children with Latin and Greek and highfalutin' notions of rights and political power, and hell will be to pay.

On the other hand, in the South, here is land and fertile land, in vast quantities, to be had at nominal prices. Here are employers who must have skilled and faithful labor, and have it now. There is in the near future an industrial, development coming which will bring the South abreast with the new economic development of the nation and the world. Freedom must accelerate this development which slavery so long retarded. Here then is no time for a philosophy of economic or class revolution and race hatred. There must be friendship and good will between employer and employee, between black and white. They have common interests, and the matter of their future relations in politics and society can well be left for future generations and different times to solve. "Cast down your buckets where you are," cried Booker T. Washington; "In all things that are purely social you can be as separate as the fingers, yet one hand in all things essential to mutual progress."

What was needed, then, was that the Negro first should be made the intelligent laborer, the trained farmer, the skilled artisan of the South. Once he had accomplished this step in the economic world and the ladder was set for his climbing, his future would be assured, and assured on an economic foundation which would be immovable. All else in his development, if he proved himself capable of development, even to the highest, would inevitably follow. Let us have, therefore, not colleges but schools to teach the technique of industry and to make men learn by doing.

These were the opposing arguments. They were real arguments. They were set forth by earnest men, white and black, philanthropist and teacher, statesman and seer. The controversy waxed bitter. The disputants came to rival organizations, to severe social pressure, to anger and even to blows. Newspapers were aligned for and against;

employment and promotion depended often on a Negro's attitude toward industrial education. The Negro race and their friends were split in twain by the intensity of their feeling and men were labeled and earmarked by their allegiance to one school of thought or to the other.

Today all this is past; by the majority of the older of my hearers, it is practically forgotten. By the younger, it appears merely as a vague legend. Thirty-five years, a full generation and more, have elapsed. The increase in Negro education by all measurements has been a little less than marvelous. In 1895, there were not more than 1,000 Negro students of full college grade in the United States. Today, there are over 19,000 in college and nearly 150,000 in high schools. In 1895, 60% of American Negroes, ten years of age or over, were illiterate. Today, perhaps three-fourths can read and write. The increase of Negro students in industrial and land-grant colleges has been equally large. The latter have over 16,000 students and the increasing support of the government of the States; while the great industrial schools, especially Hampton and Tuskegee, are the best endowed institutions for the education of black folk in the world.

What then has become of this controversy as to college and industrial education for Negroes? Has it been duly settled, and if it has, how has it been settled? Has it been transmuted into a new program, and if so, what is that program? In other words, what is the present norm of Negro education, represented at once by Howard University, Fisk, and Atlanta on one hand, and by Hampton Institute, Tuskegee, and the land-grant colleges on the other?

I answer once for all, the problem has not been settled. The questions raised in those days of controversy still stand in all their validity and all their pressing insistence on an answer. They have not been answered. They must be answered, and the men and women of this audience and like audiences throughout the land are the ones from whom the world demands final reply. Answers have been offered; and the present status of the problem has enormously changed, for human problems never stand still. But I must insist that the fundamental problem is still here.[27]

NOTES

1. The governor of Alabama from 1911 to 1915 actually spelled his name Emmet O'Neal, rather than O'Neil. "Alabama Governors: Emmet O'Neal," Alabama Department of Archives and History.

2. Scott and Stowe, 1916, 127–134.

3. Cripps, "Introduction," 1969, viii.

4. Du Bois refers to the Twenty-Eighth Annual Tuskegee Negro Conference, held in January 1917, which discouraged black migration from the South. Hudson, 2009, 157.

5. Du Bois, March 1917, 219.

6. Walter White, in 1923 James Weldon Johnson's assistant secretary for the NAACP, was preparing an article describing the evolution of race advocacy over the span of the early century. To that end, White asked Du Bois several questions about the differences between his thought and that of Washington. Du Bois, 1973, 265–266.

7. Du Bois, 1973, 266–267.

8. Du Bois, September 1924, 200–202.

9. Du Bois, March 1926, 216.

10. Amos, 1927.

11. Du Bois, July 1927, 159–160.

12. Du Bois, February 1929, 43–44, 65–69.

13. Moton, 1929.

14. Review of *What the Negro Thinks*, by Robert R. Moton, June 1929, 196, 210–212.

15. Du Bois, June 1931, 207.

16. *In re Strittmater*, 140 NJ Eq. 94 (1947).

17. Du Bois, 1973, 458–460.

18. As noted above, Louisa Strittmater was a woman, but Du Bois did not know that and assumed the letter came from a man.

19. Du Bois, 1973, 460–461.

20. Du Bois, 1934, 365–366.

21. Wright, 1941.

22. Review of *12 Million Black Voices*, September 1941–August 1942, 26.

23. Du Bois here refers to *Guinn v. United States*, 238 US 347 (1915), which ruled that grandfather clauses in state constitutions were unconstitutional.

24. Du Bois, "The Problem of the Twentieth Century Is the Problem of the Color Line," *Pittsburgh Courier*, 14 January 1950.

25. Du Bois here refers to Scott and Stowe, 1916; Riley, 1916; Mathews, 1948; and Graham, 1955.

26. Review of *Booker T. Washington and the Negro's Place in America*, Spring 1956, 183–185.

27. Du Bois, April 1932, 60–74.

Bibliography

Newspapers

Atlanta Constitution
Baltimore Afro-American
Boston Evening Transcript
Boston Globe
Boston Herald
Boston Morning Journal
Boston Transcript
The Broad Ax
Charleston Daily Mail
Chicago Conservator
Chicago Daily News
Chicago Journal

Chicago Tribune
Iowa State Bystander
New York Age
New York American
New York Evening Post
New York Times
Queanbeyan Age
Richmond Times Dispatch
Washington Bee
Washington Colored American
Washington Post

Archival Sources

"Alexander Crummell to Frazier Miller." 20 June 1898. Box 1. Crummell Letters. Folder 6. Alexander Crummell Papers. Schomberg Center for Research in Black Culture. New York Public Library. New York.

Armstrong Letterbooks. Hampton University Archives. Hampton, VA.

Booker T. Washington Correspondence, Sc MG 182. Schomburg Center for Research in Black Culture. New York Public Library. New York.

Booker T. Washington Papers, MSS 44669. Manuscript Division. Library of Congress. Washington, DC.

Burt Green Wilder Papers. 1841–1925. Collection Number 14-26-95. Division of Rare and Manuscript Collections. Cornell University Library. Ithaca, NY.

Hale, S.Q. "Recollections of a Confederate Private." Arrington Collection-Civil War, S.F1, D2, Folder 51. Alabama Room and Special Collections. University of West Alabama. Livingston, AL.

Harvard University. Faculty of Arts and Sciences. Student folders, ca. 1890–1995 (inclusive). Du Bois, William Edward Burghardt, AB 1890. UAIII 15.88.10 Box 120. Harvard University Archives. Cambridge, MA.

James Rudolph Garfield Papers, MS 4573. Western Reserve Historical Society. Cleveland, OH.

Jesse Edward Moorland Collection, DCLV96-A748. Moorland-Spingarn Research Center. Howard University. Washington, DC.

Lester Walton Papers, Sc MG 183. Schomburg Center for Research in Black Culture. New York Public Library. New York.

Merrill, James G. Collection 1899–1919. Fisk University Library. Special Collections and Archives. Nashville, TN.

Merriman, Daniel. Correspondence, 1892–1893. Misc. mss. boxes "M." American Antiquarian Society Manuscript Collections. Worcester, MA.

Nathan Francis Mossell Papers. 1873–1983. UPT 50 M913. University Archives and Records Center. University of Pennsylvania. Philadelphia.

Oswald Garrison Villard Papers, MS Am 1323. Houghton Library. Harvard College Library. Harvard University. Cambridge, MA.

Reminiscences of WEB Du Bois in the Columbia Oral History Archives, Rare Book and Manuscript Library. Columbia University in the City of New York. New York.

Richard Carroll Papers. 1908–1977. University South Caroliniana Society Manuscripts Collection. University of South Carolina. Columbia.

Samuel McCune Lindsay Papers, 1877–1957, MS #0785. Rare Book and Manuscript Library. Columbia University. New York.

Theodore Roosevelt Papers, MSS 38299. Manuscript Division. Library of Congress. Washington, DC.

WEB Du Bois Papers, MS 312. Special Collections and University Archives. University of Massachusetts Amherst. Amherst.

William Howard Taft Papers, MSS 42234. Manuscript Division. Library of Congress. Washington, DC.

Primary Sources

Amos, James E. *Theodore Roosevelt: Hero to His Valet* (New York: John Day Co., 1927).

"An Act to Establish a Normal School for Colored Teachers at Tuskegee." *Acts of the General Assembly of Alabama Passed at the Session of 1880–81* (Montgomery, AL: Allred and Beers, 1881), 395–396.

Aptheker, Herbert, ed. *A Documentary History of the Negro People in the United States* (New York: The Citadel Press, 1969).

Archer, William. *Through Afro-America: An English Reading of the Race Problem* (London: Chapman and Hall, Ltd., 1910).

The Atlanta Exposition and South Illustrated (Chicago, IL: Adler Art Publishing Co., 1895).

Baker, Ray Stannard. "An Ostracized Race in Ferment: Story of the Conflict of Negro Parities and Negro Leaders over Methods of Dealing with Their Own Problems." *American Magazine* 66 (May 1908): 60–70.

Barber, Jesse Max. "Southern Representation." *Voice of the Negro* 3 (April 1906): 242–243.

"Booker T. Washington." *Crisis* 11 (January 1916): 122–128.

"Booker Washington and His Race." *Outlook* 111 (24 November 1915): 700–703.

"Bravery and Hypnotism." *The Medical Press and Circular* 136 (4 March 1908): 254.

Buck, Daniel Dana. *The Progression of the Race in the United States and Canada* (Chicago, IL: Atwell Printing, 1907).

Catalogue of the Officers and Students of Atlanta University, 1903–1904 (Atlanta, GA: Atlanta University Press, 1904).

Comings, Samuel Huntington. *Pagan vs. Christian Civilizations: National Life and Permanence Dependent on Reform in Education, A Plea for Free Universal Industrial Training on a Self-Supporting Basis*. Reprinted by Nabu Press, 2011.

"Committee on the Negro 'Call' for a National Conference, February 1909." Ray Stannard Baker Papers. Manuscript Division. Library of Congress. http://myloc.gov/Exhibitions/naacp/earlyyears/Exhibit Objects/ NationalConference.aspx. Accessed 27 October 2012.

"Crime." *Crisis* 1 (April 1911): 11.

"Crime." *Crisis* 2 (May 1911): 7.

Dole, Charles F. "The Twentieth Century Club of Boston." *National Municipal Review* 3 (July 1914): 572–577.

Du Bois, W.E.B. *The Amenia Conference: An Historic Negro Gathering* (Amenia, NY: Troutbeck Leaflets Number Eight, 1925).

Du Bois, W.E.B. "Another Study in Black." *The New Review* 2 (July 1914): 410–414.

Du Bois, W.E.B. "The Appeal to Europe." *Crisis* 1 (January 1911): 9–11.

Du Bois, W.E.B. *The Autobiography of W.E.B. Du Bois: A Soliloquy on Viewing My Life from the Last Decade of Its First Century* (New York: International Publishers, 1968).

Du Bois, W.E.B. "Booker T. Washington." *Crisis* 11 (December 1915): 82.

Du Bois, W.E.B. *The Conservation of Races.* The American Negro Academy Occasional Papers. No. 2. 1897.

Du Bois, W.E.B. *The Correspondence of W.E.B. Du Bois*, vol. 1, *Selections, 1877–1934*, ed. Herbert Aptheker (Amherst: University of Massachusetts Press, 1973). Copyright © 1973 by the University of Massachusetts Press and published by the University of Massachusetts Press. Reprinted with permission.

Du Bois, W.E.B. "Credo." *Independent* 57 (6 October 1904): 787.

Du Bois, W.E.B. "A Crusade." *Crisis* 7 (March 1914): 238–239.

Du Bois, W.E.B. "Debit and Credit." *Voice of the Negro* 2 (January 1905): 677.

Du Bois, W.E.B. "The Dunbar National Bank." *Crisis* 35 (November 1928): 381–382.

Du Bois, W.E.B. *Dusk of Dawn* (New York: Harcourt Brace, 1940).

Du Bois, W.E.B. "Education and Work." *Journal of Negro Education* I (April 1932): 60–74. Reprinted with permission.

Du Bois, W.E.B. "Envy." *Crisis* 1 (January 1911): 16.

Du Bois, W.E.B. "Fifty Years of Tuskegee." *Crisis* 38 (June 1931): 207. Reprinted with permission.

Du Bois, W.E.B. "Five Million." *Crisis* 31 (March 1926): 216. Reprinted with permission.

Du Bois, W.E.B. "Foreign Comment." *Crisis* 1 (December 1910): 15.

Du Bois, W.E.B. "George Forbes of Boston: A Servant of Jew and Gentile." *Crisis* 34 (July 1927): 151–152. Reprinted with permission.

Du Bois, W.E.B. "Georgia Negroes and Their Fifty Millions of Savings." *World's Work* 18 (May 1909): 11550–11554.

Du Bois, W.E.B. "The Growth of the Niagara Movement." *Voice of the Negro* 3 (January 1906): 43–45.

Du Bois, W.E.B. "If I Had a Million Dollars: A Review of the Phelps Stokes Fund." *Crisis* 39 (November 1932): 347.

Du Bois, W.E.B. "Jefferson Davis as a Representative of Civilization." Harvard University Commencement address, 1890. In *W.E.B. Du Bois: A Reader*, ed. David Levering Lewis, 17–19 (New York: Henry Holt, 1995).

Du Bois, W.E.B. "The Laboratory in Sociology at Atlanta University." *The Annals of the American Academy of Political and Social Science* 21 (May 1903): 503–505.

Du Bois, W.E.B. "Litany of Atlanta." *Independent* 51 (11 October 1906): 856–858.

Du Bois, W.E.B. "A Little Bushel of Books." Review of *The Education of the Negro Prior to 1861*, by Carter G. Woodson (Washington, DC: Associated Publishers, 1915), *The Black Man's Burden*, by William H. Holtzclaw (New York: Neale Pub. Co., 1915), *Race Orthodoxy in the South*, by Thomas P. Bailey (New York: Neale Pub. Co., 1914), and *The Ultimate Criminal*, by Archibald H. Grimke (Washington, DC: American Negro Academy, 1915) in *Crisis* 10 (September 1915): 251–252.

Du Bois, W.E.B. "Lynchings." *Crisis* 39 (February 1932): 58.

Du Bois, W.E.B. "The Negro Race in the United States of America." In *Papers on Inter-Racial Problems Communicated to the First Universal Races Congress Held at University of London, July 26–29, 1911*, ed. G. Spiller, 348–363 (London: P.S. King & Son, 1911).

Du Bois, W.E.B. "A Negro Schoolmaster in the New South." *Atlantic Monthly* 83 (January 1899): 99–105.

Du Bois, W.E.B. "An Open Letter to Robert Russa Moton." *Crisis* 12 (July 1916): 136–137.

Du Bois, W.E.B. "The Parting of the Ways." *World Today* 6 (April 1904): 521–523.

Du Bois, W.E.B. "A Pilgrimage to The Negro Schools." *Crisis* 36 (February 1929): 43–44, 65–69. Reprinted with permission.

Du Bois, W.E.B. "A Plucky Man." *Crisis* 5 (November 1912): 16.

Du Bois, W.E.B. "Possibilities of the Negro: The Advance Guard of the Race." *Booklover's Magazine* 2 (July 1903): 3–15.

Du Bois, W.E.B. "The Problem of the Intellectual Woman." *American Magazine* 67 (January 1909): 288–290.

Du Bois, W.E.B. "The Problem of the Twentieth Century Is the Problem of the Color Line." *Pittsburgh Courier* (14 January 1950).

Du Bois, W.E.B. Review of *12 Million Black Voices: A Folk History of the Negro in the United States*, by Richard Wright (New York: Viking Press, 1941) in *The United States: 1865–1900* 1 (September 1941–August 1942): 26.

Du Bois, W.E.B. Review of *Black Manhattan*, by James Weldon Johnson (New York: A.A. Knopf, 1930) in *New York Evening Post* (12 July 1930): Section 3, 5.

Du Bois, W.E.B. Review of *Booker T. Washington and the Negro's Place in America*, by Samuel R. Spencer (Boston, MA: Little, Brown & Co., 1955) in *Science & Society* 20 (Spring 1956): 183–185.

Du Bois, W.E.B. Review of *Education in Africa: Recommendations of the African Education Committee*, 2 vols, by Thomas Jesse Jones (New York: Phelps-Stokes Fund, 1926) in *Crisis* 32 (June 1926): 86–89.

Du Bois, W.E.B. Review of *God's Trombones: Seven Negro Sermons in Verse*, by James Weldon Johnson (New York: Viking Press, 1927), *Negro Labor in the United States*, by Charles H. Wesley (New York: Vanguard Press, 1927), *Theodore Roosevelt: Hero to His Valet*, by James E. Amos (New York: John Day Co., 1927), and *Humanizing Education (A Preface to a Realistic Education)*, by Samuel Schmalhausen (New York: New Education Pub. Co., 1926) in *Crisis* 34 (July 1927): 159–160.

Du Bois, W.E.B. Review of *The Story of John Hope*, by Ridgely Torrence (New York: Macmillan Co, 1948) in *Crisis* 53 (September 1948): 270–271.

Du Bois, W.E.B. Review of *Up from Slavery: An Autobiography*, by Booker T. Washington (New York: Doubleday, Page & Co., 1901) in *The Dial* (16 July 1901): 53–55.

Du Bois, W.E.B. Review of *What the Negro Thinks*, by Robert R. Moton (Garden City, NY: Doubleday, Doran & Co., 1929), *Rope and Faggot: A Biography of Judge Lynch*, by Walter F. White (New York: A.A. Knopf, 1929), and *Black America*, by Scott Nearing (New York: Vanguard Press, 1929) in *Crisis* 36 (June 1929): 196, 210–212.

Du Bois, W.E.B. "Social Equality." *Crisis* 12 (May 1916): 30.

Du Bois, W.E.B., ed. *Some Efforts of American Negroes for Their Own Social Betterment* (Atlanta, GA: Atlanta University Press, 1898).

Du Bois, W.E.B. "Starvation and Prejudice." *Crisis* 2 (June 1911): 62–64.

Du Bois, W.E.B. "A Suggestion." *Crisis* 11 (January 1916): 135.

Du Bois, W.E.B. "Taft." *Horizon* 3 (June 1908): 1–8.

Du Bois, W.E.B. "The Talented Tenth." In *The Negro Problem: A Series of Articles by Representative American Negroes of Today*, 33–75 (New York: James Pott & Co., 1903).

Du Bois, W.E.B. "Tuskegee and Moton." *Crisis* 28 (September 1924): 200–202.

Du Bois, W.E.B. "The Tuskegee Resolutions." *Crisis* 13 (March 1917): 219.

Du Bois, W.E.B. "The Upbuilding of Black Durham: The Success of the Negroes and Their Value to a Tolerant and Helpful Southern City." *World's Work* 13 (January 1912): 334–338.

Du Bois, W.E.B. "Washington, Booker Taliaferro." In *Encyclopaedia of the Social Sciences*, ed. Edwin R.A. Seligman, vol. 15, 365–366 (New York: The Macmillan Company, 1934).

Flemming, William Henry. *Slavery and the Race Problem in the South, with Special Reference to the State of Georgia* (Boston, MA: Dana Estes & Co., 1906).

Forty-Sixth Annual Report of the American Missionary Association (New York: American Missionary Association, 1892).

Grant, Percy Stickney. "Socialism and Christianity." *North American Review* 190 (August 1909): 145–157.

Guinn v. United States, 238 US 347 (1915).

"He Helped to Found Tuskegee." *The Christian Register* 101 (8 June 1922): 19.

Hearings of the Committee on Interstate and Foreign Commerce of the House of Representatives on HR 20153, 21572, and 22133, on the Subject of Railroad Passenger Fares and Mileage Tickets (Washington, DC: Government Printing Office, 1907).

Holtzclaw, William Henry. *The Black Man's Burden* (New York: Haskell House, 1915).

In re Strittmater, 140 NJ Eq. 94 (1947).

Irvine, Alexander. "My Life Is Peonage: II, A Week with the 'Bull In the Woods'." *Appleton's Magazine* 10 (July 1907): 3–15.

"Items." *Liberia* 33 (November 1908), 57.

Johnson, James Weldon. *Black Manhattan* (New York: Knopf, 1930).

Jones, Jenkin Lloyd. Review of *Souls of Black Folk*, by W.E.B. Du Bois in *Unity* (7 May 1903): 148–149.

Knox, George L. *Slave and Freeman: The Autobiography of George L. Knox* (Lexington: University Press of Kentucky, 1979). Originally published 1895.

A Life Well Lived: In Memory of Robert Curtis Ogden (Hampton, VA: Hampton Institute Press, 1914).

"Lyman Beecher Stowe: Author, Editor, Lecturer." Traveling Culture: Circuit Chautauqua in the Twentieth Century, MSC0150. Special Collections Department. University of Iowa. Des Moines.

Mecklin, John Moffatt. *Democracy and Race Friction: A Study in Social Ethics* (Freeport, NY: Books for Libraries Press, 1914).

"Men of the Month." *Crisis* 7 (April 1914): 274–275.

"Men of the Month: Dr. Charles E. Bentley." *Crisis* 2 (May 1911): 10–11.

"Men of the Month: Gilchrist Stewart." *Crisis* 2 (August 1911): 147.

"Men of the Month: John S. Trower." *Crisis* 2 (May 1911): 10.

The Merchants Club of Chicago, 1896–1907 (Chicago, IL: Commercial Club of Chicago, 1922).

Meyer, Annie Nathan. "The Problem Before Women." *Appleton's Magazine* 13 (February 1909): 194–197.

Minutes of the General Assembly of the Presbyterian Church in the United States of America (Philadelphia, PA: Office of the General Assembly, 1915).

Moody's Manual of Railroads and Corporation Securities. Industrial Section, vol. I, A-J (New York: Poor's Publishing Co., 1922).

Morris, E.C. *Sermons, Addresses, and Reminiscences and Important Correspondence, with a Picture Gallery of Eminent Ministers and Scholars* (Nashville, TN: National Baptist Publishing Board, 1901).

Moton, Robert Russa. *Finding a Way Out: An Autobiography* (Garden City, NY: Doubleday, 1921).

Moton, Robert Russa. *What the Negro Thinks* (Garden City, NY: Doubleday, 1929).

The Negro Problem: A Series of Articles by Representative American Negroes of Today (New York: James Pott Company, 1903).

"News from the Classes: 1880." *Harvard Graduates' Magazine* 21 (September 1912): 153.

Niagara Movement, Committee of Organization. "Report on the Committee of Organization." December 1907. University of Massachusetts Amherst. Special Collections and University Archives. http://scua .library.umass.edu/digital/Du Bois/312.2.839-06-03.pdf. Accessed 2 July 2014.

Noel, Francis Regis, and Margaret Brent Downing. *The Court-House of the District of Columbia* (Washington, DC: Judd & Detweiler, 1919).

Ordfield, J.R., ed. *Civilization and Black Progress: Selected Writings of Alexander Crummell on the South* (Charlottesville: University Press of Virginia, 1995).

Ovington, Mary White. *The Walls Came Tumbling Down: An Autobiography* (New York: Harcourt, Brace, 1947).

"Pink Franklin." *Crisis* 1 (December 1910): 26.

"The Platform of the Niagara Movement." *Outlook* 84 (1 September 1906): 3–4.

Powell, Jacob W. *Bird's Eye View of the General Conference of the African Methodist Episcopal Zion Church* (Boston, MA: Lavalle Press, 1918).

Powers, Le Grand. *Census Reports, Volume V, Twelfth Census of the United States: Agriculture* (Washington, DC: United States Census Office, 1902).

"Reminiscences of W.E.B. Du Bois." NXCP89-A80. Columbia University Oral History Collection. Butler Library. Columbia University. New York.

"Represented at Minneapolis." *The League Bulletin*, League to Enforce Peace 51 (7 September 1917): 54.

Review of *The Souls of Black Folk*, by W.E.B. Du Bois (Chicago, IL: A.C. McClurg & Co., 1903) in *Outlook* 74 (11 July 1903): 669–671.

Roosevelt, Theodore. "Preface." In *Booker T. Washington: Builder of a Civilization*, by Emmett J. Scott and Lyman Beecher Stowe, ix–xv (Garden City, NY: Doubleday, Page & Co., 1916).

Rowe, E.T. *Lessons in Business: A Complete Compendium of How to Do Business by the Latest and Safest Methods* (Toronto: John A. Hertel Co., 1921).

Sanborn, Franklin Benjamin, ed. *The Life and Letters of John Brown, Liberator of Kansas and Martyr of Virginia* (Boston, MA: Roberts Brothers, 1885).

Schurz, Carl. "Can the South Solve the Negro Problem?" *McClure's Magazine* 22 (January 1904): 259–275.

Scott, Emmett J., and Lyman Beecher Stowe. *Booker T. Washington: Builder of a Civilization* (Garden City, NY: Doubleday, Page & Co., 1916).

Siebert, William Henry. *The Underground Railroad from Slavery to Freedom* (New York: Macmillan, 1899).

Sinclair, William A. *The Aftermath of Slavery: A Study of the Condition and Environment of the American Negro* (Columbia: University of South Carolina Press, 2012). Originally published 1905.

Smith, Wilford H. *The Negro's Right to Jury Representation* (Cheyney, PA: Committee of Twelve, 1910).

"Social Uplift." *Crisis* 11 (January 1916): 113.

Starr, Frederick. *Liberia: Description, History, Problems* (Chicago, IL: Frederick Starr, 1913).

Stone, Alfred Holt. "The Mulatto Factor in the Race Problem." *Atlantic Monthly* (May 1903): 658–652.

Stone, Alfred Holt. *Studies in the American Race Problem* (New York: Doubleday, Page, and Co., 1908).

Twenty-Fourth Annual Catalogue of the Tuskegee Normal and Industrial Institute, 1904–1905 (Tuskegee, AL: Tuskegee Institute, 1905).

Villard, Oswald Garrison. "An Alabama Negro School." *American Monthly Review of Reviews* 26 (December 1902): 711–714.

Villard, Oswald Garrison. *John Brown, 1800–1859: A Biography Fifty Years After* (New York: Houghton Mifflin, 1910).

Von Holst, Hermann. *John Brown* (Boston, MA: Cupples and Hurt, 1888).

Walters, Alexander. *My Life and Work* (New York: Fleming H. Revell, 1917).

Washington, Booker T. "The American Negro and His Economic Value." *International Monthly* 2 (December 1900): 672–686.

Washington, Booker T. *An Autobiography: The Story of My Life and Work* (Naperville, IL: J.L. Nichols & Co., 1901).

Washington, Booker T. "Early Life and Struggle for an Education." *Howard's American Magazine* 4 (November 1899): 3–6.

Washington, Booker T. *My Larger Education* (Garden City, NY: Doubleday, Page, & Co., 1911).

Washington, Booker T. "The Negro Doctor in the South." *The Independent* 63 (11 July 1907): 89–91.

Washington, Booker T. "The Negro in Business." *Gunton's Magazine* 20 (March 1901): 209–219.

Washington, Booker T. *The Papers of Booker T. Washington*, vol. 1, *Autobiographical Writings*, ed. Louis Harlan (Urbana: University of Illinois Press, 1972).

Washington, Booker T. *The Papers of Booker T. Washington*, vol. 2, *1860–1889*, ed. Louis Harlan (Urbana: University of Illinois Press, 1972).

Washington, Booker T. *The Papers of Booker T. Washington*, vol. 3, *1889–1895*, ed. Louis Harlan (Urbana: University of Illinois Press, 1974).

Washington, Booker T. *The Papers of Booker T. Washington*, vol. 4, *1895–1898*, ed. Louis Harlan (Urbana: University of Illinois Press, 1975).

Washington, Booker T. *The Papers of Booker T. Washington*, vol. 5, *1899–1900*, ed. Louis Harlan (Urbana: University of Illinois Press, 1977).

Washington, Booker T. *The Papers of Booker T. Washington*, vol. 6, *1901–1902*, ed. Louis Harlan (Urbana: University of Illinois Press, 1977).

Washington, Booker T. *The Papers of Booker T. Washington*, vol. 7, *1903–1904*, ed. Louis Harlan (Urbana: University of Illinois Press, 1977).

Washington, Booker T. *The Papers of Booker T. Washington*, vol. 8, *1904–1906*, ed. Louis Harlan (Urbana: University of Illinois Press, 1979).

Washington, Booker T. *The Papers of Booker T. Washington*, vol. 9, *1906–1908*, ed. Louis Harlan (Urbana: University of Illinois Press, 1980).

Washington, Booker T. *The Papers of Booker T. Washington*, vol. 10, *1909–1911*, ed. Louis Harlan (Urbana: University of Illinois Press, 1981).

Washington, Booker T. *The Papers of Booker T. Washington*, vol. 11, *1911–1912*, ed. Louis Harlan (Urbana: University of Illinois Press, 1981).

Washington, Booker T. *The Papers of Booker T. Washington*, vol. 12, *1912–1914*, ed. Louis Harlan (Urbana: University of Illinois Press, 1983).

Washington, Booker T. *The Papers of Booker T. Washington*, vol. 13, *1914–1915*, ed. Louis Harlan (Urbana: University of Illinois Press, 1984).

Washington, Booker T. "The Plucky Class." *Southern Workman* 9 (November 1880): 112.

Washington, Booker T. "A Stable as a Civilizer." *Southern Workman* 18 (April 1889): 47.

Washington, Booker T. *The Story of the Negro: The Rise of the Race from Slavery* (New York: Doubleday, Page, 1909).

Washington, Booker T. "Taking Advantage of Our Disadvantages." *A.M.E. Church Review* 10 (April 1894): 478–483.

Washington, Booker T. "To the Editor." *Southern Workman* 10 (September 1881): 94.

Washington, Booker T. "To the Editor." *Southern Workman* 10 (October 1881): 101.

Washington, Booker T. *Up from Slavery: An Autobiography* (New York: Doubleday, Page & Co., 1901).

Washington, Booker T. "The Woman Suffrage Movement." *New York Times* (20 December 1908): SM3.

Washington, Booker T. *Working with the Hands* (New York: Doubleday, Page, & Co., 1904).

Washington, Booker T., and W.E.B. Du Bois. *The Negro in the South: His Economic Progress in Relation to His Moral and Religious Development* (Philadelphia, PA: George W. Jacobs & Co., 1907).

Wells, Ida B. *Crusade for Justice: The Autobiography of Ida B. Wells*, ed. Alfreda M. Duster (Chicago, IL: University of Chicago Press, 1970).

"What Is a Good Negro." *Voice of the Negro* 1 (December 1904): 618.

"The Work in Progress." *The Railway Age* 27 (7 April 1890): 256–258.

Wright, Richard. *Twelve Million Black Voices: A Folk History of the Negro in the United States* (New York: Viking Press, 1941).

Secondary Sources

Adeleke, Tunde. *UnAfrican Americans: Nineteenth-Century Black Nationalists and the Civilizing Mission* (Lexington: University Press of Kentucky, 1998).

"Alabama Governors: Charles Henderson." Alabama Department of Archives and History. http://www.archives.state.al.us/govs_list/g_hender.html. Accessed 5 July 2014.

"Alabama Governors: Emmet O'Neal." Alabama Department of Archives and History. http://www.archives.state.al.us/govs_List/g_onealm.html. Accessed 5 July 2014.

Alexander, Adele Logan. "The American Way of Education and My Own History." Keynote Address. Ethical Culture Fieldstone School Founders Day. 2003.

Alexander, Eleanor C. *Lyrics of Sunshine and Shadow: The Tragic Courtship and Marriage of Paul Laurence Dunbar and Alice Ruth Moore* (New York: New York University Press, 2001).

Alexander, Shawn Leigh. *An Army of Lions: The Civil Rights Struggle Before the NAACP* (Philadelphia: University of Pennsylvania Press, 2012).

Anderson, Donald F. *William Howard Taft: A Conservative's Conception of the Presidency* (Ithaca, NY: Cornell University Press, 1973).

Anderson, James D. *The Education of Blacks in the South, 1860–1935* (Chapel Hill: University of North Carolina Press, 1988).

Andrews, William. *The Literary Career of Charles W. Chesnutt* (Baton Rouge: Louisiana State University Press, 1980).

Angell, Stephen Ward. *Henry McNeal Turner and African-American Religion in the South* (Knoxville: University of Tennessee, 1992).

Apiah, Kwame Anthony. *Lines of Descent: W.E.B. Du Bois and the Emergence of Identity* (Cambridge, MA: Harvard University Press, 2014).

Aptheker, Herbert. *Afro-American History: The Modern Era* (Secaucus, NJ: The Citadel Press, 1971).

Aptheker, Herbert. "Introduction." In *The Souls of Black Folk*, by W.E.B. Du Bois (Millwood, NY: Kraus-Thompson, 1973).

Ascoli, Peter M. *Julius Rosenwald: The Man Who Built Sears, Roebuck and Advanced the Cause of Black Education in the American South* (Bloomington: Indiana University Press, 2006).

Ayers, Edward L. *The Promise of the New South: Life After Reconstruction* (New York: Oxford University Press, 1992).

Bacote, Clarence. "The Negro in Georgia Politics, 1880–1908." PhD dissertation, University of Chicago, 1955.

Baldwin, Davarian L. *Chicago's New Negroes: Modernity, the Great Migration, and Black Urban Life* (Chapel Hill: University of North Carolina Press, 2007).

Bannister, Robert C. *Ray Stannard Baker: The Mind and Thought of a Progressive* (New Haven, CT: Yale University Press, 1966).

Bauerlein, Mark. "Booker T. Washington and W.E.B. Du Bois: The Origins of a Bitter Intellectual Battle." *Journal of Blacks in Higher Education* 46 (Winter 2004–2005): 106–114.

Berlin, Ira. *The Making of African America: The Four Great Migrations* (New York: Penguin, 2010).

Bernard, Emily. *Carl Van Vechten and the Harlem Renaissance: A Portrait in Black and White* (New Haven, CT: Yale University Press, 2012).

Blight, David W. *Race and Reunion: The Civil War in American Memory* (Cambridge, MA: Harvard University Press, 2001).

Boston, Michael B. *The Business Strategy of Booker T. Washington: Its Development and Implementation* (Gainesville: University Press of Florida, 2010).

Boylan, James R. *Revolutionary Lives: Anna Strunsky and William English Walling* (Amherst: University of Massachusetts Press, 1998).

Breault, Judith Colucci. *The Odyssey of a Humanitarian: Emily Howland, 1827–1929* (New York: Arno Press, 1982).

Broderick, Francis L. *W.E.B. Bu Bois: Negro Leader in a Time of Crisis* (Palo Alto, CA: Stanford University Press, 1959).

Brown, Ira V. *Lyman Abbott, Christian Evolutionist: A Study in Religious Liberalism* (Cambridge, MA: Harvard University Press, 1953).

Brown, Lois. *Pauline Elizabeth Hopkins: Black Daughter of the Revolution* (Chapel Hill: University of North Carolina Press, 2008).

Brown, Theodore M., and Elizabeth Fee. "Isaac Max Rubinow: Advocate for Social Insurance." *American Journal of Public Health* 92 (August 2002): 1224–1225.

Bruce, Dickson D. *Archibald Grimke: Portrait of a Black Independent* (Baton Rouge: Louisiana State University Press, 1993).

Brundage, W. Fitzhugh. *Lynching in the New South: Georgia and Virginia, 1880–1930* (Urbana: University of Illinois Press, 1993).

Brundage, W. Fitzhugh, ed. *Under Sentence of Death: Lynching in the South* (Chapel Hill: University of North Carolina Press, 1997).

Butcher, Philip. "George W. Cable and Booker T. Washington." *Journal of Negro Education* 17 (Autumn 1948): 462–468.

Carle, Susan D. *Defining the Struggle: National Racial Justice Organizing, 1880–1915* (New York: Oxford University Press, 2013).

Cell, John W. *The Highest Stage of White Supremacy: The Origins of Segregation in South Africa and the American South* (New York: Oxford University Press, 1982).

Clark, Herbert. "James Carroll Napier: National Negro Leader." *Tennessee Historical Quarterly* 49 (Winter 1990): 243–252.

Cohen, Naomi Wiener. *Jacob H. Schiff: A Study in American Jewish Leadership* (Hanover, NH: University Press of New England, 1999).

Cohen, William. *At Freedom's Edge: Black Mobility and the Southern White Quest for Racial Control, 1861–1915* (Baton Rouge: Louisiana State University Press, 1991).

Collins, Darrell. *Robert E. Rodes of the Army of Northern Virginia: A Biography* (New York: Savas Beatie, 2008).

Cox, Donna L. "Images of Kowaliga." *Alabama Heritage* 86 (Fall 2007): 42–43.

Cox, Thomas C. *Blacks in Topeka, Kansas, 1865–1915: A Social History* (Baton Rouge: Louisiana State University Press, 1982).

Craig, Berry. "William English Walling: Kentucky's Unknown Civil Rights Hero." *The Register of the Kentucky Historical Society* 96 (Autumn 1998): 351–376.

Creiger, Don M. *Bounder from Wales: Lloyd George's Career Before the First World War* (Columbia: University of Missouri Press, 1976).

Cripps, Thomas R. "Introduction." In *Working with the Hands*, by Booker T. Washington (New York: The Arno Press, 1969). Originally published 1904.

Crofts, Daniel W. "The Black Response to the Blair Education Bill." *Journal of Southern History* 37 (February 1971): 41–65.

Crogman, William H. *Talks for the Times* (Freeport, NY: Books for Libraries Press, 1971).

Cromwell, Adelaide M. *Unveiled Voices, Unvarnished Memories: The Cromwell Family in Slavery and Segregation, 1692–1972* (Columbia: University of Missouri Press, 2007).

Crowder, Ralph L. *John Edward Bruce: Politician, Journalist, and Self-Trained Historian of the African Diaspora* (New York: New York University Press, 2004).

Cureau, Harold G. "William H. Sheppard: Missionary to the Congo, and Collector of African Art." *Journal of Negro History* 67 (Winter 1982): 340–352.

Dailey, Maceo Crenshaw, Jr. "The Business Life of Emmett Jay Scott." *Business History Review* 77 (Winter 2003): 57–68.

Davidson, James West. *They Say: Ida B. Wells and the Reconstruction of Race* (New York: Oxford University Press, 2009).

Davis, Leroy. *A Clashing of the Soul: John Hope and the Dilemma of African American Leadership and Black Higher Education in the Early Twentieth Century* (Athens: University of Georgia Press, 1998).

Day, S. Davis. "Herbert Hoover and Racial Politics: The De Priest Incident." *Journal of Negro History* 65 (Winter 1980): 6–17.

Deegan, Mary Jo. "W.E.B. Du Bois and the Women of Hull-House, 1895–1899." *American Sociologist* 19 (Winter 1988): 301–311.

Desmond, Adrian. *Huxley, Evolution's High Priest* (London: Michael Joseph, 1998).

Desmond, Adrian. *Huxley: The Devil's Disciple* (London: Michael Joseph, 1994).

Deutsch, Stephanie. *You Need a Schoolhouse: Booker T. Washington, Julius Rosenwald, and the Building of Schools for the Segregated South* (Evanston, IL: Northwestern University Press, 2011).

"The Development of an African-American Musical Theatre, 1865–1910." *The Library of Congress: American Memory.* http://memory.loc.gov/ammem/collections/sheetmusic/brown/aasmsprs6.html. Accessed 27 October 2012.

"Dr. H.F. Gamble Passes." *Journal of the National Medical Association* 24 (November 1932): 24.

Drew, Mary E.C. *Divine Will, Restless Heart: The Life and Works of Dr. John Jefferson Smallwood* (Bloomington, IN: Xlibris, 2010).

Duncan, Russell. *Entrepreneur for Equality: Governor Rufus Bullock, Commerce, and Race in Post-Civil War Georgia* (Athens: University of Georgia Press, 1994).

Duncan, Russell. *Where Death and Glory Meet: Colonel Robert Gould Shaw and the 54th Massachusetts Infantry* (Athens: University of Georgia Press, 1999).

Emerson, Jason. *Giant in the Shadows: The Life of Robert T. Lincoln* (Evansville: Southern Illinois University Press, 2012).

Engs, Robert Francis. *Educating the Disfranchised and Disinherited: Samuel Chapman Armstrong and Hampton Institute, 1839–1893* (Knoxville: University of Tennessee Press, 1999).

Eskew, Glenn T. "Black Elitism and the Failure of Paternalism in Postbellum Georgia: The Case of Bishop Lucius Henry Holsey." In *Georgia in Black & White: Explorations in the Georgia Race Relations of a Southern State, 1865–1950*, ed. John C. Inscoe, 106–140 (Athens: University of Georgia Press, 2009).

Feimster, Crystal M. *Southern Horrors: Women and the Politics of Rape and Lynching* (Cambridge, MA: Harvard University Press, 2009).

Foner, Philip S., ed. "Is Booker T. Washington's Idea Correct?" *Journal of Negro History* LV (October 1970): 344–347.

Forth, Christopher E. "Booker T. Washington and the 1905 Niagara Movement Conference." *Journal of Negro History* 72 (Summer-Autumn 1987): 45–56.

Fox, Steven R. *The Guardian of Boston: William Monroe Trotter* (New York: Atheneum, 1971).

Fox, Steven R. *The Mirror Makers: A History of American Advertising & Its Creators* (Urbana: University of Illinois Press, 1984).

Friedman, Lawrence J. "Life in the Lion's Mouth: Another Look at Booker T. Washington." *Journal of Negro History* 59 (October 1974): 337–351.

Garraty, John A., ed. *The Barber and the Historian: The Correspondence of George A. Myers and James Ford Rhodes, 1910–1923* (Columbus: Ohio Historical Society, 1956).

Garrett, Franklin M. *Atlanta and Its Environs: A Chronicle of Its People and Events, 1880s-1930s*, vol. 2 (Athens: University of Georgia Press, 1967).

Going, Allen J. "The South and the Blair Education Bill." *Mississippi Valley Historical Review* 44 (September 1957): 267–290.

Goldenberg, Myrna Gallant. "Annie Nathan Meyer: Barnard Godmother and Gotham Gadfly." PhD dissertation, University of Maryland, 1987.

Goldman, Eric F. *Charles J. Bonaparte: Patrician Reformer, His Earlier Career* (Baltimore, MD: Johns Hopkins Press, 1943).

Goodman, Leonard S. "Gettting Started: Organization, Procedure, and Initial Business of the ICC in 1887." *Transportation Law Journal* 16 (No. 1, 1987): 7–34.

Gordon, Jacob U. *Black Leadership of Social Change* (Westport, CT: Greenwood Press, 2000).

Graham, Otis Lawrence. *The Senator and the Socialite: The True Story of America's First Black Dynasty* (New York: Harper Collins, 2006).

Graham, Shirley. *Booker T. Washington: Educator of Hand, Head, and Heart* (New York: Julian Messner, 1955).

Graybar, Lloyd J. *Albert Shaw of the "Review of Reviews": An Intellectual Biography* (Lexington: University Press of Kentucky, 1974).

Green, Dan S., and Edwin S. Driver, eds. *W.E.B. Du Bois on Sociology and the Black Community* (Chicago, IL: University of Chicago Press, 1978).

Greene, Suzanne Ellery. "Black Republicans on the Baltimore City Council, 1890–1931." *Maryland Historical Magazine* 74 (September 1979): 203–222.

Greenwood, Janette Thomas. *First Fruits of Freedom: The Migration of Former Slaves and Their Search for Equality in Worcester, Massachusetts, 1862–1900* (Chapel Hill: University of North Carolina Press, 2009).

Grosz, Agnes Smith. "The Political Career of Pinckney Benton Stewart Pinchback." *Louisiana Historical Quarterly* 27 (April 1944): 527–612.

Haney, Thomas M. "The First 100 Years: The Centennial History of Loyola University Chicago School of Law." *Loyola University Chicago Law Journal* 41 (2010): 651–725.

Harlan, Louis R. "Booker T. Washington and the National Negro Business League." In *Booker T. Washington in Perspective: The Essays of Louis R. Harlan*, ed. Raymond W. Smock, 98–109 (Jackson: University Press of Mississippi, 1988).

Harlan, Louis R. "Booker T. Washington and the Voice of the Negro, 1904–1907." *Journal of Southern History* 45 (February 1979): 45–62.

Harlan, Louis R. "Booker T. Washington in Biographical Perspective." *American Historical Review* 75 (October 1970): 1581–1599.

Harlan, Louis R. *Booker T. Washington: The Making of a Black Leader, 1856–1901* (New York: Oxford University Press, 1972).

Harlan, Louis R. *Booker T. Washington: The Wizard of Tuskegee, 1901–1915* (New York: Oxford University Press, 1983).

Harlan, Louis R. "The Secret Life of Booker T. Washington." *Journal of Southern History* 37 (August 1971): 393–416.

Harlan, Louis R. "The Southern Education Board and the Race Issue in Public Education." *Journal of Southern History* 23 (May 1957): 189–202.

Harris, Marvin. *The Rise of Anthropological Theory: A History of Theories of Culture* (Walnut Creek, CA: AltaMira Press, 2001). Originally published in 1968.

Harrison, Alferdteen, ed. *Black Exodus: The Great Migration from the American South* (Jackson: University Press of Mississippi, 1991).

Harvard College, Class of 1907: Secretary's Fourth Report (Norwood, MA: Plimpton Press, 1917).

Hawkins, Hugh, ed. *Booker T. Washington and His Critics: The Problem of Negro Leadership* (Lexington, MA: D.C. Heath and Co., 1974).

Hill, Robert A., ed. *Marcus Garvey and Universal Negro Improvement Association Papers*, vol. 5, *September 1922-August 1924* (Berkeley: University of California Press, 1986).

"History of the Congregational Church." First Congregational Christian Church. United Church of Christ. http://www.fcccmontgomery.com/histor/. Accessed 16 June 2013.

Hoffschwelle, Mary S. *The Rosenwald Schools of the American South* (Gainesville: University Press of Florida, 2006).

Hollandsworth, James G., Jr. *Portrait of a Scientific Racist: Alfred Holt Stone of Mississippi* (Baton Rouge: Louisiana State University Press, 2008).

Holloway, Jonathan Scott. *Confronting the Veil: Abram Harris Jr., E. Franklin Frazier, and Ralph Bunche, 1919–1941* (Chapel Hill: University of North Carolina Press, 2002).

Holmes, William F. *The White Chief: James Kimble Vardaman* (Baton Rouge: Louisiana State University Press, 1970).

"The Horizon." *Crisis* 27 (February 1924): 180–181.

Horne, Gerald. *Black Liberation/Red Scare: Ben Davis and the Communist Party* (Newark: University of Delaware Press, 1994).

Horne, Gerald. *W.E.B. Du Bois: A Biography* (Westport, CT: Greenwood Press, 2009).

Horner, William T. *Ohio's Kingmaker: Mark Hanna, Man and Myth* (Athens: Ohio University Press, 2010).

Hudson, Janet G. *Entangled by White Supremacy: Reform in World War I-Era South Carolina* (Lexington: University Press of Kentucky, 2009).

Hull, Gloria T. *Color, Sex, and Poetry: Three Women Writers of the Harlem Renaissance* (Bloomington: Indiana University Press, 1987).

Hurwitt, Elliott S. "Moore, Frederick Randolph." In *Encyclopedia of the Harlem Renaissance, Vol. 2, K-Y*, by eds. Cary D. Wintz and Paul Finkelman, 807–808 (New York: Routledge, 2004).

Ingram, E. Renee. "Bruce, Roscoe Conkling, Sr." In *Harlem Renaissance Lives from the African American National Biography*, by eds. Henry

Louis Gates, Jr. and Evelyn Brooks Higginbotham, 84–86 (New York: Oxford University Press, 2009).

Jastro, Morris, Jr. "William Hayes Ward (1835–1916)." *Journal of the American Oriental Society* 36 (1916): 233–241.

"John Stephens Durham (1861–1919)." US Department of State. Office of the Historian. http://history.state.gov/departmenthistory/people/durham-john-stephens. Accessed 26 June 2014.

Johnson, Marilynn S. *Street Justice: A History of Police Violence in New York City* (Boston, MA: Beacon Press, 2003).

Jones, Angela. *African American Civil Rights: Early Activism and the Niagara Movement* (Santa Barbara, CA: ABC-CLIO, 2011).

Jones, B.W. "Mary Church Terrell and the National Association of Colored Women, 1886–1901." *Journal of Negro History* 67 (1982): 20–33.

Jones, Ida E. *The Heart of the Race Problem: The Life of Kelly Miller* (Littleton, MA: Tapestry Press, 2011).

Jones, R. Clifford. *James K. Humphrey and the Sabbath-Day Adventists* (Jackson: University Press of Mississippi, 2006).

"Joseph Simeon Flipper." *Journal of Negro History* 30 (January 1945): 109–111.

Justesen, Benjamin R. *Broken Brotherhood: The Rise and Fall of the National Afro-American Council* (Carbondale: Southern Illinois University Press, 2008).

Kantrowitz, Steven. *Ben Tillman and the Reconstruction of White Supremacy* (Chapel Hill: University of North Carolina Press, 2000).

Katzman, David. *Before the Ghetto: Black Detroit in the Nineteenth Century* (Urbana: University of Illinois Press, 1975).

Kaye, Andrew M. "Colonel Roscoe Conkling Simmons and the Mechanics of Black Leadership." *Journal of American Studies* 37 (2003): 79–98.

Kilson, Martin. "The Washington and Du Bois Leadership Paradigms Reconsidered." *Annals of the American Academy of Political and Social Science* 568 (March 2000): 298–313.

Kirby, Jack Temple. *Darkness at the Dawning: Race and Reform in the Progressive South* (New York: Lippincott, 1972).

Klarman, Michael. *From Jim Crow to Civil Rights: The Supreme Court and the Struggle for Racial Equality* (New York: Oxford University Press, 2004).

Kousser, Morgan J. *Colorblind Injustice: Minority Voting Rights and the Undoing of the Second Reconstruction* (Chapel Hill: University of North Carolina Press, 1999).

Kousser, Morgan J. *The Shaping of Southern Politics: Suffrage Restriction and the Establishment of a One-Party South* (New Haven, CT: Yale University Press, 1974).

Kreiling, Albert. "The Commercialization of the Black Press and the Rise of Race News in Chicago." In *Ruthless Criticism: New Perspectives in US Communication History*, by eds. William S. Solomon and Robert W. McChesney, 176–203 (Minneapolis: University of Minnesota Press, 1993).

Kuehl, Warren F. *Hamilton Holt: Journalist, Internationalist, Educator* (Gainesville: University of Florida Press, 1960).

Lavender, David. *The Great Persuader: The Biography of Collis P. Huntington* (Boulder: University of Colorado Press, 1998).

Lawlah, John W. "George Cleveland Hall, 1864–1930." *Journal of the National Medical Association* 46 (May 1954): 207–210.

Lawrence, William. *Roger Wolcott* (Boston, MA: Houghton, Mifflin, 1902).

Leslie, LaVonne. *The History of the National Association of Colored Women's Clubs, Inc.: A Legacy of Service* (Bloomington, IN: Xlibris, 2012).

Levy, Eugene. *James Weldon Johnson: Black Leader, Black Voice* (Chicago, IL: University of Chicago Press, 1973).

Lewis, David Levering. *W.E.B. Du Bois: Biography of a Race, 1868–1919* (New York: Henry Holt and Co., 1993).

Lewis, David Levering. *W.E.B. Du Bois: The Fight for Equality and the American Century, 1919–1963* (New York: Owl Books, 2001).

"Life Memberships." *The Minute Man* 14 (May 1924), 3–4.

"Little Annie Rooney." http://www.fresnostate.edu/folklore/ballads/R774.html. Accessed 23 June 2013.

Litwack, Leon F. *Trouble in Mind: Black Southerners in the Age of Jim Crow* (New York: Vintage, 1999).

Lorenz, Alfred Lawrence. "Ralph W. Tyler: The Unknown Correspondent of World War I." *Journalism History* 31 (Spring 2005): 3–12.

Luker, Ralph. *Social Gospel in Black and White: American Racial Reform, 1885–1912* (Chapel Hill: University of North Carolina Press, 1991).

Lyght, Ernest S., and Jonathan D. Keaton. *Our Father: Where Are the Fathers?* (Nashville, TN: Abingdon Press, 2012).

Malone, Henry Thompson. *The Episcopal Church in Georgia, 1733–1957* (Atlanta, GA: Protestant Episcopal Church in the Diocese of Atlanta, 1960).

Marable, Manning. "Booker T. Washington and the Political Economy of Black Education in the United States, 1880–1915." In *A Different Vision: African American Economic Thought*, vol. 1, ed. Thomas D. Boston, 157–173 (New York: Routledge, 1997).

"Maritcha R. Lyons (1848–1929)." In *Notable Black American Women*, Book 2, ed. Jessie Carney Smith, 417–421 (Detroit, MI: Gale Research, 1996).

Mason, Herman Skip. *Politics, Civil Rights, and Law in Black Atlanta, 1870–1970* (Charleston, SC: Arcadia Publishing, 2000).

Mathews, Basil. *Booker T. Washington: Educator and Interracial Interpreter* (Cambridge, MA: Harvard University Press, 1948).

Mathews, Marcia M. *Henry Ossawa Tanner: American Artist* (Chicago, IL: University of Chicago Press, 1995).

Maurois, Andre. *The Titans: A Three-Generation Biography of the Dumas* (New York: Harper, 1957).

McClish, Glen. "Frederick Douglass and the Consequences of Rhetoric: The Interpretive Framing and Publication History of the 2 January 1893 Haiti Speeches." *Rhetorica* 30 (Issue 1, 2012): 37–73.

McFeely, William S. *Yankee Stepfather: General O.O. Howard and the Freedmen* (New Haven, CT: Yale University Press, 1968).

McMurry, Linda O. *Recorder of the Black Experience: A Biography of Monroe Nathan Work* (Baton Rouge: Louisiana State University Press, 1985).

McPhereson, James M. *The Abolitionist Legacy: From Reconstruction to the NAACP* (Princeton, NJ: Princeton University Press, 1975).

Meier, August. "Booker T. Washington and the Negro Press: With Special Reference to the Colored American Magazine." *Journal of Negro History* 38 (January 1953): 67–90.

Meier, August. *Negro Thought in America, 1880–1915: Racial Ideologies in the Age of Booker T. Washington* (Ann Arbor: University of Michigan Press, 1963).

Meier, August. "Toward a Reinterpretation of Booker T. Washington." *Journal of Southern History* 23 (May 1957): 220–227.

"Miller, Warner, (1838–1918)." *Biographical Dictionary of the United States Congress.* http://bioguide.congress.gov/scripts/biodisplay.pl?index=M000760. Accessed 2 July 2014.

Milton, Joyce. *The Yellow Kids: Foreign Correspondents in the Heyday of Yellow Journalism* (New York: Harper, 1989).

Mixon, Gregory. *The Atlanta Riot: Race, Class, and Violence in a New South City* (Gainesville: University Press of Florida, 2005).

Mixon, Gregory. "The Making of a Black Political Boss: Henry A. Rucker, 1897–1904." *Georgia Historical Quarterly* 89 (Winter 2005): 485–504.

Mjagkij, Nina. *Light in the Darkness: African Americans and the YMCA, 1852–1946* (Lexington: University Press of Kentucky, 1994).

Moore, Jacqueline M. *Booker T. Washington, W.E.B. Du Bois, and the Struggle for Racial Uplift* (Lanham, MD: SR Books, 2003).

Moore, Jacqueline M. *Leading the Race: The Transformation of the Black Elite in the Nation's Capital, 1880–1920* (Charlottesville: University Press of Virginia, 1999).

Morris, Aldon. *The Scholar Denied: W.E.B. Du Bois and the Birth of Modern Sociology* (Berkeley: University of California Press, 2015).

Moses, Wilson Jeremiah, ed. *Creative Conflict in African American Thought: Frederick Douglass, Alexander Crummell, Booker T. Washington, W.E.B. Du Bois, and Marcus Garvey* (New York: Cambridge University Press, 2004).

Moss, Alfred A., Jr. *The American Negro Academy: Voice of the Talented Tenth* (Baton Rouge: Louisiana State University Press, 1981).

Mounter, Michael Robert. "Richard Theodore Greener: The Idealist, Statesman, Scholar, and South Carolinian." PhD dissertation, University of South Carolina, 2002.

Nash, Margaret A. "Patient Persistence: The Political and Educational Values of Anna Julia Cooper and Mary Church Terrell." *Educational Studies* 35 (April 2004): 122–136.

Nelson, Paul D. *Fredrick L. McGhee: A Life on the Color Line, 1861–1912* (Minneapolis: Minnesota Historical Society Press, 2002).

Newby, Idus A. *Black Carolinians: A History of Blacks in South Carolina from 1895 to 1968* (Columbia: University of South Carolina Press, 1973).

Neyland, Leedell W. "The Educational Leadership of J.R.E. Lee." *Negro History Bulletin* 25 (January 1962): 75–78.

Noll, Mark A., and Carolyn Nystrom. *Clouds of Witnesses: Christian Voice from Africa and Asia* (Downers Grove, IL: Intervarsity Press, 2011).

Norrell, Robert J. *Up from History: The Life of Booker T. Washington* (Cambridge, MA: Belknap Press of Harvard University Press, 2009).

"Notes." *Journal of Negro History* 12 (July 1927): 563–566.

Orr, Dorothy. *A History of Education in Georgia* (Chapel Hill: University of North Carolina Press, 1950).

Pappas, Gregory. *John Dewey's Ethics: Democracy as Experience* (Bloomington: Indiana University Press, 2008).

Pendergast, Tom. *Creating the Modern Man: American Magazines and Consumer Culture, 1900–1950* (Columbia: University of Missouri Press, 2000).

Perdue, Theda. *Race and the Atlanta Cotton States Exposition of 1895* (Athens: University of Georgia Press, 2010).

Perman, Michael. *Struggle for Mastery: Disfranchisement in the South, 1888–1908* (Chapel Hill: University of North Carolina Press, 2000).

Perry, Chuck. "Atlanta Journal-Constitution." *New Georgia Encyclopedia.* http://www.georgiaencyclopedia.org/articles/arts-culture/atlanta-journal-constitution. Accessed 17 June 2014.

Perry, Mark. *Lift Up Thy Voice: The Grimke Family's Journey from Slaveholders to Civil Rights Leaders* (New York: Viking, 2001).

"Personal: Edward H. Morris." *Journal of Negro History* 28 (April 1943): 258–259.

Pitre, Merline. *Black Victory: The Rise and Fall of the White Primary in Texas* (Columbia: University of Missouri Press, 1979).

Rabinowitz, Howard N. *Southern Black Leaders of the Reconstruction Era* (Urbana: University of Illinois Press, 1982).

Rampersad, Arnold. *The Art and Imagination of W.E.B. Du Bois* (Cambridge, MA: Harvard University Press, 1976).

Reddick, L.D. "Biography." Alexander Crummell Papers Finding Aid. Schomberg Center for Research in Black Culture. New York Public Library. New York.

Reed, Jr., Adolph L. *W.E.B. Du Bois and American Political Thought: Fabianism and the Color Line* (New York: Oxford University Press, 1997).

Reed, Christopher Robert. *The Chicago NAACP and the Rise of Black Professional Leadership* (Bloomington: Indiana University Press, 1997).

Riley, B.F. *The Life and Times of Booker T. Washington* (New York: Fleming H. Revell, 1916).

Riser, R. Volney. *Defying Disfranchisement: Black Voting Rights Activism in the Jim Crow South, 1890–1908* (Baton Rouge: Louisiana State University Press, 2010).

Roberts, Priscilla. "Paul D. Cravath, the First World War, and the Anglophile Internationalist Tradition." *Australian Journal of Politics & History* 51 (June 2005): 194–215.

Ross, B. Joyce. *J.E. Spingarn and the Rise of the NAACP, 1911–1939* (New York: Atheneum, 1972).

Rudwick, Elliot. *WEB Du Bois: Propagandist of the Negro Protest* (New York: Athaneum, 1968).

Rudwick, Elliott M. *W.E.B. Du Bois: A Study in Minority Group Leadership* (Philadelphia: University of Pennsylvania Press, 1961).

Scarborough, William Sanders. *The Autobiography of William Sanders Scarborough: An American Journey from Slavery to Scholarship*, ed. M.V. Ronnick (Detroit, MI: Wayne State University Press, 2005).

Schneider, Mark. *Boston Confronts Jim Crow, 1890–1920* (Boston, MA: Northeastern University Press, 1997).

Schroeder, Alan. *Booker T. Washington: Educator and Racial Spokesman* (New York: Infoplease Publishing, 2005).

Schweninger, Lee. *The Writings of Celia Parker Woolley (1848–1918): Literary Activist* (Lewiston, NY: Edwin Mellen Press, 1998).

Sewell, George. "Morris Brown College: Legacy of Wesley John Gaines." *Crisis* 88 (April 1981): 133–136.

Shaw, Stephanie J. *W.E.B. Du Bois and "The Souls of Black Folk"* (Chapel Hill: University of North Carolina Press, 2013).

Shutter, Marion Daniel, ed. *History of Minneapolis, Gateway to the Northwest*, vol. 2, *Biographical* (Chicago, IL: S.J. Clarke, 1923).

Silag, Bill, Susan Koch-Bridgford, and Hal Chase, eds. *Outside in: African American History in Iowa, 1838–2000* (Des Moines: Reflections of Iowa, 2001).

Simpson, Anne Key. *Hard Trials: The Life and Music of Harry T. Burleigh* (Metuchen, NJ: The Scarecrow Press, 1990).

Smith, Eric Ledell. "Asking for Justice and Fair Play: African American State Legislators and Civil Rights in Early Twentieth-Century Pennsylvania." *Pennsylvania History* 63 (Spring 1996): 169–203.

Smith, John David. "No Negro Is Upon the Program: Blacks and the Montgomery Race Conference of 1900." In *A Mythic Land Apart: Reassessing Southerners and Their History*, by eds. John David Smith and Thomas H. Appleton, 125–150 (Westport, CT: Greenwood, 1997).

Smith, Woodruff D. *Politics and the Sciences of Culture in Germany, 1840–1920* (New York: Oxford University Press, 1991).

Smock, Raymond. *Booker T. Washington: Black Leadership in the Age of Jim Crow* (Chicago, IL: Ivan R. Dee, 2009).

Sollors, Werner, Caldwell Titcomb, and Thomas H. Underwood, eds. *Blacks at Harvard: A Documentary History of African-American Experience at Harvard and Radcliffe* (New York: New York University Press, 1993).

"Some Chicagoans of Note." *Crisis* 10 (September 1915): 37–38.

Strickland, Arvarh E. "Booker T. Washington: The Myth and the Man." *Reviews in American History* (December 1973): 559–564.

Stutman, Craig M. "Reconstruction in the Mind of W.E.B. Du Bois: Myth, Memory, and the Meaning of American Democracy." PhD dissertation, Temple University, 2008.

Suggs, Henry Lewis, ed. *The Black Press in the Middle West, 1865–1985* (Westport, CT: Greenwood Press, 1996).

Sullivan, Patricia. *Lift Every Voice: The NAACP and the Making of the Civil Rights Movement* (New York: New Press, 2010).

Sweeny, W. Allison. *History of the African American Soldier* (Phnom Penh: Keith Brooks Publishing, 2010).

Sylvander, Carolyn Wedin. *Jessie Redmon Fauset: Black American Writer* (Albany, NY: Whitston, 1981).

Sznajderman, Michael, and Leah Rawls Atkins. "William Benson and the Kowaliga School." *Alabama Heritage* 76 (Spring 2005): 24–25.

Thornbrough, Emma Lou. "The National Afro-American League, 1887–1908." *Journal of Southern History* 27 (November 1961): 494–512.

Thornbrough, Emma Lou. *T. Thomas Fortune: Militant Journalist* (Chicago, IL: University of Chicago Press, 1972).

Tolnay, Stewart E., and E.M. Beck. *A Festival of Violence: An Analysis of Southern Lynchings, 1882–1930* (Urbana: University of Illinois Press, 1995).

Towns, George A. "Phylon Profile XVI: Horace Bumstead, Atlanta University President (1886–1907)." *Phylon* 9 (2nd Qtr., 1948): 109–114.

Trefousse, Hans L. *Carl Schurz: A Biography* (Knoxville: University of Tennessee Press, 1982).

Trotter, Joe William, Jr. *The Great Migration in Historical Perspective: New Dimensions of Race, Class, and Gender* (Bloomington: Indiana University Press, 1991).

Van Notten, Eleonore. *Wallace Thurman's Harlem Renaissance* (Amsterdam: Rodopi, 1994).

Van Pelt, John Robert. "John Wesley Edward Bowen." *Journal of Negro History* 19 (April 1934): 217–221.

Vine, Phyllis. *One Man's Castle: Clarence Darrow in Defense of the American Dream* (New York: Amistad, 2005).

Waldrep, Christopher, ed. *Lynching in America: A History in Documents* (New York: New York University Press, 2006).

Waldrep, Christopher. *The Many Faces of Judge Lynch: Extralegal Violence and Punishment in America* (New York: Palgrave, 2004).

Wanklyn, Harriet. *Friedrich Ratzel: A Biographical Memoir and Bibliography* (New York: Cambridge University Press, 1961).

Weaver, John D. *The Brownsville Raid* (College Station: Texas A&M University Press, 1992). Originally published 1970.

Weiner, Melissa F. *Power, Protest, and the Public Schools: Jewish and African American Struggles in New York City* (Piscataway, NJ: Rutgers University Press, 2010).

Wilder, Craig Steven. *A Covenant with Color: Race and Social Power in Brooklyn, 1636–1990* (New York: Columbia University Press, 2000).

Wilkerson, Isabel. *The Warmth of Other Suns: The Epic Story of America's Great Migration* (New York: Random House, 2010).

Willard, George-Anne. "Charles Lee Coon (1868–1927): North Carolina Crusader for Educational Reform." PhD dissertation, University of North Carolina at Chapel Hill, 1974.

"William Henry Ferris." *Journal of Negro History* 26 (October 1941): 549–550.

Williams, Douglas Arnell. *David A. Williston: The First Professional African American Landscape Architect and His Campus Designs for Historically Black Colleges and Universities* (Ithaca, NY: Cornell University Press, 2002).

Williams, Jr., Vernon J. "A Gifted Amateur: The Case of George Washington Ellis." *American Anthropologist* 104 (June 2002): 544–550.

Williamson, Joel. *The Crucible of Race: Black-White Relations in the American South Since Emancipation* (New York: Oxford University Press, 1984).

Wintz, Cary D., ed. *African American Political Thought, 1890–1930: Washington, Du Bois, Garvey, and Randolph* (Armonk, NY: M.E. Sharpe, 1996).

Wolters, Raymond. *Du Bois and His Rivals* (Columbia: University of Missouri Press, 2003).

Wood, Amy Louise. *Lynching and Spectacle: Witnessing Racial Violence in America, 1890–1940* (Chapel Hill: University of North Carolina Press, 2009).

Woodfield, James. *English Theatre in Translation, 1881–1914* (Totowa, NJ: Barnes & Noble, 1984).

Woodward, C. Vann. *Origins of the New South, 1877–1913* (Baton Rouge: Louisiana State University Press, 1951).

Woodward, C. Vann. *The Strange Career of Jim Crow* (New York: Oxford University Press, 1955).

Wright, John A. *Discovering African American St. Louis: A Guide to Historic Sites* (St. Louis: Missouri Historical Society Press, 2002).

Zimmerman, Andrew. *Alabama in Africa: Booker T. Washington, the German Empire, and the Globalization of the New South* (Princeton, NJ: Princeton University Press, 2012).

Zipser, Arthur, and Pearl Zipser. *Fire and Grace: The Life of Rose Pastor Stokes* (Athens: University of Georgia Press, 1989).

Index

About the Author

THOMAS AIELLO is associate professor of history and African American studies at the Valdosta State University.

OTHER BOOKS BY THOMAS AIELLO

History

Jim Crow's Last Stand: Nonunanimous Criminal Jury Verdicts In Louisiana (2015)
Model Airplanes Are Decadent and Depraved: The Glue-Sniffing Epidemic of the 1960s (2015)
The Devil's Messages: Language and Contested Space in Twentieth-Century America (2013)
The Kings of Casino Park: Race and Race Baseball in the Lost Season of 1932, Monroe, LA (2011)
Bayou Classic: The Grambling-Southern Football Rivalry (2010)

Fiction

On Carpentry (2011)
Saint Norman (2002)
Womb of Monsters (2001)

Edited

Kerlin, Robert T. *The Voice of the Negro (1919)* (2013)
Lawson, David. *Paul Morphy: The Pride and Sorrow of Chess* (2010)
Burley, Dan. *Dan Burley's Jive* (2009)